**Check-in, check-out :
managing hotel operations**

D0583983

SEVENTH EDITION

Check-In
Check-Out
Managing Hotel Operations

Gary K. Vallen
Northern Arizona University

• • •

Jerome J. Vallen
University of Nevada, Las Vegas, Emeritus

PEARSON

Prentice
Hall

Upper Saddle River, New Jersey 07458

Library of Congress Cataloging-in-Publication Data

Vallen, Gary K.
    Check-in, check-out: managing hotel operations / Gary K. Vallen,
      Jerome J. Vallen. — 7th ed.
      p. cm.
    Includes bibliographical references.
    ISBN 0-13-112682-2
    1. Hotel management.   2. Motel management.   I. Vallen, Jerome J.
  II. Title.
    TX911.3.M27V352 2005
    647.94'068—dc22

                                      2004000991

Executive Editor: Vernon R. Anthony
Editorial Assistant: Beth Dyke
Production Editor: Patty Donovan, Pine Tree Composition, Inc.
Production Liaison: Adele Kupchik
Director of Manufacturing and Production: Bruce Johnson
Managing Editor: Mary Carnis
Manufacturing Buyer: Cathleen Petersen
Creative Director: Cheryl Asherman
Senior Marketing Manager: Ryan DeGrote
Marketing Assistant: Elizabeth Farrell
Formatting and Interior Design: Pine Tree Composition, Inc.
Printing and Binding: R.R. Donnelley & Sons
Cover Design Coordinator: Mary E. Siener
Cover Designer: Michael L. Ginsberg
Cover Photograph: Paul Warchol Photography
The architect for the lobby is: The Rockwell Group
The hotel is: W Hotel, Union Square, NY

Pearson Education LTD
Pearson Education Singapore, Pte. Ltd.
Pearson Education, Canada, Ltd
Pearson Education—Japan
Pearson Education Australia PTY, Limited
Pearson Educaçion de Mexico, S.A. De C.V.
Pearson Education Malaysia, Pte. Ltd.
PEARSON Prentice Hall

10 9 8 7 6 5 4 3 2 1
ISBN 0-13-112682-2

• • •

To fathers and sons who work together

Brief Contents

• • •

Contents

• • •

List of Exhibits

• • •

➤ PART II   *The Reservation Process*   127

CHAPTER 4 ➤ *Global Reservations Technologies*   129

CHAPTER 5 ➤ *Individual and Group Reservation*   169

➤ PART IV The Hotel Revenue Cycle 383

CHAPTER 10 ➤ Billing the Guest Folio 385

CHAPTER 11 ➤ Cash Transactions 425

CHAPTER 12 ➤ Credit and the City Ledger 469

➤ PART V Technology 513

CHAPTER 13 ➤ The Night Audit 515

Preface

• • •

Welcome to the seventh edition of *Check-In Check-Out*, a hotel management text. Like the previous editions, which span 30 years, this release is current and complete. The work has kept step with each new, unfolding development in a business that is dynamic and challenging. In keeping with the book's tradition, there are no shortcuts, no superficial changes. The rewrite is complete. Accuracy, currency, and depth of coverage have been and continue to be the hallmarks of this lodging management text.

Sales of guest rooms is the industry's largest income producer as well as its most profitable operating segment. Because the success of this critical department depends on the support of other units, some external to the organization, the discussion focuses on a broad view of lodging management. References throughout the chapters range from human resources to engineering; from accounting to telephone systems; from credit cards to email communications; from legal matters to travel agents; from environmental issues to global distribution systems; from spas to hurdle pricing. Lodging management is an integral part of the world of business. The book's contents provide for that.

Previous users will find new resources: Web site addresses is one example. Researchers will find expanded references: A definitive glossary is one example. Students will find in-depth coverage of content offered in no other hotel textbook: The impact of other events on lodging's future, such as Web reservations, is one example. Operating managers will find answers to the how to: How to empower employees to settle complaints is one example.

Welcome to the latest edition of a tradition in hotel operations and education.

About the Authors

• • •

Coauthored texts are not unusual unless the authors are father and son. Jerry Vallen, the father, launched the book in 1974. Gary Vallen, the son, pursued several degrees and a professional career before becoming a joint author of the fourth edition.

►**Dr. Gary K. Vallen** is a full professor in the School of Hotel and Restaurant Management at Northern Arizona University. He joined that program in 1988 as one of its founding faculty, bringing 16 years of industry experience to the classroom. Part of that resume included vice president and assistant general manager of a casino, hotel sales manager, financial and operational analyst, and associate manager for private clubs.

Dr. Vallen received his undergraduate degree in hotel administration at the University of Nevada, Las Vegas. Despite the long hours of industry, he simultaneously worked and earned an MBA at the University of Nevada, Reno. His Ed.D. degree with an emphasis in hospitality education (Northern Arizona University) was earned after he began teaching. In addition to *Check-In, Check-Out*, Dr. Vallen coauthored *An Introduction to Hospitality Management* and has published over three dozen refereed articles and conference proceedings. He is on the editorial boards of six professional journals.

Professor Vallen operates *Gary Vallen Hospitality Consultants*, which specializes in hosted casino nights for clients of destination management companies and in visitor analyses for festivals, fairs, rodeos, and ski slopes. He has developed and carried out numerous secret-shopper evaluations for both hotels and restaurants. The Southwest location has enabled him to assist many Native American groups, including the Hopi and Navajo, but he is also well known for his rural tourism expertise.

►**Dr. Jerome J. Vallen** was the founding Dean of the College of Hotel Administration, University of Nevada, Las Vegas, and served in that capacity for 22 years. He is now professor emeritus/dean emeritus. Jerry Vallen returned to the classroom for a short period before taking an assignment as founding dean of the Australian International Hotel School, Canberra.

After earning a baccalaureate degree at Cornell, he entered the hotel industry, carrying with him the food experience gained from the family's small chain of four restaurants. For several years, this author taught and worked in industry. Dr. Vallen earned a master's degree in educational administration (St. Lawrence University) and a doctoral degree from Cornell's School of Hotel Administration.

He has coauthored a book on hotel management and edited a work on the legal basis for obtaining a gaming license in Nevada. Professor Vallen has served as a consulting editor for textbook publishers; a traveling consultant to the U.S. Department of Commerce that has carried him to over three dozen countries; an outside examiner for the University of the West Indies; president of a consulting company; member of the board of several private companies and public entities; and president and chairman of the Council on Hotel, Restaurant and Institutional Education (CHRIE).

Such diverse groups as the University Alumni Association, the Educational Foundation of the National Restaurant Association, and the Educational Institute of the American Hotel & Lodging Association have honored him. So has CHRIE, with its prestigious H.B. Meek Award. Jerome Vallen has been cited in the *Congressional Record* and named among the 100 most important Las Vegans of the 20th century.

The Hotel Industry

Whatever the title, *lodging, innkeeping, the hotel business,* ours is an amazingly resilient industry. It flourishes because it adopts and adapts easily and quickly to changing circumstances. Associating with it is an exhilarating experience even if one ignores the treasures of its very long history and focuses just on the present. Except for an occasional historical glance, that's what this text does: focuses on managing for the present and the likely future of the lodging industry.

The early part of the 20th century was a period of heavy manufacturing and mass production as giant manufacturers sought economies of scale. The middle of the 20th century witnessed a second period of consolidation, driven this time by administrative and financial processes. Among those conglomerates was ITT, which eventually merged its Sheraton Hotels brand into a still more recent consolidator, Starwood Lodging Trust. A third wave of consolidation, this time for the service industries, got underway as the new century approached.

Globalization is a major part of this most recent theme. As business and industry crisscross the oceans into foreign lands, services become as important as products. Recognizable logos, such as Hilton's, drive sales and profits from services as do the brand names of manufactured goods, such as Coca-Cola.

Unit I examines this need for identification and the contradictions that surround it. Industry leaders recognize the consumers' preference for well-known brands, so they stress choice and variety. Unfortunately, they confuse the lodging buyer by offering too wide a range of facilities, accommodations, prices, and locations. An uncountable and confusing number of brands, subbrands, and allied brands compete, sometimes within the very same enterprise. Consolidation is part of the cause. It has swept over the industry. Company 1 absorbs company 2, and eventually the weaker brand disappears. Renaissance, for example, gobbled up Stouffers, and that name is no more. Will the same happen to Sheraton and Westin, great chain names now under the umbrella of Starwood?

The trend is international as well as domestic. America's famous Holiday Inn brand has gone through several ownership changes and corporate names to emerge now as part of Six Continents, a British firm.

Chapters 1 and 2 of this opening unit trace some of the forces that are changing the lodging industry. This sets the foundation for the operational issues treated in the balance of the text. Chapter 3 explains how the industry structures itself to deliver the exciting new products that enable it to retain a dynamic and competitive position.

CHAPTER 1

The Traditional Hotel Industry

Outline

Scope of the Industry
Historical Origin
Understanding the Hotel Business
Traditional Classifications

Resources and Challenges
Resources
Challenges

➤ SCOPE OF THE INDUSTRY

Historical Origin

Ancient travelers relied on the hospitality of their hosts for both accommodations and security. Hotelkeeping has its origin in that culture of hospitality. That's why both words, *hotel* and *hospitality*, have the same Latin root, *hospitium*. As the number of pilgrims and tourists and merchants increased and as their routes became predictable, personal courtesy gave way to commercial enterprise. Hotelkeeping has flourished through centuries of change because it has continued adapting its forms and services to the ever-changing demands of its guests. Modern hotels strive to maintain their traditions of hospitality and security even as they play a greater role in the social, political, economic, and cultural life of every community.

Travel was an individual endeavor at first: a solitary traveler on foot or horseback. Then came others: a loose band of pilgrims or a small coach of strangers. Travel was a rare experience because it was slow and dangerous. Few could afford the luxury, and fewer still were free enough politically to move about. Change has come rapidly. Travel is now a group activity as much as an individual one.

For centuries, hotels remained small, offering only a handful of rooms. Early guests shared accommodations with both the innkeeper's family and with total strangers. The Industrial Revolution wrought changes: in structures—steel to build high-rise buildings; in ownership—corporations to replace family proprietorships and management; and in transportation—railroads, autos, and airplanes to displace the stagecoach. Creative marketing augmented by broader political and economic freedoms were the final elements in the creation of modern tourism.

Hotels of today with their exciting architecture (see Exhibit 1–1) have become destination in themselves. That wasn't always the case. The historical role of innkeeping was one of response. So long as the traveler's course, method of transportation, and travel time were fixed, there was no need to differentiate the inn. Innkeepers located their facility along the traveler's route and waited for the business. That was true as recently as 50 years ago when roadside motels (see Chapter 2, Exhibit 2–3) dotted the U.S. highways. The range and quality of the accommodations reflected the innkeeper's inclination, not that of the guest. Shelter, rest, food, and lodging were the products of those earlier hotels. Lodging is still the basic commodity, but many hotels no longer offer food. Tomorrow may be another story altogether. There may come a time when neither rooms nor food is the industry's basic commodity, and hotels will play a different role.

➤*Palaces of the People.*   Magnificent hotels were built in the United States between the Civil War and World War I. They were like palaces in their size and splendor. But unlike the hotels of Europe, which catered to the aristocracy of the 19th century, American hotels served as home and office, meeting site, and social gathering place for guests from all walks of life. Hence, they were called *palaces of the people.*[1]

Inns or taverns were colonial America's earliest hotels. Adopting the word *hotel,* which comes from *hotel garni* (French for large, furnished mansion), signaled a shift from an industry based on roadside accommodations to those located within the

---

[1]Daniel Boorstin, *The American National Experience,* Chapter 18, "Palaces of the People" (New York: Random House, 1967); and Arthur White, *Palaces of the People* (Marlboro, NJ: Taplinger Publishing Co., Inc., 1970).

Exhibit 1–1   The new designs and exciting architecture of recently built hotels have become attractions in and of themselves. *Courtesy of the Westin Diplomat Resort & Spa, Hollywood, Florida.*

cities.[2] The first hotel built in Washington, DC, in 1793, was the palatial Union Public House. Its structure and name (*Public* House) were representative of the palaces of the people.

The U.S. currency was strong in the 20th century. After World War II, American businesses, including the lodging industry, expanded around the globe. They carried with them the American culture and the American way of business. The situation reversed in the 1980s when the dollar weakened and foreign businesses and foreign hotel companies made counterbalancing inroads into North America. Hotelkeeping became a multinational industry, binding the world's cultures through these back-and-forth investments and through the tourism that ebbs and flows with economic and political changes.

Travel and tourism, of which hotels are a part, help drive the economic engines of growth but are especially critical to the tourism earnings of developing countries. Because development goes hand in hand with construction, hotels and other tourism elements (roads, airports, etc.) have a huge economic impact even in economies as diversified as that of the United States. Some blockbuster resort projects have cost in excess of $1.5 billion! Together, tourism and construction accelerate both the economic rise and the economic downturn of tourist areas.

[2]In Australia, *hotel* means a bar or pub; in India and Pakistan, it indicates a restaurant.

➤*The Service Culture.*   Although the dates may not coincide exactly, the 21st century is likely to be known as the century of technology. Similarly, the 18th century was the agricultural age; the 19th century, the industrial age, and the 20th century, the age of service, or the service society. During the last decades of the 20th century, the sale of services grew faster than the sale of products. Medicine, banking, law, education, retailing, and hotelkeeping carry that service label.

All businesses, lodging included, do not offer the same level of customer service. The hotel industry has responded rapidly and innovatively to a growing demand for choice. So, although we speak of one industry, lodging has many, many parts, with service to the guest probably the only commonality. It is so broad an endeavor worldwide, divided into so many pieces and reflecting so many cultures, that a single definition is not possible. Several widely accepted measures are used, however, to understand what the lodging industry is about.

Understanding the Hotel Business

➤*A Cyclical Industry.*   The hotel industry is cyclical. It goes through wide swings, from periods of very good times to periods of very bad times. Hotels lag the general economy, falling later than the general decline, but also recovering later. Consequently, the number of hotels and the number of hotel rooms vary over time, shifting up and down as the cycle moves through its loops. That's what happened beginning in the early 1980s. Revisions in federal tax law and the collapse of the real estate market (remember, hotel buildings are pieces of real estate) brought the cycle to a devastating low—a low that lasted for well over a decade. Then came a slow reversal in the cycle. By the mid-1990s, hotel construction began to reappear. That upward momentum accelerated as the 1990 decade was closing.

About three years are needed between planning and opening a hotel, longer if there are special zoning, financing, or environmental issues. Openings take longer during financial downturns. Over half the planned projects are never built, and those that are have fewer rooms than originally planned. Therefore, the building boom that followed the upward cycle of the late 1990s was not readily evident until the close of the century and the beginning of the new millennium.

Recovery was halted suddenly in 2001 by the attack on the Twin Towers of the World Trade Center in New York City. The entire travel industry experienced a major interruption of the upward trend with those tragic events. Such an abrupt downturn had not occurred since 1973 when the oil embargo brought the travel industry and much of the industrialized world to its knees.

A better, long-term perspective of the industry comes about every 10 years when the Bureau of the Census responds to the constitutional requirement of a national count. Part of that census is the *SC Series*, which deals with the lodging industry.

➤*How Hotels Count and Measure.*   The 1997 census of hotels (www.census.gov), which was issued in 2002, reported on several widely followed statistics. There were approximately 56,200 properties in the United States with some 3.5 million rooms. Hotels employed about 1,700,000 workers in 1997. (Curiously, this census identifies casino hotels separately within the total.) Other agencies and organizations also count. As one would expect from so dynamic an industry, none of the figures agree. They are close, considering the 5-year time lag between the governmental reports and those of, say, the American Hotel & Lodging Association (AH&LA), previously called the American Hotel & Motel Association (AH&MA).

The AH&LA's *2002 Annual Report* lists 41,400 hotels in the United States of 15 rooms or more. These 4.2 million rooms require a workforce of 1.9 million. Parenthetically, both the Bureau of the Census and the AH&LA estimate approximately 0.5 employees per room. Other estimates come from the World Tourism Organization (WTO), Smith Travel Research, the International Hotel Association (IHA), and from private companies such as PKF Consulting and PricewaterhouseCoopers, both firms with specialities in the lodging and casino businesses. The actual numbers can never be exact because the industry is in constant flux. Estimating the cost of a typical room at $100,000 (and that's how the industry quotes value, by per-room building cost or resale price) suggests the worth of all hotel property at well over $300 billion. There is no way that a simple description of the lodging industry could emerge from that size and diversity.

Occupancy.   The previous discussions of business cycles and room numbers come together to measure the economic health of the lodging industry. An improved business environment encourages construction of new hotels, adding more rooms to the marketplace. Declining business accelerates the removal of antiquated and worn-out hotel rooms. These old hotels are kept in place during the preceding boom when there aren't enough rooms, but fall to the wrecker's ball as the lack of guests (customers) makes such properties less competitive. At any given time, the room count reflects the mathematics of the new and the old (see Exhibit 1–2).

Number of Rooms Available for Sale Nationwide[a]					
Year	*2001*[b]	*2002*[b]	*2003*[b]	*2004*	*2005*
Rooms Available at Year's Start (Last Year's Close)	3,910	3,970	3,990	4,040	4,110
Plus					
Rooms Completed[c]	110	80	70	100	120
Total	4,020	4,050	4,060	4,140	4,230
Less					
Rooms Removed[c]	50	60	20	30	20
Rooms Available for Sale at Year's End (Next Year's Start)	3,970	3,990	4,040	4,110	4,210
Approximate Increase in Supply	1.5%	0.5%	1.3%	1.7%	2.5%

[a]In thousands; add 000 to each figure
[b]Values were impacted due to the events of September 11, 2001, in New York City
[c]Figures are hypothetical based on historical averages

Exhibit 1–2   *The number of rooms available for sale* each year is the net of last year's closing count, plus new construction, minus rooms lost (through demolition or nonhotel use). This closing balance is the denominator of the fraction used to compute the national percentage of occupancy (number of rooms sold ÷ *number of rooms available for sale*). Values are hypothetical.

During declining cycles, more rooms are available for sale, but fewer guests are buying. During upward cycles, more guests are buying, but fewer rooms are available. Demand by customers is measured by the number of rooms that guests buy. This is called the *number of rooms occupied* or *the number of rooms sold*. This information is counted every night by every hotel. Although the total number of rooms in the world is an estimate at best, hotel managers know accurately the number of rooms in their particular hotels. Whether for the nation, for the region, or for the one hotel, that number is called the *number of rooms available for sale*.

The relationship between the number of rooms actually sold (demand) and the number of rooms available for sale (supply) is a barometer of the industry's health. It is a closely watched value. This relationship (or ratio) between the two values asks, How well did the hotel sell rooms in relation to the number of rooms that it could have sold? That's a big mouthful to say all the time, so the industry uses a shortcut, calling the relationship the *percentage of occupancy*, or just *occupancy*, or sometimes, *occupancy percent*.

The occupancy calculation is a simple division represented by a fraction in which the number of rooms sold is divided by the number of rooms available for sale and expressed as a percentage (see Exhibit 1–3):

$$\frac{\text{number of rooms sold}}{\text{number of rooms available for sale}}$$

Occupancy can be computed by one hotel for one night, one month, or one year. Citywide occupancy, regional occupancy (the Northeast, for example), or national occupancy (see Exhibit 1–4) can be, and are, tracked by hotels, consulting companies, convention bureaus, and state tourism offices. Of course, the figures become less accurate as the breadth of the count broadens from the individual property to a worldwide count. We saw earlier that there is no agreement even in counting the number of rooms available for sale. Nevertheless, everyone becomes engrossed in occupancy figures when companies such as Sheraton announce that a 1% rise in occupancy represents a $25 million improvement in profits. Andrew Young, mayor of Atlanta for eight years, phrased it from a different perspective, telling a group of hotel professionals that each 1% rise in hotel occupancy resulted in 400 new jobs for his city![3]

Sales per Occupied Room.   Occupancy measures the hotel's "share of the market," so it measures *quantity*. The *quality* of the business being done is measured by the amount received for each room sold, *sales per occupied room*. Sales per occupied room goes by another, more commonly used name, *average daily rate* (ADR). ADR is the second of several ways that hotels count and measure. It too is computed with a ratio or fraction:

$$\frac{\text{room sales (measured in dollars)}}{\text{number of rooms sold}}$$

Note that the number of rooms sold (or occupied) appears in both formulas (see Exhibit 1–3).

---

[3]*Hotels & Restaurants International*, June 1989, p. 40, quoting John Kapioltas, then Sheraton's Chief Executive Officer; and Andrew Young, keynote speech, CHRIE, Washington, DC, August 12, 1996.

Given	Number of rooms in the hotel available for sale	800
	Number of rooms in the hotel	820
	Number of rooms sold to guests	600
	Number of dollars received from guests for rooms	$48,000
	Number of employees on staff	500
	Number of guests	700

Computations

Percentage of occupancy is 75%.

$$\frac{\text{number of rooms sold (to guests)}}{\text{number of rooms (in the hotel) available for sale}} = \frac{600}{800} = \frac{3}{4} = 75\%$$

Sales per occupied room (average daily rate, ADR) is $80.00.

$$\frac{\text{room sales (as measured in dollars)}}{\text{number of rooms sold (to guests)}} = \frac{\$48,000}{600} = \$80.00$$

Sales per available room (RevPar) is $60.00.

$$\frac{\text{room sales (as measured in dollars)}}{\text{number of rooms (in the hotel) available for sale}} = \frac{\$48,000}{800} = \$60.00$$

Mathematical check:

$$\text{ADR} \times \text{occupancy} = \text{RevPar} \qquad \$80 \times 0.75 = \$60.00$$

Number of employees per guest room is 0.625.

$$\frac{\text{number of employees (on staff)}}{\text{number of rooms (in the hotel) available for sale}} = \frac{500}{800} = 0.625$$

Percentage of double occupancy is 16.6%

$$\frac{\text{number of guests} - \text{number of rooms sold}}{\text{number of rooms sold}} = \frac{700-600}{600} = 16.6\%$$

Exhibit 1–3   The hotel industry tracks several measures and ratios whose computations are shown. Bed (or guest or sleeper) occupancy percentage (number of beds sold ÷ number of beds available) is often substituted for room occupancy outside of the United States. (Bed occupancy of 50% approximates room occupancy of 70%.)

The health of the hotel business depends on a combination of occupancy and price. Normally, price (ADR) increases as occupancy percentage increases. That is, the more the customers want rooms, the higher the rate they'll pay. As the industry goes through a declining cycle, it is sometimes possible to keep the ADR climbing for a short time, sometimes even faster than the consumer price index, even as occupancy is falling. That's true for both an individual property and the industry as a whole. As more vacancies occur, prices (ADR) begin to level off because front-office managers reduce rates to maintain higher occupancies. How well they do their job of filling rooms without cutting prices is what the next measure measures.

RevPar (Revenue per Available Room).   RevPar is an old industry standby that has reemerged recently as a far more important value than it was 25 years ago when it

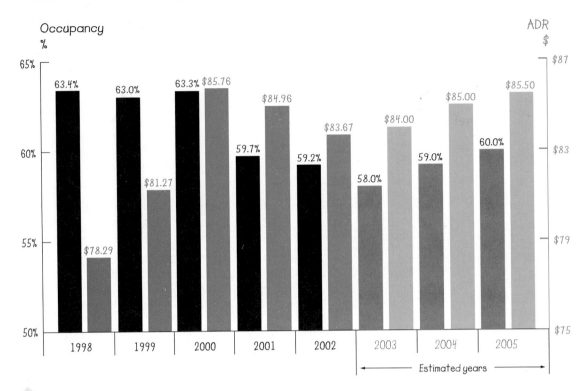

Exhibit 1–4   Industry watchers track average daily rate (ADR) and percentage of occupancy (%) in order to evaluate lodging's economic health. (RevPar, another statistic, is merely the average daily rate multiplied by the percentage of occupancy.) The final decade of the millennium was one of the most profitable periods in hotel history. Decline was first noted as the century closed, 1998 and 1999. Both business and leisure travel were impacted again by terrorism at the start of the new century. Recovery was delayed until 2004.

Values for the years 2003 to 2005 are author's estimates. Values for 1998 to 2002 are the *Courtesy of Smith Travel Research, Henderson, Tennessee.*

had a different name, *average rate per available room.*[4] Yield management has come onto the scene during that time. Yield management balances demand and price. Normally, as guest demand (occupancy) falls, price (room rate) declines. One hears that old standby, "hotels fill from the bottom up," meaning that guests elect lower rates when an empty house allows it. The superior manager strives to stabilize or even increase both price and occupancy, especially during dips in the cycle. RevPar (sometimes written as REVPAR) measures that performance. It measures revenue (or sales) per room relative to the total room inventory available. In contrast, ADR measures revenue per room relative to the number of rooms actually sold.

Exhibit 1–3 illustrates the computation. Keep in mind that room revenue and room sales are two different terms for the same value! So the fraction is:

$$\frac{\text{room revenue}}{\text{number of rooms available for sale}}$$

[4]Average rate per available room was the terminology that appeared in the first four editions of this book. The concept and the name fell into disuse only to reemerge as RevPar. Similarly, the average daily rate was originally called average room rate, a name that was gradually replaced beginning about 1980 because some thought it to mean the rate the hotel was charging.

Since RevPar involves both price and occupancy, the mathematics of the three ratios is interlocked. Multiplying the ADR by occupancy results in RevPar (see Exhibit 1–3). If nothing else, it is a good means of checking the arithmetic. Under debate is what figure to use as the denominator of the RevPar fraction. The illustration uses number of rooms *available* for sale. However, some rooms may not be *available*. Rooms may be out of order, out of inventory, in use for hotel purposes, rented as office space, and so on. To measure management's ability to use all its rooms, some argue that the denominator should be the absolute number of rooms (the total in the house), not merely those available for sale. Using the larger denominator, (total) number of rooms, results in a smaller RevPar, and that reflects less well on the management team.

Double Occupancy.   More business travelers are sharing rooms as corporate management focuses on cost-cutting. Moreover, two to a room is standard procedure at company meetings and conventions because it promotes professional friendships. Double occupancy, which refers to any room in which there is more than one person, increases per-room revenue, since there is an additional charge for the second and third occupants. Hence, families, skiers, tour groups, and similar double-up travelers boost the double occupancy figures (see Exhibit 1–3), calculated as:

$$\frac{\text{number or guests } - \text{ number of rooms occupied}}{\text{number of rooms occupied}}$$

High double occupancy skews room revenue, and hence ADR, upward. Similarly, counting *comp* (complimentary) rooms, which are occupied rooms whose charges have been waived, skews the occupancy percentage. (Many hotels do not count comps.) If comp rooms are counted as occupied, occupancy percentage rises. Of course, ADR will then fall, since the same room income would be spread among more rooms. RevPar would be unaffected because the denominator of its fraction—rooms available for sale—remains unchanged.

Just as the averages of individual hotels can be skewed, so too can the averages of the entire industry. Any computation of *average* is impacted by extreme numbers. National or regional occupancy, ADR, and RevPar figures are influenced by the large hotels, which tend to provide more information and more extreme data than do hotels of 50 rooms or less.

Break-even Point.   To break even is to have neither profit nor loss. At the break-even point, inflows from revenues exactly match outflows for costs. A large portion of a hotel's costs are fixed expenses: the payment of debt on the funds borrowed to erect the building, for example. Reducing fixed costs such as interest rates drops the amount of occupancy needed to break even. Similarly, raising the ADR, or doing more food and beverage sales, increases the flow of income. More income per room sold, a higher RevPar, means that a smaller percentage of occupancy is needed to pay off the costs, to break even.

Break-even points are important because there are no profits until that point is reached. Until the business pays its fixed expenses (interest, for example), its semifixed expenses (power, for example), and its variable expenses (wages, for example), there are no profits. But once that point is reached, profits accumulate quickly. Each dollar before the break-even point has a mission: pay off the debt, pay the electricity, pay the employee. Each dollar after the break-even point has a lesser mission because fixed expenses no longer need to be paid! Even some of the semifixed expenses have been met.

Therefore, each dollar beyond the break-even point has a very large portion earmarked as profit.

Break-even points are expressed in occupancy percentage, and this value has been dropping over the past decades as the industry focused on costs and revenues. Better hotel design and better financing have held costs in check. Changes in market mix and higher room rates have improved revenues. Taken together over a quarter century, they have brought a drop in the break-even point from occupancy percentages in the mid-70s to the mid-60s to the current high-50s. It's a good sign for the long-term economic health of the lodging industry.

➤ *Special Characteristics of the Hotel Business.*   The room manager's ability to maximize the number of rooms sold or to increase the ADR obtained is limited by several characteristics special to the lodging business. Some of these peculiarities are also found in other industries, chiefly among the airlines.

Perishability.   Even the industry's newest recruit knows that a room left unsold tonight cannot be sold again. Empty hotel rooms, like empty airline seats or unsold television commercials, cannot be shelved, cannot be stored, cannot be saved, and cannot be used again.

Location.   Ellsworth Statler (Statler Hotels were purchased by Hilton) coined the expression "Location, location, location" to emphasize its importance to the hotel. Good economic locations are difficult to find in urban America. Changing neighborhoods and shifting markets sometimes doom a hotel whose original location was good. Unlike the airline seat, there is no way to change a hotel's location. So management has learned to depend less on desirable real estate and more on marketing and sales; less on drive-by or walk-in traffic and more on central reservation systems.

Fixed Supply.   Not only is the location of the hotel fixed but so is its supply of (the number of) rooms. Airlines can adjust the number of seats by adding or removing planes from the route. With hotels, what you see is what you get.

High Operating Costs.   Unlike manufacturing industries, which offset labor with large capital investments, hotels are both capital- and labor-intensive. The result is high fixed costs (a *large nut* in the jargon of the industry), which continue whether or not the hotel has business. Thus, a high percentage of occupancy is needed just to break even.

Seasonality.   Throwing away the key is a traditional practice when a new hotel is opened. The act signifies that the hotel never closes. Yet hotelkeeping, even for commercial hotels, is a very seasonal business. The cyclical dip strikes the commercial hotel every seven days as it struggles to offset poor weekend business. The federal holiday law, which assigned Mondays to national holidays, reinforces the negative pattern of the commercial hotel.

Occupancy computations must account for this weekend phenomenon. Especially so since the business traveler—the one who is not in the hotel during the weekends—still accounts for the majority of the lodging industry's business. Given the usual profile of the commercial, urban hotel (see Exhibit 1–5), national occupancy percentages in the high 70s and 80s remain an elusive goal.

Annual cycles compound the problem. Commercial business is down even in midweek between Thanksgiving and New Year's Day and from May through Labor Day. But Christmas Day has been rising.

Monday	100%
Tuesday	100
Wednesday	90
Thursday	90
Friday	40
Saturday	20
Sunday	20
Total	460%
Average per 7 days	66%

Exhibit 1–5   Commercial, downtown hotels cycle through weekend downturns, which make it difficult to achieve annual occupancies over 80%. Airline fares, which reflect Saturday night stays, work to the advantage of convention hotels if groups can be convinced to meet on weekends. Smith Travel Research now tracks U.S. occupancy daily as well as monthly.

The ultimate solution is difficult to comprehend. Hotels in urban areas may someday operate on the same five-day week that their customers, their employees, and their suppliers do. They will respond to corporate demand cycles by closing the hotel on weekends and holidays. Managers will no longer symbolically "throw away the key."

The resort pattern is the opposite of the commercial pattern. Weekends are busy and midweek less so. The slack period of the commercial hotel is the very season of the resort. At one time, resorts opened Memorial Day and closed Labor Day. This 100-day pattern made the hotel's success dependent on the weather. Two weeks of rain are devastating when the break-even point is 80 days of near-full occupancy.

Although the dates of the winter season differ, there are still only 100 days between December 17 and March 15.

Both winter and summer resorts have extended their seasons with groups, conferences, and special activities. Hotels that operate on the four-day season may be worse off now than those on the four-season year. At least the latter have a higher double occupancy.

Traditional Classifications

The inns of old evolved from private homes. Today's hotel, even the mom-and-pop variety, is not represented as anyone's home. It is either a point of destination or an accommodation for those in transit. Yesterday's tavern offered the family meal to all who came. Dining today is a created experience in design, decor, and menu. The old inn was almost indistinguishable from its neighbors. Today's edifice is a sharp contrast in style and packaging.

Although the basic concepts of food, shelter, and hospitality remain, their means of delivery have changed. These changes have been marked by shifting terminology: hostel, tavern, public house, inn, guest house, hotel, resort, motel, motor lodge, motor inn, bed and breakfast, airtel, boatel, hometel, skytel, and condotel.

The industry's trade association has experienced a similar shift. Over time, the American Hotel Association became the American Hotel & Motel Association and, just recently, the American Hotel & Lodging Association. "Lodging" was chosen because new hotel types have appeared, as we shall see a few pages ahead.

Despite the speed of change, several traditional classifications have withstood the test of time: size, class, type and plan. Some have more objective measures than others. None are self-excluding: Hotels can fall into every category or into only some. Moreover, there are degrees of belonging. One property may be well within a classification, whereas another may exhibit only some of the characteristics. Each category has an impact on the scope and function of the front office.

▶*Size.*   The number of available rooms (the figure used to compute occupancy; see Exhibit 1–3) is the standard measure of size. Other possibilities (acres of land, number of employees, gross dollar sales, or net profits) are just not used. Of course, there's a relationship between the number of rooms and these other measures.

Although counting the number of available rooms seems to be a rather objective measure, there is uncertainty even here. Often, more rooms are advertised than are actually available for sale. Older hotels have rooms that are just not salable in modern times. Even newer properties lose guest-room inventory to permanent rentals, office space, and storage as unanticipated needs become evident. Generally, the older the hotel, the fewer the available rooms in relation to total rooms:

$$\frac{\text{Number of Guest Rooms Available for Sale}}{\text{Total Guest Rooms Originally Constructed}}$$

Hotels are grouped by size for purposes of study (including by the Bureau of the Census), for financial reporting and for membership dues. A quick and easy classification identifies hotels of over 300 rooms as large; hotels between 100 and 300 rooms as average; and those of less than 100 rooms as small. Recently, the AH&LA boosted its "small" category from 100 to 150 rooms, reporting less than 27% of its membership in that small category. The Small Business Administration (SBA) has defined "small" for hotels seeking government loans as businesses doing $3 million or less in annual receipts. (For comparison, consider an 80-room hotel with a 70% occupancy and an average room rate of $90. That would produce annual sales of $1,839,600 from just room sales; $80 \times .70 \times \$90 \times 365$ days/year.)

Visualizing such small properties as *the* lodging industry is difficult when one thinks of famous hotels such as the Waldorf-Astoria (1,852 rooms) or the New Otani in Tokyo (2,057 rooms); see Exhibit 1–6. More typical is the city of Atlanta. With 450 properties and approximately 67,000 rooms, it averages only 150 rooms per hotel. Small hotels are common wherever family rather than corporate ownership prevails. That's the case in Europe and Japan, where the shift to chain control has but recently started.

Mom-and-Pop Motels.   Attempts to distinguish hotels from motels and motor inns (motor hotels and motor lodges) by size were abandoned long ago.[5] Actually, no one cares, although there are scattered jurisdictions that still insist the distinction appear on exterior signs. Motels are autocentric, oriented to auto travel, with outside entrances that accommodate privacy and self-service. Lobby-entry hotels with interior corridors are less private but improve security.

Several factors account for the decline in the 60,000 family-owned-and-operated motels that were doing business in the 1960s. The costs of construction and the ability

---

[5]An early definition was offered by Howard E. Morgan, *The Motel Industry in the United States: Small Business in Transition* (Tucson, AZ: Bureau of Business and Public Research, University of Arizona, 1964).

Hotel	Number of Rooms[a]	Location
MGM Grand[c]	5,000	Las Vegas
Luxor[d]	4,475	Las Vegas
Excalibur[d]	4,025	Las Vegas
Bellagio[c]	3,775	Las Vegas
Circus Circus[d]	3,750	Las Vegas
Flamingo[b]	3,525	Las Vegas
Mandalay Bay[d]	3,300	Las Vegas
Mirage[c]	3,050	Las Vegas
Venetian	3,050	Las Vegas
Monte Carlo	3,025	Las Vegas
TI (Treasure Island)[c]	3,000	Las Vegas
Las Vegas Hilton[b]	2,950	Las Vegas
Paris[b]	2,925	Las Vegas
Opryland Hotel[e]	2,900	Nashville
Bally's[b]	2,825	Las Vegas
Aladdin	2,600	Las Vegas
Imperial Palace	2,600	Las Vegas
Hilton Hawaiian Village	2,550	Honolulu
Stardust	2,475	Las Vegas
Caesars Palace[b]	2,450	Las Vegas
New York, New York[c]	2,200	Las Vegas
Caribbean Beach	2,100	Orlando
Riviera	2,100	Las Vegas
New York Hilton	2,050	New York

[a]Figures rounded to 25 rooms
[b]Companies owned by Caesars Palace
[c]Companies owned by MGM Grand
[d]Companies owned by Mandalay Bay
[e]Gaylord Entertainment Co. is quietly dropping its Opryland Hotel name outside of Tennessee

Exhibit 1–6   The largest (over 2,000 rooms) hotels in the United States are concentrated in Las Vegas, evidencing the importance of casino gaming in the resort business. The Opryland Hotel bills itself as the largest U.S. hotel outside of Las Vegas.

to finance head a list of hurdles that the mom-and-pop establishments cannot overcome. They cannot purchase in quantity; they cannot advertise widely; they cannot budget management talent at the same level as larger competitors or chain/franchised properties can. The mom-and-pop survives in the same manner that other small businesses do. Guests receive the personal attention that is not possible with larger organizations. Labor costs are very low because the family babysits 24 hours per day, 7 days per week, 365 days per year, or 24/7/365.

►*Class.*   What makes a hotel first class? Or third class, for that matter? Often, "class" is just sensed; there is nothing measurable to quantify it. Two objective measures are used as indicators of class, but these are far from perfect. One approach uses the ADR; the other relies on rating systems.

Average Daily Rate (ADR).   The price that guests pay for a room is the best criterion of class. Delivering elegance and service costs money. Large rooms, costly construction, and expensive furnishings mean larger finance costs, depreciation, taxes, power usage, and so on. All of these are recovered by higher room rates. If towels are elegantly large and thick, the higher costs of purchase and laundering (by weight) are recovered by higher room rates. Similarly, a high level of maintenance, 24-hour room service, sauna baths, and other extras represent both a better class of hotel and higher room rates.

Average daily rate has been increasing (see Exhibit 1–4). But the increase does not necessarily measure greater service or elegance (that is, class) across the industry, or even at an individual property. A higher ADR is needed to recover increased operating costs (labor, energy, interest, etc.). Furthermore, properties in small towns have a different measure than their big-city cousins. A $50 rate in Los Angeles conjures up a totally different class of hotel than does the same $50 rate in a small rural town. However, at a given time and with a judicious concern for size, type, and location of the hotel, the ADR seems to be a fair measure of class. Published rates allow us to classify the nation's hotels (see Exhibit 1–7).

Full Service to Limited Service.   Hotel/motel facilities are as diverse as the traveling public. Handling this enormous range of guests has created a heterogeneous industry, from the plush, full-service high-rise to the squat, limited-service motel. On the one hand is a group of operator–investors who maintain that guests want nothing more than a room with a good mattress and a clean bath. Guests get along nicely without swimming pools, lobbies, or closets, according to this viewpoint. This hotelier offers limited service at a limited charge. There is such a market, of course, served by the $50 to $60 room rate of the budget motel.

One hundred and eighty degrees away is the full-service upscale hotel. Not only does this hotel include superior facilities, it also offers a full complement of services. Limited service means guest rooms only, with some vending machines or perhaps a nearby restaurant to service several competing properties. Full service adds a menu of dining options and a range of extras, including lounges, in-room newspapers, and specialties such as swimming pools, exercise facilities, and a wide range of telecommunications. Expense-account business executives patronize the full-service hotels, although something less costly may do nicely when they travel as family members.

Between the two extremes lies the bulk of the industry, adding services where competition requires and costs allow, paring them as market shifts and acceptable self-service equipment appear. In Chapters 2 and 3 we introduce these newer innovations to hotelkeeping. Among them is the all-suite hotel. Commercial and leisure guests alike have been attracted to all-suite accommodations such as Marriott's Residence Inns or Promus's Embassy Suites. By locating on less costly real estate and reducing the amount of public space, all-suites offer more guest room space at lower prices than at the luxury hotels. All-suites are closer to the limited-service hotel than to the full-service hotel.

Number of Employees.   *Full-service* and *limited-service* refer as much to the size of the staff as to the physical property or amenities offered. Thus, the number of employees per guest room

$$\frac{\text{Number of Employees on Staff}}{\text{Number of Rooms Available for Sale}}$$

becomes another measure of class (see Exhibit 1–3).

CLASSIFICATION OF HOTELS BY AVERAGE DAILY ROOM RATE

Deluxe Hotels (typical room rate: $600 plus/night)
Fairmont Hotels
Four Seasons Hotels
Ritz-Carlton Hotels

Upper Upscale Hotels (typical room rate: $400/night)
Le Meridien Hoels
Sofitel Hotels
W Hotels

Upscale Hotels (typical room rate: $300/night)
Hyatt Hotels
Marriott Hotels
Omni Hotels

Midprice Hotels with Food (typical room rate: $100/night)
Four Points (Sheraton)
Garden Inns (Hilton)
Best Western

Midprice Hotels without Food (typical room rate: $80/night)
Amerisuites
Hampton Inns
La Quinta

Economy Hotels (typical room rate: $60/night)
Baymont Inns and Suites
Red Roof Inns
Super 8

Budget Inns (typical room rate: $50/night)
EconoLodge
Microtel
Motel 6

Exhibit 1–7   Average daily rate can be used to categorize hotels, since room rate is one measure of class. The trade press often reports on these seven classifications.

Budget properties, which have no restaurants, no bars, no room service, and no convention space, score as low as 0.25 employees per guest room. An 80-room hotel might have as few as 20 persons on staff. There's a limit to how small the staff can shrink. Regardless of the number of rooms, the desk must be staffed every hour of the day and night. Round the clock coverage is a requirement under common law if the property holds itself out as a hotel. Workers need days off. There's housekeeping staff, perhaps laundry workers, a night security watch, someone for repairs and mainte-nance; all must be counted.

The size of the hotel matters only after that basic staffing guide is met. A hotel of 60 rooms may have almost as many workers as one twice its size. Housekeeping would be the big difference. If a housekeeper can clean 15 rooms per shift, three or four additional employees are needed to do the extra 60 rooms if occupancy is around, say, 80%. Other staff members at the desk, the manager, the housekeeper, maintenance and grounds, the accountant, and so on, might number almost the same for each property.

The in-between class of hotel uses an in-between number of employees. That ratio ranges from 0.5 (one-half) an employee per room to as much as a 1:1 ratio. Depending on the services offered, a 300-room hotel could have as few as 150 employees or as many as 250 or so. The number is most likely to be about 200 to 225 if there's food service and a bar that needs staffing.

Full-service hotels staff a full complement of departments, including bell service, restaurants, turn-down bed service, and telecommunications persons, among others. Hotels with theater shows, acres of grounds to be maintained, casinos, and 24-hour services require extra personnel and have still higher ratios, perhaps 1.5 employees per guest room. A 1,000-room hotel/casino operating fully over 24 hours could easily have 1,250 to 1,500 employees.

Asian properties offer the best in service. Labor is less costly, so the number of employees per room is the world's highest. At the Bangkok Shangri-La, for example, 1,073 staff members handle 697 rooms, a ratio of 1.5:1. Hong Kong's Peninsula Hotel ranks better still with a staff of 655 for its 300 rooms, better than 2:1.

Hotels provide job opportunities everywhere for low wage-scale employees. The 1.7 to 1.9 million U.S. hotel workers pales in comparison to the World Travel and Tourism Council's Prediction that 13% of European jobs (about 27,000,000 workers!) will be in the travel industry by 2008.

Rating Systems. Rating systems, formal and informal, government-run and privately developed, are also used to identify the class of hotel. Standardization is somewhat effective within each country but less so across boundaries, although most members of the World Tourism Organization have adopted the WTO's five recommended classifications. Top is deluxe (or luxury) class, then first class, which is not top-of-the-line despite its name, followed by tourist class, sometimes called economy or second class. Third and fourth classes, which usually have no private baths, centralized heat, or even carpeting, are not for international tourists.

Each country implements its own categories. Local inspectors tend to be quite subjective in their ratings. If there is a pool on the premises, it will meet standards whether or not it is clean. An elevator adds to the ratings whether or not it works. Government rating systems also fall prey to bribery, politics, and bickering within the trade association.

International travelers soon learn to limit stays in Africa or the Middle East to deluxe properties and to discount the deluxe category that many Caribbean properties give themselves. However, in Europe, first class is a perfectly acceptable level.

WORLDWIDE.   Worldwide there are almost 100 rating systems that range from the self-evaluation plan of Switzerland to the mandatory grading of South Africa. Some are tied to taxes and tax incentives. Many French and Italian hotels, for example, are intentionally underrated to save taxes.

Europe's four- and five-star hotels always have restaurants and bars; those with three stars may or may not. Two-star properties almost never do. *Garni* means that no restaurant is available, but a continental breakfast is usually served. In England, *hotel garni* is the U.S. version of bed and breakfast.

Stars are not used everywhere. Britain uses ticks for grading holiday parks (upscale caravan parks), and before the war there, Yugoslavia had an alphabetical system. Coffee pots and even feathers (Caribbean) have been used. The Irish Tourist Board lists facilities rather than a subjective ranking of quality. This approach—listing, not ranking accommodations—is consistent with all of the European Community. European directories identify which properties have elevators, air conditioning, laundries, and so on. They also classify by location: seaside/countryside; small town/large city. European auto associations add an extra by identifying privately owned versus government-run hotels.

The Swiss Hotel Association now uses five criteria instead of the single measure (price), which was its original category for classification. The Swiss system is unique because it is a private organization evaluating itself. Mexican hotels are also trade-association graded using the WTO's five classes, plus a luxury class, Gran Turismo or Gran Especial.

Spain has standardized the rating system of its *paradors* ("stopping places") despite the great differences in physical facilities and furnishings. The government-operated chain of nearly 100 inns maintains approximately one-third at the four-star level. All but a few of the remaining group are two- or three-star properties.

Japanese *ryokans,* which are traditional inns, are rated according to the excellence of their guest rooms, kitchens, baths, and—of all things to Western values—gardens. These very traditional hotels serve two meals, which are often taken in the uncluttered guest room that opens onto those gardens. There are an estimated 75,000 *ryokans,* of which about 1,000 have been registered by the Japanese Travel Bureau as appropriate for international guests.

Like Japan, Korea has fine, Western-style hotels at top international standards. It also has budget-priced lodgings called *yogwans* (or inns). Unlike the *ryokans,* most *yogwans* have Western-style accommodations, including private baths. Upscale *yogwans* can be identified because their names end in *jang* or *chang.*

The United Kingdom probably has the largest number of rating systems by the greatest range of organizations. Among them are the National Tourist Board (NTB), the Automobile Association (AA), the Royal Automobile Club (RAC), and commercial enterprises such as Egon Ronay and the better known Michelin. The ratings are by crowns (NTB) and stars (both the AA and the RAC) and pavilions or small buildings (Michelin). Each classification is then subdivided by grades or percentage marks. Thus the AA might rate a property as Four Star, 65%.

THE U.S. EXPERIENCE.   Unlike the United Kingdom, which uses both government and private rating systems, only private enterprise ranks U.S. hotels. Mobil and the American Automobile Association (AAA) are the major competitors, although Michelin, which is very popular in Europe, has U.S. guidebooks. Zagat concentrates on restaurant guides, and just recently on hotel classifications. J. D. Powers, famous for its ratings of other consumer experiences, has recently put toes into the rating waters, as have several Web sites. There are many other publications: bed-and-breakfast guides, geographic guides, magazine guides, even one by the NAACP, but their coverage is narrower. Individual hotel chains have internal rating systems that are by-products of their efforts to attract different market segments, but consumers may not recognize the distinction. For example, Choice Hotels International has Clarion Hotels, Resorts and Suites; Comfort Inns and Suites; Econo Lodges; Flag Inns; MainStay Suites; Quality Inns, Hotels and Suites; Rodeway Inns; and Sleep Inns.

Membership in Preferred Hotels, a loosely knit affiliation of independent hotels, requires ratings of superior or above from one of the recognized services. So just belonging to Preferred gives the property a superior-plus rating.

Mobil uses stars; AAA uses diamonds. *Mobil's Travel Guide* covers North America; the *AAA Tour Book* includes Mexico and the Caribbean. Both organizations are stingy with their five-level ratings, although each looks at some 25,000 properties annually. Mobil gives lower scores overall. Both companies field inspectors, who make onsite visits, often at the request of the hotel company. AAA inspectors identify themselves as they leave; Mobil's inspectors do not. Evaluations are based on written standards (see Exhibit 1–8), not consumer ballots, so some guests complain that what the rating systems require is not always what the customer wants.

Focus meetings between the AH&LA and the AAA have produced new rating procedures that include summary evaluations given to management. Mobil refuses to disclose why stars are added or removed. Still, it is reported that a top rating by the Mobil guide can boost business by 20%! Similarly, as much as 40% of small hotel volume may be attributed to the AAA guide. AAA includes information for travelers disabled by vision, hearing, mobility, and dexterity impairments. That's something the Scottish Tourist Bureau has done for some time, using three categories of accessibility.

Not all guides are consumer oriented. Several list conference and meeting facilities, an American specialty. Others are important to travel agents and meeting planners. Among the publications that focus on the trade are the *Official Meeting Facilities Guide* and the *Hotel & Travel Index*. The *Official Hotel Guide (OHG)*, whose ratings are favored by the cruise lines, uses subjective assessments of service as well as objecting listings of actual accommodations.

We may eventually see a new environmental rating. Research from the United States Travel Data Center indicates a willingness of guests to pay more for environmentally friendly lodgings (EFLs). EFL could be another criterion for, or a completely separate rating from, the usual standards.

▶*Type.*   Size, class, now type, and plan (discussed next) are the four traditional classifications describing the lodging industry. Type is subdivided into commercial hotels, resort hotels, and residential hotels. Like the distinctions between hotel and motel, all definitions within the lodging industry have begun to blur. Traditional designations do not always provide the best descriptions for a changing industry. They make no provision for new concepts such as conference centers or condominium hotels. A host of other new concepts has appeared in recent times, and they are classified in the emerging patterns of Chapter 2.

Commercial Hotels.   Commercial hotels (see Exhibit 1–9), also called transient hotels, make up the largest category of American hotels. They service short-term guests who are transient (temporary) and chiefly, but not exclusively, business travelers. Conventioneers, engineers, salespersons, consultants, and small businesspersons form the core of the customer base. Commercial guests are considered the backbone of the lodging industry. They are equally important to the urban property and the roadside motor hotel. The leisure market—for example, an overnight stay pre- or post-cruise, or tour-related occupancy—is an important element in the mix.

A true commercial hotel is located close to its market—the business community, which means an urban area. As the population center has left the downtown area, so has the commercial hotel. Arterial highways, research parks, business parks, airports,

Exhibit 1–8 List of criteria used in rating U.S. hotels, where rankings are usually made in diamonds and stars. Other symbols are used elsewhere. Unlike the privately owned systems of the United States, foreign rating systems are often government directed.

★ ★ ★ ★ ★

The key criteria for every rating are cleanliness, maintenance, quality of furnishings and physical appointments, service, and the degree of luxury offered. There are some regional differences, as customers have different expectations for a historic inn in northern New England, a dude ranch in the Southwest, and a hotel in the center of a major city.

★

One-star establishments should be clean and comfortable and worth the prices charged when compared to other accommodations in the area. If they are below average in price, they may receive a checkmark for good value in addition to the one star. They offer a minimum of services. There may not be 24-hour front desk or phone service; there may be no restaurant; the furniture will not be luxurious. Housekeeping and maintenance should be good; service should be courteous; but luxury will not be part of the package.

★ ★

Two-star accommodations have more to offer than one-star and will include some, but not necessarily all, of the following: better-quality furniture, larger bedrooms, restaurant on the premises, color TV in all rooms, direct-dial phones, room service, swimming pool. Luxury will usually be lacking, but cleanliness and comfort are essential.

★ ★ ★

Three-star motels and hotels include all of the facilities and services mentioned in the preceding paragraph. If some are lacking, and the place receives three stars, it means that some other amenities are truly outstanding. A three-star establishment should offer a very pleasant travel experience to every customer.

★ ★ ★ ★

Four-star and five-star hotels and motels make up a very small percentage (less than 2%) of the total number of places listed; therefore they all deserve the description of "oustanding." Bedrooms should be larger than average; furniture should be of high quality; all of the essential extra services should be offered; personnel should be well trained, courteous, and anxious to please. Because the standards of quality are high, prices will often be higher than average. A stay in a four-star hotel or motel should be memorable. No place will be awarded four or five stars if there is a pattern of complaints from customers, regardless of the luxury offered.

★ ★ ★ ★ ★

The few five-star awards go to those places which go beyond comfort and service to deserve the description "one of the best in the country." A superior restaurant is required, although it may not be rated as highly as the accommodations. Twice-daily maid service is standard in these establishments. Lobbies will be places of beauty, often furnished in antiques. If there are grounds surrounding the building, they will be meticulously groomed and landscaped. Each guest will be made to feel that he or she is a Very Important Person to the employees.

Exhibit 1–9   Urban hotels serve several markets, but chiefly business and convention guests. Location, location, location is critical to the commercial hotel. If not downtown—the illustration is New York City at 45th and Broadway; the hotel has 1,919 rooms—commercial hotels favor business parks or research centers. *Courtesy of New York Marriott Marquis, New York, New York.*

and even suburban shopping centers have become favorite locations. This helps explain the poor weekend occupancy (businesspersons are not working) of the urban hotel (see Exhibit 1–5). Attempts to offset this weekend decline with tourists, conventions, and special promotions have been only moderately successful.

Transient hotels are usually full-service hotels. Businesspersons are expense-account travelers who want (and can afford) four- and five-star accommodations. Lately, the travel offices of many businesses have begun to monitor travel costs more closely. Travel costs do affect a business's bottom line! Furthermore, Congress has enacted several restrictions on the amount that may be taken as tax-deductible meal costs (currently 50%).

From suite hotels to upgraded budgets, everyone is after business travelers, even though they are value shopping more diligently than ever before. Still, the commercial hotel remains the business center, catering to the various groups that have been enumerated, hosting trade shows, and serving as company training centers and meeting places.

Residential Hotels. In contrast to transient, commercial guests, residential guests take up permanent quarters. This creates a different legal relationship between the guest and the landlord, and may be formalized with a lease. In some locales, the room occupancy tax is not payable for a residential guest in a transient hotel.

Some residential hotels accommodate transient guests, and many transient hotels have permanent guests, with and without leases. The Waldorf-Astoria (New York City) is a good example of this combination: its Towers house permanent, often famous guests. About two-thirds of all U.S. hotels reported both transient and permanent guests in the last census.

Almost 10% of New York City's 63,000 hotel rooms are occupied by permanent guests. The Big Apple is one of several cities that still has rent control or rent stabilization. Many of these residential guests pay less than $20/day (New York's ADR is over $200) because they moved in during the 1940s and 1950s. In contrast, a company that licenses the Ritz-Carlton's name offers luxurious residential accommodations, The Residences at The Ritz-Carlton, atop its New York, Boston, and Washington properties.

Extended-Stay Hotels. Extended-stay facilities offer more than a mere hotel room but are not the same genre as residential hotels, which connote permanency. Extended stay merely means long term.

Extensive travel and suitcase living quickly lose their glamour. Something different is needed for those persons moving locations or having extended business assignments away from homes and home offices. Keeping workers comfortable and productive takes more than a traditional hotel room. Extended-stay hotels provide kitchens, grocery outlets, office space, office equipment, fireplaces, exercise rooms, laundry facilities, and more—even secretarial support—but all with maid service.

The extended-stay hotel goes all out to make the stay-away as comfortable as possible. The all-suite hotel had its origin in this segment of the travel market. The all-suite/extended-stay distinction is blurred today because the same building caters to the long-term business traveler and to the other market segments (families, in-room meetings, interviews) to which the all-suite appeals.

Resort Hotels. Transient hotels cater to commercial guests, residential hotels to permanent guests, and resort hotels to social guests—at least traditionally they do (see Exhibit 1–10).

Economics has forced resorts to lengthen their operating period from the traditional summer or winter season to year-round operations. Resorts have marketed to the group and convention delegate at the expense of their social guest. As this began happening, the commercial hotel shifted its design and markets toward the resort concept, dulling once again the distinctions between types. What emerged is a mixed-use resort. Sometimes these resorts are found in residential areas as part of a master-planned community.

Many believe that the modified resort is the hotel of the future. It is in keeping with the nation's move toward increased recreation and compatible with the casual air that characterizes the vacationer. Unlike the formality of the vacationer of an earlier time, today's guest is a participant. Skiing, golfing, boating, and a host of other activities are at the core of the successful resort.

THE MEGARESORT. Megaresorts are large, self-contained resorts. Entertainment and recreational facilities are so numerous and varied that guests need not leave the property during their entire stay. Every facility is offered under one roof. Size distinguishes the megaresort from other self-contained properties, such as the Sandals' resorts of the Caribbean. Indeed, cruise ships can be seen as a special type of megaresort.

Exhibit 1–10   Resorts have expanded their markets beyond the "social guests" that persisted through the middle of the 20th century. Amenities, including executive conference centers, spas, tennis clubs, marinas, and more—even a private island—appeal to groups as well as to leisure guests. *Courtesy of the Sagamore, Bolton Landing, New York.*

Although megaresorts are a feature of Las Vegas (see Exhibit 1–6), they are not limited to that location. The 900-room Marriott Desert Springs and Spa near Palm Springs, California, and Hilton's Hawaiian Village on Oahu (over 2,500 rooms) also represent this genre.

Single-feature, specialty resorts have also proven quiet successful. They appeared even earlier than the hotel industry's general move toward segmentation. Tennis clubs (all types of sports clubs), spas, and health resorts ("diet farms") have opened and flourished (see Exhibit 1–11). Club Meditérranée became the prototype of a new style of resort: one that features an all-inclusive price, with tips included.

America's changing demographics (age distribution) is certain to impact the type and variety of resort hotels. The wealthy baby-boom generation is moving toward retirement, and its children, generation X (or echo boomers), are reaching economic maturity. Condominium resorts are a favorite of the parents; all-inclusive resorts are a favorite of the offspring. In every case, weather and location play key roles. Geography is to the resort as commerce is to the transient hotel and population is to the residential property.

►*Plan.*   Room rates are based, in part, on the plan being offered. The plan identifies which meals, if any, are included in the rate. Obviously, rates are higher when meals are included. Classification by plan offers more certainty than the other

SPECIALTY HOTELS THAT FIT NO GENERAL CATEGORY

COUPLES ONLY
  Gay Groups
  Honeymoon Resorts
  Singles

DUDE RANCHES

ECO-LODGES
  Safari Lodges
  Wilderness Lodges

FLOATING HOTELS
  House Boats

GRAND DAMES
  Great ladies with years of reputation

HISTORICALLY LISTED AND PROTECTED
  National Trust

ICE HOTELS (Iceland)

KOSHER HOTELS
  Jewish Diet
  Muslim Diet

LUXURY CAMPING

NATIVE AMERICAN

NUDIST COLONIES (CAMPS)

YURTS (Tent Hotels)

UNDERWATER HOTELS

Exhibit 1–11   In searching for speciality market niches, hoteliers have created unique facilities that do not fall within the lodging industry's traditional classifications.

three classifications of size, class, or type. Either meals are included, or they are not. With few exceptions, hotels in the United States operate on the European plan: no meals.

European Plan.   Rates quoted as European plan (EP) include room accommodations only. Meals taken in the dining room are charged at menu prices. Evidence of the widespread use of the European plan is its lack of designation. Guests are not told, "This is the European plan"; it is assumed unless otherwise stated.

CONTINENTAL PLAN (CONTINENTAL BREAKFAST).   More than any other meal, traveler's eat breakfast in the hotel. European hotels often include a limited breakfast with the European plan. This continental breakfast (mainland Europe being the continent), which consists of coffee or hot chocolate, a roll, and a bit of cheese (cold meat or fish in Holland and Norway), is on the wane in Europe even as it gets a boost in North America. All-suite hotels have gained popularity by including free breakfasts as part of their marketing approach. It is a revival of America's view of the continental plan, which took form in the no-restaurant format of the 1950s motel. In-room coffee makers, coffee in the lobby, or coffee and sweet rolls in the small proprietor's kitchen were all touted as continental breakfast.

Continental breakfast still has other meanings. A coffee urn with sweet rolls and juice left in the lobby when the dining room closes is often called a continental breakfast. A similar setup at a group registration desk or at the rear of a meeting room during a speaker's talk appears on the program as continental breakfast. Juice is included in the United States or when the delegates are Americans, but it is not usually served elsewhere.

In some parts of the world, this abbreviated breakfast is called a bed-breakfast. That should not be confused with the Bermuda plan, which includes a full breakfast in the rate. A very hearty breakfast called an English breakfast is served in Ireland and the United Kingdom. It includes cereal, eggs with a choice of meat, toast with butter and jam, tea and coffee, but no juice. However, unlike the Bermuda plan, it is rarely included in the room rate quote.

Café complet, a midmorning or afternoon coffee snack, is mistakenly called a continental breakfast. The distinction is neither the time of day nor the menu items, but the manner of payment. *Café complet* is not included in the room rate.

The appearance of late afternoon tea as a pleasant supplement to the overworked happy hour is certain to bring further confusion in terminology. Many top U.S. hotels and cruise lines have latched onto that quintessential British ritual, afternoon tea. Delicate sandwiches and small sweets served with tea, or even sherry, comprise this light snack. It is not to be confused with high tea, which is a supper, a substantial meal almost always served with meat. High tea is a rarity today, even in British hotels.

American Plan.   Rates quoted under the American plan (AP) include room and all three meals: breakfast, luncheon, and dinner. The American plan, which is occasionally called *bed and board,* had its origin in colonial America, when all guests ate at a common table with the host's family. The plan was still in use when the affluent resorts of the Northeast began operating in the late 1800s. They adopted and held onto the plan until World War II.

New England's resorts retained the American plan for the same reason that the colonial innkeeper offered it in the first place. Both were isolated, so there was no place else to eat. Better roads and better cars gave guests the mobility that spelled the end of the plan.

Europe's full *pension* (pen'-si-own) is almost equivalent to the American plan. Breakfast is the big difference. Full *pension* includes an abbreviated continental breakfast, not the complete breakfast of the American plan. To market the American plan to international guests, European hotels rely on the more descriptive "inclusive terms." The *pension* of Europe is the guest house or boardinghouse of Britain and the United States, with residential hotels in Europe using the term *en pension. Pensiones* are usually longer-stay facilities with limited services, so guests become members of an extended family.

ADAPTATIONS OF THE AMERICAN PLAN.   Many guests see the American plan in a negative way. They believe it is too restrictive because they must be at the hotel for meals at a given hour, and because it is too costly. Everyone pays the same price regardless of what is eaten. Good market managers rarely use the term American plan, although the option is used more frequently than supposed. Cruise ships provide American-plan dining, but they don't use that terminology.

Neither do all-inclusive resorts. Although the all-inclusive is not as popular in the United States as it is in the Caribbean, it is still marketed as an *all-inclusive* rate. Of course, drinks, activities, and even tips are then included as well as American plan meals.

A *dine-around* plan is another variation. Hotels offering the American plan (regardless of what it is called) allow guests to dine at other hotels in the vicinity. Sometimes the "other" hotels are members of the same chain, and sometimes there is a cooperative consortium of competing properties that understand the marketing value of the option.

Conference centers operate the American plan almost exclusively, but they call it by another name: CMP, complete meeting package. Room rate includes room, meals, coffee breaks, meeting setups, and gratuities—similar to the ship-board cruise or the Caribbean all-inclusive plan. Of the rate quoted, 60% might be attributed to rooms, 33% to food and beverage, and the remaining 7% to meeting rooms and audio-visual facilities. But that is an internal decision, not necessarily communicated to the guest.

MODIFIED AMERICAN PLAN.   The modified American plan (MAP) is an astute compromise offered by some hotels, including those running a full American plan. The hotel retains some of the AP advantages, and the guest feels less restricted. Guests get breakfast and dinner as part of the room rate quote, but not luncheon. This opens the middle of the day for a flexible schedule of activities. Guests need not return for an inconveniently scheduled luncheon nor suffer the cost of a missed meal. The hotel retains the obvious benefits of a captive market for the dinner hour. In an effort to make the difference clear, some APs are now called FAP—full American plan.

Half-pension or *demi-pension* (DP) is the European equivalent of the MAP. It includes breakfast and one other meal along with the lodgings. Granting either luncheon or dinner gives the foreign guest the same flexibility of scheduling offered with the modified American plan.

▶*Variations on the Themes.*   The hotel business is a dynamic industry run by clever hoteliers who innovate by modifying the standard into something different even as the basic industry remains unchanged (see Exhibit 1–11).

Bed and Breakfast (B&B).   Bed and breakfast surged onto the American scene so strongly that one might think it a whole new concept in hotelkeeping. It's hardly that. Bed and breakfast in the United States takes its cue from the British B&B, the Italian *pensiones*, and the German *zimmer frei* (room available)—lodging and breakfast offered by families in their own homes. The Japanese B&B is *minshuku*.

B&B is a modern version of the 1930s roominghouse, once called the tourist home. The bed and breakfast was reborn for much the same reasons as its Depression-era predecessor—the landlord's need to supplement income and the lodger's hunt for less costly accommodations. For some innkeepers, it is an adventure, and for others, a hobby. The acceptability of the B&B gets a boost from the experience of a generation of owner–renters sharing living accommodations and time-share facilities.

Under the plan, guests take rooms with private families, who often furnish camaraderie along with the mandatory breakfast. The lack of privacy—shared bath, conversation at breakfast—forces the host and guest into a level of intimacy that brings new friendships along with the business relationship.

Like the rest of the industry, change is part of the B&B's vocabulary, and no one definition fits all the parts. There are many subcategories because the business is very individualized and localized. The B&B changes identity as it moves across the country. The B&B Inn, for example, is a product of California. It is a large version (over half the B&Bs in the United States are 8 rooms or less) and is usually the owner's primary occupation. Another subcategory, the Country B&B, is an upscale boardinghouse because it serves all meals, not just breakfast. Country B&Bs have their origin in New England. Between the coasts are a variety of facilities serving their local markets (see Exhibit 1–12). Like other small businesses, B&Bs often lack staying power. Results can be ruinous where zoning laws prohibit even a "rooms-for-let" notice in the window. One positive sign is the new Yellow Pages listing of B&B referral organizations under "B&B" rather than under their previous category of "hotels, motels, and tourist homes."

In one way, B&Bs are no different from other American hotels. They fight for business and rely on themselves for referrals. In Europe and Japan, government tourist agencies make B&B referrals and even rate them by price and accommodations. The French call them *café-couette* (coffee and quilt), and their rating system uses three to six coffee pots instead of stars. Since the U.S. government has never entered the tourist-rating business, several private rating and referral systems have emerged. Like the B&Bs themselves, these rating/referral systems come and go quickly, for they too lack staying power.

Boutique Hotels. Boutique hotels are a unique species that have their origin in very small inns (20 to 40 rooms, perhaps) but with all the amenities of a fine hotel without the size and bustle: sort of a grown-up B&B. Although they have become much larger now, they are still very fashionable, meaning they are found in good urban locations, in the "in places" of London, San Francisco, and New York, all of which necessitates higher room rates. At one time, they were called *urban inns,* or *European-style hotels,* or in Britain, *baby grand hotels.*

The very nature of the boutique hotel—that it is something different—precludes a single definition. The term has been attributed to Steve Rubell, one of the founders of New York City's Studio 54, but the concept predated him. Asked for a description of

Exhibit 1–12   Bed and breakfasts (B&B) operate under a variety of names. *B&B inns* are popular on the west coast; *Country B&Bs* are popular in New England. In between are many wonderful stopping places with award-winning breakfasts and distinctive guest rooms. *Courtesy of The Inn at 410, Flagstaff, Arizona.*

his hotel, The Morgans, Rubell said that other hotels were large department stores, but Morgans is a small boutique. Other definitions hold that a boutique hotel is simply "cool" or "hip" or "chic." The term depends on one's age, because each room and each hotel is different. Boutiques suggest something different, very eclectic, always with flair, funky, artsy (see Exhibit 1–13).

Ian Schrager, Rubell's partner, began developing the boutique in New York City. The concept spread rapidly, with Starwood Hotels introducing the W (for warm, welcoming, and witty) Hotels and Marriott redeveloping its Renaissance Chain with a face-lift into the unexpected. The brand hotel chains have entered the fray because boutique hotels have had higher RevPar and occupancy figures (lower break-evens) than their more traditional cousins. The question remains whether a branded chain can deliver the unexpected and the quirky, which are the hallmarks of a boutique. Can a hotel be both mainstream and boutique? Can hotels larger than 100 to 150 rooms with banquet and meeting space maintain the connection that boutiques develop between guests and staff? (W Hotel's flagship is the New York W with 722 rooms.) Perhaps there is a second-generation boutique hotel coming, one with both style and substance. Meredian Hotels use the term *Art and Tech:* hotels that can be provocative and still provide the basics.

Exhibit 1–13   Boutique hotels, which started as a fad, have become a distinct segment of the American hotel market. They achieved this by breaking the stereotype of the chain property. This California example well represents the genre. *Courtesy of the Georgian Hotel, Santa Monica, California.*

Trophy Hotels.   Trophy hotels are those hotels that add to the owner's reputation, similar to a trophy on the shelf. Many *grande dames*[6] of the hotel business have such wonderful reputations and historical lineage that hoteliers acquire them just to claim ownership. Some are profitable, ongoing properties, such as Denver's Brown Palace. But many trophy hotels struggle during economic dips, although they may be profitable during up-cycles. Listing these unique buildings in the National Register of Historic Places provides some helpful tax relief if the hotel is a historical site or if the boutique hotel results from a historical conversion, as it sometimes does.

RESOURCES AND CHALLENGES
Resources

➤ SUMMARY

The lodging industry continues to play an important role in the development of commerce and culture even as it undergoes rapid changes. Despite the introduction of many new lodging types, the industry retains its traditional measures of success: occupancy (%), average daily rate (ADR), and revenue per available room (RevPar).

To maximize the values of these measures, management must overcome several limitations that are inherent in the hotel business. These include a highly perishable product, an unmovable location, a fixed supply of inventory, a high break-even point, and seasonal operating periods. In addition, hotel-keeping is a cyclical industry, with long up and down waves that sometimes last a decade: tough hurdles all.

Understanding the industry's traditional identifications (size, class, type, and plan) helps in identifying the new permutations (all-suite, B&B, boutique) that keep the industry economically sound and exciting as a career. Competition sharpens the new direction, and rating systems keep the individual hotel attuned. As the changes continue, new classifications and new categories are needed. Those identities are provided in Chapter 2.

➤ WEB SITES

American Hotel & Lodging Association (AH& LA).–Lodging industry's chief trade association: http://www.ahla.com and its information site, http://www.ahla.com/infocenter/lip_02.htm

U.S. Census.–Counts the nation's lodging establishments: http://www.census.gov

R. K. Miller & Associates.–Provides lodging industry research: http://www.rkmillerinc.com

Smith Travel Research.–Provides lodging industry research: http://www.smithtravel.com

Realtime Hotel Reports.–Provides lodging industry research: http://www.hotelreports.com

Web Site Assignment

Using references cited in the Web site (or elsewhere), update the chapter's information for the current year. Provide values for the United States for the number of hotels, the number of rooms, the percentage of occupancy, the average daily rate, and the revenue per available room. Cite your source.

[6]*Grande dames* is French for ladies of aristocratic bearing—hence elegant, grand hotels.

➤ INTERESTING TIDBITS

➤ The AH&LA, American Hotel & Lodging Association—always use the ampersand, (&), not the word *and*—is not a membership organization in the true sense of the word. It is an affiliation of 50 state and two city hotel associations (New York and Washington, DC). Individual hotel properties are members of the state associations, and the state associations are members of the AH&LA. Hotel companies such as Hilton cannot be members; only the individual properties of the company can belong, affiliated through their state memberships. Nevertheless, the AH&LA reports that some

1.7 million hotel rooms in 13,000 hotels hold membership.

➤ The Burj al-Arab Hotel in Dubai, United Arab Emirates, is reported to be the tallest hotel in the world. It is higher than Paris's Eiffel Tower and just 200 feet short of New York City's Empire State Building. Some suites sell for $20,000 per night. Tallest in the United States is Westin's Peachtree Hotel in Atlanta, Georgia.

➤ *House* is often used professionally as a substitute for *hotel,* as in; "Is the house full tonight?"

➤ READING REFERENCE

The Boutique Hotel. Susan Abramsom & Marcie Stuchin. Weimar, TX: Culinary and Hospitality Industry Publications Service, 2001. Describes how the design of the boutique hotel fits into urban areas.

"High Five." *USA Today,* May 5, 2000, p. 1D. Describes what it takes for a *grande dame,* a great, old hotel, to earn a 5-diamond/5-star rating.

Challenges

➤ TRUE/FALSE

Questions that are partially false should be marked false (F).

___ 1. "Hotels fill from the bottom up" is a professional saying that means guests prefer rooms on lower floors—where fire ladders can reach—over rooms on higher floors.

___ 2. A publicity release from Dallas, Texas, stated there were 1,400 staff members in a new 1,844-room convention property. That seems about right.

___ 3. As a member of the United Nations, the United States adheres to the hotel rating system adopted by the World Tourism Organization.

___ 4. Although there are exceptions, American hotels generally operate on the American plan and European hotels, on the European plan.

___ 5. Transient hotels cater chiefly to business travelers, and that's why the term *commercial hotel* is also used.

➤ PROBLEMS

1. A natural disaster such as an earthquake or man-made disaster like the attack on the World Trade Center has an immediate effect on hotel occupancy. Explain step by step how you would estimate the loss in room income to New York City's hotels

when approached by the news media. (*Hint:* New York City has an estimated 63,000 rooms. Use figures and values from Chapter 1 and/or make assumptions; assumptions should be identified.)

2. Create a checklist with two dozen objective listings that could be used by an evaluator inspecting guest rooms for a national rating system.

3. Explain where the hotel industry is in its economic cycle. Be specific. Is it at the bottom of the trough? The highest point of its rise? Somewhere in between? If so, moving in what direction? Submit evidence to support your position.

4. Give three to five examples of each type of expense that is used to determine the cost portion of a hotel's break-even point: fixed expenses; semifixed expenses; variable expenses.

5. How many rooms does the MGM Grand Hotel need to sell annually if it budgets operations on an annual occupancy of 82%? (*Hint:* See Exhibit 1–6.)

6. Using information contained in Chapter 1, justify or challenge the statement of Andrew Young, the former mayor of Atlanta, who said that a 1% rise in room occupancy creates 400 new jobs for that city. (*Hint:* You will need to know the approximate number of rooms in the city and an estimate of the staff-to-room ratio.)

➤ ANSWERS TO TRUE/FALSE QUIZ

1. False. It means that guests buy the least expensive rooms when they are available, when occupancy is low.

2. True. 1,844 rooms ÷ 1,400 employees = 1.3 employees per room; within range for a convention hotel.

3. False. U.S. hotels are rated by private, not governmental, agencies.

4. False. Most hotels worldwide, including the United States, operate on the European plan.

5. True. Business hotels, commercial hotels, and transient hotels reference the same type of hotel: that oriented toward the business traveler.

The Modern Hotel Industry

Outline

Chapter 1 explained the origins of the lodging industry. It is to the credit of that industry that the traditional structures of Chapter 1 no longer suffice. Changes in society, travel, and business have been matched by new developments in lodging. At one time, hotels served primarily as the storage arm of transportation: locating along travelers's routes, waiting for potential guests to tire and to rest. Today's guests find an array of routes to a variety of destinations for a range of purposes. The hotel industry has had to re-create itself again and again to meet these modern demands. New patterns have appeared, and this chapters examines four of them: product, market, ownership, and management.

➤ NEW PRODUCT PATTERNS

At first inspection, the ups and downs of the business cycle (see Chapter 1) seem to impact negatively on the hotel business. That's certainly true for many hotels caught in the downward draft. But it is less so for the overall industry. Forced from complacency by falling occupancies, astute innkeepers invent new products to rekindle the demands of a fickle public. Business is sustained by a variety of new subparts. No longer does one size fit all. At first, this process was called *brand stretching*; later, *segmentation*.[1] To counter falling occupancies, upscale hotels moved vertically downward (stretched their brands) into midscale operations. Marriott introduced Fairfield Inns, for example. Midscale chains moved both ways. Choice Hotels stepped up with its Clarion brand and down with its Sleep Inns (see Exhibit 2–1).

Other chains segmented horizontally. Holiday Inn Hotels launched a new brand, Crowne Plaza, moving from traditional highway locations to compete in urban markets against the likes of Sheraton and Hyatt. Commercial chains even entered the resort business. Some of these changes brought new products to market; others merely put new faces onto older properties whose logos were no longer an asset.

The momentum accelerated, and the entire industry began offering new variations as a means of servicing specific guest needs and meeting marketplace demands. Segmentation is only the latest adaptation from an industry that responds to new conditions with dynamic innovations. Lodging has changed from small, family-owned businesses located along the byways and highways of colonial America into the 21st-century hotel with its variety of sizes, ownership patterns, locations, structures, and activities (see Exhibit 2–2).

Segmentation, Brand, and Image

Segmenting the industry has caused a good deal of confusion for both industry executives and hotel customers. The issue has been muddled by the creation of many new lodging designs and many new name brands. Unfortunately, putting a collection of similar hotels—or even worse, dissimilar hotels—under one name does not automatically create a brand. Customer recognition is what defines the brand. Hotel companies pour advertising dollars into creating that brand recognition. Brands are identified by their names and logos. Most hotel chains have several brands, some of which have been created and many of which have been acquired. There's no advantage to multiple

---

[1] The lodging industry uses *segmentation* to mean product differentiation; that is, different products. The word has an almost opposite meaning in general marketing terminology: developing a product for just one market segment.

BRAND NAMES				
Company Name	*Low End*	*Midscale*	*Upscale*	*Suites*
Choice Hotels International	Comfort Inn Econo Lodge Rodeway Inn Sleep Inn	Quality	Clarion	Comfort Suites MainStay Suites Sleep Inn Suites
Marriott International	Fairfield Inn	Courtyard Residence Inn	Marriott Hotels Ramada International Renaissance Ritz-Carlton	ExecuStay Marriott Suites Renaissance Suites SpringHill Suites TownePlace Suites
Six Continents[a]	Holiday Inn Express	Holiday Inn Posthouse	Crowne Plaza Inter-Continental	Staybridge Suites

[a]Formerly Bass Hotels and Resorts
Note: Read horizontally, not vertically, because brand comparison is valid only for other brands within the same chain. It is not intended for comparisons between companies. Choice's midscale brand, for example, is not equated to Marriott's midscale brand. (The list is incomplete.)

Exhibit 2–1   Hotel brands have been stretched in every direction as each hotel company searches for additional business segments. Cutting the market so thin confuses the buying public, which cannot track the numerous hotel names (see also Exhibits 2–7 and 2–13) and their differently named frequent-guest programs.

brands unless the company can sell the customer on the differences and values among the brands.

▶ ***Brand Equity.***   *Brand equity* is the value inherent in the shopper's recognition of the hotel brand. There is equity (value) in the brand only if that recognition carries a positive image. The guest may recognize a hotel logo but have a negative feeling about the brand. There is no brand equity if guests know the brand but will not stay. (In the United States, the Travelodge name is a good example of brand recognition with weak brand equity.) Equity develops when hoteliers identify promising segments of the lodging industry, promote their brands within those segments, and deliver an image that appeals to the marketplace. Basic to developing brand equity from mere brand recognition are four criteria: instant identification (the Marriott name comes immediately to mind); broad distribution (Holiday Inn Hotels is the best example); consistent quality (Hampton Inns has achieved that reputation); and level of service (Four Seasons tops the list).

Price (rate) is the offset to brand equity. With so many choices, guest loyalty often depends on nothing more than the rate quoted. Hotel rooms have become a commodity, much like wheat or oil. Brand managers fight an uphill battle as Web sites such as Priceline.com focus the buyer's attention on price, not brand.

A Segmented Industry	
Segmented by Activity	**Segmented by Plan**
Casino hotel	American plan
Convention hotel	Continental plan
Dude ranch	European plan
Segmented by Financing	**Segmented by Price (ADR)**
Public corporation	Deluxe (Above $100)
Private individual	Midrange ($50–$90)
REIT	Budget ($35–$50)
Segmented by Location	**Segmented by Ratings**
Airport	Five-star
Highway	Four-star
Seaside	Three-star
Segmented by Management	**Segmented by Service**
Chain	Full service
Management company	Moderate service
Self-managed	Self-service
Segmented by Markets	**Segmented by Structure**
Business	High rise
Groups	Low rise
Leisure	Outside corridor
Segmented Miscellaneously	**Segmented by Type**
Collar	Commercial
Hostel	Residential
Mixed-use	Resort
Segmented by Ownership	**Segmented by Use**
Chain	Bed and breakfast
Condominium	Extended-stay
Mom-and-pop	Health spa

New Product Segments

In many cases, segmentation merely adds new faces to older properties whose logos
no longer have equity, although they often retain brand recognition. Other efforts are
more dramatic, putting entirely new products onto the market. Among the new,
broader categories are economy (budget, or limited-service) hotels, all-suite hotels,
and a variety of new developments in casinos, spas, and conference centers. This chapter visits each.

▶*Economy (Budget, or Limited-Service) Hotels.*   The original budget hotels were motor courts (1930s), very limited roadside facilities with no services (see
Exhibit 2–3). Then came Kemmons Wilson's Holiday Inn Hotels. He founded this
chain as clean, no-frill accommodations. Existing motor-court operators saw the inns
differently; saw them as *amenity creep.*

Amenities and Amenity Creep.   The history of lodging's budget segment is the
story of amenity creep. An amenity is a special extra that a hotel provides in an effort

Exhibit 2–3   Tourist courts predated the highway hotel/motel that originated (1952) with Kemmons Wilson's Holiday Inn chain, now operated by Six Continents PLC (formerly Bass PLC) of the United Kingdom (see also Exhibit 2–11).

to distinguish itself from competitors. After a time, guests expect the amenity. No longer do they view the extra product or service as anything special. Other hotel chains are then forced to provide as standard service what the industry previously viewed as something special. So the old amenity creeps into standard service, and a new round of amenities is forced upon the industry.

Little by little, small rooms grew larger. Direct-dial telephones were installed where there had been none. Free television replaced coin-operated sets; then remote controls were added. Expensive but infrequently used swimming pools were everywhere. Air-conditioning, in-room coffeemakers, and two wash basins to the room became standard. Guest rooms supplies such as three varieties of soap, combs, and lotions joined the rush of extras. Estimates place the cost of these toiletries at over $10 per room per night.

Each upgrade pushed room rates higher. Hotel companies that started in the economy segment (Holiday Inn, Ramada) found themselves in the midrange. Undoubtedly, personal egos played a role in upgrading the chains. So did the introduction of franchising. Franchise fees are based on room revenues. As amenity creep pushes up room revenues, franchise fees to the parent company also increase.

How Budgets Compete.   As room rates inch upward, new chains fill the void at the lower end. (Some date the start of this rotation from 1964, when Motel 6 entered the market. By 1999, Motel 6—now owned by Accor—had interior corridors, improved heating and air-conditioning, and upgraded baths. Amenity creep had set in.) New budget entries forego some amenities, but many amenities (telephone, remote television, acceptance of credit cards—even breakfasts and frequent-stay programs) are now seen as basic services. Today's budgets are competing with fewer bathroom amenities, better values in construction, and attention to operations and management.

Newer and newer rounds of economy chains employ newer and newer techniques. Rooms smaller than the standard 300 to 325 square feet are being offered now. (Microtel rooms are 178 square feet.) The chains are selecting less costly land, and they are building on smaller sites, 1.5 acres or less for 100 rooms. Nonbasic amenities such as pools, lobbies, meeting space, and restaurants have been eliminated once again. (Providing free continental breakfasts is actually less costly than operating a restaurant that loses money. Besides, budget hotels/motels are almost always located near outlets of national restaurant chains, with one restaurant often serving several competitors.)

The latest round of budget hotels/motels has focused on savings in design and construction. Economy is coming from standardized architectural plans and from using a limited number of qualified builders. Structures have low ceilings and improved insulation. Costs of initial construction have been reduced, and so have later operating expenses.

Some budgets employ fewer than 20 employees per 100 rooms, almost 60% less than the traditional figures suggested in Chapter 1. Eliminating the dining room is just one technique for reducing labor. Hanging guest room furniture and providing a shower but not a tub increase the productivity of the housekeeping department. Automating telephone calls and assigning extra duties (including laundry operations) to the night clerk improve productivity on that side of the house.

Planned savings like these require new, well-designed facilities. And these were built—and succeeded—during and despite the economic dips that began the decades of both the 1990s and the 2000s. Because it takes about 250 properties to ensure market identification, some emerging chains acquired old mom-and-pop operations at fire-sale prices in order to quickly establish themselves as viable budget operators. Days Inns was chief among them.

Hard Budgets.   The economy group has been lodging's fastest growing segment during the past two decades. It outperformed the other segments during both the down cycles and the upswings. Generalizations about budget hotels are hard to sustain because, like the whole of the lodging industry, they lack a single identity. They themselves are divided.

The entire low-end segment is called economy, budget, limited-service, or simply low-end. All are euphemisms for inexpensive. Adding confusion is a jumble of names and affiliations. There are upscale budgets—what an oxymoronic term—(La Quinta, for example), intermediate budgets (Red Roof Inns, for example), and low-end budgets (Super 8 Motels, for example). At one time it was thought that Microtel, a chain of low-end budget hotels, might become the generic name for all budgets. The term would be used in lowercase letters, *microtel.*

Hard budget, including capsule rooms and truck-stop accommodations, is a fourth category of economy hotels. Hard budgets are located at airports and at the hundreds of truck stops that dot the interstate highways. Airports in Los Angeles and Honolulu offer rooms of 75 square feet (25 to 30% of a normal-sized room) for rest, showers, and stopovers between flights. Interestingly, France has a large number of hard budgets, reflecting perhaps its high payroll taxes and the need to minimize labor use.

Capsule rooms, which are somewhat like railroad sleeping berths, are smaller still, some as small as 5 feet by 5 feet, with headroom only to sit. Capsule rooms were an innovation of the Japanese. Although larger in dimension, self-service hotels—get your own linens and make your own beds—also fall into the hard budget category. Rooms are cleaned only between guests, and no other services are offered.

▶**All-Suite Hotels.**   Each segment of the industry offers something unique. Boutique hotels, discussed in Chapter 1, emphasize soft attributes (fashion and spas) over hard values (room size and meeting space). Budget hotels offer rooms at half price. Two rooms for the price of one is the all-suite appeal. Although all-suites no longer emphasize the original concept of an extended-stay or suite hotel, the basic market appeal, two for one, remains. All-suite investors find their own appeal: inexpensive construction, easier financing, higher weekend occupancy, and good profits.

Suite hotels were the brainchild of Robert Wooley, who created the first chain, Granada Royale Hometel. The idea was born in Phoenix in 1969, but it grew up in the years of the Texas oil boom. Extended-stay facilities were important to the transient oil economy. The idea was innovative—some say the best in a generation—but it borrowed from the traditional: the apartment hotel and the residential hotel.

The all-suite concept flourished after Holiday Inn acquired the Hometel brand. Holiday became the nation's largest all-suite chain, with two brands, Embassy Suites and Residence Inn. Embassy Suites, which was and is top-of-the-line, was spun off from Holiday Inn to Promus (1990) when the Holiday Inn Corporation was broken apart. (Hilton bought Promus in 1999, acquiring Embassy Suites as part of the deal.) Residence Inn was sold in 1987 to Marriott when Holiday Inn was in need of cash. Holiday Inn (now part of Six Continents PLC, which changed its name from Bass PLC) recently reentered the all-suite market with its Staybridge brand.

All-suites brought attractive returns to investors, who flocked to the segment with new names, new operators, and new products. Some companies both franchised and operated the new brands; some only operated; and some only franchised. All tried to broaden their brands. Choice Hotels cut back but still has three brands: Comfort Suites, MainStay Suites, and Sleep Inn Suites. Marriott has gone the other way, adding to its two brands: Marriott Suites, which are transient accommodations; and Residence Inns, which are extended-stay accommodations. Now Marriott has more than a handful, including ExecuStay Suites, Fairfield Suites, Marriott Suites, Renaissance Suites, Residence Inns, SpringHill Suites, and TownePlace Suites (see Exhibit 2–1).

Separate living–sleeping accommodations (see Chapter 3, Exhibit 3–18) are attractive to personnel conducting interviews, to women executives, and to others who require private space outside the intimacy of a bedroom. That's why the market shifted away from just extended-stay use. The living space contains a sofa bed and sometimes a second bath. That opened still another market: traveling families seeking economical accommodations.

Despite all-suites' tilt toward transient accommodations, two subdivisions, extended stay and corporate housing, continue to market the segment's original appeal.

Extended Stay.   Extended stay (5 nights or more—18 nights is the average stay) was the original concept of the all-suite hotel, and corporate users were the target market. The annual expenditure of extended-stay guests is four to five times that of transient guests, who stay but a night or two. Better to sell four weeks to one guest than 28 room nights to, say, 20 guests. Consequently, extended-stay hotels have higher occupancies than the norm and lower ADRs. Higher occupancy requires a good revenue management system (see Chapter 4), but problems are minimized by reduced room turnover and by the ability to accept transient guests.

Business travelers are not the only market. Families who are relocating, military personnel awaiting new housing, training/educational sessions, and employees on long-term but not permanent field assignments, such as movie crews, federal agents, or utility workers, expand the market base and still allow for a sprinkling of leisure families. Having restaurants nearby is a plus. Several extended-stay chains close the desk and lock the door overnight. That might prove troublesome in court cases that hinge on the "always-open" definition of a hotel.

The kitchenette is to the all-suite as the swimming pool is to the motel. Everyone looks for the amenity, but few use it. The search for attractive amenities and new ideas is an exciting part of the hotel business because even old, recycled ideas—all-suites as corporate housing—have a modern twist.

Corporate Housing.   The original all-suite concept is reemerging under a new name, corporate housing. This marriage of traditional hotels, apartment hotels, and all-suite hotels appeals to businesses that send many travelers to one city. The company takes a long-term lease on an apartment, but one that provides the services of a hotel. All departments of the corporation (sales, marketing, human resources, engineering) stay at the same corporate unit. Until recently, such accommodations were part of hotels or apartment buildings. Now, new buildings, which some communities consider to be housing, not transient accommodations, are being explored. Housing, in contrast to hotels, is exempt from room taxes and is permitted in areas not zoned for hotels. The tax exemption appeals to investors, as does the operational efficiency of having one dedicated building rather than many units scattered throughout the city.

▶*Other Hotel Segments.*   The dynamic nature of the hotel business—out with the old; in with the new—has kept it viable and changing. Elderhostel programs have brought hotels and universities together. Children's camps, the other end of the age spectrum, even give frequent-stay credits to kids (Camp Hyatt, Hyatt Hotels). A new hotel identification, *collar hotels*, has been coined by the beltway roads, which collar the city and bring businesses and hotels from high-rent, downtown locations to the open spaces of the suburbs. Even casinos are locating in nontraditional settings.

Casino Hotels.   The casino hotel has shaken up the established industry as nothing before in this generation. As legalized gaming (gambling) spreads, this unique type of destination resort shows signs of becoming the lodging industry's most important player. This comes as no surprise when viewed in dollars and cents. For example, $800 million annually is generated by just the food division of the MGM Mirage chain! That's more than many restaurant chains earn. The Venetian Hotel in Las Vegas is another example. It needs $1.2 million per day (yes, per day) to meet the break-even point discussed in Chapter 1.[2]

The operating focus of casino hotels differs from that of traditional hotels. Gaming revenue (called win), not room sales, is the major income producer. Therefore, having rooms occupied (having potential casino players in house) is sometimes more important than the price at which those rooms are sold. For the same reason (to get more players), single and double occupancy rates are the same. Food and beverage are sometimes viewed as loss leaders—low prices attract traffic into the casino.

Hotels with casinos are nothing new to the United States. Gaming has gone in and out of favor since the first raffle to raise money for the Continental Army. It has

---

[2]Megan Rowe, "Know When To Hold." *Hotels.* September 2001, p. 48; and "Venetian," *Las Vegas Sun.* January 3, 1999, p. 5E.

swept across the land again because of recent changes in the national psyche. Gaming is viewed now as another type of entertainment rather than as a vice. Tax revenues earned directly from gaming and indirectly from the tourism spurred by the presence of casinos have become essential to the economies of many states. That dollar flow has shut out opponents arguing against the casino industry. The biggest surprise, perhaps, has been the location of these new resorts. Biloxi, Mississippi (the heart of the Bible Belt); Deadwood City, South Dakota (a worn-out mining area); Ledyard, Connecticut (home of the Pequot Indian Nation); and more recently Detroit, Michigan (a rust-belt location) have become major tourist destinations.

Conference Centers.   Conference centers are specialized "hotels" that surfaced in the 1960s. What began in renovated mansions soon morphed to highly specialized and designed facilities that have attracted big names: Doubletree, Hilton, Marriott, and others. Even so, there are only about 150 conference centers in the United States in contrast to the 60,000 odd hotels. Unlike convention hotels, conference centers usually take no transient guests. Food service is also restricted to inhouse groups. Catering to this special market, conference centers provide a complete line of audiovisual materials, special seminar rooms and theaters, closed-circuit television with interactive teleconferencing, and simultaneous translation capabilities.

The special design of the meeting facilities distinguishes conference centers from other meeting places (see Exhibits 2–4 and 2–5). That distinction is not always understood by conference planners. Conference centers are not necessarily separate facilities—the Sheraton New York has a small conference center within the hotel—but they do have permanent and dedicated meeting space. At least 60% of the space must be dedicated if the facility wants membership in the International Association of Conference Centers. Hotel space is not dedicated because its function changes from meetings, to banquets, to trade shows, to dances (see Exhibit 2–5).

Other operational differences distinguish the conference center from the hotel. Double occupancy is higher. Even top-level senior managers are doubled up. Two to a room encourages greater familiarity, which is one goal of conference planners. Lower management and upper management get to know one another.

Rates at conference centers are bundled. Room, food, and beverage are quoted as one figure. Conference centers call this quote a *corporate meeting package* (CMP), but it is a variation of the all-inclusive American Plan. CMP is a modern version of the American Plan because the conference center is a modern marriage of the convention hotel and the traditional resort. When physically combined, a five-day workweek in the conference facility can be followed by a two-day weekend in the resort complex. Like convention hotels, conference centers are plagued by low weekend occupancy. Some have been forced to look at social guests to fill the hole. Growth in conference centers is apt to be in university conference centers; in nonresidential conference centers, perhaps in city centers or Silicon Valleys; and in special conference facilities built within convention hotels.

Spas.   Spas are mineral springs or curative waters. Spas were known and used as far back as the Romans, who "took the waters" in the city of Spa, Belgium. As the resorts of New England developed around mineral springs and curative waters, the resorts themselves became known as spas.

Today's spas are far different from those of the Romans or of even such famous spas as Saratoga (Springs) in New York State. White Sulphur Springs, West Virginia, and its bubbling fountains were widely known even in the Colonial period. These spas and others, like the Broadmoor in Colorado Springs, were sought initially for their

Exhibit 2–4   Conference centers blend pleasant surroundings with high-tech facilities and dedicated meeting space. Hotels that compete for this market segment do so with multiuse space (see Exhibit 2–5). *Courtesy of Barton Creek Resort, Austin, Texas.*

Exhibit 2–5　　The versatile space of convention hotels accommodates meetings and banquets, trade shows and weddings, proms and seminars, and more in contrast to the dedicated space of the conference center illustrated in Exhibit 2–4. *Courtesy of Radisson Hotel Orlando, Orlando, Florida.*

restorative properties and their promises as fountains-of-youth. It wasn't long before the spas became playgrounds for the rich and socially well placed. Horse racing, cricket matches, casinos, cycling, water sports, and other entertainment gradually replaced water as the main attraction at these still well-known landmarks.[3]

Early spas were focused on the health aspects of the actual waters, which limited their location. Modern spas are built anywhere, because water is not the attraction, although health remains at issue. Today's spa evokes an almost religious fervor of health, exercise, massage, and diet. Even so, spa operators do not allow gyms within the same operation. The energy and noise of a gym change the ambience, introducing hard work into an otherwise hedonistic (self-indulgent and pleasurable) experience. Stress reduction—there is no competition—is cited as the spa's primary appeal.

The growth of the industry can be explained simply: Spas are profitable. Travelers expect them and, unlike swimming pools and kitchenettes, use them, even paying handsomely for the right. The business breaks down into three categories: the spa-destination resort; a resort with all amenities, including a spa (see Exhibit 2–6); and the day spa, which may not even be in a hotel. Hoteliers originally outsourced their spa operations because they lacked expertise. Direct control means more profits, so spa departments with full-time employees have begun appearing.

➤ NEW MARKET PATTERNS

Whereas yesterday's travelers were happy enough just to find shelter and food, today's tourists need to be wooed and won. Whereas the guests of old stopped automatically at the only available hostel, their modern counterparts select from competitive offerings with many attractive inducements. An explosion of choice has taken place around the globe in all the goods and services that customers buy. Consumers are offered a rich selection of products, from bottled water to investment options. Such is also the case for lodging, which has joined the movement by introducing the new array of products that were just discussed. Now the problem is to entice the guest in.

[3]Morrissey's Club House at Saratoga was a famous casino. The carved top of the Saratoga Trunk, named for the Saratoga Spa, was designed to accommodate the elaborate wardrobe of ruffles, bustles, parasols, and petticoats that ladies brought to the resort.

Exhibit 2–6   Spas are new, profitable amenities that both resort and nonresort properties have added. Modern spas no longer rely on the curative waters from which the term originated. Health, exercise, massage, diet, and stress reduction are today's attractions. This new profit center may be leased (outsourced) to third parties. Spa etiquette preserves the quiet: Cell phones are prohibited. *Courtesy of Hotel Hershey, Hershey, Pennsylvania.*

Marketing to the Individual Guest

Hotels zero in on particular market segments (niches) as their chief sources of business. Similarly, guests go to a particular hotel because they find there the kind of accommodations and services that they seek. So the guest's very presence at a hotel tells us much about both the hotel and the guest.

►***The Guest Profile.***   Guests stay at hotels under different circumstances. Consequently, what appeals to one guest may be of indifference to another. Indeed, the same guest displays different responses during separate stays. The guest has a different profile as a businessperson than as a tourist. The single traveler has different expectations when returning as part of a business group or as part of a family unit. Looking at the guest under various circumstances enables the hotelier to build and manage for a variety of market segments.

Guest profiles have been developed by trade associations, governmental agencies, rating firms, purveyors, external consultants, magazines, and the hotel companies themselves.[4] The typical study focuses on demographic profiles. Age, income and job, gender, residence, education, and the number of travelers in the party are all determinable with a good degree of accuracy. Knowing the guests is the starting point for servicing them.

Some patterns take their lead from profiles less measurable than demographics. Developers differentiate between what have been called upstairs/downstairs buyers. *Upstairs buyers* are more oriented toward the room. These guests want large sleeping and bathing facilities and comfortable work space. For this, they will sacrifice theme restaurants, bars, banquet facilities, and exercise rooms. Not so the *downstairs guests*, who want public space above all else. Women are upstairs buyers; men tend toward the downstairs.

Extended-stay guests attempt to recreate a little of their home in the guest room. They bring personal items such as pillows, photos, stuffed animals, and personal toiletries. Very long-term guests even rearrange the furniture. Kitchenettes are used, but mostly for breakfast or for snacks, less often for dinner preparation. The extended-stay guest wants work space and good lighting. So does the business traveler.

Business/Leisure Travelers.   Businesspersons need to be at a given place at a given time. Therefore, price is less important—not unimportant, but less important—to the business guest than to the leisure traveler. Businessmen and women are not apt to cancel a trip because of high rates, and they are not apt to make a trip because of low rates. Theirs is an *inelastic* market—there is very little change in demand from a change in price. The response from leisure guests is more dramatic: High rates repel them and low rates attract them. By responding to price changes, leisure guests represent a more *elastic* market.

All guests demonstrate some degree of elasticity. Even leisure guests may be inelastic, they just have to be there—a wedding, a funeral, and so on. Business guests may be elastic, rescheduling or postponing their meetings. Companies with travel desks, which schedule and buy travel (air, hotels, and car rentals) for their personnel, are more price sensitive. With someone other than the traveler doing the planning, businesses have shifted toward the elastic side. This shift helps explain the buyer's focus on the value of all-suite hotels.

Business guests are mostly men; tourists are mostly couples. Almost everyone watches television from the bed. Business travelers use the telephone, the shower, and the TV movie channel more than leisure travelers do. Tourists hold the edge on the pool and other recreational facilities. Leisure tourists tend to be 5 to 10 years older than businesspersons. They make reservations less often and pay less for their rooms than business travelers do.

Businesswomen present still another profile pattern. They are among the fastest-growing segment of the commercial hotel market, numbering about one-third of all business travelers. The latter description is a demographic measure. How best to please that market is uncertain. That's a psychographic factor. Psychographic profiles detail personality traits, desires, and inner motivations. Every demographic or psychographic profile is necessarily flawed because no individual guest is ever 100% of the composite study. Besides, as we explain in the next section, the guest who stays at the hotel (the one whose profile the industry develops) is often not the person who bought the room initially. Male business travelers make their own arrangements more often than do female business travelers.

---

[4]The typical business guest has been profiled as male, age 25 to 44, holding a white-collar job with a salary in the mid-$50,000 range. He is a solitary traveler who comes by air, holds a reservation, and pays about $70 per night.

Business travelers, male and female alike, use the room as an office. It is no surprise then that surveys indicate a comfortable desk and desk chair are high priorities. Telephones, extra lines for email and fax, and business centers with secretarial support are top "necessities" for business travelers. Women executives (upstairs buyers) rank in-room coffeemakers almost as important as work space; men (downstairs buyers) rank coffeemakers at the bottom of the list.

Some leisure guests are out for a change of experience rather than the leisure of lie-in-the-sun beach and ocean. This niche searches for a change of pace, not for idle leisure. Hiking, mountain climbing, planting trees, rafting, and archeological digs are the sort of leisure activities that many resorts are offering and many vacationers are buying. Guests are willing to pay handsomely for these out-of-the-ordinary experiences.

The economy market is just the opposite. Price-sensitive guests form the core of the budget customers. Who are they? Government employees on a fixed per diem (per day) allowance make up one segment. Retirees, whose time is more flexible than their budgets, will go to the less convenient and less costly locations that economy properties require. Family vacationers and small-business persons sensitive to travel costs help round out this segment. International guests, who have different expectations than domestic travelers, are also part of the budget market, especially when the U.S. dollar is strong.

The International Guest.   Globalization requires special attention to the profile of the international guest. Foreign visitors are big business. The World Tourism Organization (WTO) forecasts 102 million visitors to the United States by 2020. Since they spend more time and more money reaching their destinations, international guests stay longer than do domestic guests. Typically, theirs is a six-day visit, nearly twice the usual domestic stay. International visitors to the United States help the nation's balance of trade, representing some $50 billion in export equivalence.

Japanese visitors to Hawaii spend three times that of the U.S. tourist to Hawaii. Japanese visitors almost always tour in groups, even when they are honeymooning. Office groups (women), ski groups (men), business groups (rarely women), and silver groups (retired couples) are the profiles of the Japanese traveler. Hotels seeking foreign guests need to provide accommodations (Japanese, for example, want bedroom slippers provided), and meals, especially breakfasts, that cater to the tastes of their international patrons.

▶*The New Amenities.*   "Don't sleep with amenity creep" was the 1980 slogan of the hard-budget Microtel.

Traditional amenities (swimming pools, for example) are now viewed as basic services. Bathroom amenities (numerous deodorant soaps, toothbrushes, cotton balls) and historical amenities (shoehorns, sewing kits) have been deemphasized as cost-cutting measures. Amenities remain important marketing devices, however, so new ones continuously take hold. Sometimes, they're practical amenities such as ironing boards, hair dryers, safes that hold laptops, and coffeemakers. Often, they are just opulent: Jacuzzi tubs, air purifiers, towel warmers, sound generators, and more. To the business traveler, electronics is the best amenity.

High-tech, in-room amenities range from the frivolous to the essential: from bedside gadgets that operate the drapes to dual telephone lines, in-room faxes, and electronic check in and check out. Joining the list are electronic keys, in-room private voice mail messaging, and data ports. Telephone access without fees is a welcomed amenity. Providing these self-service amenities has allowed hotels to close expensive business centers or outsource the service at unattended but dedicated centers accessed by credit cards.

Each hotel has its own version of an amenity. One offers a pet for company overnight; another a free shoeshine; a third a jogging map. Baby accommodations—

Travelodge has a "Sleepy Bear" room; others loan baby toys or offer special infant menus—have been introduced as more working and leisure parents tote children along. Alarm clocks promote a good night's sleep so long as guests are confident they'll ring. Cocooning is aided by good room service, new pillow styles and mattresses, and improved black-out drapes. What about a free telephone call home to reassure the family?

Frequent-Guest Reward Programs. Almost half of Marriott's room nights are from guests who belong to its frequent-guest program (FGP), Marriott Honored Guest Awards. Marriott's is one of many FGPs offered at all price ranges. Hyatt's Gold Passport and Hilton's HHonors Club are two other examples of high-end programs. La Quinta's Returns is an example at the low end. In between are Priority Club by Six Continents Hotels (Holiday Inn) and Best Western's Gold Crown Club.[5]

No one is really certain whether FGPs or the airlines' frequent-flier programs (FFPs) actually increase business. It's difficult to determine when all competitors bestow similar rewards. FGPs and FFPs are so alike that hotels and airlines have merged their awards; points earned with one can be used with the other. Competition has forced some hotel companies to give both airline and hotel points for the same visit! Guests win again as the chains gather more brands under one umbrella (see Exhibit 2–7).

SELECTIVE HOTEL CHAINS AND THEIR BRANDS

ACCOR (approximately 3,300 hotels with 370,000 rooms)

ETAP Hotels	Motel 6
Coralia Hotels	Novotel
Hotel FORMULE1	Red Roof
ibis	Hotel Sofitel
Mecure	

CENDANT[a] (approximately 6,600 hotels with 550,000 rooms)

AmeriHost	Knights Inn
Cuendet	Ramada
Days Inn	Super 8
Fairfield	Travelodge
Holiday Cottages	Villager
Howard Johnson	Wingate

HILTON (approximately 1,750 hotels with 300,000 guest rooms)

Conrad	Hampton
Doubletree	Harrison
Embassy	Hilton
Garden Inns	Homewood

STARWOOD (approximately 750 hotels with 230,000 rooms)

Four Points by Sheraton	St. Regis
Luxury Collection	W
Sheraton	Westin

[a]Cendant also participates in global reservation systems: Galileo; Travel and Cheap Tickets; WizCom.

Exhibit 2–7 Hotel consolidation and brand acquisition continue apace as the large chains both acquire and create new brands. Just these four chains control some 1.5 million rooms!

[5]These are registered trademarks.

These costly programs, estimated at over $10 per room per night, have a positive side as well. Vast amounts of information help hotels profile their guests, who, by identifying themselves, signal their travel and personal habits. Hotel companies do a better marketing job with these demographic and preferential profiles. Some chains boast of membership rosters with 2 million names. Gifts and prizes are the inducements that entice guests to give up this personal information.

Gifts range from the simple to the expensive. Many are services that are available even to nonmembers under certain circumstances. Among them are check cashing, room upgrade, daily newspaper, late check out, express check in and check out, toll-free reservation number, and guaranteed rates. Other gifts are specials: room discounts, discounts with travel partners such as airlines, auto-rental companies, or local tourist companies; health club membership; and free accommodations in exotic destinations. Tie-ins with credit-card companies often mean double or triple points earned.

Some hotels, sensing the guests' travel fatigue, offer premiums rather than more travel-related awards. U.S. Savings bonds, upscale gifts from spacial catalogs, and paid memberships in national organizations have all been tried. Facing tough competition from the larger chains, Adam's Mark Hotels uses cash, mailed directly to the guests, as its rewards. Below the surface is an ethical issue. Hard-core FGP participants are usually traveling on expense accounts. The companies paying the bills may look less favorably at premiums paid to their employees, especially if those employees book at higher rates than could be obtained elsewhere.

Despite costs and other issues, no one is daring enough to close a program. The hotel chain that first cancels its FGP will have some brave, and some say foolish, executives. Airlines with their FFPs are caught in the same dilemma. In fact, it was the chairman of American Airlines, Robert Crandall, who invented FFPs. The solution remains elusive for both industries.

A New Look at an Old Amenity.   Foodservice is innkeeping's oldest amenity. Yet hotel dining rooms are not favored by the traveling public. They certainly are not profitable for the host hotel. Nevertheless, industry watchers were amazed when motels and economy hotels and then all-suites eliminated restaurants. Many felt it to be a poor business decision. After all, travelers had to eat. The decision proved to be just the opposite, because alternatives were offered.

All-suite hotels provide free breakfasts, the Continental plan of Chapter 1, and the one meal that almost all travelers take in the hotel. Indeed, several surveys indicate that breakfast is one amenity for which guests are willing to pay extra. Those hotels without foodservice, chiefly economy properties, solve the problem by locating near freestanding restaurants.

Hotels have entered into partnerships, some formal and some informal agreements, with either restaurant chains or well-reputed local operators. Often the result is a cluster. Three, four, or five brand-name hotels are built around the brand-name restaurant. (Howard Johnson tried this idea without success as early as the 1950s.) Working with these neighboring restaurants to accommodate their guests, even with room service in some cases, hotels are able to close nonprofitable food outlets and improve their earnings picture.

The next move, one that is going on right now, was to invite these independent restaurants into the hotel building. Larger hotels have done that. Hamburger, chicken, and pizza franchises have opened in the lobbies—usually with street access also—of some very major hotels. Not only do they offer the type of foodservice that today's traveler prefers, but they pay rent as well!

Even hoteliers who have not given up their dining facilities have borrowed a page from the successful restauranteurs. Pizza and other fast foods are being offered by hotels. Some are using catchy new names, while others are holding onto corporate logos.

➤*Nonguest Buyers.*   The price paid for many hotel rooms is negotiated by third parties (usually legal persons: companies and corporations) who are not guests and have no intention of becoming guests. Similarly, many rooms are sold to persons who never occupy them! These "nonguest" buyers act as intermediaries for the actual occupants. In later chapters, which deal with reservations and room rates, we sharpen the distinctions. Nonguest buyers are part of the modern marketing structure that has developed as a means of selling hotel rooms. Of course, each layer adds costs that must be recovered in the room rate. Nonguest buyers add an additional layer of organization between the hotel and the guest/occupant. As a result, hotels are not selling hotel rooms as much as they are trying to buy guests from these new marketing channels.

Because of their negotiating strength, nonguest buyers such as the American Automobile Association (AAA) and the American Association of Retired Persons (AARP) haggle with hotel chains over price. They obtain special rates for their members, although the hotel doesn't know who those members are until they arrive and claim the room. So widespread is the practice that almost every hotel entertains the request for discount, whether negotiated or not, in order to stay competitive.

Special travel clubs—Amoco Traveler and Encore Travel Club are among the best known—have arranged similar discounts for their members. The clubs specialize in second-night-free deals.

Another side of the reservation picture is the third party as an actual buyer, not merely a rate negotiator. Business travel arrangements are often made by company travel desks, which may or may not be part of the traveler's firm. Either way, reducing travel costs is the mission of these tough negotiators. The range of third-party buyers is broadened further by the list that is detailed in the next section of the chapter. Group tours, incentive firms, and wholesalers are making huge space commitments, but someone else actually uses the room.

Similarly, travel agents commit the hotel to room bookings—but the travel agents don't come; their clients do. Franchisees rely heavily on the franchise reservation system, but the system is just another third party, which the franchisor may not even own! In every instance, the guest who actually arrives is different from the third party who made the reservation.

Airlines and auto-rental companies are also in the business of booking reservations. New companies are springing up locally, nationally, and internationally to reserve, buy, and resell hotel rooms. Each of these interposes a third party between the guest and the hotel.

Marketing to the Group

Seeking out and servicing group business is one of the major distinctions between modern hotelkeeping and the historic wayside inn. Selling hotel space, which is a post-World War II activity, concentrates on attracting group business. One group sale secures dozens, hundreds, or even thousands of room nights. With group business, the hotel is a destination site rather than a transient accommodation. As with individual travelers, groups come both as tourists (leisure guests) and as businesspersons (commercial guests).

▶ *Tourist/Leisure Groups.* Rising disposable income and broader travel horizons have made travel appealing to every level of society. As the relative cost of travel and accommodations declines, the market potential grows ever larger. The travel and hotel industries have finally embarked on the same kind of mass production that has brought increased efficiency to the manufacturing industries. The delay was unavoidable because the large hotel is of recent origin, and only the large hotel is interested in and able to service large groups.

The Tour Package. A new entrepreneur, the wholesaler—another third party, another nonguest buyer—has emerged in the past 25 years to handle the mass movement of leisure guests. Entrepreneurs are risk takers, and wholesalers are certainly that! Wholesalers buy blocks of rooms (commitments to take so many rooms for so many nights) from the hotel, blocks of seats from the airlines, and blocks of seats from the bus company. Then the wholesalers try to sell their packages, which now include transportation, ground handling, and baggage along with whatever else they are able to get without cost from the hotel (see Exhibit 2–8).

Quantity buying gives the wholesaler a good airline price. Special room and meal rates are negotiated with the hotel under the same umbrella—quantity discounts. With the promise of year-round, back-to-back charters, the hotel sales manager and accountant sharpen their pencils. One sale books hundreds of rooms. One correspondence confirms all the reservations. One billing closes the books. There is no commission to credit-card companies, and there is a minimum loss from bad debts. It is a bargain buy for the traveler, a profitable venture for the wholesaler, and a basic occupancy for the hotel (see discussion of yield management, Chapter 4), which also gets free advertising.

Group tours are packaged in a variety of wrappings, some reminiscent of the old American plan. Transportation, room, food, beverage, entertainment, tips, and baggage are offered for one fixed price. (Unlike the all-inclusive plan, not all items—not every meal or every drink—are included, so the hotel stands to gain from additional business outside the package.) Often, the wholesaler can sell the entire package for less than the guest's cost of the airfare alone. That's because the wholesaler has bought in large quantities, thereby earning sharp discounts from the hotel and the airline.

The wholesaler also benefits from *breakage*. Every guest does not use every part of the package. Some may not play golf. Others may not use the drink coupon in the lounge. Others may skip the buffet that is included in the package in preference for a specialty meal that they pay for separately. If the guest does not use the service, the hotel is not paid. Still, the item was computed in setting the package price. That small gain per guest, multiplied by many guests, accrues to the wholesaler as breakage.

The guest gains too, buying services at a fraction of their separate, individual costs. The travel industry, hotels included, gain as well because mass marketing has introduced many new customers to travel. Inexperienced guests find comfort in the safety and security of the group; experienced travelers find irrefutable savings in group travel. The downside is a loss of guest identity. Even the hotel staff senses a reduced responsibility when guests buy and pay through a third party.

Almost any hotel can host a tourist group if it can attract the group to the site. It must meet the price of a very competitive market to appeal to the wholesaler, and it must be large enough to accommodate the group and still handle its other guests. Hotels in out-of-the-way places cater to bus groups. They're a broader market because the number of guests is smaller and almost any hotel can handle them. With bus tours, hotels provide a mix of destination and transient service because after touring the area, the bus moves on, usually after one night.

Vacations—Round the Nation

With the Vallen Chain

⊟V

A Vallen Corporation Property

$ 497.20	$667.50	$733.33
In Las Vegas	**In Orlando**	**In Maui**
Round Trip Air	Round Trip Air	Round Trip Air from LA
4 Days/3 Nights	4 Days/3 Nights	5 Nights/4 Days
HOTEL PARADISE	HOTEL CARTOON	THE VALLEN MAUI
Taxes Included	Room Upgrade If Available	6th Night Free
Airport Transfers	$40 Daily Car Rental	Includes Full Breakfast
Free Gaming Lesson	Nonstop Flights from Major Cities	Guaranteed Ocean View or Suite

---

$515.00	$417.76
In New York City	**In Boston**
4 Days/3 Nights	4 Days/3 Nights
2 Broadway Shows	Bottle Champagne Nightly
THE BIGGEST APPLE	FREEDOM TRAIL HOTEL
Apple Before Bed	Guided Walking Tour of Historic Boston
One Breakfast-in-Bed	$25/Day Food or Beverage Credit
City Bus Tour	Surprise Amenity

CALL: 1-888-555-5555 OR YOUR TRAVEL PROFESSIONAL

Rates are quoted per person, double occupancy and are available until September 30. Unless otherwise stated, taxes and service charges are not included. Las Vegas offering is good Mondays to Thursdays only. All vacations earn Club Vallen points. Air trips, where included, require specific flights on carriers of the company's choosing. Other restrictions may apply. The company strives for accuracy but will not be held responsible for errors or omissions in this advertisement.

Exhibit 2–8   Sample of print advertising used by this hypothetical tour operator, *Vacations–Round the Nation*, to sell packaged vacations. Buying in quantity, which puts the wholesaler at risk, enables it to negotiate reduced prices from hotels and airlines and to resell at prices less than the sum of the individual parts.

The Inclusive Tour (IT) Package.   First, an explanatory note: This IT package is marketed to individual guests. Therefore, it should have been discussed under that topic, "Marketing to the Individual Guest." It has been repositioned here as part of "Marketing to the Group" because it is best understood as a modification of the wholesaler's tour package, just discussed. Unlike the wholesaler's package, which requires numerous buyers to make it profitable, the hotel's IT package is directed toward individual couples or small groups of friends.

The popularity of the wholesaler's package did not escape the notice of hoteliers. "Why give all the profits to the wholesaler?" hotel managers asked. Because wholesale tour packages are very risky, involving air and land transportation costs outside the hotel's control, hotel ITs eliminate the transportation, and with it the risk. What is left is exactly what the hotel normally packages for the wholesaler. Hotels now sell hotel tour packages, no transportation, which they sweeten with free extras not normally made available to the wholesaler. The basics remain in the hotel's package: room, meals, drinks. Hotel packages add "free" use of the tennis court (or putting green, swimming pool, playground, shuffleboard, or table tennis, etc.) and free admission to the theater (or formal garden, exhibit, animal habitat, spas, or exhibition matches, etc.). The products that the hotel includes look even better if small fees are normally paid for such services or admissions. Casino hotels often include one free play on the tables.

With ITs of its own, breakage accrues to the hotel, not to the wholesaler, who is no longer in the picture. Both wholesalers and hotels market directly to the public through

Exhibit 2–9   Inclusive tour packages (rooms; some food, drinks and entertainment) that hotels offer are similar to the wholesaler's package, Exhibit 2–8, except for transportation. Hotel packages compete with individual room sales, so they are offered and withdrawn by the hotel as occupancy dictates under a yield management system (see Chapter 4).

the media (see Exhibit 2–9). At other times they sell through travel agents. Then, of course, the travel agency collects its standard 10% commission. Since packages do not separate room charges from other charges, the commission is paid on the full value of the package, whereas normally, the commission is paid on the room rate only.

One hotel may offer several packages. Each package (a weekend package, a winter package, a golf package, and so on) is aimed toward a different market niche and includes different items at various prices. Hotel ITs must be marketed carefully because the hotel competes with itself. IT packages are discounted rooms with extra services at lower prices than the room alone sells for. Later chapters dealing with yield management and room rates raise again this issue of self-competition.

▶*Business/Commercial Groups.* Our fondness for forming into groups has produced an astonishing number of organizations. People come together under many umbrellas: business, union, fraternal, social, historical, veteran, health and medical, educational, religious, scientific, political, service, athletic, and on without end. For short, the industry uses the acronym SMURF: societies, medical, university, religious, fraternal, or sometimes SMERF: social, military, educational, religious, fraternal. Each classification translates into numerous organizations, societies, clubs, and associations. Each of them meets, holds shows, and stages conventions. Functioning at local, state, regional, national, and international levels, these groups offer business to a variety of destination facilities.

Conventions. Conventioneers assemble to promote their common purposes. These aims are as diverse as the list of associations that hold conventions (see Chapter 5, Exhibit 5–15). Meetings, speeches, papers, and talks are given on a range of topics during the gathering of two, three, or four days. Some are professional and some merely entertaining. The members also interact individually, discussing common goals and problems. Professional conventions may serve as formal or informal job-placement forums.

Both urban and resort properties vie for convention business as the growth of mixed-use facilities spreads. To be competitive, the convention hotel must provide a range of self-contained facilities. Meeting space with appropriate furnishings and equipment and food facilities large enough to accommodate the groups at banquets are the minimum facilities needed (see Exhibit 2–5). Conventioneers are a captive audience for the program and the planned activities. The more complete the property, the more appealing the site.

Sports activities, a change of scenery, and isolation from the hubbub of busy cities are touted by a resort's sales department. Urban properties compete with theaters, museums, and historical locations. Urban areas may have the advantage of publicly financed convention halls (see Exhibit 2–10).

Hotels sometimes combine facilities with those of nearby competitors when the convention size is too large for one property. Although not the rule, conventions of 50,000 to 100,000 delegates have been recorded, usually when combined with trade shows.

Trade Shows. Trade shows are exhibits of product lines shown by purveyors to potential buyers. Conventions and trade shows are often held together. Shows require a great deal of space, particularly if the displays are large pieces of machinery or equipment (see Exhibit 2–10). Space requirements and the difficulty of handling such products limit shows to a small number of hotels. The city convention bureau has a role here. It builds halls to accommodate the exhibits, leaving the housing and guest service to the local hotels.

Exhibits of small goods (a perfume show or a jewelry show are two examples) can be housed almost anywhere. They do not need public convention halls of

Exhibit 2–10   Public convention centers solicit and house trade shows whose delegates might number in the tens of thousands. What is good for the local hotel business has a major economic impact on the whole community. That value approximates $800 daily for each delegate (see Chapter 5, Exhibit 5–10) during the three- or four-day convention. *Courtesy of Las Vegas Convention and Visitors Authority, Las Vegas, Nevada.*

1,000,000 and more square feet. Hotels with limited exhibit space can still accommodate trade shows by carefully choosing what market segments to pursue. Although less common, assigning several sleeping floors to such a trade show and converting guest rooms into individual exhibit spaces is still done by hotels with no dedicated meeting areas. Then the exhibitor occupies the exhibit room as a registered guest.

The Single Entity. The single entity group is neither a tour package nor a convention/trade show. As its name implies, *single entity* has an adhesive that binds its members together. Attendees already belong to "the" group (a company, an orchestra, a college football team) before they come to the hotel. The unit (the company, the orchestra, the college football team) makes the reservation, and the unit pays the bill. The single entity stays together during the engagement: They hold meetings; they perform; they play ball.

Although the visiting athletic team is the best example of a single entity, hotels cater to a wide range of other groups. There are company sales and technical meetings, new product line showings, traveling concert groups, annual high-school graduation trips, and others. Hotel/casinos have their own form of the single entity, the gambling junket. High-rollers are brought in to the hotel for several days of entertainment and play.

The tour group offers a contrast. Tour group members have no previous relationships; they come together only for the trip. Each member pays the wholesaler a share of the cost. With an entity, the single entity pays costs, not the individual members/players. The tour group dissolves after the trip; not so, the single entity. The hotel negotiates with the (team) manager of the single entity, himself a team member, whereas the tour group negotiator is a businessperson out for profit. Both commit to a block (group) of rooms, and both pay for that block.

Similar differences exist with convention/trade shows. Convention attendees represent a wide range of companies or associations. Their only likeness is their common interest in the subject matter. There is no single entity. Each conventioneer comes and goes without concern for the schedule of other delegates, whom he or she may or may not know. The room block has been made by an organizer, often a trade show manager or association president, but each attendee makes his or her own individual reservation, and each pays the hotel his or her own bill.

Incentive Tours.   Incentive tours are special kinds of single entities. Many businesses run incentive programs to encourage sales and production workers to improve output. A cash bonus, a prize, or an incentive trip—for example, a free vacation for two to a destination resort—is the reward for those who meet the announced goals.

Hotels like to book incentive tours because all the participants are winners and only the best accommodations are chosen. Unfortunately, the deals for these facilities are frequently negotiated through intermediaries—incentive (tour) companies, which have emerged as still another nonguest buyer in the sale and distribution of hotel rooms. Incentive companies negotiate for hotel rooms and deliver them to clients, the companies holding the incentive programs. Often, the incentive companies are also the consultants handling the clients' incentive programs.

Incentive companies represent many client-enterprises. This gives the incentive companies a great deal of leverage when they negotiate with the hotel. Everyone bargains tough when accommodations for several groups are at stake. It is the very same pressure that hotels face when dealing with the quantity purchases of the tour-package companies. Price and quality are the differences: Cost is critical for the wholesaler, quality for the incentive buyer.

Tours, be they single entity, incentive, or as yet unnamed, are the group markets of tomorrow. One can foresee a growth of vertical integration with one large holding company owning the means of transportation, reservation system, tour wholesaler, incentive company, and hotel/resort. U.S. airlines might move in that direction again when the airlines recover. (At one time, U.S. railroads and later the nation's airlines owned numerous hotels. These destination hotels hosted the guests that the transportation companies were trying to promote as passengers.) JAL and ANA, both Japanese carriers, have owned destination hotels for some time. The incentive is simply profits. One hotel room sold as part of an integrated sale that includes travel agent, airline, hotel, and entertainment fees is worth many times more than a single room sale made by a standalone hotel. Cendant has several of the elements currently in place.

➤ NEW OWNERSHIP PATTERNS

The changes in guests and markets that have just been reviewed have taken place at the same time that ownership structures and methods of raising money have changed. New management patterns, discussed in the final section of the chapter, have appeared as well, adding to the dynamics of the industry.

The State of the Industry

Historically, the inn was a family affair with the host-guest relationship paramount. That circumstance began to change after World War II (early 1950s) when ownership and management became separate activities. Those who owned the hotel did not operate it. Those who operated the hotel did not own it! As the separation widened, the famous hotel chains concentrated on managing both their own hotels and those belonging to others. Those who owned the buildings and the lands on which the hotels stood were concerned more with the hotels as properties, pieces of real estate. Income taxes, depreciation, rent, and financing are more important to owners than are day-to-day operational problems. That difference brought huge changes in the lodging industry.

▶*Churning and Turmoil.*   Chapter 1 explained the industry's cyclical nature, good and bad times that come rolling in on the waves of change. The cycle is really more dramatic than that, more like churning and turmoil, because events come quickly and unforeseen. For this generation of hoteliers, the story begins in the 1970s.

A serious downturn was caused in large part by a change in the income-tax law. Its original provision encouraged an upward spiral in real-estate values, including hotel real estate. Speculators began buying and trading properties, including hotel buildings. Then Congress repealed the tax advantages. Suddenly, there was no profit in buying and selling buildings that had been run up in price many times over. Earnings from rents, room sales in hotel cases, were insufficient to pay mortgage debt. Estimates place about two-thirds of the nation's hotels in financial distress.

The collapse of the general (and hotel) real-estate market fell heavily upon the banks that had made the mortgage loans. Banks, which now owned the closed hotels, were themselves closed, and their assets (thousands of hotel rooms among them) were assumed by an arm of the federal government, the Resolution Trust Corporation (RBC). The RBC conducted a fire sale, selling hotels at substantial discounts from their original loan values. Many hotel owners were hurt, but the recovery began after years of churning and turmoil.

The recovery brought optimism to hoteliers for the first time in better than a decade. Business travel was increasing and occupancy improving. Low inflation kept borrowing costs and operating expenses steady. Most important of all, distressed hotels had either gone out of business (reducing supply) or had been repurchased during bankruptcy sales at low per-room costs. This meant lower debt and easier repayment of the mortgage loan even if sales were flat—which they weren't; demand actually increased. Since repentant lenders and disappointed speculators had not yet rushed back in to build, room supply was restricted. With increased demand and restricted supply, room rates as well as room occupancy began rising. The industry was healthy again.

The turnaround gained momentum from the early 1990s onward and lasted for 10 years. As operating costs declined, the industry's break-even occupancy fell to less than 60%. Profits soared. By 2000, new construction began hinting of another cycle of overbuilding and a new downward spin. But before the characteristic cycle began anew, the nation was hit by the events of September 11, 2001, in New York City. The whole country, but especially the travel and tourism business, experienced sudden churning and unforeseen turmoil. New issues surfaced as the lodging industry struggled to offset a dip for which it was completely unprepared. Deep discounting on Web sites wreaked havoc on RevPar (occupancy × rate) even as group business declined and attrition rates soared.

➤*A Consolidating Industry.* Consolidation—bigger hotel companies and fewer of them—has been an ongoing strategy of the lodging industry (see Exhibit 2–11). Whether the cycle was up or down, the big guys got bigger. Acquisitions of competitors has enable the surviving hotel chains to broaden their brands, add more rooms, and expand their market lines.

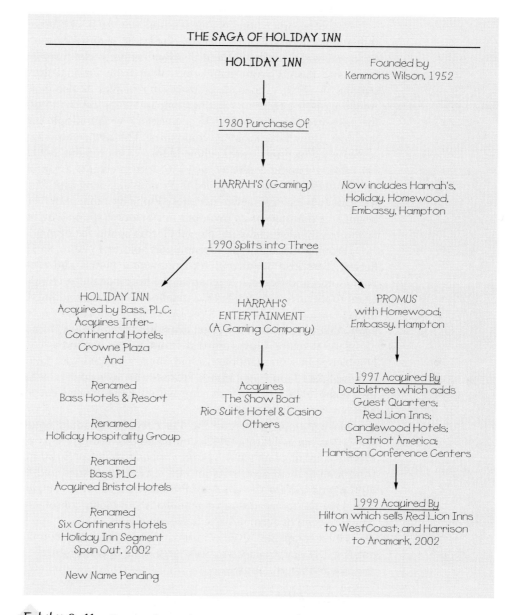

Exhibit 2–11   Promus began its own expansion after it was spun off as a division of Holiday Inn. First, it freed itself from its gaming element, Harrah's. Then Promus, which already had Homewood Suites, Embassy Suites, and Hampton Inns, acquired Doubletree and its subdivisions, Guest Quarters and Red Lion. Hilton took over the whole group in 2000. The story of Holiday Inn, one of America's icons, has been linked to Bass PLC of the United Kingdom since 1990.

Consolidation through acquisition has been possible in part because the stock market shares of the big chains have high values. (The stock market increased its evaluation of the hotel industry by 500% during the upswing of the 1990s!) Using stock as currency rather than using cash (money) facilitates the acquisition of smaller companies. REITs (real-estate investment trusts), which are discussed later in the chapter, have facilitated the consolidation movement. The success of REITs, which own the hotel real estate, accounts in part for the rising price of hotel stocks.

Acquiring other hotel chains is a function of stock market evaluations, but consolidation is more than a stock market game. Consolidation promises economies of scale and larger marketing and distribution networks for the chains. Growth comes faster and flashier from acquisitions than from internal growth. Buying instead of building produces immediate increases in revenues. It also makes good business sense. Acquiring hotels from an existing company costs less than building new ones. During the past several years, over 100 acquisitions with multiple brands have consolidated into just a few large holding companies. The ownership saga of the Promus brand serves as a blueprint for the whole industry (see Exhibit 2–11). Holiday Inn acquired Harrah's, a gaming company, in 1980. It then created a gaming division within Holiday Inn named Promus. Included in Promus's gaming unit were divisions of the original Holiday Inn (Homewood Suites, Embassy Suites, and Hampton Inns). Promus began an expansion of its own, but not before it spun away both its gaming division, now a freestanding company named Harrah's, and the original Holiday Inn chain.

(Promus's Holiday Inn division was sold in 1990 to Bass, Great Britain's largest brewer. Bass also acquired Inter-Continental Hotels and renamed its hotel division Bass Hotels and Resorts. It renamed the hotels again to Holiday Hospitality and then again to its current name, Six Continents Hotels, after adding Bristol Hotels and Staybridge Suites to its package. Bass, by whatever its current name, is reorganizing once again, divesting itself of the hotel division as the text goes to press.)

Several major moves hurtled Promus into a good-sized chain. It merged with Doubletree in 1997. Doubletree had already merged with Guest Quarters (1993) and acquired Red Lion Inns (1996). Promus also formed a joint venture to develop Candlewood Hotels and a partnership with a REIT named Patriot America Hospitality, which owned Wyndham Hotels.

Having gulped down all the lesser fry, Promus had become a big fish by 1999. But not as big as Hilton, which continued the feeding frenzy that year by swallowing Promus and all of its parts. Hilton anticipated almost $100 million in savings, partly from folding these properties into its reservation system and frequent-guest program. Hilton paid less for the whole of Promus than Promus's single acquisition of Doubletree. Like the mom-and-pop minnows before them, consolidation appears to be hastening the end of even mid-size hotel companies.

Hotel companies, even consolidated ones, look tiny compared to international giants such as, say, Coca-Cola. Still, large-scale operations make it easier to compete nationally and internationally.

➤ *The Global Village.* The appearance of the global village (shorthand for shrinking political differences and interlocking economic activity worldwide) has encouraged business interests to cross national borders and major oceans. Innkeeping has participated along with almost every other type of business. Consolidation is caused, in part, by the realities of the global marketplace.

The direction of business flow often depends on the value of international currencies. Foreign investors who want to buy U.S. hotels need to have U.S. dollars. Before they can buy the hotels, they must buy the dollars. When the dollar is weak, fewer units of the strong foreign currency are needed to buy the necessary greenbacks. This makes the purchase price an attractive bargain to international buyers with strong currencies.

After World War II (1950s), the U.S. dollar was the world's strongest currency. That made foreign hotels inexpensive to American buyers, so U.S. chains went overseas. Twenty-five years later (late-1970s) the situation reversed. The dollar had weakened, so foreign chains saw great bargains and entered the U.S. hotel market. Twenty years later (late-1990s), the situation reversed again, and U.S. hotelkeepers were active internationally once more.

There is more to global participation than currencies. Companies go international to acquire a foothold on another continent, to acquire assets (management talent or reservation systems) that they do not yet have, and to open new markets for their brands. Consumers prefer branded products, seeking the security and certainty of a brand they know. That works for U.S. travelers going abroad and for international travelers coming to the United States. At both ends, they see the brand that has been promoted in their own homeland.

Political stability is another factor. Foreign investors may face serious financial loss from political uncertainty. Better to invest elsewhere even if the price is higher than risk loss from confiscation of the hotel. The United States is attractive to foreign investors because the loss from political uncertainty is unlikely. That's especially important to non-American developers who not only differentiate more sharply the operating hotel from the real estate but have a longer business horizon than do U.S. domestic companies.

Global Village Examples.   Hotel companies compete in a vast area that stretches across the globe. European companies operate in North America; North American companies in Asia; Asian companies in Europe. There are many examples of this global outreach. Here are two interesting ones.

Stouffer Hotels, which was once based in Ohio, owned and operated upscale hotels across North America. Stouffer was acquired by Nestlé, a Swiss company. The 15,000-room chain was later sold by Nestlé to the Cheng Yu-Tung family, which also owned a controlling interest in New World Development Company. New World, a large hotel conglomerate, based in Hong Kong, was the parent company of a one-time U.S. chain, Ramada Inns. U.S. Ramada was sold to Prime Motor Inns, International. Ramada had an upscale brand, Renaissance Hotels. The upscale Renaissance properties fit Stouffer's image, but Renaissance was a better known brand outside the United States. New World folded Stouffer into Renaissance and the Stouffer brand disappeared. More recently, Marriott International (Washington, DC) outbid Doubletree Inns (Phoenix) and purchased the Renaissance Group. Over several years, the deals involved North America, Europe, and Asia.

The second illustration references the previous discussion of Harrah's, Bass, and Inter-Continental Hotels (ICH) several pages back. ICH has been in business almost 75 years. It was originally owned by the now-defunct Pan American Airlines (Pan Am). In need of cash, Pan Am sold the chain to Grand Metropolitan of Great Britain, a competitor of Bass. In 1988, Grand Metropolitan sold the chain to Japan's retail and leisure conglomerate, the Seibu Saison Group, with the Scandinavian airline, SAS, taking 40% of the deal. Almost as an aside, ICH also entered into a joint venture with Hong-Kong–based Dynasty Group. Once again, the chain was sold, this time back to Britain, to Bass PLC, which beat out Marriott and four other interested bidders. Undoubtedly, the strength of the British pound and the weakness of the Japanese yen contributed to the timing, 1998. Under Bass, ICH was teamed with Holiday Inn. Originally named Holiday Hospitality, the chain was renamed Bass PLC. Another change took place in 2001. Bass PLC sold its name and trademark, but not its hotels, to Interbrew. The Bass name went with the sale, so the hotel chain had to be renamed once again: Six Continents Hotels (see Exhibit 2–11). Six Continents Hotels reflects the broad reach of ICH and its frequent guest program of the same name. Renaming the corporation doesn't impact brand identity: The individual hotels retain the Holiday Inn or the ICH name.

ICH's parents have been the Americans, the Chinese, the English, the Japanese, and the Scandinavians! Globalization has been at work, but it isn't limited to the hotel segment of travel. Airlines and travel agencies have intraglobal connections. The marketplace requires it. Over 100,000 U.S. groups meet overseas annually. Still unclear is what impact there will be on globalization from Europe's new currency, the Euro, or from the destruction of the Twin Towers in New York City.

Name changes such as ICH's have kept pace with globalization. Best Western became Best Western International; Quality Inns became Choice Hotels International. Hotels operate easily across national borders even without a global name. Paris-based Accor has spread into 30 countries, including a strong presence in the United States with its Motel 6 and Red Roof brands.

Ownership and Financing Alternatives

Early inns were family homesteads. The buildings were under the direct control of the innkeepers, so the hotel was owned and managed by the same party. This arrangement became more difficult as the size of the hotel grew. Large hotels required large sums of money, sums beyond the means of most families. Gradually, the financing of the hotel building separated from the operation of the hotel. This movement accelerated as the modern corporation matured. More recently, financing hotels has become a very creative undertaking.

➤*Individual Ownership.*   There are still plenty of individually owned hotels. Best Western International is an affiliation of individual hotel owners. Owning a single hotel or even several hotels is not the same as maintaining a family homestead. Physically, of course, the family doesn't live there, but more to the point, the financing rarely comes from within the family. There are instances still when loans to build or buy come from the extended family: uncles and aunts; cousins and grandparents. More often, the money is borrowed from public sources.

The small, local hotel may get equity (ownership) money from prominent professional and businesspersons, who want to invest both for profit and community pride. Investment groups, entrepreneurs, hotel companies, and franchise companies are examples of the more likely investors. In all cases, investors also seek borrowed money to complete the deal. Small business loans can be financed through local and regional banks. Under the federal government's Small Business Administration and the Department of Agriculture's Business and Industry Loan Guarantee Program, a federal guarantee is possible for some portion of the loan. Small borrowers can find loan money more easily when 80% or so is guaranteed to the lending bank by one of these agencies.

As projects grow larger, more equity money is needed and the effort shifts from Main Street to Wall Street. The public corporation becomes the likely source of invested capital and the means by which borrowed capital is obtained. Large amounts of borrowed money rely on bigger, money-center banks or on insurance companies or pension funds. Some pension funds invest directly, others do so through mutual funds. Foreign investors are always a possibility. The 1980s–1990s downturn in hotel prices saw companies that normally only franchise begin to buy and own—Choice Hotels, for example—because prices were so low. About the same time, a new financing vehicle, the REIT, emerged to energize the market once again.

➤*Real Estate Investment Trusts (REITs).*   REITs are one way to own hotels or other real estate (apartment buildings, office buildings, shopping malls, etc.). Although the concept has been around for several decades, it was "rediscovered" during the late 1980s. A flow of new investment came from the REITs and accounted for much of the recovery that sustained the hotel industry during its great 1990s upturn.

REITs are public companies that raise capital through the sale of stock. Individual investors easily buy or sell small pieces of hotel ownership through the stock market. The REIT uses these funds along with borrowed funds to acquire hotels. Risk is spread among many hotels and many investors.

Prior to 2001, there were several legislative limitations placed on REITs. They were not permitted to be in any business other than real-estate ownership. A REIT (Host Marriott or Hospitality Properties Trust, for example) could own a hotel, but not operate it. A REIT could neither rent furniture nor provide other services to its tenants. REITs could not have earnings from rooms, food, or beverage sales. One big advantage offset these disadvantages: REITs pay no income taxes so long as 95% of their taxable income (90% under the new law) is returned to shareholders. That increases the REIT's appeal to the typical stock market investor who may know nothing about, and care even less about, hotel ownership or operations.

Some restrictions, but not the tax advantage, were lifted by the REIT Modernization Act, (RMA) effective January 1, 2001. The RMA allows REITs to lease (rent) operations of the hotel to a subsidiary company (a division of the REIT itself). Now both the ownership (the landlord) and the lessee (the renter) are one. Heretofore, the leasing corporation, which did pay income taxes, was technically a nonrelated company. Often, it was formed separately by individuals who were executives of or who sat on the board of the REIT. There were two conflicting interests with the old arrangement. One was the personal conflict that came from REIT individuals owning the leasing company. There was also the conflict between the REIT, which was paid rent based on total revenue, and the lessee, the tenant, which was focused on net profits. Now the landlord company is also the tenant (the leasing corporation), and it deals directly with the management company. Under RMA, the management company remains a third party and collects a negotiated management fee.

Entrepreneurship is the essence of the change. The old REITs were rent collectors; the new REITs can sell services through subsidiary corporations that pay income taxes, as do most other companies, so-called C-Corporations.

➤*Condominiums and Timeshares.*   Both condominiums (condos) and timeshares (interval ownerships; vacation ownerships) have their origins in destination resorts. The industry's catchphrase is "Build where Vacationers go." Condos, which predate timeshare intervals by some 20 years, are an American invention. Timeshares originated in Europe, but North America is a far larger market now. Ski resorts such as Aspen and Stowe were the birthplaces of condo developments. U.S. timeshares began in the sunshine coasts of Florida and Hawaii. Both segments are in a pattern of consolidation similar to the pattern driving the hotel industry. Moreover, there's a shift taking place in consumer preferences. Buyers are investing more heavily in interval ownerships now that the unethical practices of timesharing have been addressed. They are switching from permanent condo owners to part-time interval owners. As that shift takes place, the interests of the hotel industry change from occasional managers to active developers.

Condominium Ownership.   Despite some surface similarities, there are differences in the two options. The confusion comes from their physical appearance. They look alike. Condominium units were first offered as real estate purchases, and they are that still. As real estate, condos were nurtured in an income-tax environment that no longer exists. Today's owner buys for rental income, perhaps for hopes of real estate appreciation, most likely for personal and family use, only somewhat for tax advantages. Guests own condominiums as they own any home. Common space and common grounds are also owned, but as part of the group association. Each unit is complete with all the amenities, kitchen and general family space included. Owners furnish their units and maintain them according to personal preferences.

Since the owners are not always on-property, units may be placed in a common rental pool. This requires on-site management to rent and service the units. Profits, if any, are paid to the owners on a pro rata basis. The complex might be part of a large resort facility that is operated by a well-known hotel chain or management company. Or, the condo owners might employ their own staff to operate and manage the units.

There are endless permutations to the basic plan. In its simplest form, the guest owns the condominium, reserves so many days per year for personal use, and—if the guest wishes—places the unit into the rental pool for the balance of the time.

Actually, condos are an unusual mix of functions. The owners finance the facility for the developer; then they occupy the units as guests, sometimes guests of themselves, since they also hire the management company that services their stay. Mixed use may prove to be the hotel of the future. On the one property would be transient hotel rooms, all-suite extended-stay facilities, condos, and timesharing units.

Buying the Timeshare.   Unlike condominium deals, the first timeshares were not real-estate purchases. One did not *buy* the unit, so there was no property deed. One bought only the *right to use* the unit for so many days each year over a fixed period: hence the term *interval ownership*. "Buy a lifetime of vacations at today's prices" is a popular slogan today. An earlier favorite was, "Don't rent for a night; purchase a week forever"—and some contracts were forever: upward to 40 years. At the end of the contract, the developer—not the guest who had paid for many years—owned the property. In contrast, condo owners took title from the start.

Timeshare started out with a sleazy reputation. Sales without titles were not considered real-estate sales, so none of the 50 states regulated the industry. Numerous consumer complaints about misrepresentation and unethical pressure forced the real-estate commissioners of the most heavily impacted states to regulate the industry. That brought credibility to vacation ownership and encouraged the entry of well-reputed hotel companies (see Exhibit 2–12). Their presence and their aversion to the "hard sell" further reassured the buying public, so there are now about 2.5 million timeshare owners.

Changing the name from timeshares to *interval ownerships, vacation clubs, vacation ownerships,* or *fractionals* contributed to the turnaround. Very expensive timeshares use very expensive names, such as *private residence clubs.*

Names aside, timeshares remain a poor real-estate investment. Getting out from the contract is almost impossible; resale is practically unknown. Over 2% of buyers eventually give the unit back to the developer. eBay often lists units that cost in the

Timeshare Companies

Brand Names	Parent Company
Carlson Vacation Ownership	Carlson (Radisson)
Disney Vacation Clubs	Disney
Fairfield Communities	Cendant
Four Seasons Residence Clubs	Four Seasons
Grand Vacations	Hilton[a]
Horizons	Marriott[b]
Hyatt Vacation Ownership	Hyatt
Marriott Vacation Clubs	Marriott
Resort Condominiums International	Cendant
Ritz-Carlton	Marriott
St. Regis	Starwood
Trendwest Resorts	JELD-WEN
Vistana[c]	Starwood

[a]Hilton also has Hampton Vacation and Embassy Vacation.
[b]Marriott also operates urban timeshares, the Custom House (Boston), for example.
[c]Recently renamed Starwood Vacation Ownership

Exhibit 2–12   A baker's dozen, arranged alphabetically, of the nation's best-known vacation clubs, also called timeshares or fractional ownerships. This hotel segment, which was once clouded in suspicion and distrust, is now a profitable branch of the industry's largest hotel chains. Marriott was the leader, entering the timeshare business in 1984.

thousands of dollars for resale in the hundreds of dollars. The other major negative, coming for the same vacation to the same place for the same dates for 30 years, has been alleviated by two types of exchange arrangements.

EXCHANGES. Exchange clubs developed almost at the start of the timeshare industry. Like the industry itself, they matured to provide a legitimate service to a booming audience. Resort Condominiums International (RCI), a division of Cendant, and Interval International (II) are two of the better known names. For a fee, supplemented by the timeshare owner's deposit of his or her facility into the exchange pool, accommodations can be traded provided both resorts are affiliates of the program. RCI advertises access to about 3,500 resorts in 90 countries; II about 2,000 affiliates in 70 countries. Swapping accommodations is very high on the list of desirables for most fractional buyers.

The importance of exchanging facilities was not lost on the hotel industry. Two types of exchanges have developed among the companies listed in Exhibit 2–12. The first allows timeshare guests to exchange their vacation ownership time with other divisions of the hotel company or even for plane tickets. The plan builds on the hotels' frequent-guest programs. Disney adds a special incentive, allowing Vacation Club owners to exchange units for cruises!

The second exchange integrates resorts with timeshare facilities. Sometimes, they are side by side; sometimes, the two are in one building. Guests may be offered free or discounted mini-vacations at the resort provided they listen to a timeshare sales pitch. A complementary synergy takes place when transient guests are housed in unoccupied interval units. The marriage is a strong one. The hotel offers the infrastructure (restaurants, spas, golf) that the fractional facility lacks. The large party and the long-term stay of the timeshare residents offsets the less consistent base of the hotel's clientele.

Selling the Timeshare. Timeshares and condos are financing alternatives, additional sources of capital for the developer. Converting existing resorts or parts thereof was the initial phase in timeshare development. The funds were used to upgrade and refurbish, or they were used to pay off debt. Sometimes, the dollars went into the owner's pocket. This "conversion" phase didn't succeed, because buyers want more than a renovated hotel room. New timeshare construction often starts by serving transient guests in extended-stay accommodations that contain kitchens, master and second bedrooms, and a living room. Dual marketing of transient and timeshare carries the project during the difficult developmental phase.

The developer tries to sell each unit 50 times per year, once each week. An 80-unit timeshare might then have as many as 4,000 participants annually. For this illustration, a lucky developer could reap $80,000,000 to finance the project if all the units are presold at, say, an average price of $20,000 per unit per week. (The more desirable the period of use, in-season versus off-season versus shoulder season, the higher the initial timeshare cost.) That's a substantial amount of up-front money even if a mere percentage is sold, which is usually the case. In practice, two weeks or more is held back for maintenance. States such as California forbid the sale of a full 52 weeks. Unlike the condo, where repair and maintenance are the responsibility of the owner, timeshare repairs, services, and furnishings are supplied by the developer. Of course, additional housekeeping fees—called T&T (that is, trash and towels)—and maintenance fees are charged during the weekly occupancy of each holder. Timeshare members are not responsible for furnishing the space, which may be nothing more than a single converted guest room. Currently, timeshare associations do not enjoy tax-exempt status.

With the legitimacy of the industry has come innovative changes. The first was the *deeded timeshare*, where buyers actually take title, just as they do with condominiums. Deeded timeshares can be resold (but not easily), gifted, exchanged, willed, or rented. They may even appreciate in value. But that is so unlikely that suggesting it to new buyers is forbidden by the American Resort Development Association, the timeshare industry's trade group. Limiting the number of participants is another idea being tested. Rather than 50 buyers per unit, the property is sold in, say, eight-week blocks to, say, six buyers. Rotating weeks is yet another innovation. It takes advantage of the two- to four-week break in the schedule. Buyers rotate throughout the years, so no one buys the best times and no one the worst. Of course, it might take a decade to get a one-time chance at Christmas or the Fourth of July weekend.

Fractional ownerships have grown very popular with both the buyer and the developer. Their use has spilled over from resorts to private aircraft and cruise ships, which are selling suites through interval ownership. Urban hotels such as the New York Hilton are enlarging on the residential aspect of commercial hotels (see Chapter 1) by introducing timeshares to the Big Apple.

▶*Joint Ventures and Strategic Alliances.* Joint ventures are similar to partnerships created by two or more individuals. However, with joint ventures, the individuals are not persons. They are one of several entities. Joint ventures are partnerships of corporations, of existing partnerships, or even of governments. For example, privately owned Radisson Hotels formed a three-way venture with the Russian Ministry for Foreign Tourism and a publicly owned business-center company, Americon. The new entity opened the 430-room Radisson Slavjanskaya in Moscow about 10 years ago.

Canadian Pacific Hotels' union with Fairmont Hotels is another joint-venture example. After the merger, Canadian Pacific held 67% of the new company, and two other entities held the balance. Maritz Wolff (a joint partnership) and Kingdom Hotels (Prince Alwaleed's corporation with interests in Fairmont Hotels) each own 16.5%.

Marriott and Cendant formed a joint venture in 2002 to further develop and expand the Ramada and Days Inn brands in the United States. Marriott contributed Ramada; Cendant, Days Inns.

Rising costs (land and construction) and huge enterprises (megaresorts and developments) make joint ventures, which are usually financial marriages, logical unions. On the other hand, strategic partnerships tap the capabilities of different organizations. The explosion in gambling serves as a good example. Gaming management is a skill that new types of developers (native American tribes, municipalities, business development agencies) lack. Still, they want the benefits of casino ownership. Strategic partnerships bring the skills of gaming management companies to organizations that provide the sites, the licenses, and the political muscle. The $2.5 billion development of Atlantic City's marina was possible because of a joint venture that involved several casino companies and political entities.

➤ NEW MANAGEMENT PATTERNS

Our historical review has made clear that the era of the small innkeeper and the individual entrepreneur is waning. Erecting large, expensive buildings and competing in international markets require the management talent and the capital funding that only large, public companies—the hotel chains—can provide.

Chains

The very act of traveling evokes the unknown, the strange, the unfamiliar. Within such an environment, travelers must select a rather personal service—a bed for the night. Examining or evaluating the experience beforehand is not possible. The hotel's reputation or its membership in a chain or affiliated group become the primary reason for the guest's selection.

Overseas, the environment is stranger still. Brand recognition is even more critical to the selection. That is why U.S. hotels developed abroad when the United States dominated the world's business scene. With international trade now more evenly balanced, foreign chains are appearing in the United States for the same reasons.

The combination of brand recognition and the inherent strengths of size and savvy management account for the chains' popularity and growth—and grow they have. The AH&LA publishes an annual *Directory of Hotel & Motel Companies* (chains). It defines a chain as any group of two or more properties operated under a common name (see Exhibit 2–13). Chain-controlled hotels now dominate the U.S. hotel industry. Some 75% of hotel rooms are under the umbrella of one chain or another. That figure was only 37% in the early 1970s, and there are almost 10,000 additional hotels today!

Modern business practices give chains an enormous operating advantage. Among their basic strengths are (1) expertise in site selection, (2) access to capital, (3) economies of scale (purchasing, advertising, reservations, etc.), (4) appeal to the best management talent, and (5) brand recognition.

As this chapter has stressed, hotel chains are no longer hotel builders. Just as often, the builders are not the owners, and the owners are not hoteliers. So it is to the

Hotel Chains

Brand Names	Parent Company
Best Western	Membership of Independents
Choice Hotels	Choice Hotels International
Days Inns	Cendant
Disney	Walt Disney World Resorts
Doubletree	Hilton
Hilton	Hilton
Holiday Inn	Six Continents
Hyatt Hotels Corporation	Hyatt
Inter-Continental (Hotels and Resorts)	Six Continents
Marriott	Marriott Hotels, Resorts and Suites
Ritz-Carlton	Marriott
Sheraton	Starwood
Westin	Starwood

Exhibit 2–13   A baker's dozen, arranged alphabetically, of the nation's best-known hotel names. Some chains *own* their hotels, some *operate* management contracts, some have *leased* properties, and some *license* (franchise) their name. Many do all four. Some are owned by other companies.

hotel chain that the builder/developers and owners turn for management skills. It is these very same skills that institutional lenders trust for the repayment of their loans. Obviously then, successful enterprises involve mutually supportive skills from several participants.

▶*Parties to the Deal.*   Five different parties are involved in the development and operation of a hotel. The confusion is compounded when one of the participants wears two or three hats. The *developer* (party number 1) sees the opportunity and puts the plan together. That developer could be one of the hotel chains, Marriott, for example. The hotel might be part of a larger development—one element in a shopping mall, or a business park, or a timeshare in a resort complex.

Financing is arranged from a bank, insurance company, government agency, pension plan, or other source. The *financier* is party number 2. As with all the participants, financing could come in total or in part from one or more of the other parties. The developer or the hotel management company might participate in the lending but more likely in the equity.

The equity—that is, the *ownership*—is party number 3. This party could be any of the others, a public corporation, a joint venture between one or more of the parties, or a separate entity making a passive investment.

If none of the participants is familiar to the consuming public as a hotel company, there will be no brand recognition. Then it is desirable that the group that manages the operation—the *management company* (party number 4)—has a recognizable logo. If the management company does not have a strong marketing presence, a franchise is licensed from a company (party number 5) that does.

Hotel chains (see Exhibit 2–13) are likely to be a combination of all five parties. They help with development and financing, hold a piece of the ownership equity, and supply management talent. Chains provide the critical name recognition and the essential reservation system. Whereas the chain might be part of all five parties in a big development, small-town projects use several different parties. The local business community may be the developer/owner but look elsewhere for the financing, the management, and the franchise.

➤*Consortia and Membership Organizations.*   The growth of chains and franchises, with their interlocking reservation systems and easy identifications, put independent operators at a competitive disadvantage. For a long time, independent hotels struggled to maintain their freedom. Of late, the question has shifted from "if and when to affiliate" to "how to choose the right organization."

Even European hotels, which are chiefly small family inns (about three-fourths of which are independent), have begun examining possible affiliations. Affiliation for these fiercely independent hoteliers reflects the pressure of globalization and the appearance overseas of the American franchise.

Reservation referrals are cooperative organizations initially designed to provide only one common service: marketing. Centralized reservations, standardized quality, joint advertising, and a recognizable brand with a logo are the limited objectives of most referral groups. This enables the individual property to compete but still maintain its independence. There is no interlocking management, no group buying, no common financing—nothing but a unified sales effort. Unlike the franchise contract, which is discussed soon, individual identity is encouraged. For example, although rooms must meet certain standards, the building's configuration is not prescribed.

Best Western International is by far the best known membership/referral group. Each of its 4,000 properties in some 100 countries is individually owned. Members have voting status for the board of directors that operates the association. By maintaining standards, quality accommodations, and fair pricing, Best Western provides the traveling public with consistency among the properties, whose uniqueness reflects the individual ownership that is still maintained.

Preferred Hotels and Resorts Worldwide is a different type of membership group. Its rates are at the other end of the price scale from Best Western. Although both are international in scope, Preferred's membership has been less than 150 hotels. Recently, it created a new holding company, IndeCorp Corporation, with several wholly owned brands. Preferred is now one of those brand. Under IndeCorp's umbrella are other independent brands such as Golden Tulip, Summit Hotels and Resorts, and Sterling Hotels and Resorts. By developing brands, IndeCorp emphasizes its consortium strategy with now nearly 1,000 hotels. The Sagamore Resort (see Chapter 1, Exhibit 1–10) is a member of Preferred Hotels & Resorts Worldwide.

Consolidation of the consortia follows the general consolidation movement of the whole industry. Leading Hotels of the World, which had been the largest consortium of the luxury independents, less than 500 members, also began consolidating with the addition of the Leading Small Hotels group of 70 hotels. It is likely that competition may force the consortia to move beyond mere branding to begin managing, even owning, hotels. They say that their structures already emulate Accor, Bass, and Marriott.

Management Contracts and Management Companies

➤*Management Contracts.*   A management contract is an agreement between a hotel owner and a management company (see Exhibit 2–14). The contract is a complex legal instrument by which the management company operates the hotel within the conditions set down by the contract. For this, the owner pays the management company a fee of 2% to 4% of revenues. Fees are paid whether or not there are earn-

Hotel Management Companies

Name of Management Company	Approximate Number of	
	Properties	Guest Rooms
Boykin Management Company	20	5,000
John Q. Hammons Hotels	50	13,000
Interstate Hotels Corporation	160	30,000
Janus Hotels and Resorts	50	8,000
Lane Hospitality	30	6,000
Lodgian	120	22,500
MeriStar Hotels & Resorts	220	50,000
Prime Hospitality Corporation	210	28,000
Richfield Hospitality Services	40	11,000
Sage Hospitality Resources	50	8,500
Tishman Hotel Corporation	10	7,500
Westmount Hospitality Group	300	34,000
Winegardner & Hammons	30	7,500

Note: Because of rapid industry consolidation, numbers are rounded to best estimates at the time of publication.

Exhibit 2–14   A baker's dozen, arranged alphabetically, of the nations best-known hotel management companies. Even so, there is little name recognition. The 13 hotel companies have about 1,300 properties (an average of 100 hotels each company). They manage approximately 100,000 rooms (an average of about 80 rooms per property). Competition has forced many management companies into equity participation.

ings. Profits, if any, belong to the owner, but so do the losses. Since management fees are paid whether or not the property is profitable, management companies enjoy rapid expansion with little invested capital and almost no risk. Besides, most contracts provide incentive fees for the management company of 10%–25% of operating profit if and when the hotel turns profitable.

Contracts can be negotiated at any time. If early in the project's development, the management company may provide advice on construction, on systems, on financing, and so on. When times were bad, owners accepted many restrictive terms in the contract in order to secure the management company's services. An improving economy has shifted the advantage. Lenders have disposed of their excess hotel inventory, and hotels have turned profitable. Simultaneously, the number of management companies has increased. This tight competition has forced concessions from the management companies as they bid for contracts. Owning companies are able to negotiate shorter contracts, less costly fees, and more capital investments from management companies.

▶*Management Companies.*   The separation of hotel management from hotel ownership coincided with the industry's search for public monies with which to build ever-larger and more costly hotels. Professional management is critical to success when hotel owners are not operators themselves. It is enough that owners know to seek quality management.

Three separate but similar events accelerated the professionalism of lodging managers and contributed to the creation of management companies. The causes behind the events were different, but the results were the same. Lenders (usually banks) took control of hotels because owners were unable to repay mortgage loans. Bankers dislike holding physical assets, so they sell them off as quickly as possible. Knowing that the resale value of a hotel is much higher if the business is still in operation, banks hired management companies to run the defunct hotels. The Great Depression (1930s) was the first time the majority of the nation's hotels went bankrupt. It happened again during the oil embargo of the 1973, and again more recently during the collapse of the banking system (1980s). Poor times for the hotel business are good times for management companies.

A pure management company is almost unknown now. Companies like those in Exhibit 2–14 have equity (ownership) stakes in the properties they manage. They wouldn't get the contract otherwise. A bigger change has come from consolidation. Chains, which have their own management talent, have taken over many hotels that would otherwise be operating under management contracts. The number of independent properties that require management talent is declining even as the number of management companies is growing.

REITs add another issue to management contracts. Earlier, the chapter pointed out that REITs may not manage the hotels they own. That limitation was retained by the REIT Modernization Act even though it loosened another REIT restriction. Effective 2001, REITs, which own hotels, may also own the leasing company, which rents the hotel from the REIT. It is this leasing company that employs the management company.

►*Leases.*   Management contracts and lease contracts are almost opposite views of the industry's health. One or the other becomes popular depending on the position of the economic cycle. Leases are popular when times are good.

Hotels once owned the real estate and managed the operation. Owning real estate takes large sums of invested equity and significant risks from borrowing. As hoteliers became more sophisticated about finance (1960s), sale-and-leaseback became popular. The hotel company would sell the building to outside investors. The new investors would then lease (rent) the operation of the hotel back to the very hotel company that had sold the the real estate. Since the operation was profitable, both parties won. The operating companies (predecessors to some of the chains of Exhibit 2–13) had profits after they paid the lease rent, and the owning company had a fixed flow of rental income with which it could secure the borrowing. The lease's long and successful history gives precedent to current REIT arrangements.

Management contracts gain popularity when the industry goes into a slump. The operating company cannot visualize any operating profits, so it steps back from lease arrangements. The owning company still has a hotel that needs management skills. It hires the management company, paying the company a management fee as prescribed by the management contract. Incentives are paid to the management company if it produces profits through increased sales or reduced costs.

The dynamics of hotelkeeping allow for a variety of possibilities. Some hotel companies own and operate hotels. Sometimes, it is as a joint venture. Some hotel companies manage for a fee but contribute some of the equity (ownership). Some hotel companies just manage. Franchising is another option: Cendant just franchises.

►*Franchises.*   Franchising is not a new idea, nor is it unique to the hotel industry. Tires, speedy printing, diet clinics, and more are all franchised these days. With a franchise, the buyer (called the *franchisee*) acquires rights from the seller (called the *franchisor*). Those rights give the franchisee exclusive use (a franchise) of the name, the product, and the system of the franchisor within a given geographic area. Buying a franchise enables the small businessperson to operate as an independent but still have the benefits of membership in the chain.

The franchisee pays a variety of fees to adopt the name and trademark of the franchisor (see Exhibit 2–15). In addition to an initial signing fee, the franchisee pays so much per room per night throughout the life of the contract. But that's not all. The franchisee also pays a rental for the company sign, a fee to access the reservation system, and a per reservation fee for each room booked. In addition, the franchisee buys amenities from the parent company in order to get the franchise logo. Extra fees are charged for required training and for participating in the frequent-guest program. Competition has encouraged some management companies to pay all or part of the owner's franchising costs in order to win the management contract.

Franchise fees have almost doubled during the past 20 years. They now represent 9% to 10% of room sales—some 8% of sales from all sources. The impact is significant because net earnings from all departments is only in the 20% range. (Franchise expenses fees are already included in that calculation.) If net earnings are only 20% of sales, franchise fees represent a good chunk of operating costs. On the other hand, brand affiliation may add 10 percentage points to occupancy and $10 or more to ADR. That, too, is a significant amount.

With those fees come a variety of services. How many and which services depend on which franchise is purchased. The most extensive franchise might include feasibil-

Representative Franchise Fees[a]

Fee	Representative Terms	Alternative Terms
Application[b]	The greater of $45,000 *or* $400 times the number of rooms	A lesser fixed amount plus a per-room fee over, say, the first 75 rooms
Royalty	4%–6% of room revenue	3% of gross revenue; *or a* minium per night, say, $5
Advertising/ Marketing	1.5%–3.5% of room revenue	2% of gross revenue; *or a* minimum per night, say, $1 per room
Training	0.5% of gross revenue plus cost of attending school	None; franchisee bears all schooling costs for employees sent away
Reservation	3% of room revenue plus $2–$5/reservation	$8–$10/reservation; *or a* minimum per night, say, $8 per room

[a]Other possibilities include email costs, global reservation costs, termination costs, accounting charges, and participation in frequent-guest promotions.
[b]All or some (90%–95%) of the application fee is returned if the application is not approved.

Exhibit 2–15   Hotel franchisors (franchise sellers) charge franchisees (franchise buyers) a variety of fees that might total as much as 8% to 10% of gross sales!

ity studies, site selection advice, financing support, design and planning, mass purchasing, management consultations, advertising, and systems design. The central reservation system, discussed in Chapter 4, is the major reason by far that franchisees sign up. Estimates place the number of reservations coming through the system as high as 30% of the chain's total reservations and upward of 50% of all reservations for individual properties.

The Franchise and the Flag.   Hotel franchising probably began during the late 19th century. Cesar Ritz—*ritzy* now means the finest in luxurious accommodations—gave his name to a small number of hotels whose management he supervised. Kemmons Wilson made the next advance in hotel franchising with the development of the Holiday Inn chain.

Franchising is all about the brand recognition discussed earlier in the chapter. The franchisor is able to deliver immediate brand identity by selling its "flag" to the franchisee. Franchisee and parent company are so alike that guests do not distinguish between them. The physical hotels look identical. It's the ownership and management structures that differ. The chain (the franchisor) does not own the franchise property, the operator (the franchisee) does. The franchisor does not manage the property, the franchisee does. If the franchisee elects not to manage, it could hire the franchisor as its management company under a separate management contract. Or instead, it could hire an entirely different management company. So now another party, the franchisor (the franchise company), has been added to the interaction of the developer, the owner, the lender, and the management company.

Each flag denotes a certain type of facility in the buyer's mind. A franchisee intent on developing long-stay facilities wouldn't shop for a franchise flying the flag of, say, a budget property such as Holiday Inn Express.

Once acquired, changing flags—canceling the franchise contract—is difficult and expensive because most contracts favor the franchisors. Many franchisees are small, family-owned businesses, whereas the franchisor is a multifaceted company. Competition and court decisions have helped balance the interests of the franchisees against those who write the contracts, the franchisors. Franchise advisory committees, which are assertive groups of franchise members (sometimes within each brand, sometimes across the brands) are also at work.[6] Publicity generated by these groups has helped garner the support of the more sensitive franchisors. Among the defining issues are

1. Defense from competing franchises within the supposedly protected area, especially as consolidation among franchisors puts many heretofore competing brands under one umbrella and on the same reservation platform;
2. Unexpected upgrade demands by the franchisor, particularly when the franchisee sells the hotel;
3. High liquidation damages when the franchisee tries to change flags.

Despite the negatives, buying a franchise flag is equally popular with both large absentee owners and small owner/operators. Branding is essential for attracting the transient traveler who may never come that way again. Franchising's recent success in Europe reaffirms the worth of the concept.

---

[6]Asian American Hotel Owners Association (AAHOA), a mildly militant organization of small (family-owned) hoteliers, has been especially effective in fighting for the rights of the franchisee.

RESOURCES AND CHALLENGES
Resources

➤ SUMMARY

The 21st century opened with the hotel business at the peak of its cycle, in part because of the industry's willingness to try things new. New products were tested using new marketing approaches; new ownership patterns were introduced calling for new management structures. Strategic changes such as these require rapid and decisive moves to meet the intense competition head-on. Many new flags (brands) are flying even as consolidation shrinks the number of, and grows the size of, surviving hotel companies.

Shifts in the lodging industry take place within the global village, where ideas and innovations move swiftly between continents. Their speed and direction depend, in large measure, on the relative strengths of currencies. Hoteliers worldwide know that name recognition attracts the transient traveler. High fees notwithstanding, franchising is one concept that has jumped the oceans to further consolidate lodging and make it a true global industry.

For now, the inelastic business market continues to underpin the basic business of hotelkeeping. Many predict that the rapidly growing elastic market of tourism and leisure will soon replace the business traveler as lodging's major guest profile.

The 21st century will build on the dynamic changes in products, markets, financing, and operations that continue to reshape this ancient industry.

➤ WEB SITES

Cendant.–World's largest hotel franchisor: http://www.cendant.com

Choice Hotels.–Most Choice brands are at the low end: http://www.choicehotels.com

Hilton–Most Hilton brands are upscale: http://www.hilton.com

Hotel & Motel Management–Trade periodical: http://www.hotelmotel.com

Red Roof.–Part of the French chain, Accor: http://www.redroof.com

Web Site Assignment.

1. Reference the *Franchise Fee Calculator*, which *HVS International* has placed on the Web site of the magazine *Hotel & Motel Management*.

2. Select a franchise for your 120-room hotel, which has an ADR of $66 and an occupancy of 60%. Make your decision by contrasting two choices from the Web sites listed above (or from any other hotel company—see the Web Index; see also Exhibits 2–1 and 2–7) using 2 years of computations. Assume every required figure grows by 3% per year.

3. List any other assumptions that you make in reaching your decision and explain why you selected that particular franchise company.

RESOURCES AND CHALLENGES
Resources

➤ SUMMARY

The 21st century opened with the hotel business at the peak of its cycle, in part because of the industry's willingness to try things new. New products were tested using new marketing approaches; new ownership patterns were introduced calling for new management structures. Strategic changes such as these require rapid and decisive moves to meet the intense competition head-on. Many new flags (brands) are flying even as consolidation shrinks the number of, and grows the size of, surviving hotel companies.

Shifts in the lodging industry take place within the global village, where ideas and innovations move swiftly between continents. Their speed and direction depend, in large measure, on the relative strengths of currencies. Hoteliers worldwide know that name recognition attracts the transient traveler. High fees notwithstanding, franchising is one concept that has jumped the oceans to further consolidate lodging and make it a true global industry.

For now, the inelastic business market continues to underpin the basic business of hotelkeeping. Many predict that the rapidly growing elastic market of tourism and leisure will soon replace the business traveler as lodging's major guest profile.

The 21st century will build on the dynamic changes in products, markets, financing, and operations that continue to reshape this ancient industry.

➤ WEB SITES

Cendant.–World's largest hotel franchisor: http://www.cendant.com

Choice Hotels.–Most Choice brands are at the low end: http://www.choicehotels.com

Hilton–Most Hilton brands are upscale: http://www.hilton.com

Hotel & Motel Management–Trade periodical: http://www.hotelmotel.com

Red Roof.–Part of the French chain, Accor: http://www.redroof.com

Web Site Assignment.

1. Reference the *Franchise Fee Calculator*, which *HVS International* has placed on the Web site of the magazine *Hotel & Motel Management.*

2. Select a franchise for your 120-room hotel, which has an ADR of $66 and an occupancy of 60%. Make your decision by contrasting two choices from the Web sites listed above (or from any other hotel company—see the Web Index; see also Exhibits 2–1 and 2–7) using 2 years of computations. Assume every required figure grows by 3% per year.

3. List any other assumptions that you make in reaching your decision and explain why you selected that particular franchise company.

Three separate but similar events accelerated the professionalism of lodging managers and contributed to the creation of management companies. The causes behind the events were different, but the results were the same. Lenders (usually banks) took control of hotels because owners were unable to repay mortgage loans. Bankers dislike holding physical assets, so they sell them off as quickly as possible. Knowing that the resale value of a hotel is much higher if the business is still in operation, banks hired management companies to run the defunct hotels. The Great Depression (1930s) was the first time the majority of the nation's hotels went bankrupt. It happened again during the oil embargo of the 1973, and again more recently during the collapse of the banking system (1980s). Poor times for the hotel business are good times for management companies.

A pure management company is almost unknown now. Companies like those in Exhibit 2–14 have equity (ownership) stakes in the properties they manage. They wouldn't get the contract otherwise. A bigger change has come from consolidation. Chains, which have their own management talent, have taken over many hotels that would otherwise be operating under management contracts. The number of independent properties that require management talent is declining even as the number of management companies is growing.

REITs add another issue to management contracts. Earlier, the chapter pointed out that REITs may not manage the hotels they own. That limitation was retained by the REIT Modernization Act even though it loosened another REIT restriction. Effective 2001, REITs, which own hotels, may also own the leasing company, which rents the hotel from the REIT. It is this leasing company that employs the management company.

➤**Leases.** Management contracts and lease contracts are almost opposite views of the industry's health. One or the other becomes popular depending on the position of the economic cycle. Leases are popular when times are good.

Hotels once owned the real estate and managed the operation. Owning real estate takes large sums of invested equity and significant risks from borrowing. As hoteliers became more sophisticated about finance (1960s), sale-and-leaseback became popular. The hotel company would sell the building to outside investors. The new investors would then lease (rent) the operation of the hotel back to the very hotel company that had sold the the real estate. Since the operation was profitable, both parties won. The operating companies (predecessors to some of the chains of Exhibit 2–13) had profits after they paid the lease rent, and the owning company had a fixed flow of rental income with which it could secure the borrowing. The lease's long and successful history gives precedent to current REIT arrangements.

Management contracts gain popularity when the industry goes into a slump. The operating company cannot visualize any operating profits, so it steps back from lease arrangements. The owning company still has a hotel that needs management skills. It hires the management company, paying the company a management fee as prescribed by the management contract. Incentives are paid to the management company if it produces profits through increased sales or reduced costs.

The dynamics of hotelkeeping allow for a variety of possibilities. Some hotel companies own and operate hotels. Sometimes, it is as a joint venture. Some hotel companies manage for a fee but contribute some of the equity (ownership). Some hotel companies just manage. Franchising is another option: Cendant just franchises.

➤**Franchises.** Franchising is not a new idea, nor is it unique to the hotel industry. Tires, speedy printing, diet clinics, and more are all franchised these days. With a franchise, the buyer (called the *franchisee*) acquires rights from the seller (called the *franchisor*). Those rights give the franchisee exclusive use (a franchise) of the name, the product, and the system of the franchisor within a given geographic area. Buying a franchise enables the small businessperson to operate as an independent but still have the benefits of membership in the chain.

The franchisee pays a variety of fees to adopt the name and trademark of the franchisor (see Exhibit 2–15). In addition to an initial signing fee, the franchisee pays so much per room per night throughout the life of the contract. But that's not all. The franchisee also pays a rental for the company sign, a fee to access the reservation system, and a per reservation fee for each room booked. In addition, the franchisee buys amenities from the parent company in order to get the franchise logo. Extra fees are charged for required training and for participating in the frequent-guest program. Competition has encouraged some management companies to pay all or part of the owner's franchising costs in order to win the management contract.

Franchise fees have almost doubled during the past 20 years. They now represent 9% to 10% of room sales—some 8% of sales from all sources. The impact is significant because net earnings from all departments is only in the 20% range. (Franchise expenses fees are already included in that calculation.) If net earnings are only 20% of sales, franchise fees represent a good chunk of operating costs. On the other hand, brand affiliation may add 10 percentage points to occupancy and $10 or more to ADR. That, too, is a significant amount.

With those fees come a variety of services. How many and which services depend on which franchise is purchased. The most extensive franchise might include feasibil-

Representative Franchise Fees[a]

Fee	Representative Terms	Alternative Terms
Application[b]	The greater of $45,000 *or* $400 times the number of rooms	A lesser fixed amount plus a per-room fee over, say, the first 75 rooms
Royalty	4%–6% of room revenue	3% of gross revenue; *or* a minium per night, say, $5
Advertising/ Marketing	1.5%–3.5% of room revenue	2% of gross revenue; *or* a minimum per night, say, $1 per room
Training	0.5% of gross revenue plus cost of attending school	None; franchisee bears all schooling costs for employees sent away
Reservation	3% of room revenue plus $2–$5/reservation	$8–$10/reservation; *or* a minimum per night, say, $8 per room

[a]Other possibilities include email costs, global reservation costs, termination costs, accounting charges, and participation in frequent-guest promotions.
[b]All or some (90%–95%) of the application fee is returned if the application is not approved.

Exhibit 2–15   Hotel franchisors (franchise sellers) charge franchisees (franchise buyers) a variety of fees that might total as much as 8% to 10% of gross sales!

ity studies, site selection advice, financing support, design and planning, mass purchasing, management consultations, advertising, and systems design. The central reservation system, discussed in Chapter 4, is the major reason by far that franchisees sign up. Estimates place the number of reservations coming through the system as high as 30% of the chain's total reservations and upward of 50% of all reservations for individual properties.

The Franchise and the Flag.   Hotel franchising probably began during the late 19th century. Cesar Ritz—*ritzy* now means the finest in luxurious accommodations—gave his name to a small number of hotels whose management he supervised. Kemmons Wilson made the next advance in hotel franchising with the development of the Holiday Inn chain.

Franchising is all about the brand recognition discussed earlier in the chapter. The franchisor is able to deliver immediate brand identity by selling its "flag" to the franchisee. Franchisee and parent company are so alike that guests do not distinguish between them. The physical hotels look identical. It's the ownership and management structures that differ. The chain (the franchisor) does not own the franchise property, the operator (the franchisee) does. The franchisor does not manage the property, the franchisee does. If the franchisee elects not to manage, it could hire the franchisor as its management company under a separate management contract. Or instead, it could hire an entirely different management company. So now another party, the franchisor (the franchise company), has been added to the interaction of the developer, the owner, the lender, and the management company.

Each flag denotes a certain type of facility in the buyer's mind. A franchisee intent on developing long-stay facilities wouldn't shop for a franchise flying the flag of, say, a budget property such as Holiday Inn Express.

Once acquired, changing flags—canceling the franchise contract—is difficult and expensive because most contracts favor the franchisors. Many franchisees are small, family-owned businesses, whereas the franchisor is a multifaceted company. Competition and court decisions have helped balance the interests of the franchisees against those who write the contracts, the franchisors. Franchise advisory committees, which are assertive groups of franchise members (sometimes within each brand, sometimes across the brands) are also at work.[6] Publicity generated by these groups has helped garner the support of the more sensitive franchisors. Among the defining issues are

1. Defense from competing franchises within the supposedly protected area, especially as consolidation among franchisors puts many heretofore competing brands under one umbrella and on the same reservation platform;

2. Unexpected upgrade demands by the franchisor, particularly when the franchisee sells the hotel;

3. High liquidation damages when the franchisee tries to change flags.

Despite the negatives, buying a franchise flag is equally popular with both large absentee owners and small owner/operators. Branding is essential for attracting the transient traveler who may never come that way again. Franchising's recent success in Europe reaffirms the worth of the concept.

[6]Asian American Hotel Owners Association (AAHOA), a mildly militant organization of small (family-owned) hoteliers, has been especially effective in fighting for the rights of the franchisee.

➤ *INTERESTING TIDBITS*

- ➤ A *rule of thumb* is a general principle based on experience rather than on scientific testing. The "36/12 rule" emphasizes the importance of long-stay, repeat guests in the belief that 36% of the industry's room nights come from 12% of guest stays. (See also Chapter 9, "Role of the Room Rate," specifically the section "The Building Cost Rate.")

- ➤ Few single women patronized the nation's very early taverns. As that market developed, pushed along by the fight for the right to vote (post–Civil War, 1870s) and their call to the labor force (World War II, 1940s), commercial hotels set aside floors restricted to women guests. Some even had special entrances for women. A few hotels served female guests exclusively. History was revisited when the London Hilton reinvented the women's floor (2002). Extra security, in-room amenities, and female employees are the special appeals of the women's floor.

➤ *READING REFERENCES*

"Magic Fingers Lost Its Touch Long Ago, But Not For Mr. Gill." *The Wall Street Journal*, April 9, 2002, p. A1. The "Magic Finger Bed" was an important amenity of the 1960s and 1970s. As part of Motel 6's amenity creep (see page 46), the chain recently dropped this amenity. It still survives in some motels, as this very readable article relates. *The Wall Street Journal*: http://www.WSJ.com.

"Timeshare Report." Featured in issues of *Hotel & Motel Management*.

Challenges

➤ *TRUE/FALSE*

Questions that are partially false should be marked false (F).

___ 1. If, as some say, hotels are a commodity much like wheat and oil, the buyer/guest will focus on price in preference to brand.

___ 2. Amenity creep is the concern of health and safety inspectors, who force the closing of hotels when management fails to remedy the condition.

___ 3. Boutique hotels emphasize "soft" attributes (fashion, for example), whereas traditional hotels sell "hard" values (large sleeping rooms, for example).

___ 4. Hotel planners must pay attention to the differences between "upstairs buyers," for whom the room and its amenities are most important, and "downstairs buyers," who give preference to public space such as restaurants and bars.

___ 5. Elasticity of the marketplace refers to the degree that demand increases when room rates (prices) are increased or decreases when room rates are decreased.

➤ PROBLEMS

1. Using the trade press, your own management skills, or Web sites, prepare a list of six amenities, other than those cited in the text, that hoteliers use to attract business. *Hint*: Start the list with "free parking."

2. Identify the advantages and disadvantages to the personal career of a student who takes a job after graduation with a Hilton Inns franchise and passes up an offer from Hilton Hotels, the parent company.

3. Why is Best Western International not listed among the large management companies of Exhibit 2–14? After all, Best Western has some 300,000 rooms in its brand! Explain in detail.

4. Someone once said, "If you try to be all things to every guest, you'll likely end up as every guest's second choice." Is that an accurate statement? Why or why not? Answer with special attention to the segmentation of the industry's product line.

5. A traveler driving along Interstate 36 stops at two different hotels on successive evenings. Explain, and differentiate between, the signs posted by the front desk in terms of the text discussion about ownership, management, franchising, and joint ventures.
   Hotel A: This Hampton Inn is owned by Jerome J. Vallen and Sons, Inc., under license from Promus. Richfield Hotel Management.
   Hotel B: This Hampton Inn is owned by Promus. Jerome J. Vallen, General Manager.

6. Obtain a copy of a management contract from a local hotel, or review a book in the library on hotel management contracts. Discuss three terms (for example, life of the contract, payment, maintenance of the property, or investment by the management company) that intrigue you.

➤ ANSWERS TO TRUE/FALSE QUIZ

1. True. If hoteliers are unable to differentiate their hotels from others, and if the guest therefore sees no differences between them, the selection is likely to be based primarily on price.

2. False. Guests see amenities as "extras," something special that others do not offer. When everyone offers that extra, it's no longer special; it's expected. So a new amenity must be introduced: It creeps in.

3. True. In an effort to attract the new genre of travelers that appeared with the dotcom revolution, boutique hotels emphasize different values, some of which are soft; that is, hard to measure.

4. True. Certain guest types prefer certain attributes over those preferred by other guest types, and the hotel's market pretty much determines which is which.

5. False. Elasticity of the marketplace refers to the degree that demand changes (increases or decreases) when room rates (prices) increase or decrease.

The Structure
of the Hotel Industry

Outline

Price (room rate) is one reason that guests pick a particular hotel. Were each hotel the same as every other, price and price alone would determine that selection. That's how basic commodities (gasoline at the pump) are marketed: on price. Dollars and cents govern whenever buyers cannot distinguish one product from another. Fortunately, the business of lodging is not so threatened. For one, there are the dynamics discussed in Chapters 1 and 2: New products, new markets, new segments, and new innovations differentiate one hotel from another. Now Chapter 3 and later Chapter 7 look at the most telling of all the differences: the estimated 2 million persons who manage and staff the nation's 4,000,000 rooms.

Hotel service could never become a commodity, because there is a vast number of daily interactions between staff and visitors (see Chapter 7), which could never be standardized. The idea is further negated by the multicultural nature of both the workforce and the revolving customer base. Besides, the lodging business has a historical tradition of service. Unlike other industries that have but recently "discovered" the customer, hotel staffers have long been attuned to personalized service, the very converse of a commodity!

Carrying out this service mandate is exceedingly difficult. Earlier chapters described one of the hurdles: Ownership interests (real estate) and management interests (operations) frequently differ. Real-estate appreciation, the goal of ownership, is not always compatible with operating profits, the goal of management. The first focuses on asset management; the other on customer management—and managing for the customer begins with managing for the staff. Moreover, customer management, or service, is not an absolute. It's not delivered equally within the huge variety of operations, segments, markets, and locations that fall under the single umbrella called lodging. Service can be viewed best within the unique product of the individual hotel. Although there are many commonalities within lodging, every hotel is unique in one manner or another.

Physical differences are the most visible. The ski lodge has individual cottages or condos hidden in the woods. Resorts offer low-rise buildings scattered around the swimming pool and beach (see Chapter 1, Exhibit 1–10). How different are these designs from the urban, commercial giant squeezed by high land costs into a narrow, high-rise configuration (see Chapter 1, Exhibit 1–9).

The organizational structure can be just as unique, although not nearly as visible. Each operation takes form from basic organizational patterns common to the whole industry. Still, one does not expect the 1,000-room, chain-operated convention hotel to be much like the mom-and-pop highway hotel; nor the all-suite, long-stay property to take its structure from the native-American casino operation. All these differ, of course, from the structure of the conference center and the hard-budget economy and the boutique hotel.

Differences notwithstanding, both the building structure and the organizational structure adhere to basic blueprints. Although differences distinguish the properties, fundamentals remain the same. Organizations are constructed around guest services; sleeping rooms are built to nurture guest sensibilities. This chapter explores both structures.

➤ THE ORGANIZATIONAL STRUCTURE

Hotels employ a vast number of people with a variety of skills. Among them are plumbers and accountants, bartenders and cooks, groundskeepers and water purification experts, computer troubleshooters and telecommunication specialists. The larger the hotel, the more specialized are the tasks. Indeed, some hotels have larger resident populations than do many small towns.

Each hotel organizes this diversified workforce in different ways. Human and physical resources are combined to achieve company goals in the most efficient manner. Although each organization takes a unique form, the patterns that emerge are based on the industry's best practices.

Hotel organizations follow the pattern of other businesses or social institutions. The workforce is separated into specialized departments. Each is entrusted with a share of duties and services. Good management works to minimize the differences that invariably arise among the various departments. Poor performance in one department undermines the best efforts of all. Coordinating the whole, unifying the specialties, and directing joint efforts is the job of the general manager. General managers get the authority they need from the ownership interests of the management company, which may be, but rarely is, the same corporation that owns the building.

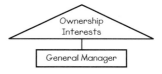

Ownership

From atop the pyramid, ownership oversees the unfolding organization (see Exhibit 3–1). Ownership is itself organized, most likely as a corporation, which is a legal person. Even individual hoteliers who own and manage family-owned businesses incorporate. Corporations are owned, in turn, by a variety of individuals. The corporation could be formed by a small group promoting a local hotel or by an international consortium operating across the globe. Control could be in the hands of one person or a family, or could be vested in as many as the 800,000,000 (eight hundred million!) shares authorized for the Marriott Corporation.[1]

One corporation might own other corporations, either as the sole owner or the major shareholder of the subsidiary corporation(s). That's Marriott relationship with its Ritz-Carlton, Renaissance Hotels, and Residence Inns divisions.

As legal persons, corporations have all the rights and responsibilities of individuals. They buy and sell hotels; they hire managers; they pay taxes; they borrow; they operate hotels. Corporations are favored because the individuals who own the corporation are not liable for corporate debts. Investors have limited liability. If the hotel fails, owners lose their investments, but they are not responsible for unpaid bank loans or food and beverage accounts owed by the corporation to the butcher or grocer. The corporate "person" is the one responsible.

Chapter 2 suggested other ownership forms. Among them are sole proprietorships, REITs, partnerships, or even corporate syndicates called joint ventures or strategic alliances.

The company that owns the building may or may not be organized similarly to the company that operates the hotel. But both anticipate a profitable operation and look to the general manager to make it happen.

[1]2001 Annual Report, Marriott International, Inc. Washington, D.C., p. 32. (Cendant has 2 billion shares authorized!)

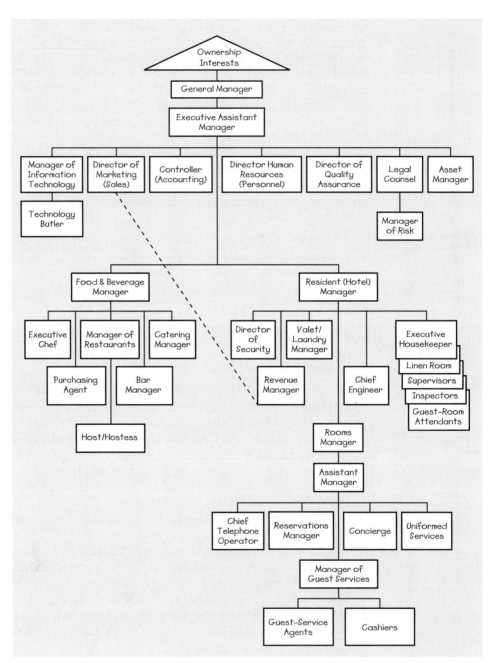

Exhibit 3–1   The organizational structure of American hotels is changing almost as rapidly as their architectural designs. Flatter organizations (fewer supervisory levels) notwithstanding, new positions are being added. Among them are managers (or directors) of quality assurance, information technology, and revenue management. The chart is not complete except for the resident manager's line, which is the thrust of the chapter and the text.

The General Manager

Management titles vary from hotel to hotel just as their organizations do. Large hotel chains use titles at the corporate level similar to other American businesses: CEO (chief executive officer); CFO (chief financial officer); COO (chief operating officer).

General manager (GM or *The* GM) is the favored title at the unit level—the operating hotel. If the GM is an executive of the corporation that owns or operates the hotel, his or her title might reflect that: *president* (of the corporation) *and general manager* (of the hotel). Owner-manager is used for a GM who actually owns the hotel. Standing alone, the title of general manager indicates no ownership interests. The GM is simply the employee most responsible to ownership, corporate or otherwise, and the one person accountable for the full scope of the operation. Total responsibility for all that happens in every department rests with the GM.

The GM deals either directly with ownership or indirectly through layers of corporate levels and titles: area vice president for operations; regional director of marketing; food and beverage manager, eastern division.

GM's with large organizations rely on an assistant, the *executive assistant manager*. Like the general manager, the executive assistant has complete jurisdiction over the entire house. That distinguishes the position from that of the *assistant manager,* which is a rooms department position (see Exhibit 3–1). Large hotels may use several assistant managers to cover the desk around the clock.

"Around the clock" because hotels never close: 7/24/365 places great demands on the time and energy of hotel executives. The work week, which is limited for operative employees by federal and state labor laws or labor contracts, is open ended for management. The burden is heavy on every department head as well as on the GM. An *executive-on-duty* program offers relief for all executives and their assistants. Slow periods (such as nights, weekends, and holidays at commercial hotels) are covered by rotating the entire management staff. Every department head of Exhibit 3–1 takes a turn as GM with responsibility for every department. The reservoir of management talent is deepened; the experience of the individual manager is broadened; and family time is strengthened.

➤*From Host to Executive.* The many changes that previous chapters recounted have impacted on the post of general manager. During the period of one-person ownership, general managers personified their hotels. The GM of the era was either the actual owner or a representative who stood in the owner's place. He (and in those days, the position was invariably held by a man) was known as "Mine Host." His name was part of the advertising, his personality part of the aura, his presence part of the hotel's very identity. Hotels were smaller, and the manager often visited with arriving and departing guests. The property reflected the host's qualities, the personality, the leadership, the essence of this very special person (see Exhibit 3–2).

Exhibit 3–2   The shift from hotel host to hotel manager is described lightly in this well-known ditty, which the authors have changed to modernize the phrasing. Time has not changed the numerous disciplines required of the modern general manager, even as qualifications shift back and forth between generalist and specialist.

What Has Become of Our Genial Hosts?

What was it in bygone days
That served the famous hoteliers?
Smiles and friendships, *bon mots* and more.
To know them, guests flocked through the door.

Schooled in the fine art of conversation
Made hotelkeeping an endless vacation,
Chatting and supping and drinking one's fill
While the cream of society fattened the till.

What has become of our Genial Hosts?
Alas, conditions have altered their posts.
They rarely see their fashionable clients.
Their careers have become mathematical science.

Occupancies, percentages, rooms income,
Wages, break-even, taxes, and then some!
Their carefree pasts have become archaic.
The innkeepers' life is today algebraic.

Each acts like an Einstein, a judge, and a foreman,
A housekeeper, a chef, an art critic, a doorman.
And there on the desk, a great volume about
Front-office management, titled *Check-In Check-Out*.

Consultants and salespersons vie for a visit
Then the new decorator with the latest what-is-it.
They're umpires and referees; they pacify all
From the board of directors to the charity ball.

And leaving the office, they find in the corridors
Anxious sales staffers and tired night auditors.
And if that's not enough, alack and egad
There's always the competitor's TV ad!

What's to be done about REITS and franchisees,
And what about the competition overseas?
Consolidation? Segmentation?
Rising prices of electrification?

Hearing the reverberations about minimum wage
Helped bring the change from host to sage.
Entertainment centers, computerization, what more?
Environmental concerns and a concierge floor.

What has become of our Genial Hosts?
What else: they're figments, relics, ghosts.
And when will they rest from their toil so hard?
When they hang o'er their tombs a "Do Not Disturb" card.

In contrast, today,

". . . the amount of time spent with customers versus budgets is totally reversed. In fact, one room clerk working at a hotel for more than six months . . . [said] she had never seen the general manager [at] the front desk!"[2]

GMs of an earlier period put their marks on properties because they were in one location for a long time. Not so today when the company's need for the special talents of a particular manager often means frequent transfers. Guests have also changed: Mass marketing and one-time arrivals make Mine Host less relevant. Executive talents now focus on a growing list of nonguest issues. Hence, many observers worry that "the business of hotels is no longer the hotel business."

Salaries and Benefits.   Outsiders still believe that the GM's job is all about meeting celebrities and enjoying free dining and drinks. But another night out for cocktails and dinner is not a hotelier's idea of a nice evening. Studies of general managers—and hotel GMs are a heavily studied group—indicate that their work weeks range between 50 and 65 hours. The same studies point out the importance of having people skills. While there are often calls for socializing and the skills that go with being an important community personage, having people skills refers chiefly to the management of the hotel's human resources. It's a job made more difficult by the staff's dependence on tips and gratuities. A large portion of the hotel staff is paid minimum wage, which accounts in part for the high rate of employee turnover.

Many hotels supplement the basic salary of wage-earning employees with incentive bonuses and rewards. The same is true for general managers who receive incentives that range between 20% and 40% of annual salary. GM salaries are dependent on three different criteria: the size of the hotel in rooms, the dollar volume of business done in gross revenue, and the average daily rate (ADR) earned by the property. Great variations in these three measures account for the large spread in annual management salaries, ranging from $40,000 to $250,000. The median salary for managers of large hotels is about $150,000 plus incentives of 20 to 25%.

GM salary packages are negotiated. Housing (no rent, telephone, or utility bills) for the manager and family might be added to the cash salary and bonus/incentive. Family meals in the dining room may be included. Free laundry and dry cleaning are common benefits. Membership fees for local clubs and associations are appropriate if the manager is expected to be a very visible community leader. Stock options (shares of stock sold to the executive at reduced prices) is another fringe benefit, an advantage of the corporate structure. The issue of what is fair compensation faces the whole business community, not that of hotels alone.

"Professional courtesy," by which one hotelier extends comp (free) accommodations to traveling executives of other hotels, is an extra benefit, but certainly not a negotiated one.

▶*Support Departments.*   Hotel managers contend with an ever-growing list of issues that require special knowledge and expertise (see Exhibit 3–2). Large hotels support the GM with experts in specialized fields of law, employment, environment, taxes, marketing, technology, and more (see Exhibit 3–1). If the GM carries a corporate title, so may these staff members. A president and general manager may have, for example, a vice president of marketing rather than a director of marketing. Remember

---

[2]Jeff Weinstein. "Old-Fashioned Hotelkeeping." *Hotels,* February 2001, p. 5.

that even if there is no separate management company, the operating hotel is also a corporation, often a subsidiary corporation of the chain that carries the name.

Staff positions support the operating departments as well as the general manager. The rooms manager, for example, looks to human resources for help in filling job vacancies; to sales for help in filling rooms; and to accounting for help in credit-card control and settlement. Staff members even make guest contact on occasion. Accounting, for example, may contact guests about unpaid accounts.

▶*The Food and Beverage (F&B) Department.*   Unlike the advisory nature of the support staff, the *food and beverage manager* has direct operating responsibility. F&B is one of the hotel's two major line departments (see Exhibit 3–1). The rooms department, which is the thrust of this text, is the other.

Food and beverage is subdivided into several operating units. Food preparation is headed by a *chef,* and food service by a *manager of restaurants,* which large properties may title *maitre d' hotel.* Parties and banquets are handled by a *catering manager* (or banquet manager), although this position is sometimes assigned to the marketing department. All beverage outlets, including banquet bars, report to a *bar manager.*

The importance of the food and beverage department has been eroding during the past half century. F&B, which accounted for nearly half of the lodging industry's revenue in the 1960s, about equal with rooms, now contributes only 20% of total sales (see Exhibit 3–3). This industrywide statistic reflects the large number of lodging units that no longer have food service. But food revenues have declined even in full-service hotels. Declines in dollar volume and in the number of food outlets have reshuffled organizational charts. Many middle management positions (bar manager and restaurant manager, for example) and their assistants have been eliminated. In fact, middle management posts have been deleted in almost every department of the hotel. Fewer managers available means that either decisions are pushed onto the operating employee—and Chapter 7 examines this issue—or responsibilities are broadened for the managers who remain.

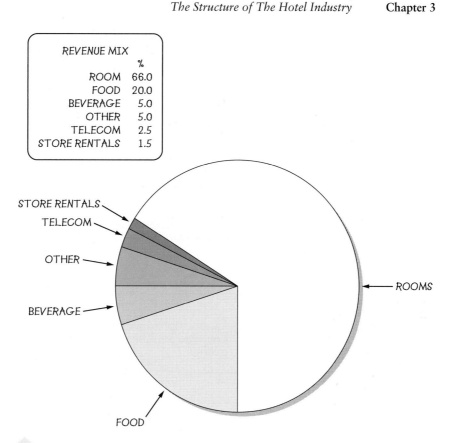

REVENUE MIX	
	%
ROOM	66.0
FOOD	20.0
BEVERAGE	5.0
OTHER	5.0
TELECOM	2.5
STORE RENTALS	1.5

Exhibit 3–3   Rooms is the largest revenue earner industrywide (remember, many small hotels have no food and beverage service) as well as the hotel's most profitable department, approaching $0.70 on the dollar. The percentage of nonroom revenues is higher in resorts that offer miscellaneous services such as spas, golf, and tennis.

The Hotel (or Resident) Manager

The *hotel manager,* also called the *house manager* or *resident manager,* is the front-of-the-house counterpart to the food and beverage manager. All operating departments other than food and beverage report to this position. Exhibit 3–1 outlines the divisions of the front of the house at a large hotel. Every department that services guests directly falls within the purview of the hotel manager. Finding employees capable of dealing with such face-to-face contacts is one major challenge of the job. Coordinating—presenting the services of several different departments as those of one company—is another (see Exhibit 3–4).

MANAGER, GUEST SERVICES

JOB DESCRIPTION

DIVISION: Gardens
DEPARTMENT: Guest Services
REPORTS TO: General Manager
STATUS: Exempt

JOB SUMMARY

The Guest Services Manager is responsible for ensuring the operation of the Front Office in an attentive, friendly, efficient and courteous manner, providing all guests with quality service prior to and throughout their stay, while maximizing room revenue and occupancy.

QUALIFICATION STANDARDS

Education & Experience:
At least 5 years of progressive experience in a hotel or a related field; or a 2-year college degree and 3 or more years of related experience; or a 4-year college degree and at least 1 year of related experience.
Previous supervisory responsibility preferred.

Physical requirements:
- Long hours sometimes required.
- Light work - Exerting up to 20 pounds of force occasionally, and/or up to 10 pounds of force frequently or constantly to lift, carry, push, pull or otherwise move objects.
- Must have a valid driver's license from the applicable state.

Mental requirements:
- Must be able to convey information and ideas clearly.
- Must be able to evaluate and select among alternative courses of action quickly and accurately.
- Must work well in stressful, high pressure situations.
- Must maintain composure and objectivity under pressure.
- Must be effective in handling problems in the workplace, including anticipating, preventing, identifying and solving problems as necessary.
- Must have the ability to assimilate complex information, data, etc., from disparate sources and consider, adjust or modify to meet the constraints of the particular need.
- Must be effective at listening to, understanding, and clarifying the concerns and issues raised by co-workers and guests.
- Must be able to work with and understand financial information and data, and basic arithmetic functions.

DUTIES & FUNCTIONS

Essential:
- Approach all encounters with guests and employees in an attentive, friendly, courteous and service-oriented manner.

Manager, Guest Services, Page 1

Exhibit 3–4   The guest-service manager, by whatever title (front-desk manager, rooms manager), has a broad range of responsibilities. They are described here in detail. *Courtesy of Wyndham Hotels & Resorts, Dallas, Texas.*

DUTIES & FUNCTIONS (cont.)

Essential (continued)

- Maintain regular attendance in compliance with Wyndham standards, as required by scheduling which will vary according to the needs of the hotel.
- Maintain high standards of personal appearance and grooming, which include wearing the proper uniform and name tag when working.
- Comply at all times with Wyndham standards and regulations to encourage safe and efficient hotel operations.
- Maintain a warm and friendly demeanor at all times.
- Establish and maintain attentive, friendly, courteous and efficient hospitality at the Front Desk.
- Respond to all guests requests, problems, complaints and/or accidents presented at the Front Desk or through Reservations, in an attentive, courteous and efficient manner. Follow up to ensure guest satisfaction.
- Motivate, coach, counsel and discipline all Guest Services personnel according to Wyndham S.O.P.'s.
- Ensure compliance to Wyndham Standard of the Week training, using the steps to effective training according to Wyndham standards.
- Prepare and conduct all Guest Services interviews and follow hiring procedures according to Wyndham S.O.P.'s.
- Conduct all 90 day and annual Guest Service employee performance appraisals according to S.O.P.'s.
- Develop employee morale and ensure training of Guest Services personnel.
- Maximize room revenue and occupancy by reviewing status daily. Analyze rate efficiency, monitor credit report and maintain close observation of daily house count.
- Attend all required Rooms Merchandizing meetings with all appropriate reports and documentation necessary to establish select sell guidelines and implement appropriate restrictions.
- Supervise the Night Audit function and monitor the House Charge Worksheet and Flash Report for accuracy.
- Participate in required M.O.D. program as scheduled.
- Ensure all end of the month report dates are met, i.e., Central Reservations, Market Segment, WynClub, AAdvantage, etc.
- Review Guest Services staff's worked hours for payroll compilation and submit to Accounting on a timely basis.
- Prepare employee Schedule according to business forecast, payroll budget guidelines and productivity requirements. Present with Wage Progress Report to General Manager weekly.
- Ensure that no-show revenue is maximized through consistent and accurate billing.
- Maintain Wyndham S.O.P.'s regarding Purchase Orders, vouchering of invoices and checkbook accounting.
- Ensure that Wage Progress, Productivity and the Ten Day Forecast are completed on a timely basis according to Wyndham S.O.P.'s.
- Maintain a professional working relationship and promote open lines of communication with managers, employees and other departments.
- Work closely with Accounting on follow-up items, i.e., returned checks, rejected credit cards, employee discrepancies, etc.
- Operate all aspects of the Front Office computer system, including software maintenance, report generation and analysis, and simple programming.
- Monitor proper operation of the P.B.X. console and ensure that employees maintain Wyndham S.O.P.'s in its use.
- Monitor the process of taking reservations ensuring that Wyndham courtesy and upselling techniques are maintained.
- Greet and welcome all guests approaching the Front Desk in accordance with Wyndham S.O.P.'s.
- Ensure implementation of all Wyndham policies and house rules. Understand hospitality terms.
- Operate pagers and radios efficiently and professionally in communicating with departmental staff. Ensure the proper use of radio etiquette within the department.

Manager, Guest Services, Page 2

Exhibit 3–4   *Continued.*

DUTIES & FUNCTIONS (cont.)

Essential (continued)
- Coordinate all aspects of the ongoing implementation of the Wyndham Way philosophy of service.
- Ensure correct and accurate cash handling at the Front Desk.
- Attend monthly all-employee meetings and any other functions required by management.
- Attend weekly staff meeting and provide training on a rotational basis using steps to effective training according to Wyndham standards.
- Perform any other duties as requested by the General Manager.
- Obtain all necessary information when taking room reservations.
- Ensure delivery of all messages, packages, and mail in a timely and professional manner.
- Be aware of all rates, packages and promotions currently under way.
- Follow and enforce all Wyndham hotel credit policies.
- Ensure that employees are, at all times, attentive, friendly, helpful and courteous to all guests, managers and other employees.
- Ensure participation by department in Wyndham Way monthly meeting.
- Focus the Guest Services and Housekeeping Departments on their role in contributing to the Guest Service Index (G.S.I.).

Marginal:
- Monitor all V.I.P.'s, special guests and requests.
- Maintain required pars of all front office and stationary supplies.
- Review daily Front Office work and activity reports generated by Night Audit.
- Review Front Office log book and Guest Request log on a daily basis.
- Assist the General Manager and Engineering Department in implementing and maintaining emergency procedures.
- Be familiar with all corporate sponsored programs such as airline mileage, Triple Upgrade, or V.I.P. programs, and the standards and procedures for each.
- Coordinate and maintain records for WynStar Program with the Wyndham Way Committee.
- Maintain an organized and comprehensive filing system with documentation of purchases, vouchering, schedules, forecasts, reports and tracking logs.
- Conduct meetings according to Wyndham standards as required by management.
- Perform, as necessary, all duties of Assistant Guest Services Manager.
- Other duties as required.

I HAVE READ AND UNDERSTAND THE JOB DESCRIPTION AS STATED ABOVE AND ACCEPT THAT ANY OF THE TASKS MAY BE MODIFIED OR CHANGED. I ACCEPT RESPONSIBILITY FOR KNOWING THE MODIFICATIONS AND / OR CHANGES IN THIS JOB DESCRIPTION. I CAN PERFORM THE ESSENTIAL FUNCTIONS OF THIS JOB AS LISTED ABOVE, WITH OR WITHOUT REASONABLE ACCOMMODATION.

_____   _____
Employee Signature   Date   Supervisor Signature   Date

Exhibit 3–4   *Continued.*

In keeping with the industry's move toward flatter organizations (fewer management levels between top management and the employee on the spot), small hotels operate without a hotel manager. Small hotels have fewer operating departments—no F&B, perhaps—and fewer staff positions clamoring for the GM's time. Without intervening management levels, the heads of rooms, housekeeping, and security have the GM as their immediate supervisor.

For our larger-hotel illustration, these important departments remain with the hotel or house manager. He or she supervises a broad sweep of support positions, not merely rooms. Included are the departments of engineering (maintenance), laundry, valet, security, revenue control, housekeeping, credit, business center, shop rentals, concierge, pool, spa, and more. (Exhibit 3–1 is not complete.)

Later sections of this chapter deal with the rooms department in detail. First, we visit with two other important segments of the house manager's responsibility: housekeeping and security.

▶*Housekeeping.*　　Responsibility for the delivery of the hotel's basic product, a clean room, rests unconditionally with this department. Yet it has never enjoyed the status afforded other units within the orbit of the resident manager. The explanation lies in part on the productive nature of the physical job: servicing guests rooms and cleaning public space. Besides, floor housekeepers usually work in isolation, while other front-of-the-house positions enjoy a rich social environment.

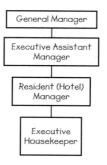

Floor housekeepers or *guest-room attendants* are among the hotel's poorest paid employees. Tips, which supplement the minimum salary of other low-wage jobs, are less available to the housekeeping crew. Therefore, the job attracts the least educated, particularly those with a limited knowledge of English—often recent immigrants. It is no surprise, then, that simple clerical duties—completing request forms for minor in-room maintenance—add to job stress. Without salable skills, housekeepers face another large negative: a great deal of part-time/call-in work. As occupancy falls, housekeeping jobs disappear. So uncertainty about the weekly pay check is piled atop physical labor and low status.

Nothing in this list of issues takes away from the amazing job that's done each day in hotels around the world. Cleanliness—the very essence of what the hotel sells and a prime factor in winning high ratings from agencies such as AAA—is achieved at a superb level of delivery because the housekeeping crew is hardworking and carefully supervised. A lack of language skills does not lessen one's motivation; minimum salary does not mean minimum commitment. But these factors, when combined with a high rate of employee turnover, do make the management job more difficult.

Organization and Duties of the Department.   *Housekeeper* is the title of this important departmental manager. In small hotels, the position requires the housekeeper to clean rooms as well as to supervise. *Working housekeeper* may then be the job title. Large hotels favor *executive housekeeper*. (Similar titles are found in the kitchen: *working chef* and *executive chef*).

Reorganization after reorganization continues throughout the industry as hoteliers try to stay ahead of business and social changes. The location of housekeeping within the overall organization has been in flux more than any other department. Responsibilities are added or deleted depending on the inclination of the general manager and the capabilities of the current housekeeper. Traditionally, housekeepers (women) have risen in the ranks from guest-room attendants. More recently, the position has been recognized for the management skills required. After all, housekeeping is the largest department in the hotel.[3] This recognition has opened the competition to professional managers, men as well as women, who have never worked the floor.

Housekeeping may or may not have responsibility for the laundry and valet departments. Housekeeping may or may not have responsibility for guest-room design and decor. Housekeeping may or may not have responsibility for swimming pools, outdoor ponds, and waterfalls with or without fish. Housekeeping may or may not have responsibility for upholsterers, painters and locksmiths. To emphasize housekeeping, some GMs have the department report directly to them; others hold to the more traditional resident-manager reporting line. Such variations account for differences among organizational structures even though there is one standard: Every hotel has a housekeeper.

Housekeeping is charged with the general cleanliness of guest rooms, corridors, and public spaces such as lobbies and restrooms. Special attendants may be assigned to employee locker rooms, guest bathhouses and spas, or other amenities special to the particular hotel. Housekeeping in the food and beverage department, including the banquet floor, is not normally the responsibility of the housekeeping department, but it may be. If not, the job is assigned to the stewar*d* (not stewar*t*), a food and beverage supervisor not shown in Exhibit 3–1.

Guest-room attendants service 12 to 18 rooms per day,[4] taking about 30 minutes per room (see Exhibit 3–19). Check-out rooms being readied for new occupants require more time to prepare than do stay-over rooms. Some hotels use two-person teams, hoping to offset job isolation and improve productivity. Housemen are available to help with heavier work, including wall- and window-washing, carpet vacuuming and shampooing, and moving furniture. Several of these jobs, window-washing in particular, may be outsourced to specialty firms. Housemen (or special "runners") move clean and soiled linens between the maids' closets on the guest floors (see Exhibit 3–15 adjacent to room 11) and the laundry.

A wide variety of guest supplies (shampoos and other amenities), cleaning supplies (rags and cleansers), and small equipment (buckets and vacuums) necessitates a careful control of inventory. Help is available from the accounting department, which usually assigns a number for each item based on occupancy patterns. Thus, so many bars of soap are ordered if occupancy for the quarter (of a year) is running at, say,

---

[3]The housekeeping staff of the 4,000-room Excalibur Hotel, Las Vegas, numbers 750 persons.
[4]Housekeeping crews were cut dramatically during the post–September 11 decline in occupancy. Many hotels assigned 20 to 24 rooms per housekeeper. With less than 20 minutes available per room, occupied rooms received less attention. Linens were not changed; amenities were not stocked; vacuuming and bathroom cleaning were curtailed.

68%. Replacements, which may be purchased directly by the housekeeper or through the hotel's purchasing department, are charged against the housekeeper's budget.

Other departmental duties include monitoring sick guests, lost-and-found property,[5] and linen control. Counting and weighing linens (about 9 pounds per midrange room) are important if the hotel has no laundry. Outside laundries base charges on linen count and weight. Moreover, many hotels rent their linen from the laundry company. Other chores include dry cleaning drapes and bedspreads, disinfecting after animal occupancy, pest control, and the difficult cleanups that follow fire and death. Linen repair is handled by a seamstress who works in the *linen room*, the central office–complex of the housekeeper. This person also fits and maintains uniforms for staff across the entire hotel. All uniformed personnel visit the linen room to trade soiled uniforms for fresh ones.

Coordination between the front desk and the housekeeping department is essential. Hundreds of persons arrive and depart daily. Rooms must be serviced quickly to placate waiting guests and maximize room revenue. A *floor supervisor* or *floor housekeeper* inspects (hence also *inspectress*) and approves rooms recently vacated and cleaned by the guest-room attendant. The room is held *on-change* by the front desk until approved by the inspection. Rooms must be reclassified from on-change to *ready* before guest occupancy, although waiting guests may be assigned on-change rooms before they clear inspection.

Continuous training and supervision are important elements of housekeeping management. Security awareness should be high on the list of topics, because most property losses (both the hotels' and the guests') originate in guest rooms. This makes guest-room attendants and floor supervisors the first line of security defense. Unfortunately, it also places them in the first line of suspicion; they have the master keys. It's a matter of self-interest for everyone on the floor to abide by basic security principles: to watch for suspicious persons; to keep floor closets locked; to secure master keys, which access the rooms (see Chapter 14), by attaching them to their persons with retractable cords. Properly trained guest-room attendants will never, ever open doors for guests without keys or allow guests to enter open rooms. That's why security training teaches housekeepers who are working a room to block open doors with their carts. Equally important, room attendants must report suspicious activity in the corridors or unusual items (burglary tools, printing paraphernalia, etc.) in the rooms.

As we shall see in the following sections, housekeeping is but one arm of hotel security.

►*Security.*   Automation and social changes have shrunk the size of several departments under the hotel managers' control. Security has been an exception. Larger budgets have allowed for more personnel and equipment. They are lodging's response to greater liability claims and rising insurance costs as street crime enters the lobbies and corridors of even the most fashionable hotels.

The scope and purpose of hotel security has changed. From the single house detective or watchman walking a nightly fire patrol—adequate for the 1950s and 1960s—hotel security has matured to match present-day demands. Vigilance increased after the Persian Gulf War (1991) and moved to the forefront of all govern-

---

[5]The lost-and-found department of Chicago's 2,000-room Hyatt Regency finds 113 pieces of underclothing, 31 pairs of eyeglasses, 30 cell phones, and 2 sets of dentures in a typical month. Jeff Higley. "Chicago hotel's lost and found department has Hart." *H&MM*, November 6, 2000, p.142.

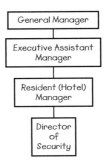

mental and business activities after the destruction of the Twin Towers, which included Marriott's hotel at the World Trade Center (2001). Parts of the industry responded to these events with knee-jerk decisions. Some refused to accept or hold guest baggage at the bell desk. Package delivery as well as some loading dock deliveries were subjected to inspection and x-rays. Auto trunks were examined before cars were garage parked. Baggage had to be removed directly from guest rooms; corridor pick-up was no longer allowed even for large tour groups.

More reasonable, permanent changes were being initiated long before the 1990s. The lodging industry was forced to re-examine its overall security because of several widely publicized events. At the top of that list was the 1971 in-room rape of a well-known Hollywood actress. That occurred just as the industry was promoting travel for unaccompanied women. Then came exposés by the press attacking the quality of hotel security even though crime rates in hotels are much lower than in the surrounding cities. Disastrous fires in Las Vegas focused attention on hotel fire safety, sprinkler systems, and evacuation plans. British tourists were targeted in southern Florida in a series of ugly incidents that required government intervention.

The lodging industry first responded with basic security measures and then moved toward professionalizing its security forces. Better, not merely more, security measures were implemented. First came the widespread installation of electronic locks (see Chapter 14), observation ports (peepholes in corridor doors), and better fire protection, including public address outlets in guest rooms. Perimeter lighting was improved. Smoke alarms and sprinkler systems were mandated. Properties that failed to comply suffered downgrades by rating agencies such as AAA and lost their franchise affiliations.[6]

A second phase of equipment upgrades is currently underway. It reflects improvements in security equipment of all types. CCTV (closed-circuit television) with improved video cameras enables one security person to monitor a vast array of corridors, parking areas, and public space. Special in-room alarms for the hearing and visually handicapped are being installed. Upgraded telephone and radio communications add to efficiency. Remote card readers control access to hotel facilities such as pools and garage gates. Perhaps biometric room systems, which are now in the pipeline, will serve as the room keys of the future. In the meantime, simple decisions such as sharing perimeter patrols with nearby competitors produce results.

An open, candid approach to the problem has been another shift in policy. Heretofore, lodging executives rarely spoke of security. Plain-clothes personnel were favored over uniforms. Today, hotels go for visibility: uniforms or distinctive blazers

---

[6]Sheraton reportedly defranchised 215 properties in the early 1990s.

in the lobbies, by the elevators—no floor access without a room key—and on patrol. Not all personnel switched to uniforms. Many still dress fashionably in keeping with their prior backgrounds as FBI agents, army intelligence officers, and police investigators, many with degrees in criminology.

Security's Charge. Good security has strong market appeal—guests want to feel safe, but that's not its major charge. Security has always had two basic responsibilities. It is charged with the protection of persons (guests and staff) and of property, including the hotel's property. In one respect, the hotel is also a person. Its well-being suffers substantially from the poor reputation that arises from security incidents, and even more so from the bungling of personnel trying to handle the situation. Many lawsuits have their origin in the failure of security and/or the desk to respond compassionately and professionally to guest injuries or losses.

Protecting persons has a higher priority than protecting property. However, loss of property far outweighs (by a factor almost as large as 9 to 1) attacks on persons. Property losses come from several directions. Petty theft of towels and other furnishings, even televisions and clocks that are not secured to the tabletop, can be attributed to both employees and guests. Employees are believed to be the single greatest source of hotel larceny, but guests often take home more than memories. Small items, especially those at convention booths (for example, sports card memorabilia), are more difficult to secure than large items such as garaged autos. Pilferage is significant enough for some hotels to tag property with innocuous looking logos. These minute circuit-containing tags track the hotel's property—and why not, when one large chain estimates the loss of just towels from guest and staff at over $3,000,000 annually!

Theft against guests is not all employee theft. There are professional thieves who specialize in hotels. They know how easy it is to obtain room keys from the desk or from the guests' belongings around the pool. Guests are not all innocent. Some lose their valuables and accuse the hotel, and others pretend a loss for insurance purposes.

Risk preparedness and crisis management have shifted the focus and structure of hotel security. Large chains have added a manager (even a vice president) of loss prevention. Petty thieves, pickpockets, and prostitutes still demand attention, but many new flash points have been added to the basic assignment of loss prevention. Security now umbrellas and trains for a whole range of emergencies, including hazardous materials; bomb threats; fire; gas leaks; terrorism; riots and crowd control; elevator failures; CPR and medical emergencies, including food poisoning; and guest lawsuits. Security has focused more attention than ever before on risk management, on workman's compensation injuries, and on compliance with ADA, Americans with Disabilities Act (see Chapter 7). In certain locales, Hong Kong for one, hotel security even prepares for cyclones, tornados, and floods. Loss of electric power is a closer-to-home contingency.

Security handles plenty of other tasks as well. It helps the credit manager with lockouts and luggage liens. It handles drunks and prostitutes (*night birds*). It maintains records and logs that become vital if cases go to court. Security works with police in robbery, murder, and suicide cases. It interfaces with insurance companies about accidents and claims.

A greater openness about security has enlisted guests into the campaign. In-room notices alert guests to first-level security: Look through the peephole; lock the corridor doors, sliding doors, and adjoining-room doors. Guests are urged to use front-office or in-room safes (see Chapter 14) for valuables since temptation and opportunity are the most recognized reasons for guest theft.

Evacuation routes are now standard postings on the inside of corridor doors, and lobby signs warn against elevator use during fires. Following examples set in the Far East, fire-exit signs have been relocated near the floor where they are visible to guests crawling under the smoke.

Competitors have also been enlisted. Governmental agencies, which might see cooperation between competing marketing departments as restraint of trade, endorse industry-wide cooperation in security. When one hotel is hit, the entire community is alerted. The likelihood of apprehending the felon increases because thieves generally work one area before moving on. Convention and visitor bureaus are part of the network. Convention crowds of tens of thousands have always created medical emergencies and petty theft. But their very size may now make them targets for coercion. Smaller, second- or third-tier convention cities are less visible and may benefit from World-Trade-Center anxiety.

Public safety, which had never been a priority in the selection of convention sites, has become a major consideration. There is increased sensitivity to booth security. Convention halls use explosive-sniffing dogs, metal detectors, package searches, and ramp control to bolster security. Off-duty police are being recruited to act as convention security. New paragraphs are hurriedly being added to standardized convention contracts to reflect the growing concern with public safety (and with ADA). New provisions for unexpected and disruptive events, force majeure *(forz ma-zhoer)*, are redefining what had been previously understood to be acts of God. Tour companies and associations are adding additional reasons for canceling group bookings or reducing room commitments without penalty.

Hotel security has moved up the organizational ladder in importance, even as other departments (bells and telephone) have been downsized. However, it functions as it always has. It acts first as a deterrent, then as a restraint, and only rarely as a police force. Hotel security must remain an iron hand in a velvet glove.

▶*Other Departments.*   Note was taken previously of the hotel manager's very broad responsibilities. He or she manages all of the hotel's operating departments except food and beverage. This includes the numerous tenants who rent space. Among them are stores and shops (florists, beauticians, men's wear, etc.), allied businesses (airline or tour desks), and commercial firms that may take office space. The business center may be owned by the hotel, or it may be another tenant. Negotiating the lease and rental contracts falls to the office of the hotel manager supported by hotel staff positions in law and accounting.

Thousands of people pass through the hotel each week. Medical emergencies must be anticipated and preparations put in place. That's another responsibility for the hotel manager, although the assignment may be delegated, perhaps to the concierge. Many large cities have some form of *HotelDocs,* a private medical service. The physicians come without charge to the hotel; ill travelers pay for the care as they would at home.

The *facilities manager,* if the hotel has one, is likely located within the hotel manager's control. The post reports either directly to the house manager or indirectly as a member of the engineering or housekeeping departments. A facilities manager is responsible for all of the physical plant, from the engine room to the gardens. The job oversees maintenance and repair, and new construction. Employee health and safety and even technology may be subject to oversight by the facilities manager.

The Rooms Manager

Full-service operations require some of the hotel manager's responsibilities to be moved down the organizational line. Rooms, which might include housekeeping, is then assigned to the next management level, the *rooms manager*. Reservations, telephone, concierge, and uniformed services are among the departments reporting to the rooms manager, as is the front desk. If the management load is still too heavy, the rooms manager may delegate oversight of the desk to another line officer, the *front-office manager*. This manager assumes control over the front desk proper, including guest-service agents (front-office clerks), credit, cashiers, mail, messages, and information. The position of front-office manager is discussed shortly.

Few hotels need so many executives for the front of the house. This chapter recognizes that by including duties of all three positions in the job description of Exhibit 3–4. Whatever the management titles, Exhibit 3–4 illustrates the need for skill in dealing with people (both staff and guests) and signals the importance of attention to detail that is expected in the rooms division.

▶*Room Reservations.*   Reservations are requests for rooms from prospective guests who intend to arrive sometime in the future. The inquiries are received, processed, and confirmed by the reservations department, which is supervised by a *reservations manager*.

Reservations arrive by letter, fax, and email, and occasionally directly across the desk. Most often, they are made by telephone. Inquiries do come to the hotel's reservation office directly from the guest, but it's more likely that the requests come through the central reservation office of the chain or franchise, the toll-free numbers. As other, independent agencies enter the reservation stream (Chapter 4 explains the procedure in detail), the number of direct reservation department/guest contacts decline. To some extent, the onsite reservation department becomes less important. Small hotels eliminate reservations entirely by assigning the job to guest-service agents, as do larger hotels during off-hours. The importance of the guest's initial contact with the hotel is sometimes overlooked. Reservation clerks must have a strong telephone personality, must be good salespersons, and must have adequate knowledge of the hotel and the community. After all, the quality of the disembodied voice is all the potential guest has to make an initial judgment.

The reservation department keeps records of who is arriving, at what time, and for how long. The information, including the type of facilities wanted, must be communicated to the front-desk clerk in anticipation of the guest's arrival. Tracking the number of rooms sold and the number still available for sale is the biggest responsibility of the reservation department. Groups and individual guests must be balanced to achieve a full house (100% occupancy) without overselling, which means not committing more rooms than are available. Reservations are maintained on a day-to-day basis for a year and in less detail for as much as three to five years ahead. Computerization has made the job easier and the decisions more accurate, as explained in Chapter 5.

▶*The Uniformed Services.*   The ranks of the service department (or uniformed services, or bell department) are on the wane. At one time, this department included baggage porters, transportation clerks, pages, and elevator operators for both guest and service cars. Now it is organized around bellpersons and door attendants, and even their numbers are decreasing. Several reasons explain the decline.

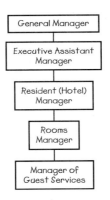

Changes in travel habits and licensing requirements have eliminated the service department's role in travel arrangements. Furthermore, guests need less help because they travel with less luggage. Stays are shorter, baggage is lighter, and self-service is part of American life. Wheeled suitcases enable guests to handle their own baggage during the bulk of their journey. Why, then, should they seek help to ride an elevator up several floors? Fewer tips translate into less job appeal and a smaller workforce in the uniformed services department.

Tips are declining even among guests who do use bell service. Bringing ice, for example, a time-honored assignment, is no longer a "front" call because refrigerators are in the rooms or self-service ice machines are on the floor. Group arrivals and departures are among the service department's best moneymakers because a contractual charge is made by the sales department for each bag in and each bag out. Funds are collected by the hotel and distributed to the bells whether or not guests use the service. Tips are high priority for housekeepers as well. To encourage gratuities, they leave envelopes and messages: "This room has been serviced by N̲A̲M̲E̲." Some are more blatant: "If you wish to leave a gratuity, please use this envelope."

The decline in the number of uniformed employees has another explanation: management cost-cutting. Today, everyone must be paid minimum wage, whereas tips alone constituted the salary of an earlier era. Reducing the staff cuts labor costs and with them fringe benefits, which add as much as one-third more to direct labor costs. So the hotel that services the entrance door around the clock is rare, and the motor hotel without any of the uniformed services is the norm. In urban properties with separate parking, someone needs to be at the door to handle garaging and other auto services. Few urban hotels own their own parking spaces. They lease the space or have an outside contractor take a parking concession. (This outsourcing is still another explanation for today's smaller uniformed staff.)

If bell services are available, they will be the guest's first contact with the hotel. Whether it's a door attendant, a bellperson, or the airport van driver (also a member of the department), the first impression will stick. The condition of the uniform, the personality of the individual, and the quality of the greeting tells the new arrival about the condition of the hotel and the level of its service (see Chapter 8, Exhibit 8–15). In this respect, the industry's human resources departments usually do a better job hiring staff for the door and the bells than for the van.

With guest arrivals and departures as their main function, bellpersons can be scheduled at a ratio of 1 bellhop per 65 anticipated hourly arrivals/departures. If they exist at all in small hotels, the bellstaff may also handle room service, lobby cleaning, and pool maintenance along with their other duties.

The title of the modern service department head is *manager of services*, or *superintendent of services*, not nearly as romantic as the more traditional terms, *bell captain*, or its shortened version, *captain*. Some services that were previously handled by the captain have migrated to the desk of the concierge. With them has gone a flow of money, since tour bookings and auto rentals represent a commission to the desk that books them.

▶ ***Concierge.***   Not many U.S. hotels have a *concierge*; it's a new rooms position that has appeared in larger, upscale, U.S. properties. The concierge has long been popular overseas, especially in France.[7] (In Great Britain, where the front office is called the front hall, the concierge is the head hall porter.) Like a French idiom, translating the nuances of the job into Americanese leaves something to be desired. Many guests are uncertain what the position does, let alone how to pronounce it (*kon syerzh*).

The word comes from the Latin *con servus*, meaning "with service." Other translations offered are "fellow slave" or, more to the point, "building guard." According to the French, the *Comte de Cierges* (Count of Cierge) was in charge of the prisons, making him the keeper of the keys under the French monarchs.[8] Thus, the European concierge appeared as a door attendant (building guard) and from that to the keeper of the keys, porter, and provider of various services.

These duties are still part of the European concierge's job, particularly in small hotels. Controlling the keys enables the concierge to watch the comings and goings of guests and thus to furnish a bit of extra protection and information. This is not the

---

[7]The International Union of Concierges was founded in Paris, France, in 1952 and in the United States in 1978. Members wear the Golden Keys (Les Clefs d'Or) that are their symbol of professionalism.

[8]The prison in Paris's Palais de Justice is the Conciergerie prison. Marie Antoinette was imprisoned there during the French Revolution.

American interpretation of the job, except when a hotel offers a concierge floor, or luxury floor. Even then, the added security is a secondary objective.

The keeper of the door, the lobby concierge (see Exhibit 3–5), provides all types of miscellaneous information and a variety of personal, but minor, services. Information and service shape the basic description of the concierge's job. Travel information, messages, tickets and reservations to a broad range of events, babysitters, language

Exhibit 3–5   To assure accessibility, this concierge is located in the lobby. Some hotels limit this service to concierge floors, which offer other extra services at a higher room rate. The pleasant working conditions and the aura of confident service are highlighted in this lobby photo. *Courtesy of the Wynfrey Hotel, Birmingham, Alabama.*

translation, and secretarial sources all fall within the purview of the concierge. Guests may ask the concierge to arrange for pet care, to provide extra chairs, to arrange flower delivery, to find lost items, to get medical care in an emergency, to recommend hair stylists, anything (see Exhibit 3–6).

As hotels retrench some services and automate others, the post of concierge becomes increasingly important. Guests can no longer turn to transportation desks, floor clerks, and elevator operators for questions and services. Those jobs no longer exist. Many of the gratuities that previously went to the uniformed staff have been redirected to the concierge desk. For services rendered, a concierge may be tipped by the guest and commissioned by the service company (theater, rentals, etc.).

A play on words has created the job of *compcierge,* in which *comp* stands for computer. A compcierge comes in two forms. The first is a *technology butler:* a technician or information technology (IT) expert who provides technology assistance to guests and conventioneers. The second form of compcierge is a computerized console that provides information about the local scene. Guests turn to the computer for directional information, theaters, restaurants, and similar listings. A computerized compcierge can stand alone or support a concierge's desk by freeing the live concierge for more complicated services.

The Concierge Floor.   The concierge floor is one amenity not discussed in Chapter 2. It is an extra service facility available at an extra charge. The concierge

Exhibit 3–6
Concierges offer an almost unlimited list of services, ranging from A to Z.

A...	as in	Art supplies and restoration
B...	as in	Babysitting services for vacating parents
C...	as in	Churches for all denominations
D...	as in	Dinner reservations at sold-out restaurants
E...	as in	Errand and courier services for speedy delivery
F...	as in	Flowers for that special occasion
G...	as in	Galleries for antiques and arts
H...	as in	Helicopter services
I...	as in	Interpreters for an international symposium
J...	as in	Jewelers from whom one can buy with confidence
K...	as in	Kennels for a cherished pet
L...	as in	Libraries for source materials
M...	as in	Maps to navigate the city or the subway
N...	as in	Newspapers from distant cities and foreign countries
O...	as in	Orchestra tickets at the last minute
P...	as in	Photographers for that spcial occasion
Q...	as in	Queries that no one else can answer
R...	as in	Restaurants of every specialty
S...	as in	Scuba diving sites and services
T...	as in	Transportation: air; auto; bus; limo; taxi; train
U...	as in	Umbrellas on a rainy day
V...	as in	Virtual reality equipment
W...	as in	Wedding chapels
X...	as in	Xeroxing a last-minute report
Y...	as in	Yoga demonstrations and instructions
Z...	as in	Zoo directions for an outing with the children

service is limited to guests on that special sleeping floor. Continental breakfast and evening cocktails are usually provided. As a premium floor, there are other extras. A terrycloth robe is furnished for the bath, shoes are shined, rooms are larger, arrival and departure procedures are expedited, and security is enhanced.

Access to the floor is limited and requires a special key for the elevator. The concierge is usually seated by the elevator, adding security as the floor clerk's position did before World War II.

All the upscale chains have concierge floors. Hilton calls its concierge floors Towers after the famed Waldorf-Astoria Towers, which is part of the Hilton chain. Hyatt uses Regency club; Radisson, Plaza Club. Add these names to the frequent-guest programs, and the confusion of name segmentation increases dramatically.

The Asian entry into the U.S. hotel business has brought pleasant additions to the concierge service. A floor butler, or floor steward, is available around the clock to handle personal services, including unpacking. Upscale Asian hotels have room bells or switches on the bed console to summon the butler.

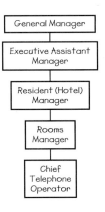

▶ *Telephone.*   Hotels have oodles of telephones! Many guest rooms have two; some have three with one in the bathroom. It is not unusual for a large hotel to have more phones than a small town has. Even as the number of instruments was growing, the size of the hotel's telephone department was shrinking. Computerization and social changes have reduced personnel in the telephone department just as automation and social changes have reduced the size of the bell department. Chapter 14 provides a complete picture of changes in the communications industry and their impact on the lodging industry.

There are fewer telephone operators because local and long-distance calls are handled by direct-dial, automatic equipment. Similarly, calls between guest rooms or from guest rooms to hotel departments, room service for example, no longer require an operator to complete the call. Electronic billing automatically records the telephone company's charges on the guest's electronic bill, eliminating the old position of charge operator.

In no other department of the hotel has the introduction of costly and complex equipment been so rapid and so complete, and worked so well. Supervising the few employees left in the department is the head telephone operator, called the *chief operator* or *telephone supervisor*. Depending on size, there might be an assistant or shift supervisor.

Operators may still answer incoming calls and direct them to their proper destinations. The caller's sole contact with the property is the disembodied voice of the telephone operator, so incoming calls must be handled professionally and pleasantly. Some hotels still have incoming messages taken by the operator. More and more, the operator doesn't answer incoming calls and doesn't take messages. Incoming calls are handled by an electronic menu from which the caller chooses a service.

If the service chosen involves a guest or guest room, the electronic voice says, "Press 1," and the operator intercedes to protect guest security, since hotels never give out the room or telephone numbers of registered guests. Automation takes over again once the operator connects the incoming call to the guest's room. The system allows the caller to leave a message on the guest's telephone mailbox. Direct access assures both privacy and accuracy. Telephone operators no longer transcribe messages by trying to interpret the many accents that make up the calling public. Guests no longer look quizzically at an operator's scribbled handwriting. Automated telephone systems provide better service despite the annoyance of listening to the electronic operator.

Even morning wake-up calls have been automated, although the number of wake-up calls has been reduced by furnishing an alarm clock in each guest room. Some guests still prefer the assurance of human intervention, so the telephone operator provides it with a morning wake-up call, but even that is automated.

Manager of Guest Services

The organizational structure of a full-service hotel calls for one final level of management, the *front-office manager* or *manager of guest services. Assistant managers* might support this position during each shift, or a senior room clerk might do the job. With so complete a structure, job responsibilities grow narrower down the organizational ladder. Front-office managers control the immediate front-office staff, but the importance of the job makes it a pivotal assignment.

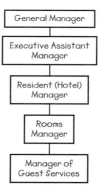

▶**Structure of the Front Office.**   Physically, the front office is an easily identifiable area of the lobby. Functionally, it is much less so despite constant reference to it as the "hub" and "heart" of the hotel. The overuse of such terms should not detract from the real importance of the front office. It is, in fact, the nerve center of guest activity: the very face of the hotel. Through it flow communications with every other department; from it emanate instructions for the service of the guest; to it come charges for final billing and settlement.

Organizational interdependence is not the only reason for the preeminent position of the front office. It is equally a matter of economics. Room sales produce about two-thirds of the hotel's total revenue (see Exhibit 3–3), more than food, beverage, and telephone combined.[9] For budget hotels, room sales account for almost 100% of sales. For others, much of the food and beverage sales originate in meetings and conventions, whose search for site selections begins with rooms. Furthermore, rooms is a more profitable department than are the other operating units. Each room-sale dollar produces about $0.73 in departmental profit. Profit for food and beverage combined averages out to about $0.21.

Guests relate to the front office, and this adds to its importance. Guests who rarely see their housekeepers, who never see the cook, who deal with sales only on occasion, know the hotel by its desk. They are received at the desk and they depart from the desk. It is toward the desk that guests direct complaints and from the desk that they expect remedies. Guest identification, as much as profit or interdepartmental dependence, accounts for management's overriding concern with the front office.

Better to define the front office as a bundle of duties and guest services rather than as a fixed area located behind the lobby desk. Some divisions of the front office—reservations, for example—can be located elsewhere without affecting their membership in the front-office structure. Computerization's instant communication has reduced the need for all front-office segments to be within physical hailing distance of one another.

Someone once said that the front office was so named because it was close to the front door. Simple enough, but many hotels have substituted the term *guest-service area* in an effort to better define the role of the front office. By extension, the front-office manager becomes the *manager of guest services* (see Exhibit 3–4). Retitled accordingly, front-office clerks become *guest-service agents*. Whatever their names, front-office managers and their agents serve the desk for the guest's convenience.

Working Hours.   Hotels never close. The legal definition of a hotel requires that they do not. Therefore, work schedules must provide around-the-clock staffing, at least at the front desk. Other departments (personnel or accounting) work a more normal workweek. Work schedules must also provide for the peaks and valleys that bring daily, sometimes hourly, fluctuations to the volume at the desk.

THE SHIFT (OR WATCH).   Most desk employees work an eight-hour shift, five days per week, with two successive days off, which creates three equal shifts per day. Sickness, vacation time, and days off are covered by others, some of whom work part time. Although there are variations, especially in resort areas, the model of Exhibit 3–7 follows the pattern of other industries.

Day shift	7:30 AM–3:30 PM
Swing shift	3:30 PM–11:30 PM
Graveyard shift	11:30 PM–7:30 AM

Exhibit 3–7   Typical working hours at a hotel's front office. Overlapping jobs are often scheduled in 15 to 30 minute intervals to ensure consistency during shift changes.

---

[9]The sequence is different in casino hotels, where gaming revenue accounts for 60% of gross and rooms only 15%. Food is 12%; beverage 9%; other 4%.

The day shift is preferred by most employees because it follows the usual work-day. Bellpersons opt for the swing shift, when arrivals and tips are the heaviest. Even senior front-office clerks choose the swing shift if tips are customary, as they especially are at resorts.

The graveyard shift has the least guest activity, but it is during this shift that the night audit is completed. The night audit is more specialized than the other front-office duties. Thus, night auditors cannot take advantage of the general policy that allows senior employees to select their shifts. Few workers prefer graveyard, which is one explanation for the shortage of night auditors.

A special effort is needed to maintain morale during the graveyard watch. Graveyard work should be covered by formal policies. Employees must know that they are not locked into a career of night work. They are rotated when openings appear in the more desirable shifts. In the meantime, salary supplements are paid for night work, and careful attention is paid to night meals in those hotels where the kitchen staff tends to shortchange the night crew's menu.

Rotating personnel and shifts whenever possible, and where union contracts allow, enables employees to know one another. It also reduces the chance of collusion among employees who always work together. Sometimes day and swing shifts are switched en masse. This is done at the start of each month as employees' days off allow. It is unwise to make the switch on two successive workdays. The swing shift would close at 11:30 PM, and the same employees would report for the day shift at 7:30 the following morning. Not only is this a burdensome procedure in a large city, where employees need commuting time, but it may also be illegal under state labor laws. Shift rotations should always follow the clock: day, evening, graveyard, off; day, evening, and so on.

Most front-office positions follow the same work pattern. Cashiers, clerks, and even supervisors change shifts in concert. A 15-minute overlap offers a continuity that is lost with an abrupt change of shifts. If there are several persons in each job, individuals could leave in 15-minute intervals. If not, complementary jobs could be changed every quarter hour. Cashiers might change at 3 PM and guest-service agents at 3:15 PM, for example.

THE SPLIT SHIFT.   Split shifts require employees to report for work, get off, and then return for a second shift the same day (see Exhibit 3–8, Employee A). Wage-and-hour laws, unionization, and just plain distance have almost eliminated use of the split shift. Isolated, seasonal resorts may still employ it if state labor laws exempt seasonal workers, in which case it is not limited to the front desk. The kitchen, dining room, and linen room also schedule that way. Commuting time is not an issue when seasonal employees live on the premises or nearby.

Employee A	7:00 AM–12:30 PM
Employee B	12:30 PM–6:30 PM
Employee A	6:30 PM–11:00 PM
Night Auditor	11:00 PM–7:00 AM

Exhibit 3–8   The split shift (or split watch) is used at seasonal resorts if labor laws allow, and if commuting time is negated by on-premise housing. Employees A and B swap shifts weekly.

The split shift offers real advantages for a small property where only one person staffs the desk. Employees need not be relieved for meals. They eat either before or after their shifts. Exhibit 3–8 illustrates the long and short days of the arrangement. Employees A and B, but not the night auditor, customarily switch shifts daily or weekly.

Resorts that do turndowns—replacing bath towels and preparing the bed for use—may require the room attendant to return in the evening for a variation of the split shift. Upscale properties handle turndowns by bringing in a second shift. That's when the night attendant leaves chocolate on the pillow.

FORECAST SCHEDULING.   Building a weekly or biweekly work schedule is part science and part art; both improve through experience. A forecast of room occupancy, which the reservation department completes (see Chapter 6), is the starting point. Manpower needs can be projected once the number of rooms occupied has been estimated. New computer programs match demand to the proper number of staff and even to the days-off/days-on preferences of the individuals.

Each hotel has its own design and logistical issues. Is there cross-training among front-office positions? Are bells supported with a concierge's desk? Do most rooms fill from walk-ins or from reservation business? Does housekeeping change linen daily even for stay-overs? Answering such questions enables management to set numerical standards for each department. The ratios vary with the size of the house and the level of luxury (ADR). If, as suggested earlier, one bellhop is needed per 65 anticipated hourly arrivals (or one guest-room attendant is needed per 13 rooms, or one guest-service agent is needed per 60 rooms occupied), the total labor force is quickly calculated. Experience for each house then dictates what hours or overlapping times to schedule the crews, taking into account the mix of full-time and part-time staff.

With forecasting and advance scheduling, employees are given their days off during the slowest part of the week. Several may be off on one day, and none on a busy day. Part-time personnel can cover peak periods, or hours of the workday may be staggered. Each technique is designed to minimize payroll costs and maximize desk coverage when required.

The amount of help needed varies during the day and even within the same shift. Cashiers are busy in the morning handling check outs and are less busy in the afternoon when the guest-service agents are busy with arrivals. Cashiers at a commercial hotel are slower on Mondays, when agents are busier, and busier on Thursdays, when agents are slower. An employee can be hired as a cashier for some days and as a clerk for others. Computer terminals are interchangeable, so agents can respond to traffic patterns, acting as either receptionist or cashier. Two job descriptions are then reduced to one.

Design of the Lobby.   Lobby use and lobby design have gone through several roller-coaster phases. Today, even economy and midscale properties are rethinking their lobby environment. Computerization of the front desk, which is within the lobby, accounts for part of the change. Information technology reduced the mountain of paper and much of the clutter that typified the old. It also shrunk the amount of floor space that the desk required and with it the old-fashioned, bank-teller look. Today's desk is compact and efficient (see Exhibit 3–9).

Exhibit 3–9   The modern front desk of a medium-sized hotel is open to the lobby to encourage a sense of welcome and enhance security. The work level is lower than the desk level to reduce fatigue and encourage eye contact. *Courtesy of Jerome B. Temple and* Lodging Magazine.

New designs brought renewed activity to once sterile lobbies; many had no chairs! Action and eye appeal have re-created the lobby (see Exhibits 3–10 and 3–11) into the same important gathering place that it was a century ago.[10]

A well-designed lobby appears as if it were a town center. Modern lobbies are great for networking. Small furniture groupings assure privacy for cell-phone use and intimacy for cocktail gatherings. Big tables, large sofas, and heavy, overstuffed chairs have been replaced with smaller, more comfortable and eye-appealing settings. Women travelers prefer a lobby bar over a lounge bar, so hotels have enlarged their offerings with food and beverage service, afternoon tea, and continental breakfast. Adding an unusual feature or exciting landmark creates a popular meeting place for appointments. All this and jazz bands too fit within lobbies that are structured around the basics: baggage, desk, food and beverage, restrooms, seating and telephones.

New or old, the lobby must provide easy access to the front office. Although the front office's architectural footprint has shrunk, new designs and images have made the desk more user-friendly than ever before.

Design of the Desk.   The standard front-desk counter is about 45 inches high and approximately 40 to 42 inches across. The working space on the employee's side of the desk is lower by 6 inches or so (see Exhibit 3–9). Reducing the height of the workspace enables the guest-service agent to carry out clerical duties comfortably. It also drops the equipment below the guest's eye level, improving face-to-face interaction between the parties. The desk's running length is determined by the number of guest rooms: 6 feet long or so to as much as 100 feet or more in some very large houses.

---

[10]President Ulysses Grant (1869–1877) frequently walked from the White House to the Willard, now an Inter-Continental Hotel, to have a cigar and a drink. Petitioners waiting to argue their constituents' positions hovered in the lobby—thus, the term *lobbyists*.

Exhibit 3–10
The once sterile and uninviting lobby has been revitalized as a dining spot and social center. Hyatt Hotels pioneered the movement with its atrium concept. *Courtesy of Hyatt Regency Atlanta, Atlanta, Georgia.*

Exhibit 3–11
The stogy front desk is "getting a life" as it moves into the lobby, where registration pods make guest-staff interactions more accessible and more hospitable. *Courtesy of Delta Hotels, Toronto, Ontario, Canada.*

Registration pods, which are nonstandard front desks, are gaining popularity with new properties. Conversion costs are high, so pods, where both the guest and agent are seated in the lobby (see Exhibit 3–11), are limited to new construction. The setting is far less adversarial than the traditional cross-the-desk barrier. Agents easily walk into the lobby to greet guests, to handle luggage, or to clarify directions. Registration pods have improved access for the handicapped, strengthening the industry's response to the Americans with Disabilities Act. With careful training, the new design develops desk personnel into strong salespersons and greeters. In so doing, it changes the ambience of the desk and the sense of the lobby.

Some front desks are nudged into lobby corners; others become the lobby's focal point. Whichever it is, the security of both employees and guests must be balanced with the desk's design and location. Employees, especially cashiers, must be secured (see Exhibits 3–12 and 3–13). Guest security is enhanced when front-office personnel have an unobstructed view of the lobby and elevator doors. Atrium hotels add a small bit of extra security because all entry doors are in full view.

Internal communication is another consideration in the design. Despite the many new marvels in telecommunications, face-to-face interaction at the desk remains an important means of handling the day's business. Most designs center the guest-service agent at the hub of activity (see Exhibits 3–12 and 3–13). From this advantageous position, agents coordinate the flow of business from reservations to departures. Groups are an exception. Hotels with large tour groups (sometimes called "tour houses") often build satellite lobbies where busloads of arrivals can be accommodated without interfering with the normal front-office traffic.

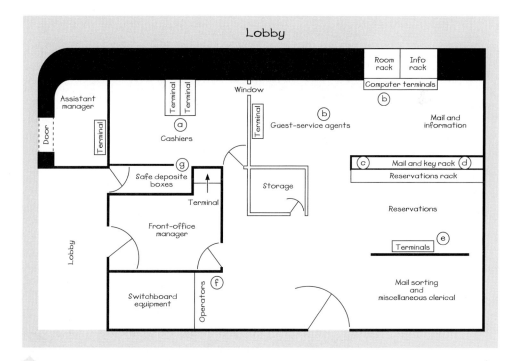

Exhibit 3–12   This schematic is not to scale, but it illustrates the design of a typical front office. Letter references key the positions and equipment to Exhibit 3–13, which illustrates a front office before the advent of property management systems (computerization).

Exhibit 3–13
This schematic is not
to scale, but it illus-
trates the design,
equipment, and po-
sitions at a front of-
fice before the
advent of property
management systems
(computerization).
Compare to Exhibit
3–12. *Courtesy of
Wilcox Interna-
tional, Inc., Division
of American Hotel
Register Co., North-
brook, Illinois.*

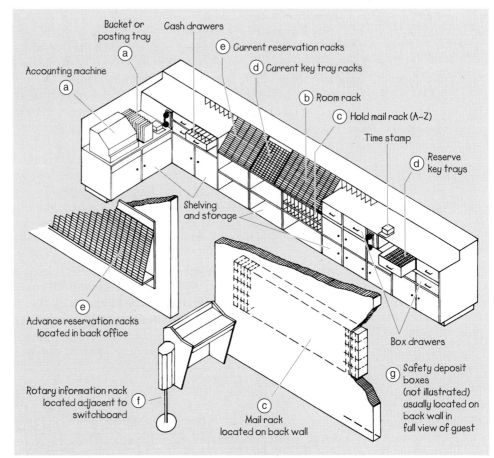

The desk must meet two objectives. It must provide a practical workspace and must incorporate an aesthetic design. Using lighting, form, and materials, architects must convey the image of the hotel: comfortable, open, organized, and professional—the very traits of guest-service agents themselves.

▶*Guest-Service Agents.*   Different titles have attempted to describe the importance of the next organizational level. *Room clerk* and *front-office clerk*, America's long-time favorites, have been replaced generally with *guest-service agent*. *Receptionist* is the term favored outside the United States.

Titles aside, guest-service agents have a host of duties concentrated in four functions: room sales, guest relations, records, and coordination (see Exhibit 3–14). Agents bring together the commitments made by reservations, the availability delivered by housekeeping, the minor repairs that so annoy guests, and the billing and collection required by accounting. Room clerks adjust minor problems and buffer management from the first blasts of major complaints. They are expected to achieve the company's ADR goals by selling up (see Chapter 8). Thus, the guest-service agent is part salesperson, part psychologist, part accountant, and part manager.

As the hotel's first-line employees, agents must carry out policies that have been established—too often without input from the desk—at higher levels. Room clerks

face a wide range of difficult person-to-person situations, most of which are not of their doing. For example,

1. Late-departing guests face a management-dictated surcharge.
2. Early arriving guests want their room, but none is available because check-out rooms have not yet be cleaned.
3. Laundry has lost a guest's best skirt.
4. Room-service breakfast never came.

Exhibit 3–14 The job of guest-service agent (room clerk) is broad, requiring persons with good people skills, good organizational skills, and good communication skills. Guests with positive experiences at the desk generally report positive impressions with the hotel.

Job Title: Guest-Service Agent

The hotel is personified by its agents. They receive the guests, service them throughout their stay, and handle their departures with efficiency and aplomb. A guest-service agent

Acts as host(ess) and receptionist.
Accepts reservations.
Quotes rates and sells rooms.
Keeps records of vacant and occupied rooms.
Registers arrivals and assigns them rooms.
Ascertains creditworthiness of hotel guests.
Controls and issues keys.
Coordinates activities with both the bellservice department and the housekeeping department.
Helps protect the guest's person, and the guest's and the hotel's property.
Responds to guest inquiries and gives information about and directions to the hotel and the locale.
Dates, sorts, and files incoming mail, messages, packages, and telegrams.
Receives and acts on guest complaints.
Maintains guest bills by posting charges and credits to individual guest accounts.
Collects in cash or credit from departing guests.
Uses computer equipment as well as telephones, telewriters, pneumatic tubes, switchboards, and video display terminals.

5. Important papers went missing in the dining room.

6. The hotel's airport bus just blew a gasket.

Unhappy guests focus on the guest-service agent. Where else would they go but to a "guest-service" agent! The situation is frustrating and stressful because the solution is more often than not out of the agent's control. Rigid policy curbs the clerk's discretion. (Chapter 7 discusses employee empowerment, which cushions this limitation.) Also, many issues are outside the desk's province. Agents must communicate with housekeeping, plead with engineering, find someone in food and beverage, or implement an arrangement made by sales and marketing. Decisions do not come promptly, and waiting guests are not patient.

Flatter and flatter organizations, which eliminate intervening management positions, always leave the guest-service agent in place. Unfortunately, this implication of importance is not always accompanied by a balance of authority or by a salary that compensates for the importance of the job done. Many years ago, a well-known hotelier noted that hotels spend large sums on building design and upgrade but never improve the position of the hotel's most visible employee, the guest-service agent/cashier.

➤*Cashiers.*   Although cashiers work in the front office, they are actually members of the accounting department, so they struggle with two reporting lines. The guest-service manager (front-office manager) directs all but the accounting work. The controller or accounting supervisor (often titled the *general cashier*) oversees the money side of the job. This reporting structure survives, although it is contrary to a basic rule of organization: Everyone should have but one boss.

Reorganization of the industry's front offices has blended the duties of the cashier into those of the guest-service agent. Both jobs are being rolled into one position except in large hotels. For money matters, the reporting line still flows through the general cashier.

Posting charges (recording them on guest bills), presenting final statements, resolving protests by departing guests, and handling cash and credit-card transactions are the major duties of hotel cashiers. Other services once included check cashing and loans— that is, cash advances. Changes in the way hotels do business have eliminated these banking services. Not only do hotels refuse to cash checks, they are unlikely to accept them in payment of the bill. Cash loans are limited to small payments made for guests; paid-outs for employee tips are the most common. Even guest service to safe deposit boxes (see Exhibit 3–12) has diminished as in-room safes have been installed (see Chapter 14).

As the guest-service agent is usually the guest's first contact with the front office, so the cashier is usually the guest's last. At one time, the cashier's window was a major source of guest irritation. Long lines and lengthy delays were the causes. Not so any more. Computerization allows guests to use one of several forms of express checkout (see Chapter 13). As guests became accustomed to and began to prefer checking out themselves, and as hotels reined in the various financial services that the cashier had previously rendered, it became possible to eliminate separate cashier positions. Many hotels have started to do so.

➤ THE BUILDING STRUCTURE

The chapter introduction pointed out the similarities between a hotel's organizational structure and the structure of the building that is the hotel. Every hotel offers guest rooms, and every hotel has an organization to deliver that product. Still, it is the differences—differences in the physical building and differences in the delivery system—

that distinguish one hotel from another. These differences explain the industry's segmentation into many parts.

The Old Versus the New

Differentiating between hotels that were built before midcentury and those built since World War II is not difficult to do. Today's hotels take far more land—have a *large footprint* in real estate terminology—because they are more open and because the individual rooms are so much larger. Exhibits 3–15 and 3–16 make the contrast clear. Some very famous hotels in the old design still exist. Best known among them are New York's Waldorf-Astoria, Chicago's Drake, and Cleveland's Renaissance.

Exhibit 3–16 represents the open design of the world's new hotels. The rectangular room shape is standard in almost every corner of the globe. Compare this design to the strange shapes and sizes of Exhibit 3–15, rooms 30 to 36, for example. It took a dozen different room rates to distinguish the variety of rooms in these older hotels. Three to five rate classes do the job today because room designs have been standardized, easing the front desk's job of quoting rates and assigning rooms.

Room sizes have increased over the decades. Size means square footage, and square footage is part of construction costs and hence of room rate (see Building Cost Rate, Chapter 9). Larger rooms translate into higher room rates. Although modern rooms are larger overall than those of 50 to 75 years ago, hotels of different classes still offer different sized rooms.

➤***The Old: Inside Rooms.***   Rooms 58 to 97 in Exhibit 3–15 form a U-shape of inside rooms around a light court. As illustrated, inside rooms are enclosed by wings of the building. Contrast this inside view to the view of any of the outside rooms in Exhibit 3–16.

The view from the very inside rooms is down toward the roof on the lower floor, which is often dirty and unsightly. Inside rooms are affected by the changing position of the sun, which casts shadows into these rooms even early in the day. Inside room design has all but disappeared, upgraded to outside rooms, just as the semiprivate (shared) bathroom of the 1930 to 1950 era has been an upgraded to the private bath.

➤***The New: Suites and All-Suites.***   The traditional suite is a parlor (living room/sitting room) with one or more bedrooms, as illustrated in the floor plan of a modern hotel (Exhibit 3–17) and by room numbers 72 to 74 in an older hotel (Exhibit 3–15). The traditional definition, a full wall—that is, separate rooms—is being challenged by new designs that use a low divider wall or even furniture to separate large accommodations (600 to 700 square feet) into "two rooms." Holiday Inn's Staybridge Suites accomplishes the division by designing the living part of the room at right angles to the sleeping portion.

Larger suites add second and third bedrooms and additional living space. Very luxurious accommodations include kitchens and formal dining rooms, saunas or swimming pools, and even libraries. Most basic suites contain wet bars and several bathrooms. Balconies and patios (*lanai* suites) are common amenities. In the proper climate, suites have fireplaces. For a truly opulent experience, some hotels, especially casino hotels, offer two-floor suites. So does America's heartland: The two-floor suite of the Netherland Plaza offers a panoramic view of Cincinnati.[11] Such amenities

---

[11]The two-floor Governor's Suite of the Fontainebleau Hilton (Miami Beach) is 20,000 square feet (the size of a dozen average homes) and has five bathrooms.

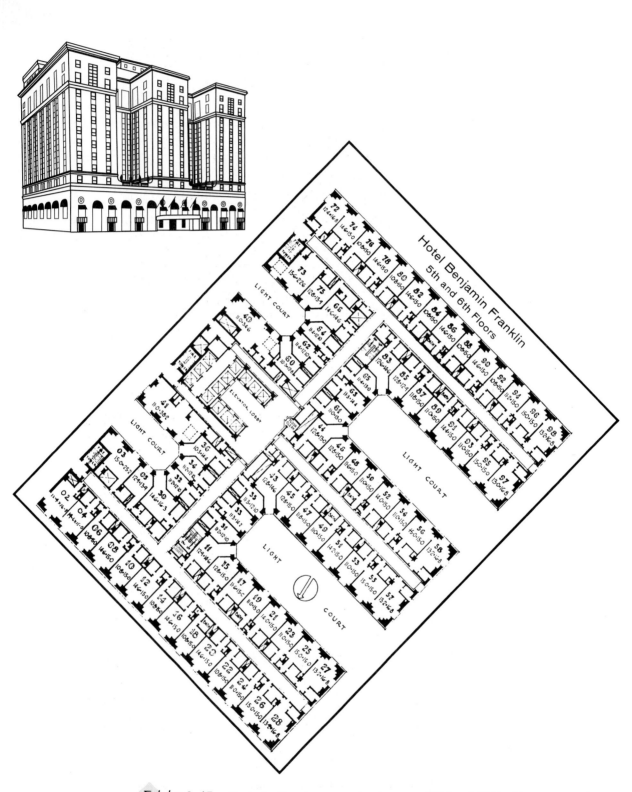

Exhibit 3–15   Typical of hotel construction between 1925 and 1945, this once upscale commercial hotel had guest rooms smaller than today's budget inns. Light courts designed to maximize land use created odd-shaped rooms: 44, 61, and 63. Note the floor closets (for linens and engineering supplies) on the corners, adjacent to rooms 11, 30, 66, and so on.

The Sofitel is a commercial hotel providing its business center and banquet/meeting facilites on the 3rd floor. Note the stairwell and the extra elevators for the banquet floor, but not for the sleeping floors.

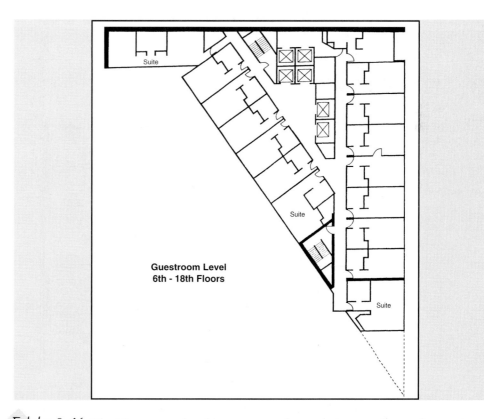

**Guestroom Level
6th - 18th Floors**

Exhibit 3–16 The 21st-century hotel has a sweep of open design even in an urban setting. Unlike the prototype of an earlier century (see Exhibit 3–15), guest rooms are standardized in shape and size. *Courtesy of the Sofitel Chicago Water Tower Hotel, Chicago, Illinois.*

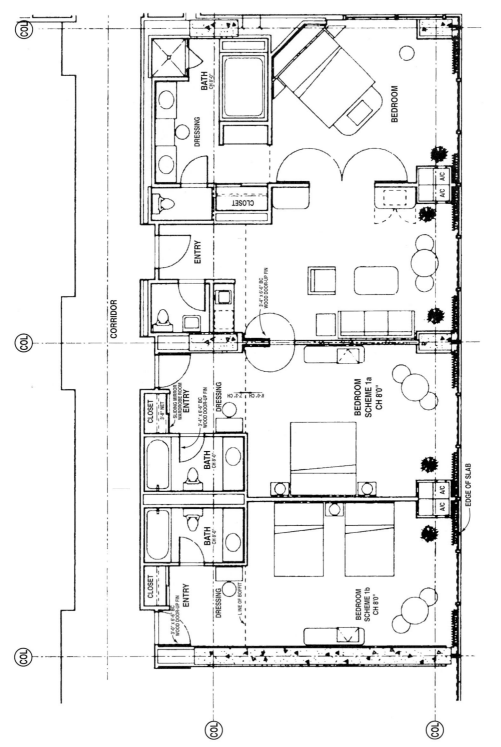

TYP END SUITE & GUEST ROOM PLAN
SCALE: 1/4" = 1'-0"

Courtesy: Mirage hotel, Las Vegas NV.

Exhibit 3–17 Folding doors separate the parlor and bedroom of this one-bedroom suite (two rooms on the right). On the left are two adjoining rooms, but the suite can be enlarged by unlocking the one connecting door. Note the back-to-back plumbing and air-conditioning (A/C) shafts. *Courtesy of the Mirage Hotel, Las Vegas, Nevada.*

stretch the average 300-square-foot room upward to 1,500 square feet (approximately 140 square meters) and more.

Speciality suites are often named instead of numbered. *Bridal suite, presidential suite,* and *penthouse suite* are popular designations. Historical figures or local references may be used to emphasize the hotel's theme: *The Kit Carson Suite,* for example.

All-suite hotels are another product altogether. They are designed for a different market and a different use (see Exhibit 3–18). All-suites compete against standard hotel rooms, not against hotel suites. To compensate for the extra square footage offered by the all-suite unit, public space is reduced. Forty percent of the typical hotel building is allocated to public areas. The all-suite hotel cuts that figure back by at least half.

All-suite and standard hotels alike employ a building technique that was invented by Ellsworth Statler in 1923. Back-to-back utility shafts reduce the amount of runs for piping, electrical, heating, and communication lines. There is economy in both the initial construction and continuing maintenance. It is not always possible, but kitchenettes, baths, and wet bars should be so constructed. Exhibits 3–15, 3–16, and 3–17 show the baths back to back.

➤*Corner Rooms.*   Corner rooms are the most desirable rooms on the floor. They provide double exposure—that is, they face two directions—and therefore command a premium price. To enhance the rate differential, corner rooms get preferential treatment from the architects. They are usually larger and are often part of a suite. Corner rooms are an integral part of older hotels because the sharp angles of the floor plans create them (see Exhibit 3–15). Modern hotels have fewer building corners and thus fewer corner rooms. Of course, round buildings, and some hotels are built that way, have none at all.

➤*Motor Inns.*   The highway hotel is a child of the motel and a grandchild to the earliest tourist court (see Chapter 2, Exhibit 2–3). Its lineage has given it its own, unique design. Although not widely applauded by architects, the simple floor plans

Exhibit 3–18   The large square footage of all-suite facilities is appealing both to the transient traveler and to the long-stay guest to whom the concept was originally marketed. Either a fold-out chair or a sofa bed in the parlor provides extra sleeping accommodations. All-suites are the fastest growing segment of the hotel market. *Courtesy of Candlewood Hotel Company, Wichita, Kansas.*

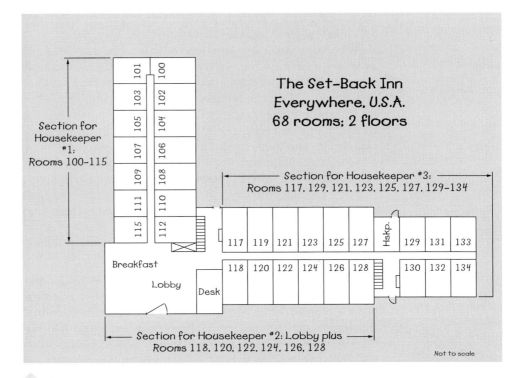

Exhibit 3–19   The typical design of a small, often two-story motor inn of 50 to 75 rooms is represented in this prototype. Ownership may still be mom-and-pop, but most motels are flagged with a franchise identity. The design anticipates three housekeepers per floor at full occupancy.

(see Exhibit 3–19) provide easy access to outside parking, which is the market that the motor inn serves.

Room rates are at the lower end of the industry's spectrum because both land and construction costs are closely watched. Land costs are kept in check by carefully selecting locations. Construction costs are kept in check by building low-rise, one- or two-floor buildings, and designing a single strip of housing, simply a long rectangle. Building a U- or L-shape (see Exhibit 3–19) helps with exterior appeal. First impressions are important because much of the traffic is due to impulse buying rather then advanced reservations. Attractive exteriors can be achieved with landscaping, facing materials on the building, and color. First impressions are fixed by the entry, both the driveway and the port-cochère. Cleanliness and maintenance of grounds, windows, and outdoor signs set the guest's expectations.

Numbering for Identification

Everyone uses the guest-room number for identification. Certainly, guests depend on the number to locate themselves. Desk personnel address guests by name, but within the front office, identification is always by number and then, if at all, by guest name. Hotel rooms are identified first by floor number and then by room number.

➤*Floor Numbering.*   Floors are numbered sequentially in ascending order, but most Western hotels omit floor 13. New York City's Plaza Hotel is an exception:

It has both a 13th floor and a room 13. Numbering systems reflect the culture of the hotel's location. Four is to the Orient as 13 is to the Occident. One never finds four in Asia as a room number, and sometimes not even numbers that add to four. Asian guests should never be assigned to rooms with unlucky numbers. Seven is a lucky number in the United States, as it is, along with six, in the Far East.

Americans number the first sleeping floor as floor one regardless of the number of levels between it and the ground. Mezzanine, upper-ground floor, and shopping level are interspersed without any standard order. The sequence adds an array of nonnumerical elevator buttons that confuse anyone who isn't a lifetime employee of the hotel. *M* is for mezzanine; *MM* is for the second mezzanine floor. Try to decipher *LM*, *SB*, and *S2* (lower mezzanine, subbasement, and subbasement 2).

The rest of the world begins numbering with the ground floor as floor number one. Even without the intermediary floors, what would be the 10th floor in the United States would be the 11th floor elsewhere.

A different numbering system needs to be used if the hotel is comprised of several low-rise buildings. Identically numbering each low rise unit of, say, three or four stories is one technique. Then each building is given a different name, and the keys for each are color coded. Others prefer to number the floors sequentially, moving in order from one building to the next. Guests get confused because only one unit has its ground floor numbered as floor one. Ground floors of the other units will have numbers in the teens or even 20s.

Hotels that have two or three towers have the same options. Either the towers are differentiated by name (the river tower) or direction (the east tower) with room numbers identical in each, or the floors are numbered sequentially with the bottom floor of the second tower using the next floor number in sequence.

▶ *Room Numbering.*   Assigning numbers to rooms is far more arbitrary than going up floor levels. Each hotel has a unique design, and that design determines where to begin numbering and what sequence to use. Sequential numbering is not even possible in an old floor plan like the one in Exhibit 3–15—too many corridors run at right angles to one another. Even one as simple as Exhibit 3–19 offers choices.

Rooms are numbered odd and even along opposite sides of the corridor. The numbering might begin at the elevator bay and progress upward as the sequence marches down the corridor: 101, 103, 105 along one side; 102, 104, 106, and so on along the other. Of course, there is no rule that requires this. An atrium hotel such as the old Anatole in Dallas has rooms on only one side of the corridor and the numbering is sequential. All-suite hotel rooms are numbered in the usual manner because every room in the hotel is a suite.

Different floor designs present different numbering problems and require good signage. If the elevator empties into the center of the sleeping floor, the logic of any system begins to break down. The numbering system gets very confusing when a new wing or ell is added to the original structure. Rarely is the entire floor, old rooms and new, renumbered in sequence. The new wing may be numbered sequentially from the old, without concern about the interface with the old numbers. Sometimes the old numbers are duplicated in the new wing by adding an identifying suffix or prefix, like *N* for north wing.

Care in using certain numbers such as four and nine applies equally to room numbering as to floor numbering, as mentioned earlier. In Asia, correct positioning is also important. Many hoteliers there employ a fung shui (or feng shui) master who helps position the location of everything from doors and windows to desks and files and helps decide the most auspicious date to open a new hotel, a new dining room, or whatever.

Adjoining or Connecting Rooms.   Rooms that abut along the corridor are said to be adjoining rooms. Using the numerical sequence discussed above, 101, 103, and 105 would be adjoining rooms, as would 102, 104, and 106. If there is direct room-to-room access (a door between the rooms) without using the corridor (Exhibit 3–15, rooms 53, 55, and 57), the rooms are said to be connecting. Obviously, every connecting room adjoins, but not every adjoining room connects.

►*Elevators.*   The first hotel elevator, almost the first elevator anywhere, was installed in 1859 in New York City's Fifth Avenue Hotel. Elevators facilitated the growth of skyscrapers, so naturally hotels became enthusiastic buyers. Early concerns dealt with lighting, ventilation, and safety. Elevators were manually operated by the bell staff until the first automatic elevator was introduced in the 1950s. Then, job losses became the intermediate concern. Sixty years later, focus has shifted to the role of the elevator in a rejuvenated lobby.

How to make the elevator fun is a concern of both elevator manufacturers and elevator buyers. The atrium elevator (see Exhibit 3–10) was the first step in highlighting its contribution to guest service and its central role in the lobby. More recently, televisions with cartoons have replace Muzak music (Le Parker Meridien Hotel in New York City).

Transparent side walls (Chambers Hotel in New York City), advertisements, and even transparent walls that present a view of the building's innards have been used in an effort to distract guests during the few claustrophobic moments they must spend in an elevator. Elevator speeds can be adjusted for smooth starts and stops or for a rapid jump from stop to full speed in just 4 seconds. Everything is open to testing so long as elevators remain an awkward ride with a dozen strangers huddled together.

Also at issue is the distance from the desk to the lobby elevator and from the elevator landings to the guest rooms. New hotel designs minimize these distances and, optimally, still maintain some oversight of elevator traffic from the front desk. The 2,600-room Aladdin Hotel (Las Vegas) includes a dual elevator core that puts all guest rooms within seven doors of any elevator. Often overlooked are the loud voices and other noises associated with guests exiting elevators. Room design and door insulation must anticipate this problem.

Room Shape and Size

The guest room is the hotel's product. Therefore, its shape and size are critical to customer satisfaction. Size, especially, separates the industry into its several classes. Small rooms are associated with hard budget properties, huge rooms with deluxe accommodations. As the rate discussion in Chapter 9 points out, setting the different rate classes within the hotel also depends in part on the differences in the physical rooms.

►*Room Shape.*   There has been little overall change in the shape of guest rooms.[12] As concave, square, and round structures are built, corresponding changes occur in the interior shapes and dimensions. Research may eventually show advantages in guest satisfaction or in reduced wear from certain shapes. Until then, the parallelogram remains the classic favorite, with the depth of the room approximately

---

[12]The W Sydney Hotel (Australia) was converted from a 100-year old wool warehouse and required 33 different shapes for its 104 rooms.

twice the width. The first increases in room size are made by adding to the depth. Width is improved next by increasing from 12 or 13 feet to 16 feet, which is a luxury-class room.

Other shapes, which might look interesting from the outside, present certain internal problems. A round building of small diameter produces rooms without parallel walls. The outer wall is circular, and the inner walls are angled to accommodate the bath and the central service core within the limited cross section of the small diameter.

The presence of full or false balconies and French or sliding doors gives a sense of spaciousness to any room. Balconies are often part of a facade that adds interest to the outside of a building.

➤*Room Size.* Room shape is an architectural decision primarily; room size is derived from financial and marketing factors. Although the trend has been toward larger and larger rooms, the economy segment has capitalized on smaller accommodations and smaller rates.

In the final analysis, the market determines the rate structure and consequently the average room size and its furnishings. That market varies from hotel to hotel, so that the twin double beds of the family-oriented hotel might be inappropriate to a property servicing the business traveler.

A comparison of international accommodations illustrates the danger of trying to identify hotels as one industry. Japan's smallest budget rooms, called *capsule rooms,* are nothing more than sleeping accommodations. Guests change in a common locker area and crawl into a capsule approximately 5 feet high, 5 feet wide, and less than 7 feet long. That is less than 40 square feet (not even 4 square meters).[13] Most hard budgets are larger. The Ibis chain, a European entry into the budget market, builds rooms of approximately 130 square feet (approximately 12 square meters). Econo Lodges and Super 8s have rooms of almost 200 square feet (nearly 19 square meters).

The surprise comes when comparisons are made between today's budget accommodations and the rooms of the Benjamin Franklin hotel (Exhibit 3–15), which was a first-class facility in its era. The 150- to 175-square-foot room of the prosperous 1920s was smaller than many of today's economy facilities, such as Choice Hotels International's Sleep Inn, at 210 square feet.

The Far East contributes to the other end of the scale as well. It has many of the world's opulent hotels, with large rooms and many extras. Hong Kong's Shangri-La Hotel offers a 500-square-foot facility (bath included). That size is immediately recognized as super luxury. (Guests do not get a feeling of luxury until the room size passes 400 square feet.)

The Four Seasons in New York City (370 rooms) compares favorably with luxury properties worldwide. Its rooms are 600 square feet (about 55.75 square meters), including a 120-square-foot bath. The standard American room measures between 250 and 350 square feet (approximately 23.3 to 32.5 square meters). So the Ramada International, another New York City hotel, is right on target at 350 square feet.

It's not enough to multiply the size of the room by the number of rooms to get the hotel's total square footage. Provisions must be made for service areas, public space, lobbies, offices, corridors, and so on. That requires almost a doubling of the total square feet needed for just the guest rooms. Even then, allowances must be made for

---

[13]One square foot (ft^2) = 0.093 square meters (m^2). To convert square meters into square feet, divide 0.093 into the number of square feet. To convert square feet into square meters, divide 10.76 (the reciprocal) into the number of square feet.

the size, type, and class of hotel. A full-service, convention property might require a total of 900 to 1,200 square feet per guest room, although the room itself is only 350 to 400 square feet. An economy property with no public space might get by with as little as 600 total square feet per guest room, of which the room itself is 250 to 275 square feet. All of this bears on the amount of land needed to erect the property.

All-suite hotels provide a contrast in size, both to one another and in comparison with standard nonsuite properties. All-suite properties are segmented into economy, midmarket, and upscale: Room size is the major difference. Guest Quarters pioneered the extended-stay hotel with a 650-square-foot unit. All-suite hotels include bedroom, parlor, bath, and kitchenette, making a unit rather than a room the standard of measure. The budget room of AmeriSuites is about 380 square feet; Park Suites measure some 480 square feet. Fireplaces carry Homewood Suites to 550 square feet. Extended-stay suites that range from 400 to 650 square feet equate to the size of a standard apartment in many large U.S. cities!

How the Room Is Used.   Hotel chains build models to test guest acceptance and preview costs before proceeding with a new concept or with a major renovation of an existing property. The disproportionately high cost of building just one model room is offset by identification of design and furnishing flaws before the major project gets under way. For one thing, more thought is focused on how the room will be used.

Different kinds of guests use rooms in different ways. Within the same dimensions, a destination hotel furnishes proportionately more storage space than a transient property. A transient property allocates more space to sleeping and less to the living area than a destination facility. Such would be the case with New York City hotels, where the average daily use of the room is eight hours. Very cold or very hot climates increase usage of the room.

The use of the room dictates the type of furnishings. A destination resort wouldn't need a desk, but business travelers use their rooms as offices. Hotel rooms serve as company offices in developing countries and are furnished as such. It is no surprise that surveys of business guests give high priority to a comfortable work environment. Business guests need access to dedicated telephone lines. Hotels that provide them have been able to reduce their commitment to expensive business centers with live secretarial support. Specific requirements by business guests reduce their elasticity and make them more dependent on the hotel that meets their needs. Hotels must then decide the value of these expensive installations in attracting a single segment of the market.

Designers have become quite successful in making small rooms look larger. For example, nightstands can be eliminated by mounting bedside lamps on the wall. Mirrors do a good job of creating a perception of space. Wall-to-wall draperies and fewer patterned materials throughout the room add to the feeling of roominess. Designers also use mirrors and balconies to expand the sense of space. Nevertheless, it takes about 20 additional square feet (1.86 square meters) before the occupant notices the larger size. That's the point where a rate increase could be justified if spaciousness is the only basis for the increase.

Clearly, there is no standard room. The hotel industry is moving in several directions at once. Miniprices use module units and measure 12 feet from center to center. Luxury operations opt for 15-foot centers and lengths of 30 to 35 feet. (The standard carpet sizes of 12 and 15 feet dictate the dimensions unless the plan calls for a custom job.) Costs of energy, borrowed money, and labor limit expansion even as competition pushes for more space. Comparisons, therefore, begin with the marketplace.

Bed and Bath

The increasing size of the bed—Americans are getting bigger—accounts in part for the increased size of the guest room. The new role of the bathroom—as a weapon in the competition wars—also contributes to the creep in total square footage.

►*The Bed.*   Bed types, bed coverings, and bed sizes vary across the world and across time. Quilted bedding appeared in Japan about 1500. It is most certain that the nomads of the Middle East were using some form of stuffing in animal skins (early futons) to ease their sleep even earlier than the 16th Century. The modern American hotel room has gone through periods which favored, first, the double bed and then twin beds. Neither of these are popular today. The queen and king have taken over. If today's hotel wants a room with two beds, it opts for queen–doubles rather than traditional twin beds. Of course, larger beds mean larger rooms. Larger rooms mean higher construction costs and, hence, higher room rates.

Beds are being lowered as well as lengthened. The usual height of the mattress and box spring is 22 to 24 inches, in contrast to the average chair of some 17 inches. Lowering the bed to 17 inches makes the room appear larger because all the pieces are on the same horizontal plane. It also makes the bed easier to sit on, and lower hotel beds are used for that purpose. Adequate seating is needed to reduce the otherwise heavy wear on mattresses when beds are used as chairs. It is a real conflict: Lowered beds make the room appear larger, but the mattresses don't last as long. Mattress life can be extended substantially if the mattress is rotated and turned on a regular schedule of four times per year. Good housekeeping departments do this as part of their quarterly deep cleaning. The position of the mattress is tracked by a system of arrows attached to the side of the mattress.

If every hotel room were a replica of every other room, room assignments would be greatly eased. Every one would get the same room configuration, and the major decision for the desk would be which floor and what location within the floor. Although modern hotels are headed that way, as the earlier discussion on floor plans indicated, the front office still needs some shorthand symbols for designating different bedding and accommodations. These symbols, which were critical when hotels used room racks (see Chapter 13, Exhibit 13–7), have been carried over into computer equipment.

Bed Sizes and Bed Symbols.   The professional termminology that describes the room's capacity is often confused with the types and kinds of beds with which the room is furnished. To a hotelier, for example, a "single" is a room occupied by a solitary guest. However, that person could be in one of several beds, including a single bed or a double bed. *Single* and *double* refer with equal ambiguity to (1) the room rate, (2) the number of guests housed in the room, (3) the number of persons the room is capable of accommodating, or (4) the size and type of the beds. It is possible to have a single occupant in a double bed being charged a single rate although the room is designated as a double, meaning that it could accommodate two persons.

A single occupant in a queen double sometimes needs assurance that no additional charge is being made for the unused bed. The single-room configuration—that is, one single bed for one person—is unknown today. Thus, to the innkeeper, "single" means single occupancy or single rate.

Single Bed.   A single bed, symbol S, sleeps one person. A true single is 36 by 75 inches, but is very rarely used; it is simply too small. Instead, the rare single room (room for one person) is furnished with a single twin or, most likely, one double bed.

When the room is furnished with one twin, the symbol S is used, when furnished with a double bed, the symbol is D. Single beds must measure at least 39 by 72 inches to win an AAA rating.

TWIN BEDS.   A twin room, symbol T, contains two beds each accommodating one person. (Two persons could also be roomed in a double, a queen, or a king bed). Twins measure 39 by 75 inches each and use linen 72 by 108 inches. The 75-inch mattress has been replaced in all bed sizes with a longer length, called a California length. The 39-inch width remains with the twin, but the length has been stretched to between 79 and 84 inches. Additional inches are added to the linen length as well.

Because of their flexibility, twins once accounted for 60 to 70% of total available rooms. The trend shifted as twins were replaced by double–doubles, and then queens, and then by queen–doubles. Single business travelers actually prefer a two-bedded room: one for sleeping and one for spreading papers.

Because the double–double and queen–double sleep four persons, they are also called *quads* or *family rooms*. Motel owners will offer couples queen–doubles at reduced rates with the stipulation that only one bed be used. A survey done some time ago by Sheraton's franchise division showed that the second bed of a double–double or queen–double was used about 15% of the time.

DOUBLE BED.   D is the symbol for double bed. The width ranges from 54 to 57 inches, and that's an important 3 inches. Like the twin bed, the length of the double has been stretching from 75 inches to the California 80-inch or more length. Linen sizes would be 90 to 93 inches wide and 113 inches long with a California mattress. Half a double bed is about 28 inches or so, narrower even than the single. That alone explains the double's loss of popularity among guests who are getting ever larger and heavier.

QUEEN AND KING BEDS.   Queen and king beds (symbols Q and K) are extra wide (60 and 72 inches, respectively) and extra long. They made popular the California length, which has also been called a *European king*. Although designed for two, three or four persons might squeeze in when the room is taken as a family room.

Both beds require larger rooms, since the critical distance of at least 3 feet between the foot of the bed and the furniture (called case goods) remains a requirement. Larger sheets, 108 by 122.5 inches, are also needed. Since laundry costs are calculated by weight, larger sheets mean larger laundry bills. A larger room with extra laundry costs can only mean a higher room rate even without consideration for the extra, up-front costs of the larger bed, mattress, and linen.

HOLLYWOOD BED.   Two beds joined by a common headboard is called a hollywood bed. Hollywoods use the symbol of the twins, T, since that's what they are. They are difficult beds to make, because the room attendant cannot get between them. To overcome this, the beds are placed on rollers and swung apart, resulting in rapid carpet wear. Because the total dimension of these beds is 78 by 75 inches (two twins), they can be converted into a king by replacing the two mattresses with one king mattress laid across both springs.

STUDIO BED (ROOM).   A studio bed is a sofa by day and a bed by night. During the day, the bed is slipcovered and the pillows are stored in the backrest. There is neither headboard nor footboard once the sofa is pulled away from the backrest to create the bed. Today's guest room serves a dual bedroom–living room function, so studio rooms should be popular with business guests. They once were. Studios are not popular anymore because the beds are not comfortable and the all-suite hotel serves the same dual purpose.

The studio room, once called an executive room, has been used to redo small, single rooms in older hotels. *UP,* undersized parlor, is one of the symbols once used for studios. In Europe, a parlor that has no sleeping facilities is called a salon.

SLEIGH BED.　Any bed can be a sleigh bed, so named because of the sleigh-like shape of the headboard and footboard. There is no change to the integral part of the bed. The use of the sleigh shape is a designer's choice. It adds no special characteristic to the bed's sleeping qualities. (See Chapter 7 for a discussion of the bed as part of the hotel's basic service.)

DAYBED.　Adding sleigh ends to a twin bed converts it to a daybed. Daybeds were once common additions to the family living room. They've made a comeback both in the home and in larger hotel rooms. Daybeds are like studio beds except they are additions to the hotel room rather than basic furnishings, as they were in the heyday of the studio room. Both daybeds and studio beds are better as beds than as sofas. At 39 inches, they're too wide for sitting. Removing the pillows converts a daybed into a sleeping bed, but without the struggle often associated with converting a sofa bed.

SOFA BED.　A sofa bed is similar in function to a studio bed. It is a sofa first of all, which makes sitting more comfortable. It is usually 17 inches off the floor, whereas the studio bed may be as high as 22 inches. Unlike the studio bed, which rolls away from its frame, the sofa bed opens in accordion fashion from the seat. Since it unfolds, the sofa bed is less convenient and requires more space than the studio.

Parlors are generally equipped with sofa beds as part of a suite (see Exhibit 3–17), but a studio "bed" is usually a room unto itself. Sofa beds can be single, double, or even queen size, although the single is more like a three-quarter bed (48 by 75 inches).

Sofa beds were once called *hide-a-beds,* and thus carry an H designation. Large rooms that contain both standard beds and hide-a-beds are junior suites. Rooms in all-suite hotels offer a sofa bed in the parlor portion of the unit (see Exhibit 3–18).

ROLLAWAY BED (COT).　A cot or rollaway is a portable utility bed that is added to the usual room furnishings on a temporary basis. A rollaway sleeps one person, and a comfortable one measures 34 by 75 inches and uses twin sheets. Cots usually come smaller—30 by 72 inches, with linen 63 by 99 inches.

Setting up cots is costly in housekeeping time, primarily because the cots are rarely located conveniently. Cot storage never seems to be high in the designer's priority, which should estimate one rollaway (mobile sleeper) per 20 guest rooms.

CRIB.　Cribs for babies are rolled into the room on an as-needed basis similar to the call for rollaway beds. Deaths from unsafe cribs have made them a sensitive safety issue. Not that infants have died in hotels, but the issue was raised by a Consumer Product Safety Commission study that reported most hotel cribs were unsafe. Infants could (*could,* not *did*) catch their heads between the slats, between the mattress and the bed frame, or in cutouts in the headboards and footboards. A bigger danger is posed by the use of regular-sized sheets on a crib mattress. A call for better general maintenance (loose parts, protruding screws, broken slats) applies to rollaway beds as well as to cribs.

WATER BED.　In two decades, water beds jumped from a novelty to a hot item and then fell back again. The bed is rarely found in hotel rooms, although it offers an alternative to inner-spring and foam mattresses. Water beds have a long history, dating back to pre-Christian, nomadic tribes, which filled goatskins with water. Their use was rediscovered by a Californian who first tried starch and gelatin as fillers. The water bed is still primarily a phenomenon of the western states.

FUTON.   The Japanese futon, which is a cotton-quilted bed, is another addition to the American sleeping design. Futons come in regular mattress sizes. The thick layers of batting are easily stored and readily adapted to service as a couch or bed.

MURPHY BED.   Like many other copyrighted brands that identify generic products, *Murphy bed* has come to mean any fold-up wallbed. The popularity of fold-up-into-the-wall beds waxes and wanes. They're great for dormitories, but are not now in widespread use in the commercial lodging industry. Disappearing by day and appearing at night improves on the dual use of the guest room. With the bed folded, the room is usable as a meeting place or for the commercial display of goods. Fold-up beds have an edge on studio rooms because the bed is far more comfortable. One needs to look far, indeed, to find either of the two in commercial use.

And for the future? Possibly air beds—warm air cushions that support the sleeper without bed frame, mattress, or linen. What a revolutionary thing that will be! In the meantime, there is apt to be an increasing degree of choice. One day, guests will pick from a variety of mattresses: foam, spring, hard, soft, orthopedic, adjustable, vibrating, flotation, and futons.

▶**The Bath.**   *Bath* is the industry's jargon for bathroom; it is not the bathing facility. Bath is not the bathtub. Located in the bath are the toilet (or water closet), the sink (or lavatory), and the tub (or bathtub) and shower. The hotel bath has undergone many changes throughout this century, but its position as a sound barrier between the room and the corridor remains. That location, abutting the corridor (see Exhibits 3–16 and 3–17), saves construction costs and leaves the desirable outside wall for windows or balconies. In more recent years, modular construction of the bath has gained some popularity. The bath is prefabricated away from the construction site and installed as one unit. Modular construction reduces the number of building trades required on the construction site and, some say, improves the quality of the work.

The bath accounts for about 20% of the room size. Thus, the baths in hard budget inns measure about 35 square feet and in midrange properties about 70 square feet. The luxurious Four Seasons, mentioned earlier, has a bath of 120 square feet. What a contrast this is to the hotel of a century ago, when public baths served whole floors or entire wings. (Very early hotels had all their baths in the basements because the mechanics of pumping water to higher floors was not yet in place.)

Stall showers, which occupy little space, gained favor as old hotels converted from rooms without baths. They fit easily into old, large closets or corners of renovated rooms. Tub and shower combinations were installed next when lifestyles changed again. Having both meets the cultural needs of all guests. The Japanese, for example, definitely favor tubs, just as they choose twin beds over all other choices. The bidet, which is installed in many other countries, has not found acceptance in the American home and thus not in the American hotel.

Upscale properties have cut back on low-cost amenities such as soap and shampoo. Strangely, they have gone all out in building larger bathrooms with expensive appointments: in-floor scales, in-bath telephones, electric shoeshine equipment, adjustable no-fog mirrors, and plush bathrobes. The Palmer House Hilton in Chicago, which was renovated several years ago, has 300 guest rooms with his-and-her bathrooms. The same Four Seasons mentioned above features bathtubs that fill in 1 minute!

Not only is the bath larger, but the ancillary space has grown as well. Dressing areas and second lavatories outside the bath proper have also increased the overall dimensions. Replacing closets with open hanger space has helped compensate. Consolidating furniture also saves space. One vertical piece incorporates several horizontal space users. Into armoires, for example, have gone television sets, bars and refrigerators, writing desks with telephones, and several drawers for clothing. Reflected in the new design is the two-night stay and garment-bag luggage of today's traveler.

RESOURCES AND CHALLENGES
Resources

➤ SUMMARY

Hotel architects have given the industry two important structures. One, the building, is designed to attract travelers and provide comfort. The other, the organization, is designed to service guests and earn their loyalty. Both forms are in change: adding wings and upgraded baths on the one hand and improving personnel and services on the other.

Good building designs recognize the diverse needs of consumers. Not all hotels offer the same accommodations. That variety provides a broad range of facilities, each designed to attract portions of the traveling public. Hard-budget hotels, for example, have rooms of 150 square-feet; rooms in upscale hotels exceed 600 square feet. (Square meters are used outside the United States, where 0.093 square meters [m^2] equals one square foot [ft^2].)

Good organizational designs are equally dynamic: changing as customer demand, technology, and service require. Today's guests are less inclined to pay for or wait for individualized care, opting instead for a measure of self-service. Less service has slashed the ranks of the uniformed services even as automation has reduced the size of the telephone department, and electronics, such as self-check in and check out, have altered the duties of the front office.

Hotel security is one department that is growing both in size and responsibility. Recent events have focused everyone's attention on security. Although hotels are not insurers of guest safety, they must exercise reasonable care to protect guests and their property. The hotel industry has responded with better trained personnel and larger security departments. Prevention and deterrence reduce the number of security incidents and, equally important, document those that are unavoidable.

Some organizational changes have shifted assignments as much as they have altered responsibilities or department size. In this respect, reservations is probably the most dynamic of all front-office departments. The text examines reservations in the next three chapters.

➤ WEB SITES

Concierge in a computer–Lobby technology to replace the human concierge: http://www.compcierge.com

Consumer Products Safety Commission–Booklet on *Hotel and Motel Crib and Play Yard Checklist:* http://www.cpsc.gov/cpscpub/pubs/cribsafe.html

International Executive Housekeepers Association, Inc.–Professional association of housekeepers in many industries: http://www.ieha.org

Meetings & Conventions Magazine–Trade periodical with articles on convention security: http://www.meetings-convenonventions@ntmllc.com

SafePlace Corporation–Private company providing safety accreditation for hotels: http://www.safeplace.com

State department security alerts: http://www:travel.state.gov

Web Site Assignment

Using these and other Web sites or periodicals, prepare a list of no less than five items for

1. security measures that hotels have recently undertaken in response to the heightened alert of American business and society; or

2. steps undertaken by management to increase the efficiency and improve the position of floor housekeepers.

➤ INTERESTING TIDBITS

➤ When corporations have thousands of individual shareholders (54,656 for Marriott as of January 31, 2002) and as many as 800,000,000 shares authorized (see footnote 1), control of a company can be maintained with far less than a majority of the shares. For example, J. W. Marriott, Jr., Chairman of the Board and CEO, holds just 31,000,000 shares, approximately 12.7% of the 242,000,000 shares issued (and about 4% of the shares authorized) but still controls the public company that carries the family name.

➤ *New Hotels for Global Nomads* was the first museum exhibit (Spring 2003 at the Smithsonian's Cooper-Hewitt Design Museum, New York City) to feature the architecture and design of lodging facilities.

Highlighted within the exhibit were *tourbus hotels,* proposed for Rome to accommodate that special bus market, and the 202-room Burj al-Arab Hotel in Dubai (see "Interesting Tidbits" of Chapter 1).

➤ It is difficult to get housekeepers, who do not read and write very well, to submit maintenance work orders. The remedy has two parts. First is the form. It must contain a preprinted list of everyday repairs. Housekeepers need only write the room number and a simple checkmark next to the repair. Second is a contest. A specific work order in a sealed envelope is posted on the housekeeping bulletin board. Any housekeeper who summits the same work order that day receives a cash award.

➤ READING REFERENCES

"The Challenge of Multi-Department Management for Future Hospitality Graduates." John Williams and Frederick DeMicco. *Journal of Hospitality and Tourism Education,* 10(1), 1998. Available: http://www.publications@chrie.org; http://www.chrie.org.

"From Clerk to Guest Service Agent." FIU Review. Spring 1988, p. 42.

Hotel, a work of fiction by Arthur Hailey, includes a negative view of the stereotyped hotel security officer but provides a picture of duties assigned to some of the hotel's staff. (See problem 1 of this chapter.)

"The Hotel Organization of the Future: Capitalizing on Change is Prelude to Success." Roger S. Cline. Arthur Andersen: Ideas and Trends on Line. Available: http://www.hotel-online.com.

Occupational Outlook Handbook. Provides career information, including job descriptions, working conditions, and potential earnings for many industries, including lodging.

Washington, D.C. U.S. Department of Labor, 2002, periodically revised.

Challenges

➤ *TRUE/FALSE*

Questions that are partially false should be marked false (F).

___ 1. The number of part-time and call-in employees that a hotel needs on a daily basis is determined by forecasts of occupancy and standards of productivity.

___ 2. The rooms department produces the largest volume of sales, but food and beverage earn the largest profit per dollar of sale (approximately $0.50 for each $1 sold).

___ 3. Hotels are especially sensitive to good security because a hotel is an insurer of the guest's safety and personal goods.

___ 4. The actual size of a projected hotel can be determined easily by multiplying the number of guest rooms by the square footage of each room.

___ 5. Most hotels are incorporated separately, although they belong to a single chain.

➤ *PROBLEMS*

1. With special attention to front-office activities, prepare a list of duties carried out by one (or more) of the fictional staff in the book *Hotel* by Arthur Hailey (Garden City, NY: Doubleday & Company, Inc., 1965; also available through Bantam Books).

2. Using information provided in this chapter or acquired elsewhere, sketch to approximate scale a typical room with furnishings that Choice Hotels might be building in Europe. (That requires dimensions to be in meters and square meters.) Above the drawing list the several assumptions as 1, 2, 3, . . . *n* that your drawing relies upon. Cite references external to the text if used.

3. Using information provided in this book or acquired elsewhere, *estimate* the total square feet of New York City's Four Seasons Hotel. Show the several mathematical steps and label all of your figures.

4. Either as part of your travels this term or as part of a field trip, contrast the size, shape, bedding, price, and characteristics of two or more hotel rooms. Discuss.

5. Interview a hotel manager or a front-office employee. From the information obtained, construct the organizational chart of the front office, and prepare a description of any one front-office job, using Exhibits 3–4 and 3–6 as a guide.

6. Using the typical occupancy pattern of an urban hotel (see Chapter 1, Exhibit 1–5), plot the biweekly work schedule for the desk of a 300-room hotel that has separate room clerk and cashier positions. The switchboard is not at the desk. Strive for efficient coverage with minimum payroll costs. All full-time employees receive two successive days off and work an eight-hour day, five days per week.

➤ *ANSWERS TO TRUE/FALSE QUIZ*

1. True. It's the combination of volume (say, 300 occupied rooms forecasted) and productivity (say, 15 rooms per housekeeper) that sets the payroll needs (20 housekeepers) for every department from food servers to bellhops.

2. False. Room sales produce both the largest dollar volume of any hotel department and the largest profit per dollar sale (approximately $0.70)

3. False. Hotels are not insurers of guest safety or personal goods, but the hotel must exercise reasonable care to protect both persons and goods.

4. False. That is the beginning of the computation. To that preliminary total must be added extra areas for corridors, floor closets, machinery, fire exits, public space (lobbies, convention space, banquet rooms), and more.

5. True. Each hotel is a separate corporation within a separate corporation within the parent corporation. Thus, one finds the New York Sheraton, a corporation, owned by the Sheraton chain, a corporation that is owned in turn by the Cendant Corporation.

The Reservations Process

Chapter 4
Global Reservations Technologies
Chapter 5
Individual and Group Reservations
Chapter 6
Forecasting Availability and Overbooking

From the largest chains to the smallest independent operations, significant investment is being made year after year in better, faster, and more enhanced reservations technologies. Whether the investment is tens of thousands of dollars for an independent property or tens of millions of dollars for a chainwide system, the goal remains the same—to increase the accuracy, accessibility, and breadth of reservations venues for the property(s).

For the chain (or consortium of chains), the simple toll-free telephone reservations centers developed 40 years ago remain the foundation of the reservations process. However, through last-room availability technology, central reservations agents are now more informed and up to the minute in terms of space availability, rate structures, and even the ability to visualize (through CD-ROM) each of the chain's properties. Through seamless connectivity technology, travel agents, airlines, and Internet providers offer additional options for making and taking a reservation. In almost all cases, the reservations are made in real time, directly to the chain's individual property being reserved. This saves the central reservation system (CRS) the task of forwarding reservations to the individual property and the property the task of updating its system with each CRS reservation received.

For the customer, these new technological enhancements lend ease, variety, and accessibility to the reservations process. In addition, the increasing sophistication of yield management technology is making the cost of a hotel room a real bargain for guests who are able to travel during the off-season, on the spur of the moment, or for those who are able to plan trip dates far in advance.

CHAPTER 4
Global Reservations Technologies

Outline

Rapid advancements in technology have changed—to the very core—the manner by which reservations are booked. Where just a few short years ago a hotel's posted available rooms were manually adjusted and sold on a daily (even hourly) basis, today's rooms are sold electronically through a myriad of channels with little or no human interaction (see Exhibit 4–1). That represents a substantial change in methodology over a few short years. What does the future hold for hotel reservations? Imagine the following rather futuristic scenario:

> Heading to the airport for a hastily scheduled business meeting, a technologically savvy corporate businessman accesses the Internet on his handheld personal digital assistant (PDA). Through the PDA, he checks availability at his favorite New York City hotel, discovers that rooms availability is tight, but manages to reserve a Parlor Queen room for $345 that night. His credit-card guarantee is transmitted automatically, and the return confirmation number is conveniently stored in the PDA for later retrieval. A room reservation in hand, our corporate executive visibly relaxes as his taxi enters the airport's unloading zone.

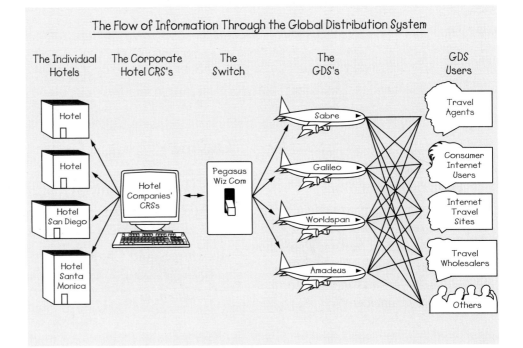

Exhibit 4–1   The Global Distribution System is enormous in scope. Each of the four airline GDS systems processes roughly 100 billion transactions per year and about 300 million requests for information per day! Galileo alone, for example, is connected to 45,000 hotel properties, 43,000 travel agencies, 500 airlines, 40 car-rental companies, 360 tour operators, and all of the world's major cruise lines.

The flow of information works like this: The supply-side of the flow begins with the hotel where information (rate and availability) flows to the switches. The switches provide that information to all four Airline GDSs. Travel agents, consumer Internet users, Internet travel sites, travel wholesalers, and a myriad of other end users (still to be invented) access the information through the GDSs. The demand side of the flow works in the opposite direction with the resulting room reservation finally coming to rest in the hotel's reservations system. *Source: Hotel & Motel Management Magazine.*

Several hours later, this futuristic scenario continues as our business traveler arrives at the Holiday Inn Wall Street. Literally, the moment he steps foot into the hotel's lobby, his digital cell phone alerts him that a message is waiting. The text message on his telephone asks if he would like to proceed with electronic check-in. No wonder he loves this hotel. Of course he readily agrees, and simply types "yes" into his cell phone and enters a preprogrammed personal identification number (PIN). Then, in one last attempt to up-sell to the guest, the hotel's property management system prompts him with several additional room-rate options. He decides to treat himself to an Executive King Suite for $425 and indicates as much on the cell phone.

As he walks across the lobby (secretly boasting because he's avoiding the growing check-in queue), his text message provides him the room number and even directions to the room (not that he needs directions—after all, this is his favorite hotel). As he exits the elevator, the hotel's short-range radio-wave technology senses him and prompts his telephone by again requesting his PIN. As he approaches the guestroom (within say 15 or 20 feet), the door automatically unlocks itself.

What a truly seamless series of transactions our corporate guest experienced. Each transaction was fully electronic—both paperless and faceless (no printed receipts or mailed confirmations, and no one-to-one or guest-to-employee interactions). Quite futuristic, you must agree! But wait . . . that technology is already in place at many hotels across America today. Everything mentioned in the above scenario is available technology accessed regularly by today's corporate guests (see Exhibit 4–2). The future is here!

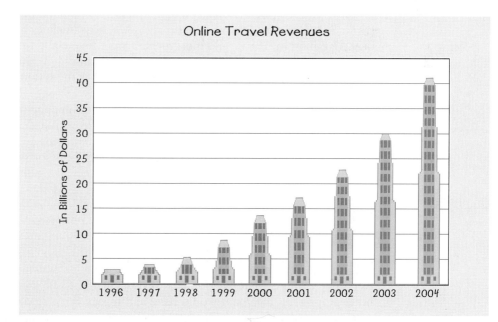

Exhibit 4–2   Between 1996 and 1999, online travel reservations grew at roughly 43% per year. In year 2000, online travel reservations grew 64% (to roughly $13 billion) over 1999. Even with a 33% growth after year 2000, online travel revenues could reach a staggering $41 billion per year by 2004!

➤ GLOBAL DISTRIBUTION

A complete understanding of today's complicated reservations technologies requires a look back to the beginning. In the beginning, even before the advent of Holidex (the lodging industry's first CRS, or Central Reservations System),[1] the airline industry was developing its own reservations systems. These airline systems proved to be an efficient and low-cost means for taking reservations. Based on these early airline successes, the lodging industry soon followed suit.

It is interesting to note that the lodging industry has historically followed airlines reservations technology ever since. The airlines have generally been the developers and investors in new systems, while the lodging industry has demonstrated itself to be somewhat more conservative. By choosing to wait on the sidelines in the early stages of development, hotel chains have ultimately saved money by taking advantage of existing technologies and systems.

The Airline Systems

In the early 1960s, airlines began developing electronic reservations systems to ease the process for booking airline seats by inhouse airline reservations clerks. Within a decade, the first airline reservations systems were being placed in travel agency offices. This was the first link in today's global distribution system networks.

You see, it makes sense to let someone else book the reservation. Why have the travel agent call the airline to book a reservation when we have the technology to place the reservations system terminal right in the travel agent's office? In addition, since the travel agent is a one-stop source for hotel and rental car reservations too, the new airline systems soon transformed into global networks.

It wasn't long before every possible airline had its hand in some reservations network. But these networks were expensive (American Airlines alone had invested well over $1 billion by 1985), and most airlines were financially or strategically forced to join together in developing CRS networks (see Exhibit 4–3). An excellent example of such a network is Worldspan, which joined together the systems originally owned by Northwest, Delta, and TWA airlines.

Back in the 1970s, some of the most expensive components of airline CRSs were the individual terminals placed in travel agency offices. As such, larger agencies with access to more potential bookings received more terminals from the various airlines than did smaller agencies. A travel agency with a large assortment of different airline terminals had more options than did a smaller agency. This difference in size and accessibility to airlines became even more pronounced as the airlines began offering hotel rooms and rental car bookings directly through their systems. Larger agencies were now able to sell a complete trip through one automated terminal; smaller agencies still needed to book most components of their reservations by telephone.

Smaller travel agents weren't the only ones left out of the picture. Many major lodging chains were not connected to airline reservation systems either. Although they were able to join, some lodging chains thought the costs were prohibitive. A single hotel property in the chain would have had to pay three separate commissions for a single reservation: The hotel would have to pay the travel agent a 10% (or higher)

---

[1]Sheraton Hotels introduced its central reservations system shortly after the Holidex system was introduced by Holiday Inns (1965). But Sheraton was the first major chain to offer a toll-free telephone number to its customers.

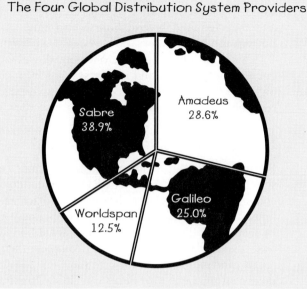

The Four Global Distribution System Providers

Exhibit 4–3   It is difficult to keep up with the changing ownerships and affiliations of the four GDS providers. Sabre, the largest of the four, was the only GDS wholly owned by one airline (American Airlines). However, American Airlines spun off Sabre in 1996 and now owns a piece of Worldspan (along with Delta and Northwest Airlines). Amadeus (originally a partnership with Air France, Iberia, Lufthansa, and Continental Airlines) grew to its number two standing by purchasing System One (owned mostly by Continental Airlines) in 1998. Galileo was purchased by Cendant Corporation in 2001 for a whopping $2.9 billion!

Here is another interesting tidbit. While Sabre owns Travelocity.com, Amadeus owns OneTravel.com, and Galileo owns Trip.com; Worldspan does not own an Internet consumer travel site. Because of their strategy—staying out of the e-commerce competition game—Worldspan has become the largest processor of Internet bookings!

commission; the airline would take a fee for access to the airline reservations system; and the hotel chain would take its normal fee for booking through the chain's central reservations office (CRO). Those chains that chose not to join the airline reservations system were still available to the travel agent by telephone, but telephone reservations were more time consuming and therefore less popular with travel agents.

To address this problem, many hotel chains began providing more efficient telephone reservation services to travel agents. In an attempt to encourage telephone bookings, hotel chains established private toll-free numbers exclusively for travel agents. These private phone numbers were staffed by experienced reservationists who could answer questions and book reservations quickly. As efficient as this may sound, to many agents the telephone approach was still not as appealing as the direct-access airline computer terminal.

Another issue that was apparent during these years was the fact that the hotel information listed on the airline reservations system was old news. Just as the hotel chain's CRO was not full-duplex (online, real-time) at this stage, neither was the airline system. Hotels still needed to close availability when only a few rooms remained (lest they be oversold), they were still not able to alter rates at a moment's notice, and they were still only able to offer a few basic rate categories. In fact, many airline reservations systems only allowed a set number of changes to hotel information per day, and they required several hours' lead time. As a result, the risk of overbooking through the airline reservations system was high.

With the old-fashioned, one-way downloading of rates and availability (half-duplex), hotel chains and airline systems were constantly updating information. Not only was that labor intensive and prone to errors, but it created time lags between the creation of new data and its appearance on the CRS.

Seamless Connectivity

By the late 1980s, the quantity of transactions between the airline global distribution systems (GDSs) and the hotel CROs[2] began outpacing the unsophisticated half-duplex communication interfaces that were in place at the time. Half-duplex systems (also known as *type B* systems) were basically one-way communication. A message would be sent in one direction, the response would be sent some time later. These type B systems required the travel agent to complete their rooms requests (or airline seats or rental cars) and forward them to the CRS. Minutes or even hours later, they received their confirmation. This delay was costly, frustrating, and prone to numerous errors and overbooking mistakes.

The introduction of full-duplex (also known as *type A*) communication in 1989 was a first step in solving this problem. Type A communication provided immediate confirmation of reservations requests (usually within about 7 seconds) and up-to-date rates and availabilities between the GDS and the CRO. Full-duplex communication between the GDS and CRS was an important landmark on the road to seamless connectivity. However, one key player was still not in the game—the hotel. The big question at this point was how the hotels themselves communicated their rooms inventory information to the chains' CROs.

▶**Last-Room Availability.**   The old-fashioned central reservations offices of the 1960s through 1980s required constant manual updating of room availability between the hotel and the CRO. The hotel inhouse reservations department was responsible for manually tracking the number of rooms sold by the CRO and calculating how many rooms still remained available for a given date. The CRO would continue blindly selling rooms until it was notified by the hotel to close room sales. In other words, the CRO never knew how many rooms were available at the individual property; it only knew that the hotel was still listing rooms available.

This placed an important responsibility on the inhouse reservations manager to notify the CRO when room availability was tightening. This notification became an exercise in timing and forecasting; as often as not, mistakes were made. Sometimes the hotel's inhouse reservations manager closed rooms with the CRO too early; other times, rooms were closed too late. If the hotel closed rooms with the CRO too early, there were still rooms available for sale and those remaining rooms became the responsibility of the inhouse reservations department. Many times, the reservations department did not have enough inhouse reservation activity and the date would come and go with several rooms remaining unsold. On the other hand, if the inhouse reservations manager closed the rooms too late, the hotel was overbooked.

---

[2]Hotel central reservations offices (CROs) are also commonly referred to as central reservations systems (CRSs). These two terms are interchangeable.

Commonly referred to as last-room availability systems, today's CRSs offer on-line, two-way communication with all affiliated hotels in the chain. No longer a hit-and-miss game of guessing when the last room will be sold, modern CRSs can literally sell the very last room at any hotel. This is because the CRS now has real-time information about the actual status of rooms at every hotel within the system. This is a significantly more efficient system because it allows the CRS more opportunities to sell every room without either underselling or overselling the hotel.

In addition, last-room availability technology is a necessary first step in providing an automated yield management system to the chain. Without online, full-duplex communication, a hotel's room rates are difficult to update. In fact, some older systems required the hotel to publish rates 18 months in advance without allowing changes throughout the entire year. The hotel literally had to forecast its levels of business and live with those forecasts no matter what might occur. As a result, the only way a hotel could alter its rates upward or downward during busy or slow periods was to close room availability with the CRO. Once closed, all rooms had to be sold through the inhouse system, and this was the only way rates could be changed as warranted. Today's online, last room availability systems allow the property to update rates with the CRS as often as necessary.

➤*Electronic Switch Technology.*   The road to seamless connectivity was now almost complete. At roughly the same time last-room-availability technology was being introduced between individual hotels and their respective CROs, another brick was being paved between airline GDSs and travel agents. To understand why this brick needed laying, look back to the 1970s.

It was in the mid-1970s that the first airline reservations terminals were being placed in travel agency offices. As more airline reservations systems became available, more terminals were placed with travel agencies. Although that sounds good, this may be an example of when more is not necessarily better.

You see, a travel agent was now faced with numerous terminals and systems to learn and choose from. Not only did that mean memorizing a different set of codes for, say, American Airlines' Sabre system as opposed to United Airlines' Apollo system, but it also took up increased space at the travel agency. It was not necessarily more efficient to have more terminals, and travel agents often found themselves spending valuable time moving from terminal to terminal to research rates, dates, and availability.

It took a new innovation, switch technology, to get all the companies speaking the same language. Today, there are several major electronic switches available. One system, THISCO, was developed by 11 major lodging chains (Best Western, Choice, Days Inns, Hilton, Holiday, Hyatt, La Quinta, Marriott, Ramada, Sheraton, and Forte) in conjunction with Rupert Murdoch's electronic publishing division. THISCO, which stands for The Hotel Industry Switching Company, was introduced in the early 1990s.

Switch technology functions like a clearinghouse. All reservations transactions are processed through the switch. The travel agent now needs access to just one terminal to communicate reservations requests and confirmations to literally any of thousands of airlines, hotels, car rentals, and other related products.

All of the benefits to the travel agent and hotel that accrue through last-room-availability systems are becoming available through airline reservations systems. Now, the travel agent is literally looking at the same hotel reservation data as the inhouse reservationist; if there are special rates or packages, the travel agent can quote them as readily as the hotel's inhouse reservationist. This is adding a new level of credibility to travel agents, who have often complained that their outdated data made them look unprofessional to the customer.

Another major advantage of the switch is that it enables the travel agent to learn just one set of procedures and to input just one set of codes. Switch technology functions as a translator as well as a real-time communicator. It translates codes into one hotel central reservations system or another. Now, when the agent is interested in booking a room with, say, two queens, the agent does not need to remember the exact input code. One chain might identify two queens with a QQ code, another chain might use 2Q or DQ for double queen. The electronic switch allows the user one system of codes and translates that information across each chain's particular CRS language.

The introduction of the switch has allowed seamless connectivity across the spectrum of reservations. Now travel agents, airline reservationists, hotel central reservation agents, and inhouse hotel reservations clerks access the same information at the same speed. So too do Internet applications access the same information. All reservations are made in real time and update the rooms inventory the moment the reservation is confirmed.

Application Service Providers

The historical evolution of CRSs from stand-alone call centers in the mid-1960s to today's seamlessly connected, last-room-availability GDSs has only been possible at a substantial price. Because of the heavy investment required, not all hotel chains are in the same place today in terms of their respective levels of sophistication.

Last-room-availability software requires an ability to integrate all of the chain's hundreds (if not thousands) of individual hotel property management systems. In terms of property management systems, some chains are still dealing with the mistakes they made decades ago. Mistakes like allowing each hotel—franchised or corporate-owned—to select its own property management system hardware and software are still proving costly to lodging chains in a number of ways. That's because different hardware and software applications across each property in the chain require either new investment to bring like products to all properties or a myriad of programming changes to get all systems speaking roughly the same language. It is this challenge facing hotel chains that has lent itself to the successful introduction of application service providers (ASPs). Application service providers are software companies (Pegasus' RezView and Swan's Unirez are two such examples) that offer a suite of software applications via Internet-based access. No longer is it necessary for a hotel chain to purchase and maintain specific property management system hardware and software for each affiliated hotel. Rather, through an Internet Web site, each hotel runs off the same suite of software by simply using any Internet-ready computer—even a laptop!

Generally, ASPs offer four primary functions in their arsenal of applications: a CRS, GDS connectivity, connections to "alternate" distribution systems, and Internet reservations. Hotels simply subscribe to the system, and all property-specific data is stored off-property in ASP-maintained warehouses (see Exhibit 4–4).

As you might imagine, numerous benefits are associated with ASP applications. Hotel chains do not have to make large capital investments in hardware and software. Nor do they have to employ a fleet of specialized software engineers to maintain the system and program new applications. Because every hotel uses the same software, multiple versions of poorly integrated applications are avoided. Best of all, new software enhancements are implemented immediately at the ASP site and available to all users instantaneously!

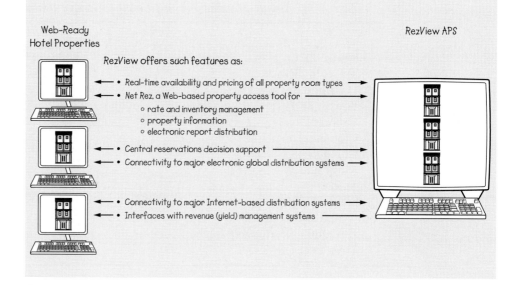

Exhibit 4–4   Features Provided Through an Application Service Provider—The Pegasus Solutions' "RezView" Model

Pegasus Solutions is the lodging industry's oldest (and most popular) provider of ASP Central Reservations software. Its ASP application, known as RezView, is utilized by more than 10,000 hotels, representing 71 brands and 2 million rooms worldwide. *Source: Hotel & Motel Management.*

▶*Single-Image Inventory.*   The biggest benefit associated with ASP applications is single-image inventory. Similar in concept to last-room-availability, single-image inventory allows all users to feed from the same database. One inventory—price and availability—is viewed by the GDS, central reservations call centers, and Internet-based distribution systems. The result is a lower error rate in reservations bookings and a resulting improvement in overall customer service (see Exhibits 4–5 and 4–6).

Although last-room-availability and single-image inventory (also known as *true integration*) appear quite similar, they are fundamentally different. The difference revolves around the fact that last-room-availability uses property management system inventory for its information. Historically, CRSs have interfaced with property management systems to determine availability and pricing. With single-image inventory, all reservations applications as well as property management system applications look at the same database and draw from the same well of information.

As such, the rooms inventory can become available for others to access. One result of having an accessible inventory is an overall savings on reservations commissions. Imagine negotiating a special corporate rate with Pepsi, for example. Rather than having Pepsi book its special rates through a travel agent (and paying commissions to the travel agent and fees to the GDS and other distribution system providers), the hotel could provide Pepsi a unique access code. All reservations booked against the inventory using this special code would be virtually commission-free!

Online Sales Revenues by Category/Industry	
	Year 2002
Category	Online Sales (est.)
Travel Industries	$11.7 billion
PC Computer Hardware	$6.4 billion
Books and Related Products	$3.7 billion
Grocery Goods	$3.5 billion
Clothing Apparel	$2.8 billion
Computer Software	$2.4 billion
Music and Videos	$2.2 billion
Ticketing	$1.8 billion
Specialty Gift Items	$1.4 billion
Health and Beauty	$1.2 billion
Consumer Electronics	$0.8 billion
Toys	$0.6 billion

Exhibit 4–5   In the late 1990s, for the first time in the history of the Internet, online travel purchases outpaced online personal computer purchases to become the leading Internet sales category. And travel bookings never looked back, continuing to grow at a rate faster than any other. That's because online travel bookings make sense—according to Internet experts, the travel industry is a natural for online bookings. Through the Internet, clients can readily compare prices, amenities, and other features before making their purchase decision.

But hotel bookings lag behind airline bookings in terms of online purchases. This is due, in part, to the fact that hotel bookings are more complicated for the average consumer—air is the simplest online purchase, followed by rental cars, with hotels coming up third for "ease of use." As such, just one out of every three or so Internet air bookings is accompanied by a related hotel booking. *Sources: Jupiter Communications, Wall Street Journal Europe, and Business News.*

Similarly, access to inventory can be made available to corporate or tour and travel group room blocks, giving groups the ability to develop their own rooming lists. Groups can then manipulate their room blocks, change names as often as needed, and simply send the hotel a completed rooming list at the touch of a button.

Taking the Reservation

With the growing importance of the GDS will come changes to the way reservations are taken. Even as we write these words, the telephone and travel agents seem to be growing less important to the reservations process. Conversely, Web sites and online bookings are growing ever more important. Only the future can tell what changes await the various players in the ever-changing reservations landscape (see Exhibit 4–9).

▶ *The Changing Role of the Travel Agent.*   On August 30, 2001, almost every travel agent office in America closed for part of the day as a symbol of protest. The travel agents' National Day of Awareness was designed to alert consumers to the

- Over two-thirds of all Internet hotel bookings are for rooms selling below $100 per night.
- While the ADR for hotel rooms has been growing at roughly 7% per year, online Internet hotel room rates have been growing more slowly—only 5% per year.
- Hotel rooms booked over the Internet sell for an average 21% lower rate than hotel rooms booked through other GDS channels.
- For rooms selling for $301 and higher, the Internet actually sells a higher ADR than for hotel rooms booked through other GDS channels.
- The average length of stay for Internet hotel room bookings is 2.1 nights. Hotel rooms booked through other GDS channels have an average length of stay of 2.2 nights.

Exhibit 4–6   Some Interesting Facts Related to Internet Hotel Bookings *Source: Lodging Magazine's Lodging Trends/Pegasus Report.*

substantial airline commission changes impacting the travel agent industry. Until just a few months before their day of protest, travel agents were generously paid by the airline industry. They enjoyed a mutually beneficial relationship that created a market in which travel agents were the number one method for consumer airline ticket purchases. Those days are gone forever.

Where travel agents previously received a respectable 10% airline commission, by August 2001, they had lost much ground, and it was still eroding before their very eyes. Imagine this: Historical commissions on, let's say, a $1,500 round-trip, first-class domestic ticket used to be a sizable $150 to the booking travel agent. That commission has slowly eroded—in 1995, Delta Airlines started the trend with a $50 cap on its 10% domestic commissions. Two years later, the airlines cut the commission rate to 8%, and then in 1998, instituted a first-ever $100 commission cap on international tickets. In 1999, most airlines cut domestic and international commissions to just 5%. Then, in August 2001, American Airlines (and its subsidiary TWA Airlines) reduced the $50 cap on domestic ticket commissions to just $20! Within days, United, Delta, Northwest, US Airways, America West, Continental, and America Trans Air (ATA) all followed with their own reduced commissions.

You can certainly imagine how devastating that was for the travel agent industry. Their bread and butter has always been airline ticket commissions, and now (using our $150 commission example above), their commissions have been reduced from $150 to just $20. Yet, bad as that may sound, in 2002, they lost even that paltry sum when most major airlines simply stopped paying commissions altogether!

Why Such Changes?   The reasons for such drastic changes are many. Some cite increased airline costs before and after various airline mergers as the main catalyst for reducing commissions. After all, when operating costs are high and competitive pressures keep tickets low, one sure way to save 10% is to simply eliminate commissions. Others suggest airline mergers have created an anti-consumer airline cartel with substantially reduced competition. Reduced competition means less consumer

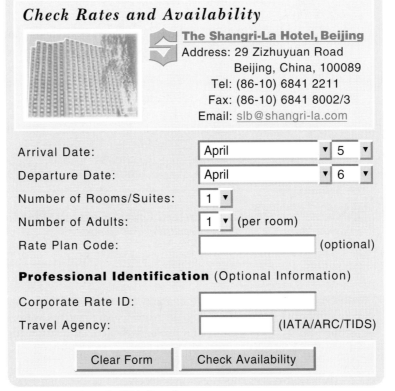

Exhibit 4–7a   Making reservations online is as easy as it is widespread (see Exhibit 4–2). This Shangri-La Hotels and Resorts online reservation form walks the guest through the process step by step. First we pulled up www.shangri-la.com. Then we selected Beijing, China and clicked on reservations. At that point, an availability screen popped up (Exhibit 4–7A). Once availability was assured, we were given a choice of many different room types and rates. Each room type was described, including rate; room description; bed type; and amenities; such as computer modem outlet, hairdryer, minibar, voice mail, and even shoe shine availability. Once we selected our room type, a "required fields" screen pulled up for us to complete and send the reservation (Exhibit 4–7B). *Courtesy of Shangri-La Hotels and Resorts, Hong Kong.*

air travel options and therefore fewer reasons to visit travel agents. Still others blame the attacks on the World Trade Center and the resulting reduction in consumer air travel immediately following September 11, 2001. However, travel agent airline ticket commissions had already received a number of reductions prior to the terrorist attacks.

Whatever the reasoning, certainly the airline industry has been successful in moving consumers away from travel agent bookings toward self-directed Internet bookings in recent years. Attractive and easy-to-use airline Web sites have helped simplify the do-it-yourself process. Discounts, double frequent flier miles, and Internet-only specials have also played a critical role in motivating consumers to visit airline Web sites.

Reservation Request

Reservation Information

The Shangri-La Hotel, Beijing
Address: 29 Zizhuyuan Road
Beijing, China, 100089

Tel: (86-10) 6841 2211
Fax: (86-10) 6841 8002/3
Email: slb@shangri-la.com

Arrival Date: Friday, April 5, 20__
Departure Date: Saturday, April 6, 20__
Daily Rate: 200.00 United States Dollars
(Per night subject to applicable tax and service charges)

Number of Rooms/Suites: 1
Number of Adults: 1

Rate and Policy Information:
SHANGRI-LA HOTELS WORLD'S FINEST CHOICE *SG*
Guarantee Policy:
CREDIT CARDS: AX VI CA DC JC VS MC
Cancellation Policy:
ONE NIGHT CXLN CHARGE AND TAX
Deposit Policy:
DEP CREDIT CARDS: AX VI CA DC JC VS MC

To confirm your reservation, please complete the booking request information below.
*Required Information

Customer Information:

*First Name: [   ]
*Last Name: [   ]
*Telephone: [   ]
*Email Address: [   ]

(Please double check your email address before submitting your information as your confirmation will be sent to this address.)

Billing Information:

*Street Address: [   ]
[   ]
[   ]
[   ]
*City: [   ]
*State/Province: [Choose a State ▼] (Required only for the United States and Canada)
*Postal/ZIP Code: [   ] (Required only for the United States and Canada)
*Country: [Choose a Country ▼]

Credit Information: (A credit card number is required to confirm/guarantee your reservation.)
*Credit Card Type: [Choose Card Type ▼]
*Card Number: [   ]
*Expiration (MM/YY): [   ]

Special Request Information:
Please indicate any additional request for your reservation such as: bed type, number of beds or smoking preference. Please note that this request is not guaranteed until check-in.
Comments: [   ]

[Clear Form]   [Reserve Now]

Exhibit 4–7b

Changes Still to Come. Where there were once 500,000 travel agencies across the world, since 1995 and with increasing frequency, the travel agent industry has experienced numerous bankruptcies and has watched hoards of agencies go out of business. The biggest change for consumers has been an increased fee structure—no longer are travel agents working exclusively on commission (at least with regard to airline commissions), and as such, it is very common for consumers to now pay travel agents a $10 to $25 per airline ticket booking fee.

Travel agents are not the only ones to implement new booking fee structures. In a move quite similar to the elimination of travel agent commissions in early 2002, most airlines have also reduced or eliminated commissions to Internet travel sites (Travelocity, Orbitz, etc.). Like the travel agent industry, the Internet travel site industry has been vocal in calling such actions predatory and anti-competitive. Where airlines had generally been paying such travel sites a 5% commission (with a maximum ticket payout cap of $10), most are now paying no commission at all. Therefore, like the travel agent industry, many Internet travel sites are now adding a surcharge to help cover costs and earn a profit.

Some experts suggest these changes are designed to reduce competition and that they will ultimately hurt the consumer. Having to pay a fee for booking a ticket at a travel Web site will likely move customers away from travel site comparison shopping and send them directly to the airline sites. Indeed, many consumers who think they are shopping wholesale travel Web sites may be surprised to know who really owns such sites (see Exhibit 4–3).

It is hard to predict what such changes will mean to travel agents, consumers, travel Web sites, the airline industry, and the hotel industry, but we can make a few conjectures. Travel agents will attract consumers from higher economic strata. These consumers will appreciate (and pay for) higher levels of service. The travel agents' expertise with regard to travel options, ease and convenience with regard to one-stop shopping, and familiarity with the customer's unique needs and wants are the products they sell. As the travel agent industry evolves, larger agencies will absorb smaller ones. The resulting few mega-agencies will undoubtedly carry more clout then we see today in terms of price/fee negotiations, wholesale travel prices, Internet Web sites, and so on.

▶ *The Hotel–Travel Agent Relationship.*   While some experts are predicting a similar reduction or ultimate elimination of travel agent commissions in the hotel industry, that seems doubtful. After all, there are literally tens of thousands of hotels compared with maybe a dozen airlines. Choose a community to visit for a few nights, and you'll be faced with selecting from numerous competing hotel properties (and other complimentary options like camping, bed and breakfasts, hostels, etc.). Even hotels working within the same chain or brand are, in essence, in competition with each other for limited travel dollars. Hotels therefore cannot afford to limit their chances of selling rooms by limiting the global distribution options they have in place. This discussion is expanded later under the section "Automated Revenue Management Systems."

Travel agents are one of the major sources of hotel reservations. Travel agent bookings represent about 15% of all hotel rooms booked. Hotels pay a 10% commission (the same commission percentage the airlines paid prior to 1995)—more in off-seasons to generate volume—for all rooms booked by a travel agency. Fees are not governmentally regulated. Amounts paid vary from property to property and even within the same property over time. *Overrides,* additional points of 10 to 15%, are paid to encourage high levels of business from one agency.

Guests pay no direct charge to the agency for its service, although some agencies have started to charge service fees for all services (not just for commission-less airline ticket bookings). Two areas of contention emerge from this relationship. One is a marketing problem, the other a bookkeeping problem.

Actually, there are several marketing problems. Hotels complain that travel agencies (TAs) send business chiefly during the hotel's busy periods. Additional reservations are not needed then, and certainly not if they require a commission. According to the agents, hotels befriend them only when there is low business and tend to ignore them and their customers—who incidentally are also hotel guests—as soon as volume recovers.

If the travel agent's repeat bookings are few and widely spaced, commission checks are small. Hotels find the cost of processing such checks greater than the commission. Hotels also have problems with some bookings when they originate with unknown agencies whose credit status is unproven. For these and for other accounting reasons that are reviewed in a later chapter, commission payments are not as prompt as TAs would like them to be. It is prompt, accurate payment that heads the agenda of every travel agency–hotel meeting.

Other key topics include the hotel's willingness to honor reservations and the reliability of its reservation system, including the frequency of overbooking. TAs are frustrated by these issues and by uncollected commissions, which they maintain total as much as half of all debt due.

The macro view is rosier. Lodging industry payments to the travel industry increase each and every year. Hotels pay billions of dollars annually to the hundreds of thousands of individual agencies. Unfortunately for the client, those payments dictate which hotel the agency selects. If the guest has no preference (many do not), the hotel that pays commissions promptly will be the one the agency selects.

The system operates through a patchwork of informal relationships. Few formal agreements are in place. Many hoteliers believe that they are in direct competition with the travel agent, fighting for the same business and paying a commission to boot. That kind of thinking is being supported by the appearance of powerful mega-agencies and consortiums of agencies. Large-volume dealers stand toe-to-toe with national hotel chains. By securing the travel contracts of small and large corporations, these mega-agencies squeeze discounted rates from the national hotel chains anxious to get or retain a piece of the business.

Inhouse Reservations Center. No matter what their affiliation or level of automation, all hotels have some system for accepting direct or inhouse reservations. In certain properties, the number of inhouse reservations is quite minimal. In other operations, however, the bulk of hotel rooms are sold through the inhouse reservations center. This is especially true with nonaffiliated, independent hotels where there is no CRS or where the CRS represents a small percentage of all reservations (see Exhibit 4–8).

Direct or inhouse reservations are also taken in quantity by hotels with large group sales business. Such business is generated by the hotel's own sales department, and those bookings bypass the CRS. For this reason, inhouse reservationists have been incorporated into the sales departments of several hotel chains.

Experienced shoppers often call the hotel directly. The inhouse reservationist is more informed about the property. He or she has one hotel, whereas the CRS agent has hundreds or even thousands. If the hotel is full, reservations might be refused by the central reservation office but still be accepted on site.

A reservations manager, or supervisor, heads the inhouse department, which might number as many as a dozen persons. Large operations permit a degree of specialization, but the size scales downward until the room clerk alone carries out the function in smaller properties. Reports and room status computations may be the responsibility of one group of employees, and others may tend solely to tour groups. More often, several of these jobs are combined into one or two positions.

Exhibit 4–8   Hotels pay numerous commissions on each hotel reservation booked. For example, let's say a person visits a travel agent to book a ski trip. The travel agent (that's the first commission the hotel pays) books the lodging reservation through one of the switch companies (that's the second commission), which in turn is routed through an airline global distribution network (that's the third commission) to the hotel chain's CRO (that's the fourth commission) and ultimately to the ski hotel.

In an effort to save on all these commissions, hotels are looking to the Internet and developing their own Web sites to attract customers directly to their in-house reservations (and bypass the costly commissions). A great idea, but relatively few hotels actually take reservations directly through their independent Web sites. Instead, either their Web sites link to the chain's CRO (resulting in a commission) or the hotel's Web page provides information only, and not online reservations capabilities (Also known as "unbookable"). This exhibit shows a popular independent resort in Arizona. In spite of the attractiveness and sophistication of the Web page, you'll notice the guest cannot check availability nor book a room online—it still requires a call (or email) to the property. *Courtesy of Rio Rico Resort and Country Club*

➤*Central Reservations System.*   The central reservations system (CRS) has historically been referred to as the central reservations office (CRO). Although there is a distinction between these two terms, today's jargon has made them almost fully interchangeable. Most managers refer to their central reservations center as the CRS.

In reality, the CRS is the entire system, including all of the link-ups, software, switches, and nuances described in this chapter. The CRO is the hotel chain's portion of this overall system. The CRO is the actual office or site at which the chain's reservationists operate (see Exhibit 4–9).

Historically, most chains maintained one CRO. Guests accessed the office simply by dialing the toll-free number the chain advertised. It was not uncommon for one CRO to receive several million phone calls per year. That is a lot of telephone activity!

Therefore, CROs needed to locate in an area with a great capacity for telephone volume. This area was the Midwest. The Midwest, especially Omaha, Nebraska, developed into a major central reservations' hub because of the excess telephone equipment in the area. The Bell System had unused capacity as a result of the massive defense grid built to accommodate the armed forces. With a promise of exceptionally good service and the support of the telephone system, hotel companies began opening reservation centers in the late 1960s. This created a specialized labor pool, making the area even more attractive.

Even today, midwestern cities such as Omaha and Kansas City house a large percentage of the nation's CROs. However, as call volumes rose in the 1980s, most chains found themselves establishing several CROs scattered nationwide and even globally (England and India have both become major worldwide call center regions). Today, the numbers are staggering. Some of the larger lodging chains boast over 2 million calls per month and book well in excess of 1 million reservations per month (see Exhibit 4–9).

Processing the Call.   Reservation agents receive the incoming calls and usually process them in 2 to 3 minutes. They are assisted with sophisticated telephone switching equipment. During busy call volume periods, automated telephone systems answer the call and may segregate the caller according to a variety of options. The caller is asked to listen to the options and then select by pressing a specific number on the telephone keypad. Large chains use the telephone system to segregate callers according to the hotel brand in which they are most interested. Another common way to separate callers is according to whether their reservation is for a domestic hotel property, a European hotel, an Asian property, a Latin American operation, and so on.

Once callers have been properly routed, they may be placed on hold for the next available reservationist. During the holding period, a recording provides information about the chain, special discount periods, new hotel construction, and the like. In recent years, more and more recordings recommend callers visit the Web site to save time and view special Internet-only discounts. Automatic call distributor equipment eventually routes the telephone call to the next available reservationist.

Time is money, with labor and telephone lines the primary costs of CROs. So the reservation manager battles to reduce the time allotted to each call. A sign in one office read: "Talk time yesterday 1.8 (meaning minutes). During the last hour, 2.2. This hour, 2.1." Actually, more sophisticated devices are available. Some computer-management systems monitor each agent, providing data on the number of calls taken, the time used per call taken, and the amount of postcall time needed to complete the reservation. However, employee evaluations must not be judged on time alone. Systems often evaluate the percentage of the agent's calls that result in firm bookings and the relationship of the agent's average room rate to the average being sold by the entire center (office).

Exhibit 4–9a   Exhibit 4–9b shows a sample reservations screen from Best Western International's proprietary Lynx reservations system (version 9.2.0). Exhibit 4–9a shows reservations workstations at Best Western International's Beardsley Operations Center in Phoenix, Arizona. This is one of five international reservations centers operated by BWI. It also operates centers in Glendale, Arizona (on the campus of Glendale Community College); Dublin, Ireland; Milan, Italy; and Sydney, Australia.

The Beardsley Operations Center is BWI's largest, with 425 reservations agents during peak staffing periods. Best Western International handles about 6.4 million domestic (including Canada) calls per year (total call volume) and another 1 million calls internationally. Total call volume includes all calls—reservations, customer service, questions, problems, cancellations, and so on. Roughly 38% to 40% of total call volume is converted into actual reservations. *Courtesy of Best Western International, Inc., Phoenix, Arizona.*

Remember, Res centers charge a fee for each reservation booked. Since the center is usually a separate subsidiary of the corporate parent, even company-owned properties pay the fee of several dollars per booking. Franchisees often pay more than just the booking fee. A monthly fee on each room plus a percent of gross rooms sales may also be charged. Franchisees complain about the fee schedule, but the reservation system is the major attraction of franchising.

▶*The Hotel Representative.*   Although less common than in years past, hotels might maintain sales offices in distant cities, sending reservations from these offices to the hotel. Casino hotels usually maintain such offices in nearby cities: New York for Atlantic City, Los Angeles for Las Vegas. Reservations are among the services provided.

Hotels also establish their presence in other locations through the use of a representative (rep). This person, or company, functions much as the traditional product representative, as a spokesperson and salesperson for many noncompeting brands. Utell International is one well-known rep.

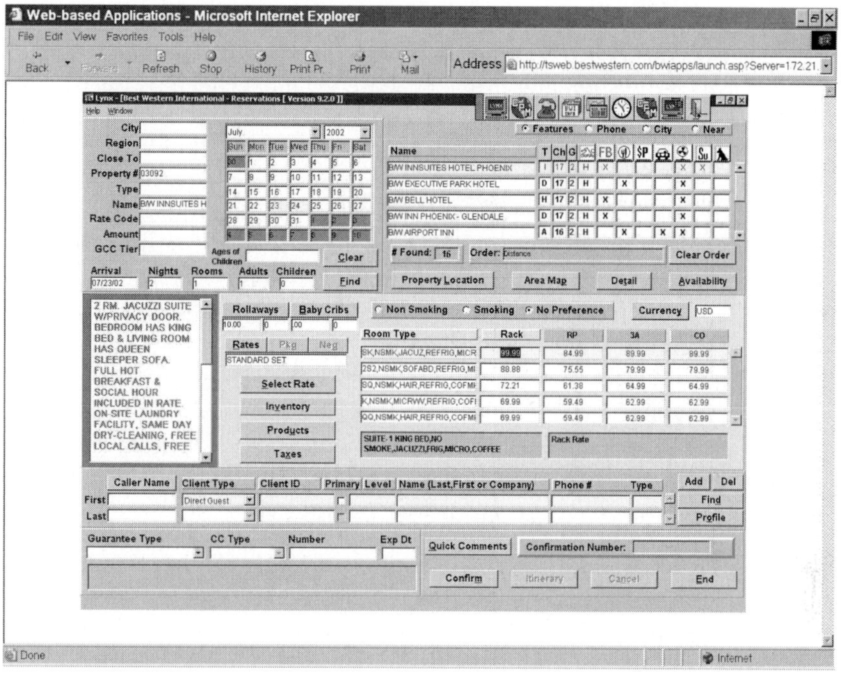

Exhibit 4–9b

When many noncompetitors (same-quality hotels from separate cities) associate with one particular rep, another alternative emerges: The independents band together to market the membership under one umbrella. Preferred Hotels and Resorts and Leading Hotels of the World are good examples of this group. These are sometimes not-for-profit affiliations.

The rep and the hotel negotiate a fee schedule, although a fee plus commission is not unusual. There is also likely an initial membership fee. For that charge, the rep provides many sales and marketing services, including trade-show representation. Most important, the rep provides the central reservation office that the independent hotel lacks. Some international reps even service chains because the international rep provides language operators overseas and settles with travel agents in the currency of the local area. These are capabilities that the chain reservation office may not have.

Technology, with its access to travel agencies, transportation facilities, and company travel departments, is the key to the reservation business. Reps maintain their own systems, which they interface electronically with one or more GDSs, something quite difficult for the independent hotel to do.

▶*Independent Reservation Services.* Membership in a CRS is one of the major advantages that chain-affiliated properties have over independent operations. The CRS provides each affiliated property access to sophisticated airline distribution systems, tens of thousands of travel agents, a convenient toll-free telephone number for potential customers, automated rate and inventory data, and a wealth of other automated benefits. Yet CRSs are extremely expensive, and the cost of developing a CRS is prohibitive for most small chains and independent operations.

Smaller chains can provide better guest service at a lesser cost by leasing the reservation service. Leasing from an independent reservation service is commonly referred to as *outsourcing*. It makes sense for independent properties and small and new lodging chains. For hotel rep companies—Utell International, for example—the move is a natural extension of their primary role and should represent economies for each of their clients. UtellVision is a computerized reservation system for Utell member hotels. The system displays two screens simultaneously. The top screen is a series of high-resolution pictures of the member hotel and maps of the surrounding areas; on the bottom is an on-line reservations availability screen.

Independent hotels and small chains that join a private reservation service expect to gain efficiency and economies of scale, and they generally do experience a number of money-saving benefits. They save significant investment in hardware and software by joining rather than developing their own system. They save operating and training costs. Reservation processing is more efficient due to the massive computer capacity of the independent reservation service. And salesmanship is enhanced by joining a group of professionally trained agents. If the independent reservation service is also an ASP, even more benefits are available to the small chain—the property management system database is Web-accessible, single-imaging allows all users access to the same information, and yield management decisions can be made on a chainwide basis—refer to the discussion on ASPs earlier in this chapter (see Exhibit 4–4).

Hotel chains have tried other, less dramatic restructuring in their search for electronic links and economies of scale. Various affiliations have been tested as a means of broadening the market and spreading operating costs over a wider base. The affiliates have been other travel and lodging companies, but the umbrella has often been that of an independent entrepreneur. Some, like the Caribbean Hotel Reservation Service, have tried to develop space banks for an entire geographic area. Others are operated for one specific group: business travelers in luxury hotels, for example. Still others are quasipublic agencies such as tourist or convention bureaus. One such example, offered by the San Francisco Convention & Visitors Bureau, is a hotline (1-888 Stay-N-SF) listing over 70 of the city's finest hotel operations!

Other Trends in Electronic Reservations

They say that in just one day, the average American adult is exposed to more information than a person living 100 years ago might have been exposed to in a lifetime. That statistical analogy speaks volumes in terms of the speed and quantity of information available today. And the trend will certainly continue. For example, the average processing power of a personal computer is expected to grow 1,000-fold over the next five years. In addition, information storage and retrieval capabilities of PCs are anticipated to grow at a compounded rate of 60% per year for the next five years. With these rapid advancements, CROs are facing increasing opportunities for unique and more effective ways of performing their businesses. From voice recognition to "mapping" software, the future is anyone's guess.

➤*Voice Recognition.*   Amazing progress has been achieved in the area of automated voice recognition. Currently there are systems in place that can recognize tens of thousands of words spoken by a host of various users. Dragon Systems' NaturallySpeaking and IBM's Via Voice are the two leading personal computer applications. Each can recognize tens of thousands of words (more than 50,000) with virtually 99% accuracy (after a few minutes of training and the use of an acoustic optimizer).

We are probably not far from a time when straightforward rooms reservations are routinely handled electronically by voice-recognition and voice-synthesis (talking) systems. Indeed, thousands of voice-recognition systems are now at work across a myriad of other industries. AT&T uses voice recognition to assist the processing of directory assistance calls. Physicians' offices use voice recognition for transcribing detailed medical records. Business corporations use voice recognition for dictating letters.

The biggest argument in favor of such a laborsaving system is the overall repetitiveness of the reservationist's job. As unique as each reservation might seem, there are more commonalities than differences. Each reservation communicates the city, date, room rate and type, and other basic data. These are functions that a computer system could logically handle. In fact, the simplest of all voice-recognition software applications utilizes a "command" system. This system recognizes several hundred words from a preprogrammed list of possible commands. On what day of the week a guest is traveling (7 possible words), the date of departure (31 possible words), type of credit-card guarantee (roughly 6 to 10 possible words), and credit-card number (10 possible words) are some of the common reservations commands a computer might easily recognize.

The voice-recognition reservations program would generate a series of questions for the guest to answer. With each response, the program would acknowledge the answer, allow the guest to make changes as necessary, and generate a new series of questions based on the previous response. In those situations where the computer could not recognize the guest's voice due to a strong accent or other impairment, a fail-safe system would be in place—the guest might press the zero button twice on the telephone keypad, for example, to alert an operator that personal assistance was needed. One of our favorite voice-recognition CROs in place today is operated by American Airlines—give it a try at 1-800-433-7300. When American's reservationists are busy, the system probes the key elements of the guest's flight information. It does a fantastic job of understanding originating airport, destination airport, day of travel, time of travel, and so on.

Such computer systems can check availability, quote rates, suggest alternative dates, and thank the guest in a manner similar to the reservationist. Of course, such a system would be significantly less personal than dealing with an actual reservationist. On the other hand, it would surely be less expensive in terms of labor costs, and the computer system would never call in sick!

➤*Mapping Capabilities.*   As GDSs gain sophistication, options that were previously unavailable (or manually performed) are increasingly being automated. One example of an old manual format now available as an automated system enhancement is *mapping*.

Commonplace requests such as a hotel's physical address, its distance from a popular destination, or specific travel directions were once manual tasks. Central reservations agents, representing chains of hundreds or thousands of hotels, were required to look up such information in databases provided by member properties. This was a slow and generally inefficient method.

Today, modern mapping functions can provide comprehensive geographical, pictorial, and textual information about every member property. Best Western was the first company of its size to offer a mapping feature with its new CRS. Now central reservations agents have immediate access to geographically related questions about property locations, mileage, travel times, and so on. For a chance to experience mapping functions first-hand, refer to the "Resources and Challenges" section at the end of this chapter. It lists five Web sites that feature state-of-the-art mapping capabilities.

Indeed, guests can retrieve the same information themselves automatically by calling any of the chain's 3,400 hotels worldwide. A call to the hotel's toll-free number from any location allows customers to determine the Best Western hotel that is closest to their desired destination and get specific directions to the property.

▶*Guest History Databases.*   Another benefit of the GDS is the ability for hotels to share guest history information. Database information is currently utilized only within chains. As the switch technology improves, guest history data may actually be shared across chains.

Even within the chain, hotels rarely take advantage of their wealth of data. Yet, most property management systems allow a guest history function. Standard information required for the reservation becomes a marketing tool, if properly administered. After all, the hotel already knows the guest's name and address, the dates of the last visit, the rate paid, the room type, the number of guests, and the method of payment. Add a bit of marketing information such as the type of discount package purchased, the special rate or promotion used, and whether the reservation was midweek or was a weekend getaway package, and the manager has an enormous amount of marketing data. For a more thorough understanding of guest history, refer to Chapter 5.

From guest history databases to voice recognition, automation is changing the GDS and the way in which hoteliers manage the reservations process.

➤ AUTOMATED REVENUE MANAGEMENT SYSTEMS

An increasingly competitive and complex lodging industry has also changed the way hoteliers sell reservations. Rather than the old goal of simply "placing heads in beds," today's hoteliers need to selectively place the right heads into the right beds at the right price. You see, despite the large number of rooms that are available on an annual basis, every reservation request is not accepted. The decision depends on space and rate ranges available for the specific dates. An occupancy forecast determines the space situation for the day or days in question. Even if only one day of the sequence is closed, the reservation may be refused and an alternative arrangement offered. This is unfortunate if the declined reservation represented a request for a number of days. It is especially unfortunate if the period in question has only one sold-out date. Then the hotel is essentially trading a profitable, long-term reservation against a potential overbooking situation for one sold-out date. In many cases, the reservationist may do just that, and override the system to book this type of reservation. Obviously, such a decision would be considered on a case-by-case basis.

In other situations, the salesmanship of the reservationist comes into play. The telephone provides a two-way conversation during which the reservationist can gauge the behavior of the guest. Some guests can be convinced to reserve their chosen date at a slightly higher nightly rate. Other guests' minds can be changed toward a slower occupancy period with the offer of reduced rates.

In any case, guests who cannot be accommodated represent lost revenues. The reservationist attempts to salvage lost reservations in a number of ways—offering premium rates during almost sold-out periods, offering different dates when rates are not as high, or even offering another sister property of the same chain in a nearby community. When all else fails, the reservationist can only thank the caller and ask him or her to try again another time.

Requests for accommodations are sometimes denied even if the house is not full. Most of the hotel's advertised packages are refused if the forecast shows that the house is likely to fill at standard rack rates. The inverse of this is also true. Reservationists must be taught to sell discounted packages or other reduced rates (weekend, commercial, governmental) only on request or when encountering rate resistance.

With a full house, requests from travel agents, to whom the hotel pays a commission, may be regretted. A low priority is assigned to requests from agents who are slow in paying. All reservations are refused if the caller has a poor credit rating, regardless of the occupancy forecast. Busy hotels give preference to higher-paying multiple-occupancy requests over single occupancy.

Casino hotels give preferential treatment to those who are likely to gamble, even to the extent of granting them free accommodations in preference to paying guests who don't play. Noncasino hotels do the same, allotting their scarce space to reservations from certain areas or markets that the hotel is trying to develop.

The Yield Management Revolution

Revenue management, the act of controlling rates and restricting occupancies in an effort to maximize gross rooms revenue, is most commonly referred to as *yield management*. In its simplest form, yield management has been around for decades. Any seasoned manager who increased room rates as occupancy for a given date rose, or who quoted higher rates for holidays and special event periods, or who saved the last few room nights for extended-stay reservations was using yield management. It is not the practice of yield management that is new, it is the incorporation of revenue managers into dedicated senior staff positions and the automation of yield management into complex property management systems that is new.

Organizations were downsized and labor costs reduced during the low cycle of the early 1990s. Despite the squeeze on profits, many hotels added revenue managers (or yield managers) to their organizations (see Exhibit 3–1). The move was easily justified by the revenue offset. Some 15 to 25% of recent ADR growth has been attributed to yield management, the specialty of these new managers. Thus, a 400-room property with an overall 10% increase in ADR from, say, $118 to $129.80 could attribute about $2 of the nearly $12 increase directly to the new yield team. Assuming 70% occupancy, that produces some $200,000 annually (400 rooms × 70% 365 days × $2). That's a wonderful return on the costs of yield management hardware, software, and related wages!

▶*A Brief History of Yield Management.* As with other businesses, price (hotel room rate) is a major factor in the decision to purchase one product (one hotel) over another. That is especially true in light of the sharper guest segmentation the industry has experienced over the last decade. Yield management works best when there are distinct market segments to attract. It is the price sensitivity of these market segments that made yield management practices successful in the first place.

The Airlines' Role. Lodging has adopted yield management concepts from the airlines. Airline rate discounting was widespread in the early 1980s, and that contributed to the array of prices that the airlines found difficult to track. They began experimenting with adjusted rates based on demand forecasts. Discounted tickets purchased far in advance were used to establish a minimum level of seat occupancy and to forecast overall demand. Low and seasonal periods were also discounted. As the plane filled and departure time neared, higher and higher fares were charged. Full price was eventually charged for the remaining seats—a price that would have been virtually impossible to charge when the plane was empty.

Airlines and hotels are much alike. Both have a relatively fixed supply of product (seats and rooms), and both have products that perish with the passage of time. In the 1980s, airlines had one extra edge—large computer capability. It takes the capacity of these large systems to simultaneously track occupancy (seat or room) and the variety of price options that both industries market.

Price-sensitive concepts have been employed by hoteliers for a long, long time. Refining the practices and developing them into a program with rules and triggers, with a knowledge base and a strategy, awaited the superior computer capability of the airlines. Today, most major lodging chains have developed automated yield management systems that rival the best of the airline systems.

Market Demand.   Airlines and hotels did differ in one respect—their view of the guest. Hotels had previously operated on the belief that their customer was not a discretionary traveler. The guest who came, hoteliers felt, was someone who had to come. Guests did not come merely because the price was reduced enough to lure them into the purchase. Urban hotels, which cater to the least flexible guest, the commercial traveler, first evidenced the change. In desperate need of weekend business, these properties began to market weekend specials to discretionary buyers. The march to yield management had begun.

You see, yield management has an economic rationale. It assumes that all customers are price conscious—that they are aware of the existence of and the significance of price variations. Furthermore, it assumes that customers are price sensitive—that their buying habits respond to increases and decreases in price.

All things being equal, the guest is motivated by lower prices. Theoretically, when a similar room type is available for a significantly lower rate at an otherwise equal hotel, the guest will select the lower-priced accommodations. In addition, guests who might not have left home at the rack rate are inclined to visit hotels when rates are low. As a result, low-occupancy periods are generally accompanied by lower average room rates.

Each customer class has different degrees of price consciousness and price sensitivity. Earlier discussions on segmentation (see Chapter 2) indicated the wide range of guests to whom the industry appeals. In simple terms, these are the business (corporate) class, the leisure (transient) guest, and the group (tour) buyer.

Corporate Guests.   The business or corporate customer is less sensitive to price—not unaware of price, just less sensitive to it. Businesspersons must travel when the need arises; they will not go merely because the price is reduced.

Business arrangements may be made only a few days or hours before arrival (see Exhibit 4–10). Location is very important, both to save travel time and to present the proper image. Business travelers need to be near the business center, which means high-priced real estate and high room rates. These travelers are away from home a good deal. They seek and probably merit a higher level of comfort than the occasional leisure traveler. In summary, business guests pay higher rates because they are less price sensitive. They have to stay in a specific location at a given time, and that arrangement is often made suddenly, with little advance planning, and therefore little opportunity to obtain discounted rates.

Leisure Guests.   The leisure guest, as the name implies, is 180 degrees removed from the corporate traveler. With leisure guests, lead time is long. Reservation bookings are well planned, with adequate time to shop for the best room rates. This class of guest is flexible as to the time of the trip, the destination of the trip, and the stopping places. These guests may not even use a hotel. High prices might drive them into

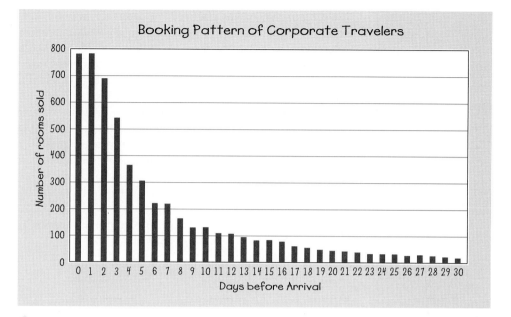

Exhibit 4–10   A 30-day booking pattern for corporate travelers. Although some corporate guests book 30 (or more) days in advance, the majority reserve rooms within a few days of arrival. This 275-room hotel receives approximately 60% of its business from corporate guests.

camping or park facilities. Poor price value might send them to the homes of friends or family. When prices of accommodations, fuel, toll roads, and gasoline are too high, this guest may just stay home.

Leisure travelers have been the major beneficiaries of the yield management approach offered by both the airline and the hotel industries. The leisure travelers' flexibility with regard to travel dates and itineraries allows them to take advantage of deep discounting during off-season and slow demand periods. It is not uncommon to find hotel rooms discounted between 50 and 80% during slow periods. A $250 hotel room in Australia's Kakadu National Park in the tropics, for example, may cost only $100 or so during the rainy season; a $400 golf package in Palm Springs may be discounted to $175 in the heat of the summer.

Group Guests.   *Group business,* the last of the three general classifications, exhibits characteristics from both of the other two categories. That's because the group market forms from components of the business and leisure classifications. From the leisure category come social, fraternal, and hobby associations, sometimes called SMERF's (social, military, educational, religious, and fraternal). From the business segment come professional, union, and governmental groups.

Both types of groups—leisure and business—have their own idiosyncrasies. Generally, business-oriented groups are sensitive to date and place while being less sensitive to rate. That is because business groups usually meet the same week every year. Leisure-oriented groups are more rate sensitive and therefore tend to be somewhat flexible with regard to date and place. Profits can be increased if the sales department, based on good forecasting, can steer the business to the right (right for the hotel) time, place, and rate.

Yield management has changed the interface between the sales department and the group buyer. Based on information from the yield management program, the sales department and/or the revenue manager must decide to take the business, reject the business, or try to negotiate a different time at a different rate. Saturday arrival for a group might actually prove more profitable at $90 per night, for example, than a Monday arrival (which replaces high rate corporate guests) at $115 per night. A well-programmed yield management system should provide the answer. (A more detailed discussion of group business and related automation is available in Chapter 5.)

At issue is whether the discounted room rates requested by the group, plus the value of the group's meeting room and banquet business, is valued at more or less than the forecasted income from normal guests who will be turned away. Yield management systems can answer that question. The discretionary decisions still remain for the salespersons to evaluate. For example, is other new business likely to spin off from this meeting? Is this a single event, or are we doing business with a meeting planner who controls 100 or more meetings per year?

Yield management means that function rooms are no longer booked on a first-come, first-served basis. Neither are guest rooms; there must be a price–occupancy mix.

▶ *Tools for Measuring Results.*   The task facing the revenue (yield) manager is formidable. Each day represents a new challenge in terms of maximizing both average daily rate and occupancy, and the amount of information available to the revenue manager grows each year. It is no longer enough to understand your own hotel's rate and occupancy for a given period of time; today you must understand how your performance measures against your hotel's *competitive market set*—all competing hotels based on geography (they are proximate to your property) and/or quality or price (they offer a similar product or are similarly priced).

Gone are the days when revenue managers drove past their competitors' hotels and counted parked cars to gauge approximate occupancies. Gone are the days when the front-desk staff made a series of telephone calls to competing properties as an exercise in guessing how many rooms they still had available and for what rates. Instead, today's sophisticated hotels have access to an incredible assortment of reports and subscription services that provide a wealth of previously unavailable data. Thanks almost exclusively to the GDS, there is literally more information available to a well-connected revenue manager than anyone could ever use. You see, information is the by-product of inventorying and selling rooms, and some of the biggest providers of subscription information services are the very providers who sell millions of rooms each year—the GDS (see Exhibit 4–11).

Let's look at some of the most popular reports.

PHASER Complete Access Reports.   Provided by a company called Travel-CLICK, the *PHASER Report* is one of several popular formats available through this company. TravelCLICK is the preeminent provider of digital media and data solutions to the travel industry. By offering hotels and other travel suppliers detailed competitive reports, TravelCLICK helps hotels position themselves more aggressively within their marketplace.

TravelCLICK pulls its competitive information directly from the GDS (from Sabre and other GDSs), which is used by more than 480,000 (about 98%) of the world's travel agents. The report breaks the hotel rates into two categories, GDS and CRS, and the report looks for the lowest available rate in each of these areas. *PHASER Complete Access Reports* provide hotel managers with a custom-designed

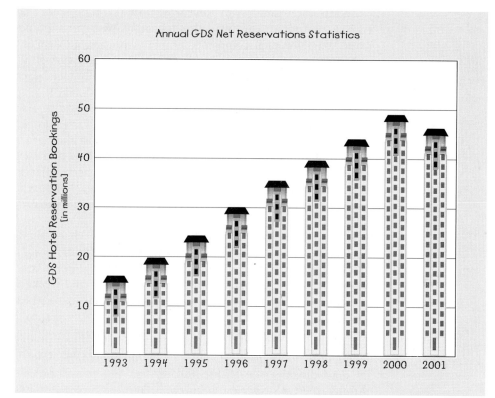

Exhibit 4–11   The Hotel Electronic Distribution Network Association (HEDNA) is a not-for-profit trade association whose worldwide membership includes executives and managers from over 200 of the most influential companies in the hotel distribution industry. Founded in 1991, all of HEDNA's activities are intended to stimulate the booking of hotel rooms through the use of GDSs, the Internet, and other electronic means.

Each year, HEDNA conducts a poll of GDSs to gather their net hotel bookings. The GDSs polled in 2000 were Amadeus, Galileo, Sabre, SAHARA, and Worldspan. *Courtesy of HEDNA, Alexandria, Virginia.*

look at their own hotel as it compares with the competitive market set. Hotel managers can select the competing hotels they wish included in their market set and set the length of time they wish covered in each particular report.

Other features of this report include highlighted rates that have risen or dropped by a user defined amount (e.g., +/− $10), total hotel availability status by day in both the GDS and CRS, and details for every rate offered in the CRS by room type across each competitive hotel during the selected time period.

Smith Travel Research's STAR Reports.   Founded in 1985 as an independent research firm, Smith Travel Research (STR) is one of the industry's leaders in providing accurate information and analyses to the lodging industry. With the most comprehensive database of hotel performance information ever compiled, STR has developed a variety of products and services to meet the needs of hotel revenue managers.

Although many reports used by revenue managers display future data (rates for a set of dates in the near future), *STAR Reports* are based entirely on historical data. This report answers the following questions: How well did I do in terms of average daily rate, occupancy, and RevPar against my competitors last week? Last month? Last year? Another key distinction is that *STAR Reports* do not share specific performance data for each competing property. Rather, all data is couched in aggregate, summary findings. In other words, a hotel can see how well it performed against the competitive market set of hotels, but cannot see how well each competing hotel performed individually (only as a set of hotels).

There are actually a series of *STAR Reports* providing a variety of ways of looking at historical data. The *STAR Trend Report,* for example, compares occupancy, ADR, and RevPar for a manager's property against the competitive market set for a series of months in the past. This report also provides an index (a measure of market penetration) that shows how well a manager's property performed against the competition (on a scale where 1.0 is performing exactly "on-market," a manager would hope to see numbers like 1.2 or 1.3, suggesting his or her property performed 20 or 30% better than the market average).

The *STAR Competitive Set Positioning Report* shares similar data as listed above, but places the manager's property in rank order against competing hotels in the market set. The *DaySTAR Weekday/Weekend Report* compares competitive hotels by their success in filling rooms during the midweek and weekends. A number of other *STAR Reports* are available as well. In fact, revenue managers are excited about a new report still under development that compares how well their hotel performs against the competition in terms of transient versus group room bookings.

Travel Information Management Services (TIMS).   The *TIMS Report* also pulls its data directly from Sabre through an automated process. Rates are gathered through the CRS seamless connection, and the report displays discounts and lowest available rates for all hotels in the competitive market set.

Hotelligence Report.   This is another popular report available through Travel-CLICK (see *PHASER Complete Access Reports* above). Not only does this report provide a wealth of information unavailable in other reports, but it is an extremely attractive report as well (see Exhibit 4–12). It compares a manager's rooms available with those available in the competitive market set. This establishes market share, and much of the report then compares actual history with theoretical market share. Data for the *Hotelligence Report* comes directly from Galileo, Sabre, and Worldspan—and the information from these three sources can be viewed both individually and in aggregate.

Specifically, the report compares room-nights sold for the manager's hotel against room-nights sold across the competitive set. Again, if the manager's hotel exceeds the theoretical market share, the report will show a market penetration of greater than 1.0. Similar statistics are available comparing overall revenue (yield) in the competitive set of hotels as well as average daily rate. Another thing this report does quite well is to show growth trends for current periods against similar periods the previous year.

Expedia Competitive Price Grid Report.   For hotels that sell rooms through Expedia, this has become a valuable report. The primary reason a hotel wants to see the rates it is listing in Expedia as well as the rates listed by its competitors is to manage its own hotel-direct Web site. You see, the revenue manager must be certain best available rates listed on Expedia are not substantially lower than best available rates listed on the hotel's own Web site. If Expedia is significantly lower, the hotel is shooting itself in the foot by training its future guests to visit other Web sites (Expedia, for example) as opposed to visiting its own hotel-direct Web site. Remember, the hotel saves commission fees when it encourages guests to book rooms through the hotel's own Web site.

THE HOTELLIGENCE REPORT

Data Solutions for the Digital World

Subscriber	Vendor Code	GDS	Total Rooms	Data Exists													Fair Share
				J-0	F-0	M-0	A-0	M-0	J-0	J-0	A-0	S-0	O-0	N-0	D-0	J-0	
The Premiere Hotel	TC	Galileo		Y	Y	Y	Y	Y	Y	Y	Y	Y	Y	Y	Y	Y	
First Avenue	TC	SABRE	168	Y	Y	Y	Y	Y	Y	Y	Y	Y	Y	Y	Y	Y	11.4%
Chicago, IL 60601	TC	Worldspan		Y	Y	Y	Y	Y	Y	Y	Y	Y	Y	Y	Y	Y	

Competitive Set

Subscriber	Vendor Code	GDS	Total Rooms	Data Exists													Fair Share
Luxury Suites	AM	Galileo		Y	Y	Y	Y	Y	Y	Y	Y	Y	Y	Y	Y	Y	
392 Hampshire Blvd.	AM	SABRE	121	Y	Y	Y	Y	Y	Y	Y	Y	Y	Y	Y	Y	Y	8.2%
Chicago, IL 60601	AM	Worldspan		Y	Y	Y	Y	Y	Y	Y	Y	Y	Y	Y	Y	Y	
Presidential Towers	PS	Galileo		Y	Y	Y	Y	Y	Y	Y	Y	Y	Y	Y	Y	Y	
6457 Washington Square	PS	SABRE	154	Y	Y	Y	Y	Y	Y	Y	Y	Y	Y	Y	Y	Y	10.4%
Chicago, IL 60601	PS	Worldspan		Y	Y	Y	Y	Y	Y	Y	Y	Y	Y	Y	Y	Y	
Executive Suites	EX	Galileo		Y	Y	Y	Y	Y	Y	Y	Y	Y	Y	Y	Y	Y	
893 Circle Bend	EX	SABRE	370	Y	Y	Y	Y	Y	Y	Y	Y	Y	Y	Y	Y	Y	25.0%
Chicago, IL 60601	XE	Worldspan		Y	Y	Y	Y	Y	Y	Y	Y	Y	Y	Y	Y	Y	
Capitol Towers	RR	Galileo		Y	Y	Y	Y	Y	Y	Y	Y	Y	Y	Y	Y	Y	
3000 Wilson Avenue	RR	SABRE	140	Y	Y	Y	Y	Y	Y	Y	Y	Y	Y	Y	Y	Y	9.5%
Chicago, IL 60601	RR	Worldspan		Y	Y	Y	Y	Y	Y	Y	Y	Y	Y	Y	Y	Y	
The Tower	TT	Galileo		Y	Y	Y	Y	Y	Y	Y	Y	Y	Y	Y	Y	Y	
4101 Hurst Avenue	TT	SABRE	237	Y	Y	Y	Y	Y	Y	Y	Y	Y	Y	Y	Y	Y	16.0%
Chicago, IL 60601	TT	Worldspan		Y	Y	Y	Y	Y	Y	Y	Y	Y	Y	Y	Y	Y	
Regal Plaza	RQ	Galileo		Y	Y	Y	Y	Y	Y	Y	Y	Y	Y	Y	Y	Y	
632 Forbes Avenue	RQ	SABRE	288	Y	Y	Y	Y	Y	Y	Y	Y	Y	Y	Y	Y	Y	19.5%
Chicago, IL 60563	RQ	Worldspan		Y	Y	Y	Y	Y	Y	Y	Y	Y	Y	Y	Y	Y	

Exhibit 4–12a   TravelCLICK's Hotelligence Report helps hotel executives make high-impact strategic and operational decisions as well as improve revenue management performance through the major GDSs. These reports are extremely useful for developing effective sales and marketing programs based on competitive information, evaluating the impact of promotional offers, and conducting performance benchmarking to fine-tune products and services.

The Hotelligence Report is 13-pages long—shown here are the first two pages. The first page displays the subscriber hotel (the fictitious Premiere Hotel), lists competing hotels (Luxury Suites, etc.), and shows that information is available for each property across the dates shown (indicated by Y, as in Yes).

The second page displays the Premiere Hotel's fair market share (11.4%) as compared with its competitive set. However, you'll notice it sold far more rooms (market penetration) than suggested by its fair share—it sold 1.549 rooms for every one room it "should" have been able to sell against its competition. However, you will also note that the Premiere Hotel did less well when it comes to average room rate (bottom left corner of page 2). *Courtesy of TravelCLICK.*

Notes: Galileo figures include reservations made through Galileo and Apollo. Sabre figures include reservations made through Abacus and Axess. Total rooms are used from the TravelCLICK hotel database. All reservations displayed on the following pages are net of cancels in each GDS. Each reservation represents a stay which occurred during the month shown on the report (date of arrival). "Y" signifies that the hotel received at least one booking from the respective GDS during the month. Fair Share is calculated using the Total Rooms from the TravelCLICK hotel database.

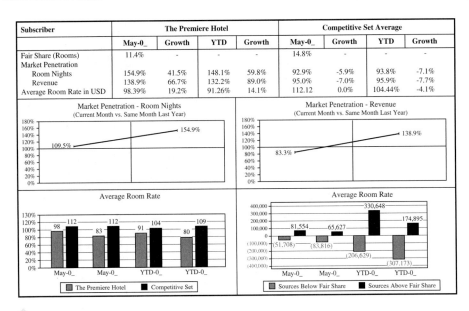

Subscriber	The Premiere Hotel				Competitive Set Average			
	May-0_	Growth	YTD	Growth	May-0_	Growth	YTD	Growth
Fair Share (Rooms)	11.4%	-	-	-	14.8%	-	-	-
Market Penetration								
Room Nights	154.9%	41.5%	148.1%	59.8%	92.9%	-5.9%	93.8%	-7.1%
Revenue	138.9%	66.7%	132.2%	89.0%	95.0%	-7.0%	95.9%	-7.7%
Average Room Rate in USD	98.39%	19.2%	91.26%	14.1%	112.12	0.0%	104.44%	-4.1%

Exhibit 4–12b

Other Reports. Listed here are several other popular reports used by today's revenue managers:

Sabre.Net Reports

Hotel Information Service (HIS) Reports

CheckRate

TrendFx

▶*Price–Occupancy Mix.* Yield is calculated by multiplying occupancy (let's say 65% for a 250-room hotel) by average daily rate (let's say that the ADR is $75.00). In this example, yield is $12,187.50 per day. Yield can be increased by raising rates when occupancy (demand) is high. Rates are raised by refusing packages, requiring minimum lengths of stay, and charging groups full rate without discounts. When occupancy (demand) is low, prices are dropped by promoting the packages, seeking out the price-sensitive groups, and creating special promotional rates. That's the dichotomy of the lodging industry; when times are good (high occupancy), they are very good (because with high occupancy comes high rate). Conversely, when times are bad (low demand), times are very bad (because all of the hotel's competitors are also lowering their prices).

Since yield is the product of the two elements, equilibrium is obtainable by increasing one factor when the other decreases. Exhibit 4–14 illustrates the mathematics. Yield in all three cases appears to be identical. With the same room revenue, a management choice between high ADR or high occupancy needs to be made.

All managers will not view the values in Exhibit 4–14 as being equal. Some would prefer the higher occupancy over the higher rate. Higher occupancy means more persons. More guests translate into more food and beverage revenue, more telephone use, more calls for laundry and dry cleaning. More guests mean more greens fees, more amusement park admissions, or more money spent in the casino. For these reasons, some hotels charge the same rate for occupancy by one or two persons.

Exhibit 4–13   The inviting main pool of the Doubletree La Posada Resort. This three-star and three-diamond property operating in Scottsdale, Arizona, includes in its competitive set such Scottsdale properties as Hilton Scottsdale Resort and Villas, Sunburst Resort, Doubletree Paradise Valley Resort, and Millennium at McCormick. Its competitive set ranges over many square miles and, interestingly, includes two other properties (Hilton Scottsdale Resort and Villas and Doubletree Paradise Valley Resort) licensed by the same Hilton Hotels Corporation that licenses the Doubletree La Posada Resort! *Courtesy of Doubletree La Posada Resort, Scottsdale, Arizona.*

Hotel	Average Daily Rate	Percent Occupancy	Monthly Gross Yield	Potential Revenue	Yield Percentage
A	$ 75	65.00	$377,812.50	$620,000	60.9
B	100	48.75	377,812.50	620,000	60.9
C	50	97.50	377,812.50	620,000	60.9

Exhibit 4–14   Price–occupancy mix: Yield is the product of occupancy times rate. Management decides whether a higher rate (ADR) or a higher occupancy is preferable. This exhibit assumes 250 rooms and a 31-day month. Potential revenue assumes 100% occupancy at an $80 ideal rate.

A different group of operators would prefer to strengthen their ADR. These managers feel that ADR is the barometer of a property's service and quality levels. With the lower occupancy that accompanies higher ADR, hotels save on variable costs like power, wear and tear on furniture and equipment, and reduced levels of staffing.

Clearly, price–occupancy mix is not a simple, single decision. Dropping rates to increase occupancy might not be the choice of every manager. Indeed, the manager might take that option at one hotel but not at another. Variations in the facilities of the hotel, in its client base, and in the perspective of its management will determine the policies to be applied.

Revenue per Available Room.   Yield is usually expressed in terms of gross revenue per day, per month or per year (see Exhibit 4–14). However, there is a special advantage to quoting yield in terms of revenue per available room (RevPar). RevPar (see also Chapter 1) combines occupancy and average daily rate into a single number. Continuing the illustration: A 250-room hotel at 65% occupancy and $75 ADR produces revenue per available room (RevPar) of $48.75 (65% × $75).

Before the popularization of RevPar in the mid 1990s, hotel managers tended toward one of the two camps described above. They migrated either toward higher occupancies or toward higher ADRs. Managers who work toward maximizing RevPar, however, must seek a balance or equilibrium between occupancy and rate (see Exhibit 4–15).

The only difference between calculating yield and RevPar is that yield incorporates the number of hotel rooms into the calculation, whereas RevPar looks at revenue per available room. In fact, if you take RevPar for any given day and multiply it by the number of rooms available in the hotel, the product is that day's yield. To demon-

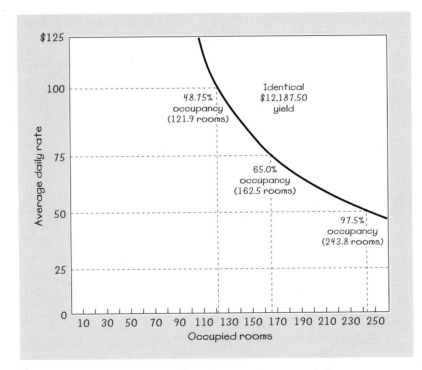

Exhibit 4–15   Referring to Exhibit 4–14, this graph demonstrates the infinite number of points that make up the daily yield curve.

strate, take the $48.75 RevPar found above in our ongoing example and multiply it by the 250 rooms available. The product is the same $12,187.50 yield calculated several paragraphs above in the price–occupancy mix discussion.

The RevPar calculation is also beneficial to management as a quick-and-dirty glimpse into the hotel's success on any given day. If the hotel knows its fixed costs on a per room per day basis (fixed costs include administrative salaries, mortgage debt, fixed franchise fees, and insurance, to name a few), it can quickly gauge how much, if any, of the RevPar can be contributed toward variable costs and profits. In our ongoing example, if RevPar is $48.75 and fixed costs are $23.25, then $25.50 per available room can be contributed toward variable costs and profit. Management can readily see how well the hotel performed on that given day.

Automated Yield Management Systems

As far back as 1998, a study of hotel sales and marketing departments found that 80% of hotels were using yield management technology to assist their decision process when booking group business.[3] The figure begins to approach 100% when individual hotel room nights booked through chains or large independent properties are included. Certainly by today's standards, yield management is an expense worth incurring.

Automated yield or revenue management systems are tools that aid management decision making. Indeed, in the absence of management, these systems can automatically change rates, restrict rooms availability, and monitor reservation activity. Here's a brief list of the functions generally attributable to yield management systems. The yield management system:

> ➤ Establishes and monitors the hotel's rate structure
> ➤ Continually monitors reservations activity and sets inventory controls as needed (even in the absence of management approval)
> ➤ Aids rate negotiations with travel wholesalers and group bookings
> ➤ Monitors and restricts the number of reservations that can be taken for any particular room night or room rate/room type
> ➤ Allows reservationists the tools necessary to be salespersons rather than mere order-takers
> ➤ Matches the right room product and rate with customers' needs and sensitivities

Profits increase in all hotels that implement automated yield management systems. Certain properties, however, fare better than others. Generally, a property needs to have several characteristics in place to experience high returns on its investment in a yield management system. Some of these characteristics include a demand for rooms that can easily be segmented into distinct markets (see Exhibit 4–16), a long lead time for some types of reservations, a variety of room types and associated rates, and high-occupancy/low-occupancy periods throughout the year.

➤ ***Artificial Intelligence Systems.*** Yield management systems allow for instantaneous response to changing conditions. Seven days a week, 24 hours a day, the system compares actual performance with forecasted assumptions and adjusts rates accordingly. To make these changes, advanced computer systems utilize either stan-

---

[3]In a 1998 study, PKF Consulting found that 83.7% of sales and marketing departments utilize automated rooms inventory controls and 79.8% of sales and marketing departments utilize yield management technology.

Data for the 250-Room Hurdle Hotel			
	Discounted Rooms	Corporate Guests	Rack Rate
Normal rate structure	$60	$120	$150
Normal room allocations	75	100	75
Current rooms demand			
Monday (hurdle price is $150)	60	100	57
Tuesday (hurdle price is $120)	53	82	48
Wednesday (hurdle price is $60)	34	51	22

Exhibit 4–16   Inventory nesting prevents higher-priced categories of rooms from being closed when lower-priced categories remain open. Hurdle pricing assumes that each business day has a theoretical rate floor against which reservation requests must be evaluated.

dard logical functions or state-of-the-art artificial intelligence operations. Artificial intelligence (AI) or expert systems use stored data that has been developed over a period of time to form rules that govern yield management decisions.

Today's expert systems are truly artificial intelligence. They literally think through demand, formulate decisions, and provide the user with an opportunity to talk with the computer. Below is a list of the special features generally found in an expert yield management system. The expert system:

1. Is able to deal not just with quantitative facts but with qualitative data as well

2. Includes an analysis of incomplete data when formulating a decision

3. Explains to the user how a given conclusion was reached

4. Allows a two-way communication interface with the user

5. Applies programmable rules and triggers to its set of facts

6. Can override basic rules and triggers when additional decision criteria warrant

7. Maintains a database of historical facts, including:

➤ Demand for similar periods over a number of past years

➤ Room-nights lost (regrets) through both in-house reservations and chain (toll-free) sources over a number of past years

➤ Changes to demand (by various market segments) as forecasted reservations dates close in

➤ The ratio and demand for transient (leisure) room-nights versus corporate room-nights over a number of past years

➤ The demand for group room blocks (and the ratio of group room block "pickups") over a number of past years

➤*Rules and Triggers.*   The computer compares actual reservation activity with budgeted forecasts. When a particular date or period falls outside the rules for that time frame, the computer flags it. Once flagged, most systems will print a management report identifying periods that are exceptions to the forecast. In addition, expert systems will automatically change rates and other sales tools. The immediacy of the expert system is a major advantage. Hundreds and even thousands of dollars may be lost in the time it takes management to approve a given rate change. The expert system acts first and takes questions later.

To establish rules or triggers for the system to use, management must first segment the room count into market types. For example, a typical 250-room property might block 25 rooms for discounting to government guests or IT packages, 50 rooms for transient (leisure) guests, 100 rooms for business (corporate) customers, and the remaining 75 rooms for sale to tours, conventions, or rack rate (see Exhibit 4–16).

Different guidelines are then placed on each of these market segments. To illustrate, assume that management expects 25% of the transient room block to fill by, say, 181 days out (days before arrival). It also expects that 91 days before arrival, transient rooms will be 60% sold, and by 61 days out, the entire block will be 90% reserved. These are the parameters that management has forecasted for transient rooms; its expectations for business rooms would be quite different. Once these triggers are identified, they are programmed into the yield management system. The computer then evaluates the effects of changing demand and acts accordingly. If, for example, 181 days out the transient room block is 35% reserved, the computer would flag the date as a potentially busy period and increase rates for all remaining rooms. How much the rates increase is also subject to advanced programming.

▶*Centralized Yield Management.*   As the trend toward seamless connectivity, single-imaging, last room availability, and centralized property management systems (ASP's) becomes more prevalent, so too is the trend toward centrally driven corporate yield management systems. At the outset, centralized yield management systems look much the same. As rooms are sold through in-house reservations (at the property) or the CRO, changes in inventory are automatically reflected in the centralized yield management system. As room types or dates begin to fill, the centralized system changes rates and inventory restrictions for the individual property. Similarly, if property-level management wishes to tap into its own yield statistics and manually alter rates or restrictions, nothing prevents that.

What appears quite similar on the surface actually affords the chain and individual property unique advantages. Through centralized yield management, the entire GDS becomes a yield management tool. In essence, the in-house property management system, the CRS, and the GDS are all reading from the same page. The chain can run a whole series of reports, which improves its understanding of certain market segments, lodging categories, dates, and trends (see Exhibits 4–12 and 4–13). Price-sensitive group room blocks can be moved to sister properties across the chain rather than being lost because one hotel in one particular city was not able to meet their price on a given date.

▶*Yield Management Controls.*   Aside from simply adjusting the room rate, hotels have several other tools with which they work. One common tool is *boxing* the date. Boxing dates (means reservations) on either side of the boxed day are not allowed to spill into that date. For example, if Wednesday, April 7, is anticipated as a heavy arrival date, we might box it. Rooms sold for Monday or Tuesday must check out by Wednesday; rooms sold for Thursday or Friday cannot arrive a day earlier. Dates are blocked in anticipation of a mass of arrivals, usually a convention or group movement, that could not be accommodated through the normal flow of departures. With such heavy arrivals, no one is permitted to check in before that day and stay through the boxed day, even though there is more than enough space on those previous days.

Another tool available to the reservations department is closing a specific date to arrival. Dates that are closed to arrival allow the guest to stay through by arriving on a previous date. Closed to arrival (CTA) is utilized as a technique for improving occupancy on preceding nights before a major holiday or event.

A final example of reservations sales tools is the minimum length of stay (MLOS). This technique is designed to improve occupancy on nights preceding and following a major event or holiday by requiring guests to book a minimum number of nights. For example, if New Year's Eve has a three-day minimum length of stay, the hotel will probably improve occupancies on December 30 and January 1.

Nests and Hurdles. Also known as *bid pricing, hurdle pricing,* or *inventory nesting,* this sophisticated yield management approach takes normal room allocations to a new level. Referring to Exhibit 4–16, let's assume that the Hurdle Hotel is experiencing an unusually high demand for corporate rooms and has sold out of the $120 rate (Monday) while still offering discounted and rack rate rooms. It would make little sense to turn down a corporate reservation request at $120 while still accepting discounted rooms at $60, but that is exactly what might happen if rooms allocations are not continually monitored. That's where inventory nesting comes in. By incorporating a set of nesting rules, the property can ensure that high-rate rooms are never closed for sale when lower-rate rooms are still open.

The newest trend in nesting does away with the old concept of rooms allocations by market segment. Instead, a minimum rate, or *hurdle point,* is established for each day. Reservations with a value above the hurdle are accepted, reservations with a value below the hurdle are rejected. In Exhibit 4–16, if the hurdle point were set at or below $60, all room types would be available. If the hurdle were raised to $100, the discounted rooms would be closed while corporate and rack rates remained available.

Rather than selling rooms according to unreserved market segment allocations, the hurdle concept sells rooms based on total property demand. When demand is low, the hurdle price is low. When demand is high, the hurdle price is high. In essence, the hurdle price represents the theoretical price of the last room expected to sell that day. If the hotel expects to fill, the hurdle point might be set at full rack rate. A person making a reservation who is only willing to pay a lower rate is worth less to the hotel than the future value of the last room, and therefore such a reservation would be denied.

The real beauty of hurdle pricing is that hurdles can be added for subsequent days. For example, in Exhibit 4–16, let's say that the hotel is close to full on Monday (hurdle point $150), somewhat less full on Tuesday (hurdle point $120), and wide open for Wednesday (hurdle point just $60). A guest wishing to stay Monday for one night only would need to pay $150 to get a reservation for the night. However, a guest checking in on Monday for three nights would get the benefit of averaging the hurdles for those three nights. By adding $150 for the first night plus $120 for the second and $60 for the third night, this three-night reservation would pay a rate of $110 per night or possibly a different rate for each of three nights ($150, $120, and $60, respectively).

Fenced Rates. A relatively new addition to the list of reservations sales tools has recently migrated to hotels from the airline industry. Fences or *fenced rates* are logical rules or restrictions that provide a series of options to the guest. Guests are not forced to select these options; their rate is determined by which (if any) options they choose.

As with yield management systems themselves, the airlines originated fenced rates. Examples of airline fenced rates might include the passenger who chose a lower but nonrefundable fare, a customer who purchased the ticket at least 21 days in advance to receive a special rate, or someone who stayed over on a Saturday night to take full advantage of the best price.

Fenced rates are relatively new to the lodging industry. However, the few chains using them seem quite satisfied with their results. It will probably be standard practice in the future to offer discounts for advanced purchases and nonrefundable and nonchangeable reservations.

RESOURCES AND CHALLENGES
Resources

➤ *SUMMARY*

Sophisticated automation is changing the method in which reservations are requested and accepted. Never before have hotels had reservations coming into their properties from so many varied directions. The introduction of last room availability technology has started a revolution in hotel reservations management.

Last room availability is real-time communication between CROs and property-level reservations systems. With last room availability, the entire GDS can identify room types and rates at a member hotel and can literally sell to the very last available room. Electronic switch technology has afforded the industry increased access to member hotels. Travel agents, airlines, and subscription on-line services are all able to electronically access a property's reservations system.

With yield or revenue management (yield equals average room rate times the number of rooms sold), room prices change as a function of lead time and demand. Vacationing families, tour groups, and seniors often know as far as one year in advance their exact date and location of travel. These customers generally book early enough to take advantage of special discounts or packages; yield management works to their advantage. Conversely, corporate travelers frequently book accommodations at the last moment. In their case, yield management works against them by charging maximum rates to last-minute bookings when the hotel is nearing full occupancy.

➤ *WEB SITES*

Mapping functions have become increasingly powerful tools in recent years. They are powerful not only because they offer integrated mapping software, but also because they attract and hold guests within the hotel chain. Best Western, for example, uses software that maps out a guest's trip and finds available Best Western hotels along the way. Take a look at the mapping software available at each of the following sites:

➤ http://www.bestwestern.com
➤ http://www.hawthorn.com
➤ http://www.mytrip.com
➤ http://www.away.com
➤ http://www.vacationcoach.com

Now, choose any of the Web sites listed above and plan a trip using the following criteria. Start the trip by automobile from your current university or community college town. Plan a trip lasting at least three nights. Identify at least three separate hotels in which you will stay during the trip (optional—make fictitious online reservations for each hotel). Identify at least three famous sights or attractions (historical, cultural, natural, etc.) you will visit over the three or more days. Print a map showing your travel itinerary with each hotel location and each attraction highlighted.

➤ INTERESTING TIDBITS

➤ While the Internet is clearly an important source of hotel reservations, not all hospitality organizations are equipped to handle such transactions. Only 78% of large hotel companies are able to handle reservations through their Web sites. Even fewer smaller hotel companies (55%) can handle reservations through their Web sites. Source: *Lodging Hospitality*.

➤ There are 500 million empty hotel room-nights per year in the United States. This provides huge opportunities for mass discounters and last-minute Web site purchases. Source: *Lodging Magazine*.

➤ A big trend with online bookings is something known as *opaque* pricing (pioneered by Priceline.com). This trend appeals to price-sensitive shoppers who are more interested in steep discounts than in specific hotel brands. Hoteliers also like this trend because it does not compromise their rate integrity. Source: *Lodging Magazine*.

➤ Although they've been a longtime holdout, luxury hotels are finally starting to offer shopper deals on the Internet. With savings of 50% or more below rack rates, try such sites as http://www.allluxuryhotels.com or http://www.LuxRes.com.

➤ READING REFERENCES

1. "An Analysis of Web Reservation facilities in the Top 50 International Hotel Chains." Peter O'Connor and Patrick Horan. *International Journal of Hospitality Information Technology, 1*(1), 1999: 77–85.

2. Any research developed by the Hotel Electronic Distribution Network Association (HEDNA). Available at HEDNA.org.

Challenges

➤ TRUE/FALSE

Questions that are partially false should be marked false (F).

___ 1. The airline industry was smart, waiting until the hotel industry (primarily Holiday Inns in the early years) developed central reservations systems and worked out all the problems. Then the airline industry "borrowed" the existing technology and developed their own automated reservation systems.

___ 2. The concept of last room availability (saving the last room until at least midnight each night) was initially started in Washington, D.C. There, hotels catering to Congressional leaders were paid a small nightly fee to keep accommodations available for VIP's until at least midnight.

___ 3. As of the year 2002, travel agents were no longer paid a commission (of any size) for booking domestic air travel on most of the major airline carriers.

___ 4. Central reservations offices have experienced higher and higher call volume in recent years. Most experts suggest this is partly due to the Internet. Guests first check the Internet for prices and then call the CRS to actually book the rooms.

___ 5. In terms of yield management, experts generally consider leisure (transient) guests to be more rate-sensitive while corporate guests are generally considered to be more date-sensitive.

➤ QUESTIONS AND PROBLEMS

1. On busy nights, it is not uncommon for a front-office manager to remove several rooms from availability. Usually, the manager creates a fictitious reservation, thereby "selling" the rooms and removing them from availability. By holding onto a few rooms, the manager feels in a better position to accommodate a special guest or request when the hotel is sold out.

   Granted that the reason management holds rooms may be very honorable, do you believe this practice undermines the very basis of last room availability technology? Explain your answer.

2. Central reservations systems are extremely expensive. Research and development, equipment, and staffing can easily run into hundreds of millions of dollars. How has this prohibitive cost structure changed the hotel industry? How will it change business in the future? And what options are available to the smaller and startup chains in the industry?

3. Several studies indicate quite clearly that reservation calls made to a travel agent, or to the res center, or directly to the hotel may result in three different rate quotes for the same accommodations at the same period of time. Explain.

4. Discuss the merits of higher rates with lower occupancy versus lower rates with higher occupancy if you were the manager of (a) a budget economy property, (b) a commercial convention property, or (c) an upscale resort property.

5. Yield management programs often discount rates to the benefit of one segment of guests but charge full rack rate to others who book at the last moment. With attention to the rewards and penalties that such policies carry, discuss a proposed policy that (a) deeply discounts rates for noncancellable reservations made 30 days in advance and (b) discounts rates for standby guests who are willing to wait until 7 PM for vacancies.

6. Develop a list of fenced rate restriction possibilities. This list may include those currently used by airlines, or create your own possible restrictions.

➤ ANSWERS TO TRUE/FALSE QUIZ

1. False. This statement is exactly the opposite of the right answer. It was, in fact, the airline industry that first developed central reservations systems.

2. False. Last room availability refers to full-duplex communication between each property and the CRO. In such systems, the central reservations office can access real-time rooms inventory for each property in the chain.

3. True. The airline industry began reducing their customary 10% commissions in 1995. By 2002, most major U.S. carriers suspended all domestic commissions. Travel agents will have to look elsewhere for income.

4. False. Central reservations offices have seen a substantial drop in call volume. The Internet is certainly responsible. Internet hotel bookings have been growing at a compounded rate, year after year.

5. True. Corporate guests need to travel when they are scheduled, and will therefore pay whatever the prevailing rate. Leisure guests are more flexible and will book with further lead time in the hope of finding a less expensive date.

Individual and Group Reservations

Outline

The discussion in Chapter 4 suggests the telephone is growing less important as a source of hotel reservations. That is true from an absolute perspective—total telephone reservations are down as a percentage of all hotel reservations. Today, almost six out of every 10 business travelers use the Internet to plan some aspect of their business travel (and three of every 10 business travelers actually purchase online travel services). The percentages for leisure travelers are quite comparable (about half go online to plan some aspect of their upcoming vacations).

The impact of this change is awesome. As telephone reservations continue to decline in ratio, the industry will surely see more layoffs and closures at central reservations offices (there have already been CRO closures across the industry due primarily to reduced call volume). Yet in spite of this change in popularity (or possibly because of this change), telephones are still an integral part of the overall hotel reservations landscape. The industry has seen a renewed vigor in its focus on telephone call centers. Proper training of telephone reservationists and corporate investment in telephone call center systems (hardware and software) are more critical today than ever before.

➤ COMPONENTS OF THE RESERVATION

Awash in technology, it is easy for a CRO to lose sight of its basic task—customer service. After running the potential guest through a gauntlet of automated telephone queries, telephone keypad number punching, recorded instructions, and on-hold background messages or music, the reservations agent can easily forget there is a real human being on the other end of the telephone. To avoid this oversight, one chain actually pastes pictures of real customers on the office walls to remind central reservations agents that real people are on the other end of the telephone!

Certainly there is good reason for such automated telephone systems. Asking the guest to select instructions in English (press '1'), Spanish (press '2'), or some other language (press '3') segregates callers to language-specific reservationists (see Exhibits 5–1A and 5–1B). Further instructions may separate callers by domestic reservations (press '1') versus international reservations (press '2'). Even more sophisticated systems can electronically ask the caller to state his or her city of choice, dates of travel, and number of guests in the party (refer to the discussion of voice recognition in Chapter 4).

For all the benefits such technology provides the call center, one axiom is abundantly clear—the fastest reservation is not always the best reservation. Some years ago, in a study of a major lodging chain's reservation office, agents experimented with changing their initial telephone greeting from the rushed monotone so often associated with call centers to a warmer, friendlier greeting.[1] The results were astounding. Customers responded positively to the inviting greeting they received, and their perceptions of the CRO improved dramatically (ultimately, the reservations booking rate should improve as well). It took very little extra time for the reservationist to be nice and to "smile" through the telephone. The friendlier greetings added a mere 300 extra seconds (5 minutes) to each reservationist's day.

Today's hotel guests, whether corporate, leisure, or group, face more lodging choices than ever before. With so many options available, central reservations offices (and inhouse reservations centers) are realizing that a well-trained reservations agent makes a significant difference in guest satisfaction, booking rates, and return business.

[1]Information related to the study of central reservations offices can be found in the June 1997 issue of *Lodging Magazine*.

TigerTalk for Innkeepers

Correspond with Guests in their Own Language

1. Select language of guest: [French ▼]
2. Enter [TO:] guest's e-mail address and [FROM:] your TigerTalk code.
3. Click on "Check Box" of every theme (Guest ID, Room Availability, Innkeeper's Response),
   and item within a theme that you wish to include.
4. Type in data or select option for each item to be included.
5. Preview e-mail any time you wish by clicking on "Preview" button.
6. From preview page, send e-mail in selected language, or return to edit.

TO: (e-mail address)   **FROM:** (Your TigerTalk Code)
[Gary.Vallen@NAU.edu]   [TT001]

☑ **Guest ID**

Title: [Mr. ▼]   Last Name: [Reservation]   First Name: [Trial]

☑ **Room Availability**

Arrival Date: Number of Nights   Number of Rooms
[July ▼] [4 ▼] [2004 ▼]   [1]   [1 ▼]

Room .... Adults .... Children   Type .... Beds ....   Smoking or Not
...1................. [2 ▼] .... [0 ▼]   [deluxe ▼] .... [1 king ▼]   [No Smoking ▼]
...2................. [0 ▼] .... [0 ▼]   [standard ▼] .... [single ▼]   [No Smoking ▼]
...3................. [0 ▼] .... [0 ▼]   [standard ▼] .... [single ▼]   [No Smoking ▼]

☑ **Innkeeper's Response**

☑ We can accommodate your room needs at the following rate
☐ We cannot meet your exact needs, but can offer the closest at the following rate
☑ Room 1: [100]   [Euro ▼]   Plus [10] % Tax and [10] % Service
☐ Room 2: [   ]
☐ Room 3: [   ]
☑ Breakfast ☐ Lunch ☐ Dinner included   Quote No. [123456]
☑ Please see description of our facilities at: [http://pretendhotel.com]

☑ Your reservation has been made.   Reservation No. [123456]
☑ Please confirm reservation with
    ☑ [100]   [Euro ▼]   ☐ Cheque/Money order by mail   ☐ Credit card info by fax
☑ Please see conditions for confirmation at: [http://pretendhotel.com]
☑ Your reservation has been confirmed
☑ Please advise of estimated arrival time

☐ Your reservation has been changed according to new room needs
☐ Sorry we cannot accommodate your room needs as requested
☐ Your reservation has been cancelled   Cancellation No. [   ]
☐ Please see conditions for cancellation at: [http://]

[Preview]   [Clear All]

A multilingual e-mail service for innkeepers worldwide by **Cyber Tigers Online**

Copyright 2001–2003 Cyber Tigers, Inc.

Exhibit 5–1a   Here is an interesting exhibit—multilanguage reservations capabilities using Cyber Tigers recent release of TigerTalk for Innkeepers. As non-English–speaking Internet users are projected to overtake English speakers as the majority in the next several years, the market for effective email in multilingual and cross-cultural environments is growing rapidly. TigerTalk is a fast and free business-to-business (B2B) email service on the Web with near-flawless translations and little or no typing. TigerTalk is based on two main premises: Keyboard input and word processing in nonalphabetic languages such as Chinese can be cumbersome, and most routine reservations correspondence revolves around a limited list of basic elements. Using TigerTalk, guests can make reservations with very little keyboard typing. Rather, most input uses preprogrammed translations of key elements (e.g., check boxes).

The most popular languages currently used are English, Spanish, Japanese, and German (in that order). But TigerTalk is currently available in English, Spanish, Japanese, German, Chinese, French, Korean, Polish, and Russian (with more to follow). Exhibit 5–1A shows a basic input screen (in English). You can then see the return email confirmation to the guest in both English and the requested language (French in this case; Exhibit 5–1B). To try TigerTalk for yourself, visit www.cyber-tigers.com. *Courtesy of Cyber Tigers, Inc., Chicago, Illinois.*

To: innkeeper@usa.com
From: voyageur@france.net
Subject: e-mail via
          TigerTalk for Travelers[sm]

This e-mail has been converted from
FRENCH to ENGLISH using
TigerTalk for Travelers
(http://www.cyber-tigers.com/ttt.html)

Hello inkeeper@usa.com,

Arrival Date: July 14, 2004
Number of Nights: 3
Number of Rooms: 1
Room 1: 2 Adult(s)
Superior category
1 queen bed(s)
No Smoking

Please inform of room availability
and quote rate.

Please reply in FRENCH. You can do so
by using TigerTalk for Innkeepers[sm] at
http://www.cyber-tigers.com/innen.html

[Return to Edit] [Send Mail]

À: voyageur@france.net
De: innkeeper@usa.com
Subject: e-mail via
          TigerTalk for Travelers[sm]

Bonjour voyageur@france.net

Nous pouvons vous accueillir comme
vous avez demandé au tarif suivant:
Chambre 1: 200 Etats-Unis Dollars
plus 5% tax
Petit Déjeuner compris
Devis N°: 12345

Date d'arrivée: 14 juillet 2004
Nombre de nuits: 3
Nombre de chambres: 1
Chambre 1: 2 Adulte(s)
Supérieur catégorie
1 grand lit(s)
Non fumeur

Pour écrire en français et envoyer en
anglais, employez s'il vous plaît
TigerTalk for Travelers a
http://www.cyber-tigers.com/tttfr.html.

Merci!

[Return to Edit] [Send Mail]

Exhibit 5–1b

Technology can get the average reservation down to 180 seconds, but a speedy "businesslike" attitude does not necessarily translate into a successful reservation!

Seasoned reservations managers realize that effective communication skills are more important than basic computer skills. Poorly trained reservations agents miss potential sales by failing to understand the guests' needs. Taking a step away from the rushed script allows the agent to develop a communicative information-gathering posture that may uncover personal information (needs) that can ultimately lead to the sale. Reservationists must realize that price is not the only factor that guests use in determining where to stay. Patiently answering questions, skillfully diffusing objections, and building personal rapport with the customer may prove as important to the decision process as the price of the room.

Training reservations agents to be salespersons is the key to success in the new millennium. That's because collecting the guest's reservation data is pretty much the same for all lodging chains. It's easy, too: Basic reservation content and each question that needs to be asked is right there on the reservations agent's computer screen. The computer literally prompts the agent through each step of the reservation (see Exhibit 5–2).

Information Contained in the Reservation

The computer not only provides rapid input, it also prompts the reservationist to ask essential questions. As one question is completed, the lighted computer cursor automatically moves to the beginning of the next question. In this way, essential information cannot be overlooked. In fact, if the reservationist attempts to enter an incomplete reservation into the system, the computer audibly beeps and the cursor blinks at the beginning of the incomplete information field.

Exhibit 5–2   All reservation screens are basically alike. They seek the same information in roughly the same order. See if you can identify which fields are essential and which are non-essential. (ADR is an abbreviation for address.)

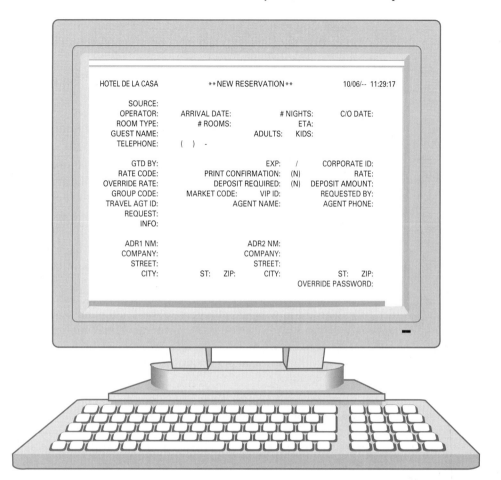

```
HOTEL DE LA CASA              **NEW RESERVATION**           10/06/--  11:29:17

            SOURCE:
          OPERATOR:         ARRIVAL DATE:          # NIGHTS:       C/O DATE:
         ROOM TYPE:            # ROOMS:               ETA:
        GUEST NAME:                        ADULTS:    KIDS:
         TELEPHONE:         (    )   -


            GTD BY:                            EXP:     /        CORPORATE ID:
         RATE CODE:              PRINT CONFIRMATION:   (N)               RATE:
      OVERRIDE RATE:              DEPOSIT REQUIRED:    (N)     DEPOSIT AMOUNT:
        GROUP CODE:         MARKET CODE:      VIP ID:            REQUESTED BY:
      TRAVEL AGT ID:                 AGENT NAME:                  AGENT PHONE:
           REQUEST:
              INFO:


          ADR1 NM:                          ADR2 NM:
          COMPANY:                          COMPANY:
           STREET:                           STREET:
             CITY:         ST:    ZIP:          CITY:                ST:    ZIP:
                                                     OVERRIDE PASSWORD:
```

This text refers to system-mandated data as *essential* reservation data. Such information is absolutely required before the computer system will accept the input screen and move the reservation to the next stage. Nonmandated data is called *nonessential* because the system does not absolutely require this information in order to continue with the reservation—an example of nonessential data is smoking versus nonsmoking room preference. Smoking preference is generally not mandated by computer systems, yet it is certainly considered of paramount importance to those guests averse to cigarette smoke. Therefore, though data may technically be nonessential to the CRS, it is not necessarily unimportant to arriving guests. Refer to Exhibit 5–2 for a glimpse at a sample reservation screen. See if you can identify which queries are essential (mandated) and which are nonessential.

➤*Essential Reservation Data.*   The reservation process and especially the information obtained during the reservation are designed to improve the effectiveness of the front office. The facts communicated through the reservation form a valuable starting point from which the front-desk clerk can understand the guest's needs. Corporate guests may be placed away from the lobby in a quieter area of the hotel, while guests traveling with children may be roomed near the swimming pool. Late arrivals (see "Nonessential Reservation Data" later in this chapter) are noted on the reservation screen so the front desk is better informed should it need to make difficult overbooking and walked guest decisions. Address information is collected so that the hotel can contact the guest for marketing or billing purposes or in the event the guest leaves behind a personal item (see Exhibit 5–2).

Arrival and Departure Dates.   In the reservations centers for national chains, the questions of arrival and departure dates come third, after "What city?" and "What hotel?" Telephone time is not used to gather the details that follow unless the clerk is certain that space is available at the time and place requested.

Number of Nights.   This bit of redundancy forestalls later problems if the guest's count of nights is not in agreement with the time between the arrival and departure dates. A common miscommunication occurs when the guest counts the departure day in the number of nights. Many systems ask simply for the date of arrival (say, October 2) followed by a question related to number of nights (say, four nights). Then, the reservationist verifies information with the guest by replying, "So we have you checking out on October 6, is that correct?"

Number of Persons.   The number of persons in the party and its structure help to clarify the kind of facilities needed. Two unrelated persons need two beds; a married couple could get by with one bed. Are there children? Is a crib required? A rollaway bed? Many hotels charge an extra fee for the second, third, and fourth persons in a room. This extra revenue contributes substantial profit to the bottom line and is easily justified when one considers the added utilities, linens, breakfast, and other items used by the extra person(s). See Chapter 9 for an additional discussion of double occupancy rates.

Number of Rooms Required.   Based on the size of the party and the types of rooms the hotel has available, additional rooms may be required. Most reservationists are authorized to handle requests for up to 10 rooms or so. As the number of required rooms increases above 10, the hotel's group sales department usually becomes involved.

Type of Rooms Required.   The question of room type is closely linked to the rate the guest is willing to pay. As the room type increases in luxury, the corresponding rate increases as well. Although the specific rate the guest wants to pay is the real question being asked, the reservationist certainly can't just offer a series of rates. That would be gauche. Instead, the reservationist offers a series of room types.

Generally, the reservationist attempts to sell from the top down. This is accomplished by offering the guest the most expensive room type first and then waiting for the guest to agree or decline before moving down to offer the next most expensive room type (see Chapter 8).

Corporate Affiliation.   Commercial hotels are very concerned with identifying all corporate guest reservations. The average corporate guest represents far more room nights than does the average leisure guest. In addition, corporate guests usually book their rooms with less lead time (and as such pay a higher average rate) than do leisure guests (see the yield management discussion in Chapter 4). As such, reservation data related to the guest's corporate affiliation is essential to the success of many commercial properties. In fact, asking the guest's corporate affiliation is often the first step in determining the rate to quote. Many corporate guests have negotiated a prearranged nightly room rate. Other corporate guests—usually less regular travelers to that particular hotel or region—are subject to the hotel's regular corporate rate.

Price.   The reservation (the sale) could be lost by the rate quotation. The agent may have no negotiating room if the yield management system has eliminated lower-priced options. Quoting the price is not enough. Distinctions between the prices must be accompanied by descriptive matter intended to entice the buyer to the better rate.

Name.   The guest's name has become more important in recent years. In the past, the name was used for alphabetical filing of the reservation and was one of several means (confirmation number, date of arrival, etc.) by which the reservations agent or front-desk clerk could access the guest's reservation record.

Sophisticated reservation systems now use the customer's name as a means of gaining efficiency, saving time, and generating guest loyalty. Many systems integrate guest history into the reservations system. As the guest's name is entered into the reservation, a screen pops up for repeat customers showing the guest's address and phone; rate, room type, and number of nights stayed during the last visit(s); and other essential and nonessential information. With most information already in the system, the reservations clerk simply verifies that this is the same guest and asks if the information is still accurate. Refer to the discussion of guest history databases later in this chapter.

Quality of the Reservation.   The three quality types of reservations available—nonguaranteed, guaranteed, or advance deposit—are determined either by the guest or the reservationist. The reservationist, for example, may be restricted from accepting nonguaranteed reservations as a function of policy or unusually high business levels for the hotel. Similarly, the guest may not have a credit card with which to guarantee the reservation or may have a card but not be inclined to use it. In either case, the reservation may fail to materialize because of disagreement at this stage in the process. See Chapter 6 for a complete discussion of the quality of the reservation.

➤***Nonessential Reservation Data.***   Depending on the reservation system in place and/or the amount of reservation activity occurring in the reservation center at the time of the call, certain reservation information may not necessarily be required for each reservation. This less important information is categorized as nonessential or "nice-to-know" data. Examples of nonessential information include estimated time of arrival, special guest requests or needs, discounts or affiliations, and smoking or nonsmoking room preference.

Although essential information must be complete for a reservation to be accepted into the computer system, nonessential information is not required. The computer will allow the input of a completed reservation into the system when nonessential data is missing. In fact, some computer screens display essential data in one color while displaying nonessential data in a secondary color. If time permits, the reservationist may request this additional data. Otherwise, it is often overlooked.

Overlooked, maybe. But just because the central reservations system doesn't mandate certain data as required fields before accepting the reservation does not necessarily mean the data is unimportant. As mentioned earlier, nonmandated information (smoking preference, for example) is still of critical importance to guest satisfaction!

Estimated Time of Arrival.   By knowing the guests' estimated time of arrival (ETA), the hotel can properly schedule front-desk clerks to assist with check-in, van drivers to retrieve guests from the airport, and bellpersons to room them. More important, hotels that are filling to capacity can be certain to save rooms for guests who are going to be especially late.

ETA plays its most critical role in such overbooked situations. When the hotel is oversold, front-desk receptionists refer to the incoming guests' ETAs. A room is usually held for guests who provide late arrival information at the time of reservation. But later in the evening, guests with no ETA (or worse yet, guests with an early ETA but who arrive quite a bit later) are anticipated as no-shows, and their respective rooms are released to other overbooked reservations. See Chapter 6 for a complete discussion of overbooking.

Special Requests.   Guest requests or needs run the gamut from simple, rather nonessential requests to extremely essential guest needs. That is why most reservationists provide guests with an opportunity to request any other items of importance before the close of the reservation process. If the request is essential (for example, a handicapped guest requesting a specially equipped room), the guest is usually certain to state the need. In other cases, the request (ocean view, near the Smith's room, below fifth floor) may be forgotten by the reservationist and the guest. That is the responsibility of the front-desk clerk—to handle each request on a case-by-case basis at the time of check in. Indeed, reservationists generally explain, "I'll note your request on the reservation, but I cannot promise you will get it." See Exhibit 5–3.

Discounts or Affiliations.   Corporate, AAA (American Automobile Association), AARP (American Association of Retired Persons), or similar discounts or affiliations are usually handled during the room type and rate discussion earlier in the reservation. In fact, many such organizations (AARP, for example) require the guest to state his or her discount as a part of the reservation process. In such cases, the discount is void if the guest forgets to request it at the time of reservation. See Chapter 9 for a complete discussion of room-rate discounts.

Smoking Preference.   What was once merely a special request has become a standard reservation input field on many systems. Smoking preferences play an important role in guest-room satisfaction. Smokers and nonsmokers alike are very committed to their particular preferences. As such, practically all domestic hotels offer smoking and nonsmoking rooms for their guests' comfort. Some properties offer entire nonsmoking floors, and one small chain even experimented with complete nonsmoking properties.

With such a focus on smoking in today's society, it is surprising that the guests' smoking preference is still classified as nonessential reservation data. Given the amount of guest satisfaction and comfort riding on the smoking preference, it is even more curious that hotel reservations departments do not guarantee the smoking status of the reserved room—yet that's the standard in the lodging industry. The guest's smoking preference is noted and the hotel tries to accommodate the request, but there are no guarantees that a smoking guest will get a smoking room, or vice versa!

Address.   The guest address and/or phone number are requested by some hotels as a matter of record. Other hotels utilize the information to mail a confirmation card or confirmation letter (see Exhibits 5–4 and 5–5). when there is sufficient lead time. In the case of third-party reservations (as when a secretary or travel agent makes the reservation), the address and phone number of the person making the reservation is also requested.

►*Confirming the Reservation.*   A letter of confirmation or a confirmation card is usually printed by the computerized property management system (or central reservations system) using the information collected during the reservation (see Exhibits 5–4 and 5–5). There is a field on the reservation screen that asks "Print Confirmation? Yes or No." The system probably defaults to "No," requiring the reservations agent to actually enter "Yes" if a confirmation needs to be mailed (see Exhibit 5–2). Some prop-

Exhibit 5–3   Be careful what you ask for . . . you just might get that room with a view. Here's a spoof on travel industry euphemisms. *Reprinted from* Last Trout in Venice: The Far-Flung Escapades of an Accidental Adventurer *by Doug Lansky, copyright 2001 by Doug Lansky. Reprinted by permission of Travelers' Tales, Inc. and the author.*

A Room With a View

It's not easy to understand travel professionals these days. And I'm not just talking about the conductors squawking gibberish over the tin-speaker public-address system on the New York City subway. Their messages are crystal clear compared to travel-brochure creators. . . Savvy travelers understand that far-flung lands don't always share the same standards.

Unfortunately, it's hard to plan a journey when you don't really know what you're getting yourself into. Before that next trip, you may want to consult this carefully researched glossary of international travel terms:

At The Hotel:

- Panoramic View: you can see the entire wall of the hotel across the alley.

- Deluxe Accommodation: end of toilet paper roll has been neatly folded to a point.

- All-Night Room Service: that's how long you'll wait for your order.

- Award Winning Hotel: has been awarded several citations from the health department.

- International Calling Available From Room: available yes, for about $12 per minute.

- Cooled by Ocean Breezes: the window is broken.

- Unrivaled Location: requires a two-hour taxi ride from the airport.

On Tour:

- Must-See: should be called might see, if the other tourists in front of you get out of the way.

- Within Walking Distance: can be reached by foot by elite Kenyan runners in less than a day

- Quaint Village: tourists outnumber locals 9 to 1.

- All-Inclusive: all except drinks, snacks, excursions, activities, and tips.

- Rain Jacket Recommended: Averages three days of sunshine per year.

Shopping and Dining:

- Where Are You From: do you come from a country with a strong currency?

- Special Price: triple what locals pay.

- Bureau De Change: will probably not charge a commission higher than the amount of money you are trying to exchange.

- Establishment Frequented by Locals: locals will try selling you roses for $5 each while you dine with other tourists.

- Tourist Menu: one meal for the price of two.

- Fully Air-Conditioned: no matter the temperature outside, the air-conditioner will be set on "turbo blast" so you can deep-freeze during your meal.

Getting Around:

- Your Luggage Will Arrive on Carousel 3: some of your luggage will arrive on carousel 3.

- Courtesy Shuttle: if it ever arrives.

- Tourist Facilities Available: gift shops within 20 yards.

- Experienced Driver: hold onto your lunch, he's been to traffic court numerous times.

erties ask the guest "Would you like us to mail you a confirmation?" Others do it as a routine activity when there is sufficient leadtime. Most properties (just over half), however, do not mail a confirmation. Instead, the reservationist closes the conversation by furnishing the caller with a confirmation number generated by the computer.

There is actually order to what appears to be random reservation numbers. First on the screen might be the scheduled arrival date, from 1 to 365. February 5, for instance, is 36. Then the individual hotel of the chain might be identified by its own code. The agent's initials sometimes follow, and identification of the reservation con-

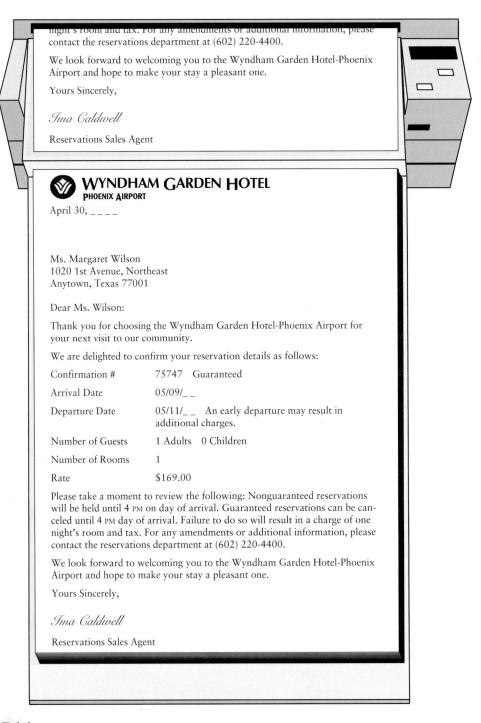

night's room and tax. For any amendments or additional information, please contact the reservations department at (602) 220-4400.

We look forward to welcoming you to the Wyndham Garden Hotel-Phoenix Airport and hope to make your stay a pleasant one.

Yours Sincerely,

Ima Caldwell

Reservations Sales Agent

WYNDHAM GARDEN HOTEL
PHOENIX AIRPORT

April 30, _ _ _ _

Ms. Margaret Wilson
1020 1st Avenue, Northeast
Anytown, Texas 77001

Dear Ms. Wilson:

Thank you for choosing the Wyndham Garden Hotel-Phoenix Airport for your next visit to our community.

We are delighted to confirm your reservation details as follows:

Confirmation #	75747 Guaranteed
Arrival Date	05/09/_ _
Departure Date	05/11/_ _ An early departure may result in additional charges.
Number of Guests	1 Adults 0 Children
Number of Rooms	1
Rate	$169.00

Please take a moment to review the following: Nonguaranteed reservations will be held until 4 PM on day of arrival. Guaranteed reservations can be canceled until 4 PM day of arrival. Failure to do so will result in a charge of one night's room and tax. For any amendments or additional information, please contact the reservations department at (602) 220-4400.

We look forward to welcoming you to the Wyndham Garden Hotel-Phoenix Airport and hope to make your stay a pleasant one.

Yours Sincerely,

Ima Caldwell

Reservations Sales Agent

Exhibit 5–4   A letter of confirmation provides the same reservation detail as a confirmation card. Such letters are not individually written—this one was prepared as an automatic function of the hotel's Fidelio PMS. *Courtesy of Wyndham Hotels & Resorts, Dallas, Texas.*

HOT WIRE HOTEL
Shocking Behavior Drive
Electric City, Washington 98765-4321

PLEASE CHECK FOR ACCURACY
Your Reservations Have Been Confirmed

Accommodations Requested

Arrival	Time	Departure	No. Guest	Room Type	Rate
6/11/	GTD	6/14/	2	DELUXE KING	120

Special Request: OCEAN VIEW   Group Affiliation: WESTERN ATHLETES CONFERENCE

PAUL D. LIGAMENT
1234 ACHILLES TENDON WAY
WOUNDED KNEE
SOUTH DAKOTA   12345-6789

We require credit to be established prior to or at registration.
For your convenience we accept the following credit cards:
VISA, MasterCard, American Express, Carte Blanche,
Diners Club, and Discover Card.

A Guaranteed Payment Reservation:
Unless canceled, you will be responsible for payment of room accommodations reserved for one night with the remaining days being canceled.

A 6:00 PM Reservation:
Room accommodations and all remaining days will be canceled at 6:00 PM unless a deposit of $100.00 per room is received in advance.

Reservation #9821-017   **Toll-Free Reservations 800-555-5555**

Check-in time is 4 PM
Check-out is 12 noon

Exhibit 5–5   As with a letter of confirmation (see Exhibit 5–4), the "confirmation card" is prepared from information collected during the reservation. Confirmation cards are preprinted with hotel information. Blank spaces (including name and address, room type, etc.) are then filled in by the computer system. Confirmation cards may be mailed as postcards. This one is designed to be stuffed into a windowed envelope.

cludes with the next confirmation number in sequence. The number, with the pieces set apart, may appear as 36 141 ABC 2366.

However that is only one possibility. Not every company follows this sequence. The reservation code might start with the first three letters in the guest's last name, and the clerk's identity might be dropped: VAL 36 141 2366. Or the number may be nothing more than the next digits in the sequence (Exhibit 5–5), accumulated by the month or year. In still other systems, the confirmation number is either completely random or is so complex it is almost impossible to decode.

Reservation Information Flow

Once entered into the system, the reservation appears electronically in a myriad of formats and printouts until the date of arrival. On that date, the reservation changes from a future reservation to an arriving reservation. On the date of arrival, the overall responsibility for the arriving or incoming reservation changes from the reservations department to the front-office staff (see Chapter 8).

An arrival list (Exhibit 5–6) is printed by the property management system each night for the following day's anticipated check ins. The transfer of data is delayed until registration. The material is keyed in by the room clerk, and the transfer completed, but only after the guest arrives. Unlike the manual rack system (Exhibit 5–7), the computerized reservation system generally does not have a supporting correspondence file. Almost all supporting data is electronic in nature. Only under unusual circumstances will there be hard-copy support. Examples of these circumstances include reservation requests by mail or fax rather than telephone.

With computerized property management systems (or a central reservations system), all the reservation information is stored in the computer's memory and can be

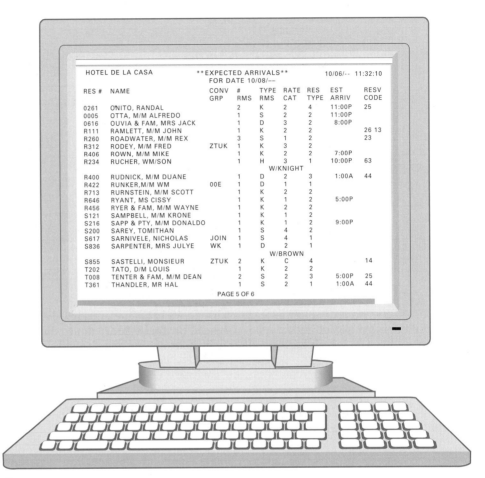

| HOTEL DE LA CASA | | **EXPECTED ARRIVALS** | | | | | 10/06/-- | 11:32:10 |
| | | FOR DATE 10/08/-- | | | | | | |

RES #	NAME	CONV GRP	# RMS	TYPE RMS	RATE CAT	RES TYPE	EST ARRIV	RESV CODE
0261	ONITO, RANDAL		2	K	2	4	11:00P	25
0005	OTTA, M/M ALFREDO		1	S	2	2	11:00P	
0616	OUVIA & FAM, MRS JACK		1	D	3	2	8:00P	
R111	RAMLETT, M/M JOHN		1	K	2	2		26 13
R260	ROADWATER, M/M REX		3	S	1	2		23
R312	RODEY, M/M FRED	ZTUK	1	K	3	2		
R406	ROWN, M/M MIKE		1	K	2	2	7:00P	
R234	RUCHER, WM/SON		1	H	3	1	10:00P	63
			W/KNIGHT					
R400	RUDNICK, M/M DUANE		1	D	2	3	1:00A	44
R422	RUNKER,M/M WM	00E	1	D	1	1		
R713	RURNSTEIN, M/M SCOTT		1	K	2	2		
R646	RYANT, MS CISSY		1	K	1	2	5:00P	
R456	RYER & FAM, M/M WAYNE		1	K	2	2		
S121	SAMPBELL, M/M KRONE		1	K	1	2		
S216	SAPP & PTY, M/M DONALDO		1	K	1	2	9:00P	
S200	SAREY, TOMITHAN		1	S	4	2		
S617	SARNIVELE, NICHOLAS	JOIN	1	S	4	1		
S836	SARPENTER, MRS JULYE	WK	1	D	2	1		
			W/BROWN					
S855	SASTELLI, MONSIEUR	ZTUK	2	K	C	4		14
T202	TATO, D/M LOUIS		1	K	2	2		
T008	TENTER & FAM, M/M DEAN		2	S	2	3	5:00P	25
T361	THANDLER, MR HAL		1	S	2	1	1:00A	44

PAGE 5 OF 6

Exhibit 5–6   Computer display of expected arrivals (reservations) list. Identical hard copies are provided on the day of arrival to the desk, the uniformed services, and even to the dining room if it is an American plan hotel. Note the estimated times of arrival and reservations codes (see Exhibit 5–8).

recalled for viewing on the computer screen if the guest name and the date of arrival are known. In a perfect world, the reservation or confirmation number would be known, and that also would bring the information forward.

Although the majority of reservations remain undisturbed until the date of arrival, a great number of reservations are changed. Common alterations to reservations include a changed date of arrival or length of stay, a changed guest name (as when an existing corporate reservation is to be claimed by a different employee), a changed room type or discount request, or a cancellation.

No matter what the alteration may be, the reservationist cannot make a change without first accessing the preexisting reservation. Only under unusual situations is the existing reservation difficult to locate. Difficulty in finding an existing reservation occurs when either the guest or reservationist has made a clerical error. Common clerical errors include incorrect date of arrival or incorrect spelling of the guest's name.

In many cases, these errors are found and rectified. In other instances, the existing reservation cannot be located. If, for some reason, the reservation cannot be found,

Exhibit 5–7   You've come a long way baby! This outdated "reservation rack" demonstrates just how far we've come (circa 1960). Actually, reservation racks are still in use in certain hotels—extremely small properties, those with a regularly disrupted power supply, and hotels operating in less sophisticated third-world countries. They're still available for purchase, too, through suppliers such as the American Hotel Register Company.

Reservation data was typed or handwritten onto slips, which were then inserted into these rack "pockets." The rack shown here had 31 days, each indicated by a black-numbered pocket. Guests arriving on a given date (say, September 7) were filed alphabetically. When that date eventually arrived, the entire rack was moved from the reservations department to the front desk.

the reservationist may actually take a new reservation. This is risky, because chances are there will now be duplicate reservations in the system.

▶*Advance Deposits.*   Guaranteeing the reservation by means of an advance deposit has grown more popular and less popular at the same time. If the request is for cash (check), the procedure has become less popular. Handling cash or checks requires a disproportionate amount of clerical time and postage relative to the economic gain.

The initial reservation procedure is similar whether or not a deposit check is requested. The reservation is confirmed, but only tentatively, since it contains dated notice that a reservation deposit is required. Two copies of the reservation confirmation may be mailed. The extra copy is to be returned with the check in the nonstamped, preaddressed envelope that is enclosed. More often than not, the hotel mails nothing. Instead, the customer is instructed to mail the deposit and to write the confirmation number on the check to ensure proper credit. With enough lead time, a receipt is usually returned to the guest. Most hoteliers, however, feel that the cost, time invested, and delay make the procedure unwarranted. This is especially true considering the widespread availability of credit cards.

Credit-Card Guarantees.   Even as requiring advance deposit checks has decreased in practice, guaranteeing by credit card is a procedure that has gained in popularity. The reservation clerk takes the credit-card number over the telephone and records it with the reservation. Nothing needs to be processed at this time. The charge will be forwarded only if the guest is a no-show, and then only if the hotel believes that collection is justified. In the usual sequence, the guest appears as expected and credit is established at registration.

Processing the credit card entails a fee that is not part of the cost of cash deposits. However, the fee isn't paid unless the charge is made. Check deposits have their own risk—they bounce.

Experienced travelers soon realize how much of a game the reservation process has become. Busy properties almost always insist on credit-card guarantees rather than on a 4 PM or 6 PM hold. Credit-card guarantees reduce the number of no-shows.

At the same time, guests know that many properties do not actually charge the card at the time of the reservation. With such properties, the guarantee is not processed until the expected night of arrival. Some unethical travelers take advantage of this practice. They provide the hotel with an inaccurate credit-card number. In this way, if they fail to show, the hotel cannot actually charge them. On the other hand, if they do arrive and their false credit-card number is challenged, they can blame it on poor communication or a clerical error: They invent the false credit-card number by changing the sequence of one or two digits on their real credit card, which makes for a fairly believable excuse. For example, if their VISA card number were 4567 890 123 456, they could simply change the number to 4567 809 123 456. Now they have a workable excuse in the event they do show up for their reservation—but a fictitious number in the event of a no-show.

Most hotel chains and individual properties are wise to this game and intercept "errors" at the time of the reservation. They accomplish this by having an automated reservations system that is interfaced directly to a credit-card clearing center. During the several minutes the guest is on the telephone with the reservationist, the credit-card number is input and an approval verification is received. If the approval is denied, the reservationist gives the guest another opportunity to read the correct credit-card number.

▶ *Cancellations.*   Cancellations require a change to the existing reservation. This is not necessarily a problem unless somehow it is improperly handled. Handling anything at the front desk in an improper manner generates problems as well as bad public relations. This is especially true with cancellations—imagine yourself in the shoes of a guest who previously cancelled the reservation. The hotel improperly recorded the cancellation and your credit-card statement now reflects a $150 no-show charge for the unoccupied room night. That is exasperating!

Encouraging cancellation calls is in the best interest of the hotel. Such calls reduce the no-show rate. Fewer no-shows generate more room revenue from walk-in guests and reduce complaints from the antiservice syndrome of overbooking (Chapter 6).

The cancellation number, which is formulated like the confirmation number (discussed earlier), is the only major difference between a cancellation call and any other reservation change. Even then, its importance is limited to guaranteed reservations. The system must protect the guest who has guaranteed the room with a credit card (or other guarantee) from being billed if the reservation is canceled in a timely manner. Nonguaranteed reservations are not generally provided with a cancellation number.

▶ *Guest History Databases.*   One of the ancillary benefits associated with the speed and accuracy of today's electronic systems has been increased data storage capabilities. Customer information, collected during the normal flow of the room reservation, can be stored in guest history databases, manipulated, and used for marketing and guest service/recognition purposes. It makes sense that the hotel's use of guest history data has risen with increased computer storage and processing capabilities.

The guest history revolution was originally fought at the individual property level. Until recently, centralizing guest history information at the corporate level was too unwieldy to justify. Guest history utilization at the property level was more manageable.

Guest history improves the most basic component of guest service: recognition. Hotels have always known that guests appreciate personal recognition. Imagine the unwavering loyalty that can be gained, then, if the guests' basic needs and requests are recognized in advance. That is the promise of guest history.

In its most common form, guest history is applied at the property level during the reservation process. The guest history function is first utilized when the reservations agent pulls up a guest's previous stay information and saves them both the burden of repeating address, credit card, and room type/rate preferences. However, guest history can accomplish far more than that. In upscale corporate and luxury properties, guest history databases often inform front-office personnel of the various likes and dislikes of the guest. Simple preferences such as ground-floor room, feather as opposed to foam pillows, extra pears in the fruit basket, and so on, go a long way toward generating loyalty and a sense of belonging.

It makes good business sense, too. Not only does the hotel gain the benefits of enhanced guest loyalty, satisfaction, and repeat visitation, but guest history databases are valuable marketing resources as well. It takes little imagination to visualize the potential a mailed marketing campaign might have when focused on certain guest history parameters. For example, a hotel facing a slow autumn might mail a special promotion to those corporate guests who visited their property at least two times last year during September and October—now *that's* pinpointing the market.

Centralized Guest History.   Beginning around 1997, the industry saw increasing centralization of guest history information. What one property in Washington, DC knew about a particular frequent corporate traveler was now becoming available through the chain's central reservations system to, say, a sister property in Olympia, Washington.

Corporate travelers have been demanding improved guest service (recognition) to compensate for rising room rates. Chains such as Marriott Hotels and Resorts, Ritz-Carlton, Preferred Hotels and Resorts, and Carlton Hospitality Worldwide saw the need to centralize guest history databanks and took an early lead in this area of automation. These chains banked on the premise that when frequent guests at one property are recognized like family in another of the chain's properties, the increased guest satisfaction translates into increased brand loyalty.

Chain guest history databases have been developed from a variety of directions. Marriott's, for example, was designed around their existing Marriott Rewards frequent guest program. Since this program was already in place across their entire spectrum of properties, Marriott thought it made sense to use Marriott Rewards as the centralized starting point. As such, when Marriott rolled out its original guest history program, it already had guest profiles from more than 9 million members.[2] However, Marriott's guest history database system initially stored only basic guest information such as bed type and smoking preference.

[2]Information related to Marriott's Automated Reservation System for Hotel Accommodations (MARSHA) can be found in the April 13, 1998, issue of *Business Travel News.*

Some of the smaller chains had an operational advantage over Marriott because of their relative size. Ritz-Carlton, for example, took the complete encyclopedia of guest history information it had developed at individual properties and integrated it into a centralized database. Ritz-Carlton calls this database its Customer Loyalty Anticipation Satisfaction System, or CLASS. Before the implementation of CLASS, regular Ritz-Carlton guests who were visiting a different Ritz-Carlton hotel for the first time would have been treated like first-timers. Now, repeat customers at one property are repeat customers at all the Ritz properties. The front-desk receptionist at the Ritz-Carlton, Buckhead, can call up the guest's latest visit (say, last month at the Ritz-Carlton, Laguna Niguel), and say, "I see in Laguna Niguel you requested a 6:30 AM wake-up call with a pot of decaffeinated coffee, skim milk, and a bagel delivered at 7 AM. Shall we provide the same for you tomorrow morning?" Wow!

Reservation Coding

The reservation's journey ends at the front desk (see Chapter 8). Sometimes the journey is long, as when the reservation was made a year in advance. In other cases, the reservation lead time is extremely short, as with reservations made minutes before arrival. In any case, the front desk is the final stopping point in the reservation's journey.

The first step in linking the reservation with the front desk is to change the status of the reservation from future reservation to arriving reservation. In a computerized system, this change occurs automatically, either as the clock strikes midnight or as a step in the night audit process.

It is at this moment that guests' special requests and needs become the concern of the front desk. Armed with the knowledge of which rooms are clean and vacant, which rooms are due to check out, and which rooms are staying over, specific room assignments are developed in accordance with guest requests. Even in an automated property, the assigning of special rooms to match special requests is a manual operation. It is the clerk, operating with good judgment, who ultimately determines which requests can be met and which requests will be declined.

▶ *Special Coding.*   Whether operating under a manual or computerized system, certain reservations are different from the rest. They may be different in their method of payment, in the guests' specific requests, in the fact that they are *commissionable* to a travel agent, in their time of arrival, or in their affiliation. Whatever the case, the front-desk clerk needs to be alert to these unique circumstances.

The difference is generally highlighted somewhere on the reservation. In an automated system, a numerical coding scheme is commonly used. In this case, advance-deposit reservations will be indicated with one code number (see Exhibit 5–8, code 40) and travel agent reservations with another code (say, code 55). Following is a brief discussion about some of these special codes. For a more complete understanding of their impact on the guest check-in process, refer to Chapter 8.

Advance Deposits.   Reservations with an advance deposit need to be specially noted. If the deposit arrived, the front-desk clerk needs to be certain to post the credit on behalf of the guest. If the deposit never arrived, the front-desk clerk will probably cancel the reservation if the hotel is nearing capacity.

Late Arrivals.   If front-desk personnel know that a given reservation is due to arrive late, they will be less likely to assume it is a no-show as the evening progresses.

Computer Code	Internal System Meaning	Actual Printout on Guest Confirmation
11	VIP	
12	Group buyer	
13	Honeymooners	
14	Comp	
20	Connecting rooms	*Connecting rooms, if possible*
21	Adjoining rooms	*Adjoining rooms, if possible*
22	Rooms on same floor	*Same floor, if possible*
23	Need individual names	*Please advise names of individuals in your party*
24	PS	*Petit suite*
25	RS	*One-bedroom suite*
26	LS	*Two-bedroom suite*
30	Send liquor	
31	Send champagne	
32	Send flowers	
33	Send gift	
34	Send fruit	
40	Require deposit	*Please send one night's deposit to guarantee your reservation*
41	Due bill	
42	No credit, require advance payment	
43	Walk-in	
44	Late arrival	*Anticipated late arrival of guest*
50	Special rate	*Special rate*
51	Airline rate	*Airline rate*
52	Press rate	*Press rate*
53	Convention rate	*Convention rate*
54	Nonconvention rate	*Convention rate applies to convention dates only*
55	Travel agency	*Travel agency*
60	Cot	*Cot will be provided*
61	Crib	*Crib will be provided*
62	Bedboard	*Bedboard will be provided*
63	Wheelchair	*Wheelchair will be provided*
70	Casino guest	
80	See correspondence for very special instructions	
99	Print special message	*(Whatever that message is)*

Exhibit 5–8   Actual listing of reservations codes from a major hotel/casino operation. Code numbers correspond to an internal system description, policy, or abbreviation. Some codes (for example, code 54) print onto a special "comments" section of the confirmation form sent the guest. Other codes (for example, code 11) are designed for inhouse use only.

Credit-Card Guarantee.   Rooms guaranteed with a national credit card are theoretically held for the guest all night long. If the guest fails to arrive, the night auditor will charge the credit card for one night's room (see Chapter 6).

Corporate Guarantee.   The right to guarantee rooms with a corporation's good credit must be prearranged with the hotel. In case of a no-show, the room charge is billed to the corporation's city ledger account (see Chapter 6).

Travel Agents.   Special-coding of travel agent (TA) reservations expedites the internal office procedure. After the guest departs, the hotel pays the travel agent's commission. (In those circumstances where the travel agent owes the hotel—an *account receivable*—the hotel bills the balance less the travel agent's commission.) When the reservation is placed, the agent identifies the agency, providing name, address, and *International Association of Travel Agents (IATA)* code number.

Reservations are confirmed to the agency, not to the guest. In some cases, the hotel lacks the guest's address until registration time. To maintain accountability with the agency, the wise hotel manager sends a notice whenever one of the TA's clients fails to appear.

VIPs.   Very important persons (VIPs) are generally coded. These may be well-known dignitaries, celebrities, other hoteliers, or important members of an association that the hotel hopes to book later. VIP designations are made by a member of management or by the sales department. *Star reservation* is also used. A *contact reservation* is a VIP that should be met (contacted) and escorted to his or her room by the management.

Riding Reservation.   Reservations for which the date of arrival is vague may be allowed to "ride." The probable date is booked and then the reservation is carried until the guest shows or an allotted period of time passes, usually less than one week. Riding reservations are seldom used. They are generally found only at resorts or for VIP reservations.

Convention Delegate.   *Group affiliation* is a better term than *convention delegate* because the members of a group need not be part of a convention. Hotels cater to tours, company delegations, wedding parties, and other groups that need to be identified. Several codes are needed when different groups are booked at one time. For a more thorough discussion of group reservations, refer to the next section of this chapter.

➤ CONVENTION AND TOUR GROUP BUSINESS

The term *group business* represents a variety of venues. Group business can range from major conventions and expositions (trade shows), to midsized corporate meetings and conferences, to smaller incentive travel packages, tour groups, and corporate retreats (see Exhibit 5–9). From large to small, group business is a major player in today's lodging industry.

For some properties, group business is almost nonexistent. Such hotels or motels may have limited or no meeting facilities, may be located in remote areas and face difficult group travel logistics, or may be so busy with leisure travel that there is no room for discounted group business. Conversely, major convention properties may derive upward of 90% of all hotel revenues from group activities. Although different types of properties have varying degrees of dependence on group business, the industry as a whole derives a significant portion of its revenues from this growing segment (see Exhibits 5–10 and 5–11).

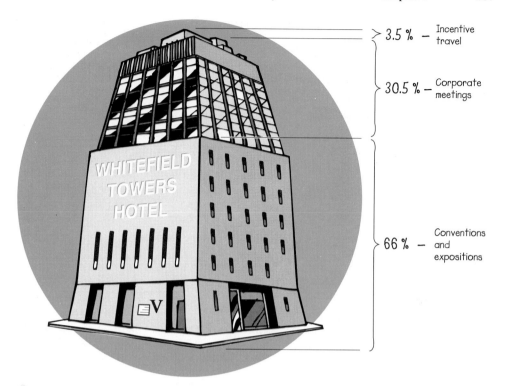

3.5 % — Incentive travel

30.5 % — Corporate meetings

66 % — Conventions and expositions

Exhibit 5–9   About two-thirds of group rooms revenue comes from conventions and expositions. The remaining one-third is composed primarily of corporate meetings (30.5%), with incentive travel (3.5%) making up the difference.

Incentive travel, tour groups, conventions, and trade shows have become mainstays of hotel sales in the United States and abroad. Such gatherings are clearly defined as group business. Business meetings and corporate retreats, though smaller in scale, are included in this broad definition.

Depending on the hotel, smaller gatherings lose the distinction of being classified and tracked as group business. A small wedding party requiring only five or seven rooms, for example, may be considered an individual rather than a group reservation. Several executives meeting in a conference room for a few days are often handled through the hotel's inhouse reservations department as individual rooms. Indeed, even a convention meeting planner visiting the property several weeks before the convention is probably handled as an individual (although complimentary) room. Technically, the meeting planner's accommodations should be tracked as part of the overall convention count.

Group reservations are handled differently from individual reservations. One difference is the central reservations office (or any of the GDS link-ups) may not be entitled to handle the group. Many chains require that group accommodations deal directly with the specific hotel property. Even at the hotel property, midsized and larger operations usually remove group reservations from the responsibility of the inhouse reservations department.

Most midsized and larger properties have a group sales department designed to handle (among other tasks) group rooms reservations. After all, depending on busi-

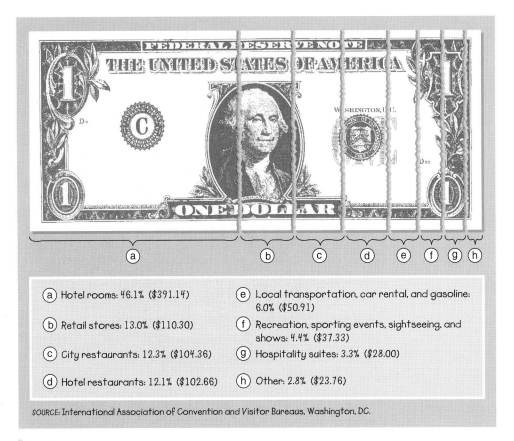

(a) Hotel rooms: 46.1% ($391.14)   (e) Local transportation, car rental, and gasoline: 6.0% ($50.91)

(b) Retail stores: 13.0% ($110.30)   (f) Recreation, sporting events, sightseeing, and shows: 4.4% ($37.33)

(c) City restaurants: 12.3% ($104.36)   (g) Hospitality suites: 3.3% ($28.00)

(d) Hotel restaurants: 12.1% ($102.66)   (h) Other: 2.8% ($23.76)

SOURCE: International Association of Convention and Visitor Bureaus, Washington, DC.

Exhibit 5–10   International conventions have a higher event expenditure per delegate ($1,088.57) than state or local conventions ($440.12). The average expenditure per delegate per convention for all conventions in the United States is $848.45. This exhibit shows how the average delegates spent their travel dollars.[3]

ness levels, policies, and property characteristics, large groups may be granted special rates and discounts. These special deals are negotiated between the group's representative and the hotel's sales manager, with final approval granted by the general manager of the property.

Because of differing policies and definitions, group business is handled and characterized differently across various hotels and chains. Therefore, it is difficult to know exactly how great is the impact of group rooms activity on the lodging industry. A fairly large number of group activities are never counted. However, the convention industry (including conventions, expositions, corporate meetings, incentive travel, and trade shows) is conservatively estimated at close to $100 billion annually in the United States alone. According to the U.S. Department of Commerce, that places the convention industry in the top 20 in comparison to all industries in the United States! Of that almost $100 billion, about 66% of the revenues come from conventions and expositions, 30.5% come from corporate meetings, and 3.5% come from incentive travel (see Exhibit 5–9). Each of these categories has its own demographics and spending patterns. Some details related to convention visitor spending are shown in Exhibits 5–10 and 5–11.

[3]Exhibits 5–10 and 5–11 assume 5% growth in spending per annum, 2000–2004.

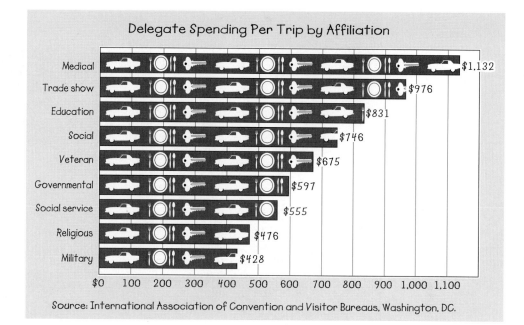

Delegate Spending Per Trip by Affiliation

Medical	$1,132
Trade show	$976
Education	$831
Social	$746
Veteran	$675
Governmental	$597
Social service	$555
Religious	$476
Military	$428

Source: International Association of Convention and Visitor Bureaus, Washington, DC.

Exhibit 5–11   Convention delegates have historically spent more per trip than corporate or leisure travelers. Depending on the type or purpose of the convention (medical vs. military), certain delegates spend more than others. (See footnote 3).

The Group Rooms Contribution

The contribution of group rooms revenues to total rooms revenues depends on the type of hotel. Some properties—conference centers, for example—are exclusively group-oriented (see Exhibits 5–12 and 5–13). Other operations choose to accommodate groups during slow periods and off-seasons (Exhibit 5–14). There are very few hotels that refuse to accommodate group business altogether.

▶*Benefits of Group Business.*   There are three distinctions that separate group business from individual corporate and leisure travelers. These distinctions represent benefits (profits) associated with selling group rooms. Even though group rooms are usually sold at a discount from rack rate (as most things purchased in quantity are sold at a discount), it is still a very profitable venture for most hotels.

However, accepting a group booking for a given date is no simple matter. It must be evaluated in terms of the group's rooms revenues and related revenues (banquets, meeting room rentals, audiovisual equipment use, etc.), as opposed to displaced transient and corporate rooms business. Whether the group business justifies displacing normal hotel business (corporate and transient rooms) is a question for the hotel's yield management team (see Chapter 4).

There are three characteristics unique to group business that affect the hotel's interest in accepting group rooms:

1. Group business is a sizable market.
2. Groups provide certain economies of scale.
3. Group delegates spend more dollars.

Exhibit 5–12   Convention and meeting facilities come in all shapes and sizes. These two examples range from a cozy roundtable conference room at the Adam's Mark Hotel in St. Louis to the 26,680-square-foot Plaza International Ballroom at the Peabody Orlando. This ballroom can seat 2,420 guests for a banquet! *Courtesy of the Adam's Mark Hotel, St. Louis, Missouri and the Peabody Orlando, Orlando, Florida. Used with permission.*

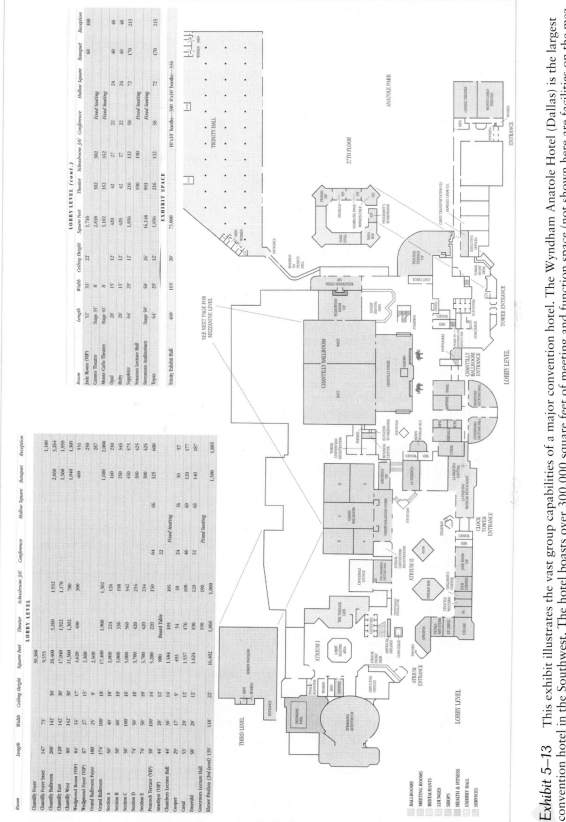

LOBBY LEVEL (cont.)

Room	Length	Width	Ceiling Height	Square Feet	Theater	Schoolroom 3'6"	Conference	Hollow Square	Banquet	Reception
Jade Room (VIP)	52'	33	22'	1,716	902	902	Fixed Seating		60	100
Cannes Theatre	Stage 35'	8		2,838	352	352	Fixed Seating			
Monte Carlo Theatre	Stage 41'	8		3,102			Fixed Seating			
Opal	28'	15'	12'	420	42	27	22	24	40	48
Ruby	28'	15'	12'	420	42	27	22	24	40	48
Sapphire	64'	29'	12'	1,856	216	132	58	72	170	213
Senators Lecture Hall					190	190	Fixed Seating			
Stemmons Auditorium	Stage 50'	50'	26'	16,148	993		Fixed Seating			
Topaz	64'	29'	12'	1,856	216	132	58	72	170	213

EXHIBIT SPACE

Room	Length	Width	Ceiling Height	Square Feet			
Trinity Exhibit Hall	469	165	20'	73,000	10'x10' booths—380	8'x10' booths—356	

LOBBY LEVEL

Room	Length	Width	Ceiling Height	Square Feet	Theater	Schoolroom 3'6"	Conference	Hollow Square	Banquet	Reception
Chantilly Foyer	147	73		50,560						1,100
Chantilly Foyer Inset	200'	73		9,555						
Chantilly Ballroom	200'	142	30	26,600	3,260	1,932			2,660	3,264
Chantilly East	120	142	30	17,040	1,922	1,170			1,560	1,959
Chantilly West	80'	142	30	11,560	1,302	780			1,040	1,305
Wedgwood Room (VIP)	84'	55'	17'	4,620	480	300			400	551
Wedgwood Foyer (VIP)	87'	27'	15'	2,160						250
Grand Ballroom Foyer	100	25	9'	2,500						287
Grand Ballroom	174'	100'	18	17,400	1,900	1,302			1,600	2,000
Section A	50'	40	18'	2,000	224	126			160	250
Section B	50'	60	18	3,000	336	198			250	565
Section C	50'	100	18	5,000	560	342			450	575
Section D	74'	50'	18	3,700	420	234			300	425
Section E	74'	50'	18'	3,700	420	234			300	425
Peacock Terrace (VIP)	58'	109'	14	5,200	220	150	Board Table		325	600
Amethyst (VIP)	44	20'	12	880			22	66		
Chambers Lecture Hall	44	36	14	1,584	105	105	64	Fixed Seating		
Cooper	29	17	9'	493	54	30	24	36	50	57
Coral	53	29	12	1,557	176	108	46	60	120	177
Emerald	58	28	12	1,624	190	120	52	66	140	187
Governors Lecture Hall					190	190	Fixed Seating			
Khmer Pavilion (3rd Level)	139	118	22'	16,492	1,860	1,080			1,500	1,885

SEE NEXT PAGE FOR
MEZZANINE LEVEL

BALLROOMS
MEETING ROOMS
RESTAURANTS
LOUNGES
SHOPS
HEALTH & FITNESS
EXHIBIT HALL
SERVICES

Exhibit 5–13 This exhibit illustrates the vast group capabilities of a major convention hotel. The Wyndham Anatole Hotel (Dallas) is the largest convention hotel in the Southwest. The hotel boasts over 300,000 square feet of meeting and function space (not shown here are facilities on the mezzanine level and in the Anatole Park). *Courtesy of the Wyndham Anatole Hotel, Dallas, Texas.*

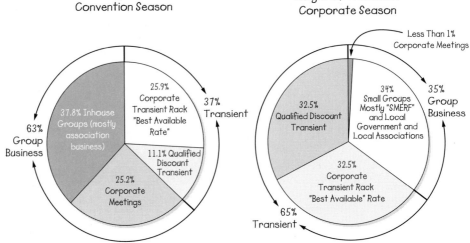

Exhibit 5–14   The lovely Doubletree La Posada Resort (see Chapter 4, Exhibit 4–13) is categorized as both a convention property and a transient resort. Depending on the time of year, this "hybrid" hotel shifts its focus from group and convention business to transient travel.

The pie chart on the left shows the operation in the height of its convention/group season (roughly January through March). The pie chart on the right shows the opposite side of the coin, when the hotel is busiest with transient travel (roughly June through August). *Courtesy of Doubletree La Posada Resort, Scottsdale, Arizona.*

The first point, group business is a sizable market, was addressed earlier in the chapter (see Exhibits 5–9 to 5–11). There is no question that group business, an almost $100 billion industry, is "sizable," and depending on the type of hotel and the market in which it operates, some properties get more than their share of group business (see Exhibit 5–14).

The second point addresses the incredible economies of scale associated with group business. *Economies of scale* is a term that denotes the economic benefits of mass production. Most items produced in mass quantities benefit from reduced per-item production costs. The same is true for the hotel industry. Selling a bulk of group rooms provides the operator with specific economies of scale. The sales department benefits from the reduced work in booking one large group as opposed to booking numerous smaller visits. The reservations department benefits from having a block of rooms set aside for the group. Even the front office, housekeeping, and uniformed services benefit from group room bookings.

With group arrivals and departures, business levels are clearly understood. With a five-day convention, for example, the front office is especially busy on the first and last days: During the first day, the front office is busy with heavy check-ins; on the last day, it is busy with check-outs. The middle days, however, are relatively slow for the front-office staff. During these slower middle days, the hotel saves labor costs by reducing its normal staffing levels. The same is true with the housekeeping and uniformed-services departments. In many hotels, the housekeeping department spends less time cleaning stayover rooms than it does cleaning check-outs. Similarly, the bell-staff is busiest when assisting guests with luggage at check-in and check-out. Uniformed-service positions are very slow during the middle days of a convention.

The third reason hotels like group business is that group delegates have a higher worth than that of individual guests. No one understands this quite as well as the casino hotels. Interacting with other conventioneers often puts group delegates in a festive mood. The trip is not just business—in many cases there is fun and excitement in the excursion. And what better way to have fun than with an all-expenses-paid trip (see Exhibits 5–10 and 5–11).

Many convention, exposition, and related group delegates are visiting the event at no personal cost. Their company or business has funded most or all of the trip. Once at the hotel, delegates have a high likelihood of spending additional money. After all, their basic expenses (meals, lodging, transportation, and convention registration) have been paid. Therefore, they buy a round of golf that they might not ordinarily purchase if they were paying for the trip on their own. They may have an extra cocktail or two and buy more expensive "call" or "premium" liquor brands. They may select a souvenir from the gift shop or even a painting from the gallery. And, of course, they might gamble a few extra (or a lot of extra) dollars. Even when delegates attend a convention at their own expense, there are favorable tax deductions that often reduce the real cost of the trip.

Casino Hotels.   Casino hotels are an interesting breed in themselves. Casino hotels generally only accept groups that have a high likelihood of gambling. All things being equal, the casino manager may prefer a group of sanitation engineers, bottling managers, or morticians over a group of doctors, lawyers, or schoolteachers. In fact, the hotel may prefer a few empty hotel rooms over a hotel full of nongamblers. Therefore, even when space is available, certain groups will be refused by casino hotels.

Assuming that the sanitation engineers are considered to be good gamblers, the casino must decide how much they are worth. The question that must always be answered is: Will the group produce more casino revenues than the individual tourists the group is displacing? If the group has a strong reputation for casino play, it will be able to negotiate a better discount than a group with a lesser (or unknown) gaming reputation.

Research shows that different delegates have different spending habits (see Exhibit 5–11). Industries in which delegates have higher annual salaries (say, physicians) usually see more spending per person during annual conventions than industries with lower annual salaries (say, military officers). This is not necessarily the case with casino gaming. With casino gaming, lower-income delegates often spend more on the casino floor than do wealthier delegates.

The reason for this dichotomy can be found in such socioeconomic factors as education, aversion to risk, moral perceptions, and any number of other reasons for which a given delegate may or may not gamble. In the example above, a casino operator may prefer the military group over the physician group if the military has a higher propensity to gamble.

Why Some Hotels Refuse Groups.   Not too many years ago, select resort operations were less inclined to accept group business than they are today. They refused group bookings for a number of reasons. The primary reason was because the group alienated nongroup guests staying at the property. That is still often the case. Staying in a hotel that is almost entirely occupied by a large group can be disconcerting to the individual, nongroup guest. Walking the halls, playing tennis, eating a meal, or sitting in the lounge can be rather self-conscious activities when the nonaffiliated guest is surrounded by loud and boisterous group delegates. Some exclusive resorts will not subject their individual guests to such an uncomfortable situation.

Hotels may be less interested in group business for several other reasons as well. Group business requires a certain investment from the hotel—there is the need for public meeting space (see Exhibits 5–12 and 5–13), audiovisual equipment, tables and chairs, food serving equipment, and so on. Also, there is the requirement of additional labor. Group hotels require a sales department staffed with one or more individuals, a convention and catering department, and food production areas. Finally, groups often negotiate discounted room rates. Hotels that find themselves in the enviable position of having strong year-round occupancy may be less interested in discounted groups.

Categories of Group Business

The need to communicate an ever-increasing amount of information has given extra strength to the convention market. Even as the information superhighway is being paved, the conventions market is larger than ever. Meeting and speaking with other delegates face to face offers certain benefits the impersonal computer, telephone, or Internet cannot provide.

Even as the convention market is growing, so is the group tour and travel market. The continued growth for this category of group business looks especially strong in light of the ever-increasing numbers of Americans over the age of 55, retired, in good health, and with plenty of discretionary dollars. Lacking the expense account and tax advantages of the conventioneer, the group tourist seeks economy above all else. Group tour and travel rates are often substantially lower than rack rates.

Whereas convention business is sold as a group and guests are handled individually, tour business is sold as a group and guests are handled as a group. One sale, one reservation, one registration,[4] one service, and one billing provide the savings on which the tour concept is built.

▶**Tour Groups.** Tour groups are very convenient for the hotel, but that convenience comes at a price. Tour operators demand deep discounts. They get them because the entire burden is on the tour operator, with only minimal risk for the hotel.

The hotel deals with one party, the group tour company or wholesaler. The wholesaler leases the bus or plane, books the rooms, commits land transportation and entertainment, and then goes out to sell the package. Historically, travel agents have been the travel wholesaler's major sales outlets. However, as the travel landscape is changing, so are the distribution systems and sources from which end users (tourists) are finding their information. The travel wholesaler then combines all purchasers (no matter what the source of their business) into one cohesive group. In so doing, the workload of the front office is reduced considerably.

As much as 40% of the tour operator's original room estimate may be lost between the start of negotiations and the date of arrival, perhaps as long as one year later. Consequently, tour operators may be given the right to *sell and report* until as close as 7 to 14 days before arrival. Sell and report, also called *status control*, allows the wholesaler or tour operator to sell rooms and report back periodically. The right to this free sell is changed to sold-out status at the discretion of the hotel's team.

---

[4]Massachusetts was the last state to pass legislation allowing preregistration of groups. Prior to 1975, each member of a group had to register separately.

Careful control is maintained over the right to sell and report because several agencies might be in that mode simultaneously. Specific dates are closed when the hotel is full and others may be closed to arrivals. Within the terms of the contract with the wholesaler, the hotel's team can alter the closeout date for the tours, asking for the final rooming list one week, four weeks, or even five weeks before arrival. Nowhere in this process is the hotel's inhouse reservation office involved. The wholesaler does all the selling. The deals are negotiated by the sales office, and the CRO is not generally involved.

▶ *Convention Groups.*   Arrangements for the convention are made by a representative, meeting planner, or committee of the organization and confirmed to the hotel with a contract of agreement. Large associations have permanent, paid executives in addition to the annually elected officers. These account executives are so numerous that they have their own organization—ASAE, the American Society of Association Executives.

If the organization is large enough to have a paid executive, he or she negotiates the arrangements with the hotel's sales staff. Details focus on many areas, including housing, meals, and meeting facilities. The organization (club, association, union) contracts with the hotel to buy meeting space (see Exhibits 5–12 and 5–13), banquet facilities, and rooms to house its own staff. It negotiates with the hotel for a block of guest rooms, but it does not pay for those rooms. Members deal individually with the hotel for accommodations.

The association sells function tickets to its membership for such events as banquets, cocktail parties, and luncheons. The money collected from these events is paid to the hotel at the negotiated price. If the association charges a higher ticket price, it will make a slight profit over the hotel's charge.

In addition, the group may also benefit from breakage (see Chapter 2) if it sells more tickets than the number of delegates who actually show for the event. On the other hand, if it guarantees a number higher than the number of delegates who show, the hotel will reap the benefit of breakage.

The organization is responsible for its own entertainment (although it may hire people through the hotel or use a destination management company, or DMC), its own speakers, films, and so on. For this, it charges the attendees a registration fee. Although some of the fee goes toward the costs of the program, the association usually profits here again.

Further gains may be made through the room rate arrangements. Sometimes organizations require the hotel to charge the attending members more than the negotiated room rate and to refund that excess to the group treasury. This raises many ethical concerns, particularly if the convention guest is unaware of the arrangement.

In no way does the association contract for rooms, except for those directly related to association headquarters, such as officers' and speakers' rooms. Room reservations are individually contracted between the hotel and each delegate. Billing is handled the same way, and collections become a personal matter between the conventioneer and the hotel.

The Threat from Discount Travel Sites.   The popularity of the Internet has made travel information more readily accessible than ever before. Broad availability of such information has affected the group travel side of the industry far more than anticipated. In the past, the group meeting planner negotiated with the hotel for the best possible convention rate, shared the headquarters hotel information—including rates—with association members and convention delegates months in advance, and assumed reservations against the group block would simply materialize. But the old way is certainly not the current way.

Discount travel sites (e.g., PriceLine.com, Expedia.com, Orbitz.com, and Last-MinuteDeals.com) have provided savvy delegates several new options. Let's create a hypothetical situation; say the fictitious Imperial Arms Hotel at a shore town in New Jersey has the American Billiards Club (ABC) convention visiting from August 3 to August 7. Delegates to the ABC convention likely made their room reservations many months ago at the group-negotiated rate of $139 per night. However, in mid-July, delegates discovered that the same rooms could be purchased over discount Internet sites for just $79 per night. It is a small sacrifice to stay outside of the convention block—Internet-booked rooms outside the convention block will not be identified with the convention and therefore will not get turn-down service, a daily convention newsletter, or the nightly conference gift—so many delegates cancel their $139 convention room reservations and booked over the Internet at $79.

But the story does not end there. If rooms at the convention headquarters hotel are $79 on the Internet, there are almost certainly other rooms in town at substantial savings as well. It turns out that the fictitious William Penn Hotel (just across the street) has rooms for only $49 on the Internet. Other delegates decide to cancel rooms at the headquarters hotel in favor of an even better rate (although they'll have to walk across the street every day) at the William Penn Hotel.

At this point, the meeting planner faces several serious issues. The availability of substantially lower rates make for not only an embarrassing situation, but a potentially costly one as well. The cost comes through group attrition (discussed in detail later in this chapter); if the convention does not generate a certain number of room nights, the difference is billable to the convention. The ABC group may potentially be liable for thousands of dollars in attrition costs because of the bargain-hunting antics of its delegates.

So what is to be done? Maybe the meeting planner should simply talk to the hotel sales department, explain what has happened in the last few days before the convention begins, and ask for a new contract and better rate. That action has been tried—it doesn't work. The hotel will stick to its guns and insist on maintaining the negotiated rate and the negotiated attritions clause.

Today's meeting planners therefore must negotiate several clauses into their contracts to combat this growing problem. One clause counts all members of the group against the guarantee. Even if members choose to stay at the hotel as unidentified delegates, if the group (ABC) can prove the members were registered with the convention, the group will receive credit against the room-night guarantee. Another response to the problem of discounted rooms is a clause in the contract stating, "No lower rates shall be offered by the hotel, through any distribution vehicle, during the contracted meeting dates, unless offered to all attendees as well."

►*Expositions and Trade Shows.*   Expositions and trade shows have many characteristics similar to conventions. In fact, trade shows are often held in conjunction with large conventions. The association (or trade-show entrepreneur) acquires space from the hotel or convention center and leases that space to exhibitors. Those managing the trade show invite guests, exhibitors, and shoppers.

The average guest stay is longer with a show because the displays, which are costly and elaborate, require setup and teardown time. Otherwise, reservation and front-office procedures are the same as for a convention or an individual guest. More city ledger charges (direct bill accounts) may occur because the exhibitors are usually large companies that request that type of settlement.

Booking the Convention

Associations book conventions and expositions as much as 5 to 10 years in advance. Extremely large conventions (100,000 delegates or more) such as the National Association of Home Builders (NAHB) or the National Restaurant Association (NRA) Trade Show may have unconfirmed bookings as far out as 20 years in advance. For small to midsized conventions, two to three years is the norm.

Initially, a blanket reservation is committed by the hotel and a rate is negotiated. For large conventions requiring more than one hotel, a citywide convention and visitor bureau (CVB) negotiates the blanket reservation on behalf of participating hotels (refer to section entitled "Convention and Visitor Bureaus" following). The blanket reservation is little more than a commitment for a set number of rooms at a set rate for a set date. There is little additional detail until at least a year in advance.

▶**Adjusting the Room Block.**   As the date approaches, some six months to a year in advance, the hotel begins to examine the blanket reservation or room block. After discussions with the association, the hotel may adjust the number of rooms required if the association predicts its convention size to grow or shrink that year. Meetings with neighboring hotels or the CVB may shed light on their management strategies with regard to the room block and the convention's ability to deliver the rooms committed. Finally, communication with other hotels where this group has previously been housed will give some sense of the group's attrition or casualty factor.

Convention hotels usually cooperate by furnishing each other historical information about the group—numbers, no-shows, and the like. They do this because conventions usually move annually. A hotel in one section of the state or nation is not competing with another if the organization has already decided to meet in another city. Similar information is available through local convention or tourist bureaus, which report to and have access to the files of the International Association of Convention and Visitor Bureaus (IACVB). The IACVB gathers data about the character and performance of each group handled by the member bureaus.

Reservation problems occur despite the best predictive efforts of the marketing and reservations departments. Association memberships change over time, and certain cities prove more or less appealing than previous sites. The casualty factor (cancellations plus no-shows) also varies from group to group, reducing the value of generalized percentage figures.

▶**Convention and Visitor Bureaus.**   Convention and visitor bureaus are publicly funded, quasi-governmental agencies found in all large and most midsized or small cities. CVBs (sometimes known as convention and visitor authorities) are a centralized entity designed to represent the city's hospitality industries. Usually, CVBs are funded by local lodging or room taxes (see Chapter 9); they may also receive some government funding and some membership dues. Because the vast amount of funding comes from lodging taxes, hotels are viewed as paying "customers" of the CVB and the CVB is, in essence, working for the betterment of the hospitality industry.

The CVB represents the city in numerous group rooms bids each year (see Exhibit 5–15). Many of these bids are made directly to the ASAE or a regional counterpart of the same. Hotel sales managers from some of the larger properties (or key properties bidding on a particular piece of business) often accompany CVB representatives on national sales trips.

Expanded Services.   In recent years, CVBs have begun vertically integrating more and more group services. Such areas as transportation services (moving delegates

SCHEDULED CONVENTIONS	Hotel	Date	Attendance
LV Merchandise/Close-Out Show	Hilton	June 2-5	30,000
5th Regimental Combat Team	Orleans	June 2-7	1,000
International Air Transport Assn.	Mandalay Bay	June 2-5	1,000
Wound Ostomy/Continence Nurses	Paris	June 2-6	3,000
American Institute of CPAs	Bellagio	June 2-5	400
New Mexico Bankers Assn.	Aladdin	June 2-5	150
Assn. of State Boards of Accountancy	Flamingo	June 2-4	150
Mechanical Contractors of America	Rio	June 3-7	600
Marine Aftermarket Accessories Expo	Hilton	June 3-6	1,000
Nat'l Military Retirees Golf Classic	Plaza	June 3-7	200
American Institute of CPAs	NY-NY	June 3-4	100
Aspen Systems Corp.	Harrah's	June 3-4	100
U.S. Department of Justice	Monte Carlo	June 3-4	60
Educational Services Institute	Monte Carlo	June 3-4	30

Exhibit 5–15   A glimpse at this convention calendar (we started randomly with June 2) gives a sense of the wide variety of associations and affiliations that meet. Note the numbers of delegates and headquarters hotels listed. *Courtesy of the Las Vegas Convention and Visitors Authority, Las Vegas, Nevada.*

to and from the airport and daily to and from the convention center), on-site registration assistance (temporary staffing of booths), database marketing (identifying who attended and from where they came), telemarketing (swaying potential delegates to attend the convention), promotion assistance (developing videos and print materials), and even special event or off-site banquet planning (managing extracurricular activities outside the convention center) are now being offered by some CVBs.

Meeting planners are generally pleased with the trend toward expanded bureau services. After all, any value-added service included with the price of convention space will ultimately make for a better convention and might even save the association money. But at what cost? Just as meeting planners are happy about the trend toward vertical integration of CVBs, independent meeting suppliers and Destination Management Companies (DMCs) are less pleased. They argue that CVBs are stepping outside their defined roles as convention and visitor bureaus. The job of the CVB, according to many meeting supply companies, is to bring business into the city. Once the CVB secures the business, independent meeting suppliers should be allowed to handle the details from there.

Certainly the CVBs' expanded role encroaches upon the independent meeting suppliers' hard-earned turf. When the CVB offers transportation services, that affects the ground-handling companies. When the CVB offers on-site registration assistance, that affects the temporary employment agencies. Others who may be affected by these expanded services include independent research and marketing consultants, video production and media print services, caterers, regional tour operators, and DMCs.

The CVBs understand the problem but often opt for the greater good to the greatest number of persons. You see, if a convention threatens to be lost to a competing city because that city is including additional services, like it or not the CVB will have to match the bid. The alternative is to let the convention, and all its associated community revenues (see Exhibit 5–10), slip away. With conventions of 10,000 delegates representing some $7,000,000 to hotels, restaurants, transportation services, theaters, and shops in a community, CVBs cannot afford to lose business for the sake of a few independent meeting planners.

The Housing Bureau.   An important division or office within the CVB is the housing bureau (or housing authority). When the CVB is successful in bidding and committing citywide rooms to groups too large to be housed by one hotel, the housing bureau becomes involved. The San Francisco CVB's housing bureau, for example, handles well over one quarter million room nights per year. It offers its services once a convention reaches 1,000 delegates in three or more hotels.

Each hotel commits rooms toward the blanket reservation and a citywide commitment is made to the association. Rates remain the prerogative of the individual properties.

Reservation request cards (Exhibit 5–16) are returned to the CVB's housing bureau rather than to the individual hotel. The bureau relays to the hotel the guest's first, second, or third choice, depending on which hotel still has space. The hotel replies to the guest and sends copies of the confirmation to the housing bureau and to the association's headquarters.

Two properties may join forces if the convention is too large for one hotel but does not need a citywide commitment. The property that booked the business becomes the headquarters site and the booking office, with the second hotel (the overflow hotel) honoring the negotiated convention rate. This practice is now considered a violation of the antitrust laws. Joint housing of delegates is permissible, but each property should negotiate its own rates.

▶ *Overflow Hotels.*   Some hotels require an advance deposit from convention delegates. This is especially true of isolated resorts where there is little chance that walk-ins will fill no-show vacancies. It is also true of overflow hotels.

Conventions are often too large to be housed in just one hotel. Therefore, the association finds additional properties to supplement the rooms available at the headquarters hotel. These supplemental properties are commonly referred to as overflow hotels.

Overflow hotels often require an advance deposit sufficient to cover the cost of all nights booked. This is because overflow properties may lose occupancy to the headquarters hotel during the second or third day of the convention. Because of cancellations and no-shows, the headquarters hotel often has vacancies at the outset of the convention. Rooms available at the headquarters hotel are very appealing to delegates housed at overflow properties. After all, for roughly the same rate, they can conveniently stay in the main hotel with all of the exciting hospitality suites and activities it has to offer.

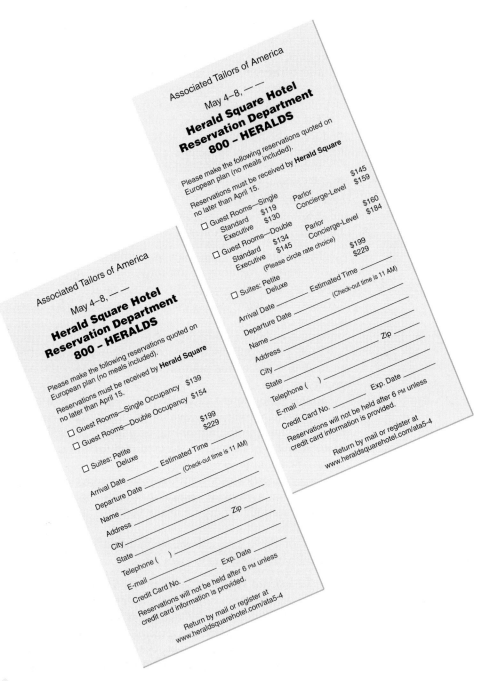

Exhibit 5–16   Here are two sample reservation request cards for individual reservations against the "Associated Tailors of America" (ATA) group room block. Note the card on the left quotes run-of-the-house (flat) rates, while the card on the right offers spread rates—one or the other would be mailed to potential delegates, depending on contracted arrangements made with ATA. In either case, rooms are quoted European plan (no meals). On the opposite side is the hotel's mailing address for insertion into a window envelope before mailing (this ensures privacy/security of guest information). Similar cards would be available for each hotel housing delegates in the citywide convention.

Therefore, overflow properties need to protect themselves against delegates who check out the second day and move to the headquarters hotel. Overflow properties sometimes protect themselves by charging full advance deposits equal to the entire number of nights the delegate initially planned to stay. They may also change their cancellation policy to reflect 48 or 72 hours advance notice.

Negotiating Convention Rates

Convention rates are a unique breed because convention organizers bargain hard to obtain the best rates they can. Yet it is the individual convention delegate who actually reaps the benefit of the discounted rate when he or she pays the room bill. The association executive or meeting planner negotiates with the hotel(s) on behalf of the convention and all its delegates. The sales manager, the director of sales, or even the general manager negotiates on behalf of the hotel.

For most conventioneers, the hotel room is the largest expense item (see Exhibit 5–10). Therefore, the convention attempts to negotiate a favorable rate so as to attract the most delegates possible. Conversely, the hotel needs to keep its profitability and yield management policies in mind as it sets rate parameters with the group.

If the convention is planned during a slow season for the hotel, the sales department is willing to negotiate. The agreed-upon room rate is also dependent on the number (and profitability) of food and beverage functions planned in association with the convention. Other factors for the hotel to consider are the makeup or demographics of the convention, whether delegates have the potential to return as regular guests, and for casino hotels, whether delegates have a propensity to gamble.

Another factor the hotel will probably consider is the *attrition factor* for each particular group. Through contacts with other properties that have housed this group in the past, the sales manager gains an understanding of the attrition or *pickup rate* for this particular group. It makes no sense for the hotel to plan 800 rooms for five nights for the Associated Tailors of America conference (see Exhibit 5–17) if they'll be lucky to actually sell 650 rooms for an average of four nights. Associations have a tendency to exaggerate the number of rooms needed by delegates. Hotels must ascertain the attrition factor or pickup rate before committing to a specific room rate.

➤**Attrition.**   The group's attrition factor and the group's pickup rate are actually reciprocals of each other. They both provide the sales department with a measurement of the number of rooms actually reserved, in comparison to the number initially set aside in the reservation room block. They just derive this measurement in slightly different ways.

The pickup rate looks at the actual number of rooms sold to convention delegates divided by the number of rooms originally blocked. For an example, let's look back to the Associated Tailors' convention. Let's assume that the blanket reservation blocked 800 rooms for five nights—that's 4,000 room-nights. However, at the close of the convention, the hotel discovered it sold only 650 rooms for an average of four nights—that's 2,600 room-nights. The pickup rate was just 65.0% (2,600 room-nights sold divided by 4,000 room-nights blocked).

Conversely, the attrition factor looks at the number of rooms that were not sold or not picked up. The attrition factor measures the remaining unsold delegate rooms by the number of rooms originally blocked. Again, let's look to the Associated Tailors' convention. If 2,600 room-nights were actually picked up against a block of 4,000 room-nights, 1,400 room-nights went unsold to convention delegates. These

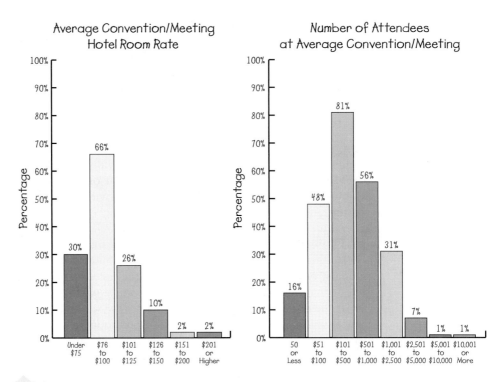

Exhibit 5–17   Here are the results of a survey distributed to convention and visitor bureaus nationwide. The data shows that the average hotel room rates associated with conventions and meetings fall between $76 and $100. The average convention size is between 101 and 500 attendees. Percentages total above 100% because CVB respondents were allowed to select more than one answer. *Source: Successful Meetings databank.*

1,400 room-nights may have ended up being sold to corporate or leisure guests, but only after the agreed-upon closeout date for accepting convention reservations (April 15 in Exhibit 5–16). The attrition factor for this group was 35.0% (1,400 room-nights unsold divided by 4,000 room-nights blocked).

Hotels Get Serious About Attrition.   Hotel attrition policies are more prevalent (and taken more seriously) than ever before. Groups that fail to fill their contracted room block (usually a 90% pick-up rate is considered acceptable—see Exhibit 5–18) are charged attrition fees ranging from a few hundred dollars to hundreds of thousands of dollars! After all, when the hotel offers reduced group room rates, it is discounting them against the group's promise to fill them. If the room nights do not materialize, the hotel's bottom line suffers.

Although attrition policies were rarely enforced a decade ago, today's attrition policies are more serious business. One of the reasons for this increased focus on attrition is the increasing availability of information to meeting planners and association executives. Email marketing and Web-based group registration provides a great deal of information in readily usable form. With online registration, attendees book their own rooms and answer their own housing questions. This releases the meeting planner from considerable administrative duties—time that can be used to ensure higher pick-up rates.

Group Room Block Attrition Calculation

	Day #1	Day#2	Day #3	Day #4	Grand Total
Rooms available for sale (this is a 400-room inventory)	395	398	396	394	
Group room block	165	210	225	195	
Net room block (allows for 10% attrition-factor per contract agreement)	149	189	203	176	
Sold against group block	152	167	177	144	
Other non-group rooms	240	194	205	224	
Total rooms sold	392	361	382	368	
Vacant rooms	3	37	14	26	
Group rooms attrition Liability (smaller of net block less group rooms sold **or** vacant rooms)	0	22	14	26	62
Times contracted (negotiated) profit margin per unsold room	$129	$129	$129	$129	
Total attrition liability	0	$2,838	$1,806	$3,354	$7,998

Exhibit 5–18   Here is an example of a room attrition calculation. This example assumes a 400-room hotel is holding a four-night group room block ranging from 165 rooms to 225 rooms per night at a negotiated $169 flat rate. It also assumes each occupied room has a variable production cost of $40; so $129 is the profit margin from each group room night. Please note the contract provides the group a courtesy 10% attrition factor before charges accrue. Also, the contract allows any group rooms sold by the hotel (to transient business) to reduce the attrition liability (in other words, the group is responsible for the lower of unsold group rooms or total hotel rooms unsold each night).

Automated attendee registration (systems like b-there.com, passkey.com, and 123sign-up.com) can alleviate costly attrition fees in several ways:

➤ Email marketing—You're attending the convention, but are your friends? Please send this email reminder to 10 of your closest associates.

➤ Targeted marketing—Which attendees who registered last year have failed to re-register this year?

➤ Cancellation tracking—Who cancelled in the past 10 days, and are any worrisome trends developing?

➤ Hotel balancing—The Omni is filled to 94% of its block (no attrition fees above 90% pick-up), yet the Radisson sits at just 74%.

➤*Comp Rooms.*   Complimentary (comp or "free") rooms are one part of the total package. Complimentary rooms for use by the association or convention are usually provided at a rate of one comp unit per 50 sold. The formula applies to tour groups as well.

Many hotels are beginning to take a hard look at how comps are earned and used. Attrition factors, no-shows, and cancellations are no longer counted in the computation. Credit is given only for the number of rooms actually sold; understays do not contribute to the count.

The use of comps is also being restricted. Comps are meant to be used by convention executives and staff during the dates of the convention and possibly several days immediately preceding or following the event. Comps are not designed for use months later as a personal vacation for the convention executive!

➤*Rate Quotes.*   Rates are quoted as flat or spread (see Exhibit 5–16). Under the *flat rate*, sometimes called *single rate*, all guests pay the same convention rate, which is usually less than the average rack rate. Except for suites, rooms are assigned on a best-available basis, called *run-of-the-house*. Some pay more for the room than its normal price, and others pay less. Run-of-the-house implies an equal distribution of room assignments. If half the rooms have an ocean view and half do not, the convention group should get a 50–50 split with a run-of-the-house rate. One Hawaiian hotel advertises "run-of-the-ocean" rates. A fair distribution includes an equitable share of standard, medium, and deluxe accommodations.

A *spread rate*, sometimes called a *sliding rate*, uses the standard rack rate distribution already in place. The level is reduced several dollars below the rack rates. Assignments are made over the entire rate spread according to individual preference and a willingness to pay. The range of wealth and interest among the attendees makes spread rates more attractive to larger groups.

➤*Selling Against the Room Block.*   As individual room requests arrive at the hotel, they are booked against the group room block. The hotel and the association reexamine the room commitment several times in the weeks leading up to the convention. Reservations received after the closeout date, 20 to 30 days before the convention starts, are accepted only if space remains—on an *availability basis only*.

Once the names and addresses are prepared, the hotel may be responsible for sending a confirmation back to each delegate. This is where the cumbersome nature of rooming lists is most apparent. The housing bureau (or meeting planner) rooming list is usually delivered to each hotel on paper, requiring the hotel to hand-enter the data into its PMS system. That's where a lot of spelling and related errors occur.

New advancements on the market take advantage of the translation capabilities of switch technology (see Chapter 4) to download the information directly from the housing bureaus to each hotel, no matter which PMS system they may be using. One of the leaders in this new technology is THISCO's UltraRes system.

➤*Unidentified Delegates.* Some delegates slip through the carefully planned system and appear to the hotel as regular guests unaffiliated with the convention. This is often accidental, but some guests deliberately trick the hotel to gain rate or room advantages (see earlier section entitled "The Threat from Discount Travel Sites").

One of two things may happen with these unidentified conventioneers: (1) the reservation might be denied (the convention block is open, but general reservations are closed), and the guest goes elsewhere; or (2) the reservation might be accepted as a nonconvention guest (both the convention room block and the nonconvention categories are open). This second option leaves the hotel with duplicate space.

The situation takes a different twist when the conventioneer accepts space outside the blanket count because all the convention spots have been filled. Once housed, this guest argues to get the special, reduced, convention rate. Too many situations like that, and the carefully balanced yield management system goes awry.

➤*IT Packages.* The inclusive tour (IT) package (Chapter 2) is the hotel's move into the lucrative group market. The hotel combines housing, food, and entertainment but no transportation to offer an appealing multiple-night stay at greatly reduced rates. The IT package affects group bookings, but it is not a type of group business.

IT packages can and do compete with convention reservations. For large conventions, the yield management committee closes the remaining rooms to all but high-priced rates. When relatively few rooms of the hotel are assigned to the convention, all rate classes remain available, including the package, priced at less, and offering more, than the convention rate. Keen convention shoppers book the IT package.

Handling Tour Group Reservations

The workload of the reservations department is affected relatively little by the demands of the tour group. Both the initial sale and its continuing follow-up rest with the hotel's marketing and sales department. That department may have a position called the *tour and travel desk*.

Yield management coordination is the major role for reservations during the time before the group arrives. Hotels doing a large tour and travel business maintain four-month horizons. Sell-and-report parameters are adjusted as forecasted demand equals, exceeds, or falls short of historical expectations.

Tour groups are almost always given shares-with rooms, since a premium is charged for single occupancy. The hotel gets a rooming list that shows each pairing. The entire block of rooms is preassigned. If the tour company brings in back-to-back groups, the very same rooms may be used again and again. Keeping the block together in the same floor or wing expedites baggage handling and reduces noise and congestion elsewhere.

Special group arrival sections, even special lobby entrances, reduce the congestion as the group arrives or departs. Transportation is by bus, even if only to the airport. These transfer costs are part of the fee and are arranged by the tour company. Bell fees for luggage-in and luggage-out are also included, levied by the hotel over and above the room charge.

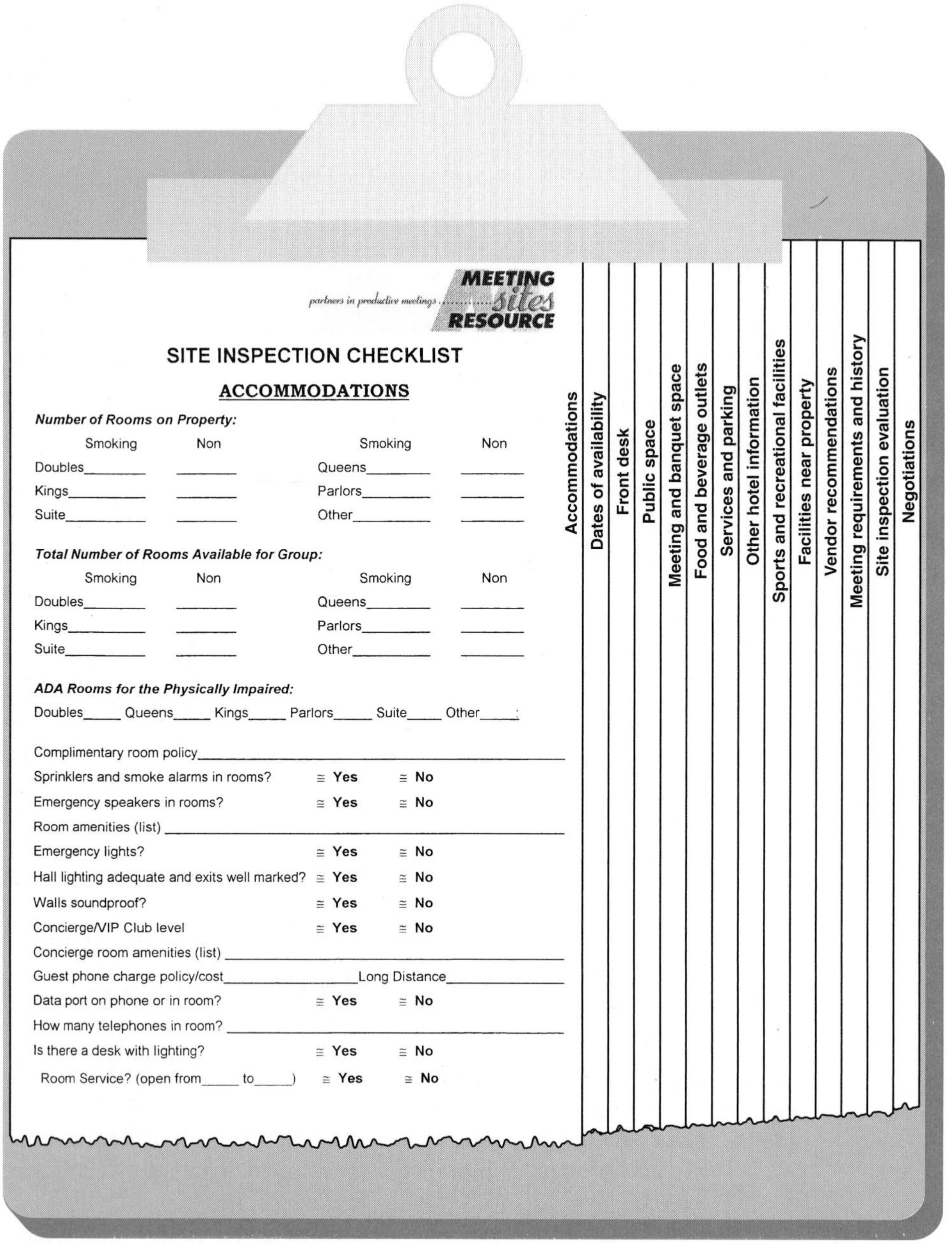

MEETING sites RESOURCE
partners in productive meetings

SITE INSPECTION CHECKLIST

ACCOMMODATIONS

Number of Rooms on Property:

	Smoking	Non		Smoking	Non
Doubles	______	______	Queens	______	______
Kings	______	______	Parlors	______	______
Suite	______	______	Other	______	______

Total Number of Rooms Available for Group:

	Smoking	Non		Smoking	Non
Doubles	______	______	Queens	______	______
Kings	______	______	Parlors	______	______
Suite	______	______	Other	______	______

ADA Rooms for the Physically Impaired:

Doubles_____ Queens_____ Kings_____ Parlors_____ Suite_____ Other_____:

Complimentary room policy______________________________

Sprinklers and smoke alarms in rooms? ≅ **Yes** ≅ **No**

Emergency speakers in rooms? ≅ **Yes** ≅ **No**

Room amenities (list) ______________________________

Emergency lights? ≅ **Yes** ≅ **No**

Hall lighting adequate and exits well marked? ≅ **Yes** ≅ **No**

Walls soundproof? ≅ **Yes** ≅ **No**

Concierge/VIP Club level ≅ **Yes** ≅ **No**

Concierge room amenities (list) ______________________________

Guest phone charge policy/cost_______________Long Distance_______________

Data port on phone or in room? ≅ **Yes** ≅ **No**

How many telephones in room? ______________________________

Is there a desk with lighting? ≅ **Yes** ≅ **No**

Room Service? (open from_____ to_____) ≅ **Yes** ≅ **No**

Accommodations | **Dates of availability** | **Front desk** | **Public space** | **Meeting and banquet space** | **Food and beverage outlets** | **Services and parking** | **Other hotel information** | **Sports and recreational facilities** | **Facilities near property** | **Vendor recommendations** | **Meeting requirements and history** | **Site inspection evaluation** | **Negotiations**

Exhibit 5–19 Association executives and professional meeting planners evaluate numerous hotels before selecting the right property for their group needs. Each hotel is evaluated for price, availability, size, ability to meet the group's unique needs, and so on. Here is a sample page (Accommodations) from a site-inspection checklist. This particular checklist has 14 pages covering a variety of categories and observations. *Courtesy of Jennifer Brown, CMP; Strategic Site Specialist, Meeting Sites Resource, Newport Beach, California.*

RESOURCES AND CHALLENGES
Resources

➤ SUMMARY

Because reservations are in a sense contractual agreements, the hotel or corporate reservationist must be careful to document all pertinent information. Some reservation information, such as the date of arrival, number of persons and type of room, and guest's name and rate, is essential to the hotel. Other information, such as estimated time of arrival, special requests, and discounts, is less important to the reservation and may therefore only be collected in certain cases or by request of the guest.

Once the reservation has been agreed upon between the customer and the hotel or the central reservations office, its journey begins. In some cases the journey is short, as with those reservations made a few hours or days before arrival, and other times it is a long journey, as with reservations made many months—even years—in advance.

Group business means different things to different hotels, but almost all properties generate some percentage of their revenue through group contracts. Group business is especially beneficial because it is a sizable market (close to $100 billion in annual sales), there are certain efficiencies (economies of scale) associated with group arrivals and departures, and group delegates generally spend more than individual guests.

Group room blocks may be negotiated years in advance and managed down to the day of arrival. Careful management of group blocks assures a high pick-up rate and little or no attrition charges accruing to the meeting planner or association executive. However, the prevalence of discount Web sites has made this task substantially more difficult.

➤ WEB SITES

Online registration and convention delegate rooming services are growing in popularity. They provide meeting planners and association executives important tools for ensuring high convention occupancy rates. Not only can attendees register for the convention, sleeping rooms, and other services online, but meeting planners can track such registrations and manipulate a variety of data designed to assist with maximizing head counts (and minimizing attrition).

The following Web sites are all vendors of registration and housing software solutions. What

tools and information do these services provide the meeting planner that would be substantially more difficult to develop without online registration?

- ➤ http://www.event411.com
- ➤ http://www.eventbookings.com
- ➤ http://www.eventregistration.com
- ➤ http://www.register123.com
- ➤ http://www.seeuthere.com

➤ INTERESTING TIDBITS

- ➤ According to a recent survey, 64% of travelers are verbally informed of the hotel's cancellation policy while booking the reservation. Additionally, 44% of hotels go a step further and actually mail a written confirmation. *Source: American Express Travel Trends Monitor.*

- ➤ Video conferencing and Web conferencing have been growing in popularity as travel alternatives. Indeed, they gained substantial popularity in the year immediately following the September 11, 2001, terrorist attacks in New York City. Video (and Web) conferences save companies on travel, per diem, ground transportation, and lodging costs by keeping participants at home or nearby in conference-enabled facilities. But a recent survey found an added bonus: Video and Web conferencing usually do not utilize the costly services of meeting planners. Instead of being professionally arranged, it appears such conferences are generally handled internally by the conference users (attendees), thereby creating a substantial cost savings.

Specifically, 69% of companies never use a meeting planner to assist with the hosting of video and Web conferences. Another 20% of companies "rarely" use a meeting planner with video and Web conferences. Some 5% range from "sometimes" to "often" in their use of meeting planners, and the remaining 5% of companies "always" use a meeting planner with video and Web conferences. *Source: Business Travel News.*

➤ READING REFERENCES

1. "The Most Contentious Clause: Why Planners, Hoteliers, and Their Respective Lawyers Continue to Battle Over How to Calculate Attrition." Loren Edelstein and Carla Benini. *Meetings & Conventions*, May 2001, pp. 46–52.

2. "When It's Smart to Turn Away Business." Bonnie Knutson, Martin Malk, and Raymond Schmidgall. *Cornell Hotel and Restaurant Administration Quarterly*, December 1995, pp. 56–61.

Challenges

➤ TRUE/FALSE QUIZ

Questions that are partially false should be marked false (F).

___ 1. Some reservation information is mandatory or essential to the reservation. The guest's date of arrival is an example of essential reservation data. Other information is nonessential and only collected when the reservationist has time to complete all computer screen fields. The guest's date of departure and number of nights required are examples of nonessential reservation data.

___ 2. As part of the cancellation process for a guaranteed reservation, the reservationist should provide the caller a cancellation number (sometimes a similar number to the confirmation number). In this way, the caller can keep a record of the cancellation. Later, should a no-show charge accidentally be made, the caller will have proof of the cancellation.

___ 3. With centralized guest history databases, a chain hotel in New York City can actually retrieve personal information (address, room type and rate, number of nights stayed, etc.) for a guest who last stayed at one of the chain's hotels in Los Angeles.

___ 4. Meeting planners or association executives who book group business (conventions, conferences, meetings, trade shows, etc.) are no longer responsible for room attrition (substantially fewer hotel room-nights sold than were originally blocked for the group) due to the government's Room Attrition Act of 1999.

___ 5. Group rooms are generally quoted as either flat rates (run-of-house) or spread rates. A hotel that offers delegates a choice—the $129 standard is available at the group rate of $99, the $169 deluxe is available at the group rate of $129, and the $199 executive parlor is available at the group rate of $149—is quoting flat rates (run-of-house).

➤ PROBLEMS

1. Many hotels are apprehensive about charging for corporate-guaranteed reservations if a business traveler fails to arrive. Even though a room was held and revenue was lost, the hotel is afraid to charge the no-show back to the corporation for fear of retaliation, alienation, and loss of future business.

    Develop a series of strict—but fair—reservations policies that protect the hotel's interests while minimizing conflicts with corporate accounts. In what instances would you charge the corporate no-show? When would you not charge?

2. The use of computerized reservations is far more efficient than the use of manual, handwritten reservations. Compare the manual reservations approach to the automated collection of guest reservation information. List as many benefits (efficiencies) created by automated reservations systems as you can.

3. As a follow-up to Problem 2, are there any disadvantages associated with automated reservations systems? Why are many reservations managers retraining agents to be more patient, friendly, and helpful? Does this retraining have anything to do with the computer age in which we live?

4. Guests generally prefer the choice associated with spread rates. Hotels find it easier to manage rooms inventory when they use flat rates. Which would you use as a hotel manager? Explain your response in detail.

5. As a prominent hotelier, you have been asked by the CVB to appear before the county commissioners during a CVB budget-review session. The commission is angry that the local CVB spends public funds to maintain a convention housing bureau and that those services are provided without a fee. Do the necessary research to provide hard facts to support your testimony in favor of the CVB.

6. The reservation of an unidentified convention delegate is treated like a corporate or leisure guest reservation. How might this lack of identifying the guest as a conventioneer affect the hotel? Could it benefit the guest? Could it hurt the guest? How will it factor into the meeting planner's attrition/pick-up rates?

➤ ANSWERS TO TRUE/FALSE QUIZ

1. False. All examples in this question are essential to the reservation. It would be impossible to effectively sell a hotel if we only knew arrival dates and never knew the number of nights intended for the reservation.

2. True. Cancellations for guaranteed reservations should always be provided a distinct cancellation number as proof the cancellation was actually made.

3. True, In fact, the New York chain hotel could look at the guest's most recent (Los Angeles) stay history and ask him if he wanted the same wake-up call (e.g., 6:30 AM) and the same breakfast (e.g., orange juice, pot of black coffee, and a dry bagel)!

4. False. Room attrition (usually calculated as less than 90% of the rooms initially blocked for the group actually having sold) has become a more critical issue for meeting planners and association executives in recent years. Hotels have become quite serious about charging groups for low occupancy. By the way, there is no such thing as the Room Attrition Act of 1999.

5. False. In fact, this hotel is quoting spread rates. If all rooms (standard, deluxe, and executive parlor) were available for a flat rate of, say, $129, then the hotel would be quoting flat rates (run-of-house). But a range of rates, as shown in the question, means the hotel quoted spread rates.

Forecasting Availability and Overbooking

Outline

In this three-chapter unit on reservations, the first chapter (Chapter 4) took us through the global distribution system, from the outset of the reservation, through its seamless channels, right into the hotel's property management system. We looked at the rapid explosion of online reservations and understood their role in yield management decisions designed to optimally fill the hotel. In Chapter 5, we considered the economics of selling blocks of group rooms (often at discounted rates) in relationship to the overall hotel rooms mix. We also examined the content of the reservation itself—what data is critical to the completion of the reservation (and what data is less essential).

But all these components of the reservations formula are dependent on one thing: an available room on the receiving end of the equation. After all, no matter how sophisticated the system that puts the guest in touch with the hotel, if no rooms are available, no reservation can be taken (or can it?). To complete our overall picture of the reservations landscape, Chapter 6 develops two distinct methods for counting and forecasting rooms available for sale.

Knowing the exact number of rooms available for sale, however, does not always answer the question, Should the hotel continue accepting reservations? There are plenty of circumstances in which a fully committed hotel continues accepting reservations when no rooms remain available for sale. In such cases, overbooking the hotel is actually less risky than it sounds. Indeed, it is often more conservative to overbook the hotel than to simply sell rooms available and wind up with numerous vacancies due to cancellations and no-shows on the day of arrival. To complete the reservations picture, Chapter 6 also addresses this overbooking dilemma.

➤ FORECASTING AVAILABLE ROOMS

The concept behind rooms inventory is simple enough. There is a one-to-one match between rooms in the hotel and rooms committed to either incoming reservations or stayover rooms. Each reservation reduces the available inventory until there are an equal number of reservations (and stayover rooms) matched with hotel rooms. At that point, the hotel is sold out.

As with most things in life, however, the simplicity of the system becomes increasingly complicated as the unique vagaries of customer contact impact the room count. Some guests stay an extra day or two in spite of their original intention to check out. Others depart a day or two earlier than anticipated due to circumstances beyond their control. Include in this growing list a few guests who cancel their reservations hours before arrival (or worse yet, guests who fail to even cancel their reservations and simply do not show up that day). Throw in another guest who arrives a day or two early and yet still expects to find room at your hotel (and it is in your best interest to accommodate early arrivals lest they cancel their future dates and stay elsewhere). Add to these circumstances the chance for human error—"Oh, I thought you said November seventeenth, not September seventeenth"—and the situation is further complicated.

The Simple, Unadjusted Room Count

It makes sense to look first at a simple room-count forecast, before incorporating the numerous complications that can affect the count. A simple room count is also called an *unadjusted* room count, because various adjustments (such as overstays, understays, cancellations, etc.) have not yet been introduced. They will be introduced later in the chapter.

In this simple form, the unadjusted room count attempts to compare the rooms available in the hotel against anticipated stayovers and expected reservation arrivals. If any rooms remain uncommitted (i.e., there are more rooms available than are committed to stayovers and reservations), they are available for sale that day.

▶*Automated Inventory Tracking Systems.* At a moment's notice, the reservations department must be able to determine the number (and types) of rooms available for sale for a given date. With such pressing urgency, reservationists do not have the luxury of subtracting stayovers and expected reservations from rooms available to determine the room count. Therefore, they need to visualize the room count in some manner.

Automated property management systems offer various status reports under the reservations module. Although status reports (see Chapter 13) are determined in part by the particular property management system, most are quite similar. Some of the standard status reports found in the reservations module include

- ▶ A 7-, 10-, or 14-day room availability report provides a window of time for which each room type is listed and the number of remaining rooms available for sale are shown by date (see Exhibit 6–6).

- ▶ A current or one-day inventory report details all rooms in the hotel and their particular status. An example of such a report is shown in Exhibit 6–1.

Business: MAY 25		1-Day Room Inventory					MAY 25 17:15:49		
				Mon MAY 25--					
Room Type	Room Cnts	Rooms Offmkt	Rooms Sold	Rooms Avail	Rates 1per	Rates 2per	Close Level	Host Status	CTA MLOS
DDSU	15	1	5	9	85.00	85.00	4	Open	
DDSN	47	13	34	0	85.00	85.00	1	Closed	
KSU	10	0	5	5	75.00	75.00	3	Open	
KSUN	33	10	19	4	75.00	75.00	3	Open	
KHCN	3	0	1	2	75.00	75.00	2	Open	
DDHN	1	0	0	1	85.00	85.00	1	Open	
KEX	1	0	0	1	85.00	85.00	1	Open	
KEXN	5	2	1	2	85.00	85.00	2	Open	
D1HN	2	0	1	1	75.00	75.00	1	Open	
Totals:	117	26	66	25	Current occupancy 72.5%				
Action: 1 = Forward 1 Day 2 = Back 1 Day									

Exhibit 6–1   An example of a one-day rooms inventory screen. This is an actual Multi-Systems, Incorporated Property Manager screen (PM Version 8.11) from a 117-room all-suite hotel. Notice that 26 rooms are off-market (out of inventory due to an in-house renovation project), 66 rooms are sold (either to incoming reservations or stayovers), and 25 rooms are available for sale. For information on CTA (closed to arrival) and MLOS (minimum length of stay), see Chapter 4. The various room types are listed in the first column from DDSU through D1HN. DD is two double beds, K is one king bed, S or SU indicates suite, EX stands for executive room-type, N means nonsmoking (in the absence of N, the room is smoking), and H or HC means handicapped accessible. *Courtesy of AmeriSuites Incorporated, Patterson, New Jersey and Multi-Systems, Inc., Phoenix, Arizona.*

➤ A reservations forecast report projects revenues and occupancies for each of several days into the future. Such a report usually displays the room and house count (number of guests in house) as well as projects the number of stayovers for each day. As the report reads further and further into the future (three to five days from today), the forecast becomes less and less accurate because it is based on each day's assumed check-outs and stayovers.

➤ A general manager's daily report looks at the current day. Group rooms picked up, guaranteed and nonguaranteed reservations, anticipated stayovers, out-of-order and out-of-inventory rooms, walk-ins, early check-outs, and more are all displayed in such a report.

➤ An arrivals list displays information about each reservation scheduled for that day's arrival. Each anticipated guest is listed alphabetically and can also be reviewed by affiliation: group reservations, travel-agent bookings, late arrivals, and so on (see Chapter 5, Exhibit 5–6).

More information may be included depending on the size of the hotel and the sophistication of the property management system.

➤*Components of the Simple Room Count.* Utilizing the information available in the property management system (see Exhibit 6–1), the first actual room count is scrutinized several days prior to the actual date of arrival. By taking a more precise look at the next several days, the reservations department prepares itself for problems that may lie ahead. In fact, several room counts may be taken throughout the actual day of arrival. Common times to readjust the day's room count are before arrivals begin (around 6 AM), just after the check-out hour (around 11 AM for many properties), and immediately before and after 6 PM for hotels that allow nonguaranteed (6 PM) reservations.

A simple room count taken during these times provides management with a true understanding of the rooms inventory status for the day. If the hotel has rooms available for sale (a plus count), it is important to know the number and types of these rooms. Armed with this information, the reservations department and the front desk can better sell the remaining rooms in the hotel. Maximum rates are charged against the last few rooms available (a yield management approach).

The hotel also needs to know when there are no rooms remaining (an even or zero count), and it is especially important to be forewarned when the hotel finds itself in an overbooking situation (a minus count)—when there are more reservations and stayovers than there are rooms available. With advance knowledge, the hotel can arrange supplementary accommodations at other hotels, alert its front-office staff to handle the sensitive situation, and encourage the reservations department to accept cancellations if and when they occur.

Even in a computerized system, where the room count is available at a moment's notice, managers still need to understand the components that form the total rooms available count. Specifically, managers wish to know the number of rooms occupied last night, rooms due to check out, and reservations due to arrive.

Committed Rooms.   The process works on commitments. The hotel is committed to guests staying over from last night and to guests due to arrive today. If the total of these (stayovers plus reservations) is less than the total number of rooms in the hotel, there is a plus count. If the hotel has more commitments than rooms available for sale, there is a minus count (overbooked).

The concept of overbooking (having a minus count) is discussed in detail later in the chapter. However, it is important to understand that it is not necessarily a mistake to overbook the hotel. Overbooking is often a strategic decision made by the reservations manager in concert with the front-office manager, the sales manager, and the general manager. The idea behind overbooking hotel rooms is much the same as the reason that airlines overbook flights. The airlines (and hotels) know that some percentage of their customers will not arrive (no-show) and others will likely cancel. Therefore, the hotel reservations department plays a guessing game by projecting a series of adjustments onto the simple room count. The goal is to overbook the hotel just enough that the projected adjustments develop into a fully occupied hotel on the day of arrival. Too conservative a projection, and the hotel has unsold rooms; too aggressive a projection, and the hotel is forced to walk overbooked guests.

Refer to Exhibits 6–2 and 6–3. Exhibit 6–2 demonstrates a simple, unadjusted room count. The simple count looks at nothing more than rooms available, rooms committed to stayovers, and rooms committed to incoming reservations. These same figures are then reused in Exhibit 6–3. Exhibit 6–3, however, demonstrates an adjusted count. By including adjustments for overstays and understays, as well as for cancellations, no-shows, and early arrivals, the numbers appear substantially different.

Given:

A 1,000-room hotel had a total of 950 rooms occupied last night. Of those 950 rooms, 300 are due to check out today. In addition, there are 325 reservations for today. There are 5 rooms out of order (OOO).

Required:

Develop a simple, unadjusted room count utilizing the given information above

Solution:

Rooms available in hotel		1,000
Occupied last night	950	
Due to check out today	300	
Equals number of stayovers		650
+ Today's reservations		325
Total rooms committed for today		975
Equals rooms available for sale		25 (with 5 OOO)

Occupancy percentage is 975 ÷ 1,000 or 97.5%.

Exhibit 6–2   A simple, unadjusted room count. This is the first of two sample problems utilizing the same basic information (also see Exhibit 6–3).

By subtracting committed rooms (650 stayovers and 325 incoming reservations) from rooms available (1,000 rooms are available despite that 5 rooms are out of order), the reservations manager knows there are 25 rooms available for sale today (1,000 minus 650 minus 325 equals 25).

Compare these results (25 rooms) with the findings from Exhibit 6–3. Although the same basic information was used for Exhibit 6–3, by incorporating a number of adjustments and projections, the end result is a substantially different room count.

Given:

A 1,000-room hotel had a total of 950 rooms occupied last night. Of those 950 rooms, 300 are due to check out today. In addition, there are 325 reservations for today. There are 5 rooms out of order (OOO). Note: This is the same information given in Exhibit 6–2.

Historical Adjustments

The hotel has developed the following historical adjustment statistics: understays, 6%; overstays, 2%; cancellations, 2%; no-shows, 5%; and early arrivals, 1%.

Required

Develop an adjusted room count utilizing the given information and historical adjustments above.

Solution

Rooms available in hotel			1,000
Occupied last night		950	
Due to check out today	300		
Understays (6%)	+ 18		
Overstays (2%)	− 6		
Equals adjusted number of rooms to check out today	312 ⟶	312	
Equals adjusted number of stayovers		638 ⟶	− 638
Today's reservations	325		
Cancellations (2%)	− 7		
No-shows (5%)	− 16		
Early arrivals (1%)	+ 3		
Equals today's adjusted reservations	305 ⟶		− 305
Adjusted total of rooms committed for sale			− 943
Adjusted number of rooms available for sale			+ 57 (with 5 OOO)

Anticipated occupancy percentage is 943 ÷ 1,000 or 94.3%.

Exhibit 6–3   An adjusted room count. This is the second of two sample problems utilizing the same basic information (see Exhibit 6–2).

Using the same figures provided in Exhibit 6–2, this room-count calculation incorporates a series of adjustments into the process. Stayover rooms, for example, are adjusted by understays (6% of rooms due to check out today) and overstays (2% of rooms due to check out today). Incoming reservations are adjusted by cancellations (2% of today's reservations), no-shows (5% of today's reservations), and early arrivals (1% of today's reservations).

The net result (57 rooms available for sale) is far different from the 25 rooms found in Exhibit 6–2.

Adjusted Room Count

Mathematics carries an aura of exactness that deceives any reservations department that relies on unadjusted figures. Most of the figures must be modified on the basis of experience. The reservations department collects data over the years, and this information establishes the basis for more precise projections. But even the adjustments change from day to day depending on the day of the week and the week of the year. Percentages change with the weather, with the type of group registered in the house, and even with the news (think September 11). Gathering the data is the first step and interpreting it is the second.

Each element in the projection can be refined over and over by using additional data or varying interpretations. Recomputing the count with these adjustments can make a substantial change in room availability (compare Exhibits 6–2 and 6–3).

►*Computing Rooms Available.* The actual number of rooms available in the hotel (1,000 rooms for the continuing example shown in Exhibits 6–2 *and* 6–3) can change from day to day. For various reasons, rooms that were available for occupancy one day may be closed to occupancy on another day. If the reason were unexpected, the removal of such rooms from inventory can have a detrimental effect on the hotel's ability to accommodate reservations.

When rooms are removed from availability, they are designated as being in one of two distinct categories: out of order or out of inventory. The difference between these classifications is of critical importance to management. The difference between out-of-order and out-of-inventory rooms impacts more than the number of rooms available for sale. One of these two categories affects the occupancy calculation (the other does not); one may play a role in management bonuses (the other does not); and for publicly traded hotel companies, one can even influence stock market prices (the other does not). The difference between out-of-order and out-of-inventory (sometimes called offline) rooms is critical.

Out-of-Order Rooms. A room placed out of order is generally repairable within a relatively short time. A minor problem such as poor TV reception, a clogged toilet, a malfunctioning minibar refrigerator, or a noisy air conditioner will usually classify a room as out of order (OOO). Out-of-order rooms pose a special problem to management because in sold-out situations they must be repaired and returned to the market quickly. In periods of low occupancy, management may wait several days before returning such rooms to inventory.

Out-of-order rooms are, by nature, minimally inoperative—the problem that placed the room out of order is slight. As a result, in some situations, out-of-order rooms may actually be sold to the public: If the hotel is facing sold-out status and the few remaining rooms are out of order, management may choose to sell these rooms "as is" for a reasonable discount. A broken TV set may warrant a $10 discount; an inoperative air conditioner may warrant a $30 discount. No out-of-order room would ever be sold if it posed a hazard to the guest.

Because out-of-order rooms can be readily repaired and returned to market, they are included in the total figure for rooms available for sale. In calculating room count statistics, out-of-order rooms are treated as if there were nothing wrong with them—they are included with marketable rooms. Similarly, when calculating occupancy percentages, out-of-order rooms are left in the denominator as if there were nothing wrong with them.

In the continuing example, note that five rooms are out of order. Because out-of-order rooms are counted in inventory, there are still 1,000 rooms available for sale in the hotel. The occupancy of 97.5% (see Exhibit 6–2) has demonstrated no change in the 1,000-room denominator.

Out-of-Inventory Rooms. Out-of-inventory rooms cannot be sold "as is." Out-of-inventory rooms have significant problems that cannot be repaired quickly. Examples of major out-of-inventory (OOI) situations might include a flood that destroyed all carpet and floorboards in a room, a fire that has blackened the walls and left a strong odor, a major renovation that leaves half of the wallpaper removed as well as no carpet or furniture, and a murder investigation in which the police have ordered the room sealed until further notice.

By their very nature, out-of-inventory rooms are not marketable. The problem that placed them out of inventory is significant enough to remove the room from marketability until it has been repaired. These rooms, therefore, are not included in the total figure for rooms available for sale. In calculating room count statistics, out-of-inventory rooms are removed from the total of rooms available for sale. Similarly, when calculating occupancy percentages, out-of-inventory rooms are subtracted from the denominator.

In the continuing example, remember there are five rooms out of order. To illustrate the points addressed above, let's see what happens if those five rooms were actually out of inventory. Remember, out-of-inventory rooms must be removed from the available rooms inventory. As a result, there will now be only 995 rooms available for sale in the hotel (1,000 rooms less 5 out of inventory). The room availability total of +25 will also change. There will now be only +20 rooms available for sale [995 rooms less (650 stayovers plus 325 reservations)]. Out-of-inventory rooms have an impact on occupancy percent as well. The rooms-sold numerator (975) remains the same, but the rooms-available-for-sale denominator would change to 995. The occupancy calculation (975 divided by 995) yields 98.0%. This is a different result from that in Exhibit 6–2, which showed 97.5%.

The distinction between out-of-order and out-of-inventory rooms is an important concept. To further illustrate the point, Exhibit 6–4 provides two sample problems. Each problem is shown in two parts (a and b). The first part of each problem shows the calculation assuming the rooms were simply out of order. The second part shows a different calculation assuming the rooms were out of inventory.

Hotel management does not take out-of-inventory rooms lightly. For one thing, such rooms artificially raise the occupancy statistic (look at Exhibit 6–4; in both cases—in all cases—out-of-inventory rooms reduce the denominator and cause a higher occupancy than would have resulted if the rooms were simply out of order). An artificially augmented occupancy statistic can have substantial consequences; management bonuses and even stock market prices are often based in part on occupancy statistics. General managers should be vigilant that out-of-inventory rooms are declared as such only when the situation truly warrants their being out of inventory.

▶ *Computing Rooms Occupied Last Night.*   Rooms occupied last night is a precise number derived during the hotel's night audit function. This figure is simply the number of rooms physically occupied on any particular night. Relatively straightforward, yes, but certain adjustments or unique situations need to be considered in order that this be the most accurate figure possible.

Certain situations may require slight adjustments to the figure in the wee hours of the night audit. One example of such an adjustment is a very late arrival (usually after midnight). If the late guest is a walk-in customer (no pre-existing reservation), the auditor adds one more room to the already computed rooms-occupied-last-night figure. If the late guest has an existing reservation, the auditor similarly adjusts the rooms-occupied figure but also needs to credit the new guest's folio with the charge likely made hours earlier when it was assumed the guest would be a no-show (see discussion on no-show guests later in this chapter).

Other considerations necessary for an accurate rooms-occupied count depend on unique hotel policies. For example, some hotels choose not to list comp (complimentary) rooms in their occupancy. As such, they are not counting comp rooms in the accounting processes for the preceding night. Therefore, the night auditor needs to remember to add

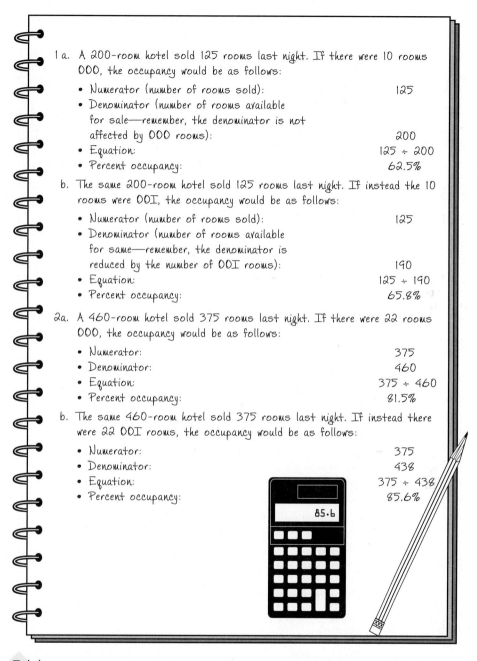

1 a. A 200-room hotel sold 125 rooms last night. If there were 10 rooms OOO, the occupancy would be as follows:

- Numerator (number of rooms sold):   125
- Denominator (number of rooms available for sale—remember, the denominator is not affected by OOO rooms):   200
- Equation: 125 ÷ 200
- Percent occupancy: 62.5%

b. The same 200-room hotel sold 125 rooms last night. If instead the 10 rooms were OOI, the occupancy would be as follows:

- Numerator (number of rooms sold):   125
- Denominator (number of rooms available for same—remember, the denominator is reduced by the number of OOI rooms):   190
- Equation: 125 ÷ 190
- Percent occupancy: 65.8%

2 a. A 460-room hotel sold 375 rooms last night. If there were 22 rooms OOO, the occupancy would be as follows:

- Numerator: 375
- Denominator: 460
- Equation: 375 ÷ 460
- Percent occupancy: 81.5%

b. The same 460-room hotel sold 375 rooms last night. If instead there were 22 OOI rooms, the occupancy would be as follows:

- Numerator: 375
- Denominator: 438
- Equation: 375 ÷ 438
- Percent occupancy: 85.6%

Exhibit 6–4   Out-of-order rooms do not affect inventory (rooms available for sale), while out-of-inventory rooms do. These two examples illustrate the difference this distinction can have on the resulting occupancy percentage. Each example is calculated two ways: First, the occupancy is calculated assuming the rooms were OOO, then the occupancy is recalculated assuming that the rooms were OOI.

all comp rooms to the rooms-occupied count. Similar errors crop up when the computer is programmed to count suites as two-room units even when the suite is not divided. The mistake comes in counting either two rooms as occupied or two rooms as checked out. Additional factors might even include unethical employees who sell rooms for cash and steal the proceeds without documenting the room sales. Such illegitimately sold rooms are usually discovered by housekeeping the following day.

▶*Computing the Number of Stayovers.*   The number of rooms scheduled to check out today is far less precise than the number occupied last night. The number of rooms due to check out is based primarily on the guests' initial plans at the time they were making their reservations. Even when a well-trained front-desk clerk reconfirms the departure date during the check-in process, changes still occur. Corporate guests may complete their business a day or two earlier (or a day or two later) than expected. Leisure guests may decide to sightsee in town a bit longer (or shorter) than originally planned. Emergencies also occur, where guests may need to catch the next flight home, regardless of their original plans.

Although these changes are difficult to project on an individual guest-by-guest basis, they generally form an historical trend over time. Although it is impossible to guess if Mr. Jones in room 2144 will stay an extra night, it is somewhat more certain to say that historically 2% of our scheduled check-outs do not depart (they overstay) after all.

Each property collects historical data with which to project its understays and overstays. This data is usually expressed in terms of a percentage of the rooms due to check out that day. For example, in Exhibit 6–3, the understay percentage is 6% (0.06 times 300 rooms due out equals 18 understays), while the overstay percentage is 2% (0.02 times 300 rooms due out equals 6 overstays). Although these are both fictitious percentages, a real hotel would develop similar statistical projections over time.

Understays.   Some guests leave earlier than the hotel expected; they are known as understays. They are also sometimes referred to as *earlys*. When calculating the number of rooms due to check out, any understays will be added to the projected check outs.

Overstays.   Some guests stay past their scheduled departure date; they are referred to as overstays. They are also sometimes known as *holdovers*. When calculating the number of rooms due to check out, any overstays will be subtracted from the projected check outs.

Occupied last night		950
Due to check out today	300	
Plus understays (6%)	+ 18	
Less overstays (2%)	− 6	
Equals adjusted number due to check out today	312	−312
Equals adjusted number of stayovers		638

By including understays and overstays in the continuing example, the number of rooms due to check out changes substantially. In the simple, unadjusted room count shown in Exhibit 6–2, the number due to check out today was 300. Once understays and overstays are included in the computation, however, that number changes to 312, as shown in the preceding table and Exhibit 6–3. Similarly, the number of stayovers (650) demonstrated in the simple, unadjusted room count of Exhibit 6–2 changes with the inclusion of understays and overstays. In Exhibit 6–2, there are 650 projected stayovers. In the preceding table and Exhibit 6–3, that number changes to 638 projected stayovers.

▶ *Computing Today's Reservations.*   Just as some departing guests change their plans and overstay or understay the scheduled visit, some expected guests do not adhere to their original reservations. Guests often cancel reservations, arrive a day or two earlier than expected, or never arrive at all. Each of these variables is assessed and adjusted according to historical data, to represent a closer approximation of reality.

No-Shows.   Some guests who hold reservations never arrive at the hotel. These guests are referred to as no-shows. No-shows may be caused by a multitude of factors. A change in business or personal plans, inclement weather or closed roads, canceled or stranded flights, illness, or death may be some of the reasons a guest fails to arrive. Indeed, it is also possible that they simply forgot they had made a reservation.

No-shows present the hotel with a unique problem—namely, it is difficult to know when to classify the reservation as a no-show. For nonguaranteed reservations, the industry standard is 6 PM. Nonguaranteed reservations that fail to arrive by 6 PM are considered no-shows, and those rooms are remarketed to walk-in guests.

Guaranteed and advance-deposit reservations are another story. The very nature of these higher-quality guaranteed or advance-deposit reservations suggests that the hotel will hold a room all night long. Therefore, it is literally impossible for a hotel front-desk clerk to determine when a specific guaranteed reservation changes from an expected arrival to a no-show. A front-desk clerk or night auditor can be fairly certain that a reservation that has not arrived by 11 PM, midnight, or 1 AM is a no-show. However, there is always the chance that the guest has been detained and will still arrive in search of the reservation.

Asking for an estimated time of arrival with the reservation is one partial solution to this problem. By documenting the guest's expected arrival time, the desk clerk is better equipped to make difficult decisions about possible no-show guests. The earlier such decisions are made, the better the hotel's chances of selling the room to a walk-in.

Cancellations.   Although cancellations mean additional work for the reservations department and the front desk, they are still infinitely better than no-shows. Guests who cancel on the day of arrival are providing the hotel an opportunity to resell the room. The earlier the cancellation is received, the better the chance of reselling the room.

Cancellation policies usually require notice at least 24 hours in advance of the reservation's arrival date. Depending on policy, cancellations made on the day of arrival may be treated like no-shows and charged one room-night. However, because cancellations (even last-minute cancellations) provide better information to the hotel than no-shows, many properties waive the one-night penalty to canceling guests. Even if the hotel charges a late cancellation fee of, say, $25, that is better for the guest than being charged one full room-night. That seems fair to all concerned, because a canceled room has more opportunity to be resold than a no-show room. As a courtesy, many corporate hotels allow business guests to cancel without penalty until 6 PM the day of arrival.

Early Arrivals.   Cancellations and no-shows reduce the number of expected arrivals. Early arrivals increase the number of expected arrivals. Early arrivals are guests who arrive at the hotel one or more days prior to their scheduled reservation date.

There are a number of reasons why a guest might arrive at the hotel in advance of the expected reservation date. For example, the reservations department may have had a different date for the reservation than the guest understood, or possibly the guest's plans changed and he or she decided to arrive one or more days early. Whatever the reason, the front office should attempt to accommodate the guest.

Even in periods of 100% occupancy, the front-office personnel strive to find accommodations for the early arrival. Not only is that good guest service, but early arrivals often represent a number of room-nights to the hotel—many early arrivals stay through the end of their originally scheduled departure. An early arrival who arrives two days early for a three-night reservation may very likely stay all five nights.

Adjusting Today's Reservations.   The continuing example in Exhibit 6–2 shows an unadjusted reservations count of 325 rooms. Assuming a cancellation rate of 2%, a no-show rate of 5%, and an early arrival rate of 1%, the numbers change significantly (see the following table and Exhibit 6–3):

Today's reservations	325
Less cancellations (2%)	− 7
Less no-shows (5%)	− 16
Plus early arrivals (1%)	+ 3
Equals adjusted number of reservations	305

A certain amount of mathematical rounding is necessary in these equations. A 2% cancellation rate with 325 reservations gives 6.5 cancellations. It is necessary to round 6.5 cancellations to 7. Similarly, no-shows round from 16.25 to 16 and early arrivals round from 3.25 to 3.

The Adjusted Result.   With all the adjustment components in place, a look at the adjusted room count (Exhibit 6–3) shows a substantial change from the simple, unadjusted room count (Exhibit 6–2). The number of stayover rooms has been adjusted from 650 to 638 because the number of rooms due to check out has been adjusted with understays and overstays. The number of expected reservations has been adjusted from 325 to 305 because of estimated cancellations, no-shows, and early arrivals.

The count of 57 rooms available for sale shown in Exhibit 6–3 is significantly higher than the count of 25 rooms available shown in Exhibit 6–2. With the same five rooms out of order, the hotel can now accept 57 rooms as walk-ins (assuming it quickly repairs the five OOO rooms).

Exhibit 6–3 could just as easily have projected a change in the opposite direction. Second-guessing the actions of the guest is the reservations department's burden. Projections are made from the historical data gathered by the property and forecasted on the basis of experience. At best, it is a composite of many previous days and may prove disastrous on any given day. A cautious projection with too few walk-ins accepted results in low occupancy and empty rooms despite guests who were turned away earlier in the day. An optimistic projection allows the desk to accept so many walk-ins that the reserved guest who arrives late in the day finds no room.

This is the dilemma of overbooking: the need, on the one hand, to maximize occupancy and profits, and the pressure, on the other hand, to keep empty rooms for reservations who may never arrive. Hotels with heavy walk-ins, similar to the airline's standbys, are more flexible than isolated properties. Selective overbooking, 5 to 15% depending on historical experience, is the hotel's major protection against no-shows, double reservations, and "guaranteed reservations" that are never paid. Conservative overbooking begins with a collection of data, made easier by a well-programmed computer and a regular update of projections.

Data collection must be structured and accurate so that the reservations office can rely on the figures. The computer can furnish the information if the database for accumulating the report was planned for in the programming. Data must be accumulated in a chronological fashion, day of the week matching day of the week. It is important for the second Tuesday in April, for instance, to match the second Tuesday in April of last year, irrespective of the calendar dates of those Tuesdays.

Dates do have importance, of course. The Fourth of July holiday is a more important date than the day on which it falls. Similarly, the days before and after such a holiday must be identified with other before and after days of previous years.

➤*Putting the Room Count to Use.*   Room forecasting starts with an annual projection and ends with an hourly report. In between are monthly, biweekly, weekly, three-day, and daily forecasts. Ten-day reports (see Exhibit 6–6) are sometimes used in place of the biweekly projections, but most reservation managers prefer to see two weekends included in a report.

Every department of a hotel uses the room count projections as a critical tool for labor planning. Each department makes sales and labor forecasts from the anticipated room count. Most departments depend on room occupancy for their own volume. This is certainly the situation with valet and laundry, room service, telephones, and uniformed services.

Housekeeping's schedule is also a function of room sales. So, too, there is a direct relation between the number of breakfasts served and the previous night's room count. Early scheduling of shifts and days off helps build good employee relations, and the two-week forecast is generally used for that purpose. A two-week lead time may be required in hotels covered by union contracts.

The reservations department should have its closest partnership with marketing and sales. Without that alliance, the property has little opportunity to maximize yield management policies. For example, how many discounted rooms has the sales department committed to wholesalers during a high-occupancy (thus, high-rate) period? The marketing department should be able to help reservations forecast no-shows, walk-ins, early arrivals, and so on, as they pertain to a particular group. Group figures differ from figures for independent guests and may vary from group to group.

Periodic Recounts.   The longer the period between the preparation of the forecast and its use, the less reliable it is. Without periodic updating, all the departments, but especially the desk, act on information that is no longer accurate. The three-day forecast permits a final push for sales and a tightening of labor schedules throughout the property to maximize occupancy and minimize costs.

By the time hourly projections are being made, responsibility has moved entirely to the front office. Overbooking problems, additional reservations, walk-ins, and stayovers are being resolved by front-office executives.

Periodic or hourly forecasts improve the system in two ways. Obviously, the information is more current (see Exhibit 6–6). Less obvious is the increased accuracy in percentage adjustments as the day wears on. Were it known, for example, that 80% of all the check-outs were usually gone by noon, a better guess of understays and overstays could be made at noon each day than at 7 AM. Similar refinements are possible with cancellation percentages, no-show factors, and so on. In fact, it is possible to improve the accuracy of no-show forecasts by separating the total reservations into three

Royal Hotel Weekly Forecast for February 3 to February 9						
	3	4	5	6	7	8	9
Rooms available for sale	1,206	1,206	1,206	1,206	1,206	1,206	1,206
Rooms occupied last night ⟶	1,121	1,190	1,193	890	480	140	611
Less anticipated departures	444	396	530	440	350	55	20
Stayovers	677	794	663	450	130	85	591
Reservations	498	386	212	25	10	501	552
Estimated out of order	3	3					
Rooms committed	1,178	1,183	875	475	140	586	1,143
Estimated walk-ins	12	10	15	5		25	63
Rooms occupied tonight ⟶	1,190	1,193	890	480	140	611	1,206
Group Arrivals							
National Water Heater Co.	80	140					
Play Tours of America			68				
Chevrolet Western Division					5	183	
PA Library Association						251	396
Chiffo-Garn wedding party							23

Exhibit 6–5   This room-availability forecast demonstrates why statistics that depend on the cumulative results of previous days' forecasts grow less reliable the further the projected horizon. Each day's values build on estimates from previous days (see arrows). If the actual number of rooms occupied in any preceding day is different than the mathematical base—and it always is—later forecasts become less and less accurate, since they begin with invalid figures.

For example, if the rooms occupied on February 3 are actually less than the 1,190 projected (less because of fewer walk-ins, more understay departures, etc.), then the rooms occupied on February 4 will also be lower than projected. After all, the count for February 4 is based upon the number of rooms occupied the night before (1,190). If the count for February 4 is lower than projected, then the count for February 5, 6, 7, and so on will also be lower than projected.

categories—advance deposit, guaranteed, and nonguaranteed—before applying a different no-show percentage to each.

Adjusting by Reservation Quality.   Returning to the continuing example illustrated in Exhibits 6–2 and 6–3, an improved adjusted room count is possible by separating nonguaranteed reservations from guaranteed and advance-deposit reservations. Instead of merely stating that 325 reservations are due in, it is more valuable to understand that, say, 100 reservations are nonguaranteed, 175 reservations are guaranteed, and 50 reservations are advance deposit.

If the hotel maintains statistical history by reservation quality or type, the accuracy of the entire projection is enhanced. In such hotels, the no-show percentage might be changed from the flat 5% for all reservation types to something more detailed. Assume that 20% of all nonguaranteed reservations are no-shows, 4% of all guaranteed reservations are no-shows, and 1% of all advance deposits are no-shows. The total number of no-shows would now change from 16 in Exhibit 6–3 to 28. This is calculated by taking 20% of 100 nonguaranteed reservations (20), plus 4% of 175 guaranteed reservations (7), plus 1% of 50 advance-deposit reservations (0.5 rounds up to 1).

Similarly, cancellations are also a function of the quality of the reservation. Cancellations are more common with guaranteed and advance deposit reservations, because such guests have an incentive to call and cancel (if the guest is not planning to arrive, he or she will save a no-show charge by calling and canceling). Likewise, cancellations are less common with nonguaranteed reservations. The guest has nothing to lose with the nonguaranteed reservation, because the reservation is basically a courtesy hold until 6 PM. Few guests take the time to notify the hotel that they are not arriving when they merely have a courtesy 6 PM hold (nonguaranteed) reservation. In our continuing example (Exhibit 6–3), let's assume 0% of all nonguaranteed reservations call to cancel, 4% of guaranteed reservations cancel, and 3% of advance-deposit reservations cancel. The total number of cancellations would now change from 7 to 9. This is calculated by taking 0% of 100 nonguaranteed reservations (0), plus 4% of 175 guaranteed reservations (7), plus 3% of 50 advance-deposit reservations (1.5 rounds up to 2).

Today's nonguaranteed reservations	100	
Today's guaranteed reservations	175	
Today's advance-deposit reservations	50	
Equals today's reservations	325	325
Less cancellations nonguaranteed reservations (0%)	−0	
Less cancellations guaranteed reservations (4%)	−7	
Less cancellations advance-deposit reservations (3%)	−2	
Equals total cancellations	−9	−9
Less no-shows nonguaranteed reservations (20%)	−20	
Less no-shows guaranteed reservations (4%)	−7	
Less no-shows advance-deposit reservations (1%)	−1	
Equals total no-shows	−28	−28
Plus early arrivals (1%)		+ 3
Equals today's adjusted reservations		291

Accuracy can also be improved by attention to the character of the market. The type of group clues the reservation department to the no-show percentage. For example, teachers are very dependable. Tour groups are nearly always full because volume is as important to the tour operator as to the innkeeper. That generalization must then be balanced by knowledge about specific tour companies. Allocations versus utilization should be computed individually on wholesalers, incentive houses, associations, and other group movers.

Market research may prove that bookings from certain localities are more or less reliable depending on transportation, weather, distance, and the kind of guest the hotel is attracting. Commercial guests have a different degree of dependability than tourists, who differ again from conventioneers or referrals. A large permanent guest population needs to be recognized in any percentage computation involving stayovers and anticipated departures.

The overall goal of any room count projection is to forecast the number of rooms available for sale. This is especially critical during high-occupancy periods. When the hotel is nearly full, it is important to forecast the number of rooms that may become available for sale due to understays, no-shows, and cancellations. By understanding the interrelationship of these adjustments, the front office has a better chance of filling the hotel.

Occupancy Forecast Report

Santa Rae Ranch
Ann Parker

Occupancy Forecast Report
For the Period from 03-JAN- to 12-JAN-
Percentages Include Out of Order and Off Market Rooms
Percentages Exclude Tentative Group Rooms

	FRI JAN-03	SAT JAN-04	SUN JAN-05	MON JAN-06	TUE JAN-07	WED JAN-08	THUR JAN-09	FRI JAN-10	SAT JAN-11	SUN JAN-12
Total Rooms	236	236	236	236	236	236	236	236	236	236
- OOO	3	2	3	3	2	2	3	1	1	0
- OFF	0	0	0	0	0	0	0	0	0	0
Rooms Available	233	234	233	233	234	234	233	235	235	236
Rooms Occupied	94	90	83	44	33	27	21	30	42	27
- Non-Group Departures	11	18	34	14	4	5	17	2	13	4
- Group Departures	12	3	14	2	2	2	0	1	5	4
+ Non-Group Arrivals	18	13	9	4	0	1	15	14	3	0
+ Group Arrivals	1	1	0	0	0	0	12	0	0	0
Net In-House	90	83	44	33	27	21	31	41	27	19
+ Estimated Pickup	0	0	0	0	0	0	0	2	2	2
+ Excess Committed	82	60	1	0	0	0	19	9	14	0
+ Tentative Grp Rooms	5	0	0	0	0	0	2	0	0	0
Net Rooms Reserved	172	143	45	33	27	21	50	52	43	21
Net Rooms Available	61	91	188	200	207	213	183	183	192	215
Non-Group										
Projected Revenue	7113.00	6527.50	3438.50	2757.50	2446.00	1810.00	1341.88	4265.37	3415.99	2913.49
Avg. Rate	103.09	101.99	88.17	95.09	97.84	86.19	70.63	137.59	162.67	171.38
Group (Reserved)										
Projected Revenue	1064.00	965.00	221.00	175.00	47.50	0.00	1148.00	1100.50	590.00	190.00
Avg. Rate	50.67	50.79	44.20	43.75	23.75	0.00	95.67	100.05	98.33	95.00
Group (Excess Committed)										
Estimated Revenue	5340.00	3925.00	20.00	0.00	0.00	0.00	1945.00	845.00	1280.00	0.00
Avg. Rate	61.38	65.42	20.00	0.00	0.00	0.00	92.62	93.89	91.43	0.00
Group (Tentative)										
Estimated Revenue	375.00	0.00	0.00	0.00	0.00	0.00	150.00	0.00	0.00	0.00
Avg. Rate	75.00	0.00	0.00	0.00	0.00	0.00	75.00	0.00	0.00	0.00
Group (Totals)										
Projected Revenue	6779.00	4890.00	241.00	175.00	47.50	0.00	3243.00	1945.50	1870.00	190.00
Avg. Rate	59.99	61.90	40.17	43.75	23.75	0.00	92.66	97.28	93.50	95.00
Totals										
Projected Revenue	13892.00	11417.50	3679.50	2932.50	2493.50	1810.00	4584.88	6210.87	5285.99	3103.49
Avg. Rate	76.33	79.84	81.77	88.86	92.35	86.19	84.91	121.78	128.93	163.34
% Occupancy Reserved	38.63	35.47	18.88	14.16	11.54	8.37	13.30	17.45	11.49	8.05
% Including Commits	73.82	61.11	19.31	14.16	11.54	8.97	21.46	21.28	17.45	8.05

	TEN/DEF	FRI JAN-03	SAT JAN-04	SUN JAN-05	MON JAN-06	TUE JAN-07	WED JAN-08	THUR JAN-09	FRI JAN-10	SAT JAN-11	SUN JAN-12
American Building Consult	DEF	30/0	20/0								
Bavarian Bakeoff	*DEF	0/1									
Bob's Bablo Island Tour	*DEF	5/4	0/3								
Brady Tours	DEF							5/0			
Cardinal Group	DEF	1/0	1/0	1/0							
Cups & China	DEF	10/0									
Honda	DEF							25/11	20/11	20/6	
MIPS	TEN	6/5	5/5								
Micro Data	TEN							2/0			
Presentations Now	DEF	5/0	5/0								
Sky Line Displays	TEN	5/0									
US Clowns Inc.	DEF	25/2	25/2								
US Water Polo Team	DEF	12/1	12/1								

* – This group's commitments must be cleaned up or all availability reports will be out of balance.

Exhibit 6–6 This computerized reservation forecast report displays a 10-day view of rooms activity. It details arrival and departure projections for individual as well as group rooms. Usually, such forecast reports also provide an estimate of each day's anticipated rooms revenues . (Note that unlike the treatment suggested by the authors, this example shows out-of-order rooms reducing rooms available. Although unusual, such a technique boosts the percentage of occupancy and so reflects better on the rooms manager.) *Courtesy of Geac Computers, Inc., Tustin, California.*

➤ OVERBOOKING

Even when hotel management boasts of reaching 100% occupancy on a given night, there are usually a few unoccupied rooms left in the hotel. The hotel shows 100% occupancy because it has sold every available room, not necessarily because every available room is physically occupied. Rooms held for guaranteed reservations provide revenue in the form of no-show charges even when the guest fails to arrive at the property. Indeed, reaching the *perfect fill* or the *perfect sell-out* (where every available room is physically occupied) is actually a relatively uncommon occurrence even in well-managed properties.

The Perfect Fill

The perfect fill is especially elusive because guests are notoriously undependable, and it just so happens that their lack of dependability creates a vacuum, requiring hotel managers to sell more rooms. That's because the adjustments we looked at in the first half of this chapter generally leave more empty rooms than they fill. In other words, the difference between adjustments that result in available rooms (no-shows, cancellations, and understays) and adjustments requiring additional rooms (overstays and early arrivals) creates, in almost all hotels, a vacuum requiring more rooms to be filled.

Let's look at that phenomenon in a different way. Selling the exact number of rooms available for sale on a given date would be a mistake. It is a mistake to assume that adjustments resulting in available rooms (no-shows, cancellations, and understays) will be balanced by adjustments requiring additional rooms (overstays and early arrivals). The reality is that adjustments resulting in available rooms far outweigh adjustments requiring additional rooms. So, managers had better oversell their properties.

Overbooking is standard practice in the lodging industry as it is in the airline industry. Overbooking means that a hotel knowingly sells more reservations than it has rooms available. When a hotel overbooks a sold-out date, it is taking a calculated risk that more guests will understay, cancel, or no-show than the number of rooms by which the hotel has overbooked. A conservative overbooking policy rarely places the hotel in a compromising situation. More aggressive overbooking, however, can force both the hotel and the unlucky guest(s) into an unpleasant situation.

Reservations Are Legal Contracts

Courts consider room reservations to be legal contracts. The request constitutes the offer, and the promise of accommodations represents the acceptance. Either the promise to pay or the actual transfer of a deposit is the third important element of a contract: consideration. Such promises may be verbal (as with a telephone confirmation) or written (as with a letter of confirmation, see Chapter 5, Exhibits 5–4 and 5–5).[1] The parties are competent; the transaction is legal; and there is a mutuality of interest. All the elements of a binding contract are in place.

---

[1]Hotel reservations are legal contracts whether they are oral (see *Dold v. Outrigger Hotel and Hawaii Hotels Operating Company*, 1972) or in writing (see *Rainbow Travel Service, Inc. v. Hilton Hotels Corp.*, 1990). Although most cases show damaged customers or tour operators suing hotels for overbooking, hotels have also been known to sue guests for their failure to arrive (*King of Prussia Enterprises, Inc. v. Greyhound Lines, Inc.*, 1978).

HOTEL OVERBOOKING SOLUTIONS

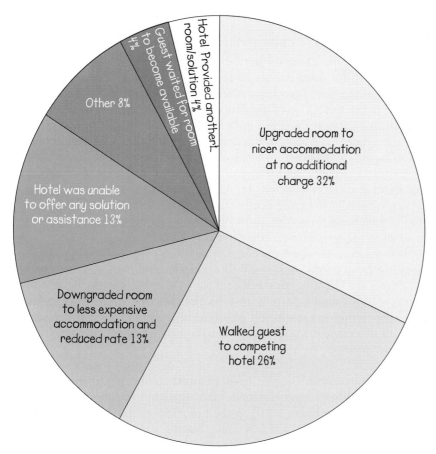

Exhibit 6–7   In a survey designed by American Express Travel Trends Monitor, an amazing 22.0% of all travelers stated they have arrived at a hotel with confirmed reservations only to find the hotel did not have a room available for them (or did not have the exact room type originally reserved). As a follow-up to that question, travelers were asked how their particular situation was handled—that information is shown in the pie-chart above.

You'll note that many of these overbooking problems were handled internally because other room types were available to accommodate the guest (solved by either upgrading the guest to a nicer room at no additional charge or downgrading the room type and adjusting the guest's rate accordingly). But a dismal 13% of these situations were poorly handled because the overbooked hotels were "unable to offer assistance!" *Source: American Express Travel Trends Monitor.*

If one party breaches the contract, the innocent party should be compensated for the injury. However, for many years, recovery by either party has generally been limited to the natural or expected costs that the parties anticipated at the time of the agreement.

There have been few legal cases involving breach of reservation contract. That is because there is little to be gained by bringing suit. If the guest breaches the contract by failing to show up for the room, the hotel may have an opportunity to resell the accommodation. Even if the room cannot be resold, the monetary loss to the hotel is minimal. Similarly, if the hotel breaches the reservation contract by failing to provide a room, the guest is free to seek accommodations elsewhere. Even if a room cannot be found, the actual cost to the guest is still quite small (possibly limited to taxi fares and telephone calls expended in search of alternative accommodations). And courts are not willing to compensate the guest for inconvenience and depression.

In very few cases (usually involving group reservations or tour operators) have negligence or fraud in room reservations been alleged and then proven. The threat remains, however, especially for those hotels that overbook as a matter of operational policy. If the complaining guest can show that the hotel consistently overbooked, there might be adequate grounds to recover in a tort action.

This is also true in cases where the plaintiff can demonstrate foreseeable damage. For example, if the hotel overbooked and walked the guest during a sold-out period in the city (say, during the Olympics or the World Series, if either were being held in the city), the hotel could reasonably foresee the difficulty the guest would have in finding an alternative room. After exhausting all possibilities, if the guest decided to sleep in his or her car and was subsequently attacked and harmed, the hotel might be found liable for significant damages.

▶*Looming Legislation.*   Severe cases of overbooking, especially in isolated resort areas where no other accommodations were available, triggered initial interest by the Federal Trade Commission (FTC) in the early 1980s. Action by the FTC was held off, in part, by the industry's decision to act. Having witnessed the restrictive regulations the government placed on the airline industry, hospitality leaders took a proactive stance. In essence, they convinced the FTC of their ability to squelch the problem by voluntarily establishing their own internal policies and regulations. Today, overbooking penalties awarded to displaced guests are remarkably similar across the major lodging chains.

Yield management may renew the government's interest—this time, probably at the state level. Several state attorneys general are again commenting that hotels are playing the same game as the airlines. Florida has already enacted such legislation. In addition to monetary penalties, the law requires the hotel to reimburse guests for prepaid reservations whether paid directly to the hotel or to a travel agency. New York requires travel agents to warn clients in the form of a rubber-stamped message that "this hotel has been known to overbook in the past" (see Exhibit 6–8).

Others at Fault.   Although states such as New York and Georgia have legislated mere refunds for unaccommodated guests, Pennsylvania, Michigan, and Florida permit punitive damages. Hawaii, Puerto Rico, and others have enacted eviction laws permitting the physical ejection of guests who overstay their reservation. That puts the ball in the hotel's court. No longer can the excuse for overbooking be laid on other guests.

The fault for overbooking is not the hotel industry's alone. Tour operators who earn commissions, conference committees who pledge room blocks, and individual

Our Pledge to You

We will not knowingly offer for rent, space on which we already have an advance deposit or credit-card guaranteed reservation from a customer. If, for any reason beyond our control, a room should not be available for a customer who has either an advance deposit reservation or a credit-card guaranteed reservation, we shall arrange for at least comparable accommodations at another hotel or motel in this area.

The Management

Exhibit 6–8   Nonoverbooking pledge. The American Hotel & Lodging Association encourages all hotels to adopt similar policies. Reading between the lines, this pledge allows the hotel to overbook nonguaranteed (6 PM) reservations. That makes sense, in light of the extremely high no-show rate associated with nonguaranteed or "courtesy-hold" reservations. According to this pledge, however, guaranteed and advance deposit reservations are not to be oversold. *Courtesy of the American Hotel & Lodging Association, Washington, DC.*

travelers who don't show are all to blame. Each, the hotel included, attempts to maximize its own position at the risk of overbooking.

Tour operators who bring planeloads of tourists to a town contribute to the overbooking problem. The group is usually divided among several hotels, with the guest's selection of a particular hotel determining the cost of the tour. The tour operator is playing the odds, estimating that a given number of guests on each plane will choose hotels in the same ratio that the tour operator has committed rooms. When too many people select one property and too few select another, the hotel is blamed for overbooking. Guests are unaware that the hotel and the tour operator had agreed on the number of rooms months before.

Convention executives must be hounded to keep their numbers current. No-shows are reduced if the number of rooms saved for the convention is adjusted to the group's history at other hotels. If possible, convention groups should pair their members at the meeting site as the individuals arrive. This reduces the number of single rooms created when previously paired delegates do not show. Failing this, the hotel can levy a compulsory room charge for no-shows.

Guests are probably the most to blame. They are notorious no-shows! Guests are known to make reservations in more than one hotel and, if they do show, change their

Sample Cancellation Policies for Discount Travel Web Sites

Discount Travel Site	Change/Cancellation Policy
Expedia.com	• Changes or cancellations are charged a $25 fee. • Cancellations or changes within 72 hours of time of arrival are charged a one-night fee.
Hotels.com	• Changes or cancellations are charged a $10 fee (recently reduced from a previous $50 fee).
Hotwire.com	• Changes or cancellations are not an option—all hotel reservations are final.
Lowestravel.com	• Changes or cancellations are always charged a fee, but the exact fee depends partly on what the hotel's individual policy requires.
Orbitz.com	• Changes or cancellations are charged no fee (other than what the hotel's individual policy requires).
Quikbook.com	• Changes or cancellations are charged no fee (other than what the hotel's individual policy requires).
Travelocity.com	• Changes or cancellations are charged a $10 fee. • Cancellations or changes within 72 hours of time of arrival are charged a one-night fee.
Trip.com	• Changes or cancellations are charged no fee (other than what the hotel's individual policy requires).

Exhibit 6–9   A sampling of hotel reservation cancellation policies for some of the biggest names in travel Web sites. One of the most punitive aspects of making such reservations is the 72-hour cancellation policy shared by several discount travel sites. Customers should be very certain they know their travel plans before making such reservations.

length of stay without notifying the desk. The reservation department is always second-guessing guests' moves, and this means occasional errors no matter how carefully previous statistics and experiences are projected.

►*Common Overbooking Policies.* The burden of *walking* an arriving guest—sending that person away—falls to the room clerk (see Exhibit 6–10). Too often management leaves it at that, making no provision to train the clerk and no provision to house the guest. Where this is a frequent affair, the staff grows immune to the protests and even finds a bit of humor in walking one guest after the other. In doing so, the staff reflects the apparent attitude of an unconcerned management. This is not the case in properties where quality assurance programs are in place (see Chapter 7). The situation is never treated lightly, even if a number of guests were walked that day.

No matter how well managed a hotel, no matter how well made the forecasts, overbooking will occur. Preplanning for overbooking reduces guest irritation and even offers some chance of retaining business.

Exhibit 6–10   An overbooked hotel is no laughing matter!

Arranging substitute accommodations elsewhere is what the clerk should do. Providing the training to anticipate the incident is what management should do. Preparation includes preliminary calls to neighboring properties as the situation becomes obvious. Many satellite properties depend on this type of overflow for business. Affiliated properties usually refer to each other before overflowing rooms business to neighboring competitors—even to the extent that a full-service chain property may walk guests to one of the same chain's budget operations and vice versa.

Managers need to be alert to unethical practices involving walked rooms. Some properties give a commission or kick back a payment to clerks of oversold properties when they refer walked guests their way. Even though the oversold hotel may specify to which properties guests can be walked, $10 or $20 from a competing operation is incentive enough to disregard the rule. Indeed, some unethical clerks may begin referring walk-in customers to the other hotel even when rooms remain available at their own property.

Significant dollars are expended when walking a guest from those properties that have a quality assurance, guest-oriented policy in place. The hotel pays the round-trip cab ride to the substitute hotel. It underwrites the cost of one or more long-distance telephone calls. It also pays the room charge, regardless of the rate, at the alternative property. Some hotels give an outright gift (champagne, fruit basket, etc.) to apologize for the inconvenience. Others give a free room on the next visit as a means of bringing back a walked guest.

Assuming that those figures are cab, $20; telephone, $7; and room rate, $73, each incident costs $100. This computation ignores the value of lost sales in the other departments. Overbooking is not an everyday affair. If three guests per night are turned away 10 times per year, the hotel spends $3,000 (3 × 10 $100) in remedies. Walking guests does not make economic sense. The cost of failing to achieve 100% occupancy on the 10 nights is certainly less expensive than the overbooking outlay, especially when goodwill is added into the equation.

Ignored in the economic computation above is the cost of public relations. The iceberg effect of one extremely unhappy guest can add up to untold costs. Plagued by bad publicity from overbooking, the Bahamas Hotel Association (BHA) formalized an areawide policy. The BHA recognized that being stranded on an isolated island without a room was not going to encourage tourism. The new policy carried the cab ride one step further, guaranteeing air taxi to another island if all accommodations in the host area were fully booked. A $20 cab ride is cheap compared with the cost of an air taxi!

Other localities have established programs to help themselves and the unaccommodated guest. Chambers of commerce or tourist authorities have set up hot lines. Many metropolitan areas have adopted a system that hooks participating properties together electronically and displays the city status on a lighted board (see Exhibit 6–11). Each morning and periodically during the day, the separate properties adjust

HOTELEX   NEW ORLEANS   AREA CODE 504

HOTELEX PO BOX 5286 REDWOOD CITY, CA 94063 **650-369-4171**	SHERATON 500 CANAL **525-2500**	HILTON 2 POYDRAS **561-0500**	HYATT RGNCY POYDRAS / LOYOLA **561-1234**	WESTIN 100 RUE IBERVILLE **566-7006**	FAIRMONT 123 BARONE **529-7111**
RADISSON 1500 CANAL **522-4500**	BOURBON ORL BOURBON / ORLEANS **523-2222**	MARRIOTT 555 CANAL **581-1000**	HLDY LE MYNE 301 RUE DAUPHINE **581-1303**	ROYAL SNSTA 300 BOURBON **586-0300**	QUEEN/CRSNT 344 CAMP **587-9700**
MONTELEONE 214 RUE ROYAL **523-3341**	CHATEAU SNSTA 800 IBERVILLE **586-0800**	BRENT HOUSE 1512 JEFFERSON HWY **835-5411**	HLDY FR QRTR 124 ROYAL **529-7211**	FR MRKT INN 501 DECATUR **561-5621**	LE PAVILLON 833 POYDRAS **581-3111**
		CROWNE PLZA 344 POYDRAS **525-9444**	INN BOURBON 541 BOURBON **524-7611**	PELHAM 444 COMMON **522-4444**	AVE PLAZA 2111 ST CHARLES **566-1212**
					FOR REPAIR CALL **1-(800) 365-3106**

HAVALEX, INC.
P.O. BOX 5286
REDWOOD CITY, CA
(650) 369-4171

CHANGE: DATE: 08/21/

FILE: NNSO897

Exhibit 6–11   Hotelex is a citywide electronic referral service provided by Havalex, Incorporated to six U.S. cities including New Orleans (shown here). Sold-out hotels refer to the lighted boxes to know which competitors still have vacancies. This proves useful when walking guests on oversold nights. The system shown here is a simple on/off system displaying rooms availability status for same day walk-ins. In Las Vegas, Havalex recently introduced a touch-screen system which displays availability for up to 14 nights at as many as 62 properties. If a guest needs, say, nine nights, the system will scan availability for all listed properties and indicate only those hotels with vacancies all nine nights. Widespread deployment of that system has been postponed, however, while the company works out various problems identified with the Las Vegas experiment. *Courtesy of Hotelex Systems, Redwood City, California.*

their availability status. Referrals are easily made by reference to the lighted board; a light on means rooms are available; a light off means that particular hotel is full. Equally important, the desk can monitor what is happening throughout the city and adjust its own walk-ins based on citywide conditions.

Clearly, steps can be taken to ease the impact of overbooking. An industrywide policy of self-policing and public relations would minimize the incidence of overbooking and diminish the outcry from those cases that do occur. Success requires the support of each hotel and chain. A visible and concerted effort may serve to ward off renewed interest by the FTC. Apparently, governmental agencies perceive the issue more strongly than does the public. An AH&LA study on customer satisfaction ranked overbooking 19th in the frequency of guest complaints against hotels. The real problem lies with properties that do nothing. They are the true culprits. Even the FTC noted that it was not overbooking per se that concerned the commission. It was what the hotel didn't do to help when the guest was turned away. The FTC was criticizing the antiservice syndrome.

Overbooking and the Antiservice Syndrome.   While the majority of hotels are proactive in preparing their employees to handle oversold days, poorly managed properties simply place the "blame" on the guest. The common antiservice approach for such hotels is to act as if the reservation never existed. The clerk's pretense is what guests find the most frustrating part of the experience. To play out the charade, the clerk consults with co-workers, massages computer keys, and examines hidden room racks. Finally comes a proclamation. To the hotel, the guest is a nonperson without a record and one for whom the hotel is not responsible.

To the dismay of the entire industry, certain properties give no attention to the matter of overbooking. They set a low priority on the loss of goodwill because they either have little repeat business or they have more business than they can handle. What is unimportant to these properties is of grave concern to the majority of hotelkeepers. The majority act to minimize the frequency of overbooking. The minority exacerbate the problem to the detriment of all.

No-Show Policies.   Any overbooking discussion invariably gets around to no-shows—people who make reservations but never arrive and never cancel. No-shows, which reach as high as 25% in some cities on occasion, run about 8% industrywide.

There is a high correlation between the incidence of no-shows and the quality of the reservation. Reservations come in three qualities. Highest is the advance deposit reservation, next is the guaranteed reservation (guaranteed to either a credit card or corporate account), and lowest quality is the nonguaranteed reservation. The higher the quality of the reservation, the lower the likelihood of no-show.

That's why hotels are less willing to accept nonguaranteed reservations (see Exhibit 6–12). Nonguaranteed reservations frequently no-show, and when they do, the hotel receives no compensation short of selling the room to a walk-in guest after the 6 PM hold. Hotels have a different option where guaranteed and advance deposit reservations are concerned.

Guaranteed and advance deposit reservations are penalized for failing to cancel or use their reservation. Guests are usually charged the cost of one room night (one room night plus tax is the common amount requested for an advance deposit). For advance deposits, it is a simple matter for the hotel to claim the deposit. With guaranteed reservations, the process is less certain. Collecting against guaranteed reservations is often quite difficult because guests are unwilling to pay the charge against their credit card or corporate account. This disagreement often results in a fight between the guest and the hotel over the amount of one night's lodging. Even when the hotel wins it loses because the guest may forever be lost as a valued customer. Exhibit 6–12 illustrates the steps a well-operated hotel must take to ensure no-show revenues are properly collected.

Cancellation Policies.   Cancellation policies are another source of irritation to guests. After taking the time to contact the hotel and cancel the reservation, many guests are told they will still be charged one room-night. Cancellation policies differ by chain, hotel, market, and destination. In addition, the cancellation policy often reflects the quantity of walk-ins experienced by the hotel. The most liberal cancellation policies allow the guest to cancel up until 6 PM on the day of arrival. Such liberal policies are generally found at corporate and chain-affiliated properties. If the guest fails to cancel within the time frame established, a one-night charge may be assessed. In contrast, many resorts and isolated destination properties mandate more stringent cancellation policies. Some request the guest to notify the hotel 24 to 48 hours in advance. Others require as much as 7 to 14 days notice. Indeed, more stringent cancellation policies may carry a weightier penalty: Some resort properties are known to charge the full prepaid stay.

The major credit-card companies mandate cancellation times for properties that guarantee reservations against their cards. Discover, MasterCard, and VISA all require properties to accept cancellations until 6 PM on the day of arrival (resort operations are given the option of requiring cancellations up to three hours earlier). American Express and Diners Club understand that different markets may require different cancellation policies. Therefore, these two companies allow hotels to establish their own cancellation times, provided that the hotels clearly explain the policies and procedures to all guests at the time of reservation. And oral descriptions are not necessarily sufficient. VISA, for one, requires written notice of cancellation policies for reservations made at least 72 hours in advance. Exhibit 6–13 charts the policies of the several credit-card companies.

Minimizing the Overbooking Problem

There are really no perfect solutions to the problem of overbooking. As long as hotels overbook to compensate for no-shows and last-minute changes in occupancy, there will always be walked guests. The answer is found not in eliminating overbooking as a management tool but rather, in minimizing the need to overbook on most occasions.

The issue boils down to this: A hotel overbooks because its guests change their minds. When guests change their minds, it often results in lower rooms occupancy than projected. Lower occupancy means less rooms revenue for the hotel. Therefore, in response to guest fickleness, the hotel has little choice but to second-guess the number of overstays, understays, cancellations, and no-shows for a given day. The operative word here is *guess.* And sometimes even the most scientific guesses go awry. That's when overbooking rears its head and guests lose confidence in the system.

Unfortunately, guests want the best of both worlds. They want the flexibility to understay or overstay as plans change, but they also want liberal cancellation and no-show policies for the times when they don't arrive. This leaves the hotel in a difficult position. If it charges a no-show guest for the unoccupied room night, the guest might never return to the hotel. If the hotel refuses a request for an overstay or tries to charge a fee to an early-departing understay, it may also create ill will. The answer is probably to be found in more restrictive reservations policies and third-party involvement.

Managing Your No-Shows

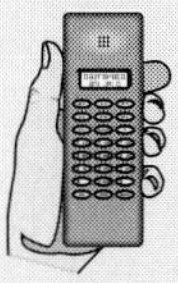

Accept only guaranteed or advance-deposit reservations. Accept very few nonguaranteed reservations.

All reservations guaranteed against credit cards should be carefully documented – name, card number, expiration, and billing address. Consider charging the card during the reservation to ensure its accuracy.

The absolute safest way to accept a credit-card guarantee is with a credit-card authorization form. The hotel faxes the form to the guest for signature, and once the form has been returned, the guaranteed reservation becomes activated.

To minimize clerical errors, train reservationists to always restate reservation details: room type, dates of arrival and departure, rate, applicable discounts, and all other pertinent information before finalizing the reservation.

Be certain reservationists explain the hotel's cancellation and no-show charge policy with each and every reservation. Some hotels go so far as to have reservationists initial a computer screen field after these policies have been explained to the guest.

Provide guests a confirmation number and recommend that they keep this number in their records.

The best way to ensure all information has been provided to the guest without dispute is to fax, email, or mail confirmation.

In the event a no-show or cancellation fee is charged, the hotel should immediately send a copy of the charge to the guest via fax, email, or mail.

Guests who cancel in an appropriate timeframe should be provided a distinct cancellation number and advised to keep the number on file.

Exhibit 6–12   Well-operated hotels take a proactive stance toward reducing their incidence of overbooking. One of the primary catalysts for overbooking is the negative impact hotels experience from no-show rooms. Here are some steps designed to minimize no-shows while maximizing the hotel's chances of recovering rooms revenue from no-show guests.

Credit-Card Company

	American Express	Diners Club	Discover Card (Novus)	MasterCard	VISA
Name of guaranteed reservations program	Assured Reservations	Confirmed Reservation Plan	Guaranteed Reservation Service	Guaranteed Reservations	VISA Reservation Service
No-show charge policy	Will support no-show charge if "assured reservation no-show" is written on signature line	Will support no-show charge if "confirmed reservation—no-show" is written on signature line	Will suport no-show charge if "no-show" is written on signature line	Will support no-show charge if "guaranteed reservation/no-show" is written on signature line	Will support no-show charge if "no-show" is written on signature line
Cancellation policy	Property may determine its own cancellation times	Cancellations by 6 PM (4 PM for resorts) on day of arrival	Cancellations by 6 PM (property may select up to three hours earlier) on day of arrival	Property may determine its own cancellation times	Cancellations by 6 PM if reservation made in past 72 hours; otherwise, property may set its own policy
Overbooking policy	Property must: • Provide and pay for room in comparable hotel for one night • Pay for one 3-minute call • Forward guest contacts to new hotel	Property must: • Provide and pay for room in comparable or better hotel for one night • Pay for one 3-minute call • Provide transportation to new hotel	Property must: • Provide and pay for room in comparable hotel for one night • Pay for one 3-minute call (if requested) • Forward guest contacts to new hotel • Provide transportation to new hotel	Property must: • Provide and pay for room in another hotel for one night • Pay for one 3-minute call • Provide transportation to new hotel • Neither hotel can charge guest for room or guaranteed reservation	Property must: • Provide and pay for room in comparable or better hotel for one night • Pay for one 3-minute call • Forward guest contacts to new hotel • Provide transportation to new hotel

Exhibit 6–13 Third-party reservation guarantees are supported by all five of the major domestic credit-card companies. If the room is guaranteed and the guest does not cancel within the established parameters, the hotel has the right to receive compensation for one night's stay. Of course, this means that the hotel must hold the room available for the guest until check-out time the following day. As long as hotels abide by the policies established by each credit-card company, they will be upheld by the credit-card companies in all but the most unusual customer chargeback disputes.

➤*Increasingly Restrictive Policies.* Certainly, the airlines are strict about their flight policies. Most tickets are nonrefundable and must be paid at the time of reservation. Courtesy (nonguaranteed) holds on reservations usually expire within 24 hours of the time they were made. No-show guests (and cancellations) face $100 "change" fees when they attempt to reuse their tickets. Indeed, unused tickets are only valid a year.

The lodging industry is slowly beginning to adopt similar policies. Merely adopting such reform, however, is not enough. The airlines went through a long period of guest education. And although the lodging industry will have a somewhat easier time educating their customers (because the airlines already broke much of the ground), competition between chains will surely affect the success of industrywide reservations policies reform.

Slowly, such changes are taking place. One chain puts its toe in the water, and soon another follows suit. Yield management fences (nonrefundable reservations, 21-day advanced purchase, and stay over Saturday night) are some of the first toes in the water (see the yield management discussion in Chapter 4). Early departure charges are also being tested.

Early Departure Fees. Several major lodging chains, including both Hyatt and Hilton, have recently experimented with early departure charges. Although not terribly costly (most guests are required to pay between $25 and $50 as an understay penalty), such fees are designed to make guests think twice before departing early. Early departure fees are also expected to improve the accuracy of the reservation on the front end; once aware of an early departure penalty, guests will probably be more conservative in estimating the number of nights they plan to stay.

As with cancellation and no-show policies, early departure or understay fees must be clearly detailed at the time of reservation booking. Credit-card companies expect properties to explain the policy in detail at the time of reservation, include a comment about the policy with mailed confirmations, and have guests sign a statement reiterating the standard during the check-in process. When these procedures are followed, credit-card companies generally support the hotel with regard to guest disputes and chargebacks (see Exhibits 6–12 and 6–13).

➤*Third-Party Guarantees.* There is some logic in removing the hotel from direct involvement with the guest when fees or penalties are involved. It is easier for the hotel to charge a credit-card company or travel agent the no-show charge than to assess it directly against the guest or the guest's corporate account. Although the guest still pays the charge in the end, the hotel is one step removed from the negative connotations associated with collecting such fees, and a third party is assigned that role.

Trip Insurance. The increasing popularity of trip or travel insurance is predicated on this same logic. By placing a third party into the equation, some of the negative feelings associated with paying a penalty are assigned elsewhere and the hotel looks a little less the bad guy.

Although few domestic hotels actually recommend travel insurance with their reservations, it is somewhat more popular in Europe. At the time of reservation, or mailed with the confirmation, is some explanation about the benefits associated with travel insurance. The benefits are simple enough: For a small fee, a third party will become responsible for cancellation, no-show, understay, or reservation change fees assessed for a given trip. The reasons the guest may change their plans are usually described with the insurance and may include illness, death, a change in business plans, or even inclement weather. Some of the more popular companies offering travel insurance include HTH Worldwide, TravelGuard, Travel Safe, and AccessAmerica.

The concept works something like this—with trip insurance, guests have no one to blame but themselves. You see, they should have purchased trip insurance (through a travel agent, tour operator, or trip insurance broker) if they thought their plans might change. Then, if they are charged a no-show, cancellation, change, or understay fee, the trip insurance will pay the cost. If they didn't buy travel insurance, how can they be mad at the hotel for charging them a fee clearly explained at the time of booking?

Credit-Card Guarantees.   Except for unusual circumstances, a credit-card is charged if the reservation has been guaranteed. Unfortunately, charging the credit card does not always equate to receiving payment. In many instances, the guest will dispute the charge.

When such disputes arise, third-party involvement by the credit-card company is necessitated. The credit-card company usually requires the guest to issue a statement in writing. Such statements as "I never made that reservation" or "I canceled that reservation well in advance" are difficult to prove.

That's why the costliest credit-card chargeback category is no-shows (see Exhibit 6–12). Hotels should arm themselves against such disputes by following standard procedures. Best Western, for example, always provides separate confirmation and cancellation numbers (unlike some chains, which simply add an "×" to the confirmation number to signify cancellation). In this way, Best Western can insist that the credit-card company ask the guest to provide the cancellation number. No cancellation number (I lost it, I threw it away, they never gave me a number), no excuse. Similarly, Best Western doesn't accept the excuse "I never made the reservation." As a company, they find that excuse questionable—after all, how did the chain get the guest's name, address, phone number, and credit-card number?

Once the statement is in hand, the third-party credit-card company usually issues a temporary credit to the guest (and an offsetting debit to the hotel). This means that, temporarily, the guest does not have to pay the charge and the hotel does not receive the income.

At this stage, the statement is copied to the hotel and the property has an opportunity to respond. Many hotels stop at this point, believing that the case will never be settled in their favor. If the hotel chooses not to respond, the guest automatically wins the decision. Even when the hotel does respond, the case is still found in favor of the guest much of the time. Some critics of the system believe that credit-card companies uphold the guests because they want to keep them as customers. That is really not the case; if the hotel follows the credit-card company's standard procedure, they should never lose a chargeback dispute (see Exhibit 6–13).

Travel Agent Guarantees.   A different type of third-party guarantee utilizes the travel agent. When a guest makes the reservation through a travel agent, the hotel removes itself from dealing directly with the customer. In the event of a no-show, the hotel receives payment directly from the travel agent. Whether or not the travel agent then charges the no-show customer is the travel agent's problem.

The only weakness with this system is that the hotel must have a credit relationship with the travel agent. In today's fast-paced travel environment, there is rarely enough lead time for the travel agent to send a check and for the hotel to clear the funds.

➤*Advance-Deposit Reservations.*   Probably the best of all methods for reducing the industrywide problem of overbooking is to encourage advance deposits. Advance-deposit reservations (also known as paid-in-advance reservations) have historically maintained the lowest percentage of no-shows. Guests who pay a substantial amount in advance (usually the first-night's room charge, although some resorts charge the entire payment up front) have a strong motive to arrive as scheduled.

However, advance-deposit reservations carry an extra clerical burden not found with other types of reservations. The reservation department, for example, has a tracking burden. If the guest responds by sending a deposit, the reservation must be changed from tentative to confirmed. If the guest doesn't respond, the reservation office must either send a reminder or cancel the reservation. Sending a reminder starts the tracking process all over again.

Handling the money, usually a check, involves bank deposits, sometimes bounced checks, and accounting records. Refunds must be made in a timely manner when cancellations are requested. Processing and writing any check represents a measurable cost of operation.

For many hotels, these operational burdens are inconsequential compared to the benefits that accrue from advance-deposit reservations. However, even those hotels using advance-deposit systems would probably switch if and when new guarantee systems become available. And that is apt to happen as new electronic systems and new innovations in money substitutes appear.

RESOURCES AND CHALLENGES
Resources

➤ SUMMARY

Accepting a reservation is really only half the battle. Tracking the reservation and forecasting house availability are also important components in the reservations' life cycle. Forecasting room availability is as much an art as it is a science. It is a simple matter to count committed rooms (those sold to stayovers and incoming reservations) as a means of forecasting the number of rooms available for walk-ins and short lead-time reservations. However, such a simple approach as counting committed rooms leaves untended a number of costly variables. Yet when the reservations manager begins to consider the potential for such variables as no-shows, cancellations, early arrivals, understays, and overstays, the art of forecasting becomes a bit like guesswork.

An error in predicting the number of cancellations and no-shows may prove disastrous to a nearly full hotel. Rooms may be overbooked, necessitating that guests be walked to a nearby property. When this is a rare occasion, the employees treat the situation with compassion and the walked guest is a satisfied one. However, when walked guests become a routine daily occurrence, the hotel is showing greed by purposely overbooking each day to compensate for the maximum potential no-shows and cancellations. In such cases, employees become jaded, guests are shown little concern, and dissatisfaction inevitably results.

In reality, the lodging industry has done a superior job reducing overbooking complaints in recent years. Partially from fear of government regulation (as with airline overbooking policies), and partially from a desire to create lasting relationships and repeat business in a highly competitive industry, few hotel overbooking complaints have become public scandals in recent years.

➤ WEB SITES

There is a wealth of information on the Web related to hotel overbooking realities and practices. Some of the information gives practical advice and recommendations to consumers, such as

> ➤ always book rooms using your credit card. Visit the following Web site and type in the words "hotel overbooking" in the search window: http://consumer.pub.findlaw.com
>
> ➤ what to do in the event you are walked ("bumped") to another hotel: http://consumer.pub.findlaw.com/nllg/TRAVELRIGHTS/
>
> ➤ horror stories of others, as with this story initially run in *USA Today* about a consul-

tant who was walked at 2 AM, and which has subsequently generated something over 2,000 responses: http://www.usatoday.com/life/cyber/tech/2002/01/04/online-hotel-complaint.htm

> ➤ overbooking debacles (the 2 AM walk) presented in a more humorous light and a few very specific overbooking policies: http://198.64.129.160/business/consumer/badhotel.htm

To find hundreds of other discussions related to hotel overbooking, visit the following site and type in the words "hotel overbooking policies" in the search window: Google.com.

➤ INTERESTING TIDBITS

> ➤ Hotels that overbook in Florida are obligated under state law to make "every effort" to find suitable accommodations for the injured party, refund the party's deposit, and potentially pay a $500 state-levied fine.
>
> ➤ In a landmark case, *Rainbow Travel Service v. Hilton Hotel Corporation* (1990), Hilton Hotels argued that their Fontainebleau Hotel was not responsible for the overbooking incident in question because it was due to factors beyond its control. Many experts believe it was the Fontainebleau Hotel's own policy manual that turned the tide of the trial against Hilton (Hilton eventually lost the trial and paid restitution to Rainbow Travel). And no doubt, that is true. The policy manual read:

Overboard

We never tell a guest we overbooked.

If an overboard situation arises, it is due to the fact that something occurred that the hotel could not prevent.

Examples:
1. Scheduled departures do not vacate their rooms.
2. Engineering problems with a room (pipe bursted, thus water leaks, air conditioning, heating out of commission, broken glass, etc.).

Always remain calm and as pleasant as possible.

➤ READING REFERENCES

"Hotel Reservation Methods—A Discriminant Analysis of Practices in English Hotels." A. Meidan and H. Chiu. *International Journal of Hospitality Management,* 14(2), 1995, pp. 195–208.

"Solving the No-Show Dilemma." S. Barth. *Lodging Hospitality,* February 2001, p. 9.

Understanding Hospitality Law. J. Jefferies and B. K. Brown. Lansing, Michigan: Educational Institute American Hotel & Lodging Association, 2001.

Challenges

➤ TRUE/FALSE

Questions that are partially false should be marked false (F).

___ 1. The term *walking* an overbooked guest means virtually the same as the term *walk-in* guest.

___ 2. A simple, unadjusted room count does not consider understays, overstays, cancellations, no-shows, or early arrivals in the calculations.

___ 3. A *perfect fill* (a sold-out night where every hotel room is physically occupied by one or more guests) is not the same thing as 100% occupancy. Therefore, it is theoretically possible for hotel management to show 100% occupancy without actually attaining a perfect fill.

___ 4. Understays and overstays both affect the room count in the same direction. They both allow the hotel to sell a few more rooms to compensate for the projected understays and/or overstays.

___ 5. Reservations are only legal contracts if the guest mails in a deposit (or has the credit card charged at the time of reservation) and the hotel returns a receipt and/or written confirmation.

➤ PROBLEMS

1. What is the difference between out-of-order and out-of-inventory rooms? Explain why one of these designations affects the occupancy count while the other has no bearing.

2. Prepare a simple unadjusted plus count from the following scenario: A 700-room hotel had 90% of its rooms occupied last night. Of those occupied rooms, 260 are due to check out today. In addition, there are 316 reservations scheduled for arrival today, and 10 rooms are currently out of order.

3. The rooms forecast committee is scheduled to meet later this afternoon. You have been asked to prepare remarks on group no-shows. Contrast the likelihood of no-shows for (a) business groups, (b) tour groups, and (c) convention groups. How would your remarks differ if the group reservation had been made by (a) the vice president of engineering, (b) an incentive travel company, or (c) a professional convention management company?

4. The rooms forecast is a tool for managers throughout the hotel; it is not for the front office alone. List and discuss how several other nonroom departments (housekeeping, food and beverage, etc.) would use the rooms forecast.

5. A chain's corporate office launches a national campaign advertising its policy of honoring every reservation. Each property is notified that overbooking will not be tolerated. What policies can be implemented at the hotel level to meet corporate goals and still generate the maximum occupancies on which professional careers are built?

6. Two hours before the noon check-out hour, a walk-in party requests five rooms. The following scrambled data have just been completed as part of the desk's hourly update. Should the front-office supervisor accept the walk-ins?

General no-show factor	10%
Rooms in the hotel	693
Group reservations due (rooms)	250
Rooms occupied last night	588
Total reservations expected today from all sources (including group rooms)	360
No-show factor for groups	2%
Understays minus overstays as a percentage of occupied rooms	8%
Early arrivals expected	2
Rooms that are out of inventory	7
Total forecasted departures for the day	211

➤ ANSWERS TO TRUE/FALSE QUIZ

1. False. Walking a guest is what the hotel must do when no rooms are available and the guest needs to be accommodated at a different hotel elsewhere in town. A walk-in guest is a person who arrives without a reservation and yet is still accommodated because rooms are available.

2. True. Simple, unadjusted room count does not consider those adjustments listed. Understays, overstays, cancellations, no-shows, and early arrivals are only considered in the adjusted room count equation.

3. True. The question defines the perfect fill correctly. Hotels can claim 100% occupancy by showing revenues from no-show and late cancellation charges even when rooms remain physically unoccupied.

4. False. Understays do increase the number of rooms available for sale on any given day. Overstays do just the opposite and decrease the number of rooms available for sale.

5. False. Although it is good advice for consumers to use a credit card when making reservations and for hotels to send (mail, fax, even email) written confirmations with hotel cancellation policies clearly detailed, they are not required for the reservation to become a legal contract. When the offer is made and accepted (even orally, by telephone) for future remuneration, a contract has been established.

PART III

Guest Service and Rate Structures

Chapter 7
Managing Guest Service

Chapter 8
The Guest Arrival, Registration, and Rooming

Chapter 9
The Role of the Room Rate

The subjects of service and price have been referenced throughout Units I and II. We know that guests choose their hotels on the basis of these two criteria, plus those of location and cleanliness. Guests give different weight to the several variables with each stay. Room rate seems to be of lesser consequence during economically "good times." Guests paid top dollar throughout the boom that closed the 20th century. Then rates fell. Even as rates declined, guests assigned them greater weight in the buying decision.

Service is more constant. One portion of service, the number of employees per guest room, does fluctuate relative to the volume of business. But as the first chapter of this unit explains, service is more than the number of housekeepers or foodservers. Service is an attitude. The quality of that attitude and the evenness in which it is delivered must be immune to the ups and downs of the economic cycle. There is a correlation, however, between the number of employees and the attitude of their service. Overworked staff become surly if they feel exploited by large staff cuts.

Good service does not replace competitive pricing. Nor does competitive price offset unsatisfactory service. Unit III brings the two together: opening the unit with the role of service and closing it with the issue of price.

CHAPTER 7

Managing Guest Service

Outline

Chapter 3 outlined the organization that structures today's hotels. It shows a top-down format because that is the reality of business systems. That supervisor–supervised relationship is not going away, but it is changing: It's softening. Beneath the change lies a realization that guest service, not clever electronics nor fancy amenities, is the essence of good hotel management. Guest service relies on and is delivered by those who are supervised, the line workers.

Guest service doesn't just happen; it must be managed—and it must be managed close to the action, not from afar. Accomplishing the shift from the traditional management-imposed culture to an employee-participative culture takes all of management's talent. It's slow, hard work. Many workers and even their immediate supervisors are not interested in taking on the job. They see guest service as management's job, not theirs. But today's innkeepers cannot be the guest's personal hosts as they were once seen to be (see Chapter 3). The task has sifted down through several organizational levels to the staffer on the floor. Getting those employees to recognize the importance of the task and the mutual interests that result from performing them is the role of managing for guest service. No easy task, that.

➤ A BRIEF HISTORY OF QUALITY MANAGEMENT

Managing quality originally meant reducing the number of manufacturing errors and improving the quality of mass-produced goods. Buyers still find inspectors' identifications in the manufactured products that they buy. This concept of quality management (QM) gradually shifted from manufactured goods to service delivery. As other measures of quality and new means of achieving it were introduced, quality management's definition changed. Thus, the broader concept of Total Quality Management (TQM) came to the service industries. It reached the hotel business with a sharper focus on quality's delivery system: service personnel. With it has come the tentative beginnings of new terminology, Customer Relations Management (CRM). For hotel managers with accounting, real estate, and marketing backgrounds, the shift was an abrupt one.

Quality Management in innkeeping gets special attention when business slumps. That happened between the late 1980s and early 1990s, a low period following the previous decade of good times. The good cycle repeated itself, running again for some 7 to 8 years beginning around 1991. Volume fell again after the events of September 11, 2001. Through it all, attention to the service deliverer, the employee, gained ground. That's evidenced in the role of the hotels' human resources (HR) departments. In two decades, hoteliers have seen the introduction, maturation, and influence of HR departments where there had been none before (see Exhibit 7–1).

Sensitivity to customer needs is not special to innkeeping. Quality service must be a standard for all businesses. In one respect, then, lodging is, like all business, just one industry among many. In other aspects, chiefly face-to-face service, hotelkeeping is not like other service industries and is very different from manufacturing.

> We are in the people business. Not the hotel business, not the real estate business. Instead of machinery, we have people. Instead of automated conveyor belts, we have people. Instead of computers that hum and print stuff, we have people. We have not come to grips with this basic concept.[1]

[1]Steven J. Belmonte, president and CEO, Ramada Franchise Systems, Inc. Talk delivered at Ramada's Annual Conference in Orlando, Florida, December 1999.

REASONS FOR THE ERA OF HUMAN RESOURCES

Realization that high touch is needed to balance high tech
Huge turnover among hotel staff (sometimes exceeding 100% annually)
Expectations and increased pressure from public, legislatures, and courts
Focus on hotel operations as well as on hotel investments
Cultural diversity in the general public and thus in the hotel workforce
Loss of supervisory management from organizational downsizing
Increased empowerment given to workers
Shortage of good job applicants at lodging's traditional salary levels

Exhibit 7–1   Before World War II, the front desk was the focus of hotel management. Food and beverage gained importance after the war. Sales and marketing ruled throughout the 1960–1970 decade. Real estate was the thrust as the century closed. The current theme is improved customer relations through human resources management.

Quality Management in Manufacturing

Globalization opens worldwide markets, but it also introduces worldwide competition. During the initial stages of globalization, fierce competition brought into question the quality of U.S.-made goods. A reputation for quality, which the United States had held since the end of World War II, passed into other hands. Nearly a quarter century elapsed before the movement reversed. A return to quality for all U.S. industries was signaled by Ford Motor Company's advertising slogan, Quality Is Job One.[2]

The now popular emphasis on quality had its U.S. origins in the manufacturing industries. The decline in the reputation of U.S.-made goods forced manufacturers to reexamine production techniques and the workers responsible for that production. U.S. manufacturing responded, but it did not originate the movement toward QM.

Some work hard at tracing the origins of the QM movement to Greek philosophers and Chinese mystics. Others attribute the entire concept to Dr. W. Edwards Deming, an American. Like so many evolving ideas, neither is all this nor all that. The Japanese, for example, invented quality control circles, which are teams of employees focusing on special issues. Many hotels have used quality circles in their QM programs. The Japanese also introduced the concept of zero defects. Zero defects are difficult enough to achieve in manufacturing, impossible to achieve in service. Zero tolerance attempts to apply the same concept to the sociocultural environment. There, too, its application has failed. Taking up the challenge, some in the hotel industry have adopted "service quality that surprises," a level as near perfection as the human element allows.

Japan and Germany have been America's primary competitors in quality. Since much of Deming's work to upgrade quality took place during the 1950s in Japan, which was infamous then for very poor workmanship, Deming remains a central figure in the whole movement. Deming urged his disciples—and that term is warranted because of the intensity of his adherents—to follow the 14 points that he promulgated. Some of his points focused on the process and the product, others on the workers and the environment.

Check-In, Check-Out does the same. First, it is a process-oriented text, dealing with how-to: how to track reservations, how to set rates, and how to improve yield

[2]Trademark of the Ford Motor Company.

management. All of this is presented in sequence with electronic technology as one means of improving the *product* and the *process*. In this manner, the book concentrates on one of Deming's concerns. Beginning with the next paragraph, the text concentrates on another of his points, the *workers* and the industrywide *environment* in which they work. Let's get on with that: job two.

Quality Management in Innkeeping

Locating this chapter on guest service right smack in the middle of the book is not accidental. It is here as a fulcrum, balancing the how-to with the other elements of quality service, the guests and the staff. Every topic that precedes this chapter and every one that follows carries a message, understood if not always expressed, about the importance of guest service throughout the hotel. Executive attention to the rooms-division employees and through these persons to the guests is essential to the management of the entire enterprise. Attending to employee issues meets another part of Deming's concept for the QM process.

Quality management has spun off other concepts, such as quality assurance (QA) and TQM. The terms seem to be interchangeable now. The essence of all three terms is that every person in the company has the opportunity, and needs the ability, to make a positive impact on the customer. Just consider the terminology. Retailers speak of *customers*, various professionals refer to *clients* or *patients*, economists cite *consumer* trends, and galleries talk of *patrons*. Only the hotel industry calls its business clients *guests*.

Hoteliers have brought many innovations into the business. Bathtubs were added to hotel accommodations before they appeared in the White House. At one time, fans, radios, televisions, elevators, telephones, clocks, and swimming pools were unique products, installed in leading properties to attract guests. They are standard expectations today. To the credit of the hotel industry, TQM is viewed similarly. Quality management was an innovation when it first came to the hotel industry. Today, it is thought to be so basic an accommodation that no hotel can operate without it. Thus, the standard of the whole industry moves upward just as it does when every hotel room has a personal computer and fax.

▶ *Examples of Quality Management.*   Hotels did not embrace QM terminology as early as manufacturing did. That fact doesn't detract from the lodging industry's long-held sensitivity to guest service. Guest service is an industry fundamental, although management's attention to it waxes and wanes. Industrywide interest in guest service peaked anew in 1992 when the Ritz-Carlton Company, a hotel management company, won the first of its two Malcolm Baldrige National Quality Awards. The award itself was new, established by Congress only five years earlier. It recognizes U.S. companies that achieve excellence by emphasizing quality. As the first hotel company to win the award, the Ritz-Carlton Company reawakened the entire industry to one of its basic tenets: Service the guests.

Winning an award in 1992 required the company to commit to excellence far earlier. Although the Ritz-Carlton Company set the pace, many other hotel companies also initiated formal QM programs. The AH&MA (now the AH&LA) held the first Quality Assurance Conference in 1988. That same year, the Educational Institute of the AH&MA published the first text on the subject, *Managing Quality Services*.[3] Both

---

[3]Stephen J. Shriver. *Managing Quality Services* (East Lansing, MI: Educational Institute of the American Hotel & Motel Association, 1988).

the conference and the text flowed from the 1981 annual meeting when the AH&MA decided to create a Quest for Quality program. From that beginning, much of the industry came on stream.

The Sheraton chain was among the earliest converts. It launched its Sheraton Guest Satisfaction System (SGSS) in 1987, some ten years before the chain was acquired by Starwood. Sheraton executives attributed part of the chain's increased occupancy and profits to the staff's heightened sensitivity to quality. The fundamentals of many QM programs are like Sheraton's were. They begin with an emphasis on hiring the right people. SGSS called it HireVision; the Ritz-Carlton Company called it Talent Plus. All programs entail training, delegation of authority to operative-level employees, and incentive awards to lubricate the smooth flow of the program's machinery. Hiring, training, delegation, and reward are the basics of all QM programs.

Sheraton is now part of Starwood Hotels & Resorts (see Chapter 2, Exhibit 2–7). The culture of Starwood has been a mixed bag. In six short years, the company acquired a very diverse set of brands. There's the upscale St. Regis on one end and Sheraton's Four Point Hotels on the other. In between are the W Hotels, which are boutique-style properties and account for some 15% of total corporate revenues. In an effort "to integrate the company spiritually and to brand a [Starwood] culture,"[4] the corporation rolled out a systemwide initiative, Six Sigma. It is part of a total reengineering designed to bring consistency to all the corporate brands. In the full meaning of *Total* Quality Management, the Six Sigma program incorporates every facet of operation from reservations to check out, from service to cleanliness.

The Ritz-Carlton Hotel Company, like its Sheraton cousin, is no longer a free-standing chain. It's a division of Marriott, which also has a mix of brands (see Chapter 2, Exhibit 2–1). In contrast to Starwood, Marriott appears to be keeping its QM programs separated. Thus, Marriott's Renaissance brand has coined its own QM program, Savvy Service. Included are 20 principles that employees—Marriott prefers to call them associates—agree to work toward and enunciate during training sessions. Savvy Service aims to capture customer attention with the unexpected. Associates offer proactive service to win from guests, by means of personalized employee attention, the same level of delight that customers find in the unexpected design of a boutique hotel.

Radisson was another early convert to QM. It began a well-structured effort to implement a guest-service training program. Called Yes I Can, the program was installed in all Radisson-owned and Radisson-franchised properties. Radisson is a member of the Carlson family. More recently, Carlson created an entirely new division called Customer Relations Management (CRM). According to its 2001/2002 *Global Report*, Carlson is trying to move customers beyond the point of simple transactions. Radisson wants a relationship that is lifelong. To achieve this, the company has introduced a single guest recognition program, Gold Point Rewards. By using this companywide currency in all of its outlets (hotels, restaurants, cruise ships, travel management, and resorts), Radisson hopes to cement permanent guest loyalty.

The early Radisson program stretched its definition of QM beyond the guest. It asked each employee to extend the same guest-oriented service to every other employee. Whether greeting or servicing a colleague, each staff member was to behave as if other staff members were guests.

---

[4]Christina Binkley. "Starwood Sets Effort to Enhance Quality and Improve Cash Flow." *Wall Street Journal*, February 5, 2001, p. PB-4.

Each chain gives the basic idea, improved guest service, its own twist. Here are several brief examples:

Ramada's original QM program, You're Somebody Special, was launched in 1987. Twenty years later, it floated a new version, Personal Best. Not only has the terminology changed, but so has the purpose. Management has designated Personal Best to be the company's very culture rather than a simple program of QM.

Doubletree, now a division of Hilton (see Chapter 2, Exhibits 2–11 and 2–13), called its efforts Continuous Improvement.

The Peabody Orlando Hotel likes Service Excellence for its QM title. It has reduced turnover through a train-the-trainer buddy system. TEAM (Training and Education of Associates by Members) includes a problem-solving board game.

Preferred Hotels has a 100-page checklist to ensure "intense, personalized understanding of guests wants and needs."

Lane Hospitality, a chain of about 35 hotels, titled its effort Employee Entrepreneurship. Employee empowerment is emphasized because Lane authorized employees to settle problems at their own organizational level.

The Arizona Biltmore took an extra step. All employees are given a small budget with which to implement their empowerment.[5]

Empowering employees has another advantage: Fewer supervisors are needed if staff members have the authority to decide on their own. But for this concept to work, better trained employees are needed to carry out the empowerment—and therefore, better salaries will need to be paid. There is no evidence yet that the hotel industry has accepted that rationale.

Whether a chain or an independent property, a conference center or a franchise company, most of the industry has adopted some form or process that could be called quality assurance. Formal quality assurance programs are expensive, ongoing, and successful only when top management is committed for the long haul. That commitment often waivers over time because, like advertising, QM costs are easily measured but results are not.

➤ WHAT IS TOTAL QUALITY (CUSTOMER RELATIONS) MANAGEMENT?

As we shall see shortly, there is no single, crystal-clear definition of QM. At its core, QM seeks the cooperation of every staff member in achieving company goals, primarily those that stress guest service and guest relationships. In that, there is nothing new; management everywhere has such intent. Quality management brings a more formal tone, a more structured approach to the task. It recognizes, moreover, that guest service has many parts. Total quality management requires attention to all, not just some, of the parts. Among them is the physical product that the hotel delivers.

The Basic Product

Guests come to hotels to sleep. They willingly overlook missing amenities and poorly decorated lobbies if sleep, the hotel's basic product, is delivered. Above all else, hotel guests expect a good night's sleep. For Total Quality Management to achieve its goals

---

[5]One of the authors experienced this when a housekeeper arranged to have the hotel limousine take him to the airport.

throughout the hotel, guests must be satisfied with the delivery of the one product that they have specifically purchased. TQM begins with the guest room. Dissatisfaction with this basic product cannot be redressed by a smiling desk clerk wearing a happy-face button as part of a structured QM program.

The search is on—there are plenty of surveys—for the room that best meets guest expectations. Hilton has experimented with 50 TLC rooms chain wide. TLC rooms—Travel, Lifestyle Centers, a takeoff of Tender, Loving Care—are configured to reduce stress among business travelers. Through design and furnishings, the rooms attempt to compensate for interrupted sleep and exercise patterns. TLC rooms provide several basics for good sleep, including blackout curtains, improved mattresses, and dual wake-up systems. (To rest well tonight, travelers must be confident about the following morning's alarm clock.) These experimental rooms also include the sublime. They have running-water calming pools, massage chairs and belts, live plants, and aroma therapy.

Even less dramatic amenities such as full-length mirrors, CD players, and in-room coffeemakers add to the guest's experience provided the guest room has met its basic commitment. To achieve minimum expectations for sleep, high standards must be set and maintained for bedding, cleanliness, temperature, and noise.

➤*Bedding.*   The proverbial good night's rest requires, above all else, a comfortable bed. Chapter 3 provided information on bed sizes. The larger beds described there provide the extra six inches of mattress (six inches longer than the average height of the sleeper) that some experts recommend.[6] King beds, which travelers favor by far, measure 80 inches by 78 inches. Those measurements produce a square-looking bed. The California or European kings are slightly smaller overall, 84 inches by 72 inches, but provide a more appealing rectangular look.

The look of the bed and the look of the room become important once comfort levels are achieved. Each age has a different look. Shag carpets, the standard of an earlier era, have been replaced along with the florals and colors that identified them: mauve, pink, and burnt-orange. Sleigh beds and striped bedspreads are the "in" decor today, at least for Sheraton. So too are white bed linens, which convey a crisp, clean look and hold up better than colors in repeated washings.

Overall, the industry gets high marks for the quality of the mattresses and springs that complete the beds. A good hotel mattress lasts as long as 8 to 10 years; a top-of-the-line mattress, up to 15 years. A good-quality queen mattress costs about $300, or just $30 to $35 per year. It makes good economic sense to buy higher priced, longer lasting, matching mattress and spring sets. Mattress quality is measured in part by the type, number, and gauge of the steel coils and the method of tying them down. A 900-coil, pillowtop mattress is being used by Westin; Wyndham has a 992-coil mattress on its king beds. Marriott has opted for a seven-inch foam mattress with a quilted top.

Housekeeping must devise a system for turning the mattresses at least four times annually (see Chapter 3), because equalizing wear ensures longer mattress life. Furnishing comfortable chairs also adds life to the bedding because guests sit on the chairs and not on the beds. Ergonomic chairs have been included in recent renovations at upscale properties. Fire-resistant bedding has reduced the number of in-room fires that result from smokers falling asleep in bed.

---

[6]Robert J. Martin and Thomas J. Jones. *Professional Management for Housekeeping Operations*, 2nd ed. (New York: John Wiley & Sons, 1992).

Linen and Pillows.   There is more to a bed than a mattress. Upgrading the sleeping experience requires close attention to the bed coverings (called the soft goods) and especially to the linen count. The standard is 180 count: 80 threads in one direction, 100 in the other. This is a durable product for the hotel and an acceptable one for the guest, who is probably using about the same count at home. Jumping to a 250-count, or even 300, as some upscale chains have done for their top sheets, makes a noticeable difference. Sheets of that count are silky smooth and luxurious. Despite the moves of keen upscale competitors, the 180-count remains the choice of most hotels.

Crawling into a bed of 250- to 300-count bottom and top sheets, plus a third sheet of 180 count to cover the blanket, is a memorable experience. But there's more. No longer will one pillow do. Several pillows, each with distinctive characteristics, including hypoallergenic ones, are on the bed or available on call. Some hotels now offer "pillow menus" with feathers and down at the top of the list. Even wedge-shaped pregnancy pillows that lift and support the abdomen are offered. The Benjamin Hotel in New York City offers 11 specialty pillows all delivered and explained by a sleep concierge! (See Exhibit 7–2.)

Lighter down blankets or comforters, which have long been used in Europe, add another dimension to lodging's "new" beds. The comforters are enclosed in pillowcase-like covers, called duvets, another European adoption. Duvets are washable; traditional bedspreads are not. Savings from dry-cleaning costs can translate into more frequent laundering. Laundered bedcovers not only feel cleaner, they are.

The Public Relations of Bedding.   Good bedding has shifted from a design and furnishing decision, which often involves pages of specifications, to a marketing and advertising strategy that also takes several pages. Westin Hotels, for one, has run multiple full-page ads about its beds and baths in the nation's leading newspapers. Westin (that is Starwood) advertises its Heavenly Bed, a Simmons Beautyrest with pillow-top mattress, and its Heavenly Bath, a dual showerhead with five adjustable jets. The pitch says "an insanely comfortable bed and a shower that engulfs you."

There is some debate over the differences, if any, between Starwood's Heavenly Bed (Westin division), its Sleigh Bed (Sheraton division), and its W bed (W Hotels division). Let the argument rage: It's a perfect publicity ploy.

Every hotel company is in the bed business (see Exhibit 7–3). Wyndham Hotels & Resorts features the Room that Performs. Marriott has the Marriott Bed; Hilton, its Sleep Tight Room; and Best Western, its Business Plus Room. They're not just pro-

Exhibit 7–2
New attention to the hotel's basic product, the bed, has prompted a range of bedding upgrades, even a sleep concierge. *Courtesy of The Benjamin, New York, New York.*

Exhibit 7–3   The quality of hotel bedding has become a major advertising point as the industry comprehends the importance of sleep and works to communicate that understanding to its guests. *Courtesy of The Benjamin, New York, New York.*

moting the beds in advertising—they're actually selling them. Westin sells as many as four per day through its special bed catalog. The Ritz-Carlton Chicago delivers an entire bed to your home if you stay in its Lakeside Suite for several nights at approximately $1,000/night. Everything in the room, including the live orchids, is for sale at the Mondrian Hotel, Los Angeles.

➤*Cleanliness.*   No architectural design is more attractive than a sparkling bed. A recent survey among American Automobile Association members who use the *Tour Book* ranked cleanliness as their top concern. Cleanliness was ahead of price, location, and amenities. A study done by Wyndham Hotels ranked stale, smelly rooms at the top of their guests' top peeves. Triple sheeting, which enclose the seldomly washed blankets between clean sheets, is the first sign of the hotel's attitude toward cleanliness. (After all, a third sheet increases laundry costs by 50%!)

Bedding must be clean! Unfortunately, clean sheets don't always look clean. There has been a shift away from ironing sheets to using a sheet of 50% cotton and 50% synthetic fiber, no-iron sheets. No-iron sheets are fine as fitted bottom sheets because the wrinkles are stretched out, providing the appearance of a smooth, ironed sheet—except fitted sheets are just not being used. They are difficult to fold and handle, require extra storage space, and tear at the corners, increasing replacement costs. Because of this, many hotels use regular, not fitted, no-iron sheets, which wrinkle and leave the impression of less-than-clean bed linen.

Cleanliness is not limited to bedding. Guests are very sensitive to the quality of housekeeping everywhere, especially in the bath. Tub/showers, toilets, sinks, and bathroom floors require special attention to remove hair and dirt. Into the corners and behind the toilets take extra care. Chrome fixtures, particularly the sink and tub drains, must be cleaned and wiped daily.

Excessive clutter in the bathroom leaves an institutional impression that offsets even the cleanest accommodations. A few simple decisions can bring order to the bath. Removing nonessentials, coffeemakers, for example, is a first step. Fewer bath amenities reduce the clutter, as do vanities at least four feet in length. A long vanity with an off-centered sink improves the look and holds bathroom essentials with a minimum of clutter.

Vacuuming, the final step in cleaning the guest room, may take place only between guests. Rooms for stayovers are not vacuumed unless the room attendant or housekeeper thinks there is need to do so. Elsewhere, the policy might be to vacuum every day, check out or not.

Overall cleanliness, inside and outside the guest room, is taken for granted. Few guests ever compliment sanitation standards on guest-comment cards, but all will complain when it's missing.

➤*Noise and Temperature.*   Noise is another explanation for the industry's failure to deliver its basic product, sleep. Even "road warriors" (business travelers who sleep away from home a great deal) complain about noisy rooms. Poor initial construction, which is not easily fixed after the fact, is high on a list of causes. Budget limitations force builders to ignore adequate sound barriers between rooms and in the utility and plumbing shafts. Back-to-back baths make for easy construction and maintenance, but play havoc in transmitting noises. In very bad cases, the plumbing is strapped inadequately, so noisy vibrations follow the opening of every faucet.

Poorly insulated rooms bring the neighbor's television set resonating into the sleeper's dreams. Everyday sounds from simple conversations to children playing come from rooms close by. Hallway noises, which include the whirr of ice-making machine motors, ice falling into buckets, ringing telephones, elevator doors, and late-to-bed revelers, add to the din. The worst noise offender is right in the room: the fan on the heating/air-conditioning system. It is as much an annoyance as the inability to control the room's temperature.

Central heating and air-conditioning systems are far superior to individual room units. Cost is, again, the determining factor. But some window units are not even temperature sensitive. They run all the time unless they're turned off completely. It's up to the sleeper to decide which is worse. Occasionally, the units don't run at all. Maintenance on the systems is minimal and on demand rather than preventative. Guests may be housed in rooms with nonworking units. Encountered occasionally are systems that deliver either heating or cooling, depending on the time of the year. No choice is available during swing months; guests get either heating or cooling, regardless of their own body temperatures.

Construction noise joins with street noise as still another QM challenge. TQM faces its toughest test when guests are roomed close to internal renovations or nearby external construction. Construction jobs always begin early in the morning. TQM requires the hotel to act. Reservations must alert the guest, and registration must remind the guest. Above all, the rate must reflect the unavoidable if the hotel is truly managing for quality.

The same kind of preventative action should be taken with all aspects of the hotel room. The Ritz-Carlton has done just that with its Care program. Care reduces the number of guest-room complaints through anticipative management. It assures, before the guest arrives, that every room has enough hangers, toilets don't leak, air-conditioners work and run quietly, and that ample pillows and towels are provided. Preventing complaints relies heavily on the hotel housekeeping inspection that Chapter 3 discussed. So the first hotel company to win the Baldrige Award for quality sees good sense in continuing TQM programs that attend to basic accommodations.

Quality Management Defined

Defining QM is as difficult a task as is delivering it. Some have tried explaining quality service by telling anecdotes, brief stories to illustrate the idea. Illustrations of this type are legend: A desk clerk makes certain that an important letter gets typed for a guest after hours; a bellperson delivers a forgotten attaché case to the airport just in time; a housekeeper takes guest laundry home to meet a deadline; a door attendant lends black shoes to a guest for a formal affair.

Despite the difficulties, formal definitions are the vogue. Everyone gives it a shot—the authors try their hand a few pages on—even if the results are incomplete. Along with hundreds of other publications, *Managing Quality Services,* cited earlier, says, "QA is a management system that ensures consistent delivery of products and services." Another puts it this way, "TQM is a way to continuously improve performance at every level of operation, in every functional area of an organization, using all available human and capital resources."[7] Both of these descriptions, which represent the general run of QA definitions, fail to emphasize the duality of the issue: QM involves both the buyer–receiver of the service and the seller–giver.

Unit I explained how segmented the hotel industry is. Its customer base is equally fragmented. Thus, the desire to deliver quality originates with innumerable sellers and many, many buyers. Each side and each member of that side sees the issue from a different perspective. No wonder variations abound in the delivery and receipt of service, and consequently in its definition. Quality service and the management of quality service have no objective measures. Definitions are necessarily vague, evalua-

---

[7]Bruce Brocka and Suzanne Brocka. *Quality Management: Implementing the Best Ideas of the Masters* (Burr Ridge, IL: Richard D. Irwin, 1992).

tions are obviously imprecise, and delivery is clearly inexact. Still, everyone knows it when they see it.

▶*The Buyer's View.*   From the guest's viewpoint, quality is the degree to which the property delivers what the guest expects. If the guest is surprised by a better stay than anticipated, the hotel is perceived as high quality. If the visit fails to meet expectations, the property is downgraded.

Advertising, word-of-mouth comments, price, previous visits and publicity create a level of expectation within the guest. Of course, that barrage of communications is received differently with different perceptions by almost every guest. Moreover, those very expectations change over time and place, even within the same guest. Influencing the guest's expectations are components that may be outside the hotel's control: a late flight, a rude cabdriver, a bad storm.

Guests hold different expectations about different hotels, even different hotels within the same chain. Quality is measured against the expectation of that particular property at that particular time more than against different hotels in different categories.

Driving up to an economy property with a loaded family van and a pet but without a reservation carries one expectation. Flying around the world to an expensive resort—a trip that a couple has planned for and saved for over many years—creates a much different level of anticipation. Coming to a busy convention property with a reservation made by the company's travel desk evokes still a third level of expectation. Each expectation must be met by the hotel with delivery at the highest level appropriate for the circumstances. Quality assurance attempts to do just that. It is a big, big order.

Consider two hypothetical properties. The first, an economy hotel offering minimal services, charges half its neighbor's rate. The neighbor, an expensive, upscale property and not a true competitor, has it all.

The economy hotel offers the following conveniences:

➤ No bellservice, but parking is convenient and many luggage carts are in the lobby.
➤ No room service, but the hotel is located near a well-known restaurant chain and has an exceptional choice of vending options.
➤ No health club, but the swimming pool is clean, open at convenient hours, and has a good supply of towels.
➤ No concierge, but the room clerk is knowledgeable and affable.

The upscale neighbor offers the following conveniences:

➤ Bellpersons, whom guests are urged to call on. But this hotel never schedules enough staff, resulting in long delays.
➤ Room service, but it is offered at limited times. This hotel suggests a pizza delivery company as an alternative.
➤ A well-reputed health club, but it is on lease, which means that this hotel charges for admission.
➤ A concierge, but the concierge has a recorded message that puts the guest on hold.

Extreme as these illustrations are, the point is obvious: Quality in the service industry is in the eyes of the beholder. Service lacks the established and measurable specifications used in manufacturing. How, then, could an agreement on the definition of service be reached if the product isn't created until it's delivered? Managing for quality, therefore, must include standards derived from the consumer's perspective. Doing so gives credence to the buyer's view of what quality service is all about. Management must first establish the systems and then the measurement standards for those systems—both to be based on the buyers' expectations. Management must also fix the procedure for achieving those standards. Successfully implemented, TQM matches the buyers' standards with the sellers' ability to deliver. When done right, the guest/buyer knows that the hotel delivers quality guest service.

▶*The Seller's View.* Like every other policy and operating practice, TQM originates with management. Either management makes deliberate decisions to implement particular ideas or it passively accepts ongoing procedures. So it is with quality assurance. Management creates and carries out a program of enhanced guest service, or there is none. Action doesn't always follow verbal support. A study of hotel general managers reported their belief in the concepts of TQM, but they downgraded its effectiveness in practice.[8]

Delivering quality requires management to focus on both employees and guests. The two are intertwined. Increasing guest services to satisfy the buyer's side of QM requires special attention to operational issues, the employees' side of QM. Staying close to the customer means stressing customer wants, ensuring consistency, remedying the mistakes that do occur, and concentrating on the whole with a passion that hints of obsession. But all of these are also operational concerns. Nothing can be accomplished without attention to the employees entrusted with the delivery.

Leadership. Adopting TQM as a company philosophy forces major changes in the definition of management. Traditionally, management is said to be a series of functions. Planning, organizing, staffing, directing, and reviewing is the classic list of management's responsibilities. Quality management adds another element—leadership. Managing as a leader requires a change in both the style of management and the composition of the workforce being managed. When both components—management and workforce—focus on delivering quality above all else, the company is said to have a *service culture.*

With a leadership style, managers shift from their traditional position of review, which requires corrective action after mistakes are made, to a proactive style of supervision. Errors must be corrected, of course, but a proactive stance aims at error avoidance. Minimizing errors, whether on a production line or a registration line, is what TQM is all about.

Total Quality Management is a pervasive term. It has come to mean almost any action designed to improve the operation. And that's just what it is: A series of small steps taken within an organizational culture that has the customer's experience as its central focus. Developing that culture requires a fundamental shift in management style. Binding employees, supervisors, and management into closer relationships takes a committed leader. Success will depend upon the degree of entrepreneurship that is created. Employees must accept their contribution to the success of the enterprise and have the power to make it happen. It will happen if management leads by balancing its authority and discipline with delegation and flexibility.

Part of the sharing of responsibility and credit is the sharing of information that once was considered confidential. Staff members must be knowledgeable about the activities of their own departments and those departments whose functions overlap.

---

[8]Robert Woods, Denny Rutherford, Raymond Schmidsall, and Michael Sciarini. "Hotel General Managers." *Cornell Hotel and Restaurant Administration Quarterly*, December 1998, p. 41.

Overlapping interests are reinforced through quality circles (QOs). Quality circles, which are discussed throughout this chapter, are employee committees. Representatives within each department and sometimes from several departments meet and work on problems. Quality circles at the front desk, for example, may have representatives from housekeeping, sales, telecommunications, and accounting. Each representative would then sit on a QO within his or her own department. Soon a network exists across the entire property. Quality assurance goals can be established to reflect the realities of the entire operation. Standards can be developed with input from other departments. Rewards for quality performance can be achievement driven.

Empowerment.   Once so much of management's guarded interests are opened to the operating staff, the next step is almost anticlimactic. Some of management's power is given away, delegated down the line. Operative employees are authorized to make their own decisions as long as these fall within the scope of the individuals' job assignments. Entrusting the employee to act responsibly requires management to give that employee the authority to take action. Giving the workforce appropriate authority is empowerment.

Empowerment locates the problem solving and decision making at the source (see Exhibit 7–4). Line employees can act effectively once they have both the information and the authority to use it. Moreover, empowering employees creates leaner and flatter organizations. The pancake-like structures make each department operate almost as a small company, with greater responsibility and accountability, under the umbrella of general management.

Empowerment doesn't just happen by fiat one day. Empowerment must have its base in employee knowledge and training. Initially, limits must apply. Limited empowerment allows the front-line staffer to choose a solution from a range of previously established guidelines (see Exhibit 7–13), and most guests see this as a fair adjustment. More senior associates may be given wider discretion (full empowerment) based on their experience and previous judgments. Whether full or limited discretion, empowerment provides a quick response to issues raised by the guest. Consulting a supervisor before acting is time consuming but might convey to the guest an impression of individualized attention.

The first response to empowerment involves individual actions by single employees. A misquoted rate is settled on the spot by the cashier as the guest checks out. Apologies for an unmade room are expressed with a small bouquet ordered by the desk attendant. Individual acts by employees bring immediate responses from the guests who experience them. But empowerment is more than guest relations.

A second and broader delegation of empowerment is that given to QOs. Originally, QOs were merely asked to identify problems and to recommend possible solutions. Where TQM has been implemented successfully, QOs are actually executing their own ideas. They have been empowered to do so. QOs tackle two types of problems. One kind deals with guest relations, usually how-to's. The group considers how to speed check ins and check outs, how to reduce errors in reservations, how to expedite group baggage handling, and more.

The second type of issues faced by QOs also has an impact on quality service, but the relationship is less guest oriented. The attention is on in-house procedures (moving linen without tying up the service elevators), cost reductions (chargebacks by credit-card companies), or operational irritations (maintenance's slow response to requests for guest-room repairs). None of these has anything to do with immediate guest service, but all of them have everything to do with QM.

GUEST QUARTERS®
SUITE HOTELS

Dear Guests:

Welcome to Guest Quarters Suite Hotels and Guest Quarters Magazine — an informative guide to this hotel's community, as well as interesting and entertaining reading on a variety of subjects.

I would like to take this opportunity to share something with you that is new and exciting at all Guest Quarters Suite Hotels. It's not a new amenity or special promotion — in fact, you can't touch or see this at all. But, when you stay at any Guest Quarters, you will sense what we are calling employee empowerment.

Employee empowerment means that at Guest Quarters, all of our employees have been trained and authorized to handle your inquiries on-the-spot. Whether it be a concern over our quality levels or a special request, Guest Quarters employees have been given the tools to make your stay flawless, without having to find a supervisor. (Of course, there are special situations which require the attention of a manager.)

Employee empowerment takes our award-winning service levels one step higher. It provides you with a more efficient and effective staff that is eager to serve you. Just as importantly, empowerment further demonstrates our confidence in our company's most valuable asset — our employees.

The results? I can't express how proud I am of how our employees have utilized empowerment. Rather than just exercise their decision-making privileges to address negative guest situations, Guest Quarters employees are going "above and beyond the call of duty" to provide unexpected touches and unanticipated acts of kindness. This is the true meaning of hospitality.

As we move forward in this decade which has been designated the "Decade of Customer Service," I am confident that Guest Quarters will continue to be one of the hotel industry's shining stars. I invite you to visit any of our 30 locations nationwide to experience impeccable service, coupled with the luxury of a suite.

Sincerely,

Richard M. Kelleher
President Guest Quarters Suite Hotels

Exhibit 7–4 Top management's support of empowerment is critical. With it, results are better than a host of amenities or an expensive advertising campaign. *Courtesy of Promus Hotel Corporation, Memphis, Tennessee. (Guest Quarters merged with Doubletree [1993], which merged with Promus [1997], which merged with Hilton [1999].)*

The Employee.   Convincing supervisors to adopt a leadership style of management is but half the battle. Customer relations management requires employees to take on responsibilities, to accept the empowerment offered. Just as some managers and supervisors oppose the transfer of their power to employees, some employees decline to accept what's offered. Many prefer not to take on what they perceive to be a management job.

Similarly, the employer's willingness to share information about the business may not be matched by the employees' interest in receiving it—or receiving it, having the capacity to understand it, or the interest to use it. Even highly motivated employees may not comprehend what is offered or what is expected. Leadership requires followers; great leadership requires inspired and motivated followers. Quality management is burdened with the development of both leaders and followers; and that must be done within a workforce of great diversity in language, education, and cultural expectations (see Exhibit 7–5).

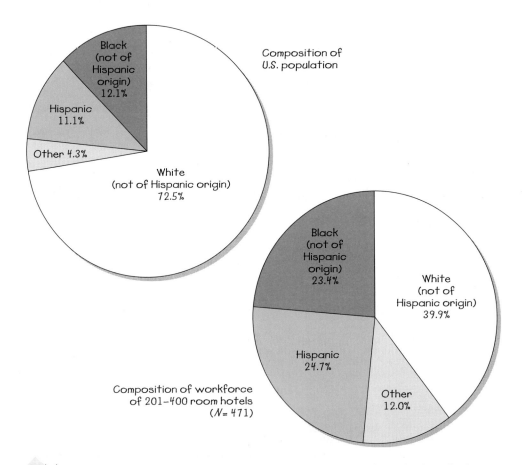

Exhibit 7–5   The workforce in American hotels differs ethnically and culturally from the makeup of the national population, which is the likely composition of the industry's customers. Managers and staff must be sensitive to expectations that differ among groups. Diversity embraces the varied cultures; affirmative action requires hiring a given number of each minority group. *Courtesy of The American Hotel Foundation, Washington, D.C.*

DIVERSITY AND TURNOVER.   The lodging industry faces two labor issues, work-force diversity and labor turnover, that are often treated as one.[9] They are because finding and retaining competent staff requires management to look across the great diversity of peoples that make up the American workforce. Moreover, as Exhibit 7–5 so clearly shows, lodging relies heavily on a nonwhite, non-Anglo workforce. Within the hotel industry, diversity is a business necessity, not a hot social issue.

The industry's continuous search for workers is a result of tight labor markets and high job turnover. Employees, and the term includes supervisors and managers as well, come and go at a costly pace. Many workers are in dead-end jobs. Boredom and monotonous repetition are blunted temporarily by moving to another property even though the new job has the same task routines. Turnover at the lowest levels of the organization, the spots where QM could shine, exceeds 200% annually in some jobs of some hotels. Every employee is replaced twice each year! Less dramatic but equally disturbing turnover occurs among managers and supervisors. Turnover feeds upon itself. Missing workers mean heavier loads for those remaining. Discontent grows so that establishing, maintaining, and improving TQM is put aside as resources are assigned to searching, finding, and replacing a turnstile staff.

Retaining workers is far less costly than replacing them. That's why retention plans, tools long used in other industries, are now finding their way into lodging. Training qualified staffers for career enhancement is one technique. Financial incentives is another—and one that has broader application. Retirement plans, year-end bonuses, and employee stock ownership are relatively new concepts for this old industry. Financial rewards such as these enable workers to build savings even though they remain in lower-end jobs. Several chains, Marriott for one, recognized this and adopted employee-participation plans years ago. Now, a shortage of applicants for low wage positions has accelerated the introduction of financial incentives throughout the industry.

Rewards, financial and otherwise, must be part of any TQM retention plan. Incentives are especially important at the front desk where TQM demands a great deal from moderately paid personnel. Chapter 9 suggests some. Although dollars and cents remain strong incentives at the operative-level, imaginative noncash rewards can be used throughout the hotel. Among them are invitations for employees to join QOs, where their ideas can get a hearing. Special cross-training sessions or second-language classes on company time go far toward retention. Building language skills adds credibility to the hotel's diversity program.

Every success should be celebrated, and every means to do so should be employed, from simple recognition such as a thank-you from the manager to incentives that bind the company and reward the individual. Employee-of-the-month is a widely used recognition. It is more effective if it carries a cash stipend and perhaps a special parking space along with a plaque on the wall and a photo in the newspaper. Some departments can accommodate flexible working hours, which may prove the best of all rewards for working parents. So, too, might job-sharing, which need not be limited to executive-style jobs. Larger hotels and local hotel consortia have taken further steps to accommodate working parents: They operate nursery schools.

Although managers, especially supervisory managers not protected under wage-and-hour laws, are not above cash rewards, the hotel industry has another incentive

---

[9]See, for example, *Turnover and Diversity in the Lodging Industry*, listed in the Reading References at the end of this chapter.

to offer: time off. Long hours on the job cause hardships in personal life for many nonhourly (so-called exempt) workers. Incentives for them may simply be an extra day off.

Good staff at all organizational levels is the thread of the quality management weave. The commitment to finding and holding those persons is reflected in the salaries paid, the training offered, and the incentives rewarded. A company that concentrates on better human resources ensures a better delivery of quality service. The effort begins with selecting and retaining the right persons.

SELECTING AND RETAINING THE RIGHT EMPLOYEE.   Managing guest services by empowering employees and enlisting their help requires a broad effort. It reaches beyond the immediate delivery of services, stretching backward to employment and forward to retention. Delivering quality service begins at the selection decision. How else can the right person be in the right place when the CRM situation requires? Hoteliers knows this, so the personnel office has been the launch site for most TQM programs.

Selecting the right employee—and TQM programs emphasize that it is *selection*, not *hiring*—is where good service begins. Imagine the impression when new hires meet the general manager who repeats that mantra: You've been "selected" because of your enthusiasm and your ability to smile when things go wrong. The industry has come to believe that it can teach technical skills, but it needs to select sensitive staff. Good service is actually intangible, not measurable, so the burden of delivery falls upon the employee who is on hand at that moment. Friendly, interactive applicants who have a sincere wish to help will solve problems of quality deficiency faster than do experienced technical workers who lack those qualities. Indeed, there are far more guest complaints about poor employee attitudes than about substandard facilities and broken TV sets.

Selecting the right person begins with searching for and finding the right pool of applicants. Personnel departments don't always clear that hurdle, because hotel job vacancies are frequent and difficult to fill. Too often, the first applicant to come is the one hired. Recruiting during good economic times takes imaginative work. Hotel companies begin with nominations from their own workforce, paying cash incentives when friends and relatives of current workers remain through a given time period. Web sites are also widely used. They're great for college recruiting, but may not reach prospective applicants for the lower-end jobs that are the most difficult to fill. Success as well as a greater diversity comes from advertising in the numerous ethnic newspapers that reach Latinos, African Americans, Koreans, and other groups. Florida Disney has gone to Puerto Rico to find staff. Early Las Vegas hotels did the same in Los Angeles. Costs skyrocket when recruiters travel and pay $1,000 to $2,000 to help new hires move and settle. No wonder everyone agrees that retention is far less costly than recruitment.[10]

Retention rates go up if new hires understand clearly what jobs they are about to take. Some properties ask the applicant to spend an hour observing the actual job. Others, like Doubletree Hotels and Resorts, go a step further. Applicants are interviewed by the very employees with whom they'll work, a practice called *peer-group hiring*. That's part of a TQM program that puts employees in decision-making roles.

---

[10]Turnover costs have been estimated at approximately $2,000 for each nonexempt (hourly) worker and approximately $6,500 for each exempt (from wage and hour laws) supervisor-manager.

Once hired, retaining the right worker, like retaining the right guest, would seem to be of the highest priority. Strangely, despite the spread in costs, retention sometimes gets less attention than the original search. Yet retaining both the recruited guest and the recruited worker is at the very heart of TQM. Induction, helping the new hire ease into the company, is a common pitfall. After a company spends many recruiting dollars, a new employee may be alienated in the very next step: entering the work door.

TRAINING.   TQM views training as an investment, not as a cost. Continuous training can be likened to a program of continually upgrading the physical plant. Both the facilities and the employees are critical to guest satisfaction. Trained staff is able to do a better job for the house and the customer. This provides personal satisfaction for the employee and develops opportunities for both long-run promotions and short-run gratuities.

Training has different purposes. One type of training improves work skills—better use of reservation computers, for example. Another type, security training, for example, widens the workers' scope of understanding beyond their immediate jobs. A third type of training enhances interpersonal skills—meeting and greeting a guest in the hall, for example. Still another purpose emphasizes the worker's personal needs: cleanliness, retirement savings, language skills. The Ritz-Carlton chain has a well-known motto: "We are ladies and gentlemen serving ladies and gentlemen." Training makes it so, since we are not all born ladies and gentlemen. Managing for service requires training in all four areas.

Employees are held responsible for their own actions. TQM doesn't overlook mistakes, but it does replace negative discipline with positive training. New directions and positive suggestions (coaching) for the next time move the system toward error avoidance. Avoiding mistakes rather than correcting them is the essence of guest service. Pledging the costs to coach and train on a continuous basis is a measure of management's commitment to a philosophy of quality service.

▶*The Authors' View.*   The entire QM culture has been summarized in a brief phrase (an aphorism) that has become a favorite of the industry. "The answer is 'yes,' now ask me the question."[11] That clearly represents the type of employee (and management) attitude that CRM programs are supposed to instill. Applications of the adage apply equally well to employee–guest interactions, employee–management interfaces, and employee–employee contacts. Under an umbrella of so broad a coverage, this brief saying offers a simple definition of total quality management.

Closer inspection proves QM culture to be very similar to the carefully cultivated culture of the concierge. With both, the attitude is expressed in Radisson's "Yes, I can!" Hotels that promote QM understand that the concierge is not a department, not even a staff. It is an attitude, the kind that one hopes all employees in a QM program hold. Hence, the first part of the authors' definition: *Quality management is an attitude that has every employee acting like a concierge. . . .*

Several times throughout this chapter the duality of quality assurance has been emphasized: The guest side (the display side) of the QM equation is balanced by the employee side (the operational side). Thus, the second phrase of the authors' definition of QM: . . . *and thinking like a manager.*

> Quality management is an attitude that has every employee acting like a concierge and thinking like a manager.

[11]Rick Van Warner attributes the aphorism to Keith Dunn, who cites Don Smith as the original source. *Nation's Restaurant News*, October 26, 1991.

Quality Management Denied

The hotel business is part of a vast hospitality industry that includes food, beverage, and entertainment facilities. Within that definition, hotel leaders see their industry as a service industry, their product as hospitality, and their customers as guests. Because this position has been verbalized so often, hotel patrons are confused by the antihospitality–antiguest–antiservice syndrome that is part of some hotels.

Guest expectations, one component of quality delivery systems, were reviewed earlier. Guests recognize that every property is not charged with the same level of product despite its grouping under the common umbrella of lodging. But guests do not understand why minimal service means antiservice, and why a lack of personnel means a lack of courtesy. Management's failure to distinguish minimal service, justified by minimal rates, from antiservice, shown by employee negativism, has lead to the antiservice syndrome that some hotels demonstrate and many guests experience.

Total Quality Management is the industry's response to antiservice. TQM programs are designed to ferret out the problems, to train for the solutions, and to reward those who demonstrate the right response. Sometimes, however, the very structure of the operation thwarts the best intentions.

➤**Who Knows Why?** Every organization develops standard operating procedures. They are to business routines as personal habits are to individual routines. Some of them are new and meaningful; some are bad and in need of change. Along with the new and the good, guests encounter the old and the useless. Like all bad habits, old and useless ways are hard to discard. Hotels that insist on keeping them irritate their guests unnecessarily and undermine the concepts of quality service (see Exhibit 7–6). To the observer, some practices seem to be almost intentional, as if inconveniencing the guest is easier than fixing the problem. Consider the following:

Who knows why?

➤ Sleepers are roused from their beds by:
alarm clocks set by previous occupants.
computerized calling systems asking for a breakfast order.
maids knocking on the door: "Never mind, just housekeeping."
running water in the neighbor's shower.

➤ Customers are assessed for:
leaving a day earlier than the four-day reservation.
incoming faxes, although incoming telephone calls are free.
late check-outs, even when occupancy is low.
gratuities when they are part of the inclusive package.

➤ Guests find:
the pool closed when they are there and open when they're away.
dining dress codes more rigid than accepted social standards.
their requests cannot be met because of some "company policy."
hotel managers taking the best parking spots.

➤ Hotels:
sell double-occupancy rooms but offer only a single key.
require bell service for individual arrivals but not for groups.

Exhibit 7–6
Who knows why?

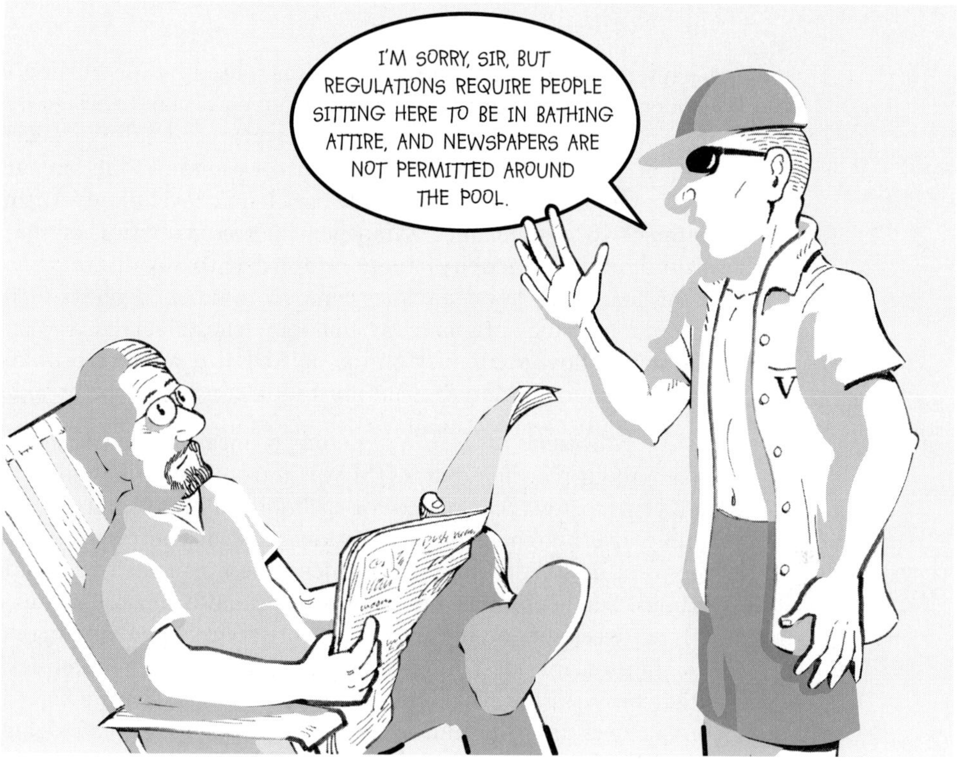

> have coffee stands that refuse service four minutes before opening time.
> impose surcharges on telephone calls paid with credit cards.
> ➤ Policies dictate:
> loud, public conversations when arrivals have no baggage.
> different rate quotes from travel agents, reservationists, and Web sites.
> no towels from the room, although there are none at the pool.
> not providing clean linens for stayovers. Is it really ecological concerns?

➤ IMPLEMENTING GUEST SERVICE

The modern hotel services mass markets. How different that is from the individualized attention that was the norm a century ago. Smiling, courteous, concerned employees working in a democratic culture have replaced the rigid, serve-food-from-the-left, clear-drinks-from-the-right, white-gloved autocracy of a past era.

Hotel companies have shifted from the formal to the informal; from pretense to expedited service; from rigid procedures to empowerment. Much of the change can be explained by the public's new attitude toward service. Aware of labor costs, functioning in a self-service environment themselves, sensitive to the employees' expectations of equality, today's guests no longer expect a servile attitude. And employees no longer deliver it. Guests do expect—and are entitled to receive during each encounter—a friendly face, an attentive ear, and a twinkling eye. After all, quality service, as previously defined, is an attitude that shines through.

Measuring Guest Service

Chapter 1 explained the several measures used by the lodging industry to evaluate its economic health. Percentage of occupancy (%) and average daily rate (ADR) are the most widely used ratios. Their values rise and fall for several reasons. Some are macroeconomic: the state of the world's economy, the strength of the national currency. Other explanations include the chain's level of advertising or the owner's commitment to maintenance. Management's contribution is the workforce. Employee attitude and productivity cannot be ascribed to any distant cause, but only to management. Startlingly good statistics come from satisfied guests served by positive employees; poor results originate in unhappy guests served by negative employees. But waiting for low occupancy and poor ADRs to warn of problems may be a matter of waiting too long. Management must look constantly for breakdowns in guest service.

▶*Moments of Truth.*   A study to measure the costs of poor service was undertaken about the time that TQM was introduced to lodging.[12] The amount of dollars and cents lost was calculated for each missed opportunity in each department. For example, overbooking, lost reservations, and discourtesy were the charges laid against the front desk. Although one incident doesn't make a bankruptcy, poor service is insidious. Single episodes mushroom from minor, miscellaneous costs to staggering totals per week, per month, per year. Antiservice comes at a high cost.

Guests and staff interact more frequently in a hotel environment than in any other business setting. Hotel employees are asked to deliver an exceptional level of service over and over and over again each day. Exhibit 7–7 highlights the cumulative impact of having one's customers in residence.

With 70% occupancy and a double occupancy of 33%, employee-guest contacts number 2,800 per day. The figure soars to over 1 million per year for a hotel of only 300 rooms! The number multiplies even faster with full-service hotels, where more op-

Exhibit 7–7
Moments of truth are the points at which the service provider and the service buyer meet eyeball to eyeball. TQM makes certain the employee does not blink because each mistake impacts the bottom line.

Number of rooms in the hotel			300
Percentage of occupancy			× .70
Number of rooms occupied each night		210	
Percentage of double occupancy			× .33
Number of guest-nights		280	
Moments of Truth			
Arrival	1		
Inquiry at the desk	1		
Bellperson	1		
Chambermaid	1		
Telephone operator	1		
Coffee shop host(ess)	1		
Server/busperson	2		
Cashier	1		
Newstand	1		
Total encounters per guest-night		× 10	
Daily number of moments of truth			2,800

[12]Stephen Hall, *Quest for Quality: Cost of Error Study* (American Hotel & Motel Association and CitiCorp Diners Club, n.d.).

erating departments mean more employees. Not only are service expectations higher at the full-service property, so are the number of service contacts.

Opportunities for meeting guest expectations—or failing to meet guest expectations—have been called "moments of truth."[13] It is during these encounters, when the service provider and the service buyer meet eyeball to eyeball, that the guest's perception of quality is set. Some say the first 10 minutes are the most critical.

How does the staff respond? Does the final guest of the shift receive the same attention as the first arrival? For many, only a smile and an appropriate greeting are needed. More is expected by the next guest: the one with the problem, the one with the complaint, the one with the special need. If the employee is empowered to act, to respond with alacrity, to evidence concern, it is a shining moment of truth.

Total quality management requires similar moments of truth between supervisors and staffers. Employees will not shine outwardly unless there is an inner glow. Supervisors will not get positive moments of truth if they always second-guess subordinates who have been empowered. Supervisors will not get positive moments of truth if staffers are irritated, say, by late work-schedule postings that frustrate personal plans. Good results from service encounters begins with a good working environment. Shining moments of truth come best from a total quality program.

➤*Quality Control Through Inspection.* Review and evaluation are essential parts of the management function. That's no less true in managing guest services than, say, in managing cash. Cash management requires standards and procedures to account for the control of money. Service management, too, has standards and procedures for maintaining quality. Quality control (QC) enables hotel companies to maintain even standards throughout all the properties of a far-flung chain. Guests rely on these standards, identifying them through corporate logos. To ensure the consistency promised by the logos, chains use inspectors to make onsite visits and evaluations.

Quality control through inspection has become an important element of TQM. Inspectors rate the condition of the physical plant as well as the responses of the employees. Some chains use their own inspectors. Others, Preferred Hotels & Resorts World Wide, for example, employ independent third parties. Visits may be announced beforehand or be made by anonymous inspectors. Either way, verbal reports are usually given to the unit managers before formal, written documents are filed with central headquarters.

Although they come for different purposes, inspectors from AAA, Mobil Travel Guide, and others are also on the road. Many properties are unaware that meeting planners are doing their own unannounced inspections before selecting a venue for the group or groups they represent.

Each chain has its own policy for appraising quality. Hilton aims for three inspections per year. Choice Hotels International sets a two-visit minimum; Super 8 Motels, four visits per property per year. Most use a point system to measure compliance with the franchise agreement. Days Inn, for example, requires 425 points to maintain minimum company standards. Cendant, which inspects three to four times per year, makes its ratings public by assigning the property one to five sunbursts in its directory. Franchise contracts differ, so franchisees have 30 to 180 days to remedy serious defaults before the franchise is canceled—and they do get canceled! Radisson culls from the bottom up, using several criteria, including the comment cards that will be discussed soon. Differences among the chains account for the variations in procedure. For example, about 90% of Radisson's hotels are franchised, compared to, say, the 75% or so of Hilton's.

---

[13]The term *moments of truth* has been attributed to Jan Carlzon, former chairman of SAS Airlines.

Quality control has many parts. One is an inspection of the physical facility. This involves a wide range of issues, from the maintenance of the grounds, to the quality of the furniture and equipment, to the cleanliness of the property. Are there holes in the carpets, burns in the bedspreads, paper in the stairwells? Check sheets used by the inspectors deal with a variety of details: working blow driers, cleanliness of air vents, number of hangers in the closet, and even the rotation of mattresses (see Exhibit 7–8).

INSPECTION REPORT

Auditor _____   Hotel _____

Identification no. _____   City _____

Date(s) _____

	Excellent	Good	Fair	Poor	Comments
Registration					
1. Waiting time		×			About 2 minutes
2. Greeting	×				Used my name in conversation
3. Friendliness		×			
4. Efficiency			×		PMS was slow
5. Staff on hand	×				Other clerks handled telephone
6. Grooming		×			Except for Grace's hair
7. Accuracy	×				
Rooming					
1. Bellperson offered				×	No, had to call housekeeping
2. Elevator wait	×				3:00 PM
3. Floor signage	×				
4. First impression			×		Not too clean; stale odor
Guest Room					
1. Hangers	×				
2. Paper products			×		Facial tissue box nearly empty
3. Sanitation			×		Shower curtains need attention
4. Desk	×				
5. Telephone and book	×				Displayed card with fees listed
6. Bed and linens		×			
7. Lighting				×	Bulb burned out, standing lamp
Services					
1. Call housekeeping		×			Delay in acquiring extra pillow
2. Send fax to self	×				Prompt, no charge to receive
3. Get maid to let in				×	Took $3 tip and let me in
4. Ask for second key		×			Clerk remembered me, or said so
5. Ask for toilet repair			×		38-minute delay

Exhibit 7–8   Secret shoppers making quality-control inspections uncover and report operating weaknesses that need management attention.

Food is tasted and drinks are sampled in all the food and beverage outlets, including room service. Large properties require several days for a full visit. Mystery shoppers, as inspectors are sometimes called, also check employee sales techniques. Does the room clerk sell up? Does the bellperson promote the facility? Does the telephone operator know the hours of the cabaret?

Security is another QC point. Both guest security (keys, locks, chains, and peepholes)[14] and internal security (staff pilferage from the hotel and theft from guests) come under scrutiny during the visit. Do bartenders ring up every sale? Does cash paid to room service waiters reach the bank deposit? Security shopping is designed to uncover dishonesty and criminal acts. That's far different from the intent of the typical inspection visit and may even require special state licensing.

Mystery shoppers are not police. Neither are they consultants or critics. They are reporters of the scene. Evaluating service and employee attitude and testing the staff's mettle during moments of truth are the purposes of quality inspections. Quality is maintained when management acts on the QC reports, using them to reinforce good habits. Training, not punishment, follows when reports are negative. When that really is the intent of the practice, the staff learns about the mystery shoppers in advance, and the inspectors' evaluation sheets are made available to all. How else will the standards that management hopes to establish be known?

Quality Guarantees

Quality guarantees (QGs) are simply assurances that the hotel will deliver on its promise of quality service, or else. . . . With QGs, the company puts its money where its advertising mouth is. Guaranteeing a satisfactory level of product and service takes gumption. It contradicts the not-my-fault phenomenon currently evident across the United States. Service guarantees take responsibility for everything that happens. Quality guarantees announce unequivocally to customers and employees alike that management is confident enough to stand behind its advertising. It is a courageous stand and a sign of management's conviction in the TQM program that it has initiated. For sure, it backfires at times! Amtrak, the nation's railroad system, dropped its satisfaction guarantee after paying $170,000 in adjustments in just one month. Information on improving service would be gathered in other ways.

Quality guarantees are not discounted room rates (see "Yield Management," Chapter 4), which are offered or discarded as occupancy declines and recovers. Quality guarantees become part of the operating philosophy of the business. They are the very essence of the operation. A potent tool like QGs should be introduced slowly and carefully. Guaranteeing quality is the ultimate goal of a TQM program, not the initial move. Guarantees almost always fail when they evolve from an advertising plan. They're almost always successful as the culmination of a carefully implemented TQM program.

Several years ago, a well-known hotel chain jumped on the QG bandwagon with a promise of "complete satisfaction." No modifiers or limiting exceptions—just complete satisfaction guaranteed. An incident arose when there was no hot water for a shower. Citing the guarantee, the guest asked for a rate adjustment. It was denied because a malfunctioning boiler was beyond the hotel's control. So much for a guarantee of complete satisfaction.

---

[14]To be approved for inclusion in AAA's lodging guide, hotel rooms must have deadbolts, automatic locking doors, and peepholes, and must provide facilities for the disabled.

Quality guarantees need to be narrowly defined at first. Once a standard is established, the guarantee can be aimed at a target and delivered accordingly. Implementing guarantees in stages, by specific expectations within certain departments as capabilities come on line, announces to guests and staff that service quality is in place. Marriott, among others, guarantees to deliver room-service breakfast within 30 minutes. Failure to do so means a free breakfast. Wrapped up in this simple promise is an advertisement, a departmental promotion, an employee empowerment, an assurance of quality, and a willingness to be measured.

Limiting the guarantee—such as the broadly used 30-minute breakfast—makes it easier to understand, easier to control, easier to measure, easier to correct, and easier to reimburse. An open-ended pledge of satisfaction *as the guest sees it* is great public relations but is open to misuse. Nevertheless, the Benjamin Hotel in New York guarantees a good night's sleep. More workable QGs might stress other time parameters: 10 minutes to bring your car from the hotel garage; 10 minutes to deliver faxes; registration within 4 minutes; drink orders served within 3 minutes. The Albuquerque Hyatt guarantees your complaint will receive "immediate action, before you leave the hotel."

Meeting planners have begun asking for and receiving service guarantees. The groups they represent guarantee room, food, and beverage numbers, so they are asking the hotels to do the same. Guarantee there will be no noise from adjacent meeting rooms. Guarantee coffee breaks will be served within 5 minutes after the session breaks. Just as the group's guarantees carry monetary penalties, so must the hotel's.

Quality guarantees are enhanced if line employees are empowered to pay off. Howard Johnson employees carry blank checks that they issue on the spot. Forcing a disgruntled guest to stew while the employee finds a manager adds to the issue even if the resolution favors the guest.

Quality guarantees are a two-edged sword. Failing to pay off after announcing a guarantee alienates guests far more than the incident itself. Guarantees must be unambiguous, limited in scope, and focused on specific objectives that are easily understood. With such guarantees, a failure to deliver is evident to all. There is no quibbling about payment, which—when made promptly—leads to guest loyalty and positive word-of-mouth advertising.

Nothing highlights operational weaknesses more than having to pay off guarantees that arise from legitimate complaints.

►*Americans with Disabilities Act.* The Americans with Disabilities Act (ADA) is a quality standard of a special nature. It was enacted into law in 1990 and became effective in 1992. The ADA provides for changes in physical structures and hiring practices to accommodate the disabled, be they guests or employees. The ADA applies to all industries, including lodging, which is covered by Title III of the act. Certain levels of quality service are guaranteed by law to some 43 million disabled Americans. Unlike the guarantees of hotel companies, the law levies stringent penalties, under civil-rights legislation, for failure to comply.

Actual enforcement with fines and penalties didn't take place for several years. Greater expectations for compliance has come with the passage of time. What previously had been resolved informally is now finding its way to the desks of many assistant U.S. attorneys. In part, the change in emphasis follows the boom in hotel construction. New facilities must be in compliance, and the law holds responsible both landlords and tenants. There have even been some efforts to add franchisors to the list. Savvy hoteliers have minimized penalties by working with private groups (for example, the Society for the Advancement of Travel for the Handicapped) to identify and correct barriers, by increasing training sessions for staff and management, and by keeping records of actions taken to comply.

The federal government's ADA and the lodging industry's QM converge on the same two subjects: Both treat guest and employee issues. The one legislates changes and the other implements them as a matter of good business. Hotel companies hired handicapped employees long before the law was enacted, although less was done to accommodate disabled guests. Radisson was an early employer of the disabled, and so was the Ritz-Carlton Company. Holiday Inn, especially its Worldwide Reservation Center, was still another. Companies like these now include ADA awareness and training as part of their quality assurance efforts. Embassy Suites calls the ADA segment of its QM program "Commandments of Disability Etiquette."

All departments of the hotel, including the rooms division, are affected by the legislation. Each responds with a different solution. Housekeepers learn to leave guest's personal belongings exactly in place. Cashiers count cash aloud, announcing which denominations are being returned. Folios and registration cards are enlarged to further help the visually handicapped. Similar alterations in procedures and space accommodate handicapped workers. Equipment might be modified or even totally replaced. Enhanced lighting, power to recharge wheelchair batteries, or other alterations are sometimes warranted. Hiring practices and other personnel procedures are often more difficult to change than the equipment or work area. Included in these special human resources needs are revised approaches to hiring, testing, job structures, position descriptions, and more.

Physical Accommodations.   Federal and state ADA laws have been confusing, frustrating, incomplete, and contradictory. It wasn't until 1997, for example, seven years after federal passage, that the rules of California and the federal government were finally reconciled. The language of the ADA is very open ended. Rules and their interpretations were to come later. For the physical plant, terms such as *undue hardship* were and still are subject to interpretation. Employers had to translate an equally ambiguous word, *disability.*

Innumerable and frivolous lawsuits hammered out, one court case at a time, the meaning of these terms and of others, such as *reasonable accommodations, readily achievable*, and *undue burden*. The interpretive load fell onto the courts because Congress failed to be specific in the legislation. Intentionally so, many say. Congress did add one quirky provision. Attorneys may collect legal fees even though plaintiffs are unable to sue for punitive damages. With an invitation like that, lawyers quickly launched a host of pesky lawsuits on American businesses, hotels included.

Recent judicial decisions have finally slowed the breakneck pace that broadened the application of the law. That said, the threat remains that ergonomic movements might be added to the disability definition. Such an extension could be disastrous for many industries, including casino hotels, which have large numbers of card dealers. Reconciling the variations between state and federal requirements is another ongoing process.

Early lawsuits and the initial attention of the lodging industry concentrated on the physical barriers because they were easy to measure and to confirm. Unlike the legislation, the operative regulations define everything in clear mathematical terms. For example, the number of handicapped parking spaces is three standard autos plus one van space per 76 to 100 parking spaces. Door thresholds must be less than 0.5 inches high; roll-in showers, a minimum of 36 by 60 inches; public rest room stalls, no less than 42 by 48 inches; drinking fountains, no higher than 36 inches from the floor.

Communications
Telephones for the hearing impaired
Public telephones at proper wheelchair height
Telecommunication devices for the deaf (TDDs)
Guest-room telephones
Visual alert to a ringing telephone
Easy dialing for those with reduced muscle control
Large telephone buttons or replacement pad
Voice-digital phone dialing

Safety Equipment
Visual alert to smoke detectors
Visual alert to door knocks, bells, and sirens
Visual or vibrating alarm clocks
Low viewports on doors
Low location of room locks
Lighted strips on stairwells
Contrasting color on glass doors and handrails
Dual handrails on ramps
Automatic door openers
Slower times on elevator door closures

Access
Handicapped parking spaces
Ramp access to and within the building
Minimum thresholds
Adequate door access
Levered hardware, or adapters

Bathroom access (see Exhibit 7–10)
Lowered drinking fountains with accessible controls
Closed-caption decoders for TV and VCR
Assisted listening systems for meetings
Mattresses on frames rather than pedestal beds
Lower light switches and thermostats
Two-level reception desks
Curb cuts in sidewalks
Eliminate high-pile carpeting
Accommodating Seeing Eye and Hearing Ear animals
Closet rods and drapery controls accessible
Extension cords for recharging wheelchairs
Lifts: elevators, vertical and incline platforms
Portable devices when facilities are not permanent
Eggcrate cushions for arthritics

Graphics
Size, color, and illumination
Braille and raised lettering in elevators
Braille and raised lettering behind guest-room doors
Recessed or projected graphics where appropriate
Verbal recitation of bill denominations when making change

Exhibit 7–9 lists a sample of other provisions that innkeepers must make to comply with the ADA.

Guest bathrooms are high on the failure-to-act list. Redoing baths is expensive, so hotels wait to comply (relying on *readily achievable* and *undue burden*) until the need for other changes is evident. Exhibit 7–10 summarizes some of those required changes. Hotels built after 1992 must set aside between 2% and 5% of their rooms for the physically, visually, and hearing impaired. Hotels that were standing before January 1993 are not required to comply with all physical standards until they undertake major renovations. What are "major" renovations for a specific hotel? Only a lawsuit will tell, and that will come after the fact.

Building roll-in showers with folding seats
Replacing faucet knobs with lever hardware
Installing grab bars in tub and toilet areas
Elevating sinks to accommodate wheelchairs
Insulating pipes on the underside of the sinks
Raising toilet seats
Lowering towel bars
Enlarging bathrooms to provide turnaround space
Providing transfer seats at the tub
Designing clearance space to get through the door
Lowering mirrors
Including hand-held showers with adjustable height bars

Exhibit 7–10   New construction and older hotels undergoing renovation require bathroom designs to meet ADA standards that accommodate disabled guests.

Innkeepers were not pleased with the passage of the ADA. Meeting architectural standards has been costly despite assurances from the bill's supporters that they wouldn't be. Much of what was feared has come true. As an offset, the ADA created a new, small source of employees (job descriptions needed to be changed) and a new guest market. There are disagreements about how much of a market. SATH, the Society for Accessible Travel & Hospitality (also the Society for the Advancement of Travelers with Handicaps) disputes some claims made by the American Hotel & Lodging Association. According to a study commissioned by the AH&LA, there is a huge surplus of ADA-standard guest rooms. Less than 20% of such rooms are in use on a given night, or so says the study.

Unquestionably, the law opened another beachhead for government similar to that which took place with the Occupational Safety and Health Act (OSHA) of 1970. Both laws have been around long enough now for anger to dissipate and efforts at compromise and compliance to be sustained.

Signage.   The ADA made innkeepers look more closely at their signage. Lack of signage or simply poor signage are irritants for all visitors, not only the handicapped. By requiring compliance for braille and raised lettering (not all visually handicapped read Braille), the law brought attention to the entire issue of good signage. The American Automobile Association joined in with its own signage requirements as part of its rating system. AAA ratings do not evaluate recreational or meeting facilities, such as the ADA's requirement of two wheelchair locations for groups of 26 to 50 persons.

Signage for the visually handicapped must be provided inside and outside elevators, on guest-room keys when requested, and on the outside of handicapped rooms. Audible elevator signals (once for up; twice for down) supplement the traditional Braille or raised numbers. Some properties are testing audio signs that are broadcast from small transmitters to the handicapped guest's receiver. The audio signal tells guests where they are and how to proceed to a room or to the elevators. Elevator locations are not always evident even to the sighted. Good signage points the way, encouraging the elderly and adults with small children to choose the safer elevator over the escalator. Signage, whether for elevators, exits, fire, or other purposes, becomes an issue of security as well as convenience.

Guests who are handicapped by other than sight rely on signs for different reasons. The wheelchair symbol used by tour books indicates the availability of special accommodations, including ramp access and accessibility to the desk, to guest rooms, to at least one food-and-beverage outlet, and of course to parking. (Police cannot enforce handicapped parking unless the international access symbol is in place both on the pavement and at eye-level.)

Good signs and directions are not special to handicapped guests. Managers must "walk" their properties, get out from their offices, and note—not just see—what guests encounter as they enter and proceed through the property as strangers. Are there fire-exit signs? If the exits are alarmed, a sign should say so. Are no-smoking rooms and floors marked? Is the entire ambiance of the hotel destroyed by a bunch of supplemental handwritten signs? Can one actually find a guest room following the posted directions? Are some rooms named rather than numbered? Are all the bulbs in electric signs functioning? Exterior signs on the building are often forgotten and lack maintenance and repair.

The alert manager should question the staff at the desk, in uniform, or on the guest floors about the location of certain sites. Employees who have no reason to be in particular areas of the hotel are often unable to direct guests to a banquet facility, the swimming pool, the spa, or the guest laundry.

Every cloud has a silver lining, and ADA's requirements have focused attention on signs as part of the overall picture of guest service.

Complaints

Complaints are another tool for directing management's attention to troubled service areas. Unfortunately, too few guests actually complain. Most merely mumble quietly, never to return. That's why those complaints that are registered must be resolved quickly and corrected for the future. Measuring customer unhappiness is like trying to compute the costs behind the moments of truth. Neither offers any mathematical accuracy, but both make many believable points.

Putting dollar values to the cost of complaints requires some assumptions. These assumptions have never been proven, but they are quoted frequently nevertheless. It is said, for example, that 10% of guests would not return to the property of their most recent stay. Using the same values as in Exhibit 7–7, a hotel would lose 21 guest-nights each day (300 rooms at 70% occupancy times the 10% loss). That totals a whopping 7,665 guest-nights per year for a 300-room hotel. Based on an assumed average daily rate of, say, $65, the failure to resolve complaints in this example would be nearly $500,000 per year (7,665 guest nights at $65). The figure stretches into the stratosphere of nearly $5 million when 3,000-room hotels such as those of Exhibit 1–6 are involved.

Some argue, moreover, that labor-intensive industries such as lodging increase productivity only by improving service encounters. The failure to do so represents additional labor costs as well as costs from lost business. Here, too, there is not much empirical evidence to support the hypothesis.

Every complaint has an impact on the bottom line, but not every complaint takes dollars to resolve. One major investigation reported just the opposite: Only one-third of all written complaints involved a financial issue. Money is more often at stake with face-to-face encounters. Exhibit 7–11 offers another tidbit: Better to spend a bit to hold that guest than to invest five times the amount soliciting a new customer.

▶*Still Another Calculation.*   Exhibit 7–11 offers still another calculation. Like the others, it begins with several widely quoted but vaguely grounded assumptions. Still, the conclusions are startling.

Loss of Guests

> 68% of nonreturning guests quit because of indifferent service.
> 32% is lost to death, relocation, competition, and poor products.

Complaints

> Less than 5% of dissatisfied guests speak out—so for every one that does there may be twenty who do not.
> Over half of the silent majority refuse to return—an iceberg floating beneath the surface.
> Noncomplaining guests do complain to friends and acquaintances.
>
>> 10 to 11 others will hear of the mishap.
>> 13% of the group will gripe to 20 others.
>
> Two-thirds of the iceberg could be won over if they were identified—about half of these could become boosters.

Costs

> It costs over $10 to write a complaint letter (including the cost of writing time, follow-up time, and postage).
>
> It costs five times more to get a new customer than to keep an existing one.

Exhibit 7–11   Widely quoted (but rarely referenced) figures emphasize the importance of a proactive stance in handling guest complaints.

Premise 1: Some 68% of nonreturning guests stay away because of indifferent service. (Deaths, relocations, competition, and poor products account for the other 32%.)

Premise 2: About 2.5% or less of dissatisfied guests actually voice their unhappiness. There is an iceberg effect here. Below the surface floats the vast bulk of complaints, never voiced and never resolved. Of this silent majority, it is said that well over half will not patronize the hotel again. Worse yet, they will tell 10 to 11 others not to do so; some tell as many as 20 others. This fact is so irrefutable in the view of many that a "rule" has been created, the 1–11–5 rule. One unhappy guest will tell 11 others, and each of the 11 will tell 5 more.

Premise 3: About two-thirds of the icebergs can be warmed and won over by resolving the complaint. About one-third of complainers can be converted from blasters to boosters if their complaints are handled quickly and properly. Implicit here is the guest's willingness to speak up. Guests will when they are very angry or when management creates an environment that encourages guests to register complaints.

➤*Preventing the Complaint.*   Identifying the reluctant complainer is a challenge. It will not be met by asking departing guests the rote question, "How was everything?" Desk personnel and managers from all operational and organizational levels must ask direct and specific questions. That means talking to guests, whether in the lobby, by the pool, or elsewhere. The dialogue may start with pleasantries: an introduction, a comment on the weather, an inquiry about the frequency of the guest's visits. But then the conversation must elicit the negatives, if there are any. "Did you use room service?" opens a chain of related questions. "How was the bed?" directs the conversation in a different direction. "Can you tell me about any especially pleasant (or unpleasant) experiences you have had here?"

Issues that flow from these solicitations are not complaints in the truest sense, but they give management direction for improving service and preempting complaints from someone else later on. More important, they bring out the guest's concerns and give the hotel the opportunity to redirect the dynamics and make friends. Many of the issues raised require no immediate actions, no costs, no allowances. They form the base for operational changes and they build the relationships that promote returning guests, especially if the questioner follows the brief interview with a letter of thanks to the candid guest.

Management must be knowledgeable if it hopes to prevent complaints. Executives who don aprons and actually work the floor, say, once a month, create more than a public-relations photo-op. They learn, for example, that the location of the dish-machine is the cause for high chinaware breakage, that the housekeeper's vacuums really don't work, and that customer service warrants the front desk's purchase of umbrellas for guest use. Managers who telephone their own hotels test departmental procedures and the disposition of their staff.

Early Warning.   Complaints can be forestalled if the staff is honest with the guest and tells it like it is. Alerting guests to bad situations allows them to decide whether or not to participate. So the reservation department explains that the pool is closed for repairs during the dates under consideration. A request for connecting rooms is impossible to promise, so the request is noted but no guarantee is made by the reservationist. And that is so stated, not just implied.

Similarly, sales executives must warn small groups about other large parties in the house during the anticipated booking period. Room service reports elevator problems and thus some delay before the order will be delivered. Room associates offer special rates in a certain wing because ongoing renovations there are noisy at times and create extra dust.

Complaint management acknowledges how the "squeaky wheel" gets the best results. Attending promptly to the squeak may mean better service for all. Observant guests often side with the hotel when an obnoxious squeaker rolls up to the desk. They will cede their priority in line to get the pest out of the way. Similarly, handling families with tired, irritable children outside the sequence actually improves service for others.

Preventing the complaint by anticipating the problem and providing unsolicited accurate information is far preferable to assuaging angry guests after the fact. Explaining the circumstances makes guests feel better about the situation and forestalls their complaints. "Housekeeping will not get to the room before luncheon, so we can accommodate your early arrival but not before 1 o'clock."

If a policy of candor works wonders in reducing complaints, the opposite is also true. Misleading information, either directly or by implication and omission, enrages guests who feel they have been cheated—as they have.

Comment Cards.   The effectiveness of guest comment cards is subject to debate. Distracters say that managers intentionally ask the wrong questions, tilting the questionnaires toward the hotel's strengths. Maybe so, but the battle to improve guest service needs every weapon that can be mustered. Comment cards are just another device for getting guest input. Like other information-gathering techniques, they have advantages and disadvantages. Innovative approaches to this old standby strengthen the instrument and improve its quality. The better the questionnaire, the more information available for managing guest services.

Hoteliers complain that guests use questionnaires to gripe. Guests do not balance the good and the bad, hoteliers protest, but concentrate their comments on operating weaknesses. Actually, that's good. Uncovering and remedying shortcomings is what TQM programs are all about. As noted earlier, too few guests ever bring their concerns to the hotel's attention. Guest comment cards help overcome the iceberg effect, the reluctance of customers to complain. Managers grumble because comment-card data, which does include a disproportion of negatives over positives, are often weighed in bonus and promotion decisions. Self-inspection helps managers recognize the tendency that many people have to explain away negative comments as simply being wrong.

Critics attack the statistical validity of comment cards based on very low response rates, typically 1% to 2% of the guest population. Long and detailed questionnaires account for some of the low numbers. Guests just won't take the time to answer. Small cards with a narrow focus, one that changes periodically, improve the overall response rate. It might be done in one of two ways. Short, themed questionnaires about a single concern—cleanliness or courtesy, for example—could be distributed throughout the entire hotel. A specialized form could be used in each department. Although not an actual questionnaire, good success is obtained with a form that asks the guest to submit requests for in-room repairs (see Exhibit 7–12).

Just asking guests to participate increases the number of returns. Some of the best results come from around the pool or during the check-out procedure, when response rates improve tenfold. Locating touch-screen terminals in the lobby near the cashier solicits direct responses from departing guests. Even here, though, the number of questions and the speed with which the guest can respond is critical to success. Strategic

Exhibit 7–12
Inviting guests to help with basic room maintenance improves the quality of the room's physical facility and provides another means of feedback to management, provided good records are maintained.

Room Maintenance

Having everything work as it's suppose to is important to your comfort and to our level of service. Please help us maintain the quality accommodations that make your stay comfortable and enjoyable. We are proud of the cleanliness and condition of this room, but items are sometimes overlooked by housekeeping or maintenance. If anything needs attention, please complete the card and leave it at the front desk or call extension 111.

Room No. _____

Please Attend To:

_____

_____

_____

Thank you,
Doug Douglas, Manager

▫**V**
A Vallen Corporation Property

placement of the equipment encourages adult use and dissuades random input from children, another criticism that is occasionally voiced.

Participation rates increase when guests have an incentive for completing the cards. The rate of return goes up with every dessert coupon or complimentary glass of wine the desk issues. (It also gets guests into the restaurant.) Similarly, room upgrades for the next visit combine incentives with room promotions. Immediate upgrades are given when the solicitation is made during registration.

Awarding prizes from a drawing of comment-card participants is another incentive for guests to complete them. It also flags the importance that the property attributes to quality assurance. Moreover, contest information enables the hotel to match guest names with comments. That isn't always possible, because some guests prefer anonymity.

Hotel companies have followed other industries by providing and advertising toll-free telephone numbers for disaffected consumers. The additional costs of doing this are balanced by the demographic data obtained. Besides, immediate attention to consumer complaints builds enormous goodwill quickly. Provided, that is, that the call is answered by an actual person, who has the ability to resolve the issue and the personality to make a friend of the caller. Like so much of the TQM concept, it is easier to create the system than it is to implement it effectively.

Every comment card or telephone call should receive an immediate and personal response from someone with authority to act. Guests then know that they are getting the highest level of attention. Telephone responses suggest a sense of urgency and often elicit further details of the incident. Carefully done, very carefully done, a letter supposedly originating with the employee involved may produce exceptional results. Far too often the hotel's response is a bland, standardized letter or a generic apology that fails to address the issues raised by the guest.

Complaints can be forestalled if management has the facts. Comment cards, direct conversations, employee inputs, and telephone hotlines help uncover unexpected problems. Recording complaints from every source on a simple spreadsheet highlights those areas or departments that appear repeatedly over time. However it is gathered, management analyzes the information for trends in operating weaknesses and strengths. A good system does more than record customer input or develop goodwill. A good system identifies both functions that are working and functions that are not.

Different information is treated differently. Management cannot always act immediately. This must be explained to employees who make suggestions or to members who sit in QOs working to improve TQM. Sometimes the issue is operational, so action can be taken immediately—adding an emergency telephone to the exercise room, for example. On other occasions, the information is strategic and involves serious budget concerns—building additional elevators, for example.

After going to great lengths to obtain information, management must assure its accuracy. Using input from comment cards for employee service awards encourages employees and their friends to complete the forms or to tell guests what to write. At other times, the forms are shortstopped somewhere. Housekeeping throws away those that are left in the rooms. Room clerks pocket those that reflect poorly, and unit managers withhold those that sound too negative. Providing postage-paid cards with the chief executive's address prevents incorrect handling and emphasizes the questionnaire's importance to the company.

Quality Circles.   Quality Circles, or quality teams, provide another method for gathering the information needed to forestall a complaint. Circles are small groups of employees who meet regularly as quasi-permanent teams to identify issues in delivering quality service. The terminology differs, but guests are occasionally added to the teams, especially at resorts. If the circle catches problems before complaints are registered, QM is working perfectly. Sometimes the remedies come after the fact, arising from management's referral of a series of complaints.

Quality circles in the service industry are very much like those in manufacturing. Small, continuous improvements—creative changes—are the goals. Spectacular breakthroughs or innovations are not customarily part of the circle's design. Consequently, the group's composition is taken from all levels and across departmental lines. Delays in room service at breakfast, for example, may prove to be housekeeping's fault—moving linen between floors ties up the elevators just when room service demand is highest!

Total quality management requires each employee to service other departments as if they were guests. A cross-departmental team, therefore, has members who are internal customers of one another. Teams may function in several capacities, or different teams may be organized for specific, corrective action. In addition, there are focus groups (short-term, one-issue teams) and ongoing self-managing units.

American culture emphasizes the individual and not the group. Circles have been very successful in some hotel environments and have flopped terribly in others. Like comment cards or lobby interviews or toll-free calls, the circle serves as another piece in the quality mosaic. It is both a source of information on which to act and a means of finding the solution with which to act.

▶*Handling the Complaint.*   Quality assurance aims for error-free service, but that is a goal more than a fact. Experience keeps a tight rein on reality, making complaint-free environments desirable but very unlikely. Only the number, timing, or place of the complaint is uncertain, not whether one will occur. As QM programs reduce the number, the remaining complaints gain in importance. Besides, not all complaints are subject to QM solutions. Systems, procedures, and training aside, the unexpected will always happen. Door attendants do lose car keys!

Preparing for Complaints.   Preparing to handle complaints begins by acknowledging their likelihood. Training programs must emphasize the probability of a complaint. Employees with a proper mindset gained through training are not caught unaware. They recognize the importance of attitude in receiving and resolving complaints. Proper preparation minimizes the impact and cost of the complaint. Preparing properly means making the best of the worst. Readying employees to receive and resolve complaints has become an integral part of QM programs.

Although the specifics differ, complaints follow a theme in each department. This gives QOs an effective role in training. Within the circle, members share their individual experiences and solutions, and the group adopts the best ideas—best practices—as departmental standards. Employee empowerment, the authority to accept responsibility and to remedy the situation, is implicit.

For front-desk employees, common themes spring from specific encounters. What is the proper response to a departing guest who protests a folio (guest bill) charge? What should be done with an irate arrival whose reservation has been sold to another? What accommodations can be made if the guest tenders a travel agent's coupon that is not acceptable to the hotel? Common situations all, playing themselves out time and again in a fixed pattern if not an exact duplication. None are rare, unexpected encounters. A series of options must be readied and employed as needed (see Exhibit 7–13).

Directing employees to kick the problem upward is an option required by certain circumstances. Even empowerment programs limit employee authority to certain deci-

Exhibit 7–13
Advanced preparations help empowered employees make the right decisions within the scope of their authority.

Hotel Anywhere, U.S.A.
Internal Memorandum

To:	Guest-Service Agents
From:	Holly Wood, Rooms Manager
Subject:	Empowerment Guidelines
Date:	January 1, 20--

Effective this date, all guest-service agents who have completed the four training hours have authority to make the following adjustments using their own discretion. Managers and supervisors are always available for consultation.

An Apology is the First Response! Apologies are free; we give away as many as necessary, but be sincere and listen carefully.

Where appropriate, verify information before acting

Issue	*Intermediate Response*	*Maximum Response*
Noisy room	Relocate, if stayover	Upgrade now or next visit; gift to the room
Incorrect rate	Correct the paperwork	Allowance for the difference; ticket to club or spa
Engineering problems: Heat and AC, TV, plumbing	Send engineer; change rooms	Upgrade; up to 25% off rate
Protest charges: Telephone	Allowance for local	Allowance for long distance
In-room film	Allowance	One per day
Valet parking	Allowance	Full amount

sion levels. Preparing employees for the complaint must include information about when and why and to whom to refer the matter. Rarely do the sessions train for the next (frequently necessary) step: What is to be done when the next level of authority is not available? Leave the fuming guest to wait . . . and wait . . . and wait?

Complaints may arise because the spread between guest expectations and service delivery widens dramatically after arrival. But complaints are not always of the hotel's doing. Hotel staff may just be the most convenient recipient of the guest's bad day. Tired and grumpy travelers, those who have done battle with family members or business associates, who have fought against canceled flights and lost luggage, may find the hotel employee—especially an inexperienced one who dither and dathers—an ideal outlet for a week of frustrations. Preparing for the complaint means understanding this.

Preparing for the complaint means putting up with drunks and being tolerant of the show-off and the braggart performing for the group. Preparing for the complaint allows one to overlook exaggerations, sarcasm, and irony. Preparing for the complaint recognizes that senior persons sometimes berate younger staff in a replay of the parent–child relationship. Preparing for the complaint means understanding that some persons can never be satisfied whatever the staff may try.

Responding to Complaints.   No complaint is trivial in the eyes of the guest. What the hotel's representative perceives as trivial often originates from a series of small, unattended-to issues that smoulder until management's casual attitude fans the fire of dissatisfaction. Suddenly, the trivial explodes into a major conflagration.

By Listening.   To bring about change, the complaint must be received and understood. Complaints are communicated only if the complainer speaks and the listener listens. It is not enough for the complaint-taker to hear passively; he or she must listen actively. Careful listening is fundamental to resolving every complaint. Full attention to the speaker moves the problem toward prompt resolution even before the explanation is complete. Experienced complaint-handlers never allow other employees, guests, or telephone calls to distract them from hearing out the complainant.

Complainers do not always begin with the real issue—which is true, of course, with many conversations. Questions are appropriate provided that they are not judgmental, but interrupting unnecessarily angers the speaker and pushes the conversation to another level of frustration before all the facts are in hand.

Listening requires good eye contact and subtle supportive body movements. Appropriate nodding, tsh-tshing, mouth expressions, and hand movements encourage the speaker and convey attention, sympathy, and understanding. It is important to remain in contact with the speaker and empathetic toward his or her experience throughout the recitation.

Guests do not like being rushed along; they want the whole story to come out. The listener must be sensitive to his or her own body language, careful that negative signals are not halting the complainer or dropping a cold blanket over the encounter. Watching for the guest's nonverbal signals helps interpret the guest's readings of one's own signals.

Attentive listening is particularly important in the resolution of accidents. Small mishaps end in court cases when the listener makes short shrift of the incident and of the person involved in the accident. Aggrieved guests want management's attention and evidence of its concern. They want a sympathetic audience to hear them out. Lawsuits are the invariable results of leaving the entire situation to the security staff. Management's representative should handle the public relations while security completes the required investigation. Together, the team must summon help and attend to any injuries. Then the investigation follows, but not in the presence of the injured party. Managers and security agents must admit no fault and promise no medical or insurance coverage. Neither should they discuss details nor quiz others staffers at the scene.

In a Proper Venue.   Complainers who grow hostile or overly upset, loud, or abusive must be removed from the lobby. Shifting to a new venue should be done as quickly as possible. Don't wait for the issue to intensify or the time committed to the situation to outgrow the lobby discussion. Perhaps the pretense can be that of comfort: Let's sit down in the office; we'll be more comfortable there, and there will be no interruptions.

Walking to the new location offers a cooling-off period. It provides an opportunity to shift the topic and to speak in more conversational tones. Walking changes the aggressive or defensive postures that one or the other might have assumed in the lobby. The office location adds to the manager's authority and prestige.

The louder the guest growls, the softer should come the response, which usually brings an immediate reaction: Loud complainers quiet down to hear replies that are given in near whispers. A harsh answer to abuse or to offensive language only elevates the complaint to a battle of personalities. Above all, the hotel wants the guest to retain dignity. Divorcing the interaction from personalities helps do that. The facts are at issue, not the persons; certainly not the employee, who may be the original target of the guest's ire.

Ultimately, the manager may refuse to discuss the issues further unless the guest modulates language and tone. The hotelier tells the complainer that he or she is being addressed politely and the listener expects the same courtesy. In a worst-case scenario, say with a drunk or drug-crazed guest, the hotel may need to call the police.

BY MAKING A RECORD.   Asking permission to record the complaint by taking notes indicates how seriously management views the matter. It also allows the guest to restate the issue and have it recorded with accuracy, at least from the guest's point of view. The hotel's representative gets an additional opportunity to express concern and sympathy as the issues are restated aloud. It also slows the conversation, helping to cool emotions. Contributing to the written report makes the complaining guest sense that already something is being done. Thus, the stage is set for resolving the problem.

Front offices maintain permanent journals of the day's activities, including complaints. These logs improve communications with later shifts since the issues often carry over. The documentation helps the participants recall the incident later, provides a basis for training, and supports legal proceedings if the matter goes that far. Serious accidents are documented again by security and by the hospital or the police, depending on circumstances.

The recordkeeping goes further. Getting the guest's folio, registration card, or reservation data helps the manager understand what happened. Calling an employee into the office or on the telephone in the guest's presence broadens the investigation, clarifies the facts, and mollifies the complainer. Employees should get as much courtesy as the guest. Training or discipline, if appropriate, is done elsewhere in private. Both the staff member and the guest should be addressed with civility, certainly using surnames and appropriate titles: Mr., Mrs., Dr., Ms.

WITH A SETTLEMENT.   Once registered, the complaint must be settled: resolved somehow and closed. The complainant expects some satisfaction or real restitution for the embarrassment. The hotel wants to keep the customer, strengthen the relationship, if possible, and send the guest forth as a booster who tells the world how fairly he or she was treated. Still, the hotel doesn't want to give away the house atoning for mistakes that caused no harm and little damage.

Apologies are free—we can give away as many as needed; and indeed, only an apology may be needed. Apologies are in order even if the complaint seems baseless or unreasonable. The effectiveness of the apology depends on the guest's reading of the manager. And that reading often reflects the importance of and the guest's involvement in the delivery of the service. A transient family views situations differently than a family celebrating an important anniversary. A business traveler's anger increases directly with the importance of the message that wasn't delivered.

Does the unhappy guest see the hotelier as truly contrite or merely mouthing niceties as a means of getting a quick solution? There are different ways of apologizing, but none are effective unless they ring true. The standard, "I am sorry, and I apologize on behalf of the hotel," goes a long way toward settling minor issues quickly and satisfactorily. "I am sorry" can take on different nuances with different levels of emphasis— "I *am* sorry"—additional words—"I am *so* sorry"—or deleted words—"I'm sorry."

Guests listen for subtle connotations in words and voice. Voices can be shaped and honed through practice to carry just the right intonations and emphases. Concern, be-

Exhibit 1–1   The new designs and exciting architecture of recently built hotels have become attractions in and of themselves. *Courtesy of the Westin Diplomat Resort & Spa, Hollywood, Florida.*

Exhibit 1–9 Urban hotels serve several markets, but chiefly business and convention guests. Location, location, location is critical to the commercial hotel. If not downtown—the illustration is New York City at 45th and Broadway; the hotel has 1,919 rooms—commercial hotels favor business parks or research centers. *Courtesy of New York Marriott Marquis, New York, New York.*

Exhibit 1–10 Resorts have expanded their markets beyond the "social guests" that persisted through the middle of the 20th century. Amenities, including executive conference centers, spas, tennis clubs, marinas, and more—even a private island—appeal to groups as well as to leisure guests. *Courtesy of the Sagamore, Bolton Landing, New York.*

Exhibit 1–12 Bed and breakfasts (B&B) operate under a variety of names. *B&B inns* are popular on the west coast; *Country B&Bs* are popular in New England. In between are many wonderful stopping places with award-winning breakfasts and distinctive guest rooms. *Courtesy of The Inn at 410, Flagstaff, Arizona.*

Exhibit 1–13 Boutique hotels, which started as a fad, have become a distinct segment of the American hotel market. They achieved this by breaking the stereotype of the chain property. This California example well represents the genre. *Courtesy of the Georgian Hotel, Santa Monica, California.*

Exhibit 2–4   Conference centers blend pleasant surroundings with high-tech facilities and dedicated meeting space. Hotels that compete for this market segment do so with multiuse space (see Exhibit 2–5). *Courtesy of Barton Creek Resort, Austin, Texas.*

Exhibit 2–5 The versatile space of convention hotels accommodates meetings and banquets, trade shows and weddings, proms and seminars, and more in contrast to the dedicated space of the conference center illustrated in Exhibit 2–4. *Courtesy of Radisson Hotel Orlando, Orlando, Florida.*

Exhibit 2–6 Spas are new, profitable amenities that both resort and nonresort properties have added. Modern spas no longer rely on the curative waters from which the term originated. Health, exercise, massage, diet, and stress reduction are today's attractions. This new profit center may be leased (outsourced) to third parties. Spa etiquette preserves the quiet: Cell phones are prohibited. *Courtesy of Hotel Hershey, Hershey, Pennsylvania.*

Exhibit 2–10 Public convention centers solicit and house trade shows whose delegates might number in the tens of thousands. What is good for the local hotel business has a major economic impact on the whole community. That value approximates $800 daily for each delegate (see Chapter 5, Exhibit 5–10) during the three- or four-day convention. *Courtesy of Las Vegas Convention and Visitors Authority, Las Vegas, Nevada.*

Exhibit 3–5 To assure accessibility, this concierge is located in the lobby. Some hotels limit this service to concierge floors, which offer other extra services at a higher room rate. The pleasant working conditions and the aura of confident service are highlighted in this lobby photo. *Courtesy of the Wynfrey Hotel, Birmingham, Alabama.*

Exhibit 3–10 The once sterile and uninviting lobby has been revitalized as a dining spot and social center. Hyatt Hotels pioneered the movement with its atrium concept. *Courtesy of Hyatt Regency Atlanta, Atlanta, Georgia.*

Exhibit 3–16 Modern architecture calls for outside rooms even in an urban setting where land costs are high. This commercial property has its business center and banquet/meeting facilities on the 3rd floor. *Courtesy of the Sofitel Chicago Water Tower Hotel, Chicago, Illinois.*

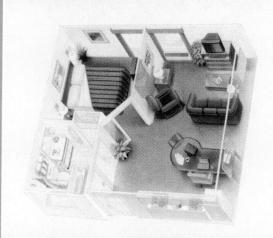

Exhibit 3–18 The large square footage of all-suite facilities is appealing both to the transient traveler and to the long-stay guest to whom the concept was originally marketed. Either a fold-out chair or a sofa bed in the parlor provides extra sleeping accommodations. All-suites are the fastest growing segment of the hotel market. *Courtesy of Candlewood Hotel Company, Wichita, Kansas.*

Exhibit 4–9a   Exhibit 4–9b shows a sample reservations screen from Best Western International's proprietary Lynx reservations system (version 9.2.0). Exhibit 4–9a shows reservations workstations at Best Western International's Beardsley Operations Center in Phoenix, Arizona. This is one of five international reservations centers operated by BWI. It also operates centers in Glendale, Arizona (on the campus of Glendale Community College); Dublin, Ireland; Milan, Italy; and Sydney, Australia. *Courtesy of Best Western International, Inc., Phoenix, Arizona.*

Exhibit 4–9b

◆ Exhibit 4–13   The inviting main pool of the Doubletree La Posada Resort. This three-star and three-diamond property operating in Scottsdale, Arizona, includes in its competitive set such Scottsdale properties as Hilton Scottsdale Resort and Villas, Sunburst Resort, Doubletree Paradise Valley Resort, and Millennium at McCormick. Its competitive set ranges over many square miles and, interestingly, includes two other properties (Hilton Scottsdale Resort and Villas and Doubletree Paradise Valley Resort) licensed by the same Hilton Hotels Corporation that licenses the Doubletree La Posada Resort! *Courtesy of Doubletree La Posada Resort, Scottsdale, Arizona.*

◆ Exhibit 7–2   New attention to the hotel's basic product, the bed, has prompted a range of bedding upgrades, even a sleep concierge. *Courtesy of The Benjamin, New York, New York.*

Exhibit 7–3 The quality of hotel bedding has become a major advertising point as the industry comprehends the importance of sleep and works to communicate that understanding to its guests. *Courtesy of The Benjamin, New York, New York.*

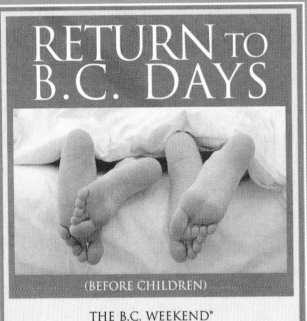

RETURN TO B.C. DAYS

(BEFORE CHILDREN)

THE B.C. WEEKEND*

$239

PER NIGHT
INCLUDES:

DELUXE STUDIO SUITE

Retreat to a weekend of divine relaxation in one of
New York's newest luxury hotels – The Benjamin. You'll enjoy
elegant accommodations, a supremely comfortable custom-made
mattress, and our pillow concierge will help you select
from 10 types of pillows for the ultimate night's sleep.

FABULOUS BRUNCH

Indulge in a delectable brunch for two at
Larry Forgione's An American Place.

LUXURY SPA

Enjoy 20% off any spa treatment at the renowned
Woodstock Spa & Wellness Center.

You can also upgrade to a one-bedroom suite for just
$50 more per night.

Call your travel consultant or 1-888-4-BENJAMIN, Ext. 303.
To learn more, take a virtual tour of The Benjamin
at www.thebenjamin.com.

THE BENJAMIN
AN EXECUTIVE SUITE HOTEL

125 East 50th Street ✦ New York, New York 10022
Manhattan East Suite Hotels
Five-globe ECOTEL® certified

*Offer subject to availability and valid weekends, effective 12/22/00 through 3/31/01. Certain restrictions
apply; taxes not included. One brunch for two per weekend stay.
Please book spa treatment at time of reservation.

Exhibit 8–2   Example of a hotel offering both doorperson and valet parking services (note the sign to the right of the doors). At the Wedgewood Hotel, doorpersons and parking attendants are one and the same. Although most small four-diamond hotels would probably not offer both services—the Wedgewood has just 51 luxury standard and executive rooms, 34 one-bedroom suites, and 4 penthouse suites—their average rate ($220–$498) is sufficient to warrant it. *Courtesy of The Wedgewood Hotel, Vancouver, British Columbia, Canada.*

The front desk of one of Orlando's busiest convention properties—The Rosen Centre Hotel. On slow check-in days, this desk works well with just one or two front-desk agents; on busy days, the desk can accommodate as many as 22 agents. Rosen Hotels & Resorts is a small chain (just seven properties, all in Orlando) with big properties (6,387 rooms in just seven hotels).

For convention business, this is one of the best places to be. Orlando's Orange County Convention Center (OCCC) boasts 1.1 million square feet of space and is ranked as one of the nation's top convention centers by *Tradeshow Weekly*. But that's old news. Today, OCCC is undergoing an expansion project to increase exhibition, meeting room, and public space to a total of 7 million square feet!! This awe-inspiring project is targeted to open in the fall of 2003.

Good business if you can get it. And Rosen Hotels & Resorts is well positioned with major convention properties flanking both sides of the OCCC! *Courtesy of Rosen Hotels & Resorts, Orlando, Florida.*

Exhibit 8–3 Here's a look at the busy front desk of the Opryland Hotel in Nashville. The Opryland is among the largest independent, un-affiliated hotels in the world. It boasts 2,884 rooms, 220 suites, and over 30 specialty shops. *Courtesy of the Opryland Hotel, Nashville, Tennessee.*

Exhibit 8–4 The Mirage Hotel and Casino in Las Vegas takes hotel front-desk design to the extreme! Hard to grow impatient waiting in line when a 20,000 gallon saltwater tank replete with full-sized sharks circling a coral reef sits just a few yards away. *Courtesy of MGM MIRAGE, Las Vegas, Nevada.*

Exhibit 8–12 Nestled in the spectacular Whitsunday Islands in the Great Barrier Reef off Australia's north Queensland coast, the Hayman Island Resort is the only facility on the island. Built with energy savings in mind, the resort's remote location practically mandates an environmentally conscious attitude. The resort grows much of its own produce, has its own power plant for electricity, and maintains its own desalination plant for fresh water. *Courtesy of Hayman Island Resort, Great Barrier Reef, Australia.*

Exhibit 11–2 Advanced ATM machines offer many more features than the standard ATM cash machines, including check cashing for personal, corporate, and payroll checks with no risk to the hotel or merchant. Risks are minimized by the Mr. Payroll ATM, which uses a security system based on facial recognition. With biometrics technology, the ATM "never forgets a face." *Courtesy of Mr. Payroll Corporation, Fort Worth, Texas.*

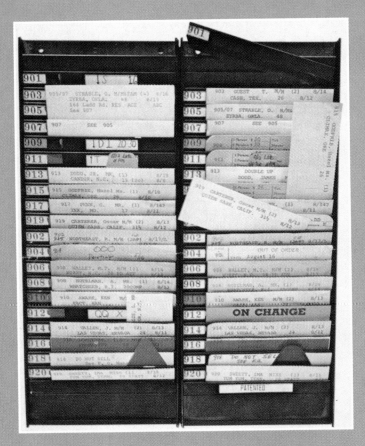

lief, and self-disparagement can be communicated irrespective of the words. Other standbys, although often repeated, have a proper place in the list of apologies: "I know how you must feel"; "Yes, that is distressing"; and "I would have done the same."

Although it is not necessary to fix blame for the incident—and doing so may be counterproductive—the hotel's staff clearly may be at fault. When pertinent, admitting as much helps to set the tone, as long as the admission doesn't include minimizing the incident or offering lame excuses. Use a simple statement about "our" mistake.

Managers who want to go beyond the apology send gifts to the room. The traditional fruit basket, or a tray with wine and cheese, or even a box of amenities serve this function. Apologies appear on the card once again.

Complaints that are settled with apologies are the least expensive kind and often prove to be the most satisfying for both sides. Subsequent telephone calls or letters reinforce the apologies that were expressed during the face-to-face encounters.

After hearing out the guest, quieting down the situation, and offering appropriate sympathy, the hotel manager must provide restitution and lay the issue to rest. The quicker the problem can be resolved, the better. That is what happens with most complaints. But serious items are not settled that easily. Smashed fenders, dentures broken on a bone, or snagged designer's dresses are not remedied on the spot. Insurance companies, or law firms in more serious instances (a fall in the tub), work their wares slowly. Nevertheless, sympathy, concern, and prompt, on-the-spot action reduce the longer-run consequences and costs.

More concrete solutions are needed when apologies are not enough. A list of options should be identified for the hotel's representative as part of the preparation process (see Exhibit 7–13). Heading the list are items that cost the hotel little or nothing, as would an upgrade. Even here, there are degrees: Should we upgrade to another level? To the concierge floor? To an expensive suite? The upgrade is offered for this visit or for another. If for another, the manager's card with a direct number—"call me personally and I'll arrange it"—reinforces the special nature of the solution. Some managers preface every offer by hinting that the arrangements are special. By implication, deviating from standard procedure recognizes the guest's importance and the hotel's desire to make things right.

Annoying but inconsequential incidents can be handled with small gifts. Tickets to an event that is being held by the hotel are welcome. Athletic contests (tennis tourneys), presentations (distinguished speakers), theater-style entertainment, and the like are almost without cost if seats are plentiful.

Admission to the hotel's club or spa, tickets to local activities such as theme parks or boat rides, or transportation to the airport in the hotel's limousine are other options. Cash refunds are the last choice, but they may be the only appropriate response. Damage to property requires reimbursement, and extraordinary circumstances necessitate an allowance against folio charges.

Usually, the situation is less serious. The guest has twice before reported an inoperative television set. Or, the guest's request to change rooms has been ignored. Or, the long delay in getting a personal check cleared for cashing is irritating and embarrassing. Complaints of this type need fast and certain action. Once the solution is resolved, a wise manager explains what is to be done and how long it will take. Better to overestimate the time—then a more rapid turnaround will impress the guest with the hotel's sincerity.

BY ASKING THE GUEST.   Guest demands soften if the episode is handled well and if the guest feels that the treatment is fair. To get that kind of response, the hotelier needs to get into the guest's head, to view the situation from the other side. If the interview appears to be moving favorably, the guest can be brought into the decision loop. Carefully, the hotel's agent elicits the guest's expectations, which often are less than the hotel's, and draws the guest into formulating the remedy. The complainer becomes part of the solution, and the process gains momentum toward a quick and satisfactory conclusion.

All of which is easier said than done. Standing near an experienced complaint-handler—listening to what is said and how it is said—is the best learning experience the manager can have. It is especially helpful if the claim is denied.

Customers are always right! Except sometimes they aren't. The first reference is to the attitude with which management hears the guest's complaint; the second reference is to the context of the complaint. Management can listen attentively, sympathize completely, and communicate caringly, but still *say no* to outrageous requests based on nonevents.

Refusing compensation—remember, apologies are always in order—may cost the customer's patronage. It is a fine judgment call, as repeat patronage may already be lost. In denying restitution, inexperienced managers resort to "company policy" as the reason. Company policy is a great turnoff! Better to explain the answer in terms of fairness, of safety, of service to other guests, of economic reality, or of past experience.

Unhappy guests may request the intervention of higher authority. If that is appropriate, the next manager must be formally introduced and the issue recapped aloud to expedite the meeting. Thereafter, the first interviewer remains silent unless questioned and allows the second conversation to progress without interruption.

Complaints that are resolved quickly and equitably make friends for the hotel. Resolved or not, management's attitude, as expressed in words and movements, goes far toward minimizing (or aggravating) the damages.

UNDER CONTRACTUAL AGREEMENTS. There is very little wiggle room for negotiating complaint settlements if guests have a pre-existing "contract" with the hotel. Too often, the public relations/advertising people put the operational/management people in just such a nonnegotiable, no-win situation. Advertisements that promise a 100% satisfaction guarantee (first offered in 1989 by Promus) allow for little discretion. The hotel has already agreed to settle for the guests' demands. If it doesn't, the company's credibility suffers immeasurably.

Recognizing the pitfalls of such open-ended pledges, hotel companies have shifted away from unequivocal guarantees to lesser promises of attention. Limited exceptions still guarantee 100% satisfaction: Breakfast in 30 minutes or it's free. Otherwise, the guarantee is 100% but only if the opportunity to remedy the shortfall fails. In other words, there's a promise to attend to the complaint. Failing that, some payment may follow.

Radisson says

Our goal at Radisson is 100% guest satisfaction. If you aren't satisfied with something, please let us know and we'll make it right or you won't pay. Please dial 0 now and tell the hotel staff what service you require or what we can do to improve your visit. If the staff is unable to satisfy you, call our corporate customer service department at 1-800-333-3333 for assistance.

The Sheraton Service Promise is

If you're not entirely satisfied, we'll take care of it. And we'll make it up to you with an instant discount, points for our rewards program, even money back. And that's a promise.[*]

[*]Service Promise applies to hotel services in the Continental U.S. and Canada and excludes group transactions. Level of compensation is at the discretion of hotel management.

RESOURCES AND CHALLENGES
Resources

➤ *SUMMARY*

TQM, total quality management, has many definitions and practices even within a single industry like lodging. TQM's goals are simple to express but difficult to implement because guest service involves two parties. Managing for the first, the guest, is not new; it is part of the industry's heritage. Bringing the second party, the employee-server, into the management process is the inspiring idea.

Attitudinal changes take place over time. Once hoteliers attended to guest needs within the accommodations that the host provided. Today's hotels furnish what the market demands, not what management wants to offer. By so doing, each company reinforces the brand image that was discussed in Chapter 2. Above all else, guests want quality rest in a physically comfortable room with service delivery in a comfortable human relations environment. As the market dictates both, the guest's perception of quality and the reality of the quality offered move closer together.

Guest satisfaction stems from the hotel's delivery of its product by courteous and empowered staff members during the many moments of truth that occur on hotel floors each day. Recognizing the employees' critical role, management is changing its methods of supervision to enlist their cooperation and initiative. Winning that commitment is an ongoing process. Empowering staff members to make decisions within their own level of authority is one of the most dramatic redefinitions of the role of the worker.

TQM has introduced new terms and new expressions. If history is any guide, the language of TQM will soon fade away. Fads in management come and go like other fashions. Carlson's recent adoption of CRM (Customer Relations Management) heralds new guest–employee terminology. Hotel managers must retain the vision behind the management of service even as such words as quality circles, quality guarantees, or even TQM itself disappear.

➤ *WEB SITES*

ADA–Compliance and checklists: http://www .usdoj.gov/crt/ada/hsurvey.pdf

Proposed rule changes: http://www:usdj.gov/crt/ ada/t2nprm94.htm

Reference: http://www.usdoj.gov/crt/ada/pubs/ reg9rpt.htm

Hilton Recruiting–Representative of industry efforts: http://www.hilton.com (click job search)

Monsterboard–Job openings listed by geography, career or interest: http://www.monster.com

National Sleep Foundation–Sleep research and sleep aids: http://www.sleepfoundation.org

Society for Accessible Travel & Hospitality: www.sath.org

Web Site Assignment

Compare six items listed on the government's ADA Web sites against a physical inspection of a local hotel (or restaurant), and report where the property is not in compliance. Include an estimated cost of reaching compliance. (With your instructor's permission, provide your report to the hotel or restaurant manager.)

➤ INTERESTING TIDBITS

➤ A good quality mattress that costs $40 to $50 per year ($400 to $500 new divided by an 8 to 10 year life) can be expensed at about $0.18 per occupant. This cost breakdown is obtained by dividing 255 days of use (365 days per year times 70% occupancy) into the $45.00 cost per year.

➤ Employees of the Inter-Continental Hotel, New York City, are empowered to use the "prescription pads" they carry to authorize free drinks for testy guests.

➤ Down, which upscale hotels use in blankets and pillows, is the first soft plumage or the underplumage of birds, usually geese (very, very expensive) or ducks (expensive).

➤ The Mandalay Bay Resort & Casino (Las Vegas) has 3,215 rooms; 128 special rooms are required if one ADA room is built per 25 regular rooms. The hotel has 178 such rooms: a ratio of 1 per 18.

➤ READING REFERENCES

"TQM in American Hotels." Deborah Breiter, and Priscilla Bloomquist. *Cornell Hotel and Restaurant Administration Quarterly*, February 1998, pp. 26–33.

Sleep and The Traveler II: The Latest Guide to Help Travelers Get the Most Out of Sleep When Traveling. Beverly Hills: Hilton Hotels Corp., 1998.

Turnover and Diversity in the Lodging Industry. Robert Woods. Denny Rutherford, Raymond Schmidgall, and Michael Sciarino. Washington, DC: American Hotel Foundation, 1998.

Service Edge: 101 Companies that Profit From Customer Care. Karl Albrecht, and Dick Schaaf. New York: Penguin, USA, 1990. Cites several hotel chains.

Challenges

➤ TRUE/FALSE

Questions that are partially false should be marked false (F).

____ 1. Some hoteliers dislike empowering employees because it requires increased supervision and therefore larger, more costly organizational structures.

____ 2. A duvet is a specially shaped bed pillow that is in demand at upscale hotels.

____ 3. The ethnic distribution (Caucasians, African Americans, Asians, etc.) of the lodging industry's workforce is almost identical to the ethnic distribution of the American population.

____ 4. Apologies are free, so the hotel should offer as many as needed to soften the complaint.

____ 5. Guaranteeing guests 100% satisfaction is the best means of developing a strong commitment from employees in the hotel's TQM program.

➤ PROBLEMS

1. Using the computer, create a simple spreadsheet showing the form and functions that management can use to summarize and analyze complaints originating within departments of the rooms divisions.

2. Prepare and briefly discuss a list of three quality guarantees that are defined narrowly enough to be communicated easily and achieved successfully: for example, room service breakfast delivered within 30 minutes. Be certain to include the penalty to be paid by the hotel if the guarantee is not met.

   a. Explain why Marriott's guarantee of breakfast is, in the words of the authors, "an advertisement, a departmental promotion, an employee empowerment, an assurance of quality, and a willingness to be measured."

3. Compute how many moments of truth occur in a full-service convention hotel of 630 rooms during a typical month. Comment.

4. From readings and personal experience, discuss six of the most difficult elements of resolving a complaint.

5. You are the hotel's liaison with the architects designing guest rooms for a new tower. Present them a list of the 10 most important items that must be provided if the hotel is to meet its obligations under the Americans with Disabilities Act.

6. List five incentives that a hotel might offer to get guests to complete a guest comment card. Make a special effort to have the incentives encourage cross-advertising, by which one department awards incentives for use in another department.

➤ ANSWERS TO TRUE/FALSE QUIZ

1. False. Empowering line workers delegates some of the supervisor's authority and responsibility down the line, reducing the amount of supervision required.

2. False. Duvets, which are beginning to appear in American hotels, are pillow-case-like covers that are washable substitutes for traditional bedspreads and are used to enclose comforters when comforters replace blankets.

3. False. The ethnic and minority distribution of the lodging workforce is skewed toward women and nonwhite males. Acknowledging that difference is a start in managing for better customer relations.

4. True. Apologies are always in order as a means of resolving complaints even if there is no fault on the hotel's part. Properly delivered, an apology may be all it takes to settle an issue.

5. False. Guarantees should be limited to narrow, measurable performances rather than to an open, unrestricted offer. Moreover, guarantees should be launched after a TQM program has been operating, when the chance of mistakes has been reduced, not as a means of achieving a TQM program.

CHAPTER 8

The Guest Arrival, Registration, and Rooming

Outline

The guest arrival process blends a wide range of hotel functions into the guest's first five or ten minutes on property. These broad functions are fairly constant across the industry—the guest arrives, registers, and arranges payment for the room, and ultimately enters the room and cursorily examines it for overall acceptability. The manner in which each hotel accomplishes these broad objectives, however, is quite varied.

The arrival process varies by guest; by hotel brand, segment, and size; and even by employee. As standard or routine as the arrival, registration, and rooming process initially appears, no two experiences are exactly alike. Guests arrive armed with a wide range of expectations—while some are seasoned, others may be novice travelers or have little experience with this particular brand or property. Similarly, each hotel provides a different experience—even properties in the same chain differ due to location, service-level, management, and other factors. Certainly, employee personalities and training influence the guest arrival experience as well.

While the broad objectives of the arrival process (arrival, registration, and rooming) remain consistent for all hotels, the actual delivery of these objectives and performance of the numerous tasks required to accomplish them is widely varied. Add to this complexity the fact that today's lodging industry has developed a number of full-service and self-service options to meet the growing variety of guests needs, and the list of potential arrival experiences grows exponentially. To illustrate the point, let's imagine two guests staying at the same downtown Los Angeles hotel. The first is a leisure guest visiting the hotel for several nights as part of an extended vacation. Knowing little about the property, this leisure guest arrives at the airport and is picked up by the hotel's shuttle, delivered to the front door, greeted by a doorperson, and escorted to the front desk. At the desk, many attributes of the hotel are explained to the leisure guest (location of the pool, hours of the dining room, the name of the duo playing in the lounge, etc.), and following registration, a bellperson shares even more information while rooming the guest. Now that's a full-service arrival complete with a number of distinct employee–guest interactions.

Change focus for a moment and follow the experience of our other hypothetical guest. This gentleman is a frequent traveler and regular corporate guest of the hotel. Upon arrival at the airport, he rents a car and drives to the property, opting to pull his own car into the parking garage rather than have it valet parked. He wheels his one piece of luggage onto the elevator, rides to the lobby, and passes directly in front of the desk on his way to a self-check-in kiosk. There, he accesses his existing reservation, scans his credit card and writes his own electronic room key, and is assigned a room number. Moments later, on his way to the room, he visibly relaxes as he considers how much he loves this hotel—even though he had not one employee–guest interaction throughout the entire arrival process.

➤ THE ARRIVING GUEST

An ideal check in goes unnoticed by the guest because all hotel and front-office functions flow smoothly. From the valet attendant who parks the car to the doorperson who greets the guest, from the front-desk personnel who handle the arrangements to the bellperson who handles the luggage, all systems work in unison. Within minutes, the guest is happily on the way to the room.

Aside from the actual reservation (which may or may not have been made by the guest), this is the guest's first opportunity to see the hotel in action. First impressions are critical, and that is why the arrival, registration, and rooming process is often referred to as a moment of truth. The front-office staff does not get a second chance to make a good first impression.

A Moment of Truth

Different segments of the lodging industry offer differing levels of service. At no time is this difference in service as pronounced as it is during arrival, registration, and rooming. Limited-service properties offer no employee interaction between the porte-cochére (the canopy in front of most hotel lobbies under which arriving guests temporarily park their vehicles) and the front desk. In a limited-service property, the guest may not see or speak with any employee other than the guest–service agent. In fact, for hotels that offer self-check-in terminals or kiosks, limited-service guests may not see any employee at all upon arrival to the hotel.

Full-service hotels, on the other hand, place several ranks of employees between the front door and the front desk (see Exhibit 8–1), and each of these encounters is a separate moment of truth, a separate opportunity for the hotel to excel (or in some situations, to fail the guest). The guest may encounter a valet parking attendant, a doorperson, and a bellperson before ever arriving at the front desk.

▶***The Valet Parking Attendant.*** The first employee that guests often encounter in a full-service hotel is the valet parking attendant. The parking attendant greets the guests as they pull their vehicles under the porte-cochère, opens their car door(s), assists with placing luggage on the curb, and takes responsibility for parking and securing the vehicle Similar services are provided to guests arriving by taxi, airport shuttle, and other means of transport (see Exhibit 8–1).

Valet parking is an amenity or service provided by many fine hotels. However, not all full-service hotels offer valet parking. It is most commonly found in urban, city-center hotels where space is at a premium and guest self-parking is inconvenient (see Exhibit 8–2).

This department is a revenue center for some hotels. By charging the guest a fee for parking each day, the valet parking department generates income to help defray the costs of maintenance and insurance on the parking lot or parking structure. The parking fee (which runs as high as $50 or $60 per day in city-center hotels) is added directly to the guest's folio or account.[1] In addition, many guests tip the attendant each time their car is returned.

Hotels may lease or subcontract the operation of this department to a private parking company. With leased operations, a private company takes the responsibility for parking the guest's car, insuring it against damage, and staffing the department. They also pay the hotel a monthly lease for the privilege of using their parking lots and garages. In such cases, the guest is often unaware that valet parking is a contracted department.

▶***The Doorperson.*** Not all full-service hotels (or even resorts for that matter) offer a doorperson. In an era of rising labor costs, that's one position easily eliminated. This is especially true when you realize that it is a non-revenue-producing department. As a result, only the finer hotels can afford to provide doorpersons. And as such, the doorperson makes a statement both about the opulence of the hotel and about its concern for providing the finest in guest service.

To many guests, no position represents the hotel quite like the doorperson. The uniformed services position of doorperson is part concierge, part bellperson, part security officer, part tour guide, and part friend all rolled into one. The doorperson may

---

[1]Parking rates for domestic Hilton Hotel properties run the highest in New York City. There, the New York Waldorf-Astoria charges $45 per day plus tax for valet parking and the New York Hilton and Towers charges $40 per day. In contrast, the San Francisco Hilton and Towers charges just $30 per day for parking. Most surprising of all, the Hong Kong Conrad (a member of the Hilton family of hotels) charges just 120 Hong Kong dollars (about $15.38 US).

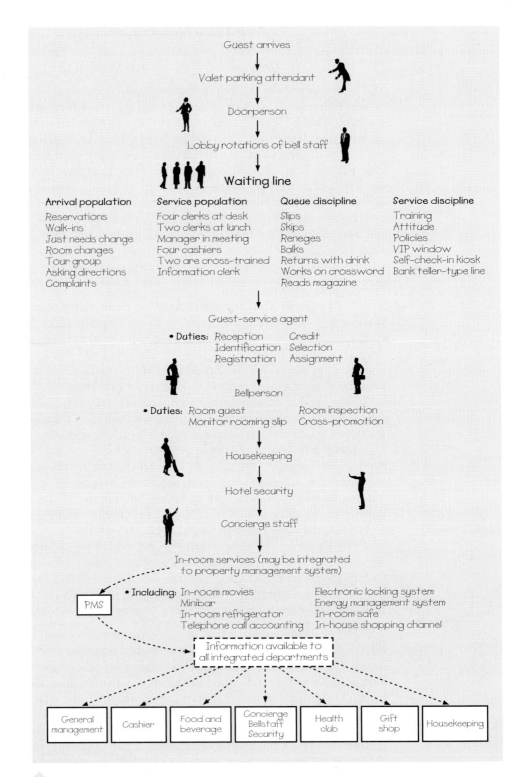

Guest arrives

↓

Valet parking attendant

↓

Doorperson

↓

Lobby rotations of bell staff

↓

Waiting line

Arrival population	Service population	Queue discipline	Service discipline
Reservations	Four clerks at desk	Slips	Training
Walk-ins	Two clerks at lunch	Skips	Attitude
Just needs change	Manager in meeting	Reneges	Policies
Room changes	Four cashiers	Balks	VIP window
Tour group	Two are cross-trained	Returns with drink	Self-check-in kiosk
Asking directions	Information clerk	Works on crossword	Bank teller-type line
Complaints		Reads magazine	

↓

Guest-service agent

- **Duties:** Reception   Credit
  Identification   Selection
  Registration   Assignment

↓

Bellperson

- **Duties:** Room guest   Room inspection
  Monitor rooming slip   Cross-promotion

↓

Housekeeping

↓

Hotel security

↓

Concierge staff

↓

In-room services (may be integrated to property management system)

PMS

- **Including:** In-room movies   Electronic locking system
  Minibar   Energy management system
  In-room refrigerator   In-room safe
  Telephone call accounting   In-house shopping channel

Information available to all integrated departments

General management	Cashier	Food and beverage	Concierge Bellstaff Security	Health club	Gift shop	Housekeeping

Exhibit 8–1   The guest arrival process is a complex choreography of departments and responsibilities. When their efforts come together seamlessly, the guest has a positive "moment of truth." Shown here is an arrival flow pattern for a full-service corporate hotel. Luxury resorts might add several functions to the flow pattern (golf, dinner reservations, or table assignments for an American plan resort). Limited-service properties might provide none of the services displayed here.

Exhibit 8–2   Example of a hotel offering both doorperson and valet parking services (note the sign to the right of the doors). At the Wedgewood Hotel, doorpersons and parking attendants are one and the same. Although most small four-diamond hotels would probably not offer both services—the Wedgewood has just 51 luxury standard and executive rooms, 34 one-bedroom suites, and 4 penthouse suites—their average rate ($220–$498) is sufficient to warrant it. *Courtesy of The Wedgewood Hotel, Vancouver, British Columbia, Canada.*

The front desk of one of Orlando's busiest convention properties—The Rosen Centre Hotel. On slow check-in days, this desk works well with just one or two front-desk agents; on busy days, the desk can accommodate as many as 22 agents. Rosen Hotels & Resorts is a small chain (just seven properties, all in Orlando) with big properties (6,387 rooms in just seven hotels).

For convention business, this is one of the best places to be. Orlando's Orange County Convention Center (OCCC) boasts 1.1 million square feet of space and is ranked as one of the nation's top convention centers by *Tradeshow Weekly*. But that's old news. Today, OCCC is undergoing an expansion project to increase exhibition, meeting room, and public space to a total of 7 million square feet!! This awe-inspiring project is targeted to open in the fall of 2003.

Good business if you can get it. And Rosen Hotels & Resorts is well positioned with major convention properties flanking both sides of the OCCC! *Courtesy of Rosen Hotels & Resorts, Orlando, Florida.*

offer the guest suggestions, point out interesting historic sites, explain difficult directions, and hail a taxi. For newly arriving guests, the doorperson assists with removing and securing luggage from the car until the bellperson retrieves it for delivery. In addition to all these tasks, the doorperson also opens doors! (See Exhibit 8–2.)

In potentially dangerous urban downtown settings, the doorperson supplements the security department by serving as an early-warning defense against suspicious nonguest "visitors" and other possibly hazardous situations. Due in large part to the doorperson's physical location at the front of the hotel, these staff members prove excellent early-warning security enhancements. Likewise, the very nature of the job, observing and greeting all who pass by, recognizing and chatting with regulars, and providing verbal suggestions and directions to those who ask, lends itself well to observation and scrutiny of would-be thieves. Certainly, all employees should be trained to observe the warning signs of suspicious visitors, but the doorperson is especially critical in watching for the following telltale signs:

➤ A person occupying a vehicle under the porte-cochère who refuses to move or has no discernable purpose for being there.

➤ A person who passes by regularly, aimlessly, or with no particular direction.

➤ A person who watches the hotel front doors or exits, or intently watches a particular employee station, or a person who intently watches another guest (especially a guest with a laptop computer or briefcase).

➤ A person carrying a suspicious package or who displays a bulge under his or her shirt or jacket.

Guest Registration

After being greeted at the curb and the front door, the guest arrives at the front desk (see Exhibit 8–1). In a small property, the desk itself is small and probably staffed with just one or two agents. Each of these agents is capable of handling the full range of functions the guest requires. In larger properties, however, the front desk may be literally hundreds of feet long, with 20 to 30 or more clerks working (see Exhibit 8–3).

In large hotels, guest receptionists or guest service agents have distinct responsibilities. During busy check-in periods, however, most other activities are placed on hold until the arriving guests—the highest priority—are handled. Arriving guests can easily tell which guest service agents are handling check-ins. For one thing, their stations are usually marked with signs reading "reception," "registration," "check-in," or "arrivals." Additionally, there may be a line (queue) of guests standing in front of each guest-service agent. For further information on waiting lines, refer to the discussion on queuing theory later in this chapter.

Two types of guests present themselves at the front desk: those with reservations and those without. Those with reservations are generally handled without problem. The agent reconfirms the accommodations requested, the guest signs the registration card, a method of payment is secured, a room is selected, and some pleasantries are exchanged. In a computerized property, the entire reception process can be handled quickly—say, in several minutes.

Guests holding reservations may encounter two problems: no record of the reservation and no space available. The arrival and reception should go quickly, even if the reservation has been misplaced, provided that space is available. As unobtrusively as possible, the clerk elicits the reservation information again and makes the assignment. No reference to the missing paperwork is made. Far more composure is necessary if the clerk is to handle an overbooking situation successfully. With proper training, the

Exhibit 8–3   Here's a look at the busy front desk of the Opryland Hotel in Nashville. The Opryland is among the largest independent, unaffiliated hotels in the world. It boasts 2,884 rooms, 220 suites, and over 30 specialty shops. *Courtesy of the Opryland Hotel, Nashville, Tennessee.*

emergency procedures described in Chapters 6 and 7 are implemented, and the moment of truth is achieved without incident.

▶*Walk-In Guests.*   The registration process is more time consuming for walk-in guests than for guests who have an existing reservation. If space is available—and it usually is (even hotels boasting 100% occupancy on a given night often have one or two unoccupied rooms)—the guest-service agent must collect the same information from the walk-in guest that the reservations department collects during a routine phone call. The difference is that now the guest is standing in front of the desk. Patiently, the agent asks about the room configuration and number of beds preferred, guests in the party, number of nights required, and so on.

Careful handling of walk-in guests is critical to the hotel's healthy bottom line. Yet, before the agent can ask questions about the party's needs, the walk-in guest is often concerned with one thing—rate. Indeed, in transient properties, the guest may literally run in and ask the "rate" question ("How much is a room?") while the car is running, the kids are fidgeting, and the spouse is losing patience. Improperly trained guest-service agents do not seize the moment and simply spit out "$129 plus tax." The potential guest turns on his or her heels and heads back out the door.

Many experts believe the hotel industry, as a whole, does a poor job focusing on the sales opportunities presented by walk-in traffic. After all, the guest is standing in front of the desk asking about rooms and rates. That places the hotel in a far more advantageous position then if the guest were on the telephone at the airport. Phoning guests have it easy; they can call one hotel after another until they find the rate they're seeking. It is far more difficult to pile back into the automobile, pull out of the driveway, and head down the street to another property.

Besides, the guest is standing in the lobby and has already been impacted by his or her first impression. If the lobby shows well, and the agent is personable, there is no reason the potential walk-in guest should turn around and leave. A well-trained agent knows that rate alone tells the guest nothing. Rather, the agent needs to describe the accommodations, explain how the hotel meets the travelers' needs (swimming pool for kids, very quiet rooms for tired corporate guests, breakfast included for price-conscious customers, etc.), and provide a list of rate options. Then, ask for the sale.

▶*Registered, Not Assigned.*   Very early arrivals, especially those who appear before the day's check-out hour, may be required to wait until a departure creates a vacancy. Even then, the room must still be cleaned. Baggage-check service is offered to all guests who must wait, and a complimentary beverage may be given to some if the hotel is responsible for the wait. In anticipation of an upcoming vacancy, the clerk may have the guest register. The account is marked RNA (registered, not assigned) and kept handy until the first appropriate departure takes place. The assignment is made but the guest is kept waiting until housekeeping reports the room ready for occupancy—guests are not sent to unmade rooms.

Guests who arrive after the room is vacated but before it has been cleaned by housekeeping—a status called *on change*—are assigned at once but not provided with a key until the room has been cleaned and inspected. This is not an RNA.

RNAs occur whenever the hotel is very full with simultaneous arrivals and departures of large conventions, or when tour groups overlap. Busy holidays cause RNAs at the type of resorts where arrivals come early and departures stay late.

Exhibit 8–4   The Mirage Hotel and Casino in Las Vegas takes hotel front-desk design to the extreme! Hard to grow impatient waiting in line when a 20,000 gallon saltwater tank replete with full-sized sharks circling a coral reef sits just a few yards away. *Courtesy of MGM MIRAGE, Las Vegas, Nevada.*

Waiting for the room is a distressing experience, especially as the hours tick away. On some occasions it may be necessary to assign guests temporary rooms, changing them to a permanent assignment later. This type of costly duplication should be avoided except in special circumstances. Most front-office systems, including computerized ones, allow RNAs to create charges even though no room identification is possible.

In corporate hotels, RNAs are less frustrating. Corporate guests who arrive early in the morning are happy to register and leave their luggage secure. They then go about their business until the workday ends later that afternoon. Upon returning to the hotel, they find their room number has been assigned and their luggage is waiting for them in the room.

Early Check-in Policies.   Generally, hotels have rooms available from the night before. Even when last night's status was "sold out," there are usually rooms available. That's because a few of last night's rooms likely were no-shows. The hotel received its revenue by billing the no-show guest, but the room itself was never occupied (for a discussion of no-shows, see Chapter 6). Therefore, a guest checking in at, say, 7 or 8 AM is likely to find a room available.

The real question is, Will the front-desk clerk allow the guest to check in? Check-in time for most hotels is between 1 and 4 PM, allowing housekeeping ample time to clean check-out rooms. A guest checking in at noon or 11 AM is no big deal, but a guest who wants access to the room at 7 or 8 AM poses a problem for some hotels—their policies do not allow early check-in without imposing a fee. Similar to a late check-out fee (for guests who stay beyond 2 or 3 PM), the idea behind an early check-in fee is that the guest is using the room for a number of hours before the start of the official "day."

Imposing such a fee does more harm than good. The guest feels cheated. Moreover, letting the guest into the room early will probably result in a few breakfast meals and some telephone revenue as well. Crowne Plaza Hotels and Resorts encourages early check-in for corporate members of its Priority Club Rewards. They advertise corporate check-ins beginning at 7 AM (and late check outs until 3 PM) without extra charge!

➤ *Waiting Lines.*   Early check-in and RNA policies do more than get the guest into the room early; they get the guest out of line too. Few check-ins occur early in the day, and therefore the front desk should accommodate such guests whenever possible. Otherwise, those guests may return during the busiest check-in times. For corporate hotels, the busiest check-in times are usually from 5 to 8 PM. The busiest check-out periods are 7 to 9 AM.

There is probably nothing more frustrating after a long day of travel than to arrive at a congested front office. From early in the morning, the traveling guest has been waiting—waiting to park the car and get a parking stub; waiting to have the airplane ticket validated and a seat assigned; waiting in the security line; waiting for the plane to begin boarding, take off, land, and deplane, and waiting to be shuttled to the hotel. Imagine the frustration walking into the lobby of your home away from home to see yet another waiting line. Indeed, that is one of the appeals of the new self-check-in kiosks, discussed later in this chapter.

It is the job of hotel management to adequately staff busy check-in periods. Hard to do, because guests can (and do) arrive at literally any hour. Add to this uncertainty the constrictions of a limited budget, union and nonunion labor laws (meal breaks and the like), employees who are not yet fully trained, sick call-ins, and the problem becomes amplified. It becomes even more exaggerated when you realize that the industry is larger and busier than ever before. How else can you check thousands of guests into a megaresort except one guest at a time?

Long Lines Equal Poor Service.   Some theorists suggest that today's guests are more impatient with check-in lines than ever before. The blame, they say, is on the computer industry, which has created a "get it now" society. Through modern technology, we can communicate at lightning speed, send documents by modem, and reach cellular phone customers wherever they happen to be. Maybe that's why guests are so impatient.

Whatever the reason guests are so impatient, it is in the hotel's best interest to minimize the wait. That is because the check-in process—and its accompanying wait in line—is one of the most critical moments of truth of the guests' stay. A long wait can ruin the check-in and ultimately the entire stay. The check-in is probably the first, or one of the first, face-to-face encounters the guest has with hotel staff. The first encounter should be memorable, and a long wait in line certainly is memorable (just not the kind of memory we wish to instill). In addition, arriving guests have little else to occupy their mind. They quickly become restless and critical of the front-office operation. You see, guests have a certain expectation with regard to the check-in process. A limited wait is reasonable, a long wait becomes synonymous with a poorly run hotel. That is especially true when there are few guests in line. When the wait is due to some hidden element, guests become indignant.

To empathize with the waiting guest, management needs to understand and train for three important factors:

1. Empty minutes go faster when the guests' time is filled with something to do. Distract and entertain them (see Exhibit 8–5).
2. For waiting guests, not knowing how long they'll be waiting is worse than knowing an estimated length of wait, even if the wait is expected to be quite long.
3. Anything the guest(s) can do to make the whole check-in process more efficient is understood and appreciated. Guests want to help.

Queuing Theory.   In the early 20th century, A. K. Erlang, a Danish mathematician, introduced a theory called *telephony*. Originally designed as a mathematical model for solving telephone traffic line usage, the theory found other applications during World War II. Each modification resulted in other names as the application changed slightly. Erlang's traffic theory has been renamed *queuing* (also spelled *queueing*) theory, congestion theory, and for its application to long customer lines, waiting line theory. Queuing theory comes from the French word *queue*, meaning to line up. The uses of this theory are manifold: toll booths, 911 calls, traffic lights, airports, parking lots, hospitals, data processing, and countless more.

Queuing theory is a mathematical tool that management uses to obtain an optimum rate of customer flow. It balances the costs of making customers wait against the costs of serving them more rapidly. Queuing theory attempts to quantify the dilemma regarding ideal levels of guest service.

Too little service and the guest waits in line, or waits on the reservation telephone line, longer than expected. Dissatisfied guests, formal complaints, a low percentage of repeat business, or lost revenue from guests who leave are the consequential losses from too little service.

Exhibit 8–5   A long queue is rarely a good thing. Waiting guests lose patience, employees feel overwhelmed, and hotel revenues suffer because guests are standing in line rather than spending money in the restaurants, lounges, and other departments. However, careful planning can take the sting out of a long queue and transform it into a carnival atmosphere. Informal policies might provide complimentary cocktail, champagne, or juice service anytime the waiting line exceeds five guests or so.

Responding to too little service (a definition that varies with the class and segment of the hotel), management adds more registration windows, more employees, more computer terminals, and self-check-in kiosks. The guest is served more rapidly but at a significant cost in labor, equipment, and lost lobby space. And herein lies the dilemma: What is the optimal point between these two extremes?—let the guest wait too long? or invest in systems and labor to eliminate the wait?

Queuing theory requires an understanding of probability statistics as well as of differential and integral calculus. Computer programs are available to do the computations. Four key elements must be quantified: arrival population, service population, queue discipline, and service discipline (see Exhibit 8–1). The quality of the assumptions and facts behind these four components dictate the level of success that the final solution takes.

ARRIVAL POPULATION.   A number of factors affect the size of the population arriving at the desk. Certain hours of the day and certain days of the week are busier arrival times than others. The quantity of group business has an impact, as does the method of handling them. Are they registered at the front desk or in a separate group registration area? All guest transactions are not the same. Guests stand in line to check in, to ask questions, to complain, to get change, and to obtain and return keys (see Exhibit 8–1).

SERVICE POPULATION.   The kind and number of available guest-service agents and their configuration behind the desk is the service population. Intrinsic to this component are several special issues. The ability of the clerks (agents), the number of clerks, and whether that figure is fixed or variable (i.e., other employees have been cross-trained to work desk check-ins), and the assignment of duties (does each position handle every request, or are there special windows for special needs?) are all elements of the service population.

QUEUE DISCIPLINE.   Queue discipline refers to the behavior exhibited by the guests who are waiting in line. This is the element that changed waiting line theory from a mathematical science to a behavioral one. Guests cry "Unfair" or "Don't cut into line" when someone who arrived after them is served before them. Skips and slips (when one guest skips or "cuts" ahead of a waiting guest, resulting in the original guest slipping further back in line) are the most infuriating of all. Additionally, queue discipline addresses the guest's reaction to the line: Does a guest refuse to join the line because of the length (a "balk")? Does a guest switch lines as the respective lengths vary? If a guest leaves the line (a "renege") after waiting for some time, is that decision determined by the length of the line, or is it a random move? Do others allow the line jumper back in? Little is really known about the behavior of hotel guests standing in line to be registered.

SERVICE DISCIPLINE.   Service discipline is the last of the four key elements. It examines the server's attitude and approach as the queue discipline questions the guest's behavior. Are guests handled on a first-come, first-served basis? How are interruptions fielded from a "one-quick-question" interloper? Is priority treatment provided for special VIPs and frequent-guest members?

Creative Solutions to Long Lines.   Responses to the problem of long waits have come from all industries. Banks have addressed the problem by implementing a single waiting line so that waiting customers don't have to be frustrated by picking the slowest clerk. Grocery chains have developed an approach that solves the problem and also serves as a marketing tool. They advertise: We'll open a new line whenever more than two customers are waiting. Fast-food chains, airlines, and many others send an employee to the rear of the line to take orders and ease the bottleneck at the cash register. Customers respond as much to the company's demonstrated concern as to the actual solution.

Some solutions can be, and have been, borrowed from other industries. The single waiting line is the most apparent. Snaking the line back on itself, as is done in theme parks, makes the line appear shorter, but it does take up costly lobby space. Telling the guest the estimated waiting time recognizes the human behavior part of waiting, but it does nothing to speed up the process. Neither does another technique, which merely assuages the guest's irritation from waiting. Borrowing from pizza-delivery philosophy, guests who wait in line longer than 5 minutes get a fun reward: complimentary cocktails, reduced room rate, or an upgrade (see Exhibit 8–5).

Radio-assisted registration has been tried, but only the largest hotels are able to work this out. Customer-service staff work the rear of the registration line or catch new guests as they enter the lobby. The reservation information is radioed to back-office computers. Moments later, the guest is directed to a special window to sign the form and pick up the key.

Separating certain guests from the regular line saves time for both those separated and for those remaining. A concierge or executive check in that accommodates special categories such as premium corporate accounts, and frequent-guest patrons are sample categories.

But some of the best ideas are the most creative. The Mirage Hotel and Casino in Las Vegas boasts a 20,000-gallon saltwater aquarium behind its front desk (Exhibit 8–4). It's hard to get bored when live sharks are swimming just a few yards in front of you. Other major hotels transform the wait into a party. They bring in jugglers, magicians, and comedians who perform for the waiting guests (see Exhibit 8–5). And of course, the amusement parks have it down to a science. Which of the following ideas can the lodging industry adopt from the theme parks?

➤ *Pre-shows:* an informative video describing various aspects of the resort and designed to run on a continuous loop

➤ *Time signs:* describing the approximate wait in line from this point forward

➤ *Live entertainers:* as with the jugglers, magicians, and comedians described above

➤ *Segmented queues:* allowing guests to see just a small section of the queue at a time to create the illusion of short lines

➤ *Video screens:* entertaining video clips of various topics, CNN News, or an in-house channel.

➤ *Interactive participation:* guests decipher codes, draw graffiti on walls, converse with robots

➤ *Themed environments:* aquariums, jungles, pyramids, and the like to give guests plenty to look at while waiting in line

➤**The Registration Card.**   As the guest approaches the front desk, a fairly standard exchange of information begins to take place. The front-desk agent begins with some common pleasantries—How are you today? Has it been a difficult travel day for you? Have you stayed with us before?—designed to make the guest feel welcome. Although some greeting is mandated in literally every hotel's front-office training manual, the length of such a greeting is partly dependent on business levels. When traffic at the desk is slow, guests frequently enjoy longer chats with staff. When other guests are waiting to be served, however, the greeting is a bit more streamlined.

In manual (nonautomated) properties, registration information is collected by handing the guest a blank registration card to complete. Today's property management systems have eliminated the need for manually collecting guest information. For the most part, information collected at registration is the same as information collected during the reservation. Automated properties preprint registration cards from the information collected at the time of reservation (see Exhibit 8–6). Now, instead of burdening the guest with completion of an entire card, the front-desk clerk merely asks the guest to verify accuracy of information and sign at the bottom of the card.

Indeed, some hotels have done away with guest signatures and registration cards altogether. If the necessary information is verified through some other means—a verbal exchange between the front-desk agent and the guest, for example—the hotel may

```
2059                M/M Paul D. Ligament    6/14/      PL          RATES DO NOT INCLUDE TAXES
Room                Name                    Depart
                                                                   Account # 1229821
DLX K N/S           Western Athletes        6/11/                  Group # WA
Type                Firm or Group           Arrive
                                                                   Deposit
ABC                 2A/1K
Clerk ID            Party


              Address          Rate Plan
                                 (160)
Street 1234 Achilles Tendon Way              ⚡ HOT WIRE HOTEL
City/State Wounded Knee, SD 00000-0000          Shocking Behavior Drive
Company Horsn Around, Inc.                       Electric City, Washington
Date Departure 6/14/                                  77777-7777
Signature Paul D. Ligament

I agree that my liability for this bill is not waived and I agree
to be held personally liable in the event that the indicated
person, company, or association fails to pay for the full
amount of the charges.                                NOTICE TO GUESTS:
                                                      This hotel keeps a fireproof safe and will not
                                                      be responsible for money, jewelry, documents,
I would like to handle my account by:                 or other articles of value unless placed therein.
                                                      Please lock your car.
  ☐ Cash/Check  ☐ MasterCard  ☐ VISA
  ☐ Diners Club  ☒ American Express
  ☐ Discover Card
```

Exhibit 8–6   With a computer-prepared registration card, all the guest need do is verify the accuracy of the information, read the disclaimers, and sign. A detailed and accurate reservation saves the hotel duplicate work. Assuming the name has been spelled properly, the address is correct, and so on, the same information collected at the time of reservation is reused again and again (on the letter of confirmation, the folio, the rooming slip, the arrivals list, etc.). In addition to a signature, hotels commonly ask the guest to confirm the rate and departure date by initialing (see initials PL) the registration card.

forego the formality of collecting a guest signature. In fact, registration is not essential to the commonlaw creation of a legal guest-hotel relationship. In several states it is not even a statutory requirement. In contrast, other countries not only require registration cards but use them as police documents. Guests furnish foreign innkeepers with passports and a great deal of personal information that has value only to the authorities (see Exhibit 8–7). Indeed, hotel registration in Brazil requires the guest to fill in the names of both mother and father. Age, gender, date of birth, next destination, previous stop, and nationality are never found with registration information collected in the United States.

Legal Release of Sensitive Registration Data.   Even without sensitive questions about age, gender, and nationality, registration documents in the United States are still ripe with data. A close examination of the guest's registration readily provides such details as name, address, and company affiliation; dates and times of arrival and departure; telephone and Internet records showing numbers dialed, times calls were placed, and duration; credit-card information; and so on. A probe of guest-history records adds frequency and dates of previous visits as well as other personal information related to hotel services, purchases, telephone records, and more.

It is this information that federal and local authorities seek in the immediate aftermath of terrorist activities and certain other localized crimes. The FBI, local police, and related authorities rapidly descended upon hotel operators following the collapse of the World Trade Center. The hotels held valuable information in the form of guest-registration cards, and authorities desperately needed that information!

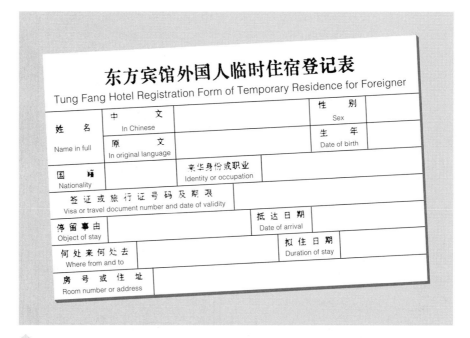

东方宾馆外国人临时住宿登记表
Tung Fang Hotel Registration Form of Temporary Residence for Foreigner

姓　名 Name in full	中　　文 In Chinese			性　　别 Sex	
	原　　文 In original language			生　　年 Date of birth	
国　籍 Nationality		来华身份或职业 Identity or occupation			
签证或旅行证号码及期限 Visa or travel document number and date of validity					
停留事由 Object of stay			抵达日期 Date of arrival		
何处来何处去 Where from and to			拟住日期 Duration of stay		
房号或住址 Room number or address					

Exhibit 8–7　　Domestic hotels would never think of asking age, sex, travel plans, or names of the guests' mother and father. Indeed, such questions would surely be construed as an illegal invasion of privacy in the United States. However, these are the types of questions asked of the guest on many foreign registration cards, including this one from the Tung Fang Hotel, Canton, People's Republic of China. In some foreign countries, the registration card can actually be used as a police document!

Yet hotel executives were hesitant to release the information. Generally, the industry has operated behind a longstanding rule of thumb that sensitive guest information can be turned over to authorities only after a subpoena or warrant has been served. (This rule has never applied to time-sensitive emergencies—the hotel wouldn't hesitate to share personal information with authorities related to a guest having a heart attack, for example).

Whether to release sensitive guest information was the conundrum in which hotel executives found themselves immediately following the September 11, 2001, attacks. Should the old standard be thrown out the window because these were time-sensitive requests? After all, providing information to authorities quickly might save lives. Or was this request for guest records to be met with the same hardline tactics as before: no information without the proper warrant and/or subpoena?

Fortunately, that question was addressed in the Anti-Terrorism Act (2001) passed within weeks of the September 11 attacks. This document gives law-enforcement authorities an emergency process for obtaining records from private entities, such as hotels. Authorities can obtain a written order in a streamlined fashion in a fraction of the time it would take for a court-ordered subpoena or warrant. By law, this written order protects hotel operators from subsequent litigation related to invasion of privacy. This approach seems to solve the dilemma—time-sensitivity versus guest privacy—for both law enforcement authorities as well as hotel operators.

Information commonly listed on registration cards is discussed in the following sections.

Number in the Party.   The number of persons (the house count) has importance for statistics that are developed during the night audit. In addition, the number of persons in the room determines the rate charged. When indicating the number of guests in the room, many hotels separate adults from children (see Exhibit 8–6). This is especially true in an American plan hotel that probably charges less for young children's meals than for adult meals.

Name and Address.   An accurate and complete name and address is needed for credit and billing and for the development of mailing lists for future sales promotions. A complete address includes such things as ZIP codes, apartment numbers, and even state of residence, for the names of many cities are common to several states. Commercial hotels often ask for the patron's business address and organizational title in addition to the residential address (see Exhibit 8–6).

Greater credit can be extended to a guest whose address has been verified through an exchange of reservation correspondence than to a walk-in. Whereas those intent on fraud will use false addresses, vacant lots, or temporary box numbers, unintentional skippers (people who forgot to check out or inadvertently left a portion of their folio unpaid) can be traced, billed, and subsequently collected from if an accurate name and address is on file.

Room Number.   Even as the hotel industry seeks higher levels of courtesy and guest service, the guest continues to be known as much by room number as by name. Once the guest is registered in the property management system and a room number has been assigned, all subsequent transactions are referenced and billed to the room number rather than to the guest's actual name. The room number is the major means of locating, identifying, tracking, and billing the guest. Even before the guest arrives, the reservation number (or with some systems a preassigned folio number) is used to locate the guest and credit advance deposits (see Exhibit 8–6).

Date of Departure.   The guest's expected date of departure is of critical importance during the check-in process. By double-checking the guest's departure plans, the front office ensures the accuracy of future room availability figures.

Many front offices require the guest to sign a statement or initial the registration card next to their date of departure (see Exhibits 8–6 and 8–8). This is especially true for busy periods when a scheduled departure is necessary to provide the room to a newly arriving reservation (see Exhibit 8–9). Of course, plans change, and some percentage of guests will invariably depart earlier or later than they originally thought. In such cases, the front office strives to accommodate the guest. There is usually no extra charge for early departures and most unscheduled stayovers are accommodated (see the section entitled "Early Departure Fees" in Chapter 6).

Discounts or Corporate Affiliations.   Another issue resolved during the check-in process is the guest's corporate affiliation or qualified discounts. The corporate affiliation (if applicable) is often logged and tracked by the front desk on behalf of the sales and marketing department. This corporate information is critical to the sales department because many companies have accounts with individual and chain properties. By tracking corporate guest visitation, the sales department is able to continue offering discounts and special rates to companies who frequent the property. Many corporations have agreements with the chain (or with an individual hotel) to stay a certain number of room nights per year. Tracking use is critical to the success of such ongoing relationships (see Exhibit 8–6).

Welcome to North Carolina

LAWS OF NORTH CAROLINA

LAW GOVERNING INNKEEPERS   (From General Statutes of North Carolina)

72-1. MUST FURNISH ACCOMMODATIONS: CONTRACTS FOR TERMINATION VALID. (a) Every innkeeper shall at all times provide suitable lodging accommodations for persons accepted as guests in his inn or hotel. (b) A written statement setting forth the time period during which a guest may occupy an assigned room, signed or initialed by the guest, shall be deemed a valid contract, and at the expiration of such time period the lodger may be restrained from entering and any property of the guest may be removed by the innkeeper without liability, except for damages to or loss of such property attributable to its removal.

72-2. LIABILITY FOR LOSS OF BAGGAGE. Innkeepers shall not be liable for loss, damage or destruction of the baggage or property of their guests except in case such loss, damage or destruction results from the failure of the innkeeper to exercise ordinary, proper and reasonable care in the custody of such baggage and property and in case of such loss, damage or destruction resulting from the negligence and want of care of the said innkeeper, he shall be liable to the owner of said baggage and property to an amount not exceeding one hundred dollars. Any guest may, however, at any time before a loss, damage or destruction of his property notify the innkeeper in writing that his property exceeds value the said sum of one hundred dollars, and shall upon demand of the innkeeper furnish him a list or schedule of the same with the value thereof, in which case the innkeeper shall be liable for the loss, damage or destruction of said property because of any negligence on his part, for the full value of the same. Proof of the loss of any such baggage, except in case of damage or destruction by fire, shall be prima facie evidence.

72-3. SAFE KEEPING OF VALUABLES. It shall be the duty of innkeepers, upon the request of any guest, to receive from said guest, and safely keep money, jewelry, and valuables to an amount not exceeding five hundred dollars; and no innkeeper shall be required to receive and take care of any money, jewelry or other valuables to a greater amount than five hundred dollars. No innkeeper shall be liable for the loss, damage or destruction of any money or jewels not so deposited.

72-4. LOSS BY FIRE. No innkeeper shall be liable for loss, damage, or destruction of any baggage or property caused by fire not resulting from the negligence of the innkeeper or by any other force of which the innkeeper had no control. Nothing herein contained shall enlarge the limit of the amount to which the innkeeper shall be liable as provided in preceding sections.

72-5. NEGLIGENCE OF GUESTS. Any innkeeper against whom claim is made for loss sustained by a guest may show that such loss resulted from the negligence of such guest or of his failure to comply with the reasonable and proper regulations of the inn.

72-6. COPIES OF THIS ARTICLE POSTED. Every innkeeper shall keep posted in every room of his house occupied by guests, and in the office, a printed copy of this article and of all regulations to the conduct of guests. This chapter shall not apply to the innkeepers, or their guests, where the innkeeper fails to keep such notice posted.

72-8. ADMITTANCE OF PETS TO HOTEL ROOMS. (a) Innkeepers may permit pets in rooms used for sleeping purposes and in adjoining rooms. Persons bringing pets into a room in which they are not permitted are in violation of this section and punishable according to subsection (d) of this section.

(b) Innkeepers allowing pets must post a sign measuring not less than five inches by seven inches at the place where guests register informing them pets are permitted in sleeping rooms and in adjoining rooms. If certain pets are permitted or prohibited, the sign must so state. If any pets are permitted, the innkeeper must maintain a minimum of ten percent (10%) of the sleeping rooms in the inn or hotel as rooms where pets are not permitted and the sign required by this subsection must also state that such rooms are available.

(c) All sleeping rooms in which the innkeeper permits pets must contain a sign measuring not less than five inches by seven inches, posted in a prominent place in the room, which shall be separate from the sign required by G.S. 72-6, stating that pets are permitted in the room, or whether certain pets are prohibited or permitted in the room, and stating that bringing pets into a room in which they are not permitted is a misdemeanor under North Carolina law punishable by a fine not to exceed five hundred dollars ($500.00), imprisonment not to exceed 30 days, or both.

(d) Any person violating the provisions of this section shall be guilty of a misdemeanor and upon conviction shall pay fine not to exceed five hundred dollars ($500.00) or be imprisoned for not more than 30 days, or both.

(e) The provisions of this section are not applicable to assistance dogs admitted to sleeping rooms and adjoining rooms under the provisions of Chapter 168 of the General Statutes.

American Hotel Register Co., Northbrook, IL 60062-7798   B6E-1029   12/94

Exhibit 8–8   Laws governing innkeepers in North Carolina are unique. Note the first statute (72-1), which requires the check-out date be signed or initialed by the guest. The last statute (72-8) allows pets in hotel rooms providing the hotel properly displays signage informing guests that pets may have stayed in the hotel and at least 10% of all rooms are set aside as pet-free rooms

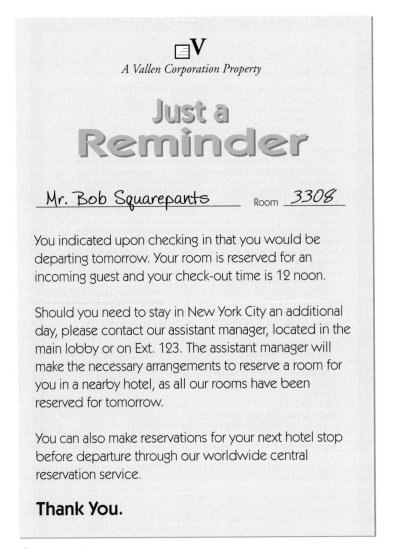

Exhibit 8–9   Check-out reminders like this may be printed on cards or letterheads and placed under the guest's door or on the pillow the night before. Reminders are used only when the hotel expects an overbooking situation the following day.

Even when a corporate guest's company has not negotiated a special room rate, the hotel is usually willing to grant a standard corporate discount. Such discounts range from 10 to 20% or higher depending on the type of hotel, the date, and season of visitation.

Even noncorporate guests may qualify for discounts. Leisure guests are often members of national or worldwide organizations such as AAA or AARP. AAA (American Automobile Association) and AARP (American Association of Retired Persons) are two of the largest membership organizations in the world. Most hotels grant AAA and/or AARP discounts to qualified guests. A complete discussion of rate discounts is found in Chapter 9.

Clerk Identification.   The front-desk clerk who checks the guest into the hotel is automatically identified in the property management system from the password the clerk used when logging onto the computer. Clerk identification is important in case a problem or other issue arises. By knowing who checked the guest in, management can return to that clerk and ask related questions. Possibly the guest was pleased with the process and complimented management on the clerk's performance. On the other hand, maybe the clerk provided an insufficient discount, was rude, or forgot to establish a method of payment (see Exhibit 8–6).

Folio Numbering. All hotels assign a unique folio number to the guest's account. In a computerized property, this account number is provided at the time of reservation. The number is assigned early in case the guest sends advance payment. The folio (or account) number references the guest's automated file just as readily as the room number or guest name (see Exhibit 8–6).

Computerized numbering serves as a control device when one employee is clerk, cashier, and supervisor all in one. It is possible for such an employee to sell the room as clerk, pocket the money as cashier, and cover the discrepancy as night auditor. When the staff grows large enough to permit a separation of duties, numeric form control becomes less important.

Another major advantage to a computerized property management system is the ease of storing records. While according to some management consultants the standard is seven years (three years for registration cards), many properties find themselves storing folios, registration cards, and accounting records for even longer periods. In an electronic hotel, storage is easy when daily records are downloaded onto tape or disk. In a manual property, storage consumes considerably more space.

Disclaimer of Innkeeper Liability. Almost every registration card carries a statement concerning the hotel's liability for the loss of guest valuables. Such a disclaimer is shown in Exhibit 8–6. The form and content of the statement are prescribed by state statute, and consequently, these vary among states. If the innkeeper meets the provisions of the statute, and public notice on the registration card is usually one such provision, liability for the loss of valuables is substantially reduced. Were it not for the dollar limits set by state legislatures, innkeepers would have unlimited liability under common law.

Common law is far more stringent than statutory law; it makes the hotel responsible in full for the value of guests' belongings. Most states, but not all, limit the innkeeper's liability to a fixed sum even when the guest uses the safe provided. Other statutes prevent recovery against the hotel if the guest fails to use the safe, provided that the hotel has complied with every provision of the law (see Exhibit 8–6). State legislatures have extended this principle of limited liability to checkrooms and to goods that are too large for the ordinary safe—salesperson's samples, for example (see Exhibit 8–10).

Notices, which must be posted in the rooms, must include the maximum rate charged for the room (see bottom Exhibit 8–10). Charges sometimes exceed that figure when a yield management system is in operation or when rates are changed frequently. The hotel may charge what it wishes, but there is a danger in not changing the permanent rate schedule that must be posted in each guest room.

Catering to Pets. Over the past 10 years or so, the number of lodging properties offering pet accommodations has increased from 30 to 65%.[2] Pet owners are becom-

---

[2]According to the AH&LA, pets are welcome in more than 23,000 U.S. lodging establishments, up from 10,000 hotels in 1994. Additional information can be found in *Accommodations Offering Facilities for Your Pet*, published by the American Automobile Association.

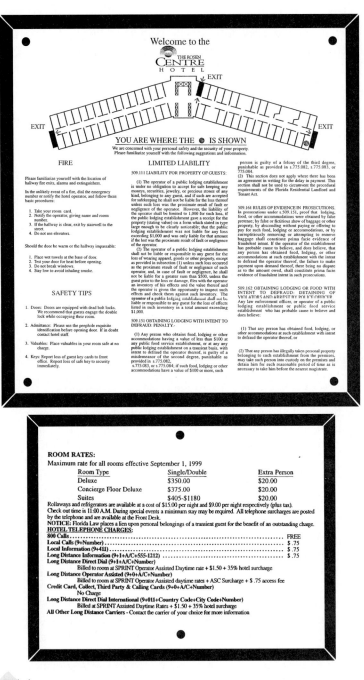

Exhibit 8–10   Most states require that limited liability notice to guests be correctly displayed in each room along with maximum room rates. When such notice is displayed, the innkeeper's liability is drastically reduced (as shown here, Florida limits innkeeper liability to between $500 and $1,000). Interestingly, Florida also adds fire and safety tips to in-room notices. *Courtesy: The Rosen Centre Hotel, Orlando, Florida.*

ing a sizable market, one not overlooked by the lodging industry. Many pet owners think "it's the cat's meow" when luxury properties cater to their pets. The Chicago Ritz-Carlton, for example, offers a gourmet room service menu for dogs and cats, a "Pet Recognition Program" that provides a treat to the guest's pet each time they visit, and even an onsite grooming and pet-walking service.

Not to be outdone, Loews Hotels has been testing "puppy pagers" at all its U.S. properties. This service offers a win-win solution to all parties involved; when a pet left alone in the room starts whining or barking, the hotel can contact the pet owner, thereby relieving not only the pet but the guests next door as well! Four Seasons Hotels and Resorts offers pet accommodations at many of its luxury properties, complete with a ceramic feeding bowl, dog biscuits, and a sleeping pillow. Holiday Inn, Ramada, Motel 6, and a growing list of other chains also accommodate guests' pets.

Catering to pets has very positive revenue potential for accommodating properties. Certain Marriott Residence Inns, for example, charge an additional $100 per stay to guests traveling with pets. Ostensibly, the $100 is a nonrefundable cleaning deposit to return the guest room to pet-free status. Hotel InterContinental in Los Angeles also charges $100 per stay. The San Ysidro Ranch in Montecito, California, charges $75 per pet. The Soho Grand in New York takes it a step farther by charging $12 for a pet toothbrush and toothpaste, $20 for a pet full-body pillow, and another $10 for pet in-room dining service—traveling with pets isn't so "ruff" after all.

Starwood Hotels & Resorts has recently developed a pet-friendly program for all its Sheraton Four Points properties. They have high hopes for pet-related revenues, even after a recent experience at their Los Angeles airport property where staff was asked to find frozen rats to feed a guest eagle (visiting as part of an Alaska tourism promotion)!

On the other side of the coin, however, registering pets does have some serious potential costs—including the discomfort of other guests. Some guests may be hypersensitive to pet dander (fur and hair) left behind even after the most through of cleanings. Guests have the right to know if pets have previously stayed in their rooms (see Exhibit 8–9). Some hotels therefore refuse all animals except seeing eye dogs, as permitted by law. Other properties limit their acceptance to small dogs (no cats) weighing less than 50 pounds.

Points of Agreement.   Even as management strives to expedite the process, extra reading matter is being added to the registration card. The content of these extra messages differs among hotels and chains. Each has different problems and legal experiences. The presence of the messages meets legal requirements, but it is doubtful whether any guest actually reads messages during the hurried moments of registration. The message may be repeated on the rooming slip or key card envelope, however, and those item(s) are left with the guest (see Exhibit 8–19).

Despite the printed comments that guests are supposed to read, legitimate misunderstandings (about the rate, the date of departure, etc.) do occur. To minimize the likelihood of misunderstandings, hotels often train front-office personnel to elicit the guest's agreement on several of the more sensitive issues.

The room rate is one such issue. Although it is bad form to mention the guest's rate aloud, it is important to reach agreement on the nightly charge before rooming the guest. Rather than discussing the rate aloud, it has become standard practice to ask the guest to initial the rate. Usually, the clerk circles the rate, passes the registration card to the guest, and asks for the guest's initials (see Exhibit 8–6). If there are any disputes about discounts or special pricing arrangements, now is the time for the guest to mention them.

Another point of agreement sometimes stressed on the registration card is the smoking status of the guest's room. Smokers and nonsmokers alike are adamant about their personal preferences. Nonsmokers want a fresh room without the stale odor of smoke; smokers want a smoking room complete with ashtrays and matchbooks.

Hotels can spend considerable funds making nonsmoking rooms truly smoke-free. Window and wall coverings, bedspreads, and carpet have never been exposed to smoke. Should a guest smoke (or allow a friend to smoke) in such a setting, it could cost the hotel hundreds of dollars to make the room smoke-free again. Therefore, nonsmokers are sometimes asked to initial the nonsmoking status (N/S in Exhibit 8–6) as a reminder to keep the room smoke-free.

Also frequently included on the registration card is a statement by which the guest agrees to stand personally liable for the bill if some third party (the company, the association, or the credit-card company) fails to pay (again, see Exhibit 8–6).

Green Hotels. The hotel's environmental conservation programs are sometimes mentioned on the registration card (though it is more likely that such programs are addressed on the rooming slip or as collateral marketing material inside the guest room—so the guest has more time to read about them). Hotels are beginning to regularly promote the "greening" of their workplace.

Not only is the greening of our industry the politically correct thing to do these days, but it is also quite profitable. It is profitable in two ways: from a marketing standpoint as well as a cost-savings one. Environmental consciousness is great for public relations and generates positive feedback from hotel guests. Although guests may be slightly inconvenienced by the green programs in place, hotels that offer such initiatives say that guests rarely complain. In fact, they become involved. By hanging-up wet towels to use again (see Exhibit 8–11), initialing an agreement to have bed linens laundered every other day,[3] and walking into a warm room because the air-conditioning adjusts to an energy-savings mode when unoccupied, the guest takes an active role in the hotel's green consciousness.

Although the more sophisticated energy, water, and waste management savings systems are usually engineered into the initial design of the facility, there are many retrofit opportunities available to hotels for little or no investment. For a discussion of automated energy management systems, see that section in Chapter 14; see also Exhibits 8–11 and 8–12).

Simple low-investment programs usually concentrate on saving money through energy and water conservation. Hotels are different from other businesses because lights stay on 24 hours a day. Merely turning off unnecessary lighting, changing 100-watt incandescent bulbs to 20-watt fluorescents, and putting exterior lighting on timers will save considerable money and help the environment. With the average hotel room spending between $5.50 and $6.00 per night on energy consumption, a simple conservation program can result in substantial savings. In fact, after some basic staff training, in-room brochures, and changing a few high-wattage light bulbs, most properties see a reduction of 30 to 50% for in-room energy consumption. For a 250-room property (with 70% occupancy), that translates to energy savings of $110,184 to $183,641 annually!

---

[3]The experience of one 291-room full-service property demonstrated savings of 6,000 gallons of water and 40 gallons of detergent per month just by laundering bed sheets every other day. And that was for an optional program in which not all guests chose to participate.

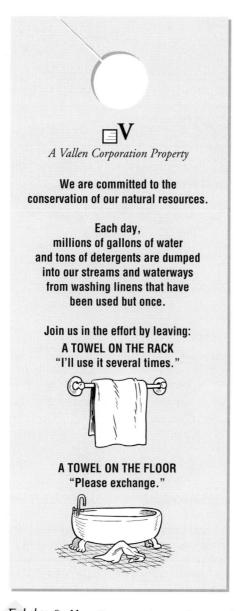

Exhibit 8–11   Conservation makes good sense for all involved. It makes economic sense for the hotel by saving money on water usage, energy consumption, and wear and tear on linens and laundry equipment. Employees find that inhouse conservation efforts save housekeeping time on stayover rooms and make them feel better about the company for which they work. Guests support environmental programs wholeheartedly—according to the U.S. Travel Data Center, 87 percent of consumers support "green" travel. After all, if nobody changes linens/towels at home every day, why should hotels?

Additionally, retrofitting guest-room showers, faucets, and toilets pays for itself quickly with the savings in water consumption. Even low- or no-investment policies such as serving water in the restaurant only upon request or laundering linens less often (see above) makes a big impact when multiplied over hundreds of guest rooms.

Exhibit 8–12   Nestled in the spectacular Whitsunday Islands in the Great Barrier Reef off Australia's north Queensland coast, the Hayman Island Resort is the only facility on the island. Built with energy savings in mind, the resort's remote location practically mandates an environmentally conscious attitude. The resort grows much of its own produce, has its own power plant for electricity, and maintains its own desalination plant for fresh water. *Courtesy of Hayman Island Resort, Great Barrier Reef, Australia.*

Here are some of the touches guests and/or employees might experience in a green, environmentally focused hotel:

- ➤ Leftover food is donated to local shelters, soup kitchens, or food centers. Food waste and scraps are composted.
- ➤ Guest room bathrooms provide refillable dispensers for soap, shampoo, conditioner, and lotion.
- ➤ Guest towels are reused and linens are changed less frequently for extended-stay guests (see Exhibit 8–11).
- ➤ Toilet tank diverters and low-flow faucets save water with little impact on guest satisfaction.
- ➤ In-room sensors turn off or lower the use of air-conditioning and heating when the guest exits the room. Some hotels have a master switch near the

front door that additionally turns off selected lights and electrical appliances (television) upon departure.

➤ Recycling bins are conveniently located near ice machines and vending areas.

➤ Rather than individually wrapped packets, banquet facilities use pitchers for milk and cream, pourers for sugar, and small serving bowls for jams, jellies, and butter.

➤ Some hotels go so far as to make laundry bags and pillowcases from old sheets, napkins and aprons from old tablecloths.

➤ COMPLETING THE REGISTRATION

At registration time, many things are going on simultaneously: The reservation is being located; the guest is being welcomed; accommodation needs are being determined, reevaluated, and checked against available inventory; some small talk is taking place; the clerk is trying to sell up; the guest's identity, including the correct spelling of the name and address, is being verified; certain public rooms or services in the hotel are being promoted; the anticipated departure date is verified; both the guest and the clerk are completing their portions of the registration card; the credit card is being validated; and mail or messages are handed over. Finally, a bellperson is called and the guest is roomed.

All this normal activity notwithstanding, the clerk must remain alert to special cases. Room clerks issue the coupons that accompany each IT package, and there could be a dozen of them. Room clerks are the point position for advertising contracts (rooms traded for advertising), for travel agency vouchers (the guest has paid the travel agency that booked the room), and for special rates. Conventions, for example, sometimes have reduced rates before and after the convention dates and sometimes they don't. And of course, if it's a mystery shopper checking in, a few more curves will be thrown at the overworked front-desk clerk (see Chapter 7).

Throughout the procedure, which could take anywhere from 1 to 15 minutes, the clerk must remain calm, dignified, and friendly. Some feel that the clerk's attitude is the most important part of the whole registration, reception, and room selection process.

The Room Selection Process

Early each morning, front-desk clerks look at the rooms they expect to have available for sale that day. Rooms that were not occupied last night are immediately available; rooms that are due to check out today will eventually be available (assuming that they actually check out; see Exhibit 8–9). By comparing the housekeeper's report against the property management system, the clerk identifies all available rooms. A determination is made at this point as to how many additional walk-ins will be accepted. The decision will be revised many times throughout the day (see the discussion in Chapter 6).

➤*Blocking Rooms.*   Every room has distinct features, and a well-trained desk clerk understands these distinctions. Not all double–doubles are the same. Some are better than others because of location, view, newer furnishings or paint, or any number of other enhancements. The task of the front desk is to align reservations with available rooms.

Blocking, or preassigning rooms to guests, ensures a high level of certainty that special requests will be accommodated. When the room count identifies a high number of rooms available for sale, few rooms will be preblocked. For example, there is no purpose in blocking a standard queen reservation when there are numerous standard queen rooms available. Conversely, when the room count is tight (few rooms available to walk-ins) all incoming reservations will be blocked against the list of available rooms. In this way, the few unblocked rooms remaining are easily identified for walk-in customers. Theoretically, the best available rooms should be saved for guests with reservations, leaving the less desirable rooms to walk-in customers. Even when there are dozens of executive kings available, for example, some are less desirable—possibly they are noisier due to their location next to elevators or the housekeeping office; maybe the view is unattractive because they overlook dumpsters, parking lots, or the roof of another building; or maybe they still have the old furniture and have not yet been renovated. Whatever the reason, less desirable rooms should be offered to walk-in guests and the better accommodations saved for those who made advance reservations.

In the event that the house count is negative (the hotel is overbooked), a priority list is established. Management-made reservations, VIPs, and guaranteed reservations head the priority list—the rest of the reservations will probably be filled on a first-come, first-served basis. Regardless of projections, a careful rooms manager always blocks special cases early in the day. Included in this category are connecting rooms, early check-ins, handicapped rooms, management-made reservations, suites, and VIPs. If the house is very crowded, even special request assignments may need to wait for check outs. The desk knows who the anticipated departures are, although it's never really certain. The desk does not know what time the departures are leaving relative to the arrival of the new guests. So special requests are assigned first to vacant rooms (if the rooms meet the requirements of the request), and then to other rooms as the guests depart.

The room numbers of the preassigned rooms are entered into the PMS. This prevents duplicate room assignments to other arrivals. It also provides immediate display for the clerk when the guest approaches and requests the reserved accommodations. Changes in the original assignments are made throughout the day as new information surfaces. If the arriving guest reports a change in the size of the party, or in the date of departure, or if the party appears before the preassigned room has been vacated, changes will need to be made.

➤*Assigning Rooms.* Whenever possible—and it's possible more than it's practiced—the agent should attempt to *sell up*—to sell the guest a higher-priced room than was originally reserved. Good selling is the key to rooms profits (see Chapter 9, Exhibit 9–18).

The best way to sell up (or up-sell) the product is to show it. At resorts, where longer stays are the norm, guests may prefer to see the room before signing in. That can be done—and has been done—with a screen monitor at the desk. With sophisticated reservations systems, the same image can be projected into the home to sell the reservation directly to the buyer via the Internet. The use of a front-desk photo album is another common (and inexpensive) way to demonstrate to the guest the various differences in room types.

Obviously, the better the clerk knows the product, the more rapidly and satisfactorily the assignment will be made. It has been jokingly said that the fewer the rooms available, the easier it is to make assignments. With few rooms, the guest must take what's offered or have nothing.

Property Management System Algorithms.   The computer uses an algorithmic function to search its memory for appropriate room assignments. Algorithms are a series of "if-then" statements by which the computer arrives at the proper response. The algorithm comes into use when the computer displays an arrival list, an over-the-credit-limit report, or similar statements. It does the same with room assignments, but the program is more sophisticated.

Suppose that a double–double is to be assigned to the arriving party. The system can be made to display the first choice (the computer's first choice), and the room is then assigned. Or, if the clerk wishes, the screen will display all the double–doubles, including those ready, those on change, and those that are out of order (see Exhibit 8–13). Management can control the display—the first double–double displayed is the one that management wants sold first, and the final room on the list is to be sold last.

Without sophisticated computer algorithms, the computer would simply display available rooms in numerical order (see Exhibit 8–13). If this were the case, the first rooms displayed (rooms numbered in the 100s, 200s, etc.) would be sold far more often than rooms with higher numbers. With computer algorithms, management controls the order in which rooms are displayed (and ultimately sold) to accomplish any of several goals: to rotate room use equally, to concentrate occupancy in newly refurbished rooms at a higher rate, to restrict wings or floors to save energy, and others.

Upgrading.   Upgrading a room assignment—giving a better accommodation for the original rate—is one technique for resolving complaints. It has other applications as well. Upgrades might be given to frequent-guest program members, to VIPs, to businesspersons from companies with negotiated corporate rates, and even to guests as a reward for patiently queuing.

Upgrades are also used if there are no rooms available at the rate reserved. In such cases, a well-trained and motivated front-desk clerk tries to up-sell the guest. More frequently, the guest is given the better room at the lower rate, but the upgrade is explained. If the differential is significant, the guest is moved the following day when the lower rate opens. The costs of moving, to both the guest and the hotel, warrant leaving the upgraded assignment for a few nights if the rate spread is small.

Did Not Stay.   A party that registers and leaves is a DNS—a did not stay. Dissatisfaction with the hotel or an incident with a staff member may precipitate the hasty departure. The guests sometimes seek remedy first, or they may leave without saying why. The cause isn't always the hotel. Emergency messages may be retrieved upon arrival, or a telephone call might come in soon after the room assignment. As a courtesy and to ensure good guest relations, usually no charge is levied if the party leaves within a reasonable time after arrival, even if the room was occupied for a short period.

As a control device, DNS guests are referred to the rooms division's supervisory staff. Upon further investigation, supervisors may uncover poorly trained employees, a weakness in the reservations system, or some other root problem as a result of the DNS complaint. Although the vast majority of DNS situations (which don't occur all that often) are legitimate, some caution is urged.

The most common DNS ruse happens when a conventioneer finds an open room at the headquarters hotel down the street. That's why caution is always urged with overflow guests housed from another hotel. Some managers actually ask the complaining DNS guest (who probably said something like "this room does not meet my standards" or "I've received an emergency call and must leave immediately") to wait a moment. The manager then phones the headquarters hotel and asks if they are holding a reservation for the guest (say Dr. Brown). If the response is "yes," the manager will explain to the DNS guest that the hotel must charge him for a one-night stay. When such guests realize their trickery has been uncovered, they usually settle down and spend the night(s) in the hotel after all.

Date: 06/06/__ 10:37

Room Number	Discrpncy	Room Type	Clean Sectn	Hskpg Credits	# of Guest	Room Status	Description
102		DDSN	R1	1	0	VACANT, CLEAN	RIVER N/S CONNECT 103
103		DDSN	R1	1	2	OCCUPIED, CLEAN	RIVER N/S CONNECT 102
105		KEX	R1	1.5	0	VACANT, CLEAN	RIVER S
106		KKEX	R1	1.5	2/2	OCCUPIED, CLEAN	RIVER S
107		KN	N1	1	2	OCCUPIED, CLEAN	POOL N/S
108		DDN	N1	1	0	VACANT, DIRTY	POOL N/S
109		KK	N1	1	2	VACANT, CLEAN, BLOCKED	POOL S
110		KEX	N1	1.5	0	VACANT, CLEAN	POOL S
111		PEXN	S1	2	0	VACANT, DIRTY	MTN VIEW N/S CONNECT 112
112		DDN	S1	1	0	VACANT, CLEAN	MTN VIEW N/S CONNECT 111
115		QSN	S1	1	0	VACANT, CLEAN	MTN VIEW N/S
116		DDSN	S1	1	2/3	OCCUPIED, CLEAN	MTN VIEW N/S
117		K	S1	1	3	VACANT, CLEAN, BLOCKED	MTN VIEW S
118		QS	S1	1	0	VACANT, CLEAN	MTN VIEW S
119		K	S1	1	2	VACANT, CLEAN, BLOCKED	MTN VIEW S
120		DD	S1	1	1	VACANT, CLEAN, BLOCKED	MTN VIEW S
121		PEXN	P1	2	1	OCCUPIED, CLEAN	SPA N/S
123		PEXN	P1	2	2	OCCUPIED, DIRTY	SPA S CONNECT 125
125		PEX	P1	2	1	VACANT, DIRTY, BLOCKED	SPA S CONNECT 123

MORE

Due check out: 30	Dirty: 67	Occupied: 114	Occupied/clean: 62
Blocked: 24	Clean: 193	Vacant: 146	Vacant/clean: 131
			Occupied/dirty: 52
			Vacant/dirty: 15

Exhibit 8–13   This room status report displays rooms in numerical sequence. Other options allow the clerk to display rooms by status (e.g., clean and vacant, occupied, on-change), room type (double-double, executive parlor, concierge-level, etc.), and other parameters (view, smoking/nonsmoking, etc.). With a sophisticated computer algorithm, the system can be programmed to display rooms in reverse numerical order, randomly, or in any unique order dictated by management. PEXN means nonsmoking, executive parlor-with Murphy bed.

Cash-Only Guests.   Although all guests are asked to establish credit at check in, few actually pay their bills in advance. Instead, most guests imprint a credit card or utilize their corporate account to establish credit against charges to be incurred during the visit. Only a small percentage of guests choose to pay cash (or a cash equivalent like a traveler's or personal check) at check in.

Under the law, hotel room charges may be demanded in advance. In addition, the law provides innkeepers with the right to hold luggage for nonpayment. This prejudgment lien is under court challenge. Rather than testing the issue, hotel keepers rely on the credit card and on their right to collect in advance.

Paid-in-advance or cash-only guests are "flagged" to prevent charges being made from other departments. Once the room is paid in advance, other departments must also collect cash for services rendered. Communicating that to the other departments often results in costly errors. You see, few hotel guests are cash-only customers. Even those who prefer to pay with cash at check out are encouraged to leave their credit card on file during the visit. In this way, explains the front-desk clerk, they can charge various expenses incurred around the property back to their hotel room account—it's far more convenient. Later they can replace the credit-card charges with cash upon check out, if that's their preference.

As such, few hotel guests are paid-in-advance customers (it is common in budget properties). Therefore, other hotel departments (restaurants, lounges, golf courses, health spas, clubhouses, gift shops, etc.) are relatively unaccustomed to dealing with cash-only guests. These other departments often forget to check their point-of-sale systems (which are usually interfaced with the property management system) to verify the guest's credit standing. In the end, they inadvertently deliver room service meals, extend access to tennis courts, and even allow merchandise charges to cash-only guests.

This places the burden of payment back on the shoulders of the front desk. A guest who has "charged" a $50 room-service meal must now pay for it. Some front-office managers will phone the guest's room and explain that a bellperson is coming up to collect payment; others leave a less intrusive message to please settle the account with the front desk. If the incident was accidental, the money is forthcoming. But those guests who were trying to defraud the hotel make themselves scarce at this point and likely never settle their account!

By the way, telephone charges are a common source of lost revenues from paid-in-advance guests. When checking in the paid-in-advance guest, with so much else on their minds, front-desk clerks sometimes forget to deactivate the in-room telephone from outgoing calls. Only during the night audit shift does the hotel then realize it has a cash-only guest owing $35.00 in long-distance charges. Certainly, the desk can't wake the guest at 2 AM, so they leave a note for the morning crew. When the morning desk staff follows up, they find that the guest has already departed.

VIP Guests.   Reservations may carry the designation VIP (very important person), SPATT (special attention required), Star Guest, or some similar code. Such codes designate the guest as an important person, requiring the clerk to provide service in keeping with the visitor's stature. The guest could be the executive officer of a large association that is considering the hotel as a convention site, a corporate officer of the hotel chain, or perhaps a travel writer.

Such a designation sometimes requires management to accompany the arriving guest to the room. It sometimes means that the guest need not register. It may also mean that no information about the guest will be given out to callers unless they are first screened.

There is a difference between a VIP and a DG (distinguished guest), according to one professional publication. The VIP represents either good publicity for the hotel or direct business, whereas the DG is honored because of position rather than economic value. Presidents, royalty, movie stars, and celebrities rate a DG designation. Meeting planners, company presidents, or committee chairpersons get the VIP treatment and then only during the tenure of their office. VIPs and DGs may be treated to comp rooms, baskets of fruit, and bottles of wine or champagne.

▶*Self-Check-in Kiosks.* Even as hotels strive to provide higher levels of guest service, automated devices enable guests to perform more front-office functions themselves. The best example of customers serving themselves is self-check-in/self-check-out terminals or kiosks. Located in the lobbies of some of the finest hotels in the world, guest-operated terminals are no longer viewed as a reduction in service. Instead, self-check-in devices provide the guest with another long-awaited option. Rather than queuing at the front desk for an undetermined length of time, today's sophisticated traveler can opt for a self-check in (see Exhibit 8–14). Not only does it save waiting in line, but the overall self-check-in process is faster too. According to

Exhibit 8–14 AutoCheck is an excellent example of a self-check-in kiosk. At the touch of a screen, this full-color system retrieves the guest reservation, verifies credit, authorizes inhouse charges, checks the guest into the property management system, assigns a room, generates a keycard, prints the room number and directions, produces amenity coupons, and activates the phone, voice mail, movie, and energy management systems. *Courtesy of Multi-Systems, Incorporated, Phoenix, Arizona.*

Hilton Hotels Corporation, the average self-check-in takes between 30 and 45 seconds. That compares quite favorably with the average check-in time at the front desk of 210 seconds (three and a half minutes).

Integrated directly into the property management system, the self-check-in/self-check-out terminal offers choices much like a guest–service agent would. The guest can select room numbers and room types from an on-line inventory of clean and available rooms. In addition, many of these machines are portable (some are even wireless), thereby allowing the hotel to strategically locate the terminal in busy areas (say, for a large group check in). Some hotels even locate the system in their shuttle vans for registration en route from the airport. Other hotels staff front-desk receptionists at airport luggage claim areas. While guests are waiting for their luggage, they can register using a hand-held terminal, and the room key is waiting upon arrival.

Prerequisites.   Most self-check-in terminals require the arriving guest to hold an advanced reservation and a valid credit, debit, or smart card. Although that is the current standard, these prerequisites are changing. Some of the newest self-check-in devices now provide an option for walk-in customers. However, the self-check-in process becomes more detailed for the walk-in guest. All of the basic information obtained during the reservation process (name, address, length of stay, etc.) must be input by the walk-in guest. Some self-check-in terminals now accept cash. These are especially popular in limited-service motels that continue to sell rooms after hours via automated terminals (see Case Study below).

Features.   Many self-check-in systems display an electronic map of the property or print room directions. In this way, guests can knowledgeably select rooms most convenient to them. In addition, it is possible for the terminal to display messages, promote certain aspects of the hotel, and even to up-sell the guest to a higher-priced room!

Most self-check-in/self-check-out terminals feature a built-in printer that provides the guest with a receipt of the transaction. This receipt may actually be used as a guest identification card during the stay. Some of the newer self-check-in systems even utilize touch-screen technology. Rather than using a keyboard or computer mouse for data entry, the guest need only touch the monitor. For example, if the computer provides a selected list of room types, the guest merely touches the list next to the room type of choice.

Self-check-in terminals also provide the guest with a room key. While some of the older systems required the guest to visit the key clerk at the front desk, most of the more recent terminals include an automated key function. At the end of the self-check-in process, the system dispenses a key or prompts the guest to remove a blank key card from the stack and swipe it through the electronic key writing slot. As an added bonus, many systems allow guests to use their personal credit cards as the room key.

Case Study.   Numerous chains have introduced self-check-in systems over the last few years. Hyatt Hotels' Touch and Go system is available at almost all of its non-resort properties. Cendant has built the AutoCheck system into every one of its Wingate Inns. The list, including Promus, Hilton, Choice, and others, continues to grow.

Choice Hotels created a whole new chain based around the premise that some guests prefer efficiency over service. This chain, MainStay Suites (all-suite properties with rates ranging from $50 to $110), doesn't even have a front desk! Instead, guests proceed to a kiosk, where they choose the language (English, Spanish, or French) with which they prefer to check in. They then select a task from one of four icons: check in, check out, other hotel services, or community information.

During the check-in process, an automated voice takes the guest through each step. The voice asks the guest to swipe the same credit card used to make the reservation. The card number then accesses the reservation particulars from the central reservation system, Choice 2001. The voice then asks a series of questions related to departure date, room preference, and rate. Once the particulars are verified, the system asks the guest to create and confirm a PIN number. This number is used to access the MainStay Suites system during the remainder of the guest's stay.

At this point, the self-check-in kiosk dispenses a key (or keys), displays a bird's-eye view of the property, and prints an advance folio. The folio reiterates the room rate, check-in and check-out dates, and the room number. It also tells the guest how to find the room and where best to park. The folio is the only place where the guest is addressed by name or room number—for security reasons, the system never displays the guest's name or room number except on printed receipts. When everything is concluded, guests press the "finish" button, and the system wishes them a nice visit.

Establishing Guest Credit

Accurate identification at check in is so important as to be mandated by many local statutes. By accurately knowing the guest, the hotel protects itself and provides a valuable service to local law enforcement agencies (refer back to "Legal Release of Sensitive Registration Data" earlier in this chapter). Information about transient visitors can be of critical importance. In Rhode Island, a guest was found murdered. The hotel had obtained no identification at check in, and it took authorities many days to identify the victim.

Proper identification also serves to protect the hotel. When cash customers are allowed to check in without producing identification, the hotel opens itself to a number of potential problems. A classic case in Arizona illustrates the point. A guest checked into a one-story motel, paid cash for the room, and signed the registration card with a phony name. In the dead of the night, the guest proceeded to load his van with all of the room's furnishings. The next day, the guest was gone, the motel room was bare, and the motel had absolutely no recourse, having failed to obtain proper identification. (And the room was truly bare. The guest had taken everything—the TV set, bed, and dresser, as well as the toilet, tub, and carpet!)

Even if the guest has no intention of stealing, securing guest identification aids the hotel in a multitude of ways. Knowing the guest's name and address allows the hotel to return lost and found items, bill and collect late charges, and maintain a valuable database.

➤*Credit Cards.*   Every registration card asks the guest to identify the method of payment (see Exhibit 8–6). If a personal or company check is the answer, credit approval must be obtained from the rooms division manager. More likely, a credit card is tendered. If there is a choice, the desk should always request the card for which the hotel has negotiated the best merchant discount fee (see Chapter 12).

With a property management system, the credit-card data is entered into the electronic folio either through the means of a credit-card reader. The terminal reads the magnetic strip and communicates that number electronically to the credit-card clearinghouse. Use of electronic credit-card scanners integrated with property management systems saves about 40 valuable seconds during the check-in process. The number can be punched in manually if the strip signal is damaged or inoperative. Back comes an authorization number (or a denial), which appears on the screen of the credit-card reader. The authorization number is the hotel's guarantee that the credit card is legitimate.

Part of the communication between the credit-card company and the hotel involves the amount of charges that will be added to the guest's balance. Limits exist for both the hotel and the individual. These "floor limits" are explained in Chapter 12. That discussion also includes the next steps in the credit-card story: processing the card at departure and collecting from the credit-card company.

➤***Back-Office Records.*** Front-office records post departmental charges incurred by the guest against the credit established at check in. Back-office records track those charges through the bank or credit-card company until payment has been received. Credit cards are just one of several records initiated by the front office but completed by the back office. Final settlement of travel agency bills clears through the back office, although the reservation and paperwork begin at the front. Frequent-guest records and frequent-flyer partnership records are another front-office/back-office relationship. The disposition of these various records is explained in Chapter 12. It is not a matter that concerns the clerk at the point of registration.

Record keeping for frequent-guest or frequent-flyer programs is a relatively new job for the front office. Although it is a feature incorporated into property management systems at most chain-affiliated hotels, guests using self-check-in terminals may still be required to visit the desk for frequent-guest credits.

➤ ROOMING THE GUEST

When the guest registration process nears completion in a full-service hotel, a bellperson arrives to escort the guest to the room. As the guest moves into the realm of the bell department, a number of critical functions are accomplished. The bellperson explains various locations and departments throughout the hotel, details a list of current hotel activities and promotions, and serves as final inspector before the guest prepares to occupy the room.

Uniformed Services

The bellstaff is part of a much larger department commonly referred to as uniformed services. Throughout the guest's visit, the uniformed services department attends to various needs and requests. Valet parking, doorpersons, concierges, hotel security, and the bell staff all play a key role in enhancing the property's image (see discussion in Chapter 3). No other department has the degree of personal one-on-one time with the guest as does uniformed services.

Like all members of uniformed services, the bellstaff are goodwill ambassadors who turn an ordinary visit into a warm and personable experience (see Exhibits 8–15 and 8–16). By developing close, professional relationships with the guest, a well-trained bellperson successfully promotes a number of hotel services. Suggestive selling and gentle persuasion are invaluable skills for a bellperson to possess.

➤***Guest Communication.*** Bellpersons, like all members of the uniformed services staff, are encouraged to engage the guest in conversation. Whenever staff members see a guest, they should make the effort to smile and at least offer a simple greeting (see Exhibit 8–16). By taking such steps, the guest comes to know and trust one or more members of the uniformed staff.

It is interesting to watch which uniformed personnel are attracted to which guests. Sometimes it is a matter of personality type or due to a relationship formed during the rooming process. Whatever the reason, many guests develop a favorite among the

Exhibit 8–15   The legendary elegance of the Fairmont Hotel, built atop San Francisco's Nob Hill in 1907, is embodied in the bell department. A large bellstand (centered in the lobby just behind the bellman standing in the photo) staffs more than 20 bellpersons for this 600-room property. *Courtesy of The Fairmont Hotel and Tower, San Francisco, California.*

bellpersons or other uniformed services staff. Such relationships, as long as they remain in the boundaries of professional behavior, are encouraged by management.

By developing such personable relationships, the bellperson is well situated to know when the guest's visit has gone awry. The bellperson can then approach the guest and solicit the complaint. Careful training places the bellperson in the critical role as bridge between the dissatisfied guest and the responsible department. When management works to keep open these lines of communication, the bellperson performs a key function in the hotel's quality assurance program (see discussion in Chapter 7).

"Wired" Bellpersons.   Generally, outfitting the bell department with inconspicuous earpieces, a voice-activated mouthpiece, and attached belt pack costs less than $100 per employee. Having direct and instantaneous communication with bell staff (along with other front-of-the-house departments) is critical, especially in upscale properties. Today's guests have less patience waiting for an employee to answer a page, find a house phone and call the desk, or answer a cell phone. Talkabout headsets are not only instantaneous, but they give the entire staff a look of crisp professionalism and service-readiness. Additionally, in this day of heightened security, they allow the bell person to perform a critical role as the mobile eyes and ears of the hotel.

In recent years, headset systems have been proliferating across the hotel industry—especially in luxury properties—at an astonishing rate. For example, The Breakers, one of the most outstanding five-star, five-diamond resorts in America, has been a believer in talkabout headset systems for a number of years. Today, it boasts over 200 headsets, enough to staff better than 10% of its workforce! Hyatt Hotels & Resorts

Among the unofficial requirements for a Four- and Five-Diamond ranking by the American Automobile Association are the following services expected of bellpersons:

All Bellpersons Must:
__ Be neatly uniformed.
__ Wear tasteful nametags where appropriate.
__ Be friendly, courteous, and helpful.
__ Be knowledgeable of hotel and surrounding area.
__ Make good eye contact with guests.
__ Acknowledge the presence of guests (e.g., when passing in corridors).

On Guest Reception:
__ Welcome guest to the hotel with friendly greeting.
__ Address guest by name (should pick up on name from desk or luggage tags) frequently.
__ Explain food and beverage department, recreational and other facilities without being asked..
__ Hang garment bag in closet.
__ Take out and set up luggage rack; suitcase should be placed on luggage rack, not on bed or floor.
__ Explain operation of lights, TV, and thermostat.
__ Offer ice at a Four-Diamond, expected to be automatic at a Five-Diamond.
__ Point out emergency exits, and safety features.
__ Offer to open or close drapes.
__ Explain any unusual features within the room.
__ Explain turn-down service.
__ Check bathroom supplies.
__ Offer additional services.

On Check Out:
__ Arrive promptly (wait should not exceed 10 minutes).
__ Check around room and in bathroom for belongings that might be left behind.
__ Offer to arrange for car delivery.[4]

Exhibit 8–16   AAA inspectors rate hotels based upon a number of criteria. Here is a general list of bellperson guidelines used for four- and five-diamond properties.

has been systematically installing these communication systems in its premier hotels, and the Ritz-Carlton Hotel Company has headset systems installed in every one of its domestic properties.

[4]This list is a general guide and should not be construed as an official set of bell department standards. The list was compiled from two sources: an article entitled "Highly Effective Bell Staff Enhances Your Property's Image," *Hotel & Resort Industry*, May 1988, pp. 84–89, and an AAA Web site: http://www.ouraaa.com/news/news/diamond/5diamondsvc.html#bellservices (1999).

▶*Uniformed Services Training.*   Although a professional dialogue is encouraged, it is often difficult to monitor and maintain. All uniformed services staff (but especially the bellperson) have ample opportunity to speak with the guest on an intimate level. By design, bellpersons have a great deal of autonomy. During the rooming process, driving the airport shuttle, and at other times, the bellperson can be with a guest(s)—and out of management's sight—for 10 or 15 minutes at a time. Therefore, it is difficult for management to know what is actually being discussed with the guest during these one-on-one conversations.

There are numerous examples of bellpersons stepping over the line of acceptable behavior. Distraught with the job, a bellperson might bad-mouth the hotel or senior management to the guest. Disappointed with the lack of gratuities that day, a bellperson might boldly ask for a more generous tip from the guest. There are even cases where bellpersons dealt drugs and prostitution to the guest! Minimizing such occurrences begins with proper hiring and continues with constant training.

Mystery Shopper Services.   Because it is so difficult to assess the bellperson's professionalism while he or she is rooming the guest, many managers stress its importance with secret shopper services. Such services work on the premise that employees act differently when they sense that management is watching. On the other hand, a secret shopper posing as a hotel guest is able to truly observe the employee's professionalism on the job.

Secret shoppers visit the property and stay one or more nights (see Chapter 7). During this time, they attempt to engage employees in a number of usual and sometimes unusual activities. Although employees are probably forewarned that secret audits may be conducted, they usually have no idea they are being observed. As a result, secret shopper services are an excellent way to monitor the effectiveness of employee training—especially in the uniformed services department.

The Bell Staff

Several innovations have affected the uniformed services department's functions and means of earning income. Self-service icemakers and vending machines on the floor, and in-room refrigerators and minibars, have reduced the kind and number of service calls that bellpersons make. Group arrivals and self-check-in kiosks, in which individuals room themselves, further reduce the service functions of this department.

▶*Rotation of Fronts.*   Tips comprise the bulk of the bell department's earnings. According to a study done by the American Hotel & Lodging Association, the bellperson's cash salary was the lowest of any hotel employee, and yet the bellperson total earnings usually exceed that of other front-office employees, including some management positions.

The bellperson who comes forward to take the rooming slip and room the guest is called a *front*. Fronts rotate in turn. The one who has just completed a front is called a *last*. Lasts are used for errands that are unlikely to produce gratuities. Cleaning the lobby is a responsibility of the last. Lasts are also assigned dead room changes, with no chance of a gratuity, such as lockouts and moves carried out in the guest's absence.

Between the front and the last, positions rotate in sequence, moving forward in the rank as each new front is called. Each position in the sequence should be represented by a particular post in the lobby. One station might be by the front door to receive incoming luggage; another across the lobby; a third by the elevators. Staffing requirements for a full-service bell department run approximately one bellperson for every 40 to 50 estimated check-ins (see Exhibit 8–15 where the Fairmont Hotel runs a ratio closer to one bellperson for every 20 check-ins).

The procedure is much less formal today. Fronts wait by the bellstand, which is visible from the front desk. As the clerk completes the registration, the front is summoned to the desk by lights or hand signals or verbally by the clerk calling "Front!" Aware of the routine, the front rarely needs prompting.

With a property management system, remote printers located at the bellstand print the rooming slips, so the bellpersons approach the guests aware of their names. By coding the printout, the desk communicates additional information (VIP, heavy luggage, etc.) to the bell department. The property management system also maintains a record of fronts.

A record of fronts assures each person a proper turn, although the sequence may be altered if a guest requests a specific person or if a last is still away on some time-consuming errand. The record, maintained at the bellcaptain's desk, tracks the crew, which is the most mobile department in the hotel. By noting the bellperson's presence on various floors at various times, the record offers protection from accusations in the event of theft or other trouble. The comings and goings of the bell staff, the purposes of their errands, and the times elapsed must all be recorded.

➤*Responsiblities of the Bell Staff.*   Depending on the level of service for the particular hotel, there may be no uniformed services department at all. In many small hotels, the bell staff is a catch-all department that performs a multitude of tasks. Small operations may ask the bellperson to drive the shuttle van, act as doorperson, make room-service calls, deliver cocktails to guests relaxing in the lobby, and even aid the front-desk staff during meal-break periods.

Certain responsibilities are outside the scope of the bell department's duties. Bellpersons do not quote rates or suggest room assignments. They call the room clerk for a second assignment whenever the guest is dissatisfied with the room.

Bellpersons, or just the captains, share in other incomes. Auto rentals, tickets to local attractions, and bus tours are available at the bell captain's desk. Each of these companies pays a commission (usually 10 to 15%) that more often accrues to the uniformed services than to the hotel. This may also hold true when the hotel contracts an outside laundry or dry cleaner for guest service.

Luggage.   The doorperson, or just as often the guest, carries in the baggage from the cab or car. It stays on the lobby floor until the guest is finished registering. The front-desk agent gives a rooming slip to the bellperson, who then takes over the guest's service. Jointly, the guest and the bellperson identify and retrieve the luggage and head toward the elevator. The guest, the bellperson, and the baggage might ride up together. Or the bellperson might leave the guest in order to transport the luggage on the service (rear) elevator, while the guest rides the guest (front) elevator. They meet at the elevator lobby on the guest's assigned floor.

Final Inspection.   Rooming guests is the primary task of the bell department. Although many individuals room themselves, it is preferable to go in the company of a staff member. Guests who are in the company of a bellperson avoid the embarrassment of walking in on an occupied room. Service personnel always knock, announce themselves, and wait before unlocking the door.

Once inside, the bellperson performs another inspection function. First, the bellperson hangs the guest's loose clothing and hefts the baggage onto the luggage rack (see Exhibit 8–16). Temperature controls are checked, and the room is inspected for cleanliness, towels, soap, toilet tissue, facial tissue, and other needs. Lights, hangers, television sets, and furnishings are examined. Special features of the hotel are explained—the spa or the operating hours of room service, for example.

Self-service items are pointed out—the ice machine, or the in-room refrigerator. Connecting doors are unlocked if the party is to share several connecting rooms. Unless there is a special request for service, the bellperson leaves the key and the rooming slip and accepts the proffered tip, if any. Before leaving, there may be a final sell for a particular dining room or lounge and a final "good day." (see Exhibit 8–16).

Group Luggage Handling.   Tour groups are easy for the bellstaff to handle and are generally quite profitable. Using the guest list furnished by the group, the desk preregisters the party (see Exhibit 8–17). Roommates, whom the tour company has identified, are assigned, and keys are readied in small envelopes for quick distribution (see Chapter 12, Exhibit 12–5). Similar key envelopes are prepared for rapid distribution to airline crews when permanent reservations have been negotiated with the airline.

The property management system can print the key envelopes (coded by groups), the rooming lists (knowing who is with whom and in which room is very important to the tour guide or the company meeting planner), identification cards for in-house use, baggage tags, and every other form needed for a successful group meeting. All of these items are derived from the same basic information, which is fed into the computer only once.

Final instructions to the tour members may be given on the bus. Communication is impossible once the captive audience is lost. Tour members are reminded that charges not included in the tour price will need to be settled individually with the hotel. A notice to that effect is also included in the key envelope (sometimes called the key packet). The envelopes are distributed in the lobby (or on the bus) by the desk, the tour coordinator, or sometimes the bellstaff. Guests find their own rooms without help from the bell department while the baggage is being unloaded from the bus.

Group baggage can be a headache as well as a backache for the uniformed services if bags are improperly marked or hard to identify. Putting some procedures in place makes the task easier. The tour company should provide each traveler with brightly colored tags to attach to the luggage before departure. The color identifies the group, expediting baggage handling in and out of the airport and the hotel. The individual's number is written on each tag, and that number corresponds to that person's place on the master rooming sheet (see Exhibit 8–17). Copies of the list should have been given to every hotel on the tour. The number, which is easier to read than a name, helps the bellstaff match the bags with room numbers.

There is another variation: Each bag can be marked with the correct room number from a computer printed list of adhesive-backed labels. The bellperson removes the room number from the printed list and slaps it on the bag for delivery.

All hotels that cater to tour and meetings business use similar techniques for delivering group baggage. Although it has the appearance of antiservice, delivering the group's luggage in bulk is really the only efficient manner for handling the task. By eliminating the one-on-one rooming of each guest, the bell department can move through luggage deliveries quickly. Aside from being escorted to their rooms, group guests don't miss much else. Information normally shared during the rooming process—hours of the restaurant, for example—is shared by a desk clerk or bellcaptain during a short presentation to the captive audience on the bus. This frees the bell

```
HMS32G        FINNERMAN              VAIL  SKI  MEADOW'S  LODGE                      2/05/

Refer
  #    GUEST NAME        ROOM   GROUP    ARRIVAL   DEPART   COMPANY LINE            # PERS
  1    ADAMS      ADAM    609   NEWMEX    2/05      2/08    NEW MEXICO ST. SKI TEAM    1
  2    BURTON     BOB     607   NEWMEX    2/05      2/08    NEW MEXICO ST. SKI TEAM    1
  3    CURTIS     CHARLES 612   NEWMEX    2/05      2/08    NEW MEXICO ST. SKI TEAM    1
  4    DILARDO    DALE    612   NEWMEX    2/05      2/08    NEW MEXICO ST. SKI TEAM    1
  5    ELAN       EVAN    616   NEWMEX    2/05      2/08    NEW MEXICO ST. SKI TEAM    1
  6    FEINSTEIN  FRED    613   NEWMEX    2/05      2/08    NEW MEXICO ST. SKI TEAM    1
  7    GRAY       GARY    604   NEWMEX    2/05      2/08    NEW MEXICO ST. SKI TEAM    1
  8    HARRIS     HARRY   606   NEWMEX    2/05      2/08    NEW MEXICO ST. SKI TEAM    1
  9    INGOLS     IAN     616   NEWMEX    2/05      2/08    NEW MEXICO ST. SKI TEAM    1
 10    JEFFREYS   JEFF    606   NEWMEX    2/05      2/08    NEW MEXICO ST. SKI TEAM    1
 11    KASTLE     KRIS    604   NEWMEX    2/05      2/08    NEW MEXICO ST. SKI TEAM    1
 12    LANGE      LOUIS   605   NEWMEX    2/05      2/08    NEW MEXICO ST. SKI TEAM    1
 13    MORRISON   MORRIS  602   NEWMEX    2/05      2/08    NEW MEXICO ST. SKI TEAM    1
 14    NORDICA    NEWT    605   NEWMEX    2/05      2/08    NEW MEXICO ST. SKI TEAM    1
 15    OLIN       ORSON   609   NEWMEX    2/05      2/08    NEW MEXICO ST. SKI TEAM    1
 16    POWELL     PAUL    607   NEWMEX    2/05      2/08    NEW MEXICO ST. SKI TEAM    1
 17    QUAIL      QUINN   618   NEWMEX    2/05      2/08    NEW MEXICO ST. SKI TEAM    1
 18    ROSSIGNOL  ROBERT  602   NEWMEX    2/05      2/08    NEW MEXICO ST. SKI TEAM    1
                                                                     TOTAL PEOPLE:   18
```

Exhibit 8–17 A group rooming list showing names (and reference numbers), room numbers assigned, arrival and departure dates, and group affiliation is initially prepared by the tour operator or meeting planner. This list serves as the reference document for baggage, billing, and group communication. Small groups such as this are regularly housed on the same floor to ease luggage handling.

department to get right to luggage deliveries. Within 30 to 45 minutes, most small and midsized groups will have received their luggage.

Group luggage is the bellpersons' bread and butter. That's because the bell department is paid a small stipend for every group guest arriving and departing that day. Group contracts include a negotiable charge commonly referred to as "baggage in and baggage out." Group baggage handling rates run as little as $2 per person in and $2 per person out, to as much as $6 per person each direction. Group baggage handling rates may be a factor of unionization (unionized bell departments may set a minimally acceptable rate), the time of year the group arrives, the room rate paid, and so on. The entire fee (both in and out) is paid at the time of contract, and a hotel that handles a lot of group business can easily supplement paychecks by several hundred dollars per bellperson per week.

▶*Rooming Slips.*   The rooming slip serves as a vehicle for communication between the front desk and both the bellperson and the guest. The bellperson uses the rooming slip to better understand the guest and the rooming situation. The slip provides the bellperson with information related to the guest's name, the guest's affiliation or corporate name (if appropriate), the room number assigned, the guest's home city (great for making small talk), and the number of nights reserved. As explained earlier, the rooming slip also serves as a support document to prove the bellperson's whereabouts during a specific period in question.

Although not intended for that purpose, the slips have been used by the Internal Revenue Service. Estimating the average tip per front and counting the number of fronts according to the rooming slips provides a fair estimate of tip income. The estimate is then compared to that reported by the employee.

Content.   The guest uses the rooming slip for two purposes: as a receipt and as guest identification. As a receipt, the rooming slip provides the guest with an additional opportunity to verify the accuracy of information. For example, the rooming slip may show that the guest's name has been misspelled. The room rate, date of check out, or some other information may also be inaccurate. Many rooming slips restate hotel disclaimers as a means of strengthening the hotel's legal relationship with the guest (see Exhibits 8–18 and 8–19).

Overseas hotels use the rooming slip as a sales tool for their own property and for local, noncompeting businesses. Few American hotels sell such advertising space. With their more extensive services and facilities, they need all the space themselves.

The American rooming slip is an interesting mix of selling, services, and legal safeguards. Depending on management's inclination, the rooming slip is either a simple slip of paper or a complete, elaborate sales tool in a variety of colors. Exhibit 8–18 lists the range of information that a hotel might try to communicate to the guest.

Color-coded rooming slips may also serve as a guest identification card. The color tells the cashiers in the bars and dining rooms whether the guest is a paid-in-advance guest, a tour group member, a VIP, and so on.

Although the guest is just arriving, check-out information and a check-out form are frequently provided in order to plan for a quick departure. Quick check out has been in place far longer than self-check-in/self-check-out terminals. Innovative departure systems that did not need computer hardware were inaugurated as early as 1975. However, they all require the guest to use a credit card or other form of advance credit.

Informative
  Floor plan of the property
  Aerial view of the property
  Emergency and fire exits
  Telephone directory of services
  Kinds of lobby shops
  Foreign language capabilities of the staff
  Airline, taxi, and limousine telephone
    numbers
  Local sites to see and things to do
  Airport bus: times of operation and rates
  Currency exchange capabilities
  Map of the city with highway designa-
    tions

Marketing
  List of restaurants: prices, hours of oper-
    ation, and menu specialties
  A message of welcome or a note of ap-
    preciation
  WATS number for other hotels in the
    chain
  Recreational facilities: tennis, golf, pool,
    sauna
  Discount coupons to area retailers and
    attractions

Regulatory
  Check-out hour and check-in hour
  Rate of gratuity applied to the room
    charge
  Regulations for visitors
  Limitations on pets

Dress code
  Availability of the safe for valuables
  Settlement of accounts
  Expectations for guaranteed reservation
    holders
  Deposit of room keys when leaving the
    property
  Fees for local, long distance, and 1-800
    calls
  Other hotel fees and surchanges

Identification
  Clerk's identifying initials
  Identification of the party: name, number
    of persons, rate, arrival and departure
    dates
  Room number
  Key code—where room access is con-
    trolled by a dial system key

Instructional
  Express check-out procedure
  Electrical capacity for appliances
  What to do in case of fire
  How to secure the room
  Notification to the desk if errors exist on
    the rooming slip
  How to operate in-room movies, Internet,
    and games; their cost
  How to operate the in-room refrigerator;
    cost
  Rate of tax applied to the room charge

Exhibit 8–18   The size and breadth of the property dictates the size and breadth of the rooming slip. Small hotels may provide the registered guest little more than a simple receipt, a key envelope, or nothing at all. Other hotels, anxious to market inhouse services, local attractions, paid advertisers, and legal disclaimers, may provide a multipage rooming booklet (see Exhibit 8–19). This exhibit demonstrates the variety of content found on rooming slips in the United States—it is an incomplete list. Can you add categories of your own?

Exhibit 8–19   Example of a rooming slip and packet presented to arriving guests at the Monte Carlo Resort & Casino. Not only are arrivals given a guest card for making room charges across the property, but they are also presented a welcome packet. Included in the packet is a property map; a few gaming, food, and beverage coupons; an express check-out form; and assorted legalistic statements. *Courtesy of Monte Carlo Resort & Casino, Las Vegas, Nevada.*

RESOURCES AND CHALLENGES
Resources

➤ SUMMARY

Arriving guests face a number of opportunities to meet members of the uniformed staff. Valet parking, the doorperson, guest service agent, and the bell department all play critical roles in the arrival process. The first impressions made by these employees create a positive (or negative) lasting effect on the guest's perception of the hotel operation.

The check-in procedure represents an especially sensitive segment of the arrival process. The front-desk agent communicates with the guest in an unscripted fashion where few rules dictate their interaction. A wise front-desk agent evaluates the guest and attempts to understand unique requirements. Too rapid a check in and the guest leaves with a sense of rudeness or having been rushed. Too slow a check in and the guest perceives inefficiency in the hotel operation. Add to this sensitivity the need for the desk agent to retrieve payment, extract additional information, get a signature on the registration card, ask credit questions, and attempt to up-sell to a higher-priced room, and the check-in process can be an intense several minutes.

The bell department spends the last moments with the arriving guest. Rooming the guest is a complex process of small talk, suggestive selling, room inspection, and overall guest service. Oh yes—bellpersons carry the luggage as well.

➤ WEB SITES

Environmentally friendly hotels stand to gain dramatically over the next few years. Hotels stand to gain customers because the majority of guests surveyed agreed they would spend more money and make additional effort in order to stay in an environmentally conscious property. Hotels stand to gain monetary savings because environmental conservatism adds up to real utilities and equipment savings. And hotels stand to gain prestige and respect because guests, employees, and management all feel better about working/staying in a globally conscious property.

Look at the five "green" hospitality industry Web sites listed and then answer the related questions below:

- ➤ http://www.greenseal.org
- ➤ http://www.enn.com (Environmental News Network)
- ➤ http://www.greenhotels.com
- ➤ http://www.greenatworkmag.com
- ➤ http://www.isdesignnet.com/ED (EnvironDesign)

Looking at the listed Web sites, find one specific example for each of the following:

1. A hotel that has boosted its occupancy or average room rate by adding a publicized environmental conservation program.

2. A hotel saving money by incorporating an environmental conservation program.

3. A hotel that boasts lower employee turnover, enhanced reputation, or some other positive publicity as a result of incorporating an environmental conservation program.

➤ INTERESTING TIDBITS

Bet you haven't heard this one . . .

A few minutes after being roomed by the bellperson, a guest picks up the in-room telephone and calls the front desk.

Guest: Help. I can't get out of this room.

Front Desk: I don't understand, sir. What's wrong? Just open the door.

Guest: Well, there are three doors. The first one opens into the bathroom. The next one opens into the closet. And the third door has a "Do Not Disturb" sign on it.

➤ READING REFERENCES

"*The Color of Money*." Sara Welch. *Successful Meetings*, March 2001, pp. 49–55.

"Late Arrivals Provide Challenge for Properties." Patricia Alisau. *Hotel & Motel Management*, September 3, 2001, p. 32.

"No More Ruffing It." Christina Binkley. *Wall Street Journal*, August 11, 2000, p. W-1.

Challenges

➤ TRUE/FALSE

____ 1. The registration process includes the exchange of personal guest information. In certain emergencies (like the terrorism experienced on 9/11), this information is critical to local police or federal investigations. Generally, hotel managers should release such information upon request of law-enforcement officials. It is not necessary to wait for a written report, court order, warrant, or subpoena, because hotel employees, managers, and owners are protected by state innkeeper statutes.

____ 2. Although personal guest information (age, sex, travel destination, and purpose for travel) is not asked on U.S. registration cards, it is common practice in many foreign countries.

____ 3. Because the federal government regulates hotels, the amount of liability a hotel faces for the loss of guests' belongings (due to theft) is the same nationwide.

____ 4. Some self-check-in kiosks actually dispense a room key and detailed property map to the guest.

____ 5. A simple discussion about queueing theory in the hospitality industry would likely include management's dilemma between providing too much front-desk staff (short lines but high labor costs) and too little front-desk staff (longer lines and dissatisfied guests).

➤ PROBLEMS

1. Reorganize the following jumbled list of events, persons, and job activities into a logical flow from start to finish of the guest arrival process:

   a. Room selection
   b. Establishing guest credit
   c. Registered, not assigned
   d. Bellperson
   e. Valet parking attendant
   f. Rotation of fronts
   g. Room assignment
   h. Obtaining guest identification
   i. Rooming slip
   j. Upgrading and/or up-selling
   k. Rooming the guest
   l. Preblocking rooms
   m. Doorperson
   n. Ice bucket filled
   o. Guest queue
   p. Registration card signature
   q. Check-out reminder
   r. Room status report
   s. AAA discount
   t. Pet deposit

2. Foreign registration cards often require significantly more personal information than is required for domestic registration cards. Some management personnel feel that this extra data amounts to an invasion of the guest's privacy. Other managers, however, believe this extra information aids the hotel in providing better security and service levels to the guest. With whom do you side? Why might a hotel legitimately need to know your future and past destinations, your mother's maiden name, and your date of birth?

3. Intentional bias can be programmed (through computer algorithms) into the room-selection sequence of a property management system. Rooms will then appear in a prescribed order rather than in sequence or at random. Certain rooms can be offered first, or not, depending on management's criteria. Give examples explaining why management might wish to decide which rooms appear in which sequence in order to direct the clerk's selection.

4. A local merchant, whose attempts to service the hotel's guest laundry and dry cleaning business have been frustrated, visits with the new rooms manager. (The laundry of this 600-room, commercial hotel does not clean personal guest items.) The conversation makes the rooms manager realize that she has never seen commission figures on any of the reports. She learns that the bellcaptain, who doesn't seem to do any work—that is, he doesn't take fronts—gets the commissions.

   The rooms manager initiates a new policy. All commissions from car rentals, bus tours, ski tickets, laundry, balloon rides, and so on, will accrue to the hotel. An unresolved issue is whether or not the money will go into the employee's welfare fund.

   A very angry bellcaptain presents himself at the office of the vice president of the rooms division. Explain with whom you agree (the rooms manager or the bellcaptain) and prepare an argument to support your opinion.

5. Some hotels upgrade corporate guests to nicer rooms when space is available. Usually, the guest need not even ask for this courtesy—it is offered as standard operating procedure. Managers of such properties believe that the corporate guest appreciates the courtesy and the nicer room. And since the room is not likely to sell anyway, why not make someone happy?

   The reverse side of this argument, however, suggests that the guest comes to expect this treatment and even feels slighted if only standard rooms are available. In addition, hotels that give upgrades away free are doing themselves a disservice in terms of up-selling corporate guests to a higher rate. After all, why should corporate guests ever select higher-priced rooms (or concierge floor rooms) when they are given at no extra charge as a matter of standard practice? How would you respond to these arguments?

6. Ten weary, footsore travelers,
　　All in a woeful plight,
　Sought shelter at a wayside inn
　　One dark and stormy night.
　"Nine beds—no more," the landlord said,
　　"Have I to offer you;
　To each of eight a single room,
　　But number nine serves two."
　A din arose. The troubled host
　　Could only scratch his head;
　For of those tired men, no two
　　Could occupy one bed.
　The puzzled host was soon at ease—
　　He was a clever man—
　And so to please his guests devised
　　The most ingenious plan:

| A | B | C | D | E | F | G | H | I |

　In a room marked A, two men were placed;
　　The third he lodged in B.
　The fourth to C was then assigned.
　　The fifth went off to D.
　In E the sixth he tucked away.
　　In F the seventh man;
　The eighth and ninth to G and H.
　　And then to A he ran.
　Wherein the host, as I have said,
　　Had lain two travelers by.
　Then taking one—the tenth and last,
　　He lodged him safe in I.
　Nine single rooms—a room for each—
　　Were made to serve for ten.
　And this it is that puzzles me
　　And many wiser men.

　　　　　　　　—Excerpted from *Hotel News*, Winnipeg, 1935.

Does it also puzzle you? How was the ingenious host able to lodge ten men in only nine rooms?

➤ ANSWERS TO TRUE/FALSE QUIZ

1. False. Hotels, their employees, and managers are not protected by innkeeper liability statutes. They are, however, protected under the new Anti-Terrorism Act (2001), which makes the request for private information (registration information) far more streamlined. Rather than waiting for a court order, warrant, or subpoena, law-enforcement officers can readily secure a written request. Hotel managers should insist on waiting for such a document before releasing a guest's personal information.

2. True. Registration cards in many foreign countries ask more detailed personal information, which would likely be deemed an invasion of privacy in the United States.

3. False. Innkeeper liability limits are established by state statutes. As such, they differ state to state.

4. True. Some self-check-in kiosks talk with the guest in an audible computer-generated voice; most dispense a room key or ask the guest to swipe a keycard from a nearby stack; many provide a detailed map of the property.

5. True. Queuing problems have been addressed through computer software applications. These programs basically seek to identify the optimum staffing levels to service an unknown arrival population. Too much staff, and labor costs are high while lines are short . . . too little staff, and lines are long while tempers are short.

CHAPTER 9

The Role
of the Room Rate

Outline

**The Room Rate's Impact
on Guest Demand**
*Hotel Room Demand
Discounts Off Rack Rate
Additional Rate Factors
Time is Money*

Determining the Proper Room Rate
Traditional Rate Calculations

Resources and Challenges
*Resources
Challenges*

The rate for which a hotel's rooms are sold communicates a great deal about the hotel. Rates higher than the market average suggest a better hotel than the norm—better either because it is newer, offers a higher level of service, has a premium location, or any number of other factors. Higher rates might also result from a better management team—a management team committed to selling its hotel at the top of the market, a management team with a careful eye toward yield management, a management team with a clearer understanding of the level of elasticity in the local market's demand, and even a management team more concerned with hotel profitability. The room rate plays a critical role in hotel prestige, demand, and profitability.

➤ THE ROOM RATE'S IMPACT ON GUEST DEMAND

In the aftermath of September 11, 2001, the lodging industry faced a slowdown in overall travel demand. This slowdown caused a momentary reduction in the relentless growth of annual hotel room rates. According to some analysts, the industry's average room rate for 2001 was $85.38, or about 1% less than the rate experienced for the year 2000 ($86.24). The impact of 9/11/01 continued into 2002 causing the industry's annual average room rate to fall to $83.67. By 2003, however, rates were back on track and again growing faster than the nation's rate of inflation. The rate of growth in room prices has held roughly steady at 6.8% per year for more than 25 years (see Chapter 1). The average room was selling for just $17.29 in 1975. It was selling for $83.67 in 2002. Twenty-five years from now (assuming room-rate growth remains steady at 6.8% annually), the average hotel room will run about $433.36 per night! How old will you be in 25 years? Will you be able to afford $433.36 per night to stay at the Holiday Inn?

Hotel Room Demand

Today, there are more hotel rooms available in the United States than ever before, but room demand is higher than ever before too. The result is a form of inflation—inflation at a microeconomic level, affecting just the travel industry. Inflation occurs when too many dollars are chasing too few goods. The result from such a dilemma is a rise in consumer prices; and the entire travel industry (hotels, air travel, rental cars, and restaurant meals, to be specific) has experienced an inflation of prices over the past several years (see Exhibit 9–1).

The amazing thing about the great economic boom of the late 1990s and the following slowdown the economy experienced in the early 2000s is that most other industries demonstrated extremely low inflation. The national Consumer Price Index (CPI) reflected low single-digit inflation during most of these years (generally 2 to 3%). Most products, the travel industry excepted, cost little more today than they did, say, five years ago—but not so with hotel rooms. Hotel rooms represent a microcosm of the overall economy—and a unique microcosm at that.

Unique, because no matter what direction the nation's economy, room rates continue to rise. In the economic boom of the late 1990s, room rates rose because increasing room demand was creating upward pressure on rates—when the economy is strong, salespeople are traveling; companies, both large and small, are hosting more lavish corporate retreats; and conferences are boasting record attendance. The leisure travel market, flush with its own sense of wealth, is also traveling more.

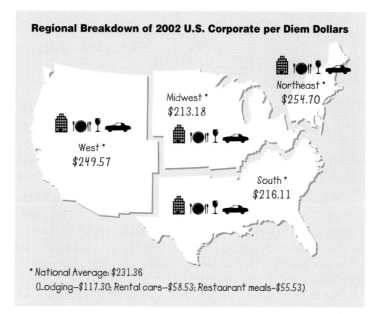

Regional Breakdown of 2002 U.S. Corporate per Diem Dollars

Northeast *
$254.70

Midwest *
$213.18

West *
$249.57

South *
$216.11

* National Average: $231.36
(Lodging—$117.30; Rental cars—$58.53; Restaurant meals—$55.53)

Exhibit 9–1   In 2002, the average daily cost of lodging, ground transportation, and food (per-diem travel costs) rose 7.4 percent—a substantial increase in light of the nation's 1.6 percent overall rate of inflation. Indeed, almost one-third of the nation's top 100 cities saw per-diem rates above $250 (compare that with just 16 percent of the top 100 cities above that threshold the previous year). *Source: 2002 Corporate Travel Index,* Business Travel News.

In slower economies, as experienced in the early 2000s, there is often a different type of pressure on room rates. Faced with lower corporate profits and depressed stock prices, public hotel companies continue to push room rates as a critical means of retaining earnings even when the market seems to be slowing. How else can you account for the continued growth of room rates through the lean years of the late 1980s and the early 2000s?

That's the uniqueness of the situation—other industries are experiencing small price increases, while the lodging industry is averaging twice the national rate of inflation. The thing about "averages," however, is that there are highs and lows. Some markets (mostly major urban areas) are seeing rate increases even higher than those described above. Other markets are stagnant in terms of room rate inflation.

►*Competition.*   Just as operating costs dictate the minimum a hotel can afford to charge, competition sets the maximum it can expect to get. External competition from neighboring facilities prescribes the general price range. Internal physical differences within the rooms determine the rate increments.

Supply and demand, the degree of saturation, and the extent of rate cutting in the community fix the rate parameters. Customers comparison shop, and hotel management should do the same. Differences in both the physical facilities and the range of services offered justify higher rates than the competition. The physical accommodations are easier to compare; they are there for the looking. Swimming pool, tennis courts, meeting rooms, restaurants, and a lobby bar head a long list of differences that give one property a competitive advantage over its neighbor. Room size, furnishings (bed and bath types), location, and exposure further differentiate the product.

The condition of the facilities can offset their competitive advantage. "Clean and neat" sends an important subliminal message. Hotels with burnt-out bulbs in exterior signage, wilted flowers in the planters, and dirty glass at the entry lose out to hotels with lesser facilities that look fresh and new.

Differences in service are more difficult to discern, but they add to the room rate charge as substantially as do other components. Twenty-four-hour room service, pool guard on duty, and an extensive training program for employees begin another, less visible list of competitive advantages. Like the capital outlays of the physical accommodations, these costs must be recaptured in the room rate as well.

▶*Room Rate Elasticity.*   Elasticity is the change in demand (rooms sold) resulting from a change in price (room rates). If demand increases with a drop in price (or decreases when price is raised), demand is elastic. If demand appears unaffected by drops or increases in price, demand is inelastic. Hotel room rate reductions in an elastic market generate new business (higher occupancy). Hotel room rate reductions in an inelastic market generate little or no new business.

The hotel industry has always believed that reductions in rate produce less new revenue than is lost from lowering the unit price, thereby suggesting that room demand is somewhat inelastic. The supposition was supported by actual experience. Room income (occupancy multiplied by average daily rate) actually rose during the low-occupancy periods of the late 1980s and again in the early 2000s because increased room rates did not drive away significant amounts of sales (occupancy). It did not, goes the reasoning, because room demand is inelastic (see Exhibit 9–2).

Elasticity of demand for hotel rooms is exceedingly complex. An inelastic property or market can actually increase rates during an economic slump with profitable results. Rate changes can be disastrous—or very beneficial—depending on the elasticity of demand for the property and market in question.

Different markets have different degrees of sensitivity. Tour properties are more elastic, and commercial demand is more inelastic. Hotels experience different degrees of elasticity throughout the year. That is what the demand pricing behind seasonal rates is all about. A given hotel may have numerous "seasons" throughout its annual cycle.

Elasticity of demand was the catalyst for major change throughout the travel industry between the 1970s and 1990s. During this period, customer profiles began to form into distinct buyer segments. The airlines—after deregulation—were the first to capitalize on the emerging distinctions between corporate travel and the leisure market. The hotel industry wasn't far behind.

This parameter shift was the beginning of a conscious attempt to segregate buyers by their price sensitivity, the concept behind yield management. Both industries discovered that demand was elastic for the leisure market and inelastic for the business segment in terms of both time and price. The group-rooms market seems to share some of the characteristics from both corporate and leisure travelers.

The art of managing these distinct markets cannot be taken lightly. Success from discounting to the leisure market (where lower rates result in incremental increases in occupancy) does not hold true with the corporate market (where lower rates are not offset with increased occupancy). Similarly, offering alternative dates to move the guest into discounted low periods of occupancy works well with the leisure market (whose vacation periods are relatively flexible) but poorly with corporate guests (whose travel dates are on a need-to-go basis). Discretionary leisure buyers may even

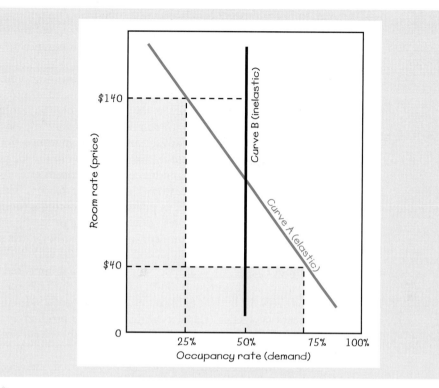

Exhibit 9–2   Curve A represents a normal elastic demand curve. The leisure market is generally considered to have elastic demand. As room rates fall, room demand from the leisure market increases. In the example diagram, when the rate is reduced from $140 to just $40, occupancy jumps from 25% to 75%. The corporate travel market, on the other hand, is considered relatively inelastic (curve B). Corporate travelers have historically been little concerned with rate, and a reduction in room price will not create much increased demand. Those days may be changing, however, as corporate travelers experiment with booking last-minute discounted rooms found on a number of Internet sites.

change location to save the lodging budget, while corporate guests are last-minute shoppers with extremely little flexibility (see Exhibit 9–2).

Complicated as this may seem, group-rooms business throws yet another dimension into the picture. Tour groups, which are usually price sensitive, take on many of the characteristics of the leisure segment—elastic in terms of rate, flexible with regard to date. Conventions, trade shows, conferences, and corporate retreats generally demonstrate the characteristics of the corporate market—inelastic with regard to rate, inflexible in terms of travel dates. But remember one thing, even an inelastic market becomes elastic at some point. There may be little or no difference in corporate occupancy when the rate fluctuates between $80 and $160. But if the rate becomes too high, say $260, some sensitivity will ultimately result. A growing trend—corporate guests finding last-minute bargains via Internet leisure travel sites—is adding a new twist to the old formula.

Rate Cutting.   According to many industry experts, there is a distinct difference between rate cutting and discounting. Rate cutting functions in an inelastic market. Unwarranted rate cuts generate new business for one property only by luring the customer away from another property. Discounting, on the other hand, attracts new customers to the industry, benefiting all properties. Discounting seeks out the stay-at-home customer, the visit-friends-or-family customer, and the let's-camp-out customer. Rate cutting aims at the guest already staying in a competitor's hotel across the road or down the boulevard.

Competitors, who are the source of the new business, counter with rate cuts, and the price war is on. A decline in price per room and in gross sales, rather than the hoped-for increase in occupancy, is the net result. Some resort localities outlaw price wars by making it a misdemeanor to post rates outside the establishment. Printed rate schedules are permitted; it is advertising on the marquee that is not allowed. Conversely, other communities actually require room rates to be posted outside the property. In such cases, the lowest and highest posted room rates on the marquee establish the rate parameters that the customer can expect to pay. This reduces the unsavory practice of "sizing up" the walk-in guest before quoting a room rate.

The long list of special rates (discussed later in the chapter) proves that not all rate variations are viewed as rate cutting. Perhaps they must merely stand the test of time. The family plan, in which all children roomed with their parents are accommodated without charge, caused dissension when it first appeared (see Exhibit 9–10). It is today a legitimate business builder. So, too, is the free room given to convention groups for every 50 or 100 paid rooms. Like any good sales inducement, special rates should create new sales (elasticity), not make the product available at a lower price. For once sold at a lower rate, it is almost impossible to get the buyer to pay the original price.

Once established, rates are not easily adjusted. Increases must be undertaken slowly if they are not to affect patronage. It does not matter that the rate was too low to begin with. Rate reductions will bring no complaints if the initial rates were too high. Opening with rates that are too high may do devastating damage before the adjustment is made. Excessive rates create bad word-of-mouth advertising that takes time and costly sales promotions to counteract.

▶*Elasticity of Lodging Taxes.*   One rate component over which hotel managers have little or no control is local lodging taxes. Also known as bed, room, or hotel taxes, these guest charges often provide significant revenues for the local municipality (see Exhibit 9–3). Operating with increasingly tight budgets, cities are lured into the easy money available from taxing out-of-towners. After all, it appears politically correct to increase the tax revenue base without actually raising the taxes charged to local citizens.

But the reality of the situation is not so straightforward. Several concerns are not initially apparent. First is the ethical debate. Many antagonists of the hotel tax believe it is wrong to charge out-of-town visitors for city services and improvements that are not tourism related. For example, how can one justify charging a bed tax that's earmarked for improving and building new schools and local sports field complexes (as shown in Exhibit 9–3)? The visitor clearly does not benefit from the taxes paid—it is taxation without representation.

Second, several careful studies have demonstrated that an increased lodging tax actually hurts the local economy. More revenue may be lost in other taxes than is actually gained in room tax. For example, New York City had the highest lodging tax in the United States (an effective 21.25% rate). In large part because of this tax rate, the city suffered a decrease in convention business by as much as 30%. With 30% fewer convention visitors, that was 30% fewer purchases of souvenirs, arts and crafts, meals and drinks, clothing, and related purchases. Each of these purchases generated tax

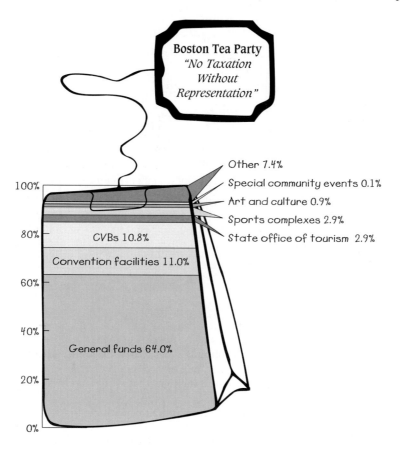

How Travel-Related Sales Taxes Are Used

Exhibit 9–3   Someday, tourists may complain "No taxation without representation" as loudly as at the Boston Tea Party. That's because travel-related taxes generate about $8 billion a year for local municipalities. Yet little of these visitor-paid taxes find their way into improved tourist-related facilities. The bulk of lodging tax revenues is deposited into community general funds and then used for urban projects with little or no relation to tourism (like maintaining a prison, as is the case in Phoenix!).

revenue (sales tax) in its own right. Therefore, an increase in the lodging tax had negative repercussions—a decrease in related sales tax revenues—for New York City. Today, New York City's lodging tax (13.25% + $2 per night) doesn't even rank in the top five cities across the United States (see Exhibit 9–4).[1]

Taxing Demand.   Although the individual traveler rarely considers the rate of local taxes, group business has become increasingly conscious of this vexing premium. Carefully negotiated group rates seem purposeless and inconsequential if the city then slaps an additional 15 to 20% levy on rates that have been shaved by just five to ten

---

[1]The International Hotel Association (IHA) published a study entitled "IHA Taxation Survey— A Comparative Survey of Taxation on the Hospitality Industry." This study offers an analysis, country by country, of the taxes levied against hotels and restaurants.

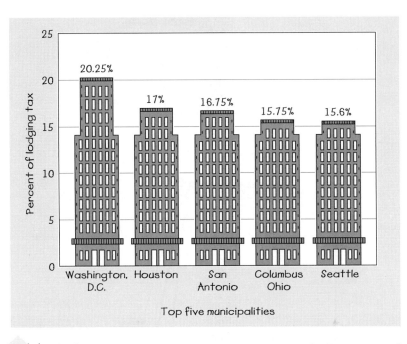

Exhibit 9–4   In rough economic times, when cities and other municipalities face budget shortfalls, hotel occupancy (lodging or bed) taxes offer an easy solution. By taxing tourists, city governments avoid the fight that would likely ensue if they raised citizens' property taxes or sales taxes.

This exhibit shows the five communities with the highest bed taxes in the United States. Across the country, the average lodging tax is 11.65%. High tax rates, yes, but not as bad as many foreign countries—Hungary charges hotel guests some 59 separate taxes totaling a whopping 39% of the hotel bill!

dollars. Bed taxes have become deterrents to the marketing efforts of numerous convention and visitor bureaus. Taxes in the 10 to 12% range seem acceptable to most consumers. Rates above 14% meet resistance among some groups and associations. Yet, Washington, D.C., Houston, and San Antonio—well recognized destinations for groups—struggle with room taxes close to 17% or higher (see Exhibit 9–4).

The trend may be changing, however. More and more hotel managers are joining together to battle rising bed taxes in their cities. By forming one cohesive and vocal group, hotel managers represent a formidable opponent to city councils bent on raising the tax. And with the domino effect that develops when fewer visitors come to the city, it is not difficult to garner additional support from local merchants.

The lodging industry stands firmly against the proliferation of bed taxes. To fight increasing taxation, various industry associations have begun conducting research and educational campaigns aimed at local politicians who see the tourism sector as an easy place to find tax revenues without actually having to face the taxpayer. This research has generated some interesting findings. Twenty-five years ago, total room taxes (state and local sales and bed taxes) were just 3 to 4% of the room charge. Today, the national average is 11.65%—better than a threefold increase (see Exhibit 9–4). The rise in bed taxes may be the highest increase in taxation of any industry in the United States, except possibly the gaming industry. The lodging industry pays about twice the tax rate imposed on most other goods and services.

Looking at 50 destinations around the globe, the World Tourism Organization (WTO) concluded, "taxes on tourism are proliferating . . . in some cases they can stifle tourism and cause a net loss in revenues for a destination." According to the WTO, roughly 73% of the destinations studied had raised tourism-related taxes over the past several years. Indeed, governments are finding creative ways to levy new taxes against tourists—more than 40 different kinds of taxes were identified, including many new ones (like environmental taxes) that had never before existed.

Similar research by the American Hotel Foundation discovered that an increase in the bed tax has negative repercussions on rooms demand (elastic rooms demand will decline when the total room rate including tax increases). A decrease in rooms demand doesn't just affect the hotel industry. Tourists and corporate travelers who stop coming can't buy meals, rent cars, take home souvenirs, or play at golf courses, to name a few complementary visitor services. In fact, a hypothetical 2% increase in the lodging tax results in a 5.1% reduction in room sales and associated visitor spending.

Discounts off Rack Rate

All hotels have a rack rate against which other pricing structures are designed (see Exhibit 9–5). A hotel's rack rate is the quoted, published rate that is theoretically charged to full-paying customers. In essence, the rack rate is the full retail rate. However, just as customers rarely pay the sticker price for a brand-new automobile, guests rarely pay the rack rate for a hotel room.

Although reservationists try to offer the customer full rack rate, shrewd guests never accept it. Corporate discounts, affiliation discounts (AAA and AARP, for example), frequent-travel discounts, advanced and nonrefundable purchases, and a host of other possibilities have all combined to erode the hotel's ability to charge full price.

Proof of discounting is most evident in the average daily rate computation. Hotels with an average rack rate of, say, $78 probably never actually attain a $78 ADR. Instead, the property's ADR is a reflection of the vast discounting taking place throughout the property. Corporate meetings, tour groups, discounted transient travelers, and corporate guests negatively affect the hotel's ability to sell rooms at rack rate. As a result, a hotel with an average rack rate of $78 probably receives an ADR closer to $68.

►*The Discounting Dilemma.* In those markets where demand is strong, competing hotels continue to push rates to new ADR heights. Hotels find it easier to sell expensive rooms, and price-sensitive guests find few properties willing to bargain on rate. This is not the case in all markets. In markets where demand is soft, the industry tears down the very prices it worked so hard to build. And like anything else, it is easier and faster to destroy than to build. In markets where discounting is rampant, the only sure winner is the customer who buys a quality product for a fraction of the price. If and when occupancy demand finally catches up to rooms supply, the industry finds itself dug into a deep hole. After becoming accustomed to discounted rates, customers perceive full rates as a very poor value.

Hotel customers are becoming increasingly aware of the room rate discount game. Travel articles tout the same mantra to all customers—shop around for your best rate. Many customers have trained themselves to ask for the discount when booking lodging accommodations. This creates the image that standard prices are unfair and that the industry needs to discount because the quality of the product does not warrant full price.

Monte Carlo
RESORT & CASINO · LAS VEGAS

NO ONE CAN OFFER OUR ROOMS AT A LOWER RATE. WE GUARANTEE IT!

Online Reservations

King

click on picture to enlarge

▢	Rooms Available. No Restrictions.
▢	Sold Out. No Rooms Available.
▢	No Arrivals. Prior Night Stay Required.
▢	Special Restrictions Apply. Call 1.888.529.4828 to Reserve.

DELUXE ROOM CALENDAR | Help
Rates listed are for deluxe rooms.

Next Four Month Calendars >>

NOVEMBER

S	M	T	W	T	F	S
					1 •	2 •
3 •	4 •	5 •	6 •	7 •	8 •	9 •
10 •	11 •	12 •	13 •	14 •	15 •	16 S/O
17 $49	18 $49	19 $49	20 $49	21 $49	22 $69	23 $89
24 $49	25 $49	26 $49	27 $49	28 $89	29 $149	30 $89

DECEMBER

S	M	T	W	T	F	S
1 $49	2 $49	3 $49	4 $49	5 $49	6 $89	7 $149
8 $59	9 $49	10 $49	11 $49	12 $49	13 $89	14 $99
15 $49	16 $49	17 $49	18 $39	19 $39	20 $49	21 $89
22 $49	23 $49	24 $59	25 $59	26 $59	27 $129	28 $149
29 $179	30 $249	31 $279				

JANUARY

S	M	T	W	T	F	S
		1 $79	2 $49	3 $99	4 $99	
5 $59	6 $59	7 $89	8 $159	9 $179	10 $179	11 $249
12 $89	13 $89	14 $89	15 $89	16 $89	17 $129	18 $179
19 $69	20 $119	21 $179	22 $189	23 $239	24 $249	25 $199
26 $119	27 $79	28 $119	29 $119	30 $149	31 $159	

FEBRUARY

S	M	T	W	T	F	S
						1 $249
2 $89	3 $119	4 $189	5 $189	6 $189	7 $199	8 $249
9 $119	10 $119	11 $119	12 $89	13 $69	14 $199	15 $279
16 $179	17 $79	18 $79	19 $119	20 $119	21 $189	22 $199
23 $69	24 $69		26 $69	27 $69	28 $149	

ARRIVAL & ROOM TYPE | Help
Rates valid for single or double occupancy.
$25.00 additional charge for each additional person.

Exhibit 9–5 In terms of fluctuating rates, the Las Vegas lodging market is probably the most volatile in the United States. The same room can change price dramatically from day to day based upon occupancy projections, group rooms inhouse, and other variables. The Monte Carlo Resort & Casino, for example, does not even print a rack rate card or brochure—it would be obsolete the moment it was printed. Requests for such information are referred to its Web site: www.montecarlo.com. *Courtesy of the Monte Carlo Resort & Casino, Las Vegas, Nevada.*

Discounting Profitability.   Room discounting is designed to increase occupancy at the cost of a lowered room rate. If the resulting occupancy increase is sufficient, it covers the lost revenues from reduced rates. In such a situation, both parties are happy—the guest pays less for the room and the hotel makes a higher profit from having created more room demand.

However appealing these potential profits are, rate discounting has a negative side as well. In fact, the whole idea of discounting rates to increase demand is somewhat suspect. Let's assume that a given hotel property was operating at an annualized occupancy of 60% with a $70 ADR. Because the property decides it wants to increase occupancy, it establishes a rate discounting program. Exhibit 9–6 shows that for this example, a 10% rate discount (second column of Exhibit 9–6) requires occupancy to rise to 66.67% in order to gross the same revenues as previously earned. That's an 11% increase in occupancy required to offset a 10% discount in price—just to gross the same revenues!

An 11% increase in occupancy may not be easy in a community experiencing, say, only a 3.0% demand growth. To accomplish an 11% increase, some other lodging operation(s) will lose customers. Herein lies the biggest problem: As competing lodging properties catch wind of your discounting program, they too will begin to discount. Ultimately, a rate war will ensue, and the only winner will be the customer who pays the reduced rate.

➤*Examples of Discounted Rates.*   Discounted or special rates come in a variety of shapes and sizes. Some merely provide a slight discount from the rack rate, as when a hotel offers a 10% price reduction for AAA or AARP members. Other special rates, such as volume discounting programs and seasonal price reductions, are quite significant, reducing the posted rate up to 50%, 75%, or even more.

The reordering of rates is part of the shakeout of segmentation. Rates are a function of supply and demand, and in a perfect economy these two variables move toward equilibrium. However, for now, *special rates*—a term that is preferable to *discounted rates*—are in. The list of those entitled to special rates is limited only by the imagination of the marketing department.

Current Occupancy (%)	Percent of Rate Discount			
	10%	15%	20%	25%
50	55.56	58.82	62.5	66.67
55	61.11	64.71	68.75	73.33
60	66.67	70.59	75.00	80.00
65	72.22	76.47	81.25	86.67
70	77.78	82.35	87.5	93.33
75	83.33	88.24	93.75	100.00

Exhibit 9–6   Shown is a rate-discounting equivalency table. Figures in columns two through five (listed as 10% through 25%) reflect the new occupancy percentages required in order to produce the same gross revenues the hotel was generating before the rate discount. For example, a hotel that discounts rates by 20% must increase occupancy from its current 65% level to 81.25%, or room revenue will fall.

A well-known comment from Randy Smith, founder and chairman of Smith Travel Research, says it all: "It's starting to dawn on the industry that reducing room rates isn't going to bring more people into the market—[reducing room rates] is just stealing the existing customers from down the street."

One hotel chain has special rates for teachers; another for students. Most have discounts for senior citizens; almost all allow children in the room with their parents at no charge. The *Worldwide Directory* of Holiday Inns advertises a sports rate for U.S. amateur and professional teams. Special introductory rates are a common tactic for launching a new hotel. The same tradition that gives police officers discounts in the coffee shop gives other uniformed groups such as the clergy and the military discounts off the room rack. And so the list grows.

Travel agents and travel writers usually get free accommodations while they are on familiarization (fam) trips. At other times, the special rate is a standard 50% discount, unless, of course, they come during the height of the busy season.

Hawaii's *kama'aina* rate (literally, kama means "person"; aina means "land"; translation is "native-born") is an interesting case of special rates. A class-action suit was filed by a Californian on the grounds that the 25% discount granted to Hawaiian residents was discriminatory. The argument was denied by the court. The judge found that "offering a discount to certain clients, patrons, or other customers based on an attempt to attract their business is [not] unlawful." The decision is important because it shows the other side of the issue. Rates that are raised to discourage business from certain persons might well be judged as discriminatory. Rates that are lowered to attract certain persons are viewed quite differently, at least by one court.

All rate discounts should be aimed at the development of new markets and should be phased out as that market stabilizes. It does not work that way in practice. Over time, many special rates become part of the established rate structure. Here are some of the more common examples of discounted rates found in most hotels:

Seasonal Rates.   Posted rack rates can be changed, or they can include seasonal variations. Season and off-season rates are quoted by most resort hotels, with incremental increases and decreases coming as the season approaches and wanes (see Exhibit 9–7). The poor weekend occupancy of urban hotels has forced them to offer a seasonal rate of sorts—a discounted weekend rate.

Hotel capacity in many resort communities is vast, able to handle great numbers of tourists during periods of peak demand. Because of this glut of hotel rooms available for high-season demand, low-season rates are often deeply discounted—so steeply in fact, that many resort properties once closed their doors during low-occupancy seasons. This practice changed some 10 or 15 years ago. Today, very few resort properties actually close for the off-season. The expense of reopening the facility, training and hiring new staff each year, and operating a skeleton crew to maintain the closed facility combined to change the economics of closing the property. Instead, resorts remain open, steeply discounting rooms to value-conscious guests.

Weather-related Discounts.   When it comes to negotiating group rates, even nature gets involved. A growing trend designed to reduce the length of the low or shoulder season at certain resorts is a weather discount factor. Credits or discounts against the rate are offered guests for each day it rains or stays unseasonably cool.

Obviously, this is risky business, and few resorts are yet offering such plans. But select Hiltons and Marriotts are currently on the bandwagon, and others are sure to follow. Indeed, at least one Marriott resort offers a "temperature guarantee" package that they have insured through Lloyd's of London!

Weekly Rates.   Weekly rates, which are less than seven times the daily rate, are offered occasionally. Improved forecasting and increased revenues in all the other departments compensate for the reduction in room revenue.

Nestled in the high Sonoran Desert foothills north of Scottsdale, the Boulders offers the enchantment of a dramatic location created by the forces of time. Spectacular rock outcroppings that captivate everyone who steps within their spell. Ancient saguaros silhouetted against the clear Sonoran sky. And a world-famous resort which blends so easily with nature that the local wildlife might never notice it was there.

The private country club features two 18-hole championship golf courses built right into the desert, as well as a tennis garden and the new Spa... which offers a variety of signature body treatments using the natural herbs of the desert along with a fully equipped cardiovascular and weight room, aerobics classes, and a variety of nature hikes and other stimulating programs.

Just a short stroll from the resort is el Pedregal, a festival-style marketplace of intriguing shops, restaurants, and galleries. And all around the Boulders in the enticing tranquility of the lush Sonoran Desert with its breathtaking natural views.

RESORT CASITAS

At The Boulders there's no such thing as a typical guest room. Instead there are 160 guest casitas shaped into the dramatic terrain, each decorated with natural wood and Mexican tile. Among the pleasures of these individual casitas are fully stocked mini-bars, a woodburning fireplace for cozy evenings, and a private patio or balcony overlooking the spectacular desert terrain.

CASITA DAILY RATES

Oct 1–Dec 8	$429	April 28–May 26	$495
Dec 9–25	$305	May 27–Sept 7	$205
Dec 26–31	%575	Sept 8–Dec 7	$495
Jan 1–Feb 14	$550	Dec 8–25	$290
Feb 15–April 27	$625	Dec 26–31	$575

PUEBLO VILLAS

Ideal for families or groups of friends who want to make themselves at home in a spacious setting, the Pueblo Villas offer all the same services and amenities as the casitas. Each Southwestern-style patio home features a fully-equipped kitchen, spacious dining area and living room, fireplace, private patio, laundry facilities and garage, with a choice of one, two or three bedrooms.

PUEBLO VILLA DAILY RATES

	1-Bedroom Plus Den	2-Bedroom	2-Bedroom Plus Den	3-Bedroom
Oct 1–Dec 8	$515	$675	$775	$1195
Dec 9–25	$365	$480	$550	$749
Dec 26–31	$690	$902	$1040	$1450
Jan 1–Feb 14	$660	$865	$995	$1095
Feb 15–April 27	$750	$985	$1130	$1245
April 28–May 26	$595	$780	$895	$985
May 27–Sept 7	$245	$320	$370	$405
Sept 8–Dec 7	$595	$780	$900	$990
Dec 8–25	$350	$455	$525	$575
Dec 26–31	$690	$905	$1040	$1145

All rates are per accommodation, subject to limited availability and do not include tax or daily service charge.

Exhibit 9–7 The Boulders Resort & Golden Door Spa in Carefree, Arizona, publishes the year's high-, mid-, and low-season rates on one brochure. Notice the wide price disparity between seasons. Add in the fact that such hotels are often more restrictive to certain discounts during high season and less restrictive during low season, and the disparity grows even wider. To illustrate the point, a low-season Resort Casita at $290 is more than twice as expensive in high-season at $625. The disparity is even more exaggerated with Pueblo Villas (high-season 3-bedroom at $1,245 is more than three times the price of the low season's $405). *Courtesy of the Boulders Resort and Golden Door Spa, Carefree, Arizona.*

Both the daily rate—assume $170—and the weekly rate—assume $1,050—are documented by the clerk. The $170 rate is charged daily until the final day, when a $30 charge is posted. In this way, the daily charge is earned until the guest meets the weekly commitment. If one-seventh of the weekly charge were posted daily, the hotel would be at a disadvantage whenever the guest left before the week was up, as frequently happens. One variation on weekly rates leaves the daily rate intact but discounts services such as valet, laundry, and greens fees.

Corporate Rates.   America's corporations do a great deal of business with the nation's hotels. Corporations and hotel chains are synergetic. Corporations have offices and plants worldwide. Employees at all levels (management, personnel, sales, engineering, accounting) travel in vast numbers. They visit the very countries and cities in which the hotel chains have opened their properties worldwide. The synergism works when the employees of a certain corporation stay in the hotels of a given chain. By guaranteeing a given number of room-nights per year, the corporation negotiates a better rate, a corporate rate, from the hotel chain.

Reducing room rates is only part of the discount. Reducing the number of rooms needed to close the deal is a more subtle form of discounting. Not many years ago, corporate rates required 1,000 room-nights per year. Recent figures place the level as low as 50.

The figures were pushed lower by the appearance of third-party negotiators rather than by the astuteness of corporate travel desks. Corporations with numbers that were too small to negotiate on their own were included under the umbrella of room consolidators. Third-party volume buyers who were in no business other than negotiating discounts with hotels (and airlines) represented numerous companies and developed a tough rate-negotiating base. Hotels responded by dealing directly with the smaller corporate accounts, bypassing the travel agents and the consolidators.

Technology has altered the corporate discount picture as well. In the past, major corporations negotiated favorable rates by promising a large annual room volume with a given chain. However, no one really counted, and room volume (actual or anticipated) was never verified. With the increasing sophistication of CRS systems, most major hotel chains are now able to accurately track a corporation's total room volume chainwide. Corporate room activity at franchised properties, parent properties, and through the CRS are all combined into a quarterly volume report. Renaissance Hotels, for example, produces quarterly reports for more than 1,800 of its major corporate accounts. These reports take the guesswork out of room rate negotiations and give both the hotel chain and the corporation an accurate picture of utilized volume.

Corporate rates are now one of the panels in the mural of discounting. But their implementation has left still another irritant between travel agents and hoteliers. Slashing rates low enough to compete for corporate business leaves the hotel little margin for paying commissions. Travel agents get no commission when they book rooms for corporate clients who have negotiated special rates with the hotel. The agent who makes the reservation to accommodate the corporate client is in a dilemma. Either book the room and get no commission or tell the corporate clients to book their own rooms.

Commercial Rates.   Commercial rates are the small hotel's answer to corporate rates. Without the global chain's size to negotiate national corporate contracts, smaller hotels make arrangements with small commercial clients. Such understandings might account for 5 or 10 room-nights per year for a manufacturer's representative or salesperson traveling on a personal expense account.

Under the commercial rate plan, a standard low rate is negotiated for the year. This standard rate provides the commercial guest with two advantages. First, the rate is guaranteed. Even during periods of high occupancy, most small hotels honor the commercial rate. Second, when demand is mild, the commercial guest is granted an upgraded accommodation at no additional charge. This small courtesy costs the hotel nothing, yet generates substantial loyalty on the part of the guest. Few hotels actually distinguish between corporate and commercial rates. The two terms are effectively synonymous.

Government Per Diems.   Federal, state, and local governments reimburse traveling employees up to a fixed dollar amount. This per-diem (per day) cap is made up of two parts: room and meals (and may include a third component—car rental). Reimbursement is made on the actual cost of the room (a receipt is required) but no more than the maximum. Anyone traveling on government business is reluctant to pay more than the per-diem room allowance, since the agency will not reimburse the excess. Meal reimbursement is a given number of dollars per day and generally requires no receipts (see Exhibits 9–1 and 9–8).

Key cities, those with higher costs of living, are given higher caps (see Exhibit 9–8). The General Services Administration (GSA) of the federal government publishes the per-diem rates that apply to federal employees. The distinct market segment covers all federal civilian employees, military personnel, and recently, cost-reimbursed federal contractors.

Difficulties may arise when the per-diem guest encounters the desk. Some chains accept the government rates, but individual properties may not. And if they do, the yield management decision may reject these heavily discounted rates for that particular period. Moreover, since per diems, like some other special rates, are on a space-available basis, some central reservations systems will not quote the rate for confirmation. *Space available* means that rooms are not confirmed until close to the date of arrival. Over all these hurdles, the guest must then prove per-diem entitlement. Without a standardized form, letter, or procedure, the individual room clerk makes a discretionary call based on whatever evidence the guest can provide.

In recent years, a controversial repeal of a previously mandated government regulation has left the lodging industry wondering what is fair in terms of per-diem rates. The debate revolves around the Hotel and Motel Fire Safety Act of 1990. This act was proposed after a U.S. Treasury agent perished in a fire at the Dupont Plaza Hotel in San Juan, Puerto Rico, on New Year's Eve 1986.

In an effort to protect government employees traveling on business, the 1990 act mandated that hotels must comply with certain smoke detector and sprinkler regulations if they wished to sell rooms to government employees traveling on per diem. Complying with this act cost the lodging industry over $1.2 billion per year! Some 17,000 hotels and motels across the country (about 38% of all hotel and motel rooms nationwide) complied with the Fire Safety Act.

These hotels made the fire safety investment because they believed that compliant properties would be the only ones allowed a piece of the lucrative government market. In late 1996, however, the government—just as it was about to begin auditing all hotels to verify their compliance with the act—pulled the plug on the policy by removing the audit requirement. Today, hotels are still urged to provide adequate fire safety protection, but the government is not auditing their actual compliance—a move that has been deemed unfair by the thousands of hotels who spent billions of dollars bringing their fire safety systems up to code in the early 1990s.

How to Use the Per-Diem Tables

The maximum rates listed in the table are prescribed by law for reimbursement of per-diem expenses incurred during official travel within CONUS (the continental United States). The amount shown in column a is the maximum that will be reimbursed for lodging expenses, including applicable taxes. The "M&IE" rate shown in column b is a fixed amount allowed for meals and incidental expenses covered by per diem. The per diem payment for lodging expenses plus the M&IE rate may not exceed the maximum per diem rate shown in column c. Seasonal rates apply during the periods indicated. Unless otherwise specified, the per diem locality is defined as "all locations within, or entirely surrounded by, the corporate limits of the key city, including independent entities located within those boundaries."

Requests for per-diem rate adjustments should be submitted by the agency headquarters office to the General Services Administration, Office of Governmentwide Policy, Attn: Travel and Transportation Management Policy Division (MTT), Washington, DC 20405. Agencies should submit their requests to GSA no later than May 1 in order for a city to be included in the annual review.

MAXIMUM PER-DIEM RATES IN THE CONTINENTAL UNITED STATES
STATE: UTAH

| | | | Column | | | |
| | | | *a* | *b* | *c* | |
Locality	County and/or Other Defined Location	Seasons (Beg-End)	Max Lodging	Local Meals Rate	Max Per Diem	Eff. Date
BULLFROG	GARFIELD	01/01-12/31	73	32 + 2	107	10/01/20__
CEDAR CITY	IRON	01/01-12/31	59	36 + 2	97	10/01/20__
DAVIS COUNTY	WEBER AND DAVIS	01/15-02/28	169	36 + 2	207	10/01/20__
DAVIS COUNTY	WEBER AND DAVIS	03/01-01/14	69	36 + 2	107	10/01/20__
LAYTON	WEBER AND DAVIS	01/15-02/28	169	36 + 2	207	10/01/20__
LAYTON	WEBER AND DAVIS	03/01-01/14	69	36 + 2	107	10/01/20__
MOAB	GRAND	03/15-10/31	90	36 + 2	128	10/01/20__
MOAB	GRAND	11/01-03/14	55	36 + 2	93	10/01/20__
OGDEN	WEBER AND DAVIS	01/15-02/28	169	36 + 2	207	10/01/20__
OGDEN	WEBER AND DAVIS	03/01-01/14	69	36 + 2	107	10/01/20__
PARK CITY	SUMMIT	04/01-12/14	79	44 + 2	125	10/01/20__
PARK CITY	SUMMIT	12/15-03/31	169	44 + 2	215	10/01/20__
PROVO	UTAH	01/15-02/28	169	40 + 2	211	10/01/20__
PROVO	UTAH	03/01-10/31	69	40 + 2	111	10/01/20__
PROVO	UTAH	11/01-01/14	60	40 + 2	102	10/01/20__
SALT LAKE CITY	SALT LAKE AND DUGWAY PROVING	01/15-02/28	169	36 + 2	207	10/01/20__
SALT LAKE CITY	SALT LAKE AND DUGWAY PROVING	03/01-01/14	75	36 + 2	113	10/01/20__

Source: GSA, Washington, DC.

Exhibit 9–8   The General Services Administration (GSA) of the U.S. government prints annual per-diem tables for official travel within CONUS (Continental United States). Annual adjustments are made to per-diem rates each October. Shown as an example is the state of Utah. See www.dtic.mil/cgi-bin/cpdrates.pl. *Source: GSA, Washington, DC.*

Employee Courtesy Rates.   Most hotel chains extend special rates to their employees as a courtesy to them when they travel to other hotels within the chain. Indeed, for the large chains, this is actually a market segment. Substantial discounts from the hotel's minimum rate plus upgrade whenever possible result in a very attractive bargain. Special rates are always provided on a space-available basis. Employee-guests are accepted only if rooms are vacant when they present themselves (some chains allow reservations a few weeks before arrival if projected occupancy is below 75% or so). The Federal Deficit Reduction Law of 1984 reinforced this by taxing the employee for the value of any free room if paying guests were turned away.

Offering complimentary or discounted employee rooms is an inexpensive way for chains to supplement their employee benefits packages. Because such rooms are provided on a space-available basis, there is little associated cost (aside from housekeeping) to providing the employee a free or deeply discounted rate. And many chains find some real benefits in increased morale and motivation as employees take advantage of the chain's discounted rooms.

In fact, some chains actually listen to their employees. They request visiting employees to fill out evaluation forms complete with comments and suggestions for improvement. If carefully monitored and tracked, such a "secret shopper" program can have enormous advantages to the chain.

It Pays to Pay Rack Rate.   Although not really a discount, some upscale chains are experimenting with added perks for guests who actually pay full rack rate. The perks include such valuable amenities as free use of a cellular telephone, limousine service to the airport and nearby shopping, free dry cleaning, and even free food items. Several Ritz-Carlton properties allow full rack–rate guests an extended check out until 6 PM. Four Seasons hotels give deluxe accommodations (a free upgrade) to rack rate guests.

Senior Citizen Rates.   Every 7 seconds, another person reaches age 50. There are currently better than 75 million Americans over the age of 50, and that number will jump to about 100 million by the year 2010. In addition to these age-related statistics, it is important to note that senior citizens (defined as 50-plus years of age by some organizations) represent the fastest-growing travel market.

Although seniors are by no means a homogeneous group, they have certain features and expectations in common. First, people over the age of 50 are the best money savers in the world. As such, when they travel (and they love to travel), they're careful with money. They try to find travel bargains, and they can find them, because they have such flexible travel schedules.

When asked about their preferences, seniors listed discounted buffet breakfasts, complimentary newspapers, and free cable television as their top lodging amenities. They also seem to appreciate hotels where grandchildren stay free, low-cholesterol and low-sodium menu items are offered, bathtub grab bars are provided, and large-digit alarm clocks and telephones are available. Chains such as Ramada Inns, Howard Johnson's, and Hilton, to name a few, are among the leaders in marketing to senior travelers.

Infinite Other Discounts.   There are an unlimited number of additional rate discounting possibilities. Large groups such as AAA, Discover Card members, or the like no longer have a monopoly on special rates. Any sized group that can produce even a few room-nights per year is negotiating discounted rates.

One growing midsized market is bank clubs. Members of credit unions or banks and holders of numerous credit cards now find discounted rates part of their incentive package. Some of these groups charge for the service, others provide it free as a means of attracting and holding bank customers.

The Entertainment Card, Quest International, and other travel clubs carry more clout today than ever before. By providing members with deep discounts (usually about half of rack rate) for traveling during off-peak periods, such clubs provide a win–win–win product. The travel club wins because it charges members a fee to join, members win by gaining access to substantial travel discounts, and hotels win when rooms fill (albeit at discounted rates) during less busy periods.

Hotels must be extremely careful, however, to limit the use of such discounts to the slower periods of the year. It's a costly mistake replacing a full-paying rack rate or corporate guest with an Entertainment Card customer on a sold-out night. On the other hand, it makes good sense to attract such deeply discounted business on nights when the hotel is unlikely to fill. Yield management is the tool for making the decision.

Auctioning is a form of discounting that is gaining popularity even at the smallest market level—the individual traveler. Auctioning allows hotels, airlines, and rental car agencies to enter a product-available database marketed directly to the traveler through technology available to the average person (see Exhibit 9–9). The guest—say, Carl Jones—decides where he is traveling to, the dates and times he wishes to travel, and any specifications (must be a four-star property, a midsized car, etc.) related to the trip. He is then asked to quote his own rate!

If a hotel, airline, and/or rental car agency informs the database that this is a reasonable offer, Jones gets the deal as bid. He never knows until the offer is accepted which airline he will fly, which hotel will accommodate him, or which rental car he will drive. If the bid is too low, Jones places a time limit on his offer and waits to see over the next few days whether the various travel components in question will respond favorably.

In recent years, companies such as Priceline.com (see Exhibit 9–9), Bid4Travel, LuxuryLink.com, and skyauction.com (to name a few) have taken inventory auctioning to new levels. By matching millions of potential buyers with millions of vacant rooms (and available rental cars, empty airline seats, etc.), travel auction companies have created a growing niche for themselves. To qualify for deep discounts, travel auction companies often require a degree of flexibility on the part of the customer (non-prime-time flight schedules and less-popular travel dates are the norm). As the popularity of travel auction Web sites continues to grow, and their contribution to total rooms and other services sold continues to rise, customers will find their purchasing clout rising as well. The result will be more peak-time and high-demand travel bookings.

▶*Complimentary Rooms.* Hotel managers should be as reluctant to give away complimentary (comp) rooms as automobile sales managers are to give away free cars. But both the perishability of the room and the low variable cost of housing an occupant change this reality. Comps are used for business promotion, as charitable giveaways, and as perks.

By custom, complimentary rates are extended to other hoteliers. The courtesy is reciprocated, resulting in an industrywide fringe benefit for owners and senior managers. Such comps rarely include food or beverage (costs are too high) even in American plan hotels. As mentioned earlier, another portion of the travel industry—travel agents and travel writers—are comped during fam trips. Deregulation permitted fam trip comps by the airlines, which have now joined the hotel industry in developing site inspection tours for the travel industry.

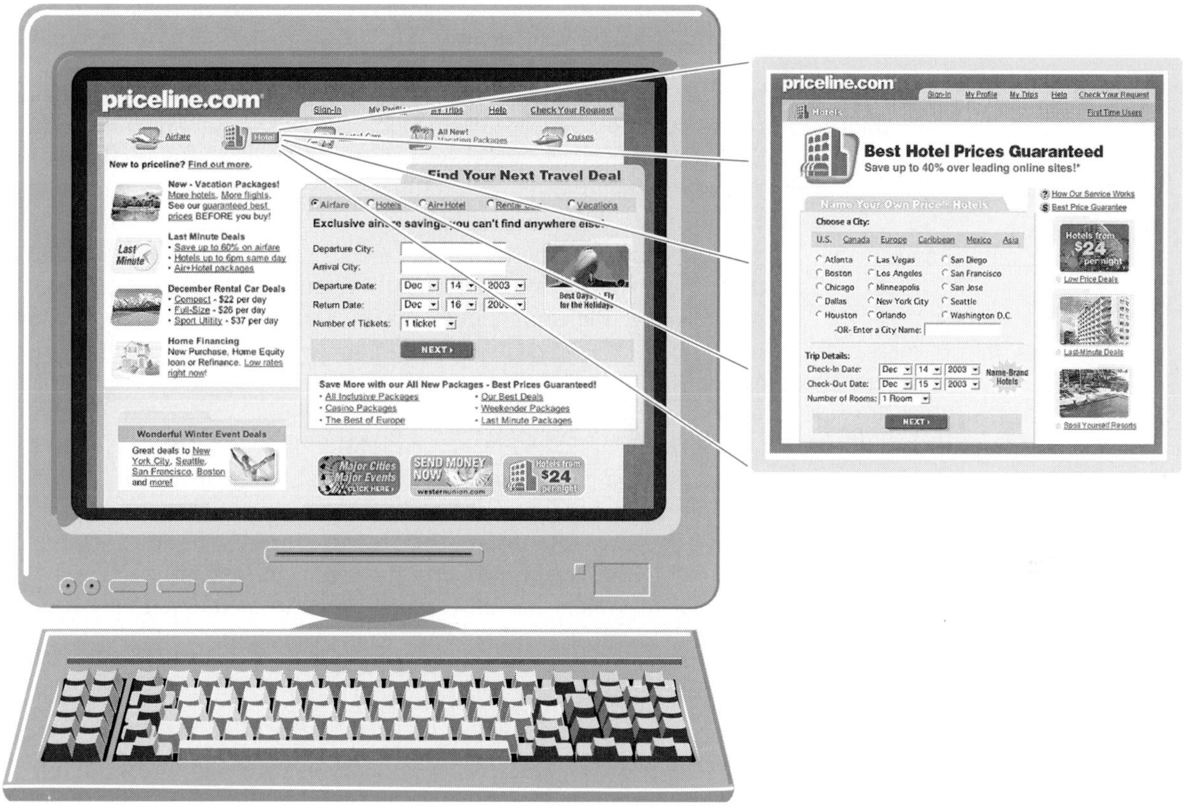

Exhibit 9–9   Since its introduction in 1998, Priceline.com has sold over 7 million hotel rooms through its online auction service. In its own words, here is how the process works:

> Every night, thousands of hotel rooms go unsold throughout the country. That's lost revenue for the hotels, and a great opportunity for priceline customers! Tell us where and when you want to go, select the hotel quality level (1–5 stars), tell us how much you want to pay, and guarantee your request with a major credit card. We'll take your offer to all the participating hotels in the city or area you select (with priceline, you'll always stay in a nationally recognized, name-brand or quality independent hotel). If your offer is accepted, we'll immediately book the room(s) you requested, at the price you want to pay!

Courtesy of priceline.com, Stamford, Connecticut.

Site inspections are also made by association executives, who are considering the property as a possible meeting place. Site visits are comped even though some association executives have been known to abuse the industry standard by using site inspection opportunities to vacation with their families. Comp rates as part of the group's meeting were discussed previously, and these are considered to be acceptable standard practice.

Comps are given to famous persons whose presence has publicity value. Comps are used as promotional tools in connection with contests in which the winners receive so many days of free accommodations. In gambling casinos, comps extend to food, beverage, and even airfare from the player's home. Parking is so difficult in Atlantic City that it too has become part of the high-roller's comp package. After all, in a brief period of table play, a high-roller can lose many times the cost of these promotions, which on close inspection prove to be surprisingly inexpensive.

Posting the Comp.   Internal control of comps is crucial! In most hotels, the night auditor is required to submit a report of comps granted each day and by whom. To that end, the actual room rate is recorded on the registration and marked "COMP." Daily, or at the end of the stay, the charge is removed from the folio with an allowance (see Chapter 10). Under this procedure, a daily room charge is made so that the room and the guest are both counted in the room and house counts. The total allowances at the end of the accounting period provide statement evidence of the cost of comps.

Some casino hotels have the comp paid by a paper transfer to another department (sales, casino, entertainment). The departmental manager has accountability, and the amount of comps appear on that departmental budget.

Recording no value at all is another method for handling free accommodations. No dollar value is charged each day and, therefore, no allowances are required to remove the charges. Neither is a permanent dollar record of comps available. Comps are not usually recorded in room and house counts under this procedure.

The night auditor prepares rate-discrepancy reports for all types of discounts and comps. They are a quick product of a property management system (see Chapter 13). The property management system has all the rack rates in memory. Every room assigned at a special rate is identified and reported to management.

Additional Rate Factors

Not all variations to the rack rate involve discounting. Some factors actually raise the room charge to a premium level above the posted rack rate or charge additional fees of some form or another. Special, high-demand, premium dates (New Year's Eve, for example) may find rooms selling for rates substantially higher than the hotel's normal rack pricing. Likewise, many hotels post additional charges for extra guests occupying the room. Another example of room prices rising above rack rates can be found in long-term group room negotiations. When the group is contracting for rooms to be delivered years into the future, inflationary issues need to be factored into the quoted rate. Other fees or additional charges increasingly evident in the past several years are the energy surcharge, "resort," and other nonroom fees.

▶**Energy and Other Nonroom Surcharges.**   Imagine spending several lovely days at a resort only to find at check-out a $10 per-day "resort fee" on your guest folio. "What is this fee?" you ask the cashier.

She replies, "We add that fee to each room for your convenience. It blends a number of services into one simple price for all rooms." As you wonder what kind of convenient services you're paying for, she continues, "Rather than add a daily fee for the newspaper, health club, and energy your room used, we simply charge $10 to all rooms."

Wow. That seems a bit underhanded—and it may well be. Currently, some states' attorney generals are examining such fees and surcharges under their Deceptive and Unfair Practices Acts.[2] In spite of the perception that these are deceptive practices, many hotels have adopted such charges in recent years.

---

[2]According to *H&MM* magazine, Florida's state attorney general is responding to a number of consumer complaints related to hotel resort fees, energy surcharges, and the like. At issue is whether such charges violate the state's Deceptive and Unfair Practices Act.

Most hotels entered the guest-room surcharge arena with energy surcharges starting in early 2001. You may remember certain states, California especially, were hit with substantial energy price increases during the winter of 2000–2001. For many such hotels, the rapid increase in energy prices was a financial nightmare resulting in 100% and 200% increases in monthly energy expenses. The Hotel del Coronado, for example, saw its $50,000 to $60,000 monthly energy bill rise to more than $200,000 per month. As another example, the Wyndham Hotel in San Diego received a $46,000 energy bill for the month of January 2001. That was substantial when taken in context—the hotel's entire energy cost for all of 2000 was just $96,000! What else could hotels do but pass these charges onto their guests?

Wyndham responded by adding a $3.50 per room-night energy surcharge for California-based hotels and $2.50 for many other Wyndhams across the country. Similarly, Starwood Hotels & Resorts Worldwide implemented a $2 per room-night energy charge across its west coast properties. A month later, it began charging such fees across all its brands (Westin, Sheraton, Four Points, St. Regis, Luxury Collection, and W Hotels) in many of its U.S. locations. Hilton, Crowne Plaza, Holiday Inns, and a multitude of other chains have similarly added energy charges to guest room folios across the country.

Resort Fees and Other Hidden Charges.   Resort fees commonly range from $5 to as high as $25 per day. The logic for such charges is that hotels can conveniently provide a range of complimentary services under one resort fee umbrella. Complimentary? Convenient? Why should guests be asked to pay for items that have historically been provided at no charge? Morning newspapers, in-room coffee, and free local telephone calls are examples of "complimentary" services for which many hotel guests are now charged. Add the health club or spa, fax and business center services, and even swimming pool maintenance, and you round out the list of items commonly included in this "convenient" fee.

The good news about such fees is that they appear to be on the decline. After these fees reached their peak in the early 2000s, many hotels decided energy surcharges, resort, and other nonroom fees are more a nuisance and source of complaint than they are a true revenue source. According to some experts, at its height, 30% of hotels may have charged some type of added service fee. By all estimates, that number is down to about 10% of all hotels. The ratio is likely much higher with resort properties, however.

Wise operators have realized the incremental revenue does not justify the loss of customer goodwill—especially when those complaints usually come at check-out, the last guest experience before exiting the property. Anyway, guests have become increasingly aware of these deceptive charges and are asking for them to be removed from their guest folios. Additionally, groups are aware of hidden fees and ask they not be included in group-rooms pricing. But the biggest factor of all may be the growing potential for legal action. States attorney generals aside, Starwood Hotels was recently hit with a $100 million class-action lawsuit because of its resort fee surcharge. The lawsuit charges the chain with defrauding guests by misrepresenting the resort fee as a type of occupancy tax.

Imagine how guests must have reacted to a now defunct policy at Westin Hotels & Resorts to add a dollar donation for charity to every guest's folio at check-out. Although the program was ostensibly "voluntary," many guests complained that they did not know it was being added and therefore were not able to request the dollar be removed from the folio. The campaign entitled Check-Out for Children was a substantial source of revenue to UNICEF.

➤*Premium Periods.*   Some hotels find themselves in the enviable position of having too much business—too much demand during certain premium periods. These premium periods are generally characterized by a national or regional holiday, major sporting event, or other sizable attraction. For example, when Indianapolis hosts the Indianapolis 500, when New Orleans celebrates the Mardi Gras, or when Los Angeles enjoys the Rose Bowl, hotel rates rise dramatically.

Premium rates are charged when normal demand significantly exceeds room supply. In such cases, hotels have been known to charge several times their standard rack rate. Such rate adjustments may be based on "gut feel" and a knowledge of what other properties are charging, or yield management software may be utilized to assist with the decision-making process.

Indeed, rate alone is not the only adjustment the guest will be forced to accept. Other standard practices include closing specific dates to arrival and requiring certain minimum lengths of stay (see Chapter 4). By carefully following such practices, a manager can extend a sold-out day—say, Super Bowl Sunday—into a sold-out weekend or three-day event.

➤*Double Occupancy.*   Double occupancy refers to the use of the room by a second guest. Traditional rules increase the single-occupancy rate by a factor (normally not twice) whenever the room is double-occupied. However, the price spread between single and double occupancy has been narrowing. One rate for one or two persons is being used more frequently because the major costs of a hotel room are fixed (debt service, taxes, depreciation). Having a second or third occupant adds relatively few incremental costs (linen, soap, tissue). As such, one charge for both single and double occupancy is gaining favor.

Convention rates are almost always negotiated with double occupancy at no extra charge. The more persons in the hotel, the more the hotel benefits from sales in other departments: banquet, bar, casino. Suite charges have also followed that pattern. The room rate is the number of rooms that comprise the suite, not the number of guests who occupy it. The room, not the guest, becomes the unit of pricing.

Several arguments support the movement toward a single room price (see Exhibit 9–10). The fewer the rate options, the less the confusion, and the more rapidly the telephone reservationist can close the sale. Price is a critical issue in package plans or tour bookings, and rates can be shaved closely because the second occupant represents a small additional expense. A third occupant adds a still smaller incremental cost. The incremental cost is almost unnoticed if the extra person(s) share existing beds. That is what makes family-plan rates attractive. An extra charge is levied if a rollaway bed, which requires extra handling and linen, is required. Suite hotels are popular because the extra hide-abed is permanently available as a sofa bed in the room.

With rollaway beds, the used bed is returned to the housekeeping office, where linens are changed and the bed is stored for its next use. With sofa beds, however, the housekeeping department must remember to look at the sofa bed linens after each guest check-out. Guests often use sofa beds during their stay and then fold the sofa bed backup before check-out as a means of straightening the room and creating more floor space. Without careful follow-through by the housekeeping department, new guests can check into a room and find the sofa bed has been previously used.

Unless the family-rate plan has been quoted, a charge is generally made for the third and subsequent occupants to a room. Even in hotels where single and double occupancy is charged the same rate, a third or fourth guest probably pays an additional fee. Usually, that added charge is a flat fee—say, $20 per extra person.

Controversy is growing among American hotelmen about the family rate plan method of basing hotel rates upon occupancy by adults only. Children of 14 years or less, accompanying their parents, are not charged for occupancy of rooms with their parents. For example, one adult and a child are charged a single rate for the double occupancy of the room. Two adults and children are charged a double rate for a room, or two single rates if two rooms are engaged. There are various other modifications of the plan, but fundamentally it represents complimentary accommodation of children below a certain age level.

At least three leading hotel chains have adopted the plan and report great success from the higher occupancy attributable to it. Why, then, the controversy? Certainly when hotel chains of the stature of the Statler, Eppley, and Pick chains favor the family rate plan, it is well on its way to becoming a standard practice for most other hotels in the country.

The controversy rests on the issue of whether this plan is a form of rate cutting—the most disagreeable word in the hotelman's language. In this era of downward adjustment from high wartime levels of occupancy, naturally hotelmen are sensitive to any indirect methods of reducing rates. No hotelman wishes to see any kind of repetition of the rate-cutting practices of the 1930s.

In an attempt to evaluate the plan in its rate-cutting connotation, we believe that most hotelmen would be hardpressed to define a rate cut in exact terms. For example, is the commercial rate to traveling men a type of rate reduction? Does a convention rate involve a hidden discount? We can remember the time when it was standard practice to compliment the wife of a traveling man, when a week's stay at a hotel resulted in having the seventh day free of charge, and when the armed forces, clergy, and diplomats got lower rates.

In our opinion, rate cutting is practiced only when hotels depart from their *regular* prices and tariff schedules in order to secure patronage from prospects who are openly shopping for the best deal in room rates. If, therefore, it is regular practice for hotels to have special rates for group business, this does not seem to represent rate cutting; and the same principle should apply to the family rate plan. If this plan becomes widely adopted—as seems very likely—then it falls into the category of any other special type of rate for special business.

In some respects the plan is a form of *pricing accommodations by rooms instead of by persons*. In many resort hotels a room is rated regardless of its occupancy by one or two persons, and a similar concept is used in apartments and apartment hotels.

Although the arguments for or against the family rate plan must be decided by hotelmen themselves, a strong point in favor of the plan is found in its adoption by other vendors of public service—the railroads and airlines. Family rates, weekday rates, seasonal rates, special-type carrier rates, etc., have been in vogue for several years. If the hotels adopt the family rate plan, it seems that they will be falling into line with a national trend rather than venturing alone into a new and untried experiment in good public relations.

Source: The Horwath Hotel Accountant.

Exhibit 9–10   A circa-1958 article discusses the controversy surrounding the family-rate plan. The article states "the plan is a form of pricing accommodations by rooms instead of by persons." Note in the third paragraph that rate-cutting (i.e., discounting) is referred to as "the most disagreeable word in the hotelman's language." Also note the names of old chains that are no longer in business.

Many hoteliers find a flat $20 fee illogical in light of the numerous room types available at the property. Where $20 may be fine for a $100 standard room, it does not seem high enough for a $150 deluxe or a $200 executive parlor. Indeed, if the hotelier can make the argument that we charge for extra guests because they cost the hotel incremental expenses, that argument is doubly true in premium rooms.

In a standard room, extra guests (whether the second, third, or fourth occupant) cost the hotel in a variety of ways, including extra water and electricity, additional amenities, more towels and linens, and of course some wear and tear. These costs are not identical from a standard room to a deluxe accommodation. Hotels outfit deluxe rooms with larger bathtubs, more expensive personal amenities, heavier-quality linens, and higher-quality furnishings. An additional person in a deluxe room has a higher incremental cost to the hotel than does an additional person in a standard room.

A flat $20 rate represents a declining percentage of the rate as the quality of the room increases. In the $100 standard, $20 reflects a 20% surcharge. Yet in the $200 executive parlor, $20 reflects only a 10% surcharge. In fact, if the $100 standard guest is willing to pay $20 for an extra occupant, it makes sense that the $200 executive-parlor guest would be equally willing to pay something like $40 for an extra guest.

Time is Money

While the actual date of arrival and departure is the primary consideration for establishing the guest charge, the number of hours of occupancy may someday play a role in rate determination. In simple terms, time is already a rate criterion in many hotels.

▶ *Arrival Time.* The day of arrival is listed on the reservation, the registration card, and the guest folio. The time of arrival is also indicated on the folio by means of an internal electronic clock operating in the property management system. Assuming that the clock is accurate, the actual minute of check in is recorded on the electronic folio.

The actual time of arrival is more critical to the American plan hotel, where billing is partially based on meals taken, than to the European plan operation. American plan arrivals are flagged with a special meal code.

The hour of arrival at a European plan hotel is less critical. An occasional complaint about the promptness of message service or a rare police inquiry might involve the arrival hour. Very, very late arrivals, such as a guest who arrives at 5 AM are the exceptions. Somewhere in the early morning hours (5 to 7 AM) comes the break between charging for the night just passed and levying the first charge for the day just starting.

Check-in hours are difficult to control. Guest arrivals are dictated haphazardly by travel connections and varying distances. Still, many hotels have established check-in hours. The termination point of a night's lodging is more controllable, so every hotel posts an official check-out hour (see Exhibit 9–11).

▶ *Departure Time.* Check-in and check-out hours are eased or enforced as occupancies fall or rise. Setting the specific check-out hour is left to each hotel. It might be established without any rationale, or it might be the same hour that nearby competitors are using. The proper hour is a balance between the guest's need to complete his or her business and the hotel's need to clean and prepare the room for the next patron.

Seasoned travelers are well aware that check-out extensions are granted by the room clerk if occupancy is light. Under current billing practices, the effort should be made cheerfully whenever the request can be accommodated. If anticipated arrivals require enforcement of the check-out hour, luggage should be stored in the checkroom for the guest's convenience.

Exhibit 9–11
Permanent bureau tent card left in each guest room. Many hotels place a similar statement on the registration card.

CHECK-OUT TIME: 1 PM

We would like to ask your cooperation in checking out by 1 PM so that we may accommodate travelers who are beginning their stay. If you require additional time, you may request a two-hour grace period (until 3 PM) from the assistant manager or the front-office manager. If you wish to check out later, we regret that there must be a $12-per-hour charge, from 3 until 5 PM, for this added service. An additional half-day rate will be charged to guests who delay their departure until between 5 PM and 8 PM. After 8 PM, a full-day rate will be charged. Of course, you are then welcome to remain until the following afternoon at 1 PM.

As an incoming guest, your comfort and convenience depend on these stipulations. We hope you will visit again soon.

Resorts are under more pressure than commercial hotels to expedite check outs. Vacationing guests try to squeeze the most from their holiday time. American plan houses usually allow the guest to remain through the luncheon hour and a reasonable time thereafter if the meal is part of the rate. Some 90% of the resorts surveyed in an AH&LA study identified their check-out hour to be between noon and 2 PM, in contrast to the 11 AM through 1 PM range used by transient hotels. These same properties assigned new arrivals on a "when-available" basis.

Special techniques in addition to that shown in Exhibit 9–11 have been tried to move the guest along. On the night before departure, the room clerk, the assistant manager, or the social host(ess) calls the room to chat and remind the guest of tomorrow's departure. Even today, this task could be assigned to a computer. A more personal touch is a note of farewell left by the room attendant who turns down the bed the night before. A less personal touch can be seen in Exhibit 9–12.

The 24-Hour Stay. Recently, some hotels have been experimenting with true 24-hour stays. There is no official check-in time and no posted check-out hour. Rather, guests explain their travel plans at the time of reservation and identify their estimated times of arrival and departure. They are then welcome to stay at the hotel an entire 24-hour period for one set room rate.

To qualify for these 24-hour programs, guests must make advance reservations and identify their estimated hours of arrival and departure at the time they make the reservation. Additionally, guests must pay rack rate—discounted packages do not qualify for the 24-hour programs.

Recently, while staying at one of the San Antonio Marriotts, I had occasion to make this request. I would be in meetings all morning, and I wasn't scheduled to leave until 3 PM. I figured I could have lunch, go back to my room and dig out my winter coat and boots, then check out.

The night before I was to leave, I made my request. The clerk asked me what time I wanted to check out. "Three o'clock," I answered.

"You can stay until three, but we'll charge you for a half-day," he said.

At first, I was stunned by the sheer greed this response implied. When I recovered, I asked whether this was an arbitrary decision on his part or a policy of the hotel.

"It's our policy," he said, defensively.

"Is it a *new* policy?" I responded, trying to keep a smile on my face, "because I've never heard of such a thing."

"No, it's not new, and I don't know what kind of hotels you've been staying in, but it's very common."

First deny my simple request, then try a subtle insult. Good thinking.

This kind of treatment would probably have bothered me in any hotel, but it seemed terribly out of place at a hotel with an otherwise extraordinarily friendly and accommodating staff.

The next day, I visited the front desk, posed the same request—hypothetically—to a different employee, and asked how he would handle it. He said he would ask how late, check to see if the room was booked, and possibly okay it based on whatever information he got from the reservations system. If he wasn't sure, he would check with someone in the back office, and they would most likely okay it. Standard operating procedure, in my experience.

Exhibit 9–12   This excerpt from "The Late Check-Out" in the March 1997 issue of *Lodging Hospitality* plays off a vague set of policies that plague our industry. Is it okay to check out late—certainly. But not too late. In most hotels, permission to check out a bit later, say 2 PM, is readily forthcoming. But 3 PM, and worse yet, 4 PM, are somehow far more difficult to attain in almost all hotels! When asked why, front-desk receptionists often respond, "Our housekeeping department goes home at that hour," or "We have your room reserved for another arrival," or similar such comments. *Written by Megan Rowe, Senior Editor, and used with permission.*

The logic behind such rate/time programs becomes more evident when you realize these programs are most likely found at airport properties. Guest arrivals (and departures) are predicated on flight schedules. As such, a hotel that will accommodate guests' unique 24-hour stays may develop a favorable reputation and earn higher market share.

Therefore, it makes sense to view these 24-hour day programs as marketing tools. They drive higher rates and hopefully attract unique customer segments who appreciate the unusual policy. Today, these programs are viewed as marketing "gimmicks," but so are any policies that differentiate a hotel from its competitor. Only time will tell if these programs are ushering in a new era of room pricing.

Incentive Rate Systems.   Incentive rate systems have been suggested as a means of expediting check outs. First, the check-out period for a normal day's charge would be established—say, between 11 AM and 1 PM. Guests who leave before 11 AM are charged less than the standard rate, and those who remain beyond 1 PM are charged more. Flexible charges of this type require a new look at the unit of service, shifting from the more traditional measure of a night's lodging to smaller blocks of time.

Unlike other service industries, hotels have given little consideration to time as a factor in rate. Arrival and departure times establish broad parameters at best. We can expect these to narrow as hotelkeepers become more concerned with the role of time in rate structuring. Taken to the other extreme, it is conceivable that the hour will eventually become the basic unit for constructing room rates. Under current practices, a stay of several hours costs as much as a full day's stay (see Exhibit 9–13).

The total length of stay may also be an issue in the guest's level of satisfaction with the hotel. Guests with few hours to visit scarcely get enough time to sleep and bathe. It is the guest with sufficient leisure hours who truly enjoys the property by taking advantage of relaxation and recreational activities (see Exhibit 9–13).

A popular journalist once observed facetiously that the length of time one spends in a hotel room is inversely proportional to the quality of that hotel room.

Guest	Rate Paid	March 15th Arrival	March 16 Departure	Total Hours Occupied
1	$225.00	1 AM (March 16)	Until 6 AM	5 Hours
2	225.00	2 PM	Until 11 AM	21 Hours
3	225.00	8 AM	Until 3 PM	31 Hours

Exhibit 9–13   Shown are three different hotel room utilization schedules. Three guests, facing substantially different travel schedules, have three unique hotel experiences. Even though each guest pays the same $225 rate, they experience three significantly different lengths of stay.

The first guest flies in very late (1 AM) and is forced to check out early the next morning (6 AM) to catch a connecting flight. The second guest exactly parallels the hotel's standard check-in and check-out times by arriving at 2 PM and checking out the next day at 11 AM. The third guest has nothing but time on his hands. By taking advantage of light occupancy and normal front-office courtesies, he asks for an early check-in (at 8 AM) and an extended late check-out (3 PM—see Exhibit 9–12).

No wonder hotels are looking more closely at hours occupied as one variable in establishing rate. These three guests paid the same rate, yet one guest occupied the room 620% more hours than another!

When you arrive at, say, 1 AM and need to get some rest for a 7 AM flight the next morning, the room will be lavish—there will be vases of roses, trays of food and drink, soft music, a Jacuzzi tub, and candlelight. Conversely, when you have no time commitments and all day to spend in the hotel, it is invariably a poor-quality establishment—there will be no restaurant or lobby, fuzzy TV reception, and a drained swimming pool!

➤*The American Plan Day.*   Meals are part of the American plan (AP) rate, as they are with the modified American plan (MAP). Accurate billing requires an accurate record of arrival and departure times. Arrivals are registered with a meal code reflecting the check-in time. For example, a guest arriving at 3 PM would be coded with arriving after lunch but before dinner.

A complete AP stay technically involves enough meals on the final day to make up for the meals missed on the arriving day. A guest arriving before dinner would be expected to depart the next day, or many days later, after lunch. Two meals, breakfast and lunch, on the departing day complete the full AP charge, since one meal, dinner, was taken on the arriving day. MAP counts meals in the same manner, except that lunch is ignored.

Guests who take more than the three meals per day pay for the extra at menu prices, or sometimes below. Sometimes, guests who miss a meal are not charged. That is why it is very important to have the total AP rate fairly distributed between the room portion and the meal portion. Meal rates are set and are standardized for everyone. Higher AP rates must reflect better rooms, since all the guests are entitled to the same menu.

AP and MAP hotels have a special charge called *tray service*. It is levied on meals taken through room service. European plan room service typically contains hidden charges or inflated prices as a means of recovering the extra service. Menu charges are greater than the usual coffee shop prices when the food is delivered to the room. This device is not available to the American plan hotel because meals being delivered to the room are not priced separately. Instead, a flat charge of several dollars per person is levied as a tray service charge.

➤*Day Rate Rooms.*   Special rates exist for stays of less than overnight. These are called *part-day rates, day rates*, or sometimes *use rates*. Day rate guests arrive and depart on the same day.

Day rates obviously make possible an occupancy of greater than 100%. Furthermore, the costs are low. Nevertheless, the industry has not fully exploited the possibilities. Sales of use rates could be marketed to suburban shoppers and to small, brief meetings. Unfortunately, better airline service has cost hotels day rate business, although capsule rooms at international airports have had some success. Airport properties have promoted their locations as central meeting places for company representatives coming from different sections of the country.

A new day rate market is becoming evident. Motels near campsites and along the roadways are attracting campers as a wayside stop during the day. A hot shower, an afternoon by the pool, and a change of pace from the vehicle are great appeals when coupled with the low day rate.

Check-in time is often early morning. Corporate guests prefer to start their meetings early, and truck drivers like to get off the highway before the 8 AM rush hour. If clean rooms remain unsold from the previous night, there is little reason to refuse day rate guests early access to the room. Indeed, they may order room-service coffee or breakfast as an added revenue bonus.

Since rooms sold for day use only are serviced and made available again for the usual overnight occupancy, the schedule of the housekeeping staff has a great deal to do with the check-out hour. If there are no night room cleaners, the day rate must end early enough to allow room servicing by the day crew. On the other hand, low occupancy would allow a day rate sale even late in the day. Nothing is lost if an additional empty room remains unmade overnight.

There are no rules as to what the hotel should charge for the day room. Some purists suggest that it must be half the standard rack rate. Others appreciate the extra revenue and are willing to charge whatever seems appropriate. Corporate hotels must remember that their day rate rooms compete with their convention and meeting facilities. A small group of executives might prefer meeting in the day rate guest room with its attached bathroom and access to room service rather than the larger impersonal convention meeting room. This can prove detrimental to the hotel if the meeting room sells for two or three times the day rate room.

➤ DETERMINING THE PROPER ROOM RATE

Because a sound room rate structure is fundamental to a profitable hotel operation, every manager is sooner or later faced with the question of what is the proper room charge. It is a matter of exceeding complexity because room rates reflect markets and costs, investments and rates of return, supply and demand, accommodations and competition, and not least of all, the quality of management.

Divided into its two major components, room rates must be large enough to cover costs and a fair return on invested capital, and reasonable enough to attract and retain the clientele to whom the operation is being marketed. The former suggests a relatively objective, structured approach that can be analyzed after the fact. The latter is more subjective, involving factors such as the amount of local competition and the condition of the economy at large. There is little sense in charging a rate less than what is needed to meet the first objective; there is little chance of getting a rate more than the competitive ceiling established by the second limitation.

Yield management, the balancing of occupancy and rate, has emerged as the number one component of rate making. Yield management has attracted attention because it introduces two new concepts to room pricing: (1) the industry is selling rooms by an inventory control system for the first time, and (2) the pricing strategy considers for the first time the customer's ability and willingness to pay. This discretionary market, with a sensitivity to price, is itself a new phenomenon (see Chapter 4).

In years past, the rate structure was built from the standpoint of internal cost considerations. Yield management has not eliminated that focus. Important as they are, customers are not the only components of price. Cost recovery and investment opportunity are reflected there as well. Depreciation and interest as well as taxes and land costs are outside the hotel–guest relationship but not external to the room charge.

The more traditional components of rate deal with recovering costs, both operating and capital. They deal with profits and break-even projections. Mixed into the equation are competition, price elasticity, and rate cutting. And in the end, the average daily rate earned by the hotel is partly determined by the ability of a reservationist or room clerk to sell up.

Traditional Rate Calculations

Hotel room rates are derived from a mix of objective measures and subjective values. Expressing room rates numerically gives the appearance of validity, but when the origins of these numbers are best-guess estimates, the results must be viewed with some measure of doubt or uncertainty.

Facts and suppositions combine together when hotel managers calculate the required room rate. As useful and respected as the following mathematical formulas may be, they are still merely an indication of the final rate. Fine-tuning the formula, establishing corporate and double occupancy prices, and adjusting the rate according to the whims of the community and the marketplace are still the role of management.

➤ ***The Hubbart Room Rate Formula.***   The Hubbart room rate formula[3] offers a standardized approach to calculating room rates. The Hubbart formula sets rates from the needs of the enterprise and not from the needs of the guests. The average rate, says the formula, should pay all expenses and leave something for the investor. Valid enough—a business that cannot do this is short-lived.

Exhibit 9–14a illustrates the mechanics of the formula. Estimated expenses are itemized and totaled. These include operational expenses by departments ($1,102,800 in the illustration), realty costs ($273,000), and depreciation ($294,750). To these expenses is added a reasonable return on the present fair value of the property: land, building, and furnishings ($414,000). From the total expense package ($2,084,550) are subtracted incomes from all sources other than room sales ($139,200). This difference ($1,945,350) represents the annual amount to be realized from room sales.

Next (see Exhibit 9–14b), an estimate of the number of rooms to be sold annually is computed. Dividing the number of estimated rooms (22,484) to be sold annually into the estimated dollars ($1,945,350) needed to cover costs and a fair return produces the average rate to be charged ($86.52). The computations are simple enough; the formula is straightforward enough. Deriving the many estimates is where the weakness lies.

Shortcomings of the Formula.   Like many such calculations, the Hubbart room rate formula is only as accurate as the assumptions on which it was projected. Several such assumptions come immediately to mind for the Hubbart formula: What percentage is "reasonable" as a fair return on investment? What occupancy rate appears most attainable? What are the cost projections for payroll, various operating departments, utilities, and administrative and general?

The formula leaves the rooms department with the final burden after profits and losses from other departments. But inefficiencies in other departments should not be covered by a high, noncompetitive room rate. Neither should unusual profits in other departments be a basis for charging room rates below what the market will bring.

There is some justification in having rooms subsidize low banquet prices if these low prices result in large convention bookings of guest rooms. (Incidentally, this is one reason why the food and banquet department should not be leased as a concession.) Similar justification could be found for using higher room rates to cover unusually high dining-room repairs and maintenance, or advertising costs. The trade-off is wise if these expenditures produce enough other business to offset lost room revenue resulting from higher room rates.

---

[3]*The Hubbart Formula for Evaluating Rate Structures of Hotel Rooms*, 1952, is available from the American Hotel & Lodging Association, 1201 New York Avenue, NW, Suite 600, Washington, D.C. 20005, and is used here with the association's permission.

				Example
Operating Expenses				
Rooms department				$467,400
Telecommunications				60,900
Administrative and general				91,200
Payroll taxes and employee benefits				178,200
Marketing, advertising, and promotion				109,800
Utility costs				138,900
Property operation, maintenance, and engineering				56,400
Total operating expenses				$1,102,800
Taxes, Insurance, and Leases				
Real estate and personal property taxes				67,200
Franchise taxes and fees				112,200
Insurance on building and contents				37,200
Leased equipment				56,400
Total taxes, insurance, and leases				$ 273,000
Depreciation (Standard Rates on Present Fair Value)	*Value*	*Rate*		
Building	$_____ at	_____ %		168,750
Furniture, fixtures, and equipment	$_____ at	_____ %		126,000
Total depreciation				$294,750
Reasonable Return on Present Fair Value of Property	*Value*	*Rate*		
Land	$_____ at	_____ %		
Building	$_____ at	_____ %		
Furniture, fixtures, and equipment	$_____ at	_____ %		
Total fair return				$ 414,000
Total				$2,084,550
Deduct—Credits from Sources Other Than Rooms				
Income from store rentals				14,850
Profits from food and beverage operations (if loss, subtract from this group)				131,400
Net income from other operated departments and miscellaneous income (loss)				(7,050)
Total credits from sources other than rooms				$ 139,200
Amount to be realized from guest-room sales to cover costs and a reasonable return on present fair value of property				$1,945,350

(a)

Exhibit 9–14a

	Example	
1. Amount to be realized from guest-room sales to cover costs and a reasonable return on present fair value of property [from part (a)]		$1,945,350
2. Number of guest rooms available for rental		88
3. Number of available rooms on annual basis (item 2 multiplied by 365)	100%	32,120
4. Less: Allowance for average vacancies	30%	9,636
5. Number of rooms to be occupied at estimated average occupancy	70%	22,484
6. Average daily rate per occupied room required to cover costs and a reasonable return on present fair value (item 1 divided by item 5)		$ 86.52

(b)

Exhibit 9–14 (a) Although the Hubbart room rate formula was first introduced in 1952, it is still the most widely used means of computing zero-based room rates. By dividing annual fixed costs, variable expenses, and a reasonable return on the property by the estimated number of rooms projected to be sold for the year, the Hubbart formula provides a fairly reliable minimum average rate calculation.
(b) Computing the denominator, the estimated number of rooms to be sold for the year, requires an occupancy projection. But it is difficult to project the occupancy before one knows the average rate to be charged—a real conundrum! *Courtesy of the American Hotel & Lodging Association, Washington, D.C.*

Additional shortcomings become apparent as the formula is studied. Among them is the projected number of rooms sold. This estimate of rooms sold is itself a function of the very rate being computed. How can a hotel estimate the number of rooms it will sell before first knowing the average rate for which it will sell each room—yet that is exactly what the Hubbart formula requires! Rate, in turn, is a function of double occupancy. Yet the increased income from double occupancy is not a component of the Hubbart formula. Neither component (the impact of rate on occupancy and the impact of double occupancy on rate) is projected.

The average rate that is computed ($86.52) is not the actual rate used by the hotel. Hotels use a number of rate classes, with various proportions of the total number of rooms assigned to each classification (see Exhibit 9–7). The actual average rate will be a weighted average of the rooms occupied. Reflected therein are the range of accommodations the hotel is offering and the guest's purchase of them based on nearby competition.

Square Foot Calculations. To compensate for the fact that the Hubbart room rate formula provides no rate detail by room type classification, some managers use a square foot calculation. The basis for this is the fact that more expensive and higher-quality guest rooms are invariably larger than standard rooms at the same property. Therefore, rather than calculating the Hubbart room rate per room sold, this variation calculates the rate on a per-square-foot basis.

To illustrate, assume that the hotel presented in Exhibit 9–14 has a total of 27,250 square feet of space in its 88 guest rooms. With occupancy of 70%, there would be an average of 19,075 square feet sold per day. With an annual required return of $1,945,350, the daily required return is $5,329.73 ($1,945,350 divided by 365 days). Therefore, each square foot of rented room space must generate $0.27941 per day ($5,329.73 divided by 19,075 square feet sold per day) or almost 28 cents in daily revenue. As a result, a 300-square-foot room would sell for $83.82 (300 square feet times $0.28) and a 450-square-foot room would sell for $125.73. Assuming that the hotel sells all room types in equal ratios to the number of rooms available in each type, this square foot calculation works as well as any other means for determining individual room type rates.

➤*The Building Cost Room Rate Formula.*   Time and repetition have created an industry axiom saying that rate can be evaluated by a simple rule of thumb (the building cost rate formula): The average room rate should equal $1 per $1,000 of construction cost. For a 200-room hotel costing $14 million (including land and land development, building, and public space but excluding furniture, fixtures, and equipment), the average rate should be $70 ($14 million ÷ 200 rooms ÷ $1,000).

The building cost yardstick is about as reliable as an old cookbook's direction to the chef: "Flavor to taste." Despite some very radical changes throughout the years, the rule is still being quoted on the theory that rising construction costs are being matched by rising room rates. Higher construction costs are a function of room size as well as building materials and labor. This generation of rooms is 100 to 200% larger than rooms were even 25 or 30 years ago.

Cost of construction (including the costs of land and land improvement) includes other factors: type of construction, location, high-rise versus low-rise buildings, and the cost of money. Luxury properties can cost five or six times as much per room as economy hotels. Land costs vary greatly across the nation. Comparing California and Arkansas is a lesson in futility. New York City may be stretching toward a $400 per-night room rate, but that is not the expectation of the manager in Dubuque, Iowa.

Economy chains have stopped advertising a minimum national rate. Each locale has its own cost basis for building, borrowing, taxing, and paying labor. Budgets aim only for a percentage rate below that of local competitors. Advertising a single rate as part of the national company logo is no longer feasible.

Increases in room construction costs are startling. Marriott's typical room cost runs between $100,000 and $200,000 today. Its figure was $8,000 in 1957. Consider what has happened in Hawaii over 20 years. Twenty years after the Mauna Kea was built at $100,000 per room, it was sold at $1 million per room! And the hotel was two decades older by that time.

The situation is the same in New York. Regent Hotels, a superluxury chain, has a 400-room hotel in New York with an average cost of $750,000 per room. With an actual average daily rate in the $400-range, the hotel is far from the $750 ADR dictated by the rule-of-thumb standard.[4]

---

[4]Although the business world regularly uses the term *rule of thumb* to denote an industry standard, one origin of this term is far from being politically correct. The expression may derive from Anglo-Saxon common law, where little more than 100 years ago, a man's wife and children were his personal property, his chattel. If he was so motivated, he could beat them, as long as the weapon he used was no larger in diameter than his thumb—hence one possible origin of the phrase.

Another origin is that of a unit of measure. The length of the thumb from knuckle to tip of a 10th Century English king named Edgar the Peaceful was a unit of measure (roughly an inch)—hence the other common explanation of the term.

The Hotel Bel-Air in Los Angeles is another hotel that breaks the mold. With only 92 rooms, the property sold for a record $110 million (or approximately $1.2 million per room) to a Japanese hotel concern. Despite its incredibly high average daily rate (about $400), the hotel earns far less than the $1,196 per average room-night that the building cost rate formula dictates.

These examples are special cases of "trophy hotels." Viewing the trophy as an art asset, which gives satisfaction and pleasure to the owner, offers some perspective on the price. Like an art piece, these eyebrow-raising prices are justified as long-term investments and by their uniqueness (location). In retrospect, the excessive prices of a generation ago have proven to be good deals.

In fact, no one actually expected the Japanese hotel company that purchased the Hotel Bel-Air to make an operating profit. Profit, if any, would come from selling the resort several years down the road. The Japanese buyer was one of four interested parties willing to bid in excess of $1 million per room for the Hotel Bel-Air. And the company that sold the hotel made an enormous profit, having purchased it just seven years earlier for $22.7 million.

Trophy hotels are extreme examples that do not set the rule for the remainder of the industry. With economy hotels costing less than $50,000 per room, and standard properties less than $80,000 per room, advocates of the rule take heart. Lower costs and lower rate figures maintain the spread between actual rate and rule-of-thumb rate close enough to keep the rule alive.

Conditions seesaw, first supporting the rule and then undermining it. The general rise in land and construction costs has been offset by improvements in design and reductions in labor force. The rise in financing costs has been offset by the lower costs of older hotels still in use. Since building costs are tied to historical prices, older hotels have lower financing costs (and probably lower real estate taxes, too) to recover. That is true, at least, until they're sold.

The building cost formula, a standard whose first known reference was in 1947, is still as roughly accurate today as it probably was back then.[5]

The Cost of Renovation.   The costs of additions, property rehabs, or new amenities such as swimming pools fall within the scope of the $1 per $1,000 rule. First, the cost of the upgrade is determined on a per room basis. The installation of an in-room air-conditioner might be priced at $1,500 per room. A general-use item such as a sauna would need a per room equivalent. The cost (assume $150,000) would be divided by the number of rooms (100) to arrive at the per unit cost.

Exhibit 9–15 illustrates an example of a major hotel renovation program. This exhibit assumes that a 200-room hotel spends $1,303,240 renovating its rooms, for an average cost of $6,516.20 per room. The problem assumes the hotel has a 12% cost of funds (interest rate). With a $6,516.20 expense per room at 12% interest and 15 years of debt repayment, $956.74 is the annualized cost of principal and interest

---

[5]An August 1995 letter to the editor of the *Cornell Hotel and Restaurant Administration Quarterly* stated that the earliest reference the author (Bjorn Hanson) could find was a 1947 publication of the *Horwath Accountant* (a newsletter from a now defunct accounting firm). The author of this newsletter (Louis Toth) stated that for the $1 per $1,000 rule of thumb to work, several things needed to be in place: (1) The rule referred only to the cost of the building, not the entire project; (2) the hotel needed to receive rents from concessionaries to cover debt service and taxes on the land itself; (3) the hotel needed a 70% occupancy; (4) the cost of FF&E could be no more than 20% of the cost of the building; and (5) income before fixed charges must be at least 55% of room sales.

1. Renovation Project Parameters

	Guest rooms: Cost per Room	Hallways: Cost per Door	Meeting Space: Cost per Square Foot	Lobby: Cost per Square Foot	F&B Outlets: Cost per Seat	Total Project
Soft costs[a]	$ 515	$ 194	$ 2	$ 3	$ 212	N/A
Hard costs[b]	3,305	755	5	18	1,342	N/A
Subtotals	$764,000	$189,800	$105,000	$73,500	$170,940	$1,303,240

2. Basic Hotel Information

- A 200-room full-service airport hotel
- 15,000 square feet of convention space
- 3,500 square feet of lobby space
- One 110-seat restaurant and bar
- 12% cost of funds interest rate
- Total renovation cost $1,303,240 (as shown above)

3. Project Cost per Average Guest Room

- $1,303,240 project divided by 200 rooms equals $6,516.20 per room.
- Assume that the $6,516.20 project cost per average room is to be repaid over 15 years at a 12% cost of funds rate.
- The combined principal and interest charge is $956.74 per room per year.

4. Impact of the Building Cost Room Rate Formula

- The $956.74 annualized cost per average room divided by $1,000 rule-of-thumb formula equals $0.96 increase per average room night sold.

---

[a]Soft costs include professional and contractor fees, sales tax, and shipping fees.
[b]Hard costs include construction costs, labor, materials, and all FF&E.

Exhibit 9–15   Figures developed in this exhibit come from an actual renovation project of a 200-room full-service hotel. Applying the $1 per $1,000 building-cost room-rate formula standard to this project results in roughly an added $0.96 in required per-room revenue.

per room per year. Therefore, the rule of thumb established in the building cost rate formula suggests that the hotel needs to charge an additional $0.96 per occupied room-night to compensate for the expense incurred when renovating its facility. With that kind of information, management can evaluate the likelihood of the additional investment being competitive in the eyes of the guest who is asked to pay the increased price.

➤*The Ideal Average Room Rate.*   The firm of Laventhol & Horwath designed the ideal average room rate as a means of testing the room rate structure. Although the L & H accounting firm is no longer in business, its ideal average room rate lives on. According to this approach, the hotel should sell an equal percentage of rooms in each rate class instead of filling from the bottom up. A 70% occupancy should mean a 70% occupancy in each rate category. Such a spread produces an average rate identical to the average rate earned when the hotel is completely full—that is, an ideal room rate.

Exhibit 9–16 illustrates the computation used to derive the ideal rate. This formula assumes that each room type (standard, executive, deluxe, and suite) fills to the same percentage of rooms sold as every other room type. Again, at a 70% hotel occupancy, 70% of the standard rooms will be sold, 70% of the executive rooms will be sold, 70% of the deluxe rooms will be sold, and 70% of the suites will be sold.

Once calculated, the manager is armed with a valuable figure, the ideal average room rate. As long as rates remain constant and the ratio of double occupancy does not change, the manager has a valid ideal rate. If the actual average rate on any given day or week is higher than the ideal average rate, the front-office staff has been doing a great job of up-selling guests. Either that, or the hotel has failed to provide a proper number of high-priced rooms. Such a hotel's market may be interested in rooms selling above the average, so room types and rates may need to be adjusted upward.

An average room rate lower than the ideal, and this is usually the case, indicates several problems. There may not be enough contrast between the low- and the high-priced rooms. Guests will take the lower rate when they are buying nothing extra for the higher rate. If the better rooms do, in fact, have certain extras—better exposure and newer furnishings—the lack of contrast between the rate categories might simply be a matter of poor selling at the front desk (discussed later in the chapter).

Check in at the front desk represents the last opportunity to up-sell the guest to a more expensive room accommodation. Good salesmanship coupled with a differentiated product gives the hotel a strong chance to increase middle-and high-priced room sales. Such comments as "I see you have reserved our standard room; do you realize for just 12 more dollars I can place you in a newly refurbished deluxe room with a complimentary continental breakfast?" go a long way toward satisfying both the guest and the bottom line.

A faulty internal rate structure is another reason that the ideal room rate might not be achieved. The options, the range of rates being offered, might not appeal to the customer. Using the ideal room rate computation, the spread between rates could be adjusted. According to the authors of the formula, increases should be concentrated in those rooms on those days for which the demand is highest. That begins with an analysis of rate categories.

Rate Categories.   The discrepancy between the rates the hotel offers and those the guests prefer can be pinpointed with a simple chart. Guest demands and the hotel offerings are plotted side by side.

Room Type	Number Rooms by Type	Percent of Double Occupancy	Single Rate	Double Rate
Standard	140	30	$ 80	$ 95
Executive	160	5	105	105
Deluxe	100	25	120	140
Suite	75	70	160	160
Total rooms	475			

Calculation Steps

1. Multiply all standard rooms (140) by their single rate ($80) to get a product of $11,200. Then take the double occupancy percentage for standard rooms (30%) times the total number of standard rooms (140) to get 42, the number of double-occupied standard rooms. Next, take the 42 double-occupied standard rooms times the differential between the single and double price ($95 double rate minus $80 single rate equals $15 differential) to get $630. Finally, add the room revenue for standard rooms calculated at the single rate ($11,200) to the additional room revenue received from standard rooms sold at the double rate ($630) to get the full-house room revenue for standard rooms, a total of $11,830.

2. Follow the same procedure for executive rooms: 160 rooms times $105 equals $16,800. The differential between single and double occupancy for executive rooms is zero, so there is no added revenue for double occupancy. The full-house room revenue for executive rooms is $16,800.

3. Follow the same procedure for deluxe rooms: 100 rooms times $120 single rate equals $12,000. In terms of double occupancy, there are 25 deluxe rooms (25% double occupancy times 100 rooms equals 25 rooms) sold at a $20 differential ($140 double rate minus $120 single rate equals $20 differential) for a total double occupancy impact of $500. The full-house room revenue for deluxe rooms is $12,500.

4. Follow the same procedure for suites: 75 rooms times $160 equals $12,000. The differential between single and double occupancy for suites is zero, so there is no added revenue for double occupancy. The full-house room revenue for suites is $12,000.

5. Add total revenues from standard rooms ($11,830), executive rooms ($16,800), deluxe rooms ($12,500), and suites ($12,000) for total revenues assuming 100% occupancy—ideal revenues. That total ($53,130) divided by rooms sold (475) is the ideal average room rate of $111.85.

No matter what the occupancy percentage, the ideal average room rate remains the same.

Try this problem again, assuming, say, 70 percent occupancy. The end result will still be an ideal average room rate of $111.85.

Exhibit 9–16   Although Laventhol & Horwath, the firm who first developed the ideal average room rate, is no longer in business, the formula remains viable. Follow these steps to develop an ideal average room rate for any hotel. *Courtesy of Laventhol & Horwath, Philadelphia.*

Guest demands are determined by a survey of registration card rates over a period of time. The survey should not include days of 100% occupancy when the guest had no rate choice. Special rate situations would also be excluded. Using elementary arithmetic, the percentage of total registrations is determined for each rate class. Exhibit 9–17 illustrates the contrast between what the guest buys and what the hotel offers. It also points to the rates that need adjustment.

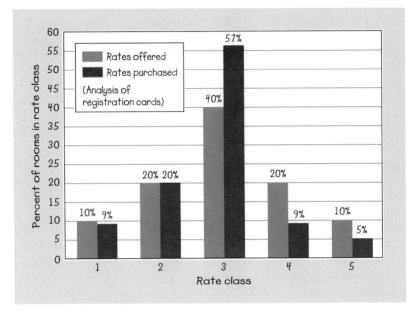

Exhibit 9–17   An analysis of registration cards, over a period of time, will reveal which room rates are purchased most regularly. This sample hotel has five rate classes, representing 10%, 20%, 40%, 20%, and 10% of all hotel rooms respectively. However, an analysis of rates purchased suggests a disproportionate percentage of guests opt for class 3 (and fewer guests than expected choose classes 4 and 5).

Exhibit 9–17 assigns 40% of the hypothetical hotel to the median room rate. Two additional categories of 20% and 10%, respectively, appear on both the lower and upper ends. It is the sad history of our industry that hotels fill from the bottom up. Lower-priced rooms are in greatest demand. This means that low occupancy is accompanied by a low average daily rate. It is felt, therefore, that there should be more categories at the lower end of the price scale. These lower categories would be bunched together, while the higher rates would be spread over fewer categories. That might be the reason that Hilton advises its franchises to concentrate on the minimum single rate as the key in competition.

▶*Up-selling Premium Accommodations.*   The room rate policy faces a moment of truth when the front-office employee and the buying public come face to face. Fashioning a room rate policy is a futile exercise unless management simultaneously prepares its staff to carry out the plan. The selling skills of reservationists and clerks are critical to the average daily rate until the house nears capacity. Since nearly full occupancy is a rare occasion, earning a consistently higher ADR on the 60 to 70% day is achieved only when a program for selling up is in place.

The hardest sell comes from the guest-service agent. A guest who approaches the desk with a reservation in hand has already decided to buy. Already committed, the new arrival is susceptible to a carefully designed and rehearsed sales effort (see Exhibit 9–18). The hardest job comes from the reservationist who doesn't even see the buyer. Too hard a sell, too firm a price, and the guest is lost early on. Teamed up, the reservationist and the room clerk deliver a one–two punch to the ADR, although they could be 1,000 miles and 30 days apart.

Mastering the Basics of Selling

---

1. Impressing the Guests

- Maintain an appealing physical appearance, including good posture. Don't lean or hang over the front desk. Bring to the job your own sense of spirit and style.
- Organize and keep the front-desk area uncluttered.
- Get to know your property's every service and accommodation type thoroughly. Make frequent forays around the property to learn firsthand about each kind and category of room so that you can better describe the facilities to potential guests.
- Memorize or keep close at hand an up-to-date list of the locations and hours of operation of all food and beverage facilities; entertainment lounges; recreational and sports rooms; and banquet, meeting, exhibit, and other public areas.
- Learn the names and office locations of the general manager and all department heads, including directors of marketing, sales, catering, convention services, and food and beverages.
- Be friendly to guests, greeting them warmly and, whenever possible, by name and title. For instance, when requesting a bellperson's service, ask him or her to take "Mr. Smith to room 340." (To ensure the guest's privacy, be discreet in mentioning the room number to the bellperson.) Call the bellperson by name as well.
- Give guests your undivided attention.
- Answer all questions completely, but concisely and accurately, based on your in-depth knowledge of hotel operations. Refrain from boasting about accommodations and services; instead, offer simple, to-the-point descriptions of features.
- Assume a polite, patient manner in explaining the various options available—for example, the size of rooms, kinds of reservations (confirmed or guaranteed), and the terms *American, European,* or *modified American plan.*

2. Winning the Guests

- Expand prospects' accommodations horizons with descriptions of the room and service possibilities awaiting them. Potential guests may think of a hotel as simply a building filled with bedrooms, but you know better. So inform them about rooms with views, rooms near the health spa, twin-bed rooms, suites, rooms furnished according to a certain historical period, or ultramodern accommodations with Jacuzzis. Lay everything out for prospects, dwelling on the positive, distinctive appeals of each choice. Throw in the tempting intangibles associated with each type of room; for instance, the prestige of having a room on the same floor as the hotel's exclusive club for special guests, or the pleasure of staying in a room equipped with a VCR or a fireplace.
- Attempt to sell a room to suit the client. Observe people and try to read their particular hankerings. If a guest is new to the hotel, a room with a nice view might be impressive. Business travelers might prefer a quiet room at the back. Guests with children, people staying for an extended visit, honeymooners, and celebrities are among those who might be interested in suites.
- Sell the room, not the rate. If a guest asks flat out for rates, avoid quoting a minimum or just one rate; instead, offer a range, portraying in detail the difference in accommodations that each rate affords.

Exhibit 9–18a   Mastering the basics of selling. Commonsense advice from the Foundation of the Hospitality Sales and Marketing Association International's pamphlet entitled *The Front Office: Turning Service into Sales. Courtesy of Hospitality Sales and Marketing Association International, New York.*

- Should a prospect look unsure or reluctant to book a room, suggest that the guest accompany a hotel employee on a walkthrough. A tour of the premises gives guests a chance to settle any doubts they might have and demonstrates the hotel's policy of goodwill and flexibility.
- Keep abreast of special sales promotions, weekend packages, and other marketing strategies, and dangle these offerings to prospects. (To make sure you're informed, you might ask your sales department to hold regularly scheduled presentations to front-office staff on their latest schemes.)
- Look for opportunities to extend the sale—there are many. If a guest mentions that he or she is hungry or arrives around mealtime, promote the hotel's dining facilities; if a guest arrives late, talk up the entertainment lounge or room service. As the person most in contact with guests throughout their stays, you are in the enviable position of being able to please both your guest and hotel management. You can delight guests merely by drawing their attention to the multitude of services your hotel offers, whether it's quick dry cleaning or a leisurely massage. And you can thrill the boss by advancing a sale and hotel revenues through your promotion of in-house features.

3. Wooing the Guests
- When a guest arrives, upgrade the reservation to a more luxurious accommodation whenever availability allows, ask whether the guest would like to make a dinner reservation, and ask whether he or she would like a wake-up call.
- Record and follow through on all wake-up call requests.
- Deliver mail and messages promptly.
- Avoid situations that keep guests waiting. For instance, if you're unable to locate a guest's reservation and a line is beginning to form on the other side of the counter, assume that the hotel has plenty of the desired accommodations available and go ahead and book the guest. Finish registering anyone else who is waiting, and then search for the missing reservation.
- Should mishaps occur, whether a reservation mix-up or a housekeeping error, handle the matter with aplomb without laying the blame on any individual employee or department.
- Dispatch each departing guest with a favorable impression of the hotel. In other words, treat the guests with care and courtesy during check out. Regardless of whether guests enjoyed their stay, they will remember only the hassles experienced at check out if you allow them to occur. Therefore, don't. That is, be sure there are useful, comprehensive procedures for dealing with guests who dispute postings and payments, and follow those procedures with assurance and professionalism.

Exhibit 9–18b   Continued

A firm sale begins with product knowledge. That's why good sales executives travel to the central reservation office to brief the operators there. On property, both the reservationists and the room clerks need continuous training about the facilities and accommodations of the hotel. This is rarely done. Few hotels ever assign 15 minutes per day for staff visits and inspections. Hotels spend millions of dollars upgrading rooms and modernizing facilities, but the room clerk never sees the changes. A simple and consistent training program assures management that reservationists and front-desk clerks know their product.

If the desk staff knows the product, a repertoire of reasons can be developed to up-sell. A 10% up-sell of $10 to $20 is not a large increment in terms of today's rate (see Exhibit 9–19). Since every dollar of the increment goes to the bottom line, it rep-

Top Dozen U.S. Cities for Hotel Room Rates

Rank	City	Average Room Rate
1.	New York City	$234.84
2.	Chicago	$196.00
3.	San Francisco	$191.56
4.	Boston	$178.10
5.	Washington, D.C.	$172.64
6.	Honolulu	$169.75
7.	New Orleans	$166.25
8.	San Jose	$166.21
9.	Oakland	$165.25
10.	Stamford	$161.42
11.	San Diego	$156.09
12.	Wilmington	$155.50

Top Dozen International Cities for Hotel Room Rates

Rank	City	Average Room Rate
1.	Monte Carlo	$379.00
2.	Kuwait	$361.00
3.	Moscow	$354.00
4.	Tel Aviv	$348.00
5.	Tokyo	$336.00
6.	Buenos Aires	$335.00
7.	Rio de Janiero	$332.00
8.	Jerusalem	$332.00
9.	London	$332.00
10.	Hong Kong	$330.00
11.	Paris	$328.00
12.	Dubai	$328.00

Source: "Corporate Traveler Index" (2000) published annually by *Business Traveler News* since 1985.

Exhibit 9–19   Even expense-account guests are reluctant to pay more for up-graded rooms, especially in international locations where the average corporate rate is practically twice that of U.S. cities. Intensive training plus incentives can remake guest-service agents into top-notch salespersons. Convincing just 10% of recalcitrant buyers to upgrade will produce incremental profits even after funding incentive bonuses for front-office staff.

By the way, New York City, with the most expensive rooms in the United States, ranks just 40th on an international scale (between Shanghai's $237 average rate and Santiago's $230 rate). *Source: "Corporate Traveler Index" (2002) published annually by* Business Traveler News *since 1985.*

resents a large annual figure, even if only a portion of the attempts are successful. The focus might be to move the commercial guest from standard service to a concierge floor. The weekend shopper of that commercial hotel needs a different approach. This discretionary buyer may turn away if the rates quoted at check in fail to reflect the package plan originally booked at the time of reservation.

Each guest looks at the incremental dollars differently, and so does the employee. Management must be cognizant that the basic room rate and especially the incremental up-sell seem excessive to employees working for an hourly wage. Part of the training must attend to the employee's frame of reference. Having some type of incentive plan for the employee does help change attitudes.

Incentives to Up-sell. Motivated room clerks are better selling tools than cut rates and giveaways. They are less expensive, too, even with an incentive-pay plan. And it takes a good incentive plan coupled with proper training to make the system work.

Incentive systems stimulate interest and emphasize the goals of management. Rewards are especially important during heavy discounting periods, when guests know that low rates are available and sales resistance is high. Unlike some other places of the world (see Exhibit 9–19), clerks in the United States do not share in any mandatory service charge. Therefore, a special cash pool is needed for incentive distributions.

Incentive systems require an accurate and easily computed formula. Flat goals can be established, or the focus can be on improvement from last year, or last month, or last week for that matter. Most front-office incentives are keyed to average daily rate. Occupancy is a factor in total revenue, which suggests other bases for setting goals.

Most systems establish a pool that is shared by the team. Individual competition is restricted to the clerks, but selling up is a function of the reservation office, the telephone operators, the bellpersons, and others. That's why the pool, with its spinoff in morale and teamwork, is preferred.

The cash pool is generated from a percentage—say, 10%—of room sales that exceed projections. Management projects either the total room sales or the average daily rate. Management projections might be based on the ideal room rate (see Exhibit 9–16) or the budget forecast. If actual sales exceed target sales, the bonus becomes payable. The bonus period is important. It must be long enough to reflect the true efforts of the team but short enough to bring the rewards within grasp.

Higher ADRs are a win–win–win situation. The clerk wins by receiving increased payroll as an incentive for up-selling. Management wins because up-selling contributes proportionally higher profits to the P & L Statement. And the guest wins by receiving exactly the room desired—this is where training is so important. The clerk isn't forcing anything on the guest that the guest doesn't want. Guests are more than ready to pay top dollar for better and better accommodations. That's been demonstrated time and again over the past decade as room rates and room quality continue to rise.

RESOURCES AND CHALLENGES
Resources

➤ SUMMARY

A proper room rate is as much a marketing tool as it is a financial instrument. That's because the room rate needs to be low enough to attract customers while being high enough to earn a reasonable profit: Easier said than done. Even in this day of sophisticated computer technology, calculating the room rate still involves plenty of guesswork and gut instincts. There is an unquantifiable psychology involved in the room rate. An attractive rate for one person may appear too high or too low to another guest. For some, high rates suggest a pretentious operation; for others, a low rate suggests poor quality.

Searching and working toward the perfect rate is difficult, indeed. Even after the rate has been determined and established, it is immediately changed. Rates fluctuate by season, they change according to room type, they vary with special guest discounts, and they shift as a function of yield management.

Although there are some well-established methods for calculating the proper rate, these should never be used to the exclusion of common sense and market demand. The Hubbart room rate formula and the building cost rate formula are two of the most common means for determining the rate. In addition, the ideal average room rate formula adds a dimension of retrospection to understanding the appropriateness of a rate in terms of the local marketplace.

➤ WEB SITES

An interesting study can be made by examining the various lodging tax rates levied by municipalities across the United States. Washington, D.C., and Houston, Texas, are the highest cities with rates of 20.25% and 17% respectively. But it is surprising to see other less-likely cities charging high lodging tax rates (Milwaukee and Cleveland, for example, both hover near 15%).

On the other end of the scale are some rather large metropolitan areas with surprisingly low rates. Wilmington, Delaware, for example, has the 12th most expensive hotel rooms in America (average rate is $155.50). Yet Wilmington's lodging tax rate is just 8.0%—a bargain by most standards. Boston is another good example. Ranked fourth for U.S. cities in terms of average room rates ($178.10), it is ranked just 38th in terms of lodging tax rates (under 10%).

Take a few moments on your own and look at some cities of personal interest. Here are a few Web sites designed to provide lodging tax rates across the United States:

➤ CRC Online uses data available through the National Conference of State Legislatures. Visit http://www.crcmich.org/ALMANAC/GOVTFINC/LOCALREVS/lodging.htm.

➤ Runzheimer International offers a number of products and links related to travel costs. Log on to its site using http://www.runzheimer.com, and then visit its "Runzheimer Guide to Daily Travel Prices" section.

➤ The General Services Administration (GSA) of the U.S. government has a site at http://www.policyworks.gov/org/main/mt/homepage/mtt/perdiem/taxesr.

➤ A partnership between the World Travel & Tourism Council and Michigan State University offers a tax barometer—an economic index report that tracks and monitors lodging and related taxes in more than 50 high-traffic destinations worldwide. You can find their site at http://www.traveltax.msu.edu/barometer/[htm. then simply place here whatever city you choose].

➤ The Travel Industry Association of America also researches lodging taxes and their impact on state economies. Visit their site at http://www.tia.org.

➤ INTERESTING TIDBITS

There are certainly a lot of pressures affecting room rates. Hotel utility, labor, financing, and related costs all continue to rise. No wonder room prices grow at rates that exceed the cost of inflation year-after-year.

Convention delegates, like other hotel guests, understand these inflationary pressures and expect to pay a room rate sizable enough for the hotel to make a profit on their group or convention. However, few convention delegates realize that part of their expensive room rate has actually become a profit center to their convention's treasury! That's right—rebates from headquarter hotels housing convention delegates are very common. The negotiated room rate for the convention often includes a percentage or flat amount that is earmarked by the hotel as a rebate to the convention's treasury.

Such rebates make sense if they help fund continental breakfasts, expensive speakers, or elaborate theme parties. Such rebates do not make sense, however, if they are kept confidential and held in secret from delegates. The type and amount of negotiated rebates certainly should be public information to all attending delegates.

➤ READING REFERENCES

The Front Office: Turning Service into Sales. New York: Hospitality Sales and Marketing Association International.

Getting Into Your Customer's Head. K. Davis. New York: Random House Times Business, 1996.

Marketing for Hospitality and Tourism, 3rd ed. P. Kotler, J. Bowen, and J. Makens. Upper Saddle River, New Jersey: Prentice-Hall, 2003.

Marketing Leadership in Hospitality: Foundations and Practices, 3rd ed. R. Lewis and R. Chambers. New York: John Wiley and Sons, 2000.

Challenges

➤ TRUE/FALSE

____ 1. It can be said that hotel rooms have a floor and ceiling with respect to the rates they can ask. The floor is the minimum that needs to be charged to cover variable costs associated with selling the room and contribute something to fixed costs and profitability. The ceiling is the maximum amount that can be charged and still remain competitive in the marketplace.

____ 2. The fact that hotel rates continue to rise at a pace faster than the rate of inflation suggests there is some level of inelasticity in terms of the lodging industry as a whole.

____ 3. Assume a brand new 200-room hotel has $15 million in construction costs, $3 million in land and land improvement costs, and $2 million in furniture, fixtures, and equipment (FF&E) costs. The building cost rate would be $90 per room, because we do not include FF&E when looking at brand new construction.

____ 4. The most expensive community in the United States in terms of lodging taxes is Los Angeles (Los Angeles County) with a whopping 24.25% lodging tax!

____ 5. Hotels and resorts often charge additional fees (sometimes called resort fees or service fees) to help defray the costs of newspapers, health clubs, in-room coffee, and so on.

➤ PROBLEMS

1. Assume that the ideal average room rate for a given property is $87.25. Month after month, however, the hotel consistently outperforms its ideal average room rate by at least $5 to $10. You are the general manager of the property, and you know you can extract much information from this data. Based on the fact that the hotel's actual ADR is consistently higher than its ideal average room rate, what do you know about the front-office staff's ability to sell rooms? What do you know about the price sensitivity of your customers? And what do you know about rate tendencies in the surrounding marketplace? Armed with this data, what type of action might you now consider?

2. Up-selling at the front desk is paramount to enhancing hotel profitability. Yet up-selling also has the potential to cause the guest discomfort and to appear pushy or aggressive. There is a fine line between professionally up-selling the room and appearing as if you are "hustling" the guest. How might you attempt to up-sell each of the following types of guests? Acting as the guest–service agent prepare a professional up-selling dialogue for each of these situations (make up your own room types and rates as necessary):

   a. Standing before you is an executive on your corporate-rate plan. He is stretching and yawning from a hard day of air travel and local meetings.

   b. About to check in is a mother with her three young children. She is alone—her husband doesn't arrive until tomorrow. The kids are obviously excited about the prospects of swimming and running around the courtyard.

   c. Two gentlemen from a recently arrived bus tour are standing in front of you. Even though the rest of the tour group is housed in standard queen doubles, these men are commenting that their room is much too small.

   d. A female executive with an extended-stay reservation is currently checking in. She comments on the fact that she must stay in your hotel for at least 10 days. How can she possibly survive 10 days away from home?

3. A commercial hotel offers a deeply discounted rate on Friday, Saturday, and Sunday nights. Discuss what should be done or said in each of the following situations:

   a. A guest arrives on Saturday but makes no mention of the special rate and seems unaware of the discount possibilities. The desk clerk charges full rack rate. On check out Monday morning, the cashier notices the full rate charged for two nights, but the guest (after reviewing her folio) says nothing.

   b. The situation is the same as that in part (a), but this time the guest does comment that she thought a discounted rate might apply.

   c. A corporate guest stays Wednesday through Wednesday on company business. He receives a slightly discounted commercial rate for all seven nights, but his rate is still much higher than the special weekend rate available to anyone off the street. He knows about the special rate and asks that his three weekend nights be reduced accordingly.

   d. Create a fourth scenario of your own.

4. Explain why hoteliers differentiate between discounting practices and rate cutting. Create a list of similarities and differences between discounting and rate cutting. Then conclude whether you believe they are substantially different activities or really two different statements for describing exactly the same practice.

5. The Hubbart room-rate formula calls for an average room rate that will cover expenses and provide a fair return to the investors. Compute that rate from the abbreviated but complete set of data that follows:

Investment (also fair market value)

Land	$ 3,000,000
Building	25,000,000
Furniture and equipment	6,000,000
Nonappropriated expenses, such as advertising, repairs, etc.	$ 1,200,000
Income from all operating departments except rooms, net of losses	$ 3,200,000
Rooms available for sale	563
Nonoperating expenses, such as insurance, taxes, and depreciation	510,000
Desired return on investment	16%
Interest on debt of $25,000,000	14%
Percentage of occupancy	71%

6. Using the data from Problem 5, compute what the typical room charge should be according to the building cost rate formula.

➤ ANSWERS TO TRUE/FALSE QUIZ

1. True. The floor (lowest point in the rate range) is the minimum the hotel can charge and still be able to recover all associated variable costs and return some additional amount toward fixed costs and profitability. The ceiling (highest point in the rate range) is the maximum the hotel can charge and still remain competitive in the marketplace.

2. True. As a whole, the lodging industry is relatively inelastic. This can most easily be seen at times of the year when all hotels in a given community raise their rates. But remember, a single hotel is relatively elastic in terms of its competitors.

3. True. The building cost rate formula does remove the cost of furniture, fixtures, and equipment when calculating the rate. So,

construction ($15 million) plus land and land improvements ($3 million) total $18 million. Divide that by 200 rooms to get $90,000 in costs per average room. Divide that by the $1,000 constant to arrive at a $90 average rate.

4. False. The most expensive community in the United States in terms of lodging taxes is actually Washington, D.C., with a 20.25% lodging tax.

5. True. Hotels and resorts do charge resort or service fees. This practice has come under growing scrutiny. Some hotels have decided to eliminate these hidden charges. Others have a liberal credit policy for any complaining guests.

PART IV

The Hotel Revenue Cycle

Chapter 10
Billing the Guest Folio

Chapter 11
Cash Transactions

Chapter 12
Credit and the City Ledger

The textbook's theme continues with this fourth unit, "The Hotel Revenue Cycle." Previous units have moved the reader along a journey which parallels the guest cycle. The first unit (Part I) actually presented the industry as a whole, providing the reader a broad understanding of the major players, ownership structures, types and classes of properties, staffing hierarchies, and basic analytical and managerial ratios and concepts. The three chapters which comprise the second unit (Part II) described the hotel reservations function. Modern telecommunications have changed the mechanics of reservation requests, and modern technologies have improved the hotel's techniques of forecasting and processing room availability. Once the reservation contract is agree upon, the hotel confirms the understanding and begins tracking the expected arrivals through its reservation system.

In Part III, the guest arrives, sometimes carrying the reservation made in Part II and sometimes unexpectedly as a walk-in. The mechanics of that arrival, including room rate decisions, rooms assignments, and the rooming process, are examined thoroughly in this middle section of the book. Here, too, are discussed the special guest-service relationships that set the tone during the arrival time (Part III) and throughout sale of services (Part IV).

The fourth unit (Part IV) brings us to the very heart of the reason hotels are in business; the sale of services (especially room sales). Selling services is only one part of this section. Recording the sales, collecting the amounts, and establishing the accounting procedures make up the content of Chapters 10, 11, and 12. In Part V, the cycle closes, and the guest checks out. There are still records to keep after the guest's departure---as there were throughout the guest's entire stay. Part IV attends to the records of the sale and Part V to the accuracy of the record.

Computerization has improved the methods for recording and reviewing the records from guest sales and services. The fundamentals of these processes are based in an accounting system whose essential rules have remained unchanged despite the speed and accuracy of computerization. In Part IV we review the basic rules of accounting and provide a simplistic and repetitive approach to understanding these concepts. This teaching technique helps the student past the hurdles of accounting credits and debits even if the reader lacks formal courses in the subject. Too often the nonaccountant rejects the accounting explanations as being too difficult. Not so with this proven approach. After reading this unit, students will realize how little accounting skill is required to be knowledgeable about front-office guest folios.

In part, the business environment for hotels is a noncash one with credit, credit cards, debit cards, and smart cards the new media of exchange. We explain this in Chapter 12. Despite the popularity and convenience of the cards, cash retains its hold on many business activities. In Chapter 11, we review the money form of cash as well as its substitutes, old standbys, such as traveler's checks and personal checks. Before we examine cash and credit cards, an overview of the entire billing process is provided in Chapter 10.

All of the preceding carries the guest (and the text) to the final stage of the sales/collection process, the audit. In Part V we emphasize the changes in audit techniques that computerized property management systems have brought. For one, they have reduced the piles of paper and make possible the megaproperties (hotels of 2,000 rooms and up) that have proliferated in the past decade.

Billing The Guest Folio

Outline

There's a tempo, a rhythm, to the flow of guests through the hotel. Reservations sound the first beat. The full swell of services begins after guests arrive and register. The melody doesn't end until they depart and settle the amounts owed. Between check-in and check-out, guests enjoy the facilities of the hotel. Selling those facilities is what the business of hotelkeeping is all about. Hotel incomes are earned from the sale of such services. How those incomes are recorded is what the chapter is all about.

1. *The Hotel's Sale of Services.* Hotels sell rooms, food, and beverage along with minor departmental services such as telephone, laundry, and in-room films (see Chapter 3, Exhibit 3–3). Full-service properties have more departments (convention services, wedding chapels, parking, spas) and need more sophisticated systems of recordkeeping.

2. *The Hotel's Method of Recording Sales.* Hotels and their customers (guests) have a different relationship than do other retailers and their customers. Hotel customers register as they arrive. Their names, addresses, credit-card numbers, and often business associations as well, are known to the innkeeper. Consequently, the sale of services can be completed without immediate payment. Unlike other retail transactions, which require immediate settlement, the merchant/hotel waits for payment. Sometimes the wait is a few days, sometimes a week. In the meantime, the amounts due are recorded on a bill, which is presented to the guest as he or she departs. Hotel professionals call that bill a *folio.*

3. *The Hotel's Method of Preparing the Customer's Bill (Folio).* The folio is an accurate and current statement of how much the guest owes the hotel. It is available at the front desk on demand. Whereas other retailers, department stores for example, send monthly statements, the hotel's statement is ready on a moment's notice. It's ready even though the exact moment of departure is unknown. Even the day of departure may be uncertain. Of course, the hotel is as anxious as the guest to have an accurate folio available. Incorrectly charged items delay the check-out procedure and create ill feelings. Charges not on the folio statement are difficult to collect after a guest has departed. Collecting these *late charges* by mail is expensive, both in administrative costs and in guest relations.

---

4. The Hotel's Method of Recording (Accounting for) Each Transaction.

Understanding the accounting rules is not essential to a clear understanding of the three other components of the chapter. Hereafter, accounting rules are set in a box like this one. Students unfamiliar with the debits and credits of accounting may choose to read these accounting fundamentals or skip them. The text will make good sense even if the accounting information is skipped.

► ACCOUNTS RECEIVABLE

Except at the retail level, most commerce is carried on without immediate payment. Businesses buy and sell to one another without a direct exchange of money. Payment is delayed until a more convenient time in order to complete the sale as quickly as possible. Hotels also work that way. Guests are not disturbed during their sleep in order to collect the room rates! Instead, charges are made to the folio and collections are made later. Guests usually settle at check-out time. During the period between the sale (room, food, beverage, etc.) and the payment (at departure), the guest owes the hotel. A customer who owes a business for services that have not been paid is known as an *account receivable*.[1]

Definition of Terms To Be Used	
Accounts Receivable (A/R)	Customers who owe for services already rendered
City Receivables	Accounts receivable who are not registered
Transient Receivables	Accounts receivable who are currently registered
Charge	The amount that the hotel asks for its service
Late Charge	Service charged to the folio after the guest has left
Folio	Guest bill; also called account card; an A/R
Ledger	Group of folios
City Ledger	A ledger of city receivables
Transient Ledger	A ledger of transient receivables; also called a rooms ledger, a front-desk ledger, a guest ledger
Posting	The process of recording a charge or credit on the folio

Types of Accounts Receivable (A/R)

Hotels have two types of accounts receivable because there are two types of hotel guests. The most obvious guest (or account receivable) is one who is currently registered and occupying a room. Oddly enough, this most visible class of guest is not the largest dollar debt (accounts receivable) that the hotel is owed. More money is owed by the second type of accounts receivable: persons or companies that owe the hotel for services but are *not* registered and *not* occupying a guest room. Registered guests are called *transient guests*; nonregistered accounts receivable are called *city guests*. Both owe the hotel for services rendered and sold. One group, the city receivables, are not even in the hotel and may never have been!

Guests can and do change categories; transient accounts receivable usually become city accounts receivable. When guests check out, leaving their transient classification, they usually settle their folios (that is, pay the bill) with a credit card. The amount owed is now a debt of the credit-card company. The hotel will be paid by a city-ledger receivable: Visa, MasterCard, Diners Club, or other credit card. Credit-card companies obviously are not registered guests occupying a room. The credit-card debt is owed by an account receivable who is not registered: a city account receivable.

▶**The Ledgers.**   There are numerous accounts receivable in both categories. Hotels as large as those in Chapter 1, Exhibit 1–6, have several thousand guests and approximately the same number of folios. Accountants call a group of folios a *ledger*. (Any group of records can be called a ledger.) Since all the parties are registered—that is, transient—guests, the folios at the front desk are viewed as one record: a transient ledger.

---

[1]Remember the spelling rule for rec*ei*vable: Place *i* before *e*, except after *c*, or when sounded like *a* as in n*ei*ghbor and w*ei*gh.

City accounts receivable are similarly combined. The total record of individual city accounts, debtors to the hotel who are not currently registered, is viewed as one record, a city ledger.

The Transient Ledger.   Transient ledger is shorthand for the transient accounts receivable ledger. Hotel professionals use other jargon to identify this particular ledger. Because the ledger (that is, the total record of debt to the hotel by registered guests) is available at the front office, it is frequently called the *front-office ledger.* Since it is made up of registered guests, it is also called the *guest ledger.* Room rates are the largest source of charges to guest folios, so *rooms ledger* is still another term used for the transient ledger.

The variety of terms used to identify the transient ledger spills over to the folios that make up this ledger. Thus, the single transient folio may be called *folio,* or *guest folio,* or *front-office folio.* Since the folio is a record of the guest's account with the hotel, the folio is also called an *account card* or *guest bill.*

The City Ledger.   There are numerous subcategories of the city ledger, as Chapter 12 explains, but there is but one general term, city ledger. That makes city-ledger references easier to remember than the variety of labels used for the transient ledger (guest ledger, rooms ledger, front-office ledger).

The guest ledger is located at the front desk, the city ledger in the accounting office. With computerization, ledgers have no real physical location. They can be accessed wherever a control terminal allows. Timing is the major difference between the two ledgers. Charges, which are the records of services rendered, are *posted* (recorded) immediately to the guest ledger since the guest might choose to leave at any time. City guests, who must establish credit in advance, are billed periodically. This permits some delay in posting city-ledger charges. Like many other businesses do, hotels bill city accounts monthly. Often, a three-day cycle is used for the first billing. These variations in timing are accommodated by different ledger forms as well as by different posting and billing procedures.

▶*What Is and Isn't Accounted For.*   Each folio is a record of the guest's debt to the hotel. Folios deal only with accounts receivable. Persons who pay cash for services, as they might in cocktail lounges and restaurants, are not billed at the front desk. It makes no difference whether the buyer is a registered guest or a stranger. There is no debt, hence no account receivable, when settlement is made immediately with dollars.

Strangers, nonguests without front-office folios, can still purchase on credit. They do so with credit cards. A credit-card purchase creates an account receivable within the city ledger, not with the guest ledger (front-office ledger). Using the credit card means the credit-card company will pay the hotel. The credit-card company is a non-registered account receivable. That's the definition of a city-ledger account. If services are purchased with a credit card by anyone, guest or nonguest, the purchaser owes the credit-card company and the credit-card company owes the hotel.

In summary, both registered guests and strangers use the hotel's facilities. Those services are paid for in one of two methods. Either they pay with cash or they charge to a credit card. People increasingly opt for the credit card.

Guests have a third option of payment, which is not open to strangers: Guests charge services to their rooms, their folios. By signing for the charge, the guest acknowledges the debt and authorizes its posting to the folio. Payment for that charge and all others on the folio comes later, usually at check-out. This chapter concentrates on this third method of settlement. Cash is treated in Chapter 11 and credit cards in Chapter 12.

The Folio: The Individual Account Receivable

Folio, bill, guest account, account card, guest account card, and guest bill are used interchangeably. Some parts of the world use *visitor accounts*. All refer to the single folio that is opened for each guest. "For each guest" is not entirely accurate, because one folio may serve several persons, as it does with a family.

Definition of Terms To Be Used	
Account	A guest's transient folio, or a city-ledger record
Asset	Something owned by the hotel (building, A/R, furniture)
Balance of the Account (or Account Balance)	The net difference between charges and credits
Cashier's Bucket (or Well or Pit)	A front-office file, sometimes recessed in the desk
Charges	Amounts owed by guests for services received
Credits	Amounts by which guests settle the charges they owe
Direct Billing	Bill goes to the entity that created it, not to a credit card
Incomes	Earnings that the hotel enjoys from the sale of services
Master Account	Front-office folio for group charges and credits
PMS	Property management system, the hotel's computer
Sales	Same as income, although technically not exactly
Split (Billing or Folios)	Distribution of charges between master account and folio

➤*Location and Filing of Folios.* Without exception, modern hotels use the computerized folios (see Exhibit 10–1) that property management systems (PMS) create. There are no physical folios because the records are in computer memory. Folio contents can be viewed on computer screens or by printing *hard copies*. Therefore, the desk needs input and output devices (keyboards, scanners, display screens, and printers) to record and access folio information.

Older, hand-prepared, pencil-and-paper folios (see Exhibit 10–2) had to be physically stored at the desk in a *cashier's well*, also called a *cashier's bucket* or *cashier's pit* (see Exhibit 10–3). Folios were separated there by heavy cardboard dividers. Guest folios were kept in room-number sequence because room numbers, even more than guest names, were and still are the major means of guest identification. Not all hotels have done away with cashier's buckets. The need still exists under some PMSs for filing paper records, but not folios, by room number.

Whether maintained electronically or by hand, the folio is the responsibility of the guest-service agent or the front-office cashier. Hand-prepared folios generated such large quantities of paper that billing clerks (or posting clerks) supported the cashier. As the chapter explains later, recording charges on the folio is now done electronically at computer terminals in the various departments providing the services (food, beverage, spa, etc.). Thus, there are fewer desk employees and fewer paper errors. As front-desk jobs are combined (see Chapter 3), guest-service agents with broader responsibilities take on what was once the job of front-office cashiers and billing clerks.

➤*Number of Folios.* The size of the hotel generally determines the number of folios in use. Essentially, one folio is the norm for each occupied room. There are ex-

```
                                              1000 NOAH VAIL
          ⊡V                                  ROTTEN PUMPKIN POND
   A Vallen Corporation Property              MASSACHUSETTS  01266
   HI-JINKS HOTEL                             1-800-555-5555

                                              RES#  43 RLG 1234      ACCT#  5941

                                              IN      11-02-        OUT    11-04-
   NAME:    Iona Carr

   ADDRESS: S.N. Eaky Rd.                     RATE  100             ROOM   444
            Mousie, KY 40288
```

DATE	DESCRIPTION	REFERENCE	CHARGES	CREDITS	BALANCE
			100.00		100.00
11/02/	ROOM	444 18-1	5.50		105.50
11/02/	ROOM TAX	444 18-2	13.98		119.48
11/03/	COFFEE SHOP	444 38-1	11.10		130.58
11/03/	TELEPHONE	444 43-2	6.00		136.58
11/03/	FAX	444 43-3	22.60		159.18
11/03/	LOUNGE	444 26-2		159.18	–0–
11/03/	VISA#1111111	444 50-4			

. . . . If you were a Vallen ⊡V Associate Member,
you would have earned 320 Club Membership points.

TRANSFER TO CITY LEDGER
I AGREE THAT MY LIABILITY FOR THIS BILL IS NOT
WAIVED, AND AGREE TO BE PERSONALLY LIABLE IF
THE INDICATED PERSON, ASSOCIATION, OR COMPANY
FAILS TO PAY ANY PART OF THESE CHARGES.

_____
SIGNATURE

For Reservations: 1-617-555-5555 • Fax: 1-617-555-5554 • E-mail: vallen@hotel.com

Exhibit 10–1   Typical computerized guest bill (folio) printed at the end of a guest's stay. Information above the double lines (reservation number, arrival and departure dates, rate and room number) has its source in reservation and/or registration data. Services rendered to this guest are recorded below the double lines, and their meanings are the focus of this chapter.

ceptions. One room with several friends would need several folios if each is to pay an equal share. A single occupant in a two-room suite would have just one folio.

City-ledger accounts are opened for nonregistered guests (individuals, companies, associations) who want credit privileges with the hotel, so the number of guest rooms isn't a factor for the city ledger. Before credit cards were widely adopted, large hotels

ROOM NO. _____409_____   **E69080**

m M/M Art E. Fishal

86 Bates Boulevard

~~Hitchcock Texas 01020~~

ROOM NO. _____409_____   **E69080**   CLERK

                                                    SB

m M/M Art E. Fishal

86 Bates Boulevard

Hitchcock, Texas 01020

ARRIVED	RATE	PERSONS	COT	REG. CARD #	PREV. INV. #	CLERK
12/23/	78	2	N/A	69080	N/A	SB

DATE	12/23/		12/24/												
BROUGHT FORWARD			99	24											
ROOM	78	–													
TAX	6	24													
RESTAURANT	15	–													
"															
TELEPHONE-LOCAL															
-LONG DISTANCE															
TELEGRAMS															
LAUNDRY & VALET															
CASH ADVANCES															
"															
NEWSPAPERS															
TRANSFERS from 407	#69081		84	24											
TOTAL DEBIT	99	24	183	48											
CASH															
ALLOWANCES															
CITY LEDGER:															
-ADVANCE DEPOSITS															
-CREDIT CARDS			183	48											
-TRANSFERS															
BALANCE FORWARD	99	24	0												

ALL ACCOUNTS ARE DUE WHEN RENDERED

Exhibit 10–2   The left and right folios illustrate two pencil-and-paper bills, each prepared with a carbon copy. They were in widespread use at one time but have been replaced by computerized folios, Exhibit 10–1. Both exhibits reflect similar information but in different formats. (Refer to this illustration again when the text explains two types of transfers: (1) Room 407 has a folio-to-folio transfer of $84.24 to room 409; (2) room 409 transfers the entire folio balance of $183.48 to the city ledger.)

had upward of a thousand city-ledger accounts. Individual accounts are not needed today because almost everyone carries a credit card. Now the bulk of the city ledger can be accounted for in a half-dozen credit-card accounts. Electronically tying city-ledger accounts to the computers of credit-card companies and banks speeds processing and reduces administrative costs.

ROOM NO. _____ 407 _____   **E69081**

𝓂 _____ Benny Fishal _____

12345 Education Avenue
Reading, Pennsylvania, 98765

ROOM NO. _____ 407 _____   **E69081**   CLERK

SB

𝓂 _____ Benny Fishal _____

12345 Education Avenue
Reading, Pennsylvania 98765

ARRIVED	RATE	PERSONS	COT	REG. CARD #	PREV. INV. #	CLERK
12/23/	78	2	N/A	69081	N/A	SB

DATE	12/23/		12/24/											
BROUGHT FORWARD			84	24										
ROOM	78	–												
TAX	6	24												
RESTAURANT														
"														
TELEPHONE-LOCAL														
-LONG DISTANCE														
TELEGRAMS														
LAUNDRY & VALET														
CASH ADVANCES														
"														
NEWSPAPERS														
TRANSFERS														
TOTAL DEBIT	84	24	84	24										
CASH														
ALLOWANCES														
CITY LEDGER:														
-ADVANCE DEPOSITS														
-CREDIT CARDS														
-TRANSFERS TO 409	*69080		84	24										
BALANCE FORWARD	84	24	0											

ALL ACCOUNTS ARE DUE WHEN RENDERED

Exhibit 10–2   *Continued*

▶**Master Accounts.** The master account is its own person, much like a business corporation has a legal identity separate from that of its individual owners. This accommodates tour companies, trade associations, convention organizations, and single-entity groups that incur charges that are not billable to any one person (see Chapter 2 for an explanation). Group services—an awards luncheon for example—are charged to this nonperson folio, the *master account*. Master accounts allow group charges to be distinguished from personal charges. These accounts are not city accounts receivable, because they represent the organization currently registered. So long as the group is in the hotel, its master account is a standard guest folio, such as Exhibit 10–4.

Exhibit 10–3   Cashier's wells (buckets or pits) separated pencil-and-paper folios by sequential room numbers. Some computerized properties still use the buckets to separate and locate preprinted folios, correspondence, or vouchers.

As with all folios, master accounts are settled at check-out. Settlement involves a joint review of the many charges by representatives of the hotel and the organization. Then the folio is transferred to the city ledger for direct billing. Obviously, then, the city ledger has more than just credit cards. Individual accounts receivable with billing to be made to the person, company, or organization (rather than through credit cards) are also part of the city ledger.

Master accounts are complex. They may number 25 pages and more. It takes telephone calls and faxes and emails to resolve what the hotel believes it is owed and what the association believes it owes. Conflicts arise over the number of persons at each function, over who signed for services, over the number of comp rooms, over sales taxes due, and so much more. Chapter 12's discussion of the city ledger explains the final billing and settlement.

How Master Accounts are Structured.   Decisions about master account billing are made well in advance of the group's arrival. Service details, credit terms, and authorized signatures are part of the negotiations between the hotel and the organization. How charges are to be distributed between individual folios and the master account is the group's decision, not the hotel's. The hotel is responsible for billing as instructed.

SINGLE-ENTITY GROUPS.   Employees gathering for company business or groups traveling together, say, to perform, are examples of single-entity groups (see Chapter 2). Charging all the room rates to a single master account is one method of billing such closely related groups.

CONVENTION GROUPS.   Unlike single-entities, convention delegates hail from many locations and companies. Delegates pay their own room and personal charges. No master account would serve for room rates, since delegates have no relationship other than their mutual attendance. However, the association staging the event has a master account for banquet costs, cocktail parties, and meeting expenses. Other gen-

**1000 NOAH VAIL
ROTTEN PUMPKIN POND
MASSACHUSETTS 01266
1-800-555-5555**

A Vallen Corporation Property
HI-JINKS HOTEL

RES#	LG 1235	ACCT#	1206
IN	5-14	OUT	5-16
RATE	MASTER	ROOM	2323

NAME: Alumni Associates of America

ADDRESS: #1 College Campus Road
Any University Town
State of Confusion 00000

DATE	DESCRIPTION	REFERENCE		CHARGES	CREDITS
5/14	BD DIRECTORS LUNCHEON	2323	38-3	550.00	
5/14	AUDIO/VISUAL	2323	50-1	100.00	
5/14	COCKTAIL RECEPTION	2323	26-2	12,000.00	
5/14	ROOM 2323	2323	18-1	200.00	
5/14	ROOM 2325	2323	18-1	200.00	
5/14	ROOM 1618/1620	2323	18-1	600.00	
5/14	ROOM TAX	2323	18-2	80.00	
5/15	BREAKFAST BAR	2323	38-4	800.00	
5/15	ROOM RENTALS	2323	38-1	1,500.00	
5/15	BUFFET LUNCHEON	2323	38-3	10,500.00	
5/15	FLAG RENTALS	2323	50-4	250.00	
5/15	ROOM 2323	2323	18-1	200.00	
5/15	ROOM 2325	2323	18-1	200.00	
5/15	ROOM 1618/1620	2323	18-1	600.00	
5/15	ROOM TAX	2323	18-2	80.00	
5/16	FULL-SERVICE BREAKFAST	2323	38-3	3,500.00	
5/16	ROOM ALLOWANCES 1/50	2323	18-6		2,000.00
5/16	ADJUSTMENT FOR FLAGS	2323	50-8		250.00
5/16	DIRECT TRANSFER	2323	C/L		29,110.00
5/16	THANK YOU				-0-

. . . . If you were a Vallen **V**ssociate Member,
you would have earned 58,220 Club Membership points.

TRANSFER TO CITY LEDGER

I AGREE THAT MY LIABILITY FOR THIS BILL IS NOT WAIVED, AND AGREE TO BE PERSONALLY LIABLE IF THE
INDICATED PERSON, ASSOCIATION, OR COMPANY FAILS TO PAY ANY PART OF THESE CHARGES.

SIGNATURE _____

For Reservations: 1-617-555-5555   •   Fax: 1-617-555-5554   •   E-mail: vallen@hotel.com

Exhibit 10–4   Master account folios accumulate charges for group events in contrast to personal folios that accumulate guest's individual expenses. Rooms charges for 2323, 2325, and 1618/1620 are for association use, either for staff or guests. Credits to settle the folio include two allowances: one room for each 50 room nights used by the group, and an adjustment with the 5/15 charge for flags. The unpaid balance is transferred to the city ledger for direct billing. (Figures are rounded for clarity.)

eral costs, such as telecommunications and room charges for employees or speakers, also go onto the master account. Such charges must be authorized by the signature of the person or persons identified during the prenegotiations.

Many master accounts are created during a large convention. Participating companies in attendance at the convention may have exhibits, employee rooms, hospitality suites, and other services that require charges to that subgroup. As affiliated or allied members, they may see public relations benefits from sponsoring a meal. Each, then, has its own master account. There is no accounting relationship to the association's master account. The hotel tracks and bills each separately.

TOUR GROUPS.   Master accounts for tour groups differ from master accounts for convention groups. Convention attendees pay their own bills. Tour-group participants pay the tour company in advance, and the tour company negotiates with the hotel. So the tour company is responsible for payment of all charges included in the package. The tour company's master account includes the room charges for everyone in the group, plus whatever else was sold with the package: meals, drinks, shows, golf, and so on. Personal expenses—those not within the package—are charged to the guest's personal folio.

Split Billing.   The distribution of the charges between the master account and the guest's personal folio is called *split billing* or *split folios*. Both the master folio (often called the *A folio*) and the guest or *B folio* are standardized forms of the types illustrated throughout the chapter. A and B are used merely to distinguish the group entity from the individual person. The A folio is the major folio where the large charges of the association, tour company or business are posted. Sometimes, the hotel itself is the A folio. Such is the case with casino comps and frequent-stay customers.

Casino Comps.   Casino hotels sometimes provide complimentary (free) accommodations to "high rollers" (big players). Split billing is used to account for the comps. To the A folio is posted all the charges that the hotel/casino will comp. Depending on the size of the guest's credit line, the comp could be for room only, or for room, food, beverage and telephone. Even the airfare might be reimbursed. Items not covered are posted to the B folio, which the guest pays at departure.

Preferred-guest Programs   Preferred-guest (or frequent-traveler) programs employ the flexibility of split billing. Two different folios are opened when a guest checks in with frequent-traveler points. The full rate of the room is charged on the A folio. On departure, the guest pays the nonroom charges, which have been posted to the B folio. The A folio is transferred to the city ledger, and either the parent company or the franchisor is billed. According to the frequent-traveler contract, one of these is now the account receivable obligated to pay the room charge.

The actual amount paid to the hotel under the preferred-guest program is always less than the rate quoted to the guest. Most programs pay full rack rate only if the occupancy of the hotel is above a given figure—90% perhaps. Below that figure—and the hotel is usually below that figure—the program reimburses the participating hotel for its operational expenses: linen, labor, and energy. So the reimbursement may be set anywhere from $20 to $50. No provision is made for recovering fixed costs such as taxes, interest, or fair wear and tear.

The burden falls heaviest on resorts. Where else would one expect the frequent traveler to use the points—at the same corporate hotels where the points were originally accumulated? Or at a luxury resort with friends and relatives? The burden of preferred-guest program redemption is especially onerous to resorts if the program reimburses, as some do, on a sliding scale based on the previous month's average daily rate. Resorts discount rooms during the off-season or the shoulder periods. This produces a low ADR. Yet the next month, when the season starts and when the frequent travelers cash in their points, the parent company reimburses on the basis of the previous month's low ADR.

Understanding Charges and Credits

Familiarization with accounting and with its system of charges and credits gives front-office associates a big assist in handling folios. The knowledge is especially helpful in understanding how front-office records (the transient ledger) interface with back-office records (the city ledger). Since many guest-service agents lack accounting knowledge, front-office forms are designed without that requirement. Exhibit 10–13, for example, uses plus (+) and minus (−) to indicate increases (charges) or decreases (credits) to folios.

Exhibits 10–5, 10–6, and 10–12 mark the differences by using two columns. One is titled "Charges" and the other "Credits." Charges for services rendered increase the guest's debt to the hotel (Exhibit 10–5, line 1, the ISLANDER Restaurant). Credits reduce the guest's debt (Exhibit 10–5, line 11, DIRECT BILL). With enough credits, the folio is paid; the balance is zero (Exhibit 10–5, final line).

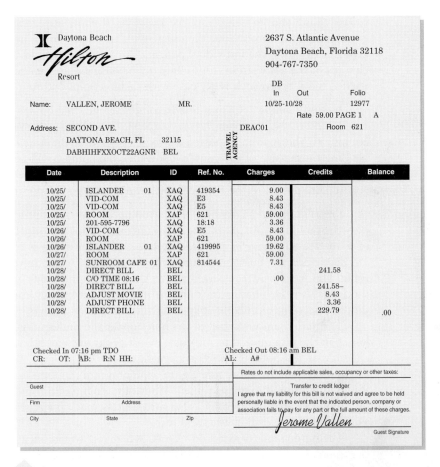

Exhibit 10–5   Debits (charges) and credits (payments) can be visualized within the traditional accounting "T," debits in the left column and credits in the right. The final entry represents a transfer to the city ledger for direct billing to the sponsoring organization, similar to Exhibit 10–4. *Courtesy of Daytona Beach Hotel Resort, Daytona Beach Florida.*

Radisson Hotel Ottawa Centre

100 Kent Street, Ottawa, Ontario, Canada K1P 5R7 Telephone (613) 238-1122

LA RONDE FINE CUISINE   **CAFE TOULOUSE**   *Lautrec's*

ROOM / CHAMBRE	NAME / NOM	RATE / TAUX	DEPARTURE / DEPART	TIME / HEURE	
2228	STEIN, FRANK N.	75.00	14/10/		ACCT# 20539

ROOM / CHAMBRE	FIRM OR GROUP / COMPAGNIE OU GROUP	PLAN	ARRIVAL / ARRIVEE		
1K1A	AMERICAN		09/10/	12:29	GROUP 6566

54	P.O. BOX 1211	DB			
	LANSING MI 90125-0012				

CLERK COMMIS	ADDRESS / ADRESSE	METHOD OF PAYMENT MODE DE PAIEMENT

DATE	REFERENCE/RÉFÉRENCE		CHARGES	CREDITS / CRÉDITS	BALANCE DUE / SOLDE DÛ
09/10	ROOM	2228, 1	75.00		
09/10	ROOM TAX	2228, 1	3.75		
10/10	TOUL POS	000000	17.12		
10/10	LNG DIST	315-386-	.57		
10/10	ROOM	2228, 1	75.00		
10/10	ROOM TAX	2228, 1	3.75		
11/10	ROOM	2228, 1	75.00		
11/10	ROOM TAX	2228, 1	3.75		
12/10	LNG DIST	315-386-	1.14		
12/10	LNG DIST	315-386-	1.14		
12/10	ROOM	2228, 1	75.00		
12/10	ROOM TAX	2228, 1	3.75		
13/10	TOUL POS	000000	9.86		
13/10	TOUL POS	000000	16.58		
13/10	ROOM	2228, 1	75.00		
13/10	ROOM TAX	2228, 1	3.75		
					440.16

FIRM / COMPAGNIE	ADDRESS / ADRESSE	I AGREE THAT MY LIABILITY FOR THIS BILL IS NOT WAIVED AND AGREE TO BE HELD PERSONALLY LIABLE IN THE EVENT THAT THE INDICATED PERSON, COMPANY OR ASSOCIATION FAILS TO PAY FOR ANY PART OR THE FULL AMOUNT OF THESE CHARGES.

CITY _____ PROV. _____ POSTAL _____
VILLE   POSTALE

ATTENTION _____

GUEST SIGNATURE X _____
SIGNATURE DU CLIENT

IL EST CONVENU QUE MA RESPONSABILITÉ DE CETTE FACTURE N'EST PAS ABROGÉE ET JE CONSENTS A L'ASSUMER DANS L'ÉVENTUALITE OU LA PERSONNE INDIQUÉE, SOCIÉTÉ OU ASSOCIATION REFUSE DE PAYER LE MONTANT EN TOTALITÉ OU EN PARTIE.

Courtesy: Radisson Hotel Ottawa Centre, Ottawa, Canada.

Exhibit 10–6   Computer-prepared folio showing the individual's group affiliation, *American*; the group's identification, 6566; the clerk's identification, 54; the guest's account number, 20539, which is often the same as the room number; and the guest's agreement for ultimate liability of the bill. The $440.16 balance must still be resolved to zero the account. *Courtesy of Radisson Hotel Ottawa Centre, Ontario, Canada.*

A third technique for distinguishing charges from credits is illustrated in Exhibits 10–10 and 10–14. Only one column is used, but credits are marked "CR." Figures that are not marked are understood to be charges. Most folio postings are charges.

> *Bracket materials are used hereafter to repeat the same discussion using accounting terminology. Explanations are complete even if the bracketed paragraphs are skipped. Students are urged to read the bracketed content for a broader understanding of the folio and its relationship to the hotel's accounting system.*

THE MEANING OF DEBITS AND CREDITS.

Accounting language speaks of debits and credits instead of charges and credits. Debits (or charges) increase the values of certain accounting records. In this chapter, the focus is on folios, which are accounts receivable. Other accounts, cash for example, are also increased with debits. Cash and accounts receivable are among the many assets (things that hotels own) that follow the same accounting rules. Accounting records, assets among them, that are increased with debits are decreased by credits.

Increases in assets, including *accounts receivable* and *cash*, are made with debits.

Decreases in assets, including *accounts receivable* and *cash*, are made with credits.

Accounting students will recognize the folio as a T-account, where debits are on the left side and credits on the right. Exhibit 10–5 is highlighted with horizontal and vertical lines to reinforce the visual similarities between an account receivable folio and an account receivable T-account.

Assets. An asset is something a business owns. Hotels own many assets, including land, buildings, furniture, and kitchen equipment. Only two of the numerous assets owned are important to the front office and its folio responsibilities. Accounts receivable, which are debts that customers owe the hotel (the hotel owns the debt), is one of those assets. Cash is the other. Cash is money: money in the bank, money at the desk, money in the bar till. Cash has become less important to the records of the front office because both guests and hotelkeepers prefer folios to be settled with credit cards.

Sales or Incomes. Hotels are in the business of selling services. It's those sales that produce incomes and eventually profits for the business. The sale of rooms is the

---

Be they guests or strangers, customers who buy services with cash in the lounge, the coffee shop, the newsstand, or other hotel departments increase the hotel's cash asset. There is no record on the guest's folio, but there is an increase (debit) to cash according to the accounting rule:

Increases in assets, including accounts receivable and *cash*, are made with debits.

Increases in incomes (sale of rooms, *food*, beverage, spa, etc.) are made with credits.

Debit: Cash   33.00
    Credit: Proper Department (room, *food*, beverage, spa, etc.)   33.00
Explanation: Sold coffee-shop meal for cash.

Hotel guests may make the same purchases by signing for the charges. That requires an entry on the folio, a debit to the asset accounts receivable.

Increases in assets, including *accounts receivable* and cash, are made with debits.

Increases in incomes (sale of rooms, *food*, beverage, spa, etc.) are made with credits.

Debit: Accounts Receivable/Guest's Folio   33.00
    Credit: Proper Department (room, *food*, beverage, spa, etc.)   33.00
Explanation: Sold coffee-shop meal on account (to registered guest).

hotel's major product. Depending on the size, class, and type of property, income is also earned from the sale of other products and services. Guest pay for these services by charging them to the folio (establishing an asset called account receivable) or paying for them with cash. Sometimes they use credit cards. The delivered product or service is the same, they're just paid for differently. The record of service is different from the record of payment, although the two records take place simultaneously, as we shall see next in the discussion of equality.

Debit/credit rules are different for sales (incomes) than for assets. Just as all assets follow one asset rule, so all incomes follow one income rule. It is an opposite rule.

> Increases in assets, including *accounts receivable* and cash, are made with debits.
>
> Increases in incomes (sales of *rooms*, food, beverage, etc.) are made with credits.

> Debit: Accounts Receivable/Guest's Folio   100
>   Credit: Proper Department (*room*, food, beverage, spa, etc.)   100
> *Explanation*: Guest occupied room.

Sometimes, but not too often, incomes are decreased. Go back mentally to the guest-management contents of Chapter 7. Assume that as a result of a serious mistake on the hotel's part, the guest's room charge is waived. The room income, which was recorded yesterday with a credit (see immediately above) must now be reversed. Allowances, which are the opposite of sales, are used to do that.

> Decreases in incomes (sales of *rooms*, food, beverage, etc.) are made with debits.
>
> Decreases in assets, including *accounts receivable* and cash, are made with *credits*.

> Debit: Proper Departmental (*room*, food, beverage, spa, etc.) Allowance   100
>   Credit: Accounts Receivable/Guest's Folio   100
> *Explanation*: Room allowance because of housekeeping failure.

The room-sale debit offsets the original room-sale credit. The net result is no charge in the guest's folio. Both postings, the sale and the sale adjustment (an allowance), appear on the folio.

EQUALITY OF DEBITS AND CREDITS

Every accounting event has two parts. This dual accounting system always requires equal dollar amounts of debits and credits. For example, two things happen when a bar bill is paid with cash. One, the hotel has more cash in the till. Two, bar sales, or bar income, has also increased. Both increase by the same dollar amount. The $33 food example several paragraphs back illustrates that equality.

If the bar drinks are charged to the room, the accounting entry changes somewhat, illustrated by the second $33 example, but the equality of debits and credits remains the same.

Reexamine the room sale and then the room adjustment discussed above, giving special attention to the equality of debits and credits — first, when the room sale was recorded, and then when the room was adjusted because of the complaint.

➤ POSTING TO ACCOUNTS RECEIVABLE

Hotels extend credit to guests. They do so because the guests' identities have been confirmed through reservations, registrations, and credit-card verifications. Except in unusual cases (see Chapter 8), guests are permitted—indeed, expected—to charge goods and services to their front-office folios. Front-office folios are the records of accounts receivable.

Most guests take advantage of the system, but some elect to buy goods and services with cash. Paying for a bar drink or a buffet breakfast with cash does not impact the folio. Folios are accounts receivable. Guests who pay with cash owe nothing, so no accounts receivables, no folio records, result from cash purchases.

Certain items, room charges or telephone calls made from the room, always sell on credit. There is no practical way for the hotel to collect cash for these sales. Telephone calls are recorded automatically on the folio by a tie-in with the telephone company. Room charges are recorded nightly by the night auditor. No one expects the room charge to be collected in cash in the middle of the night. So both are folio charges. Both are sales made on credit.

Guests may also elect to use credit cards for drinks or meals. Credit-card companies are accounts receivable too, but they are not registered; they are city-ledger receivables. Front-office folios involve transient receivables only. Neither cash purchases nor credit-card purchases appear on the front-office folios of registered guests.

Cash and credit cards especially do have a role at the front desk. They are used at check-out time to settle (pay for) the folio balance. We discuss this at the end of the chapter.

Definition of Terms to Be Used	
Allowance	Reduction of the debt owned by an account receivable
Departmental Control Sheet	Pencil-and-paper record of departmental (food, beverage, etc.) charges made to various guest rooms
Transfer	Movement of a folio balance between ledgers or guests
Zero Balance	After check-out, every folio has a balance of zero

Overview of the Billing Procedure

Electronic folios gained popularity from the mid-1980s on. Pencil-and-paper folios were the norm during the previous half-century. That period produced, first, better carbon paper and then duplicating paper without messy carbon. Stationery companies introduced packaged forms that reduced the need to write and rewrite the same information for duplicate copies. The PMS software similarly reduces redundancy. It retains information in computer memory and prints it as often as needed.

➤ *Preparing the Folio.*   Computers format the folios (see Exhibits 10–5, 10–6, etc.) as guest arrive and register. The data comes from the registration card (see Chapter 8, Exhibit 8–6) entered by the guest-service agent as the arrival procedure unfolds. The PMS can even incorporate reservation information onto the folio. In fact, some hotels prefer to use the reservation information to print the reg card or the folio the night before. One or both are then ready when the guest arrives.

Many bits of information appear on the folio. The bottom of Exhibit 10–5 indicates the time the guest arrived. The check-out time appears there when the guest leaves. More often, arrival time appears at the top of the folio, as in Exhibit 10–6. Note the arrival time is 12:29. Group affiliations are also shown. Exhibit 10–6 indicates the affiliation to be the *American* group with its billing code, Group 6566 (right side, above center).

There is common information in every folio exhibit of the chapter. Exhibit 10–6 can serve as the source. Illustrated are the room assigned (2228); the rate charged ($75); and dates of arrival and anticipated departure (9/10 and 14/10).[2] Included, of course, is the guest's name, Frank N. Stein, and address. The number of persons is usually shown, but not in Exhibit 10–6 (see Exhibit 10–9).

Folios are numbered sequentially as a means of identification and accounting control. The folio account number of Exhibit 10–6 is 20539. Folio numbers are especially important for internal control when the hotel uses pencil-and-paper folios, and almost always appear in the upper right corner, Exhibit 10–2.

As society grows more litigious, information of all kinds is being added to the folio to protect the hotel from unwarranted lawsuits. Notice of the availability of a safe for the protection of the guest's valuables is one such disclaimer. This fits better on the registration card (Chapter 8), which the guest sees on arrival, rather than on the folio, which the guest normally sees at departure.

Nearly every folio now carries at the bottom of the page a statement about liability for the bill (see Exhibit 10–1 and others). With so many persons (employers, associations, credit-card companies) other than the guests accepting the charges, hotel lawyers want to make certain that eventually someone pays. The odd part about the statement is how rarely the guest is asked to sign it.

Presenting the Bill.   Common law protects the innkeeper from fraud. Guests who are unwilling or unable to pay may be refused accommodations. Extending credit, as most hotels do, is a privilege that may be revoked at any time. Nervous credit managers do just that whenever their suspicions are aroused. The folio is printed and presented to the guest with a request for immediate payment. Even the traditional delay of paying at check-out is revoked. The entire industry has gone one step further by collecting in advance with cash (rare) or by obtaining credit-card identification.

Since most guests are not credit risks, bills are normally presented and paid at check-out time. It works that way for the vast majority of guests who stay for several nights. A folio is printed on demand as the guest departs. If there are any adjustments, an amended copy is printed for the guest to take away. Many hotels deliver the customer's initial copy under the guest-room door sometime during the previous night. If a hard copy is not needed, the folio can be viewed on a front-office monitor or more leisurely on the television in the guest room.

Long-term guests are billed weekly, and they are expected to pay promptly. Regardless of the length of the stay, folios are also rendered whenever they reach a predetermined dollar amount. The class of hotel, which reflects room rates and menu prices, determines the dollar figure that management sets as the ceiling. No charges are allowed beyond that value.

►*Communications.*   Guests buy and charge services as soon as the folio is opened, even before going to the room. That was always possible, but the computer opens the folio immediately. Pencil-and-paper systems required front-desk agents to

---

[2]In many nations, the day of the month is written before the month of the year. So it is on this Canadian folio. 9/10 is the 9th of October, not the 10th of September.

recopy the registration information onto the folio. Recopying caused long delays because it was not an agents' first priority at a busy desk.

Guests buy services from dining rooms, cocktail lounges, newsstands, room service—from all the many departments of a full-service hotel. Getting the charge information from the point of sale to the folio at the front desk is critical to the accuracy and the completeness of the billing process. Understanding how that was once done will reinforce the understanding of how it is done now.

Before the Age of Electronics.   Pencil-and-paper systems required close cooperation and fast footwork between departments. The department making the sale had to manually communicate the information to the desk and do so as quickly as possible. To illustrate, let's follow the sequence for a guest who ate breakfast in the coffee shop. By signing the restaurant check, the guest ordered the meal charged to the folio.

REMINDER: IF THE GUEST PAID WITH CASH OR CREDIT CARD, THERE IS NO FOLIO RECORD! The coffee-shop cashier was expected to check the guest's identity. That was done—but very, very rarely—with either the guest's key or an identification card (see Chapter 8).

As a precaution against the loss of this signed check, a handwritten record called a *departmental control sheet* was prepared by the departmental cashier (see Exhibit 10–7). The signed check, now called a *voucher*, was sent from the coffee shop (or any other department) to the front desk. Both the voucher and the back-up control sheet included no less than the guest's name, room number, check number, and dollar amount.

The front-office employee who received the voucher searched through the numerical sequence of the room numbers in the pit (see Exhibit 10–3). The folio was removed, and the dollar amount ($15) was posted (see Exhibit 10–2). Each posting had to be located in the correct vertical column (the date) and horizontally opposite the proper department, "RESTAURANT." The folio was refiled in the well, sequentially by room number. As part of the entire folio, the $15 was paid at check-out.

Sending the voucher to the desk was easier said than done. Hand-carried vouchers moved slowly because the coffee-shop cashier had to wait for a runner: a busperson, foodserver, or bellperson. To minimize the inconvenience of frequent calls, and also because cashiers lacked authority over runners, several vouchers were accumulated before someone was summoned, which further delayed the folio posting. Fur-

DEPARTMENT CONTROL SHEET

NAME

VOUCHER NO.	ROOM NO.	GUEST NAME	AMOUNT	MEMO
11370	409	Fishel	$ 85	
11371	1012	James	27	

KAYCO NCR FORM NO. 118   **THIS REPORT MUST BE SENT TO NIGHT AUDITOR BY 12 O'CLOCK EACH NIGHT.**

Exhibit 10–7   Segment of a departmental control sheet where guest vouchers are hand-recorded (as precaution against loss) before being dispatched to the front office for posting. Compare this procedure to the electronic communication of Exhibit 10–8.

thermore, busy runners sometimes forgetfully pocketed the voucher as they ran off to do their regular duties.

Posting were often late in arriving at the desk. Those appearing on a folio after the guest checks out, called *late charges*, are very difficult to collect. If the amount is small, the hotel doesn't even try.

Other systems were tested as the industry move toward computers. Communication between the departments and the desk relied in the interim on telephones, remote printers, and pneumatic tubes. Each had advantages and disadvantages.

With Electronic Systems.   The computer, the hotel's PMS has done away with vouchers, control sheets, runners, and late charges. Communication is electronic. The distant department is tied electronically to the front desk by means of the PMS. Cashiers in the dining rooms, lounges, and room service enter the check into an electronic cash register, called a *point-of-sale (POS) terminal* (see Exhibit 10–8). Instantaneously, the information enters computer memory. The guest's folio is always current and late charges are minimized. Moreover, the PMS gives the departmental cashiers additional capability to verify guests' identities and their right to charge.

Property management systems with point-of-sale terminals are expensive installations. Management might make an economic decision to leave certain minor departments, which generate a small amount of revenue, without POS capability. Therefore, some hotels have a mixture of electronic and pencil-and-paper systems.

Exhibit 10–8   Point-of-sale (POS) terminals are located at revenue centers (restaurants, lounges, gift shops, etc.) throughout the hotel. Each POS interfaces with the hotel's PMS, permitting cashiers at distant locations to post electronically to guest folios. The screen shown in Chapter 13, Exhibit 13–2, appears in the computer window.

Posting Charges to Accounts Receivable

Charges (increases to accounts receivable) and credits (decreases to accounts receivable) are posted (entered on the folio) to keep guest accounts current. Our discussion centers first on posting the charges and then on the meaning of each charge.

►*Understanding the Line of Posting.*   Each charge line on the folio represents two things. One is the change in the value of the account receivable. The amount the account receivable owes the hotel gets larger with each charge posting.

The purchase of goods and services are charges, and they increase the amount owed by the guest. Exhibit 10–9 illustrates several of these departmental charges.

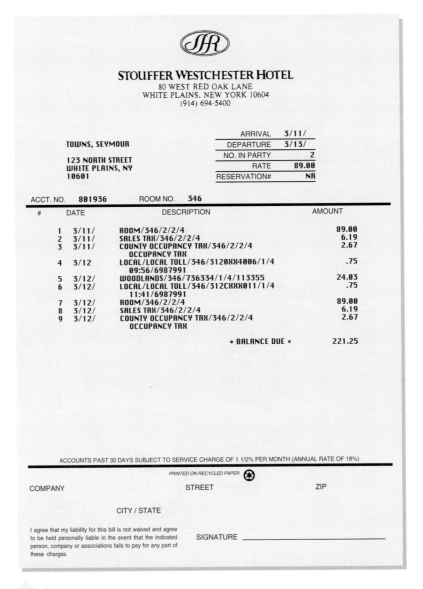

Exhibit 10–9   The format of all electronic folios is much the same, although some have two columns (debit and credit) and some only one, leaving the reader to distinguish between charges and credits. Note the sales tax postings on lines 2, 3, 8, and 9. Stouffer is no longer a hotel chain. *Courtesy of Stouffer Westchester Hotel, White Plains, New York.*

Among them are room sales (line 1, Exhibit 10–9), restaurant sales (line 5, Woodlands), and telephone calls lines 4 and 6). Each line in Exhibit 10–9 increases the debt owed by the guest/account receivable to the hotel. Note that lines 2, 3, 8, and 9 are not sales (incomes). They are taxes. That discussion is several pages ahead.

REMINDER: IF THE GUEST PAID WITH CASH OR A CREDIT CARD IN THE WOODLANDS RESTAURANT, THERE WOULD BE NO FOLIO RECORD! Folios are accounts receivable, guests who still owe. Obviously, nothing is owed when payment is made with cash or credit card.

The second, but less evident, event that each line represents is the departmental record. Charges made by the guest are sales to the departments. Each line of posting is a charge by the guest and a simultaneous record of hotel income by department. As guest account balances increase, so do the income flows from the particular departments.

Each folio illustrated in this chapter carries the same format. There is a single line record for each activity. The printed information in the center of the folio identifies the source of the income. The fact that a line of posting exists means that the account receivable is also impacted.

Examine Exhibit 10–9 or any of the other folio exhibits. Each line is read as a two-part accounting entry. One is a debit, the other the balancing credit. Since folios are accounts receivable, every folio line represents either an accounts receivable debit or an accounts receivable credit! With charges, each line is an accounts receivable debit, and the credit is to the department printed on the horizontal line.

Increase in assets, including *accounts receivable* and cash, are made with debits.

Increase in incomes (sales of *rooms, food, telephone*) are made with credits.

Increase in liabilities (debts owed to banks and *governments*) are made with credits.

Line 1   Debit accounts receivable, credit room sales for $89.
Line 2   Debit accounts receivable, credit sales taxes payable for $6.19.
Line 3   Debit accounts receivable, credit occupancy taxes payable for $2.67.
Line 4   Debit accounts receivable, credit telephone sales for $0.75.
Line 5   Debit accounts receivable, credit restaurant sales for $24.03.
Line 6   Debit accounts receivable, credit telephone sales for $0.75.
Line 7   Debit accounts receivable, credit room sales for $89.
Line 8   Debit accounts receivable, credit sales taxes payable for $6.19.
Line 9   Debit accounts receivable, credit occupancy taxes payable for $2.67.

Reference Numbers.   Exhibits 10–5, 10–6, 10–9, and 10–10 display reference numbers on each line of posting. These numbers identify departments in the hotel's chart of accounts. A chart of accounts is a coded numbering system by which the hotel classifies its records. Each department within the hotel is identified by code, but it isn't a secret code. Having codes makes record keeping easier. There is no uniform coding system among hotels, but there is consistency within the individual property and sometimes within the chain.

Consider the reference numbering of Exhibit 10–10. In the second column under the "description," the number 2315 appears on lines 2 to 11. That's the room number,

HAWAII PRINCE HOTEL

W A I K I K I

⊙ *PRINCE HOTELS*

Hawaii Prince Hotel, 100 Holomoana Street, Honolulu, Hawaii 96815
Telephone: (808) 956-1111 Facsimile: (808) 946-0811

A-STANDARD

DECAT, M/M BILL
1234 PENNSYLVANIA AVENUE
WASHINGTON, DC
56789-0000

ARRIVAL DATE 6/21
DEPARTURE 6/22
NO. IN PARTY 2
RATE 125.00

ACCOUNT NO. 67877   ROOM NO. 2315

NUMBER	DATE	DESCRIPTION		AMOUNT
1	5/31	ADV DEP VISA MASTER	4000 0000 0000 0000	$130.21CR
		1NT RM/ST TAX	67877	
2	6/21	ROOM	2315 518	$125.00
3	6/21	EXCISE TAX	2315 519	$5.21
4	6/21	ROOM TAX	2315 520	$6.25
5	6/21	LOCAL PHONE 3:57	2315 621XXX9005	$.75
6	6/21	PROMENADE DECK	2315 5996	$23.00
7	6/21	PROMENADE DECK	2315 5996	$3.00
8	6/21	PROMENADE DECK	2315 5996	$.96
9	6/22	PRINCE COURT	2315 1382	$18.00
10	6/22	PRINCE COURT	2315 1382	$2.00
11	6/22	PRINCE COURT	2315 1382	$.75
				$54.71
		* Balance Due *		

SIGNATURE

I AGREE THAT MY LIABILITY FOR THIS BILL IS NOT WAIVED AND AGREE TO BE HELD PERSONALLY LIABLE IN THE EVENT THAT THE INDICATED PERSON, COMPANY OR ASSOCIATION FAILS TO PAY FOR ANY PART OR THE FULL AMOUNT OF THESE CHARGES.

Exhibit 10–10   Line 1 of the folio illustrates an advanced deposit made by a credit card, an unusual posting. Note references to the chart of accounts in the center under "description." Each debit posting is to the room number, 2315. Equal and opposite credits are charged to their respective departments: 518, 519, and 520 are accounting codes for rooms; 5996 is beverage; and 1382 is food. The balance due will most likely be charged to the same credit card. *Courtesy of Hawaii Prince Hotel, Honolulu, Hawaii.*

the number of the account receivable being charged. In the third column is a second series of numbers, which represent the departments generating the postings. Lines 2, 3, and 4 contain the numbers 518, 519, and 520 respectively. The rooms department is identified by the number 5. Hence, 518 is room sales, 519 is room tax, and 520 is room tax for a second governmental agency.

The number 5996 appears on lines 6, 7, and 8. In this case the number 59 indicates beverage sales and 96 indicates the Promenade Deck, so 5996 is beverage sales on the Promenade Deck. The number 5997 might be beverage sales in the Prince

> Increases in assets, including *accounts receivable* and cash, are made with debits.
>
> Increases in incomes (sales of *rooms*, food and other) are made with credits.
>
> Increases in liabilities (debts owed to banks and *governments*) are made with credits.
>
> Line 2:   Debit accounts receivable, credit room sales for $125.
> Line 3:   Debit accounts receivable, credit excise taxes payable for $5.21.
> Line 4:   Debit accounts receivable, credit room taxes payable for $6.25.

Court, 5998 might be beverage sales through room service, and 5999 might be beverage sales in banquets. Line 6 is the actual sale of beverages, line 7 is the tip that the guest added to the bill, and line 8 is the tax due.

> Increases in assets, including *accounts receivable* and cash, are made with debits.
>
> Increases in incomes (sales of rooms, *beverage* and other) are made with credits.
>
> Increase in liabilities (debts to *employees* and *governments*) are made with credits.
>
> Line 6:   Debit accounts receivable, credit beverage sales for $23.
> Line 7:   Debit accounts receivable, credit tips owed to employees for $3.00.
> Line 8:   Debit accounts receivable, credit sales taxes payable for $0.96.

Food sales are similarly referenced using number 13. The number 1382 is food sales in the Prince Court. Just as beverage sales had several divisions, so might food sales: coffee shop, banquets, room service, pool snack bar, and buffet, 1383, . . . 1387.

Exhibit 10–9 follows the same concept although the presentation differs. The account receivable is identified on each line by its room number, 346, immediately after the department name. Then, just as with Exhibit 10–10, comes a series of numbers identifying the departments that generated the charge. Code 2/2/4 (lines 1, 2, and 3) represent room department charges (rooms sales and room taxes) corresponding to code number 5 of Exhibit 10–10.

The references of Exhibit 10–5 do not follow the same pattern. The ID column is quite likely the person doing the posting. The Ref. No. column may refer to the number on the voucher that gave rise to the charge. That idea is supported by the sequential numbering of the two Islander postings, 419354 on 10/25 and 419995 two days later, on 10/27.

➤ *Getting the Posting Onto the Folio.*   Charges are posted throughout the day as guests use hotel services. Often, the same charges appear repeatedly, as they do for food and telephone. Depending on the type and class of hotel, less frequent charges may be generated in a variety of minor departments. Among them might be laundry and dry cleaning; garage and parking fees; saunas and health clubs; and in-room safes, bars, and films (see Exhibit 10–5, lines 2 and 3). Full-service resorts might have sports and recreational charges for green fees, ski-lift tickets, skeet, horseback riding, and the like.

In every instance, the charge must be communicated to the desk from the distant department providing the service. Either the desk accesses the information from the computer or receives it in paper-and-pencil form. In the first case, the department uses a POS and the communication is electronic. If there is no POS, the voucher is delivered by hand, telephone, or remote printer, and the guest-service agent enters the charge into the PMS through the front-office terminal.

The Rooms Department.   Posting rooms-department charges is different than posting charges from other departments. Room charges are posted only once each day. Food, beverage, and telephone might have several daily postings. Furthermore, room charges are posted by the night auditor during the early hours of the morning. Other charges are posted as they occur throughout the day. The final difference is the location of the charge. Room sales originate at the desk, so there is no need to communicate electronically or with vouchers.

With a pencil-and-paper system, the night auditor removes each folio from the well (see Exhibit 10–3), writes the room charge and tax on each, and totals the account (see Exhibit 10–2). This is a very time-consuming and error-prone procedure.

Property management systems keep the room rates in memory, compute the taxes automatically, post and total electronically, and print on demand. With a PMS, the night auditor initiates a program that posts the room rates and taxes to all the folios, as illustrated in Exhibit 10–10, lines 2 to 4, and in other illustrations throughout the chapter.

Four exceptions, all infrequent ones, require room rates to be posted during the day rather than by the night auditor. Exception one is the day rate: Guests arrive and depart the same day—leaving before the night audit even takes place. Late check outs are another example. The previous night's room charge is posted in the normal manner by the auditor, but the premium for staying beyond the check-out hour is added by the cashier as the guest departs. It's something the auditor has no way of knowing. Situation three is a recent innovation. Guests who check out earlier than the guarantee on their reservations are compelled to pay a penalty, which is posted by the guest–service agent on duty. Again, the auditor has no way of knowing about the early departure.

Paid-in-advance guests, say those without luggage, are the final exception. Often, but not always, room charges are posted at the same time such guests make payment—that's even before they go to the room. With this procedure, guests get receipts at check in and do not return to the desk at check out, having already settled their accounts. At the time of the audit, the night auditor finds that the room rates have already been posted.

Although posted at a different time and in a different manner, room sales have the same impact as sales in other departments. All increase the amount owed by the guest, the account receivable. Most folio postings do that: increase the amount owed by the guest. The critical posting is the guest's settlement of the account. That's when the debt is paid and the account receivable is reduced to zero. *It is* always *reduced to zero.* Before examining account receivable settlements, let's review sales taxes as another of the charges (increases) to accounts receivable.

SALES TAXES.   Taxes levied on room sales by local, county, and state governments are universal to hotelkeeping (see Chapter 9). Government find taxing visitors easier than taxing residents. Making the hotel collect the tax adds insult to injury. With rare exceptions, every jurisdiction requires each room charge to be followed by one or more tax charges. The amount owed by the account receivable increases with each room sale, which belongs to the hotel, and with the room tax, which the hotel collects for the government.

Taxes collected (taxes payable) make the hotel an account receivable to the government just as the guest is an account receivable to the hotel. Logically enough, an account receivable becomes an *account payable* when situated on the other side of the owe–owed relationship. The government considers the hotel's debt as an account receivable. The hotel, which owes the amount collected from guests, considers the government an account payable. So, the amount due is labeled *taxes payable*. Exhibits 10–6, 10–9, and 10–10 reflect those tax entries.

Periodically, perhaps quarterly, the hotel pays the governmental agencies the taxes due.

WHEN TAXES ARE LEVIED ON THE GUEST

Increases in assets, including *accounts receivable* and cash, are made with debits.

Increases in incomes (sale of *rooms*, food, beverage, spa, etc.) are made with credits.

Increases in liabilities (debts to employees and *governments*) are made with credits.

Debit: Accounts Receivable/Guest's Folio	107	
Credit: Room Sales		100
Credit: Taxes Payable		7

Explanation: Collected taxes on guest's room charges.

WHEN TAXES ARE PAID BY THE HOTEL TO THE GOVERNMENT

Decreases in liabilities (debts to employees and *governments*) are made with debits.

Decreases in assets, including accounts receivable and *cash*, are made with credits.

Debit: Debit Taxes Payable	7	
Credit: Cash		7

Explanation: Paid government sums collected from guests.

Posting Settlements to Accounts Receivable

As the guest folio (an account receivable) is increased by charges, so it is decreased by credits (payments). Simply put, paying the bill by one of three means reduces the guest's obligation to the hotel.

Although charges occur and are posted numerous times throughout each day, settlement of the account usually waits until check-out time. Of course, guests can and do make payments during the stay. With reservations, payments are often made in advance, prepaid. Irrespective of when and how the payment is made, the transient folio (the guest bill, the front-office account) *must* always have a zero balance at check out! That is, total debits posted throughout the stay and total credits, whenever posted, must equal at departure. Departed guests can have no transient folio balance if they are no longer registered. The first few pages of the chapter made clear that only registered guests can have accounts in the transient ledger.

➤*Three Methods of Settling Accounts.*   Hotels have many services to sell, and they result in an array of charge postings. Payments, often called credits, are easier to track because there are only three means of settling the account debt: *There are only three methods of settling a folio.* These can be applied separately or in combinations.

1. Cash is one method, but it is used infrequently. Cash means any kind of money: bills and coin; foreign currency; domestic and international traveler's checks; personal checks; bank checks; cashier's checks; even casino chips. Payment with cash is discussed thoroughly in its own chapter, Chapter 11.

2. Allowances, reductions to the amount owed, are a second method of settlement. One study suggested that billing errors that require allowance adjustments may occur as often as one in four postings!

3. Transferring the folio balance to someone else is the third method of settlement. Credit-card transfers are the best examples. Guests move their folio balances to other accounts receivable. That is usually a credit-card company, but not always. That "person" eventually makes settlement with the hotel.

➤*Allowances.*   Just as retail stores allow the return of unsatisfactory goods, hotels give credit for poor service, misunderstandings, and mathematical errors. The retailer's exchange of merchandise is the hotel's allowance. Legitimate adjustments to guest complaints are considered so important that lease provisions usually give the hotel authority to grant allowances for unsatisfactory service by concessionaires renting space in the hotel.

Even computerized properties use paper-and-pencil allowance vouchers, also called *rebate slips*. A written record requiring an authorized signature highlights the issue both for the guest and for the company anxious to minimize errors in guest service (see Exhibit 10–11). Improving weaknesses in the operation starts with knowing what the failures are.

REBATE CREDIT			
Allowance Voucher			
Date _July 6_ ____			12501
Name _Jones L. K._		Room _1617_	
Explanation			
Laundry lost tie	23	50	
GUEST SIGNATURE _L.K. Jones_		Cashier _ABC_	
Kayco NCR Form 126 O.K. By ____			Manager

Exhibit 10–11   Allowance vouchers are numbered for accounting control. They also serve as first-line alerts to a management that is sensitive to the quality of guest service (Chapter 7) by highlighting company errors and guest complaints.

An allowance report is prepared daily as part of the night audit. As hotels empower employees (Chapter 7) to make decisions such as granting allowances, reports to management increase in importance as a control technique. Employee empowerment aside, good fiscal management requires a supervisor's signature when the value of the allowance exceeds a given amount. That limit would vary with the class of the property.

Allowances are given to adjust the bill after the fact. Problems brought to management's attention early enough will be corrected. Allowances are warranted only if it is too late to rectify the complaint. A range of circumstances require allowances: a higher room rate is posted than appears on the guest's rooming slip; a charge belongs on someone else's folio; a guest room never receives service from housekeeping; the hotel fails to deliver a basic commodity such as hot water; or a guest is given a comp.

Comp Allowances. The authority to compliment rooms or other services—the "power of the pen"—should be restricted and carefully monitored. Because comps are subject to abuse, management should require a daily comp report (see Chapter 13). Misuse starts when comp guests are not registered. Then there is nothing to report: no room count, no house count, and no room income. Proper handling of room comps starts with a daily posting of the full room rate. To allay the guest's concern, the rate is flagged on the rooming slip, "100 COMP" for example. An allowance valued at the sum total of daily folio postings is granted at the time of departure.

The allowance illustration presented under the topic of sales or incomes on page 409 is repeated here with the tax added on. If the guest stayed four nights, the first entry would be made four times, once each night, but on the folio and in folio format (see Exhibit 10–10, for example). Here, the folio entry appears in accounting form.

Increases in assets, including *accounts receivable* and cash, are made with debits.

Increases in incomes (sales of *rooms*, food, beverage, etc.) are made with credits.

Increases in liabilities (debts owed to banks and *governments*) are made with credits.

Debit: Accounts Receivable/Guest's Folio   107
    Credit: Proper Department (*room*, food, beverage, spa, etc.)   100
    Credit: Sales Taxes Payable   7
Explanation: Comp guest occupied room.

Reversing the room sale (or any other sale) with one allowance results in no charges to the guest and no room (or other) income earned by the hotel. However, a clear record of what occurred is now on the books. Some jurisdictions require room taxes to be paid on comp rooms. Sometimes the hotel pays; sometimes the comped guest pays, as illustrated next.

Decreases in incomes (sales of *rooms*, food, beverage, etc.) are made with debits.

Decreases in assets, including *accounts receivable* and cash, are made with credits.

Debit: Proper Departmental (*rooms*, food, beverage) Allowance 400
    Credit: Accounts Receivable/Guest's Folio   400
Explanation: Comped four nights (leaving guest to pay the $28 tax bill).

Allowances for Poor Service.   Accidents happen: A shirt is scorched in the laundry; a skirt is torn on a rough cocktail table. And service delivery fails: A foodserver spills coffee on a guest; a child's crib is never delivered. Service mishaps are bound to occur when servicing hundreds of visitors each day.

If the problem is caught immediately, management remedies the mistake: delivers the crib. If not caught immediately, or if the problem has no remedy (the shirt is burned), there is little to do but reimburse with an allowance. Every allowance, whether for comps or adjustments, results in reductions of both the account receivable (the guest's folio) and the departmental income. If the original charge was made to a credit card (as it might be in the lounge where the skirt was torn), the adjustment would be made to the credit card, not to the folio.

> *All allowance entries follow the same format as the room comp allowance above. The specific departmental allowance is subsituted for the room allowance of the illustration.*

Allowances to Correct Errors.   Handling small late charges is one of several clerical errors requiring correcting allowances. A late charge is posted to the folio of a guest who has already checked out. If the charge is large enough to pursue by mail, a transfer—soon to be explained—is used. If the late charge is too small to warrant the costs of collection, including guest annoyance, it is wiped off. Accounts receivable is credited and the hotel absorbs the error.

Some errors are just carelessness in posting. Exhibit 10–12 shows the allowance for $0.99 that was inadvertently posted as part of the room charge by the night auditor. Exhibit 10–5 (third line from the bottom) adjusts for a dual posting of an in-room film (lines 2 and 3).

Many errors originate in misunderstandings or lack of attention. For example, a couple arrives for several days but one spouse leaves early. Although the desk is aware of the situation, the double occupancy rate continues for the entire stay. An allowance is needed to reduce the charges by the difference between the single and double rates multiplied by the number of nights overcharged.

In theory, it should not happen, but sometimes a guest folio is carried one night beyond the actual departure day. An allowance corrects the error. This happens most frequently with one-night, paid-in-advance guests who do not bother to check out.

Every protested charge is not the hotel's error. This is why having old vouchers accessible to the cashier is helpful. (New PMS programs display vouchers from previous days, reducing the time needed to otherwise search manually.) When shown a signed voucher, guests often recall charges that they had vehemently protested only moments earlier. Large bar charges fall into this category when viewed with a sober eye the following day. This also happens when two persons share a room and one makes charges but the other pays. Especially when the first guest has already checked out is it necessary to prove to the remaining guest that the charge was made.

Although computers reduce the number of errors, they do not compensate for guest forgetfulness or for honest misunderstandings or mistakes.

Extended-stay Allowances.   Some resorts and extended-stay properties allow a rate reduction if the guest remains an extended length of time. To make certain of the guest's commitment to remain, the full daily charge is posted and not the pro rata charge of the special rate. Either an allowance is given on the final day to adjust the weekly rate or the charge of the final day is reduced to meet the special weekly total.

☐V

A Vallen Corporation Property

STATEMENT DATE
12-23-

MR. STERLING SILVERS

FOLIO NUMBER
98141 (304)

CO-NRL 7:42 AM

ACTIVITY DATE	CHARGE CODE	DESCRIPTION	CHARGES	CREDITS
12-22-	R#304	ROOM CHARGE	59.99	
12-22-	RT304	ROOM TAX	3.60	
12-23-	ARNRL	ALLOWANCE/ROOMS		.99
12-23-	MC7:43AM	MASTER CHARGE/VISA		62.60

I agree that my liability for this bill is not waived and agree to be held personally liable in the event that the indicated person, company or association fails to pay for any or the full amount of these charges. All accounts are due and payable upon receipt.

Signature: _____

BALANCE DUE
0.00

ORIGINAL

Exhibit 10–12   The folio is zeroed out (see lower right corner) using two—allowances and credit-card transfers—of the three methods of settling a folio account. Exhibit 10–14 illustrates the third option, cash payment. Note the sequential folio number on the top right.

Recording the Allowance.   Allowances, as well as the other two methods of settling an account (cash and transfers), are usually resolved at the time of departure. Once the issue has been settled, a voucher is completed and an authorized signature obtained (see Exhibit 10–11). As Chapter 7 explains, empowered employees are authorized to sign off within a given dollar range

The allowance is used with either or both of the other payments to settle the bill. Exhibit 10–12 illustrates settlement with an allowance and a credit-card transfer.

> *Using the vouchers and computer records, the accounting department, not the front desk, will charge (debit) each allowance against the department from which it originates.*

▶*Transfers.*   Like allowances and cash payments, transfers are usually, but not always, recorded as the guest checks out. A transfer simply moves the balance of one record (a front-office folio) to another record (most often a city-ledger account). The balance of the front-office folio gets smaller, usually falling to zero. The balance of the other record gets larger by the same amount.

All or part of a folio balance can be transferred. Transfers can be made between accounts in the same ledger (registered guest to registered guest in the transient ledger) or between accounts in two ledgers (registered guest in the transient ledger to city account in the city ledger). The first transfer type, registered guest to registered guest, is easier to track because both folios are available to the front-office staff. Transfers between transient folios and city accounts, usually credit-card companies, may appear incomplete to the front-office staff because the city ledger is not at the front desk. It is maintained by the accounting office.

> *Every accounting event (entry) must have equal dollar debits and credits.*

Transfer of Transient Ledger to Transient Ledger.   The two pages of Exhibit 10–2 illustrate how transfers are recorded on pencil-and-paper folios. Note that both parties have folios, and both stay one night, December 23 (the first vertical column). Both folios have room and tax charges of $84.24 ($78 + $6.24). When the new day, December 24, starts, both have beginning balances, BROUGHT FORWARD. The BROUGHT FORWARD value is larger in Room 409 than in 407 because of the restaurant charge. As the day unfolds, Room 407 gives (transfers) its balance to Room 409. Both check out before the second day ends. Room 409 pays the total amount. That total payment of $183.48 is the second of the two transfer types: transfer of transient ledger to city ledger. It is discussed next.

Room 407 clears the bill with a transfer. By so doing, the folio balances out to zero (see Exhibit 10–2). Every check out must have a zero balance: payments (the transfer) equaling charges, $84.24.

The same transfer sequence can be seen in Exhibit 10–13, line 009, illustrated on PMS folios. Guest Berger, room 301, settles his account with a credit transfer to guest Meade, room 723. Meade's account increases and Berger's decreases by the same value, $230.80. With the credit transfer, Berger's account is zeroed out (minus sign) as required of all check outs.

Transfer of Transient Ledger to City Ledger: Credit Card.   Credit cards are the most common method of settling transient folios. The guest "pays" the transient folio by transferring the balance to a credit-card account in the city ledger. The front-office cashier sees the transient folio brought to zero and leaves collection from the credit-card company to the accounting office, which is covered in Chapter 12.

Three exhibits illustrate the mechanics. Exhibit 10–12 shows a credit card used in conjunction with an allowance. The two credits of $63.59 balance the debit total of $63.59. Note the zero balance on the bottom right. Now the hotel must collect from VISA, the city-ledger account.

Similar transfers are highlighted on Exhibits 10–2 and 10–13. After the transient folio to transient folio transfer, a second transfer is made. On Exhibit 10–2, Art E. Fishal's transient folio balance, $183.48, is transferred to the credit card. Thus, Fishal's account is zeroed. Same with Exhibit 10–13, where Meade shifts the $435.85 balance to American Express.

Transfer of Transient Ledger to City Ledger: Direct.   The obsolete pencil-and-paper folio had one major advantage. Itemized for all to see were the several options that guests could use to settle their folios. Exhibit 10–2 lists them below the TOTAL DEBIT line. They are CASH (treated in the next chapter), ALLOWANCES (previously discussed), and CITY LEDGER (meaning transfers). Those are the three methods of settlement mentioned throughout this chapter.

There are several choices within the city-ledger/transfer category. They are listed in sequence in Exhibit 10–2: ADVANCE DEPOSITS (the final topic of this chapter), CREDIT CARDS (discussed immediately above), and all other TRANSFERS (the subject of the following paragraphs).

One of the "other" transfers is that of a transient folio moved to another transient folio, which was reviewed above. It is illustrated in Exhibit 10–2, where Benny Fishal's $84.24 balance is moved to the folio of Art E. Fischal, and in Exhibit 10–13, where Berger's $240.80 balance is shifted to Vincent Meade's folio.

Another of the "other" transfers involves moving folios to the city ledger, but not to a credit card. Direct city-ledger transfers are no different in form and procedure than the more common transfers to credit-card companies. The distinction lies in the city-ledger destination. With credit-card transfers, the balances move from folios to a credit-card company, such as Visa or American Express. The credit-card company sends the hotel the monies due. Direct transfers result in personal debts in the city ledger. Rather than being owed by a credit-card company, the debt is owed by an individual, a company, or an association. Such credit is almost always pre-approved. Chapter 12 contains a more complete discussion of transfers.

Master accounts are the best examples of direct city-ledger transfers. Exhibit 10–4 illustrates a transfer in which Alumni Associates shifts its transient folio to a city-ledger account of the same name. Billing is direct from the hotel to the association's headquarters. Exhibit 10–5 is the same type of transfer, but to an individual city-ledger account rather than to a company or association account.

Coupons.   Direct city-ledger transfers sometimes involve coupons. A guest who is booked by a travel agent or airline may pay the transient folio with a coupon. This is a receipt by which a third party, the travel agent, acknowledges that it has already been paid by the guest. By accepting the coupon, the hotel agrees to directly bill the travel agency or other third party. This is accomplished by transferring the transient guest's folio to the third party's account in the city ledger and billing by mail (see Chapter 12).

Skippers.   Despite improved credit-checking procedures, hotels still experience *skippers,* persons who leave (*skip*) the hotel without paying. Some skippers are accidental or the result of misunderstandings. The transient folio is transferred to the city ledger and billed. Since honest guests leave a trail of reservation and registration identification, collection takes place without difficulty.

Canadian Pacific Hotels & Resorts

Hotel Macdonald

10065 - 100 Street
Edmonton, Alberta   T5J 0N6
Tel. (403) 424-5181   Fax (403) 424-8017
G.S.T. Registration # 100769686

RECYCLED PAPER   PAPIER RECYCLÉ

ARRIVAL/ARRIVÉE	FOLIO NUMBER/No DOSSIER
WED 12 JUN	**006562**
DEPARTURE/DÉPART	BALANCE/SOLDE
FRI 14 JUN	**.00**

INTR2 KG /B 301   **FOLIO/DOSSIER**

NAME/NOM	NIGHTS/NUITS	STATUS/STATUT	DATE	TIME/HEURE	ID
Mr. Hamilton Berger	2	**Ck Out**	**14 JUN**	**1:34p**	**RV**

ADDRESS/ADRESSE   GUARANTEED BY/GARANTI PAR
                                                          AX

REMARKS/REMARQUES
CAN

LINE No. No LIGNE/	DATE	ROOM CHAMBRE	DESCRIPTION DEPARTMENT	REFERENCE RÉFÉRENCE	AMOUNT MONTANT	ID
001	12JUN	01/301	Room Charge	Rm 301	95.00+	DV
002	12JUN	01/301	Room Tax	Rm 301	4.75+	DV
003	12JUN	01/301	GST Room	Rm 301	6.65+	DV
004	13JUN	01/301	Room Charge	Rm 301	95.00+	SS
005	13JUN	01/301	Room Tax	Rm 301	4.75+	SS
006	13JUN	01/301	GST Room	Rm 301	6.65+	SS
007	14JUN	/301	Library Bar	2135	16.97+	
008	14JUN	/301	GST Library	2135	1.03+	
009	14JUN	01/301	Guest Ledger 006573 Meade, Vincent		230.80-	RV

Goods & Services Tax (GST) Summary

A	0.0000	.00	13.30+	13.30+
B	0.0000	.00	1.03+	1.03+

Grnd Tot	**216.47+**	**14.33+**	**230.80+**

Guest's signature
Signature du client X _____

I agree that my liability for this bill is not waived and I agree to be held personally liable in the event that the indicated person, company or association fails to pay for any part or the full amount of these charges. Over due balance subject to a surcharge at the rate of 1.5% per month after one month. (19.56% per annum)

Je me porte personnellement responsable du règlement total de cette noté au cas ou la compagnie, l'association ou son représentant désigné en refuserait le paiement. Les comptes en souffrance sont sujets à un intérêt de 1.5% par mois après un mois. (19.56% par annee).

Exhibit 10–13   Line 9 of both folios illustrates a transfer from room 301 (left page) to room 723. That transfer zeros the account of 301, and the guest checks out. Room 723 also checks out after making a different type of transfer, one from the guest ledger to the city ledger using an American Express credit card. Sales taxes (GST) are summarized on each folio. Note the plus (debit) and minus (credit) signs used instead of two columns. *Courtesy of Hotel McDonald, Edmonton, Alberta, Canada.*

Real skippers make their living by skipping. Their moves are intentional and deliberately planned even though the states have legislated skipping as a prima facie case of intent to defraud the innkeeper. Because it is a crime, a police report should be filed.

It often takes a day or two to verify the skip. Charges for additional room nights are posted during that period. It makes little difference, actually, since collection is rare. Once discovered, the room is checked out. The folio balance is transferred to city ledger and eventually written off as a bad debt.

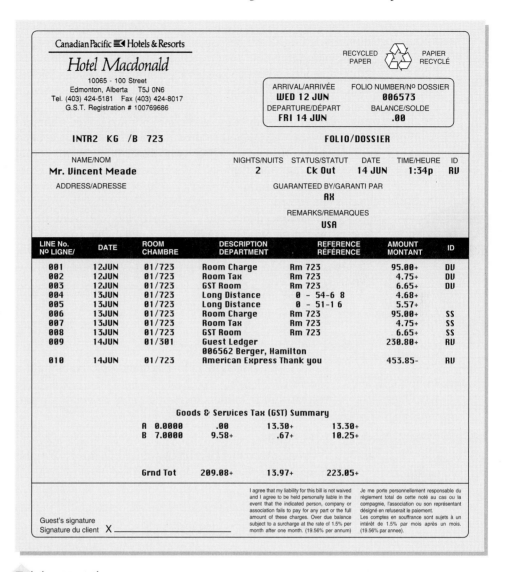

Canadian Pacific ◄ Hotels & Resorts

Hotel Macdonald

10065 - 100 Street
Edmonton, Alberta   T5J 0N6
Tel. (403) 424-5181   Fax (403) 424-8017
G.S.T. Registration # 100769686

RECYCLED PAPER / PAPIER RECYCLÉ

ARRIVAL/ARRIVÉE	FOLIO NUMBER/Nº DOSSIER
WED 12 JUN	**006573**
DEPARTURE/DÉPART	BALANCE/SOLDE
FRI 14 JUN	**.00**

INTR2 KG /B 723   **FOLIO/DOSSIER**

NAME/NOM	NIGHTS/NUITS	STATUS/STATUT	DATE	TIME/HEURE	ID
Mr. Vincent Meade	**2**	**Ck Out**	**14 JUN**	**1:34p**	**RV**

ADDRESS/ADRESSE

GUARANTEED BY/GARANTI PAR
AX

REMARKS/REMARQUES
USA

LINE No. Nº LIGNE/	DATE	ROOM CHAMBRE	DESCRIPTION DEPARTMENT	REFERENCE RÉFÉRENCE	AMOUNT MONTANT	ID
001	12JUN	01/723	Room Charge	Rm 723	95.00+	DV
002	12JUN	01/723	Room Tax	Rm 723	4.75+	DV
003	12JUN	01/723	GST Room	Rm 723	6.65+	DV
004	13JUN	01/723	Long Distance	0 - 54-6 8	4.68+	
005	13JUN	01/723	Long Distance	0 - 51-1 6	5.57+	
006	13JUN	01/723	Room Charge	Rm 723	95.00+	SS
007	13JUN	01/723	Room Tax	Rm 723	4.75+	SS
008	13JUN	01/723	GST Room	Rm 723	6.65+	SS
009	14JUN	01/301	Guest Ledger 006562 Berger, Hamilton		230.80+	RV
010	14JUN	01/723	American Express Thank you		453.85-	RV

Goods & Services Tax (GST) Summary

A	0.0000	.00	13.30+	13.30+
B	7.0000	9.58+	.67+	10.25+

Grnd Tot	**209.08+**		**13.97+**	**223.05+**

Guest's signature
Signature du client X _____

I agree that my liability for this bill is not waived and I agree to be held personally liable in the event that the indicated person, company or association fails to pay for any part or the full amount of these charges. Over due balance subject to a surcharge at the rate of 1.5% per month after one month. (19.56% per annum).

Je me porte personnellement responsable du règlement total de cette noté au cas ou la compagnie, l'association ou son représentant désigné en refuserait le paiement. Les comptes en souffrance sont sujets à un intérêt de 1.5% par mois après un mois. (19.56% par année).

Exhibit 10–13b   *Continued*

Telephone companies may rebate credit for telephone calls made by skippers and not paid. There are never too many, since the skipper has no wish to leave a traceable trail.

Transfer from City Ledger to Guest Ledger: Advanced Deposits.   Transfers of advanced deposits flow in a direction opposite to the other interledger transfers. Credit-card and direct city-ledger transfers shift the account receivable *from* the transient ledger (the front-office folio) *to* the city ledger. Billing is then made by the accounting office. Advanced deposits move the other way. The balance starts in the city ledger and moves from the city ledger to the folio in the guest ledger. Since the deposit precedes the guest's visit, the transfer usually appears on the folio's first line (see Exhibits 10–10 and 10–14, lines 1). But how does the deposit get into the city ledger to begin with?

Guaranteed reservation's require a deposit, either a credit-card deposit (see Exhibit 10–10) or a cash deposit (see Exhibit 10–14). The hotel receives the asset, either the account receivable with the credit-card company or the cash by means of a check. Note that advanced deposits in cash are rare, usually limited to resorts. Most advanced deposits are made with credit cards, but these too are rarely processed as advanced deposits. Rather, they are handled as guaranteed reservations and processed after the fact, but only if the guest does not arrive (see Chapter 6).

The hotel's obligation to provide service equal to the deposit cannot be recorded on the front-office folio. There is no front-office folio, because the guest hasn't arrived. Only registered guests have transient folios, so the hotel opens a city-ledger record called Advanced Deposits. Advanced deposits from all guests are accumulated in this one record.

With advanced deposits, the hotel has collected payments even though the guests owe nothing. This makes the hotel liable (owing) for services sometime in the future. Just as the hotel has liability for room taxes collected but not yet paid to government, so it has liability to provide paid-in-advance guests with future services.

When a cash deposit (check) is received,

> Increases in assets, including accounts receivable and *cash*, are made with debits.
> Increases in liabilities, including *debts to guests* or governments, are made with credits.

Debit: Cash
  Credit: Accounts Payable/Advanced Deposits (City Ledger)
Explanation: Cash deposit received for future arrival

The record of the hotel's city-ledger liability, advanced deposits, remains in the city ledger until the guest arrives days or weeks later. Upon arrival, the balance is transferred from the city ledger to the guest's newly opened folio in the transient ledger. As with other transfers between ledgers, guest-service agents at the front office may see only the transient-ledger half of the entry.

The deposit is applied to the arriving guest in the following accounting entry, which appears in folio format on line 1 in Exhibit 10–14.

> Decreases in liabilities, including *city-ledger debts to guests*, are made with debits.
> Increases in liabilities, including *front-office folio debts to guests*, are made with credits.

Debit: Accounts Payable/Advanced Deposits (in City Ledger)
  Credit: Accounts Receivable/Guest's Folio (in Guest Ledger)
Explanation: Guest with advance deposit arrives; liability is transferred.

30 PITT STREET
SYDNEY NSW 2000 AUSTRALIA
TELEPHONE: (02) 259 7000
FACSIMILE: (02) 252 1999
TELEX: AA127792
A.R.B.N. 003 864 908

SYDNEY
RENAISSANCE
HOTEL

GUEST	ROOM	2003
VALLEN, M/M J	RATE	170.00
EASTER PACKAGE	No. PERSONS	2
2ND AVE BEACHSIDE APPTS	FOLIO No.	152490
BURLEIGH HEADS QLD 4220	PAGE	01
	ARRIVAL	04/12/
	DEPARTURE	04/16/
CH-A BUNNY	DEPOSIT	$680.00

DATE	REFERENCE No.			DESCRIPTION	CHARGES / CREDITS
		00754		DEPOSIT	680.00CR
APR12	401	01859	99	LOCAL CALL	.70
APR12	011	02003	00	ROOM CHG	170.00
APR13	131	04071	61	BRASSERIE	22.00
APR13	401	02145	99	LOCAL CALL	.70
APR13	011	02003	00	ROOM CHG	170.00
APR14	181	02003	43	MINI BAR	2.50
APR14	011	02003	00	ROOM CHG	170.00
APR15	401	01736	99	LOCAL CALL	.70
APR15	011	02003	00	ROOM CHG	170.00
APR16	001	00001	23	PAID CASH	26.60CR
				TOTAL-DUE	.00

TRAVEL AGENCY
LOVE   TRAVEL
JENN
SH8   HIGH   ROAD
SOUTHPORT   QLD   4215

CHARGE TO

I AGREE THAT MY LIABILITY FOR THIS BILL IS NOT WAIVED AND AGREE TO BE HELD PERSONALLY LIABLE IN THE EVENT THAT THE INDICATED PERSON, COMPANY OR ASSOCIATION FAILS TO PAY FOR ANY PART OR THE FULL AMOUNT OF THESE CHARGES.

SIGNATURE

SYDNEY RENAISSANCE HOTEL - INSPIRED BY THE PAST, DESIGNED FOR THE FUTURE. sm
FOR RESERVATIONS: AUSTRALIA (008) 222 431, IN SYDNEY (02) 251 8888 • BANGKOK 02 236 0361
HONG KONG (852) 311 3666 • JAPAN (0120) 222 332, IN TOKYO (03) 3239 8303 • KUALA LUMPUR
(03) 241 4081 AND (03) 248 9008 • SEOUL (02) 555 0501

AUSTRALIA • CANADA • CARRIBEAN • CENTRAL AMERICA • CHINA • EUROPE • HONG KONG • INDIA
INDONESIA • JAPAN • KOREA • MALAYSIA • MEXICO • MIDDLE EAST • PAKISTAN • SRI LANKA
THAILAND • UK • USA   FORM No FO 001 12/92

Exhibit 10–14   This folio opens with a credit balance, a cash deposit transferred from the city ledger. Another cash payment zeros the account as the guest checks out. Cash payments like these are one of three methods for settling folios. Exhibit 10–12 illustrates the other two methods, allowances and credit cards. *Courtesy of Sydney Renaissance Hotel, Sydney, New South Wales, Australia.*

The hotel still owes the guest; the transfer has not changed that. Purchases during the guest's stay (rooms, food, and so on) are applied against the original deposit. Either the hotel still owes the guest at the end of the stay, or the guest has charged more than the original deposit. With the former, a refund is necessary, and that is explained in Chapter 11. More likely, the guest checks out owing an additional amount because deposits are usually one night's room rate only. Then the cycle begins again with payment at check-out.

Payment on checkout can be made with one of the three methods: allowances, cash (see Exhibit 10–14), or transfers (credit card or direct). Most likely, settlement will be by credit card. This moves the balance *to* the city ledger *from* the transient ledger, whereas the deposit shift had been *from* the city ledger *to* the transient ledger (see Exhibit 10–14).

RESOURCES AND CHALLENGES
Resources

➤ SUMMARY

Hotels sell their services to strangers and to registered guests. Whereas strangers must pay immediately for services like food and beverage, guests may delay payment until checkout. In the interim, guests owe the hotel; they are accounts receivable (A/R). A record of that debt, called a folio, is maintained in the front office. All the folios together are called a ledger. Hence, the billing records of registered guests are in a front-office or transient ledger. Nonregistered parties—credit-card companies, for example—may also owe the hotel. Their records are maintained in a different ledger, the city ledger, by the accounting office.

Usually, guests settle their individual folios as they checkout. That's the time they pay for all of the services (room, room taxes, food, beverage, spas, golf, etc.) that have been charged to them. Payment is by cash (rare), by allowances (for service adjustments), and by credit cards (the usual method). Credit-card settlements transfer the balance of the front-office folios to the records of the credit-card companies in the city ledger. The accounting office bills and collects from credit-card companies.

Master accounts, which track the charges of groups, are also maintained on folios. These too are transferred to the city ledger when the association or company checks out. (Every folio must have a zero balance after check out!) Master accounts are billed directly to the group's headquarters. That's different from billing credit-card companies for third-party folios. Both types of billing originate in the city ledger, having been transferred there from the front-office ledger. That discussion resumes in Chapter 12.

Hotels have not only accounts receivable, but also accounts payable. Receivables are something the hotel owns. Payables are something the hotel owes. Hotels owe governments for room taxes collected but not yet paid. Hotels owe employees for tips collected but not yet paid. Hotels owe guests with advance deposits (not common) for services not yet delivered.

➤ WEB SITES

There are many purveyors of property management systems (PMS), including the first three sites.

CSS Hotel Systems–purveyor of PMS:
   http://www:csshotelsystems.com

Data Plus, Inc.–purveyor of PMS:
   http://www.dphs.com

Galaxy Hotel Systems–subsidiary of Starwood Hotels, purveyor of PMS:
   http://www:galaxyhotelsystems.com

Hospitality Financial and Technology Professionals (HFTP)–Formerly, International Association of Hospitality Accountants; previously Hotel/Motel Accountants:
   http://www.hftp.org

Meetings and Conventions (M&C)–Trade press that features occasional articles on master accounts: http://www.meetings-conventions.com

State of Texas–Sales tax procedure for the state of Texas offers a good overview of the lodging industry's basic billing procedures: http://www.window.state.tx.us/taxinfo/audit/hotel/hotel.htm

Web Site Assignment

Using *Chapter 3* of the Web site of the State of Texas, report on any variations between the text's recommended procedure for handling sale taxes and those required for Texas hotels.

➤ INTERESTING TIDBITS

➤ A study done by Richey International and New Castle Hotels reported folios to be in error 27% of the time for small items (fax, in-room films, etc.); 32% of the time for minibars; and 17% for food-and-beverage charges. Most errors were in the guests' favor! *Hotels*, May, 1997, p. 28.

➤ When working with master accounts, meeting planners (1) demand a chronological presentation so that hotel charges can be compared to the scheduled program; (2) insist on paying the account in full, holding up tens of thousands of dollars in payment while waiting to resolve minor items; (3) reject charges for services to unauthorized signatories, even if they are officers of the company or association.

➤ Casinos comp room, food, and beverage for "high rollers," those who bet heavily and have large lines of credit. Comps for "whales," extremely wealthy high rollers, are almost limitless. It is said there are about 200 whales worldwide, although some estimates go as high as 1,000 such individuals: Persons who play $10,000 a hand. Angie Wagner, "Casinos' Save the Whales' Campaign is Succeeding," *Las Vegas Sun*, May 5, 2001.

➤ READING REFERENCES

Convention contract used by the American Red Cross to book hotel facilities: http://www:tallytown.com/redcross/form6508.pdf. (Requires Acrobat Reader on the computer.)

"Payback Time: How to Take Control of the Hotel Billing Process." Cherly-Anne Sturken. *Meetings and Conventions*, May 2002, p. 58.

"The Uniform System of Accounts for the Lodging Industry: Its Importance and Use by Hotel Managers." Ray Schmidgall and F. Kwansa. *Cornell Hotel and Restaurant Quarterly*, December 1999, p. 88.

Using Computers in Hotels, 2nd ed. Peter O'Conner. London: Cassell PLC, 2002.

Challenges

➤ TRUE/FALSE

Questions that are partially false should be marked false (F).

___ 1. Split billing is a method of settling charges on a folio by which certain amounts are settled with allowances, while other charges are settled with transfers.

___ 2. Guests who arrive late to claim their reservations (each hotel sets its own definition, but usually after 9:00 PM) are called late charges.

___ 3. Certain departmental charges (rooms, food, beverage, and telephone sales) may be posted to folios several times each day.

___ 4. Recording and classifying allowances enables management to identify weak areas of operation that need the attention of its customer-relations program.

___ 5. Point-of-sale terminals are needed in the dining rooms because every diner's charge must be posted to the folio quickly, no matter how it is paid: cash, credit card, or signature on the check.

➤ PROBLEMS

1. Differentiate the following:
   a. Debit from credit.
   b. Master account from split account.
   c. A folio from B folio.
   d. Transient guest from city guest.
   e. Charge from payment.

2. Use a word processor to replicate the folio that would be produced when the Arthur Jones family checks out. Mr. and Mrs. Jones and their infant son, George, reside at 21 Craig Drive in Hampshireville, Illinois 65065. Their reservation for three nights at $125 per night plus 5% tax was guaranteed May 17 with a $200 cash (check) deposit for one night, indicating that they will arrive late. They check in at 10 PM on June 3 and take one room (1233).
   a. Breakfast charge on June 4 is $12.90.
   b. Mrs. Jones hosts a small luncheon meeting for her company, and a $310 charge for the meeting room and meal is posted to the folio.
   c. The family decides to leave earlier than planned and notifies the desk of a 7 PM check out.
   d. A long-distance call of $8 is made.
   e. The family checks out. They raise the issue of no clean linen—the laundry had a wildcat strike—and argue for an allowance. One is given—$25. The rooms manager then charges 30% of the normal room charge for the late departure.
   f. Payment is made with an American Express card, no. 33333333333.

3. Create a pencil-and-paper folio; use Exhibit 10–2 as a guide. Post the events of Problem 2 as they would appear on a hand-prepared folio.

4. Under which of the following circumstances would management grant an allowance? How much would be the value of that allowance? What else might be done if an allowance were not granted?
   a. Guest sets the room alarm clock, but it fails to go off, which causes the guest to miss a meeting that involves thousands of dollars of commission.
   b. Same circumstance as part (a) but the guest called the telephone operator for a morning call, which wasn't made.
   c. Guest checks out and discovers the nightly room charge to be $15 more than the rate quoted two weeks earlier by the reservations center.

d. Same circumstance as part (c) but the discrepancy is discovered soon after the guest is roomed.

5. How would the following transfers be handled? (Answer either by discussion, by offering the accounting entries, or both.)

   a. A departing guest discovers that a $60 beverage charge that belongs to another guest, who is still registered, was incorrectly posted yesterday to the departing guest's account.

   b. Same circumstance as part (a) but the $60 beverage posting was made today.

   c. Same circumstance as part (a) but the other guest has departed.

   d. Two days into a guest's four-day stay, the reservation department realizes the guest's advance deposit was never transferred to the front-office account.

   e. Same circumstance as part (d) but the discovery is made by the guest, who writes to complain about the omission one week after check out.

6. Check your understanding of accounting by proving the debits and credits for each of the following situations, which were not discussed in the text.

   a. The hotel pays the quarterly sales taxes of $8,925.00 due the local government, the city of Popcorn, Indiana.

   b. The hotel receives a check from Diners Club for payment of credit-card balances due of $1,000.

   c. Same as part (b) but Diners Club withholds 4% for a fee.

   d. The hotel receives a check from its parent company for $1,500, representing the total payment due for several frequent-stay guests who used their points at your hotel. The amount of room charges generated by those guests was $5,500.

➤ ANSWERS TO TRUE/FALSE QUIZ

1. False. Split billing is the distribution of charges between master-account folios (sometimes called "A" folios) and individual, personal folios ("B" folios).

2. False. Late charges are departmental charges (sales) that arrive at the front desk too late for posting to the active folio: The guest has checked out.

3. False. Some charges may appear on the folio several times each day (food, beverage, telephone), but room charges are posted just once daily.

4. True. Good accounting requires adequate explanations for each allowance. Classifying those complaints highlights areas needing management attention.

5. False. Point-of-sale terminals expedite posting of check-signature charges only; payments made in cash or with credit card are not posted to folios even if the diner is a registered guest.

Cash Transactions

Outline

➤ *HANDLING CASH TRANSACTIONS*

Due to the ease, security, and prevalence of credit cards and debit cards, departing guests rarely pay hotel room folios with cash. Conservative estimates place cash payments during check-out at something less than 5% of the time. Cash payments are probably more common in budget or economy properties; they are even less common in corporate hotels (where employer-provided credit cards are frequently used) and resort properties (where the folio from a one-week stay might easily reach $3,000 or more).

In today's electronic age, cash is simply less convenient than credit cards, debit cards, or other forms of electronic payment. After all, compared with credit (or debit) cards, cash is bulkier, less secure, provides a less detailed transaction trail, and requires an exchange to local currencies when visiting foreign countries. For corporate guests, an added step is required when using cash—the corporate guest must either obtain a cash advance before beginning the business trip or be out-of-pocket the amount of cash expended until the company reimburses his or her travel costs. No wonder so few guests pay cash at the front desk.

In spite of the small amount of cash that changes hands over the front desk, its relative importance to the operation of the hotel is substantial. Full-service properties monitor daily cash balances in cashiers' drawers to ensure there is enough cash on hand to manage the numerous nonpayment cash transactions that regularly occur. Guests expect to cash traveler's checks, even personal checks at times. They may need to change large bills. We should expect that foreign currency conversions at U.S. hotels will increase substantially with the introduction of the euro, the single European currency. Front desks also handle cash advances to guests and provide up-front money for many hotel uses. So cash is not going to disappear into a cashless society.

Even as cash grows less popular as a means of folio settlement, its security grows more problemsome. Cash is very negotiable, easily pocketed, and a continuing target of the bad guys. Counterfeiters, bad check artists, photocopiers and short change manipulators work their wares at hotel desks. They would rather try the hotel desk than busier retail outlets. Guest-service agents handle less money than most other retailers, and are, therefore, less skilled at identifying bogus paper. When speaking of money, eternal vigilance is trite but true.

Cash Paid-Outs

Cash at the front desk flows both ways; *cash receipts* and *cash paid-outs.* In every other operational department of the hotel, cash flows in to the various departmental cashiers (cash receipts). Only at the front desk does cash flow in both directions.

Cashiers in the front office, as in all hotel departments, may receive cash as payment to settle a guest account. However, as already noted, cash is less frequently used at the front desk to settle the guest folio than it is in various other departments where the purchase is substantially less (e.g., breakfast in the dining room, a few beverages in the lounge, or a newspaper in the gift shop).

Another difference between the front office and other hotel departments is worth noting: While cashiers in other departments receive cash to settle purchases of various departmental products (e.g., breakfast, beverages, newspaper), cash transactions at the front office settle accounts receivables. Front-office cashiers have no product to sell. Conversely, outlet cashiers have no record of accounts receivable and are not able to accept payments from departing guests. Each cashier type accepts cash from guests but for different reasons.

Here is a simple formula for understanding the relationship of cash to accounts receivables:

Increases in assets, including accounts receivable and *cash,* are made with debits.

Decreases in assets, including *accounts receivable* and cash, are made with credits.

Cash paid-outs are the exclusive right of the front-office cashier. Except for tips paid to employees (waitstaff, for example), no paid-outs are ever made by cashiers in other operating departments. Paid-outs to guests are, in fact, small loans made by the front office to or on behalf of the guest. Paid-outs are debits to the guest folio and increase the amount the guest owes the hotel (accounts receivable). Similarly, the paid-out requires a cash outlay and therefore reduces the amount of cash in the front office cashier's drawer. Again,

Increases in assets, including *accounts receivable* and cash, are made with debits.

Decreases in assets, including accounts receivable and *cash,* are made with credits.

Tips to employees are the most common paid-out, but there are others as well.

➤*Tips to Employees.*   Tips are the most common cash advance. They are paid to an employee upon request of the guest. A signed check from the dining room or bar is the usual method of request. The amount of gratuity is added to the check by the guest when signing for the service. When the signed voucher reaches the front-desk clerk, the departmental charges are separated from the tip. The tip is posted under the cash advance category, not the food or beverage category. After all, the tip is not departmental income, so it must not appear under a departmental heading.

Acting on the guest's signature, the front-office cashier pays the tip to the server, who signs for the money on a cash advance voucher. The cash advance voucher is then posted to the guest's folio along with the departmental charge (food, beverage, or whatever). At the end of the shift, this paid-out appears on the cashier's balance report as a reduction to the cashier's drawer.

Since the procedure is not an unusual one, a traffic problem could develop at the front desk if employees from all over the hotel came to collect their tips. To forestall this, tips are paid by the cashiers in the various dining rooms and bars. In a way, the problem handles itself. Most tips are added to national credit cards. Charges to national credit cards do not usually come to the front office. Only charges to the guest's folio, whether there are tips or not, flow through the front-office procedure. Even a credit-card charge (restaurant, bar) made by a registered guest will not pass through the guest's folio, but rather, will be deposited as income directly by the department involved.

Front-office cashiers still process tips to front-of-the-house employees: bell, housekeeping, and delivery persons. Most hotels pay their employees' tips on receipt or at the end of the shift. This is wonderful for the employee, but it can often result in the hotel subsidizing its employee gratuities in three common ways: float (that is, the time value of money), merchant discount fees on credit cards, and potential noncollectible accounts. Granted, it may be a minimal sum of money when considered on a per employee basis, but over time (and in large properties with hundreds or thousands of employees) it can quickly add to a significant amount.

Float.   Because of the time value of money, it costs the hotel money to prepay an employee's tip before the guest's bill is paid. Yet this is exactly what happens with many paid-out tips. To illustrate the point, let's follow the payment cycle for a newly arriving guest, Diane Green.

Upon arrival, Green asks the front desk to issue a $10 tip to the bellperson as a paid-out against her folio. Because this is the first day of a lengthy visit, let's assume that Green's folio will not be settled for nine days. In this example, the hotel has ostensibly paid the bellperson with money it will not receive for nine days.

To add insult to injury, Green's bill will probably be settled by a national credit card. Certain types of credit-card companies may take weeks before they pay the hotel. It is conceivable therefore that the hotel has paid the bellperson a tip with money it will not receive for some 20 or 30 days! That is a costly employee benefit (see Exhibit 11–1).

Merchant Discount Fees.   National credit-card companies charge merchants (hotels) a fee for accepting their credit card. The merchant discount fee may range anywhere from just over 1% to just under 5%, depending on the sales volume of the hotel, the credit card in question, and a number of other variables (see Chapter 12). In Green's example, she settled the bill with an American Express card. Let's assume that the hotel pays a 2% fee for the use of American Express.

A 2% fee on all American Express card sales means that the hotel receives $98 from American Express for every $100 charged at the hotel. Therefore, American Express will only reimburse the hotel $9.80 for the bellperson's $10 tip, which the hotel has already paid in full.

Although 20 cents sounds trivial, it adds up over time and volume. After all, that's 20 cents for just one tip to one bellperson; imagine dozens of tips to possibly hundreds of employees per day (see Exhibit 11–1).

Noncollectible Accounts.   The most blatant example of subsidizing employee paid-out tips is when the guest folio becomes uncollectible. Whatever the reason for the uncollectible account, the hotel loses more than the departmental revenues. Whether the uncollectible folio was a direct bill account gone bad, a personal check with insufficient funds, or a fraudulent credit card, the hotel also loses the amount of the paid-out tip.

Some hotels attempt to recover uncollectible tips from their employees. But collecting from the employee months after the service was rendered is quite unlikely. In addition, it negatively affects morale to collect what the employee perceives as a rather trivial sum of money.

Another Look at Employee Tips.   Exhibit 11–1 demonstrates the hidden costs to the hotel of paying employee tips upon receipt. For example, while visiting the hotel, Ms. Green might charge a few meals (and tips) to her folio, she might call the front desk and ask them to pay the bellperson a tip on her behalf, and she might charge cocktails (and tip) in the lounge one evening as well. Although Ms. Green has yet to check out (and when she does, her bill might not be settled for many days), the employees will all receive their tips on the days she makes the various charges. This is a costly employee benefit for the hotel.

Yet almost all hotels conduct this practice. There really is no other way to handle employee tips without creating additional burdens. Hotels could refuse to allow guests to charge tips against their folio. Although this would save hotels the cost of the merchant discount fee, the practice would create far more ill will than it would save in expenses. Similarly, hotels could wait to pay employee tips until the guests' bills actually

Schedule of Hypothetical Costs Associated with Paying Employee Tips Upon Receipt

1. **Assumptions**
   - Hotel staffs 7 bellpersons per day, who average $20 per day in charged tips.
   - Hotel staffs 22 waitpersons and room servers per day, who average $45 per day in charged tips.
   - Hotel staffs 4 bartenders per day, who average $40 per day in charged tips.
   - Some 75% of all charged tips are paid by credit card. The average merchant discount fee for all types of credit cards is 2.25%.
   - The average time for settlement of the bill (including those who pay by credit card, those who pay by direct bill, and those who pay by cash) is 2 weeks past date of check out.
   - Approximately 0.5% of all folios are noncollectible.

2. **Float-Related Costs**
   - Total employee tips paid out per day are $140 for bellpersons, $990 for waitpersons, and $160 for bartenders. That's $1,290 for 365 days equals $470,850 per year.
   - Assuming a 9.0% internal rate of return and an average 2 weeks before collection, the hotel's cost of floating employees' tips equates to $1,629.87 per year.

3. **Merchant Discount Fees**
   - Assuming $470,850 per year in total employee tips and that 75% of all tips are paid to credit cards, the total amount of tips paid by credit cards is $353,137.50.
   - If the average merchant discount fee is 2.25%, the hotel's annual cost of paying employees tips in full (rather than discounting them) is $7,945.59.

4. **Noncollectible Accounts**
   - Assuming $470,850 per year in total employee tips and that 0.5% of all folios are noncollectible, the hotel pays employee tips of $2,354.25 but never receives payment from the guest.

5. **Grand Total Annual Costs**
   - The hotel's cost of floating employees' tips equates to $1,629.87 per year.
   - The hotel's cost of paying the employees' share of the merchant discount fees is $7,945.59.
   - The hotel's cost of paying employee tips on noncollectible accounts is $2,354.25.
   - For this hypothetical scenario, the total cost to the hotel for paying employee tips in full is $11,929.71.

Exhibit 11–1   Employee tips are customarily handled as paid-outs on the same day they are charged to folios or credit cards. This costly practice is, in fact, an employee compensation benefit and should be explained that way and so treated during wage negotiations.

cleared. This would save hotels those expenses related to both float and noncollectible accounts. It would, however, create such an accounting and tracking nightmare that it would be hard to justify. Hotels look upon tip expenses as another cost of doing business, a costly one at that.

Exhibit 11–1 assumes that a full-service hotel pays tips to bellpersons, waitpersons, and bartenders. They are but 3 of numerous commonly tipped positions (clubhouse staff, banquet staff, etc.). These and a number of other assumptions are discussed in Exhibit 11–1.

➤*Cash Loans.*　Although paid-outs against the guest folio represent money provided by the hotel on the guest's behalf (as when a tip paid to a bellman is charged against the guest's folio), they are not exactly cash loans. Actual loans to hotel guests are generally quite rare, occurring under unusual circumstances and only to those guests well known by the hotel's management. Advancing money to the guest as a paid-out (debit) against the folio runs the same costs and risks discussed above (float, credit-card merchant discount fees, and potential losses from uncollectible accounts). However, just as few hotels charge processing fees to employees who receive tips against credit cards, equally few hotels charge fees to guests desperate for a cash loan (see Exhibit 11–1).

It is now more difficult to cash a check than it was to obtain a cash loan years ago. This is especially true on weekends when banks are closed. Some hoteliers believe that it is better to have a small loan skip than to have a large check bounce, so they grant the former if forced to choose. Companies that use the hotel on a regular basis may establish "loan" arrangements for their staffs by guaranteeing the advances. Preferred-guest programs provide just such check-cashing privileges.

Third-Party Sources of Cash.　A number of new options have surfaced due partially to the hotel industry's unwillingness to act as banker for the millions of domestic and international travelers. Among these options are automatic teller machines (ATMs), credit-card advances, and expedited money order services. Each of these options provides cash to the guest without jeopardizing the hotel or putting it into a business for which it lacks expertise.

Credit-card advances (for example, Comcheck) and money order services (for example, Western Union's FlashCash) transfer the related costs and risks (float, credit-card discount fees, and potential losses from uncollectible accounts) from the hotel to the guest. In essence, guests send themselves money and pay their own costs. For example, by calling Western Union and using a national credit card, guests authorize payment to themselves. The guest gets the money, but Western Union, not the guest, is now the hotel's account receivable.

These financial services don't come free. Fees paid by the guest to the third parties range from 5 to 10%, depending on the amount and the company plan. Guests who would howl at the hotel for charging such usury pay up without a whimper.

Automatic Teller Machines (ATMs).　By far the most common method used by today's guests to obtain needed cash is the automatic teller machine (ATM). The use of ATMs (see Exhibit 11–2) is not limited to the United States: ATMs are rapidly becoming the accepted norm for quick currency worldwide. The two most popular overseas networks, Cirrus (linked to MasterCard) and Plus (linked to VISA), can be accessed by over 90% of the ATM bank cards in circulation in the United States. Another attractive benefit to using worldwide ATMs is that the ATMs' foreign exchange rate is often lower than the rate charged by local banks.

Exhibit 11–2   Advanced ATM machines offer many more features than the standard ATM cash machines, including check cashing for personal, corporate, and payroll checks with no risk to the hotel or merchant. Risks are minimized by the Mr. Payroll ATM, which uses a security system based on facial recognition. With biometrics technology, the ATM "never forgets a face." *Courtesy of Mr. Payroll Corporation, Fort Worth, Texas.*

Corporate travelers are depending more and more on ATMs. They are available 24 hours a day, 365 days a year, and with hundreds of thousands of machines available, an ATM is usually just a step away. This limits the amount of money corporate travelers need to carry for a long trip. In addition, it minimizes the risk of financial loss if the guest's wallet is stolen or lost.

Although this is the age of credit cards and electronic payments, travelers still need to carry cash for expenses such as taxicabs, tips to skycaps or bellpersons, newspapers, and incidental items. Corporate travelers have historically received cash advances prior to departing on business trips. Yet cash advances are costly, running as much as $20 or more to process each corporate travel advance because of the number of staff involved. The traveler needs to fill out the cash advance request, the manager needs to approve it, an accounts payable clerk processes it, and a financial manager cuts the final check.

In recent years, many firms have begun using ATMs exclusively. The traveler uses the corporate credit card to secure cash for the trip, getting additional cash when necessary along the way. At the end of the trip, whatever cash remains unspent can be redeposited directly back to the ATM account. Even considering the fees charged by the ATM network this is a considerably cheaper way of handling cash advances.

ATMs in Hotel Lobbies.   Lodging chains are quickly realizing the benefits associated with installing ATMs in hotel lobbies. Such chains as Choice, Crowne Plaza, Doubletree Club, Embassy Suites, Hilton, Holiday Inn, Radisson, Ramada, and Sheraton have ATMs in place in some of their hotel lobbies. Not only do these machines provide guest convenience, they have become a new revenue center for the hotel as well.

Prior to 1996, there was no incentive for hotels to install ATM machines, because banks did not charge the user a fee per transaction. Instead, all ATM network costs were paid internally by the banks themselves. In April 1996, VISA and MasterCard eased their restrictions on surcharging cash ATM transactions. Following this change in policy, ATM users began paying a surcharge ranging from roughly $2 to $5 per transaction (depending on card, location, bank, and amount of transaction).

A number of ATM manufacturers also provide hotel service contracts. In exchange for a place to install the ATM (usually in a secure high-traffic area such as the hotel lobby) and access to thousands of guests, the service provider agrees to purchase, install, and maintain the machine; load it with cash on a regular basis; and split surcharges with the hotel. Pay telephones, soda, snack, newspaper, and cigarette machines are installed under similar contracts.

Not only does the hotel benefit from this new revenue source, but it also reduces or eliminates the need for the front desk to cash personal checks. In addition, with more cash in their hands, guests may spend more in the gift shops, restaurants, bars, and casinos.

ATM's Dispense More than Cash.   The newest ATMs are fast becoming important new marketing tools for hotels and local merchants. ATMs promote products through coupons and/or on-screen graphics. Many ATMs allow a hotel to custom-design one or more coupons for the back of the guest receipt. A coupon might be worth a free drink in the bar or a free appetizer in the restaurant. In addition to this approach, ATMs can flash messages and promotional screens to the guest while waiting for the transaction to process.

Because today's hottest ATM's are wired directly to the World Wide Web, literally anything goes. Guests can pay utility bills, apply for a new car loan, or trade stocks. Indeed, the ATM can print cashier's checks, make a pitch suggesting the customer try the hotel's new credit card, even show the guest tomorrow's weather forecast. Exhibit 11–3 provides a glimpse at some of the most likely ATM possibilities.

▶*Paid-outs to Concessionaires.*   Full-service hotels often arrange for local merchants to provide guest services the hotel is unable to offer. These merchants may actually have an outlet inside the hotel (for example, a beauty salon, florist, or gift shop), or they may contract services off-premise (for example, a travel agent, valet cleaning, or a printing shop). These private vendors are commonly referred to as *concessionaires;* their shops are known as *concessions.*

The concessionaire–guest relationship often mandates that the hotel act as middleman. In circumstances where the hotel relays the goods on behalf of the guest (laundry is usually delivered to the guest's room by the bellstaff, for example) or where the concessionaire looks to the hotel for collection (say, when a guest charges her hairstyling to the room folio), the hotel is acting as an intermediary. As such, the hotel is sometimes entitled to a fee or commission for its part in the process. It is not uncommon for hotels to earn 10 to 20% of the laundry and dry cleaning revenue (the other 80 to 90% accrues to the vendor) as their share of providing laundry bags, bellstaff pickups and deliveries, storage, and collections.

The hotel also finds itself stuck in the middle when dealing with problems or complaints. When a piece of clothing has been lost or destroyed, the guest is not inter-

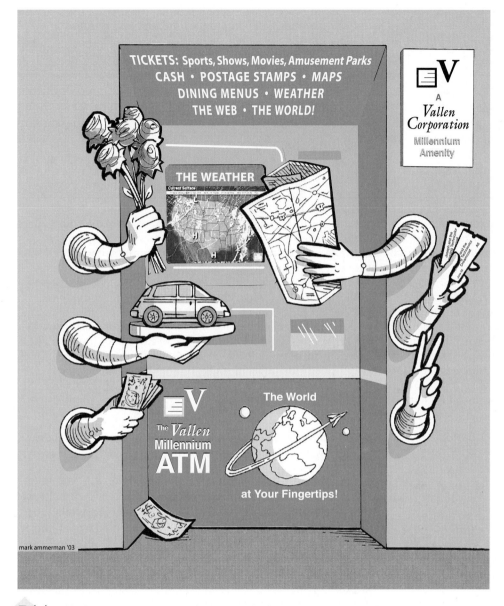

Exhibit 11–3   Because many of today's ATMs are wired directly to the World Wide Web, they provide a wide range of services. Hotels need to choose for themselves which features are most appropriate for their guests and which generate the most revenue. Tickets for sporting events and nearby shows, maps, weather forecasts, and postage stamps make sense for corporate guests and the hotel's bottom line (ticket purchases, for example, usually have a hotel commission built into the sales price). But when other guests are waiting in line to withdraw funds, time is of the essence—it makes little sense to show movie trailers (which also represent revenue to the hotel) at the expense of frustrated guests.

Company	Number of Worldwide ATMs[1]	Number of Countries in Which ATMs are Available	Appropriate Fee per Transaction
American Express	500,000+	130+ countries	2 to 5% of the transaction amount
Cirrus (MasterCard)	790,000+	100+ countries	Rates set by the issuing bank
Diners Club (in conjunction with Master Card/Cirrus ATMs)	790,000+	100+ countries	4% of the transaction amount, or $6
Plus (VISA)	800,000+	144+ countries	Rates set by the issuing bank

Exhibit 11–4   Corporate and leisure travelers have benefited in recent years with the growing number of available ATMs. This is especially true in foreign countries, where travelers gain the convenience of local currency at the touch of a button without the concern of exchanging just the right amount of money. Also, using international ATMs allows the traveler to float the currency exchange for some 20 or 30 days. During that time, the U.S. dollar may gain value against the foreign currency, more than offsetting the assessed transaction fee.

Additionally, ATM machines in hotel lobbies likely increase revenues. Cash retention is generally quite high with ATM users. In other words, some of the money dispensed to the guest through the ATM probably stays in the hotel. Research shows that 30 to 33% of cash is retained from ATMs located in large retail stores; 35 to 40% is retained from ATMs located in small retail stores; and 70 to 80% is retained from ATMs located in nightclubs. No research is yet available for hotel lobbies.

ested in learning that the laundry service is a private concession. Quality guest service dictates that the hotel solve the problem on behalf of the guest!

Accounting for Paid-outs to Concessionaires.   The hotel also acts as intermediary in terms of disbursing revenues to the concessionaire. Payment is made to the merchant when the service is completed and charged to the guest's folio as a paid-out. Specifically, the clerk debits accounts receivable (a paid-out on the guest's folio) and credits cash. The clerk then removes the cash from the drawer in the amount of the paid-out (remember, the paid-out charged the guest may be different from the amount of cash handed over to the concessionaire, because the hotel may keep a portion of the proceeds as its share of the transaction). The concessionaire then signs the paid-out voucher and the money is handed over.

At the end of the shift, the cashier's balance report reflects the reduction of cash in the money drawer. In essence, the hotel has loaned the money on behalf of the guest and awaits repayment when the guest checks out. Of course, all of the costs associated with float, credit-card discount fees, and uncollectible accounts are issues for negotiation between the hotel and the concessionaire.

Paying the concessionaire in cash each time the service is used is expensive and time consuming, for the merchant as well as for the hotel, since the concessionaire must wait for the cash and sign the paperwork. In many cases, a different plan is

[1]Exhibit 11–4 assumes an annualized growth rate for ATMs worldwide of roughly 10%. Actually, international ATMs have been growing at a more rapid rate than domestic ATMs in recent years.

arranged. The hotel bills the guest just as if the concessionaire were a department of the hotel, collects on check out, and reimburses the merchant periodically. In such cases, the guest's folio looks a bit different. Rather than reflecting a paid-out posting, the charge instead is posted to an actual department (say, laundry or valet). The net effect—the guest owes the hotel—remains unchanged.

➤*Refunds at Check Out.*   On occasion, the hotel owes the guest a refund at the conclusion of the stay. This happens for one of several reasons. Either there was a substantial deposit with the reservation, or a large payment on account was made on (or after) arrival. If the guest shortens the stay, or the hotel adjusts the rate downward, there could be a credit balance at the time of departure. Paid-in-advance guests who leave additional deposits to cover other charges to their rooms (such as for telephone calls) may also show a credit balance.

At check out, the hotel pays the guest. Zeroing the credit balance of the account requires a debit or charge entry. A paid-out voucher is prepared for the guest's signature in the amount the hotel owes. At the end of the shift, the computerized cashier's balance report subtracts the amount of the paid-out from the total cash remaining in the money drawer.

Cash is never refunded if the original payment was not made in cash! If the guest's personal credit card were the source, for example, the hotel would issue a rebate against the credit card. Similarly, large cash deposits made by the guest may not be refundable on check out. Before receiving the large cash deposit, the clerk should explain hotel policy regarding paid-outs. Some hotels restrict the size of the paid-out to, say, $100. Anything above that amount requires a check to be processed by the hotel accounting department and mailed to the guest's home. This prevents guests from depositing illegitimate traveler's checks, personal checks (discussed later in this chapter), or counterfeit money and then attempting to collect legitimate cash against that amount the following day.

Cash Receipts

We have already emphasized that cash paid-outs are limited to front-office cashiers; cashiers in other departments never make cash paid-outs. Cash paid-outs are essentially advances or loans against accounts receivable. Eventually, those advances are repaid by the guest. That normally takes place when the balance of the folio is settled, typically at check out. Guests settle their folios, as Chapter 10 stressed, in one of 4 methods: with cash, with credit card, with an allowance, or with a transfer (credit). Cash paid by the guest and received by the hotel is the thrust of this chapter. Again,

Increases in assets, including accounts receivable and *cash,* are made with debits.

Decreases in assets, including *accounts receivable* and cash, are made with credits.

➤*Cash Receipts at Check Out.*   Only a small percentage of check outs elect to settle with cash. Most guests pay by credit card or request direct billing through the city ledger. Very few use cash, traveler's checks or personal checks.

Posting cash paid to the folio has the opposite effect from posting a cash paid-out to the folio. Whereas the paid-out increases the amount owed by the guest (debit to accounts receivable), cash receipts decrease the amount owed by the guest (credit to accounts receivable). In all cases, the amount collected from the guest is the exact amount required to reduce the folio balance to zero.

It is a quick procedure: The computerized property management system maintains a cumulative balance, which indicates the amount due. Some hotels display the folio on the computer screen for the guest to scan, others deliver preprinted hard copies to all departing guests, and still others encourage self-check out via the television screen (see Chapter 14).

Whatever the method, all cashiers are trained to inquire about very recent charges that may still be unrecorded. Catching unposted telephone or breakfast charges minimizes the number of late charges, with their high rate of uncollection and guest displeasure.

➤*Cash Receipts on Account.*   Payments may be requested at any time, not just at departure. Long-term guests are billed weekly, as a means of improving the hotel's cash flow and keeping the guest as current as possible. Guests who exceed certain credit limits or guests who generate too many charges (especially items normally paid for in cash) are billed at the hotel's discretion. Sometimes, guests themselves decide to make payments against their accounts.

At check out, departing guests are given a copy of the zero-balance folio as a receipt for their cash payment. Similarly, guests who make cash payments on account are given a copy of the folio to serve as a receipt of the payment. The only difference is the timing: the folio given in the middle of the stay is probably not a zero-balance folio. In fact, paid-in-advance customers usually maintain a credit balance on their folios throughout some of the visit.

The desk is frequently faced with a guest—especially one who hasn't traveled extensively—who tries to pay on the day before departure. Because of possible late charges, the desk tries to discourage guests from making payment too early. In fact, day-early payments require special attention by the cashier, who must be certain to collect enough to cover the upcoming room-night and room tax that will not be posted until the auditor arrives. So the employee convinces the guest to wait until the next day rather than paying in full the previous day in anticipation of an early departure. Naturally, many guests find it incomprehensible that they are dissuaded from concluding their business until the next morning. This is much less a problem in modern hotels, which provide the guest with a number of rapid automatic or self-check-out options.

➤*Cash Receipts at Check In.*   All guests are asked to establish credit at check in. Most simply proffer their credit card and the desk clerk verifies it for a predetermined floor limit. Direct bill guests are not asked about credit at check in because their company has a previously established account on file with the hotel's accounting department. Only cash guests, then, are actually asked to pay their room charges up front. Cash guests include those paying with currency, traveler's checks, and personal checks (if allowed).

Unless an additional deposit is made, no other room charges are allowed against a paid-in-advance guest, who often departs the hotel without stopping at the desk. An additional room charge is made and collected each succeeding day the customer remains. Unless this is received, someone on the desk automatically checks out paid-in-advance guests by the check-out hour of the following day. Some limited-service properties may actually lock out guests who remain beyond the check-out hour. Less extreme measures, including telephone messages, are usually used to communicate with the paid-in-advance guest.

Automatic check out of a paid-in-advance guest requires coordination and communication. The front desk must be careful not to prematurely show as vacant any room that was paid in advance. Prior to automatically checking the guest out, a bellperson or housekeeper is asked to inspect the room. Only after they communicate that the room is truly empty should the front desk complete the check out.

➤*Reservation Deposit Receipts.* Just as cash is seldom used to pay the folio at the front desk, so is cash rarely used when requesting an advance deposit. Most guests simply guarantee the reservation with a credit card. Still, some hotels (particularly resorts where reservation lead time may be several months in advance) request advance deposits in order to hold the reservation. In such cases, the easiest means of collecting the deposit is simply to charge the guest's credit card upon taking the reservation.

Some properties, however, do not choose to collect deposits against guest credit cards. Who can blame them? When there is sufficient lead time, a mailed-in deposit (check or money order) has no merchant discount fee associated with it. For the hotel that collects an entire season's worth of advance deposits, this small distinction may represent thousands of dollars in savings.

Different hotels handle these deposits in different ways, usually as a function of the size and sophistication of their accounting systems. The easiest but least businesslike method assigns the check to the front-office cash drawer. There it stays, unrecorded, until the guest arrives weeks or months later. The check is then applied to a newly opened folio as if the money were just received that day. This procedure simplifies the bookkeeping, especially if there is a cancellation, but it has little additional merit even for a small hotel. Lack of a proper record and the failure to clear the check through the bank indicate poor management of both procedure and funds.

Sometimes the actual folio that is to be assigned the guest on arrival is opened when the deposit check is received. This procedure is extremely cumbersome for manual or semiautomated properties that utilize prenumbered folios. However, in computerized properties, this procedure works quite satisfactorily. That is because one major difference between manual and computerized properties is the timing as to when they assign the guest folio. In a manual property (unless a reservation deposit is received), the folio is not assigned until check in, which may be months later. In a computerized property, a folio identification number is assigned immediately, at the moment of reservation.

Establishing a City-Ledger Account. The most common method for handling reservation deposits uses the city ledger (see Chapter 12 for a complete discussion of the city ledger). An account is established in the city ledger for advance-deposit receipts. Guest deposits are credited to that account and later transferred to the folio on guest arrival.

With a city-ledger advance-deposit account, the front-office cashier sees only one side of the transfer, the credit made to the account of the arriving guest. The debit portion to the city-ledger advance-deposit account is made by the accounting office, not by the front-office cashier.

As an additional control, the reservation office keeps both the front-office cashier and the city-ledger accountant current with the names and amounts of advance deposits. Each day's anticipated list is compared to the actual arrivals, and oversights are corrected. Deposits applied that day by the front-office cashier become the basis of the city-ledger debit entry made by the accountant. Some unclaimed deposits will be returned because of timely cancellations. Others will be forfeited to pay for the rooms that were saved for the no-shows.

House Receipts and Expenses

Although the front-office cashier is primarily responsible for handling rooms-related revenues and disbursements, other responsibilities are assigned as a function of convenience. Due to the fact that the front desk is centrally located and accessible to all departments of the hotel, the cashier in the small hotel takes on a set of hotel-related cash responsibilities, both house receipts and house expenses.

▶*Assorted City- and General-ledger Receipts.* Some hotels, especially small properties that lack a full accounting staff, elect to funnel all cash and check receipts through the front office. This adds another person and record to the process, which strengthens the internal control. It also adds another set of responsibilities to the front-office cashier.

Examples of assorted city- and general-ledger receipts that are not affiliated with the rooms division include receipts for meetings or banquet functions, reimbursements or rebates for overpayment to vendors, refunds or credits from taxes, and lease revenues from merchants or concessionaires. In small hotels, the front-office cashier might serve as dining room or lounge cashier. Magazines, newspapers, and candy may be sold across the desk. Coin collections from vending machines or sales of miscellaneous items such as kitchen fat (to tallow-rendering plants) or container deposits may all flow through the front desk. Meal tickets in American-plan resorts are also commonly sold at the front desk to nonguests.

Depending on the accounting system in place, the cashier records a credit to some type of general account and a debit to cash on the front-office documentation. The specific detailing of the general account (each affected account must be updated) is later handled by the accounting department on an item-by-item basis.

▶*Assorted House Paid-outs.* Just as some of the cash receipts collected by the front-office cashier are not actually paid-in-advance guest receipts (rather they are city- or general-ledger receipts), some of the paid-outs made by the front-office cashier are not actually guest paid-outs (rather they are house paid-outs). The front-office cashier acts, on one hand, as a depository for the accounting department and, on the other hand, as the accounting department's disbursing agent.

Unlike guest paid-outs, which have an impact on the cashier's drawer, house paid-outs do not. As such, house paid-outs are not posted to the property management system—guest paid-outs most certainly are. The reason house paid-outs do not affect the cashier's drawer is because the cashier treats house paid-outs (petty cash disbursements) just like cash.

The person receiving the money (say, the bellperson who just purchased $30 worth of flour for the kitchen) signs a petty cash voucher (see Exhibit 11–5). The voucher is kept in the cashier's drawer and treated as if it were cash. It is cash, because the accounting department's general cashier will buy the petty cash voucher at some later point. The purchase of this voucher by the general cashier reimburses the front-office cashier and leaves the cash drawer intact—as if the petty cash disbursement had never been processed in the first place.

The Imprest Petty Cash Fund. If the front-office cashiers are reimbursed daily, the petty cash fund is administered by the accounting department's general cashier. If the front-office cashiers are only reimbursed when petty cash vouchers reach a sizable sum or at the end of the month, it is known as an imprest petty cash fund. An imprest fund authorizes the front-office cashier to hold petty cash vouchers in the drawer day after day.

```
┌─────────────────────────────────────────────────┐
│                   PETTY CASH                      │
│                                                   │
│  AMOUNT  16 ³⁷              Date  Dec. 18          │
│                                                   │
│  FOR  One Hotel T-shirt —                         │
│  Promotional gift to Sunshine Tours Leader        │
│                                                   │
│  CHARGE TO  Director of Sales and Marketing       │
│                                                   │
│             SIGNED  Mary Noel                     │
│  KAYCO FORM NO. 1046                              │
└─────────────────────────────────────────────────┘
```

Exhibit 11–5   Petty cash vouchers are often simple, handwritten forms. When available, a store receipt documenting the exact amount of the purchase should also be attached. *Courtesy of Kayco Systems, Lake Elsinore, California.*

The cashier holds the house petty cash vouchers until some predetermined point is reached. This point is usually a function of both time and amount. A cashier is assigned a limited bank from which to conduct all the day's transactions. If the cashier's ability to make change and serve the guest is compromised by a large petty cash holding, it is time to sell the vouchers to the general cashier. Some hotels have a specific policy when the total petty cash vouchers in a given cashier's drawer reaches, say $25, the amount must be turned over to the general cashier. Petty cash vouchers are also cleared from front-office cashiers at the end of each accounting cycle, usually the last day of the month.

A wide range of small expenditures are processed through the petty cash fund. Salary advances to good employees or termination pay to employees the hotel wants immediately off the premises might be paid by the fund. Some freight bills need immediate cash payment under ICC regulations. Stamp purchases, cash purchases from local farmers or purveyors, and other payments (see Exhibit 11–5) may be handled through the front office, especially in smaller hotels.

▶ THE CASHIER'S DAILY REPORT

Every cashier in the hotel, whether at the front office, the dining room, the bar, room service, or the snack bar, prepares a daily cash report. With the report, the cashier turns in the departmental monies. These combined funds (plus any that clear through the general cashier) constitute the hotel's daily deposit made to the bank.

The daily deposit is supported by a flow of cash records. The records of the front-office cashiers (see Exhibits 11–6 and 11–7), are first reviewed by the night auditor because they contain accounts receivable information. They are processed again the following day through the income audit. The income audit combines the front-office cash records with the records of the other departmental cashiers. This creates a support document (see Exhibit 11–8) for the bank deposit.

CASHIER: ARDELLE			REPORT DATE: 03/09/--				15:27:30

CASHIER'S BALANCE REPORT

CODE	ROOM	LAST NAME	FIRST NAME	ACCOUNT	RATE	TIME	AMOUNT
→ 0001	217	JOHNSON	LINDA	CASH	RACK	06:57:23	48.52
0026	1171	VANLAND	TOM	VISA	GRP	07:11:10	179.37
0024	678	HARRISON	GEORGE	DSCV	TOUR	07:12:12	87.50
0025	456	LENNON	JOHN	MC	TOUR	07:16:44	87.50
→ 0011	319	WILSON	BILL	CHCK	DISC	07:17:17	82.50
0011	337	ADAMS	JOHN	CHCK	RACK	07:21:50	67.21
0031	902	GREENBACKS	LOTTA	POUT	RACK	07:24:01	-17.50
0026	842	STUART	LYLE	VISA	GRP	08:10:15	161.40
0024	212	JONES	ROBERT	DSCV	DISC	08:34:20	242.59
0011	711	GREGORY	GARY	CHCK	TOUR	09:10:10	111.77
0011	315	GONNE	CONNIE	CHCK	RACK	09:44:30	96.20
0031	107	MOORE	MANNY	POUT	TOUR	10:10:15	-20.00
0025	371	ORTIZ	RAUL	MC	RACK	10:40:29	68.57
0011	211	JACKSON	ANDY	CHCK	DISC	11:04:41	46.31
0011	551	WASHINGTON	BOB	CHCK	TOUR	11:57:01	1,278.71

Exhibit 11–6   In the "account" column of this cashier's balance report are shown cash, checks, city ledger (credit cards), and paid-outs. The "code" column references the hotel's chart of accounts. Follow the arrows marking cashier Ardelle's cash guests, Johnson and Wilson, through Exhibits 11–7, 11–8, 11–9, and 11–10.

Preparing the Cashier's Report

The front-office cashier's report is much more complicated than standard cashier reports found in other departments. This is due to the two-way flow of front-office cashier's responsibilities. Remember, whereas departmental cashiers only receive payment from guests, front-office cashiers both receive funds and pay them out.

▶ ***The Cashier's Bank.***   Each cashier receives and signs for a permanent supply of cash, called the *bank*. The amount varies depending on the position and shift that the cashier works. A busy commercial hotel needs front-office banks of as much as $10,000, but the night cashier at the same hotel might get along with $250. It is partly a question of safety and partly a question of good financial management. Excessive funds should not be tied up unnecessarily; temporary increases can be made for busy periods.

A careful review of all house banks may release sizable sums for more profitable use. One major accounting firm reported that the total of a hotel's house banks and cash on hand is about 2% of total sales (about $600 per room). An excessive percentage suggests that cashiers are borrowing from their banks or that daily deposits and reimbursements are not being made, which means that extra funds are required to operate the banks. There are other reasons, of course—infrequent reimbursement of the petty cash fund, for example, which makes the fund unnecessarily large.

Cashiers lock their banks in the safe or hotel vault after each shift. The cashier's bank may not be used for personal loans. To ensure that all funds are properly held in

```
CASHIER:  ARDELLE      REPORT DATE: 03/09/--              15:28:41

                   CASHIER'S BALANCE REPORT BY CODE
```

CODE	ROOM	LAST NAME	FIRST NAME	ACCOUNT	RATE	TIME	AMOUNT
→ 0001	217	JOHNSON	LINDA	CASH	RACK	06:57:23	48.52
TOTAL	CASH		0001				48.52
→ 0011	319	WILSON	BILL	CHCK	DISC	07:17:17	82.50
0011	337	ADAMS	JOHN	CHCK	RACK	07:21:50	67.21
0011	711	GREGORY	GARY	CHCK	TOUR	09:10:10	111.77
0011	315	GONNE	CONNIE	CHCK	RACK	09:44:30	96.20
0011	211	JACKSON	ANDY	CHCK	DISC	11:04:41	46.31
0011	551	WASHINGTON	BOB	CHCK	TOUR	11:57:01	1,278.71
TOTAL	CHECKS		0011				1,682.70 ←
TOTAL	AMERICAN EXPRESS		0021				0.00
TOTAL	CARTE BLANCHE		0022				0.00
TOTAL	DINERS CLUB		0023				0.00
0024	678	HARRISON	GEORGE	DSCV	TOUR	07:12:12	87.50
0024	212	JONES	ROBERT	DSCV	DISC	08:34:20	242.59
TOTAL	DISCOVER		0024				330.09
0025	456	LENNON	JOHN	MC	TOUR	07:16:44	87.50
0025	371	ORTIZ	RAUL	MC	RACK	10:40:29	68.57
TOTAL	MASTERCARD		0025				156.07
0026	1171	VANLAND	TOM	VISA	GRP	07:11:10	179.37
0026	842	STUART	LYLE	VISA	GRP	08:10:15	161.40
TOTAL	VISA		0026				340.77
0031	902	GREENBACKS	LOTTA	POUT	RACK	07:24:01	-17.50
0031	107	MOORE	MANNY	POUT	TOUR	10:10:15	-20.00
TOTAL	PAID-OUTS		0031				-37.50

Exhibit 11–7   Cashier's report by code (the hotel's chart of accounts). This portion of the report shows payment methods against which the cashier reconciles cash, checks, charges, and paid-outs. This report shows payment activity by room number. Other reports would also be printed showing activity by department (say, telephone, restaurant, or lounge). This exhibit is the second in a series of interrelated exhibits (11–6 through 11–10) that follow the reports of cashier Ardelle.

CASH RECEIPTS SUMMARY REPORT

DEPARTMENT	CASHIER	CASH SALES	COLLECTION TRANSIENT RECEIVABLES	COLLECTION CITY LEDGER RECEIVABLES	TOTAL CASH RECEIPTS	PAID-OUTS TRANSIENT	PAID-OUTS CITY LEDGER	NET CASH RECEIPTS	ADD:OVERAGES LESS:SHORTAGES	TURN IN FOR DEPOSIT
FRONT OFFICE	ARDELLE		452.51 →	1,278.71 →	1,731.22 →	-37.50 →	0.00	1,693.72	-.76	1,692.96
FRONT OFFICE	BABETTE		1,171.14	622.50	1,793.64	-49.00	-25.00	1,719.64	1.20	1,720.84
FRONT OFFICE	CHARLES		850.19	1,460.51	2,310.70	-11.50	-5.00	2,294.20	0.00	2,294.20
FRONT OFFICE	DIANE		67.10	0.00	67.10	0.00	0.00	67.10	0.00	67.10
FRONT OFFICE	EDWARD		572.46	604.27	1,176.73	-12.90	0.00	1,163.83	-2.41	1,161.42
FRONT OFFICE	FRANCES		934.72	210.58	1,145.30	-18.65	-14.00	1,112.65	.87	1,113.52
GIFT SHOP	GARY	687.14	0.00	0.00	687.14	0.00	0.00	687.14	0.00	687.14
GIFT SHOP	HARRY	901.73	0.00	0.00	901.73	0.00	0.00	901.73	-1.47	900.26
LOUNGE	ILONA	1,262.85	0.00	0.00	1,262.85	0.00	0.00	1,262.85	1.01	1,263.86
LOUNGE	JEROME	2,411.59	0.00	0.00	2,411.59	0.00	0.00	2,411.59	0.00	2,411.59
RESTAURANT	KATE	816.44	0.00	0.00	816.44	0.00	0.00	816.44	-.25	816.19
RESTAURANT	LOUISE	1,017.55	0.00	0.00	1,017.55	0.00	0.00	1,017.55	-.61	1,016.94
SNACK BAR	MARC	469.68	0.00	0.00	469.68	0.00	0.00	469.68	2.71	472.39
SNACK BAR	NANETTE	371.02	0.00	0.00	371.02	0.00	0.00	371.02	0.00	371.02
DAILY TOTALS		7,938.00	4,048.12	4,176.57	16,162.69	-129.55	-44.00	15,989.14	.29	15,989.43

Exhibit 11–8   This cash receipts summary recaps records of all departmental cashiers and serves as the source document for the income auditors' daily bank deposit. Information shown for front-office cashier Ardelle corresponds with Exhibit 11–6, from which Washington, a city-ledger collection, appears in column 5 above. The total of the other cash collections, Johnson through Jackson, appears in column 4 as transient collections. Paid-outs (column 7) originate in the bottom three lines of Exhibit 11–7. Follow the balanced cashier report of Ardelle across a continuing series of interrelated Exhibits 11–6 through 11–10.

the cashiers' bank, the accounting office sporadically schedules surprise counts. When the cashier comes on duty, he or she will find the safe deposit box inaccessible—access to the safe deposit box requires two keys, one is the cashier's key and the other is the accounting office's master key. To open the box, the cashier needs to summon an auditor, who takes a few minutes with the cashier to count and verify the contents.

Unfortunately, common banks for several employees to share are not unusual. These are seen in every department from the bar to the front office. With shared banks, control is difficult to maintain, and responsibility almost impossible to fix. Custom and convenience seem to be the major reasons for continuing this poor practice, although it obviously requires less hotel funds to stock shared banks.

Everyone handling money should be covered by a bond. Bonds are written to cover either individual positions or as blanket coverage, whichever best meets the hotel's needs.

The bank must contain enough small bills to carry out the cashiering function. There is no value in a bank comprised of $100 bills. Two examples follow: with a $500 bank for the text discussion, and a $1,000 bank for the separate discussion of the exhibits.

▶ *Net Receipts.*   Net receipts represent the difference between what the cashier took in (receipts) and what was paid out. Since only front-office cashiers are permitted to make paid-outs, net receipts in the bar and coffee shop are the same as total receipts except when tip advances are made. Net receipts at the front office are computed by subtracting total advances (paid-outs), city and transient, from total receipts, city and transient. House paid-outs and miscellaneous receipts are not included because they're counted as cash (as discussed earlier in the chapter).

For discussion, assume the totals of the front-office cashier's balance report to be:

Receipts	
Transient receivables	$2,376.14
City receivables	422.97
Total receipts	$2,799.11
Paid-outs	
Transient ledger paid-outs	$ 107.52
City ledger paid-outs	27.50
Total paid-outs	$ 135.02
Net Receipts	
Total receipts	$2,799.11
Less paid-outs	135.02
Equals net receipts	$2,664.09

The front-office cashier accesses this information through the cashier's balance report. See Exhibits 11–6 and 11–7 for examples of a cashier's balance report. Note, however, that this current example (total receipts of $2,799.11 and total paid-outs of $135.02) does not correlate to the figures shown in Exhibits 11–6 through 11–10. For an example of a net receipts calculation using the figures found in Exhibits 11–6 and 11–7, see Exhibit 11–9.

Some balance reports provide only summary data such as that described in this section—total transient ledger receipts, total city ledger (and general ledger) receipts, total transient ledger paid-outs, and total city ledger paid-outs. Other balance reports are very complete, telling the cashier exactly how much net receipts to have in the drawer.

Whether the system provides detail for net receipts or not, this figure is a simple number to compute. In this example, net receipts are total receipts ($2,799.11) less total paid-outs ($135.02) equals $2,664.09 in net receipts.

►*Over or Short.*   No cashier is perfect. The day's close occasionally finds the cash drawer over or short. Sometimes the error is mathematical, and either the cashier finds it without help or it is uncovered later by the auditor.

Cash errors in giving change are usually beyond remedy unless they are in the house's favor. Guests may not acknowledge overpayments, but they will complain soon enough if they have been shortchanged. Restitution after the fact is possible if the cash count at the end of the shift proves this to be so.

Overages and shortages become a point of employee–management conflict in those hotels where cashiers are required to make up all shortages but turn in all overages. Better systems allow overages to offset shortages, asking only that the month's closing record balance. Both procedures encourage the cashier to reconcile at the expense of ethical standards. Shortchanging, poor addition, and altered records accommodate these management requirements. It is a better policy to have the house absorb the shortages and keep the overages. A record of individual performance is then maintained to determine if individual overages and shortages balance over the long run. They should, unless the cashier is inept or dishonest.

Over or *short* is the difference between what the cashier should have in the cash drawer and what is actually there. It is the comparison of a mathematically generated net total against a physical count of the money in the drawer. The cashier *should* have the sum of the original starting bank plus the net receipts. What money is on hand in the drawer is what the cashier *does* have. Over or short is the difference between the *should have* and the *does have*.

In our continuing example, the front-office cashier should have $3,164.09 on hand at the close of the shift. This is calculated by taking net receipts of $2,664.09 (see discussion page 443) plus starting bank ($500) equals $3,164.09.

Should Have on Hand	
Net receipts	$2,664.09
Starting bank	500.00
Total of should have	$3,164.09

Once the cashier knows how much should be in the drawer, it is a simple matter of comparing that total with the actual cash on hand. The cashier's drawer probably contains personal and traveler's checks, currency, coin, and petty cash vouchers. Credit cards are not included in this discussion of the cashier's drawer because they are often electronically deposited to the hotel's bank or handled by the accounting department as a city ledger accounts receivable. A full discussion of credit-card processes is included in Chapter 12.

Does Have on Hand	
Checks (personal and traveler's)	$2,704.60
Currency	356.00
Coin	62.13
House petty cash vouchers	42.50
Total cash on hand	$3,165.23

The cashier apparently has more in the drawer than there should be. In such a case, the cashier has an overage. If the amount of cash on hand were actually less than what there should be, the cashier would be short. The amount of the overage or shortage is simple enough to compute—just subtract the amount there should be ($3,164.09) from the amount of cash on hand ($3,165.23). The net total ($1.14) is the amount of overage. A positive net number is always an overage; a negative net number is always a shortage.

▶*The Turn-in.*   When the cashier has calculated net receipts, determined the amount there should be, and counted the actual cash in the drawer, it is a simple matter to compute the turn-in. However, in many hotels, the cashier is not responsible for counting the drawer. In such operations, cashiers are not allowed to count the drawer even if they wish to.

Cashiers who are permitted to total their receipts and count their drawers know exactly how much they are over or short. Overages can be very appealing to unscrupulous cashiers. If allowed to calculate the amount of overage, some cashiers will pocket the difference. That is troublesome, but it becomes double trouble when the cashier's calculations were in error. If the cashier bases the overage amount on an error and then steals that amount, the mistake (and the theft) is likely to be uncovered by the night auditor. This is a common way in which hotels uncover employee embezzlement.

For this reason, many hotels limit the employee's access and knowledge regarding the correct amount of the day's deposit. Instead, the employee rebuilds the starting bank with currency and coin and then deposits everything else remaining. In such operations, the front-office cashier functions no differently than a departmental cashier.

The Front-office Turn-in. The turn-in of the front-office cashier is more complicated than the turn-in of the departmental cashiers. The front-office bank is used to cash checks, make change, and advance cash as well as to accept receipts. Assume, for example, that nothing took place during the watch except check cashing. At the close of the day, the bank would contain nothing but nonnegotiable checks. It would be impossible to make change the next day with a drawer full of personal checks. So the cashier must drop or turn in all nonnegotiable items, including checks, traveler's checks, foreign funds, large bills, casino chips, cash in poor condition, vouchers for house expenses, and even refund slips for inoperative vending machines.

The objective of the cashier's turn-in is to rebuild the starting bank in the proper amount and variety of denominations to be effective during the next day's shift, and "drop" the rest of the contents of the cash drawer. Sometimes, there are enough small bills and coins in the cashier's drawer to rebuild tomorrow's bank quite easily. At other times, there are too many large denomination bills or nonnegotiable checks and paper to effectively rebuild tomorrow's bank. In such cases, the cashier must turn in all of the large bills and nonnegotiable paper, leaving tomorrow's bank short. That's OK, because the income audit staff will leave currency and coin in requested denominations for the start of tomorrow's shift. By adding these new funds to the short bank, tomorrow's drawer will be both accurate and effective.

Our continuing example helps to illustrate the concept of turn-in or drop. Remember that the cashier has a total of $3,165.23 on hand, comprised of checks ($2,704.60), currency ($356.00), coin ($62.13), and house petty cash vouchers ($42.50). The cashier must turn in all of the nonnegotiable paper, including checks ($2,704.60) and house petty cash vouchers ($42.50), which equals a $2,747.10 total turn-in.

►*Due Bank.*   At this point it is quite obvious that the cashier does not have enough small bills and coin to rebuild tomorrow's $500 starting bank. In fact, tomorrow's bank will be short by $81.87. This shortage is commonly referred to as the *due bank*. It is also known as the *due back, difference returnable, U-owe-mes,* or the *exchange.*

The due bank is calculated by subtracting the amount of money retained by the cashier, $418.13 ($356.00 in currency plus $62.13 in coin) from the amount needed to open the next day's bank, $500.

Due Bank Computation	
Original bank	$500.00
Cash on hand	418.13
Due bank	$ 81.87

Since the cashier always retains the exact bank, it is apparent that the turn-in includes the overage or allows for the shortage. The hotel, not the cashier, funds the overages and shortages. A due bank formula, which produces the same due bank figure as the simple subtraction computation, mathematically illustrates the hotel's responsibility for the over and short.

Due Bank Formula
Due bank = turn-in − (net receipts ± over or short)
Due bank = $2,747.10 − ($2,664.09 + $1.14)
Due bank = $2,747.10 − ($2,665.23)
Due bank = $81.87

To keep their banks functional, cashiers specify the coin and currency denominations of the due bank. There is little utility in a due bank of several large bills. For the very same reason, the turn-in may be increased with large bills to be exchanged for more negotiable currency. More often, the change is obtained from the general cashier before the shift closes, or from another cashier who has coins and small bills to exchange.

Exhibits 11–9 and 11–10 offer a second example complete with cashier's turn-in envelope, but with different values from the text discussion.

The Income Audit

Income auditors and general cashiers are members of the hotel's accounting department. They usually perform the income audit each morning to process the cashier drops made the preceding day. One purpose of the income audit is to verify that each department's (and indeed each shift's) cashiers have accurately dropped (turned in) the amount indicated on the deposit envelopes (see Exhibit 11–10). Although this function is performed in a vault or safe room, there are several general cashiers present and the audit may even be videotaped as an additional safeguard.

The income audit generally has two purposes: to audit the day's incomes from cash and accounts receivable sales, and to prepare the hotel's daily bank deposit.

Given

1. A starting bank of $1,000
2. The cashier's balance report shows:

Cash receipts (both transient and city ledger)	$1,731.22
Paid-outs (both transient and city ledger)	37.50

3. Count in the cash drawer at the close of the watch

Checks	$1,682.70
Currency	821.00
Coin	177.26
House vouchers	12.00
	$2,692.96

Computation

1. Net receipts (gross receipts minus advances)
   NR = $1,731.22 – $37.50 = $1,693.72
2. Overage and shortage (what should be in the drawer minus what is in the drawer)
   O&S = ($1,000 + 1,693.72) – 2,692.96 = $0.76 short
3. Turn-in (checks, vouchers, other nonnegotiable items, and all cash except the bank)
   TI = $1,682.70 + 12.00 = $1,694.70
4. Due bank (amount needed to reconstitute the bank)
   DB = $1,000 – (821.00 + 177.26) = $1.74.
5. Verification (the excess of the turn-in over the amount due)
   DB = $1,694.70 – ($1,693.72 – .76) = $1.74.

Exhibit 11–9   Preparation of Ardelle's front-office cashier report requires an understanding of the computations. Refer back to Exhibits 11–6, 11–7, and 11–8 to understand the numbers shown under "cash receipts," "paid-outs," "checks," and so on. Remember, this exhibit is based on the figures shown in the continuing series of Exhibits 11–6 to 11–10, and is *not based on the text discussion*, which provides a look at a *different* example.

$$X - (1029.44 + 1.1) = 1150.12$$

During this function, every deposit envelope from every department cashier is opened, verified, and added to the growing pile of cash, checks, traveler's checks, foreign currency, house vouchers, and so on. Every form of payment except credit cards is counted, totaled, and added to the hotel's daily deposit. Credit cards are the exception because hotels electronically deposit many national cards (for example, VISA and MasterCard). Other credit cards are billed through the city ledger (for example, American Express) placing them directly in the hands of the accounting staff.

The income audit includes both front-office cashiers (who probably calculate the exact amount of their turn-in and know shift by shift whether they are over or short) and departmental cashiers (who may or may not precalculate their turn-in before preparing the deposit envelope). In the case of departmental cashiers who rebuild their starting bank and blindly drop the rest of their money, the general cashier merely counts and verifies the contents of the drop. Whereas the general cashier attends to the actual count of the cash turned in, the income auditor focuses on the accuracy of the amounts reported by the various departmental cashiers. Together, the general cashier(s) and income auditor(s) make up the day audit team.

DEPARTMENT CASHIER'S REPORT

DAY *TUE*   DATE *3-9*

CASHIER *Ardelle*

DEPT *F.O.*

SHIFT *8:00*   A.M.☑ P.M.☐   TO   *4:00*   A.M.☐ P.M.☑

	AMOUNT	✓
CURRENCY $1.00		
" $5.00		
" $10.00		
" $20.00		
" $50.00		
" $100.00		
COIN 1¢		
" 5¢		
SILVER 10¢		
" 25¢		
" 50¢		
" $1.00		
BAR STUBS:		
PAID-OUTS:		
VOUCHERS AND CHECKS:		
New York Exchange-Wilson	82	50
Cleveland Trust-Adams	67	21
Chicago 1st Natl.-Gregory	111	77
Bank America-Gonne	96	20
Natl. Bank of St. Louis-Jackson	46	31
First Interstate-Washington	1278	71
Postage Stamp Voucher	12	—
TRAVELER'S CHECKS		
LESS SHORT		76
TOTAL AMOUNT ENCLOSED	1694	70
NET RECEIPTS WITH O & S	1692	96
DIFFERENCE	1	74

Exhibit 11–10   Cashier's envelope for preparing the "turn-in" (or "drop") at the close of the shift. Refer back to Exhibits 11–6 to 11–9 to understand the source of checks enclosed, the postage stamp voucher, the "due bank" difference of $1.74, and so on. Note that the net receipts figure includes the $.76 shortage (O & S stands for "over" and "short"). *Courtesy of Kayco Systems, Lake Elsinore, California.*

➤*Paying Off the Due Bank.*   Many cashiers turn in more money than necessary. The excess amount of their drop is the due bank. As discussed above, due banks are caused by a variety of factors: there may have been a large house paid-out that used most of the drawer's cash; there may have been too many large denomination bills and too few small ones to effectively rebuild tomorrow's starting bank; or there may have been too many checks cashed to leave sufficient money for tomorrow. Whatever the reason, the income audit staff pays each cashier's due bank from the growing pile of turned-in cash before preparing the hotel's daily deposit.

Most operations use a signature and witness system to facilitate returning the due banks to each cashier. One main cashier (often a front-office cashier) is given a series of due bank envelopes with the name of each cashier to whom the envelope is owed. The departmental cashier then signs for the sealed envelope in the presence of the main cashier and adds the contents of the envelope to the department's starting shift bank. Of course, the sealed envelopes were prepared during the cashier audit and were therefore witnessed by several general cashiers as to the correct amount sealed inside. Although simple, these signature and witness systems are generally quite effective.

➤*Paying Off the House Vouchers.*   In hotels that utilize an imprest petty cash fund, front-office cashiers are asked to hold their house vouchers until they build to some predetermined amount (say, $25). Front-office cashiers write house vouchers for a soda machine refund ($0.75), a video game refund ($0.50), and a tank of gas for the shuttle van ($19.50). These are kept in the cash drawer until they exceed the predetermined amount ($25). Even at the close of the shift, as the cashier is building tomorrow's starting bank, the vouchers are still kept by the cashier. Tomorrow, however, if the cashier writes a few more house vouchers (say, a gallon of sour cream was purchased from the grocery store for $4.59), the entire sum of all vouchers will be turned in.

In this example, the sum to be turned in by the end of the second shift is $25.34. The cashier turns in all of the house vouchers, not merely the one or two vouchers that put the total over the predetermined amount. The income audit staff counts the house vouchers as cash and credits the drop envelope with the amount of house vouchers. In some cases, a due bank may be caused by an extremely large house voucher (say, a large C.O.D. shipment arrived).

➤*Tour Package Coupons.*   Hotels that operate in busy tour and travel markets often incorporate the redemption of package coupons and certificates into their cash drawer procedures. Such coupons or certificates are found primarily in departmental cashier turn-ins, but front-office cashiers may also have an opportunity to redeem them under some circumstances.

Generally, package tours provide the guest with substantially more than just a hotel room. Breakfast each morning of the visit, two free rounds of golf, a discount in the gift shop, several free drinks, and a dinner show are all examples of products that might be included in a packaged tour. In order to identify themselves as members of the tour, guests are presented with a coupon booklet that contains redeemable certificates.

As an example, when a couple arrives at the dining room for breakfast, the waitstaff and cashier may not be aware they are tour customers. In fact, they are treated like any other customer until the end of the meal. Then, instead of paying for the breakfast in cash, credit card, or room charge, the tour couple need only redeem their complimentary breakfast coupons.

It's at this point that many accounting systems break down. Departmental cashiers forget to collect tour coupons with the same determination that they show when collecting cash. After all, the cashier thinks, the meal is complimentary; if the tour guest accidentally forgets the coupon booklet in the room, what's the harm? This overlooks the fact that someone is paying for the guest's complimentary meal (golf, drinks, or whatever). In fact, the redeemed coupon serves as documentation to the travel wholesaler for payment. Redeemed coupons are proof that goods (breakfast in this case) were exchanged and become the basis for the account receivable. That's why redeemed coupons often become part of the departmental cashier's daily turn-in.

➤*Foreign Currency.*   Foreign currency (see Exhibit 11–11) is not regularly accepted in the United States. Overseas, U.S. currency is widely accepted. Even the Canadian dollar, with its stability and similarity of value, experiences exchange problems as it moves southward from the U.S.–Canadian border. But international tourism is growing at an amazing rate, with more to come in the years ahead. More foreign currencies are being tendered across hotel desks, and more language capability is being encouraged among front-office staffs.

Nevertheless, relatively few American hotels have followed their international counterparts into the foreign-exchange business. This is a service that many U.S. hotels prefer to have done by another agency. Thus the growth in foreign-exchange facilities has been outside the hotel lobby.

Cities with large numbers of foreign visitors, such as New York and Miami, have developed adequate exchange facilities to accommodate the international tourists. These currency-exchange companies, privately owned, have been supported by local tourists bureaus, chambers of commerce, and the U.S. National Tourism Organization, all of which see the importance of the international tourist to the balance of trade. Exchange agencies allow the hotels to service the currency needs of the international guest with a reasonable ceiling on costs.

Servicing the guest is all that American hotels appear to do. It is a limited service at that—limited to a very few hotels that deal only in a few popular currencies because they have identified a well-defined international market segment for themselves. Overseas, foreign exchange is a profit center for the hotel. There is a profit to be made because both domestic and foreign hotels exchange currency at something less than the official rate. That's a double insult because even the official rate, which is determined by open market bidding, provides a spread between buy price and sell price.

Since it is not desirable to inventory money from all around the world, hotels do not provide for the reconversion of local currency into foreign funds as the visitor prepares to go home. Therefore, the hotel's concern is only with the bid rate. Money brokers quote both a buy (bid) rate and a sell (ask) rate. The desk buys foreign currency from the guest at a rate that is lower than the broker's bid rate, reselling later to the broker at the bid rate. The hotel might buy Canadian dollars, for example, at 8 cents less than it sells them for, although the official spread might be only 4 cents. The extra spread between buy and sell may be further enriched by a supplemental exchange fee. This fee, which currency dealers call *agio,* provides the hotel with additional funds to pay for bank charges or to offset unexpected variations in foreign currency value. The latter makes it especially important to process foreign currency quickly and to include it in the turn-in every day.

Obtaining daily quotes and avoiding banks that are not brokers themselves (that is, middlemen) will maximize foreign exchange profits. In fact, the hotel could become an intermediary broker by also converting funds for taxi drivers, bellpersons, and servers throughout the community in addition to its own personnel. Of course, this opens a whole new business with the large risks that accompany foreign exchange.

Country	Currency	Country	Currency
North America		**Caribbean, Bahamas, and Bermuda**	
Canada	Dollar	Bahamas	Dollar
Mexico	Peso	Bermuda	Dollar
		British Virgin Islands	Dollar
Central and South America		Curacao	Guilder
Argentina	Peso	Jamaica	Dollar
Bolivia	Boliviano	Martinique	Franc
Brazil	Real	Trinidad	Dollar
Chile	Peso	**Africa**	
Colombia	Peso	Egypt	Pound
Costa Rica	Colon	Ethiopia	Birr
Ecuador	Dollar	Ghana	Cedi
El Salvador	Colon	Libya	Dinar
Guatemala	Quetzal	Morocco	Dirham
Honduras	Lempira	South Africa	Rand
Nicaragua	Cordoba	Sudan	Dinar
Peru	New Sol	Tanzania	Shilling
Uruguay	New Peso	Zambia	Kwacha
Venezuela	Bolivar	**Mideast, Far East, and Pacific**	
		Australia	Dollar
Europe's EMU		Bahrain	Dinar
Austria (schilling), Belgium	Euro	China	Renminbi
(franc), Finland (markka),	(phased	Hong Kong	Dollar
France (franc), Germany	in 1999–	India	Rupee
(mark), Greece (drachma),	2002)	Indonesia	Rupiah
Ireland (punt), Italy (lira),		Israel	Shekel
Luxembourg (franc),		Japan	Yen
Netherlands (guilder),		Jordan	Dinar
Portugal (escudo), and Spain		Kuwait	Dinar
(peseta)		Lebanon	Pound
Other Europe		Malaysia	Ringgit
Czech Republic	Koruna	New Zealand	Dollar
Denmark	Krone	Pakistan	Rupee
Hungary	Forint	Philippines	Peso
Malta	Lira	Saudi Arabia	Riyal
Norway	Krone	Singapore	Dollar
Poland	Zloty	South Korea	Won
Russia	Ruble	Syria	Pound
Slovak Republic	Koruna	Taiwan	Dollar
Sweden	Krona	Thailand	Baht
Switzerland	Franc	Turkey	Lira
United Kingdom	Pound	United Arab Emirates	Dirham

Exhibit 11–11   Shown are most of the world's currencies. Conversion rates for major currencies are quoted in local newspapers and in *The Wall Street Journal*. See the text for additional discussion of the European Economic and Monetary Union's (EMU) euro.

If the hotel is dealing in foreign currencies, the accounting office must furnish the cashier with a table of values for each currency traded (see Exhibit 11–11). (Several airlines quote currency rates, including rates on foreign traveler's checks, as part of their reservation system service.) If currency values fluctuate over a wide range, a daily or even hourly quote is necessary to prevent substantial losses. More likely, the hotel will just refuse that particular currency.

Canadian currency poses less of a problem than most other kinds. It is similar in form, divisions, and value to the U.S. dollar. Consequently, hotels close to the border have accepted Canadian dollars at a par with the U.S. dollar. Although this practice involves an exchange cost to the hotel, it has been a good advertising and public relations gimmick that has more than offset the expense.

The EMU Euro.   In an attempt to become more competitive on a global basis and to simplify currency transactions in closely related countries, the European Economic Monetary Union (EMU) created a new form of currency. In 1999, prior to the introduction of the new euro banknotes (see Exhibit 11–12), all EMU member countries were given a choice to join the new monetary system. Several countries opted out of the euro, including Denmark, Sweden, and the United Kingdom. One other country, Greece, did not qualify to join the euro system because of significant government and public debt.

The new euro was introduced in January 1999 and became the sole currency for 12 countries (see Exhibit 11–11) by January 2002. Many experts predict that the euro will become the dominant force in international tourism, in part because the euro reflects more assets and GNP than does even the U.S. dollar.

The euro has certainly simplified matters for the lodging industry. Currency exchange rates with the euro are far less volatile and are easier to track than were the currencies of 12 separate countries. In addition, currency exchange rates among the 12 EMU countries have been eliminated, saving tourists the cost and inconvenience of exchanging various monies. But best of all, the new euro has made much of Europe seem almost borderless as tourists travel country to country with little more difficulty than Americans travel from state to state.

Although the European Union (EU) consists of 15 member states, only 12 have adopted the euro. Denmark and the United Kingdom have opt-out clauses, which implies they are not likely to adopt the euro. Sweden will join the other euro states once it has fulfilled the conditions required for membership. Currently, the 12 countries that constitute the euro area include Austria, Belgium, Finland, France, Germany, Greece, Ireland, Italy, Luxembourg, The Netherlands, Portugal, and Spain (Exhibits 11–11 and 11–12).

The euro (denoted with a € symbol) has eight coins and seven notes in circulation. While the reverse side of every euro coin is the same across all member states, the obverse side is unique to whichever EU member state printed that particular coin. No matter what obverse side might show on a particular coin, it can be used anywhere inside the 12 member states. For example, a German citizen could purchase a slice of pizza in Italy using a coin depicting the imprint of the King of Spain.

In terms of the common reverse side, all coins are minted with a map of the European Union against a background of lines to which are attached the stars of the European flag. The 1, 2, and 5 cent coins put emphasis on Europe's place in the world; the 10, 20, and 50 cent coins present the European Union as a gathering of nations. The 1 and 2 euro coins depict Europe without frontiers.

The seven euro notes, in different colors and sizes, are denominated in 500, 200, 100, 50, 20, 10, and 5 euros. Unlike euro coins, the euro notes have no national side—they are uniform throughout the euro area. Designs of the notes are symbolic of Europe's architectural heritage. Interestingly, the buildings depicted on the various notes do not represent actual structures: They are all fictitious to prevent any one country from gaining undo exposure to its monuments. Windows and gateways dominate the front side of each banknote as symbols of the spirit of openness and cooperation in the European Union. The reverse side of each banknote features a bridge from a particular age, a metaphor for communication among the people of Europe and with the rest of the world. All notes carry advanced security features (Exhibit 11–12).

Example from the Land of Nod.   Let's see what needs to be done when a guest from the Land of Nod tenders a ₦ 1,000 bill in payment of a $34 account. Each ₦ (Nod dollar) is exchanged at 5 cents U.S. money by the hotel, although the official rate may be somewhat higher—say, 5.1 cents. Therefore, the ₦ 1,000 is exchanged at $50, which is $1 less than the official rate of exchange. The cashier would return $16 U.S. in exchange for the ₦ 1,000 and the charge of $34. (Change is given only in

Exhibit 11–12   The obverse of each of the seven Euro banknotes features architectural styles from the seven ages of Europe's cultural history. The windows and gateways are symbols of the spirit of openness and cooperation in the European Union. The reverse depicts seven different European bridges. Each bill boasts a unique color, and the size of the note increases with denomination.

U.S. dollars even if the cashier has Nod dollars.) If, on the other hand, the guest had offered only a N 500 bill, the cashier would have collected an additional U.S. $9 to settle the $34 account in full. What if it were a N 2,500 bill, and the cashier had on hand 1,500 Nod dollars? What would be the change? (Answer: The cashier would give U.S. $91 in change. Remember: Foreign currency is never returned even if it's available in the cash drawer. That would give away the profit earned on the exchange rates.)

Rare indeed is the hotel that will accept a foreign check. However, if payment were made by foreign check, the hotel makes an additional charge, passing on to the guest the bank's fee for foreign exchange. The amount of the fee is a function of both the size of the check and the variation in the rate of exchange.

Foreign traveler's checks (especially Canadian traveler's checks) are more readily accepted than personal checks. Although cashiers are cautioned to use the same level of scrutiny with foreign traveler's checks as they use with U.S. traveler's checks (accepting traveler's checks is discussed in depth towards the end of this chapter), there is an additional catch. Foreign traveler's checks look identical to U.S. traveler's checks, with one simple difference: Instead of stating "Pay to the order of (name) in U.S. dollars," the foreign traveler's check states "Pay . . . in Canadian dollars" (see Exhibit 11–17), or whatever currency. Many a time has a clerk accidentally cashed a foreign traveler's check thinking it was payable in U.S. funds. This can represent a considerable loss to the hotel.

➤ CASH AND CASH EQUIVALENTS

Even as the ratio of guests' folios paid with cash and cash equivalents (traveler's checks, personal, and corporate checks) is decreasing, the incidence of counterfeiting and forgery is at an all-time high. Due to advances in technology and print quality, computers are responsible, in part, for the rise of cash-related crimes proliferating nationwide. The busy hotel, with its hundreds or thousands of new guests each day, creates the perfect haven for such crimes. That's why it is of paramount importance that managers be trained in the secure handling of cash and checks.

Hotels are likely targets for professional counterfeiters for several reasons. First, agents are often rushed with numerous small transactions, allowing the professional counterfeiter easy access and egress. Second, hotel cashiers are inundated with so many guests that they would probably have a difficult time remembering (much less describing or identifying) the professional counterfeiter.

Finally, as discussed earlier, hotels handle relatively little cash as a percentage of all sales volume. Although that may sound contradictory, counterfeiters often seek establishments that deal in little cash. That's because cashiers who handle lots of cash become very adept at spotting a phony. Conversely, hotel cashiers (who handle relatively little cash) are less prepared to spot fake currency.

Counterfeit Currency

According to the U.S. Secret Service, there may be over $1 billion in counterfeit currency in worldwide circulation. In the United States, the number is far less (about $35 million). But as the U.S. dollar has become increasingly accepted worldwide, the incidence of counterfeiting has also been rapidly increasing. You see, just as hotel front-office cashiers (who handle relatively little cash) are likely targets for counterfeiters, so are international cashiers, who probably handle even fewer

U.S. dollars. And according to the Secret Service, whereas the most popular counterfeit bill in the United States is the $20 bill, overseas the most popular counterfeit is the $100 bill!

As computer technology has improved, the counterfeiting problem has compounded. Recently, a high school student in New Mexico made $1, $5, $10, and $20 bills by scanning the real currency into her home computer and printing the money out as a school project. She then asked classmates to tell the difference, and several students later spent the currency at local stores. Another case includes a 16-year-old West Virginia boy who scanned his own portrait over Ben Franklin's and successfully passed the obviously bogus $100 note.

Virtually anyone willing to spend the few hundred dollars necessary to purchase a color printer/scanner can enter the counterfeiting business. In just four short years, computer-generated counterfeit money has risen from 0.5% (half of one percent) to over 44% of all counterfeit money in circulation.

➤*Detecting Counterfeit Currency.*   Beginning in 1996, the U.S. Treasury began issuing currency with new security features. The $100 bill (see Exhibit 11–13) was the first, followed by the $50, $20, $10, and $5 bills introduced at the rate of roughly one new bill every year. The redesigned notes take advantage of new technologies to make them more secure from counterfeiting as well as easier to recognize when passed (see Exhibit 11–14). Since the first series of notes was introduced in 1861, U.S. currency has continually evolved in an attempt to thwart counterfeit activities. Despite many previous alterations, this most recent design change is probably the most noticeable.

Exhibit 11–13 details the eight new features embedded in bills introduced since 1996. Hold a new $100, $50, $20, $10, or $5 bill to the light and notice some interesting enhancements. For example, a polymer security thread runs top to bottom down the bill, just to the left of the portrait. A watermark, to the right of the portrait, is visible from both the obverse and reverse of the bill. These two features are difficult to replicate on counterfeit bills. The most difficult of all, however, is the color-shifting ink found in the numerical denomination of the bill at the bottom right corner. Looking at it head on, the number appears green. Bringing it up under your eye and turning the bill away from you, you'll notice that the green color shifts to black. None of these three features can be successfully scanned into even the most sophisticated computer systems available today. For other security features, see Exhibit 11–13.

Other Cashier Applications.   Hotel cashiers may also be interested in a number of relatively inexpensive counterfeit detection devices that have hit the market in recent years (see Exhibit 11–15). Aside from the sophisticated security identification features readily visible to the human eye found in today's U.S. currency, these inexpensive detection devices utilize two additional technologies in their search for counterfeit currency. One of the most popular devices is a detector shaped like a marker pen made by companies such as Dri-Mark Products of New York. This pen is popular with major retailers (such as Disney) because it is simple to use. In essence, it employs a chemical reaction to indicate whether the currency in question has authentic cotton fibers. All U.S. currency is made from 100% cotton rag—there is no paper content. As such, detector pens that react with starch (found in paper products) turn counterfeit bills brown.

A second detection technology searches the bill for magnetic ink. Magnetic ink has been used by the Federal Reserve since 1932. The ink is found on the portrait and

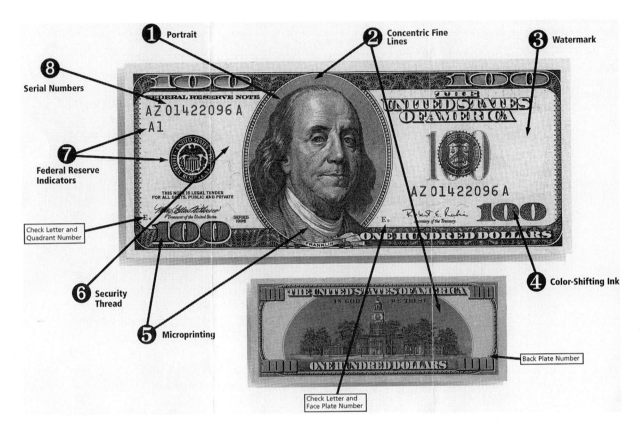

① Portrait The enlarged portrait of Benjamin Franklin is easier to recognize, while the added detail is harder to duplicate. The portrait is now off-center, providing room for a watermark and reducing wear and tear on the portrait.

② Concentric Fine Lines The fine lines printed behind both Benjamin Franklin's portrait and Independence Hall are difficult to replicate.

③ Watermark A watermark depicting Benjamin Franklin is visible from both sides when held up to a light.

④ Color-Shifting Ink The number in the lower right corner on the front of the note looks green when viewed straight on, but appears black when viewed at an angle.

⑤ Microprinting Because they're so small, microprinted words are hard to replicate. On the front of the note, "USA 100" is within the num-

ber in the lower left corner and "United States of America" is on Benjamin Franklin's coat.

⑥ Security Thread A polymer thread is embedded vertically in the paper and indicates, by its unique position, the note's denomination. The words "USA 100" on the thread can be seen from both sides of the note when held up to a bright light. Additionally, the thread glows red when held under an ultraviolet light.

⑦ Federal Reserve Indicators A new universal seal represents the entire Federal Reserve System. A letter and number beneath the left serial number identifies the issuing Federal Reserve Bank.

⑧ Serial Numbers An additional letter is added to the serial number. The unique combination of eleven numbers and letters appears twice on the front of the note.

Exhibit 11–13 In spite of the state-of-the-art security devices featured in the new U.S. currency (since 1996), it is still readily counterfeited. Similar sophisticated anticounterfeit measures can be found on the new European Union euro as well.

Department of the Treasury
United States Secret Service

Counterfeit Note Report

INSTRUCTIONS TO BANK:

1. Prepare two copies of this form for each suspected counterfeit note.

2. Submit copies of completed form with each suspected counterfeit note to your LOCAL SECRET SERVICE OFFICE.

3. If desired, an additional copy of this form should be prepared and retained for your records.

FROM: (Indicate Bank's Name and Mailing Address (include Zip Code))

DO NOT WRITE IN THIS SPACE

Telephone Number of Bank (include area code) _____

Point-of-Contact (include extension and e-mail address, if applicable) _____

Classification Number _____

FOLD HERE .... **IMPORTANT NOTICE** .... FOLD HERE

Bank tellers and persons surrendering the note should date and initial each counterfeit note with pen and ink in the border areas of the note for identification. If the person surrendering the note knows from whom he/she received it, or has a description of the passer, or his/her auto, or any other information, **TELEPHONE the local Secret Service office IMMEDIATELY** and hold the note. (The telephone number of your local Secret Service office can be found in the front cover of your telephone directory.) Otherwise, If no information is available, please mail the note to our local office on the day it is received.

DESCRIPTION OF COUNTERFEIT NOTE OR RAISED NOTE (for raised note give serial number only)

DENOMINATION	FEDERAL RESERVE BANK (Series 1996 - Letter/Number)		CHECK LETTER/QUADRANT NO.

CHECK LETTER/FACE PLATE NO.	BACK PLATE NO.	SERIES	SERIAL NUMBER

COUNTERFEIT NOTE RECEIVED FROM

NAME OF CUSTOMER / BUSINESS	DATE OF DEPOSIT
CUSTOMER'S HOME ADDRESS	CUSTOMER'S HOME PHONE A/C
	CUSTOMER'S BUSINESS PHONE A/C

NAME OF PERSON SURRENDERING AND INITIALING NOTE	NAME OF TELLER RECEIVING AND INITIALING NOTE

INFORMATION ABOUT COUNTERFEIT NOTE

DOES THE CUSTOMER HAVE ANY INFORMATION AS TO THE SOURCE OF THE COUNTERFEIT? ☐ Yes ☐ No

WAS THERE ANY SUSPICIOUS ACTIVITY? ☐ Yes ☐ No

IS THIS A NON - CUSTOMER? ☐ Yes ☐ No

REMARKS:

DISPOSITION (For Secret Service Use Only)

☐ Genuine note and SSF 1604 returned to bank (Receipt No. _____)

☐ Acknowledgement of Receipt returned to bank

☐ Other (Specify)

UNITED STATES SECRET SERVICE   **PLEASE SUBMIT TO THE LOCAL SECRET SERVICE JURISDICTIONAL FIELD OFFICE**   SSF 1604 (03/2000)
This form was electronically produced via OmniForm by USSS/ADMIN/MNO/FARS   (Previous Editions may be used.)

Exhibit 11–14   A Counterfeit Note Report must be completed and turned over along with any questionable bill(s) to the Secret Service immediately following a suspected counterfeit incident. These self-executable reports can be readily downloaded from http://www.secretservice.gov/money_receive.shtml. Here are the recommended steps that front-office cashiers should follow when encountering suspected counterfeit bills:

1. Don't return the bill to the passer. It will just encourage the person to leave the scene.
2. Delay the passer, if possible.
3. Observe the passer and any friends, colleagues, or vehicles (license numbers) to provide authorities with a description.
4. Call the police or the local office of the Secret Service.
5. Write your initials and date on the blank portion or border areas of the note, but handle the bill as little as possible (for later fingerprinting).
6. Place the bill in a clean envelope as soon as possible.
7. Surrender the note only to a properly identified police officer or Secret Service agent.

around the edges. Counterfeit currency created on copiers or printing presses lacks the magnetic ink (see Exhibit 11–15).

Whatever their approach, hotels are urged to use caution when accepting currency. Counterfeit currency can cost a hotel a considerable amount of money in a relatively short amount of time because counterfeiters usually pass a number of bills in quick succession. Counterfeit bills are like ants—you never find just one! And when the hotel finally realizes what has happened and calls the Secret Service, they are in for another shock—the counterfeit bills will be confiscated without restitution.

Check-Cashing Safeguards

Even in the smallest hotel, management cannot make every credit decision every hour of the day. Instead, it creates the policies and procedures that will minimize losses and retain customer goodwill. A credit manual or credit handbook is the usual manner of communicating management's position. Each company reflects its own approach in policies, but procedures for handling personal checks (and traveler's checks) are much alike from hotel to hotel and from handbook to handbook.

Hotels train their front-office personnel to be pleasant, courteous, and accommodating. Check scam artists are usually loud, rude, and threatening. By pushing in during rush hours, harassing the clerks who have been taught to "take it," and pressuring for service, passers of bad checks walk away with millions. Losses can be reduced when certain procedures are put in place. Risk can be reduced, yes, but not entirely eliminated—there is no foolproof system. Remember, "If you believe you have a foolproof system, you've failed to take into consideration the creativity of fools." This ad-

Exhibit 11–15   Detection devices like MoneyChecker supplement front-office training designed to recognize counterfeit currencies and related products. Detection devices are generally inexpensive and require minimal training. The least expensive (and least sophisticated) detection comes with special pens designed to change color when they contact the starch in paper counterfeits—real currency is made from cotton fibers. But inexpensive detection pens are easily thwarted by coating the fake bills in plastic (usually with a sprayed-on ScotchGuard-type product).

A slightly higher investment by the front office affords substantially improved detection in the form of UV lamps. UV lamps (like those found in the MoneyChecker) readily illuminate the color-coded security threads found in all $5, $10, $20, $50, and $100 U.S. currency bills (see Exhibit 11–13). A built-in template on all MoneyCheckers shows the location and color of each denomination's security thread. Additionally, the UV lamp can help authenticate credit cards, driver licenses, and travelers checks, many of which now boast logos or overprinted areas visible only under the specific wavelengths of UV light. *Courtesy of Angstrom Technologies, Erlanger, Kentucky.*

vice comes from Frank W. Abagnale, a well-known check counterfeiter made famous by the movie *Catch Me If You Can.*

➤*Procedures for Minimizing Fraud.*   Hotel operations are 100 times more likely to lose money to forged and fraudulent checks than they are to armed robbery! Using proper check-cashing procedures is critical to avoid significant losses from this form of theft.

As with counterfeiting, computer technology has made check-cashing forgery a simple crime for anyone to perpetrate. Basic desktop publishing and scanning equipment is all one needs to ably copy and alter personal checks. And since checks are paid by computer automation as well, the altered check will clear provided the account has sufficient funds.

Unfortunately, hotels that accept forged or worthless checks have little recourse. Banks are not responsible for losses incurred from bad checks passed against them. The hotel ends up holding the bag—prevention is the only cure.

The Old "One–Two–Three."   Prevention is as easy as one–two–three. That's because the vast majority of faulty checks can be detected by front-office cashiers with three simple observations.

First, is the check perforated? All legitimate checks are perforated on at least one side (except for the small percentage of checks that are government checks, checks printed on computer card stock, and counter checks). Because perforation equipment is so bulky and expensive, few check forgers bother with this detail.

Second, do the Federal Reserve district numbers 1 to 12 match the location of the issuing bank? Cashiers should compare the Federal Reserve district number located between the brackets along the bottom of the check with the restated district number printed (in smaller type) in the upper right-hand corner of the check (see Exhibit 11–16, item 9). Many check forgers change the Federal Reserve district numbers at the bottom of the check to a different district. In this way, the check is sent for clearing to the wrong district, gaining the forger several valuable days. Remember, if the numbers don't match, the check is a forgery.

Third, is the routing code printed in magnetic ink? The routing code found at the bottom of the check (Exhibit 11–16, item 8) must be printed in dull, flat magnetic ink. If the ink is shiny or raised, the check is a forgery.

Although these are the three critical questions for a cashier to observe, there are others. A comprehensive check-cashing checklist has been developed and is discussed later in this chapter. It provides management with a more thorough understanding of the check-cashing process.

Simple Deterrents.   Every weapon available must be employed in the battle against check fraud. Closed-circuit television in banks and photographing procedures elsewhere affirm a hotel's right to use similar equipment. Dual-lens cameras, which simultaneously record a picture of the instrument being negotiated and of the check passer, are available. Other systems allow the development of latent fingerprints without the use of ink or other messy substances. Just a sign explaining that such equipment is being used serves as a deterrent, as does a printed warning citing the penalty for passing bad checks.

Other hotels collect a check-cashing fee, which is used to offset worthless checks. The rationale of penalizing honest guests is open to debate. It would be better to adopt and enforce a stringent procedure, irritating as it is to the honest guest, than to collect an unwarranted fee. The procedure may include a telephone call at the guest's expense to

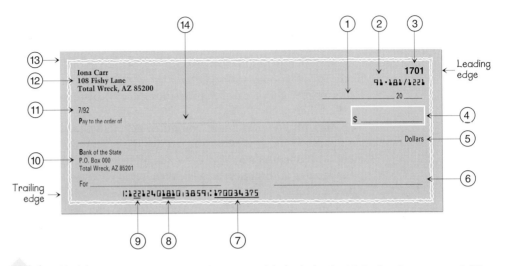

Exhibit 11–16   Fourteen locations flag a possible bad check: (1) Is the date current? (2) Do the routing numbers correspond to the magnetic numbers? (3) Has the account existed for some time? (4) Is the amount more or less than the statutory definition of grand larceny? (5) Are the values of the handwritten dollars and the numerical dollars identical? (6) Does the signature correspond to the registration card or the endorsement? (7) Are the account numbers in agreement with a bankcard that is being proffered? (8) Is the magnetic ink dull or reflective? (9) Is the number of the Federal Reserve region accurate? (10) Does the bank directory list this bank as shown? (11) When was the account established? (12) How does the maker's identity compare with the hotel's records? (13) Is the check perforated? (14) Is the payee a third party, a corporation, or cash?

his or her office or bank according to the circumstances and time of day. Using a check-cashing service may cost the guest a similar fee, but it puts the hotel in a better light.

Endorsements.   Procedural protection requires proper and immediate endorsement after the check is received. This is particularly true with open endorsements containing only the payee's name. The cashier should use a rubber stamp that reads as follows:

For Deposit Only
The ABC Hotel

The stamp should contain space for identification, credit-card number, room number, and the initials of the person approving the check.

Invariably, bank endorsements blot out much of the information recorded on the rear of the check. The data is unusable when needed most, if the check comes back. This issue, which was one that every industry faced, was addressed by Congress in 1988. The legislation that emerged assigned the first 1.5 inches from the trailing edge of the check (see Exhibit 11–15) to endorsements. In that space on the rear of the check go all the endorsements and whatever identification will fit into the area. The front of the check can still be used if more data is needed.

►*Check-Cashing Checklist.*   No single set of rules covers every circumstance, but a list of limitations and restrictions is a helpful guide to those responsible for approving checks. Such a list follows. Modifications depend on the class of hotel, the source of authority, and the circumstances surrounding the particular request:

1. Accept checks only for the amount of the bill. Be particularly alert for the cashback technique, by which cash as well as services rendered are lost.

2. Allow no one to be above suspicion on weekends, holidays, and after banking hours.

3. Refuse to accept any check that is altered, illegible, stale (older than 30 days), postdated, poorly printed, or from a third party.

4. Be suspicious of checks slightly smaller than the statutory measure of grand larceny. If $500 separates petty larceny from grand larceny in the state, a $507 check is less likely to be counterfeit than is a $496 one.

5. Compare the signature and address on the check with those on the registration card: Are they similar? Should they be? Compare the signature on the front with the endorsement on the rear. Ask the same questions!

6. Compare the age of the guest with the birth date on the driver's license. Has the license expired? Compare the person's listed height and weight, hair and eye color, and the photograph, if available, to the person standing before you. More and more state driver's licenses and identification cards are being manufactured with tamperproof technology. When identification data has been altered, the card disintegrates in some conspicuous manner. For example, with Pennsylvania's driver's licenses, the state seal disintegrates if the card has been altered.

7. Pay special attention to endorsements. Accept no conditional, circumstantial, or restrictive endorsements. Challenge endorsements that are not identical to either the printed name (in the case of a personal check) or the payee (in the case of a third-party check).

8. Require endorsements on checks paid to the bearer or to cash. Require all endorsements to be made in your presence, repeating them when the check is already endorsed.

9. Refuse a check payable to a corporation but endorsed by one of the officers seeking to cash it.

10. Obtain adequate and multiple identification and record it on the rear 1.5 inches of the trailing edge along with any other information that can help if the check is refused: address, telephone number, credit-card number, license plates, clerk's initials.

11. Verify business names in telephone directories or listings such as Dun & Bradstreet, Inc. Obtain military identification. Call local references. Request a business card.

12. Create fictitious information or names of company officers and see if the guest verifies them.

13. Make certain that the check is complete, accurate, and dated. Watch for misspellings and serial numbers of more than four digits.

14. Keep a bank directory and check the transit and routing numbers against it. Verify the name of the bank with the directory listing, giving special attention to the article "the" and the use of the ampersand (&) in place of the word *and*. "City Bank of Laurelwood" is not the same as "The City Bank of Laurelwood"; "Farmers and Merchants Bank" is not "Farmers & Merchants Bank."

15. Check for perforations. All legitimate checks have at least one side that is perforated.

16. Remember, cashier's checks (checks drawn on the bank by one of its officers) are spelled with an apostrophe *s*, are full size, never pocket size. Watch it! These checks can be stopped at the bank of issue up to 72 hours after being validated. (Trust companies issue treasurer's checks, not cashier's checks.)

17. Be cautious of certified checks, since most persons do not use them.

18. Check the signatures on bank drafts (a check drawn by a bank on its correspondent bank) with the bank directory, and verify the bank's correspondent bank at the same time.

19. Note that because of withholding, payroll checks are almost never even dollar amounts.

20. *Read* identification—don't just look at it! Ask questions: "What does your middle C stand for?" Don't offer the answer: "Is your middle name *Charles?*"

21. Determine whether the guest is registered from the same city as the one in which the bank is located.

22. Be familiar with bank locations: The 12 Federal Reserve districts are numbered from 1 in the east to 12 in the west. Locate the magnetic code on the lower left of the check. The first two digits following the bracket (|:) identify the Federal Reserve bank handling the commercial paper. Numbers greater than the 12 Federal Reserve districts are fakes. This is not true of NOW accounts or similar noncommercial checks.

23. Watch the calendar: Most bad checks are passed during the final quarter of the year, the holiday season.

24. Expect the magnetic code to be dull; shiny numbers that reflect light have been printed with other than magnetic ink. Preestablish firm limits on the value of the checks to be cashed.

25. Question emergencies. If airfare is needed to fly home unexpectedly, why can't the airline take the check?

26. Ignore evidence of identity that consists of social security cards, library cards, business cards, or voter identification cards. These are easily forged or reproduced, and they generally carry no photo.

27. Personally deliver the check to the cashier without allowing the guest to retrieve it once it has been approved.

28. Watch check numbers. Low digits mean a new account where the danger is greatest. The larger the number, the safer the check. New accounts generally begin with number 101, and 90% of all "hot" checks are written on accounts less than a year old (numbered 101–150).

29. Look for the small date on the left upper section of the check (when available). This indicates the date the account was opened.

30. Do not write the check; insist that the check be written by the guest.

31. Machine, color-copied checks can be smeared with a wet finger; real safety-paper checks cannot.

32. Remember that bank cards do not cover cash losses, only merchandise purchased. Limit check cashing to the front-desk cashiers.

33. Note that credit managers have been known to eavesdrop on guest telephone calls.

34. Ask yourself how difficult it would be to create the identification offered.

35. Compare the numerical amount of the check with the written amount.

36. Watch the value of foreign traveler's checks. Foreign checks are issued in foreign currency. Don't cash 20 marks or francs as a U.S. $20 value (see Exhibit 11–17).

Debit Cards.   Debit cards provide the hotel with immediate payment through the guest's bank account. Rather than writing a personal check, the debit card electronically debits the guest's bank account and credits the hotel's. Payment is immediate, and the risk associated with accepting personal checks is removed. For additional discussion on debit cards, refer to Chapter 12.

Exhibit 11–17   Foreign traveler's checks look similar to U.S. traveler's checks. Although there are variations in color, an unwary cashier can easily confuse currencies, potentially costing the hotel substantial losses. This is especially true when the check is payable in dollars, which are used by a number of countries, including Australia, Canada, Jamaica, Hong Kong, Singapore, and the United States (see Exhibit 11–11).

►*Traveler's Checks.* American Express (AmEx) pioneered the traveler's check, and it has retained its preeminent position ever since. VISA and MasterCard entered the field in the late 1970s and early 1980s as extensions of their credit-card business. Several banks and travel agencies round out the slate of participants. It is a competitive business. However, due primarily to the proliferation of ATM machines (discussed earlier in the chapter), the traveler's check industry has stagnated in recent years. With easy access to electronic cash, travelers feel even more secure carrying their plastic ATM cards as opposed to dozens of bulky traveler's checks. As such, the traveler's check industry stalled in the late 1990s at about $50 billion per year. It will probably decline in volume over the coming decades, even as the industry has found renewed popularity through the use of gift checks (traveler's checks given instead of cash for weddings, birthdays, etc.).

Generally, traveler's checks are purchased by the consumer prior to a trip. They are used as if they were cash, with the issuing company guaranteeing their replacement against loss or theft. The charge is usually 1%, but the checks are often issued without charge. Even without charge, there is plenty of competition for the business. Large sums of interest-free money are available for investing. The time lag (the float) between the purchase of the traveler's check and the use of the check might be months. Some 15 to 20% of traveler's check sales are never claimed. No wonder AmEx advertising encourages buyers to hold their checks for some distant emergency.

Buyers sign the checks at the time of purchase and countersign when they cash the instruments. Signature comparison is the main line of defense against fraud. Checks must be countersigned under the scrutiny of the cashier or resigned if they were initially endorsed away from the cashier's view. Some traveler's checks provide for dual countersignatures (usually to accommodate a husband and wife team), yet only one signature is required to cash the check.

Traveler's checks are very acceptable and some hotels will cash them even for non-registered guests. Other hotels are extra cautious and require additional identification or compare signatures to registration cards. Comparing signatures is all that's required. In fact, many issuing companies do not even want the cashier to ask for additional identification. That is because extra identification takes the cashier's focus away from the signature line. And the identification may also be invalid—in more than half the instances of stolen traveler's checks, the identification has also been stolen!

Prompt refund of lost or stolen checks is their major appeal. Hotel desks, with their 24-hour service, represent a logical extension of the issuing company's office system. Hilton entered into such an agreement with Bank of America. It is both a service to the guest and a marketing device for the chain.

Traveler's Checks Deterrents. The best defense is to carefully watch the guest sign the traveler's check. Cautious cashiers should never remove their eyes from the check being signed. Indeed, some cashiers never even remove their hand from the check, always holding onto one corner while the guest is signing. It is a simple matter for someone to produce a stolen traveler's check, pretend to sign it while the cashier's attention is focused elsewhere, and then quickly substitute a previously signed traveler's check with a well-forged signature.

Like their commercial brothers, traveler's checks employ a magnetic code on the lower left portion of the paper (see Exhibit 11–17). In the United States, the first digits are always 8000, which tells the clearinghouse computer that it is a traveler's check. The next portion of the code identifies the type. For example, 8000001 is Bank of America, 8000005 is American Express.

Although forgers can easily alter the clearinghouse transit codes, they cannot easily copy the high-quality, high-speed laser images major companies print in their traveler's checks. These images can be seen when holding the traveler's check to the light (don't confuse these highly detailed laser imprints with simple watermarks found in paper). MasterCard and Thomas Cook, for example, show a Greek goddess on the right side of the check. Similarly, Citicorp displays a Greek god's face on the right of the check. Bank of America uses three globes (which supplement the other globes already visible). And VISA provides a globe on the left with a dove in the upper right of the check.

American Express utilizes a somewhat different safety approach. Red dots are visible in the check if held up to the light, but a wet finger is the acid test. It will smear the check when applied to the denomination on the back left side but will not smear the back right side.

The components of this chapter—cash, cash paid-outs, and cash equivalents—represent a small percentage of the transactions that occur at the front desk. Most transactions are handled by credit card or credit transfer to a city ledger account. In Chapter 12, the focus changes to the issues of credit. Because credit cards and credit equivalents represent the lion's share of front-office transactions, poor or lazy procedures can harm front-office profitability. In Chapter 12 we explain credit-handling procedures and caution managers to treat credit transactions with the same care as cash transactions.

RESOURCES AND CHALLENGES
Resources

➤ *SUMMARY*

Even as the quantity of cash circulating in hotels declines, the need for careful cash-handling practices increases. This is especially true for front-desk cashiers because they not only receive cash but pay it out as well.

Front-office cashiers receive cash from a number of potential sources. Guests may pay cash on their room folio at check in, at check out, or in the middle of their stay. Cash is also received at the desk on behalf of other departments (as when a customer pays for a banquet) and for auxiliary revenue centers such as soda machines or video games.

Cash is paid out by the front-office cashier for a number of reasons as well. On check out, the guest who overpaid the folio may receive a refund.

Employees may receive charged tips in cash, concessionaries may receive charged purchases in cash, and guests themselves may receive cash advances against the folio. Add to this list of paid-outs the use of an imprest petty cash account and the front-office cashier's job becomes a complicated and sensitive task.

To make the job even more difficult, cashiers must remain alert to potential check-cashing, credit-card, or cash transaction frauds. Hotel front desks are favorite targets for counterfeit currency, forged checks, or stolen credit cards. Front-office managers need to carefully train cashiers to identify situations where fraudulent practices may occur.

➤ WEB SITES

The growth of ATMs has been phenomenal. In 1992, there were just 9,700 ATMs in the United States. Four years later (1996), that number had grown to 33,400. Four years later (2000), that number had grown to 158,000 ATMs in the U.S. And four years later (2004), that number was expected to grow to well above 350,000 ATMs in the United States (see Exhibits 11–2, 11–3, and 11–4).

As ATMs grow in importance and acceptability worldwide, they become an increasingly important amenity for hotel lobbies. After all, 80% of Americans carry an ATM card, and 60% of them use the card regularly (at least eight times per month). More specifically, 60% of Americans aged 25 to 34 years and 51% of Americans aged 35 to 49 years use an ATM at least eight times per month, withdrawing an average $55.00 per transaction.

Use the following Web sites to learn more about this important allied industry:

➤ http://www.rbrldn.demon.co.uk (History of the ATM industry as well as numerous research papers and projections through the year 2007. There is a charge for most research papers, but the summaries are free to read and quite interesting.)

➤ http://www.ATMmarketplace.com (Visit this Web site to see all the latest products, prices, and features.)

➤ http://www.kioskcom.com (A Web site related to ATM kiosks and related trade shows/conferences.)

➤ http://www.link.co.uk (Link Network is the world's busiest ATM switch.)

➤ http://www.worldmall.tv/debit_cards_ATM_cash_card.htm (This Web site has been developing methods for wiring cash through Western Union using ATMs—very useful for hotel guests in need of funds!)

➤ INTERESTING TIDBITS

➤ Some first-class hotels operating in cities with large international markets use transient ledger paid-outs to provide exceptional service. InterContinental Hotels & Resorts, among others, prepare small cash packets (InterContinental calls these packets by such names as Little Touches, Instant Money, and Currency Exchange Kits) for their arriving guests who have not yet had time to secure local currencies. The cost for these packets (usually in bundles worth $25 to $50) is charged to the guest folio as a paid-out, but that small attention to detail is priceless!

➤ There are currently 15 member states in the European Union (EU). These include Austria, Belgium, Finland, France, Germany, Greece, Ireland, Italy, Luxembourg, The Netherlands, Portugal, and Spain (the twelve current adopters of the euro currency). Sweden will surely be next to adopt the currency, while Denmark and the United Kingdom will probably not join the euro nations in the short run.

But the European Union is expanding. A new wave of candidates from 10 other European nations stand an excellent chance of joining the EU over the coming years. Watch for some or all of the following countries to join the EU in the near future: Cyprus, Czech Republic, Estonia, Hungary, Latvia, Lithuania, Malta, Poland, Slovakia, and Slovenia.

➤ In contrast to the European Union's mass conversion to the euro (11 member states introduced the euro on the same date in 1999), Central America has "dollarized" in a more quiet fashion. Today, quetzals, colons, balboas, and sucres (currencies of Guatemala, El Salvador, Panama, and Ecuador respectively) have all been replaced (or used in tandem) by the U.S. dollar. Similar conversions to the U.S. dollar have been taking place in South America as well.

➤ READING REFERENCES

ATM Networks. O. Kyas and G. Crawford. Upper Saddle River, New Jersey: Prentice Hall, 2002.

Catch Me If You Can: The True Story of a Real Fake. S. Redding and F. Abagnale. New York: Broadway Books, 2000.

The Dollarization Debate. D. Salvatore (J. Dean and T. Willett, Eds.) Oxford University Press, 2003.

The Euro: Evolution and Prospects. P. Arestis, A. Brown, and M. Sawyer. Northampton, MA: Edward Elgar Publishers, 2001.

Managed Floating Plus: The Great Currency Regime Debate. M. Goldstein. Published by the Institute for International Economics, 2002.

What Every Credit Card User Needs to Know: How to Protect Yourself and Your Money. H. Strong. New York: Owl Books, 1999.

Challenges

➤ TRUE/FALSE

___ 1. Front-office cashiers accept cash in two directions: They receive cash (receipts) as well as pay cash out (paid-outs). This is different from cashiers in all other departments, where cash transactions flow in just one direction. In other words, cashiers in all other departments do not make paid-outs.

___ 2. Cash settlements for hotel account balances (paid in cash) are far more common than most people realize. This is especially true in corporate hotels, where cash payments account for more than one-third of all room folio settlements.

___ 3. The front-desk cashier is often the source of imprest petty cash funds for all other departments on-property. For example, if the restaurant was running low on butter and awaiting Thursday's delivery, they could use money available through the front-desk cashier's imprest fund to purchase enough butter at the grocery store to hold them over a few days.

___ 4. To determine how much a front-office cashier might be over or short, the cashier compares the "should have" against the "do have." The amount of the cashier's "should have" is equal to the starting (opening) bank drawer plus net receipts.

___ 5. Today's U.S. currency contains a number of state-of-the-art security features designed to prevent counterfeiting. These features include, among others, a watermark visible when the bill is held to the light, a security thread whose location changes according to the denomination of the bill, and color-shifting ink.

➤ PROBLEMS

1. Industry experts suggest the amount of cash in the banks of hotel cashiers should equal some 2% of gross revenues, or about $600 per available room. For a 100-room hotel that grosses $3 million annually, this equals $60,000 in cashiers' banks.

As a new general manager, you are concerned with the sizable amount of outstanding cash in your cashiers' various banks. You know that if it were released from the banks, the cash could return significant revenues or interest income.

Be creative as you identify three distinct methods for identifying which banks have excess cash or other means for releasing some of the $60,000. However, remember to maintain cash bank security as you brainstorm new methodologies.

2. An international guest tenders $171 in U.S. funds and #2,000 from his native land to settle an outstanding account of $206.20. #s are being purchased by the hotel for 51.50 per U.S. dollar. What must the cashier do now to settle the account? Assume that the guest has more U.S. dollars; assume that he doesn't. The hotel cashier has no foreign funds in the drawer.

3. Explain how international tourism helps balance the trade deficit of the United States. How does international tourism worsen the deficit?

4. Sketch and complete a cashier's envelope for October 11 showing the details of the turn-in and the amount of due back. (City-ledger collections are handled by the accounting office. No provisions are made for cash over or short; the cashier covers both.)

Given for Problem

House bank	$1,800.00
Advances to guests	$181.15
House vouchers	$16.20
Vending machine refunds	$0.50
Received from guests	$7,109.40
Cash in the drawer exclusive of other cash listed below	$1,721.00
Traveler's checks	$2,675.00
Personal checks:	
Washington	$75.25
Lincoln	$310.00
Jefferson	$44.98
Carter	$211.90
Kennedy	$55.00
Others	$1,876.85
Bills of $100 denomination	10 each
Torn and dirty currency	$62.00
Coins	$680.14

5. Imagine that your hotel operates in a community where the incidence of counterfeiting is quite high. Develop a procedure for all front-desk cashiers in terms of accepting U.S. currency. Remember to be sensitive to the amount of time it takes to examine a bill properly and the fact that the cashier may be busy with other guests in line. Also, discuss whether the procedure should be eased for smaller denominations: $50s?, $20s? What if the cashier knows the guest from previous hotel visits? Be certain that your policy distinguishes between the newer currency (introduced in 1996) and the older currency (which will be in circulation for many years to come).

6. Some hotels prevent cashiers from knowing their net receipts. Without knowing net receipts, the cashier turns everything in from the day's drawer except the bank. If the drawer is significantly over for the shift, the cashier is none the wiser and is not tempted to steal the amount of the overage. Do you support such a policy? Are there any drawbacks to not allowing cashiers access to their net receipt figures?

➤ ANSWERS TO TRUE/FALSE QUIZ

1. True. For front-office cashiers, cash flows in two directions: receipts and paid-outs. For all other cashiers, cash flows one way—receipts.

2. False. Cash settlements for hotel account balances are actually relatively rare, probably ranging below 5%. This is especially true for corporate hotels, where almost all accounts are settled as either a transfer to the city ledger's corporate account or paid by credit card.

3. True. By signing an imprest voucher, the restaurant would secure enough funds to purchase the butter at the grocery store. The grocery receipt and any remaining change would be returned to the imprest petty cash fund.

4. True. The starting bank plus net receipts equal the "should have." Comparing that with what is actually in the drawer at the end of the shift ("do have") determines whether or not the cashier is over, short, or right on the nose.

5. True. These are all security features currently found on U.S. currency.

Credit and the City Ledger

Outline

Buying with credit—the promise to pay later—is how American business does business. Testimony to the power of credit is the 21 billion credit-card transactions that retail customers make annually. One subgroup, hotel guests, use credit cards for most of their room, food, and beverage purchases. Cash, as Chapter 11 suggests, is out of favor with both hotel guests and their hosts.

Even commercial transactions, which once were settled monthly with an exchange of business checks (cash), have given way to aggressive credit-card marketing. Corporate procurement cards (business credit cards) are now widely used. Master-Card has BusinessCard, for example,[1] but it is just one brand among some 200 commercial cards.

➤ REVIEW OF THE CITY LEDGER

Whatever the business, customers who have not yet paid for goods and services already received are called accounts receivable (A/R). Chapter 10 explained that hotels have two types of accounts receivable. Registered guests are called *front-office (transient or guest)* accounts receivable. Their debts are tracked on front-office folios. Those who owe the hotel but are not registered are known as *city* accounts receivable. Their debts are tracked separately by the accounting office.

Accounts receivable records are accumulated in ledgers. The term *ledger* survives although the records are no longer in bound books; they're computerized. Hence, the records of registered guests are grouped together in a front-office (transient or guest) ledger. Likewise, nonregistered accounts receivable are grouped in a city ledger. Individual records in the guest ledger are identified by room numbers. City-ledger accounts have no room numbers; they are not occupying rooms. Account numbers are used instead.

Most city receivables (accounts receivable who are not registered) start out as front-office receivables (accounts receivable who are registered). A registered guest usually shifts debt from the front office to the back office by using a credit card. The debt is still owed, but the transient guest has left the hotel. Once the guest is no longer registered, the debt becomes part of a city ledger. City-ledger accounts receivable include more than credit-card companies. Associations, wholesalers, travel agents, individuals, and client companies become city accounts whenever their front-office folios, often master accounts, are transferred to the city ledger for direct billing by mail.

Transferring an account from the front-office ledger to the city ledger is one of the three methods of settling a folio at check-out time. Allowances and cash, the other two methods, were discussed in Chapters 10 and 11. This chapter concludes the unit by viewing the city ledger in its entirety, broadening the discussion beyond city-ledger transfers.

➤ CARDS

Credit cards, long the domain of serious shoppers, face potential competition from a recent surge in debit-card use.

---

[1]Trademark names are used throughout the chapter. Read® adjacent to each and every registered name.

Credit Cards

For now, credit-card use continues to grow worldwide. Even Europeans, long-time cash traditionalists, have come aboard. Much like the hotel industry has done, credit-card companies continue refashioning old offerings into more appealing products. The credit revolution that began during the last half of the 20th century gains momentum still.

➤*Brief History of Hotel Credit Cards.*   Credit in innkeeping has a long tradition. It traces back to the proprietors of the Roman mansions, the Biblical inns. These early innkeepers issued negotiable tokens. They were used as money because the good faith and credit of the innkeeper guaranteed their redemption. Tokens were accepted broadly and exchanged on demand, although value fluctuated with the creditworthiness and reputation of the hotelkeeper. Paper scrip and tokens were reborn with colonial innkeepers some 2,000 years later. In between, medieval knights and noblemen used wax impressions of their signet rings to guarantee payments to their hosts. Freed from the need to carry coins, they traveled with greater ease along the dangerous roads populated by highwaymen.

Hoteliers began dabbling in credit again in 1915 when two economic power-houses, the telegraph company (Western Union) and the national railroads, issued special cards to preferred customers. With the airplane came the Air Travel Card (1936), although the birth of modern credit cards is said to be 1950. A New York attorney, supposedly embarrassed at being short of cash in an upscale restaurant, founded Diners Club that year. It was used at only 27 fashionable restaurants in New York City, but gross billing immediately reached $1 million in 1950.

America Express, which had dominated the issuance of traveler's checks since 1891, introduced the American Express (AmEx[2]) card in 1958. It too was quickly successful. Over a quarter million subscribers joined the first year. Banks entered the fray in 1960 when California-based Bank of America (B of A) launched Bank Americard. Success came again—so much so that B of A franchised the concept. Four Chicago banks introduced MasterCard in 1965. Four California banks followed suit with MasterCharge in 1967.

It wasn't long before consolidation and innovation had produced an array of products (see Exhibit 12–1). Present-day Visa International emerged from B of A's BankAmericard. Citicorp bought Diners Club in 1981, and a Chicago/California connection produced MasterCard International.

As the action heated up, hotel chains began issuing their own credit cards—but not for long. Hotel credit cards were short-lived. Costs of administration and borrowing were too high. Hotel chains were much smaller in the middle of the century, and they lacked the computer capacity and financial depth to stay the course. Besides, broad-based cards were finding more general acceptance. Many hotel chains returned to the arena through affinity-card partnerships with Visa and other international cards.

Hilton's experience is a good example of the ambivalence that the whole industry had toward credit cards. Between 1959 and 1962, Hilton twice converted its system. All Hilton and Statler cardholders (Hilton bought the Statler chain in 1954) were switched from company cards to Carte Blanche and back again to company cards only. Undoubtedly, part of the problem was Hilton's choice of Carte Blanche as the partner. Carte Blanche was a small player in the national scene and unknown interna-

---

[2]AmEx or Amex, abbreviations for American Express, is sometimes confused with Amex, an abbreviation for the American Stock Exchange. AMEX or Amexco also reference American Express.

Chronology in the Development of the Credit Card

1936	Universal Air Travel Plan consolidated and re-branded with PassAge, AirPlus and Air Travel Card to its present-day terminology of Universal Air Travel Plan. UATP is a travel card, not a consumer card. It is accepted by virtually all the world's airlines and co-brands other segments of the travel experience with MasterCard or Visa.
1950	Diner's Club focused on wealthy clientele patronizing fashionable New York restaurants.
1958	AmEx (Green) Card launched by American Express, long-time leader (1850) in the travel business.
1960	BankAmericard introduced and franchised by Bank of America.
1961	The Japanese credit card, JCB, is the largest credit-card company outside of the United States. The logo of the Japanese Credit Bureau infers an endorsement of the merchant.
1965	MasterCard founded as a joint venture of Chicago banks.
1967	MasterCharge founded as a joint venture of California banks.
1970	MasterCard and MasterCharge merge and form MasterCard International.
1975	First appearance of debit cards.
1977	BankAmericard changes its name to Visa.
1978	Carte Blanche acquired by Citigroup (Citicorp/Citibank). Still in circulation but not aggressively marketed in 25 years.
1980	First appearance of affinity cards.
1981	Citigroup adds Diners Club to its Carte Blanche network.
1981	Frequent-flier programs introduced.
1985	Discover Card is launched as a product of Sears Financial Network, which later became Novus Services. Now, Sears' National Bank issues MasterCard, and Morgan Stanley owns Novus/Discover Card.
1990	American Telephone and Telegraph (AT&T) becomes the first nonfinancial enterprise to enter the credit-card business with its Universal Card.
1998	Citigroup acquires AT&T's Universal Card, adding it to its credit-card division.
2003	T&E cards battle bank card in the courts eventually gaining access to the banking system.

Exhibit 12–1   Fifty-plus years have transformed credit cards from an idea in one man's head (Diner's Club, 1950) to a multi-billion dollar industry that has changed the way merchant/hotels and customer/guests do business.

tionally. It was acquired in 1978 by CitiCorp, now CitiGroup, which broadened the global coverage of Carte Blanche by adding Diners Club in 1981. Diners Club still has a strong international presence because it franchises outside the United States.

By the 1970s, the lodging industry had come to understand that credit cards were financial instruments, not marketing tools for hotel chains. With some relief, the industry left the credit-card business to the credit-card companies. So, another agency wedged itself between the hotel operator and the guest. There are third-party reservation agencies, third-party marketing groups, third-party telephone companies, and third-party credit-card issuers. Hilton's current credit card, for example, is a Citibank Visa card, not a Hilton-issued card. With this Hilton HHonors Visa Signature Card, users earn points in both airline miles and Hilton's frequent-guest program (FGP), including amenities such as health club admissions.

Partners With Lodging.   The credit-card industry works hand-in-glove with the lodging industry. Despite tensions between individual companies, the industries cooperate on a range of matters. Competition among the four major cards (Visa, MasterCard, AmEx, and Discover) undoubtedly accounts for part of their support. So does the mutual interests of the two industries. Reliance on each other contributes to a strong partnership. Good purveyors service their customers diligently, and that is another reason that the credit-card industry stands firmly with lodging.

Each of the major cards supports a different need. Visa's contribution is a national educational program concentrating on reservations and no-shows. Visa began underwriting the cost of related research more than a dozen years ago. MasterCard supports the Educational Institute (EI) of the American Hotel & Lodging Association (AH&LA). EI provides a broad program of studies for all levels within the lodging industry, but MasterCard's major thrust is developing service skills at the front desk. Obviously, better front-desk operations, reduce no-shows, and up-selling reservations tie the contributions of Visa and MasterCard back to their own credit-card products.

American Express has the longest affiliation, nearly 40 years. It's strong support has taken several paths, including partnering with the AH&LA in legislative affairs and contributing regularly to the American Hotel Foundation. Discover Card is a latecomer to the industry (see Exhibit 12–1). Its national contribution is yet unclear, but it is forming strong, single-company relationships.

All credit-card companies participate in the lodging industry's regional and national meetings. If nothing else, they take booths and exhibit at the trade shows. Very often, they sponsor meals and other show events, underwriting the cost of speakers, for example. (These are the kinds of activities that create the secondary master accounts discussed in Chapter 10.)

Kinds of Credit Cards

Consumer credit cards are growing increasingly alike, but they didn't start out that way. Although the number and variety of credit cards seem endless, consumer cards fall into three general categories. *Bank cards* are the most common, followed by *travel and entertainment cards* (T&Es). *Private label cards* comprise most of the third category: all others.

The credit-card industry is extremely competitive. Each of the three types was designed initially for different consumer markets. T&E cards, by their very name, were to be used chiefly for travel, leaving bank cards for local shopping. That's not so any longer. Competition has forced each to take on attributes of the other. The differences between bank cards and T&Es began blurring some time ago:

➤ Bank cards now charge annual fees, although they were initially offered without charge.

➤ T&Es, which always required merchants to wait for their reimbursements, now have express deposits.

➤ Prestige cards with high spending limits for the affluent, the initial customers of the T&Es, are everyone's game today.

Bank Cards.   Visa and MasterCard are the best-known bank cards. Bank cards are issued to anyone: depositors and nondepositors, locals and distant consumers, strong and weak debtors. Annual solicitations are estimated at more than 3 billion mailings. There are more bank cards in the United States than there are residents!

Recall that T&E cards, which marketed to the affluent customer, preceded bank cards by a decade. Bank cards entered the market by soliciting consumers unable to qualify for the more stringent credit standards of the travel and entertainment cards. Banks are in the business of lending money for interest. Banks cards are just another form of bank loan. Lower economic groups are solicited to take cards and pay them off over time. Wise cardholders make prompt payments to avoid the high finance charges, up to 1.5% per month. The banks are lending at 18% or more annually while they borrow for far less. It's a good business to be in!

Bank cards are the products of numerous banks, each competing for the same customer. But all are franchisees of either Visa or MasterCard. These associations are joint ventures of their member banks. Banks are consolidating, much as is the lodging industry. Economies of scale and reduced competition make credit cards a profitable adjunct to the banking industry and minimize the need to compete with lower interest rates.

Discover Card is a special kind of bank card because it is issued and processed through an investment bank, Morgan Stanley. Discover Card offers the ultimate reward to cardholders, cash refunds up to 1% of annual purchases. Despite its generosity and the industry's lowest merchant fees, Discover lacks the image of the snazzier cards. Both it and American Express have operated outside of the Visa/MasterCard franchise system. That may be changing, as an upcoming discussion explains.

Travel and Entertainment Cards (T&Es).   American Express is the best known T&E. Travel and entertainment cards are not divisions of banks, although Diners Club/Carte Blanche has recently become part of one, Citigroup. T&Es do not solicit marginal users in order to collect interest. Cardholders are expected to settle in full each month. Failure to do so evokes penalties, one of which is interest. So the distinction is somewhat academic. If late payments persist, the card may be revoked or some incentive may be withheld. T&E cardholders pay larger annual fees and face tougher credit checks.

Higher card fees from users—$1,000 annually for AmEx's "Black Card"—fewer bad debts (about 0.25% lower than bank cards), and higher discount fees (merchant's costs), not interest, are the T&Es' major income sources. And in those higher discount fees lie the cause of one segment of the credit-card wars, discussed shortly.

T&E's are slower than bank cards in reimbursing merchants/hotels. This provides another means of earnings, called *float*. If collection is made from cardholders on day 1 and payment to the merchants is delayed until day 11, the credit-card company has interest-free use of the money for 10 days. What is aggravating to the merchant waiting for several hundreds or even thousands of dollars is very big money to the T&E working with tens of millions of dollars. Everyone—credit-card company, merchant, business user, and consumer—chases the float. Float is one explanation for the increased use of credit cards by businesses. The business has interest-free use of the money for 30 to 60 days, between dates of purchase and payment to the credit-card company.

Private Label Cards.   Private label cards are best illustrated with the hotel's own card. Such cards have very limited use; other merchants will not accept them. Promoting customer loyalty has been their chief purpose, but the 1.5% monthly charge on overdue accounts (see Chapter 10, Exhibit 10–9) certainly helps the hotel's bottom line. Sales promotion rather than credit control has been the objective of private label cards. So where the cards do exist, credit verification is minimal. There is no urgency for the industry to return to private labels because frequent-guest programs now provide the same marketing information. Moreover, the credit-card companies, AmEx in particular, provide merchants with helpful customer analyses.

Gasoline companies (Arco, Texaco, etc.) marketed private label cards for many years. Consumers once carried a variety of gas cards as they carry a variety of credit cards today. Billing and payment were handled through the corporate gas companies. The oil embargo of the 1970s changed the retail gasoline industry dramatically and contributed to the disappearance of these private label cards.

Department stores have fared better. They still issue private label cards but have replaced their policy of selling only with company cards by now accepting national credit cards as well.

New Products.   In their continuing quest for market share, credit-card issuers have introduced many new products. Two in particular, *affinity cards* and *co-branded cards,* were big hits when first issued.

Affinity cards carry two designations: the name of the affiliated group and that of the credit-card company. Almost any organization that offers the credit-card company an extensive mailing list can affiliate. Charities, professional organizations, public-service television stations and environmental groups add their names to the already established national card. The card company gets a list of possible new card users. Affinity cards are supposed to sharpen the group's identity and get members to use the card for the benefit of the organization. To encourage membership use, the affiliated organization gets a small signing bonus, typically a few dollars for each name on the list, and a percentage of every sale, typically 0.5%. The money is used to save the whales or build homes for the needy, whatever the group's inclination.

Affinity cards failed on two counts. First, banks gave up a portion of their discount fees expecting to recover the costs with higher interest receipts. It didn't happen. Second, card users gave up rewards to benefit the group. That worked for only so long. As the quality of rewards improved, member support declined. It was one thing to waive claim to a road map or another ice chest and a totally different decision to forego larger gifts, or savings bonds, or best of all, frequent-flier points. (For 1 or 2 cents per mile, airlines sell the points to banks, which award them to credit-card users.) As rewards got better, affinity support faded, but not before some 3,000 distinctive-looking cards featuring images such as mountain goats had been issued.

Co-branded cards held a different promise, beginning with their availability to the general public. Affinity cards were limited to affiliated groups. Co-branding didn't survive as planned. Major co-branders abandoned their participation because of high costs. General Motors had co-branded with Household International to offer points toward the purchase of a GM car. Ford Motor Company did the same with Citibank's card. AT&T's no-fee-for-life card was popular, but "no fees" accounted for its early withdrawal. Liabilities grew too rapidly even for companies as large as these giants. Ford had already paid out $500 million when it exited. Almost as quickly as their boisterous appearance came their quiet demise. But co-branding remained.

Co-branded cards are especially popular with lodging companies. Hilton, Marriott, Starwood—all hotel chains—co-brand with credit-card companies. Co-branded cards carry special privileges, such as check-cashing, room upgrades, and free continental breakfasts. In the longer run, guests build equity in loyalty programs: frequent-flier accounts or FGPs, or better still, both. Key to co-branding is the value of the reward. They're not giving away autos or hotels, just points in loyalty programs. Some chains use the same points to settle complaints (see Chapter 7).

Total points increased substantially during the lodging slump that started in this century. Luring guests with more points soon built liabilities for the lodging industry that approached those of the airlines.

BROADENING THE MARKET.   New products aren't always as dramatic as affinity and co-branded cards, although they may be introduced with just as much hoopla. Basic cards have morphed into gold cards, platinum cards, titanium cards, and back to blue cards and black cards. Each is presented as a new product with different costs, different privileges, and different rewards.

Competition is keen, and the credit-card companies search continuously for that special new product. Recent lures have stretched the imagination. Visa gives free movie tickets for using its debit cards. All the major issuers now have gift cards, whose prepaid amounts can be used at almost any store. (Of course, buyers pay upfront fees.) The potential is enormous: birthdays, graduations, newborns, holidays, even employee incentives.

Minicards, which are designed to hang on key chains, are a recent gimmick, as are new shapes and different sizes. As yet, they don't all work in ATMs. Perishable cards for one-time use with Web purchases are also being tested as a fraud preventative.

Card companies offer dozens of card types. Every market segment is fair game. Procurement cards, limited-use cards, payroll cards, and central-billing cards with customized reports appeal to businesses. American Express has pushed into retailing (grocery stores and gasoline stations) by doubling the points awarded. Special campaigns are aimed at senior citizens and at college students accepting their first card.

▶*How the System Works.*   The system works because there is something in it for everyone (see Exhibit 12–2). Credit-card *users* (hotel guests) purchase goods and services without cash. Payment may be financed through the credit card or delayed until billing, 20 to 50 days later. Card *issuers* (the banks) profit through a variety of fees, which are discussed next. *Merchants*[3] (the hotels) cooperate in the system, although they foot the entire cost. But they benefit by making sales that might otherwise go elsewhere, and they do so with less risk of loss. Hotels generally have done away

---

[3]Credit-card companies have always viewed those in the travel trade as poor credit risks, but especially so after September 11, 2001. Unable to get merchant status (see Exhibit 12–3) many travel agents use preferred vendors such as ASTA (American Society of Travel Agents) or ARC (Airlines Reporting Corporation) to handle credit-card processing. The credit-card companies have allowed this.

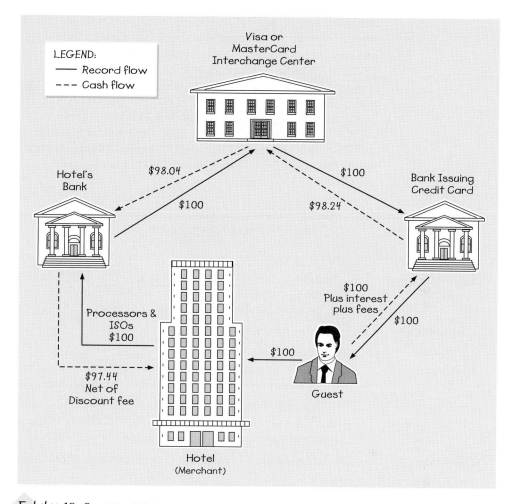

Exhibit 12–2   The full burden of settlement, 2.56% ($100–$97.44), falls on the merchant/hotel as credit-card charges clear the interchange system Transaction fees, rental equipment fees, and chargeback fees are other costs paid by the merchant. Unless customers are careful money managers, they too will contribute through late fees and interest.

with the position of credit manager. *Local banks* (the first step in processing the charges) have no float, but they earn fees for handling the transaction.

Fees.   Credit-card companies charge merchant/hotels discount fees. Bank cards charge at the lower range, 1 to 2% of the transaction; T&E's at the upper end, 3 to 5%. Card fees are no different from other business expenses—they can be negotiated. Large-volume merchants such as hotel chains negotiate smaller discount fees. Competition among rival banks and their independent sales organizations (ISOs) is so keen that even the smallest hotel dickers successfully. Besides, hotels have other banking relationships that give the merchant additional bargaining leverage. Franchise systems have a competitive edge over independents because they combine the volume of their memberships. Umbrella organizations have tried to do the same for independents, but administrative costs offset the gains from quantity discounts.

Card type (bank versus T&E) and dollar volume generated are only two of many cost components. Handling, authorization, and settlement procedures add to the merchants' (hotels') costs. Before the credit-card business grew so large, banks handled all support services. Costs have now been unbundled. The jobs of selling the merchant and servicing the merchant are handled by agents other than the banks (see Exhibit 12–3). With these services come fees: setup fees, per-transaction fees, programming fees, statement fees, authorization fees, monthly minimum charges, telecommunication costs, and lease payments. These third-party costs add 2 to 3% or more to the discount fees. Effective rates often reach 3 to 5%, even for bank cards!

Costs are higher still if credit cards are handled manually. Point-of-sale terminals in F&B outlets save processing fees. So does swiping cards through an electronic scanner during registration (see Exhibit 12–4). Waiting until later to manually verify a

CREDIT CARD TERMINOLOGY AND DEFINITIONS

Associations	Affiliations of member banks to form the MasterCard and Visa systems.
Card-processing company	Handles electronic transactions at the *POS*, which includes verifying the card, transferring the funds, and issuing approval codes. May also be an *independent service organization.*
Card-service provider	See *Merchant service provider.*
Chargeback fee	Credit-card company's charge added to the original value of a service when the charge is protested because of error or guest dispute.
Credit-card Companies	Technically, firms that appoint their own merchants and issue their own cards. Best known are American Express, Diners Club/Carte Blanche, and Discover. Generically used to include bank cards as well.
Discount rate	The percentage of each sale that the card companies charge the merchant; one of several fees, including a flat fee.
Handling	The method, manual or electronic, used to generate a sales slip.
Independent service organization	ISOs are contracted by banks to sell merchant status to businesses (hotels). May simultaneously be *card-processing companies* or may purchase wholesale services from one, reselling the services at retail.
Interchange fee	Charge paid by the merchant's bank that issued the card to compensate in part for the waiting time—float time—until payment is received.
Merchant service provider	Also called a *card-service provider.* Any company, including banks, *card-processing companies,* and *independent service organizations,* that arrange for and service *merchant status.*
MOTO	Mail order/telephone order; nonelectronic communications.
Merchant status	A business (hotel) authorized to process credit-card charges. Authorized merchants may not process cards (factor) for nonmerchants.
POS	A widely used abbreviation for point-of-sale.
Processor	See *Card-processing* company.

Exhibit 12–3   The phenomenal growth of the credit-card industry requires a host of ancillary agents to support and service the transactions. All add costs to the merchant's fee.

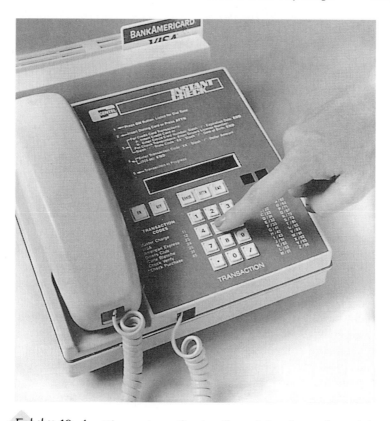

Exhibit 12–4   Electronic verification (by swiping the credit card through the horizontal reader) is faster and less costly to the merchant/hotel than is manual input by means of the touch-tone telephone. The cost of buying or renting the equipment is offset in part by savings in reduced discount fees. *Courtesy of Centel Transaction Services, Las Vegas, Nevada.*

card that the guest has already taken away incurs extra fees. All "nonmag" alternatives (manual handling, telephones, faxes, and mail) carry higher discount fees. Savings from electronic processing offset somewhat the costs of owning or leasing electronic equipment.

Another fee, a chargeback fee, is levied against the hotel when a charge is dishonored because of disputes with guests or errors in processing. The fee is an extra insult because the hotel also loses the amount charged, the original sale. Losses are compounded if the chargeback contained tips (see Chapter 11, including Exhibit 11–1).

Folio charges made by guests for purchases in lobby shops raise similar issues. At best, the hotel pays no less than the discount fee on the value of the concessionaire's charge. If there's a chargeback, the concession purchase hits the hotel again—this time for the full value of the charge. Credit-card fees and dishonored charges must always be part of a concessionaire's lease.

Interest on unpaid balances, late charges, and annual fees are card users' major costs. New, insulting fees are on the horizon. Several issuers charge for inactive accounts or for accounts that fail to make minium monthly purchases. There's an additional fee if the account is closed. Such unconscionable charges are reminiscent of the lodging industry's failed efforts at collecting for early check-outs or for reservation cancellations less than 72 hours (3 days!) in advance. Neither industry is apt to make friends.

Other Cards

Despite their placement in a chapter titled "Credit and the City Ledger," neither debit cards nor smart cards are categories of the city ledger. But they are issued by the same credit-card companies, and they do impact both hotels and guests.

▶*Debit Cards.*   Debit cards transfer funds electronically (EFT, electronic funds transfer). Money is instantaneously switched from the cardholder's bank account to the merchant/hotel's bank account. Settlement is immediate. With debit cards, there is no debt and hence no accounts receivable. Debit cards are cash settlements, as explained in Chapter 11, but cash settlements without risk from dishonest employees, from overages and shortages (no one makes change), or from bounced checks.

Debit cards are to merchants what automatic teller machines (ATMs) are to cardholders. With an ATM, the user gets the cash in hand. With online debit cards, the merchant or hotel gets cash into its account as quickly as the swiped card passes through the reader. There is no time lag, no question about the user's ability to repay, and no float. No float is a negative for the consumer, but a positive for the hotel, which doesn't wait for its money.

Use of debit cards climbed—quadrupled between 1995 and 2004—as credit-card debt burgeoned. Fear of overextending their credit encouraged consumers to pay immediately (debit card) rather than delay (credit card), even though float was lost. Credit-card companies unintentionally encouraged the change by reducing grace periods (float time dropped from 29 to 21 days), increasing late fees, and awarding loyalty points for debit-card purchases. Debit-cards mean fewer written checks, which are costly for banks to process. Theft is the major negative for debit cards. An imposter can clear out the user's entire bank account. Debit-card issuers now cover such losses as they do with credit-cards.[4]

As customers shifted toward debit cards, banks began charging them fees. Merchants were already paying fees. Merchant fees are higher if customers sign for the debit charge (about $0.60 per transaction); lower if they punch in pin numbers (about $0.15). Retailers have sued over the difference (see below, "Credit Card Wars").

Debit cards are the first step in the march toward the cashless society that futurists predict. Electronic funds transfer means savings in processing expenses, in time and paper handling, and in accounting costs for merchants, banks, and consumers. Smart cards are the next step.

▶*Smart Cards.*   Smart cards were introduced in France during the 1950s, and Europe has maintained its lead since then. Card companies in the United States are working, even cooperating, on smart-card development. Progress is slow because a universal system is essential. A hybrid card containing both a magnetic strip and a computer chip may appear during the transition.

Smart-card development began with *stored-value cards*. These *electronic purses* are a cross between cash and debit cards. Users buy the card with up-front cash. Telephone cards are the best known. The loaded card is swiped through the computerized terminals until the prepaid amount is used up. Stored value cards are popular in campus food services and are being tested by some fast-food chains. The card is either discarded or reloaded through ATMs or telephone lines.

---

[4]Fifty dollars is the maximum credit-card loss under the federal Fair Credit Billing Act. Losses from debit-card transactions are not protected by the Electronic Fund Transfer Act, which regulates debit cards.

Smart cards, the next level of sophistication, are miniature computers scarcely different in size and appearance from a standard credit card. They have an electronic chip instead of the magnetic stripe of present-day cards. That's why they're also called *digital cash* or *chip cards*. Unlike credit cards, smart cards carry a sizable quantity of storage in their microchip databases. The typical card has 8K of memory, roughly 15 pages of typed data. The memory can be accessed by card-reader devices that quickly scan and use information from the card. Smart cards are seen to be the future because they are everything in one. They are credit cards, stored-value cards, identification cards, debit cards, door keys, medical and insurance records, ATM cards, and more, all rolled into one. Smart-card use will gain momentum as Internet commerce rises and better methods are needed for paying across the Web. Smart-card use will require additional investments in equipment at the merchant/hotel level.

Retailers are already using low-level smart cards to track customer demographics and loyalties. These cards provide marketers with customer names and addresses, with purchasing patterns, income levels, and hobbies. Understanding customer habits and lifestyles enables retailers to better market products and services. Customers receive discount coupons, special advertisements, and bonus points as their payoffs.

The hotel industry has had the very same information for years. The customer's identity, company, room preference, and frequency and length of stay are available to any hotel with a property management system. Making use of the information is another issue; few hotels do, but many say they are starting. How pleased a guest would be with a birthday card from a favorite hotel, with a thank-you note for staying five times in the past three months, or with a favorite bottle of wine waiting at check in. Intense competition demands a level of service beyond the industry's norm. Smart cards and credit management will help bring that to reality.

The Card Wars

Competition has kept credit-card companies fighting to gain and hold market share. Friendly rivalry has gradually grown more intense. Small, sporadic skirmishes broke out and eventually turned into out-and-out war.

Initially, T&E cards and bank cards were very different in their cost, appeal, and services. Some were no-fee cards and some were no-limit cards (not really), but each was pitched to a different audience. Gradually they grew more alike, offering the same kinds of coverage. At one time, travel life insurance, collision insurance on rental cars, emergency cash, and waiver of the $50 base liability were the hottest new products. Soon, every card offered the same.

New card types were the first signs of friendly contention as each issuer tried to one-up the competition. Now the three big issuers each have a dozen or more consumer cards. They have developed special cards for business as well. Corporate meeting cards are among the newest. Limited-use cards, which protect a company by restricting the card's use, are already an old standby. Employee travel is the best example. Neither ATM withdrawals nor consumer purchases are allowed with limited-use cards. The cards help employees as well. Using personal cards for business travel creates excessive charges that may signal credit problems where none exist.

►*Skirmishes.*   Most battles have been between the bank cards and the T&Es, particularly AmEx. Visa and its much smaller rival, MasterCard, have also butted heads. Market share has been the battlefield, and Visa the continuing victor. It won the business of one of the world's largest banks, Citigroup, by cutting a better deal about identity: "Not just Visa; Citibank Visa." More often, however, the two have joined forces against American Express—none more egregious than their union to maintain a monopoly on debit cards, see "The Big Battles."

The Bunker Hill of the credit-card wars took place in 1988. MasterCard won a lawsuit allowing it and Visa to call their premium cards "gold cards." AmEx had claimed and marketed that term for 20 years. This early clash brought the animosity into the open. The gloves were off.

Other minor attacks were made by the bank cards against American Express. Small business were encouraged to avoid AmEx's T&E card. The bank cards supported them with an ad campaign based on "AmEx is not taken there." Some merchants accept T&Es but discourage customers from using them. AmEx fights this battle because it has a contract provision that forbids merchants from doing just that. There is no law requiring merchants to sign on, but the contract is clear: Sign on and you may not discourage the user. Most merchants protest quietly by posting T&E logos at the bottom of their credit-card displays. Grumbles aside, the number of T&E outlets grows, part of the general increase in credit-card use.

Three years after their "gold-card" victory, the bank cards won again. The restaurant industry of Boston was the battlefield for what became known as the "Boston Fee Party." A group of restauranteurs refused to accept AmEx cards. The discount rate was too high at 3.5% of sales. Bank fees were 1 to 3%. A 2% difference for an upscale restaurant doing $2.5 million per year is $50,000 out of the owner's pocket. The battle grew more tumultuous when Visa started paying legal fees for the restaurant owners. American Express capitulated, reduced fees, and increased advertising expenditures. Probably as a result, AmEx fees have generally fallen everywhere from 3 to 5% of sales (3.25% average) to 2.7 to 4% of sales (2.75% average). Helping with advertising for the Boston restaurant scene wasn't really special because American Express already promoted specific restaurants and restaurant cities.

Swirling around the main issues are many subissues. Among them is the consolidation and competition of the credit-card issuers, the big banks. This plays the big banks against the small ones as well as against each other. Two-thirds of all cards are issued by just five banks, including MBNA and Bank One (First USA).

Airlines, which pay large sums to the card companies, have reacted with two decisions. They are aggressively marketing their own card, Universal Air Travel Plan (UATP), and simultaneously laying credit-card fees onto travel agencies. Volume allows the airlines to get credit-card fees as low as 1.5%, whereas small travel agents pay 4% or more. All airlines may soon refuse to act as the merchant for tickets sold by travel agencies.

▶*The Big Battles.*   Several issues have now entered the courts. AmEx has refused to allow British Air to hand off merchant status for travel agencies and has taken the matter to law.[5] The new "hidden" fee of 3% that the bank cards have levied on overseas use has triggered its own court case.

Even as these legal struggles take shape, two far bigger battles have moved through the system. Behind them lies the animosity of the bank cards to the T&Es. The first big battle was settled when the Justice Department successfully sued the bank cards over antitrust. "Duality" was one keyword. Banks that issued one card, say, Visa, sat on the board of the other network, MasterCard, and vice versa. This stifles

---

[5]*Travel Weekly* reports that Delta Airlines "subsidized" travel agents to the tune of $190 million in 2001 by acting as their credit-card merchant. July 8, 2002, p. 1. (See footnote 3)

competition, says the government, as does the "exclusivity rule," the refusal of both networks to allow its member banks to process T&E cards. After several years, a split ruling came down. Although duality remains, U.S. banks may now issue T&E cards if they wish to do so. Foreign banks have done that for some time.

A private class-action lawsuit, not a governmental probe, has also been settled. Large retailers, including Wal-Mart Stores and Sears Roebuck & Co., sued the card networks, Visa USA and MasterCard International. Fees are the issue, and the rapid adoption of debit-cards the cause. Interestingly, Sears itself is the third largest Master-Card issuer!

The suit alleged that the credit-card companies have promoted less efficient (off-line) and hence more costly debit-card processing. Debit-card verification can be done with either PIN numbers (electronically) or signatures (manually). The suit claimed that Visa and MasterCard pressured merchants to use signatures to verify the sale, not PINs. Merchants who did not comply lost the regional credit-card connections that are essential to credit-card transactions. Merchants who do comply are stuck with higher fees. Behind it all, claimed the suit, lies MasterCard's and Visa's concern that regional debit-card processors may grow into national organizations to compete with the card companies' systems. The essential allegation claimed that using credit-card leverage has enabled the bank cards to control debit-card processing.

Visa and MasterCard have an "honor all cards" requirement. Merchants who accept the bank credit cards must accept the bank debit cards or lose credit-card rights. This promotes competition by allowing customers to choose the preferred card. Otherwise, claims Visa and MasterCard, merchants would insist on competitors' cards only. The court ruled in favor of the plaintiffs.

➤ OTHER CITY-LEDGER CATEGORIES

Credit cards are found in every city ledger because credit cards are one of the three methods of settling accounts (see Chapter 10). Depending on its market, hotels may or may not have other city-ledger accounts. Charges arise from parties (weddings, for example) or other ballroom rentals (charity dances, for example) that never register even one person. Most city-ledger postings come from registered guests who transfer their accounts from front-office folios to back-office city ledgers. For individuals, that means city-ledger credit cards. For groups and associations, that means individual city-ledger accounts, one of which is master accounts.

Master Accounts

Master accounts accumulate charges for groups. As Chapter 10 explained, master accounts are front-office folios. However, the guest is a group or association, not an individual person. Room charges, entertainment, banquets, and meeting room space are just some of the charges that master accounts accumulate. Outside vendors (florists, bands, and audio-visual rentals) are sometimes paid by the hotel and charged to the master account. Chapters 10 and 11 explain how these charges are posted to the front-office folios. Total charges are transferred to the city ledger when the event ends. Billing and collection follow.

Functions that involve hundreds of persons represent large sums of money. The hotel wants prompt payment. To ensure this, the master account folio is carefully reviewed by the client (the meeting planner, the association executive) and by the hotel (the sales manager and the accountant). Errors in master account folios may be substantial, but even meeting managers concede that they are not always in the hotel's favor. Even so, there are four common errors that irritate meeting planners. Attending to these beforehand expedites the billing, the settlement, and the eventual payment. Preventing the complaint is what good service is all about.

Error 1 is split billing. Meeting planners complain that charges are incorrectly split between master accounts and individual, personal accounts. Charges for group events should appear on the master folio and not on the personal folio of the executive who signs the tab. Front-office employees grow careless despite specific, written instructions from the client.

Error 2 is unauthorized signatures. Meeting and convention groups have many bosses. In addition to the elected board of directors, the officers, and the paid professional staff, there are informal leaders and past officers. Not all these persons are authorized to sign for charges. Meeting planners complain that unauthorized charges with unauthorized signatures appear on master accounts despite an advanced list of authorized signatures having been provided.

Error 3 is the sequence of posting. The breakfast charge of day 2 of the meeting should not appear on the folio before the dinner of day 1. Picky clients require the entire bill to be reposted to show each event in sequence. Comparisons to the original contract and to the function sheets are facilitated thereby. That pleases the meeting planner, but the hotel could have done it beforehand.

Error 4 is comp rooms. Complimentary rooms are given to the group according to a widely used formula: 1 free room-night per 50 paid room-nights. Meeting planners complain that hotels deduct the lowest room rates against the free markers instead of the highest room rates. Comp rooms go either to VIPs or to staff members working the convention. Therefore, when making the adjustment, the best rates should be comped, says the client. Specifically, if the group has a secretary in one room and a keynote speaker in another, the hotel should match the one comp room allowed against the speaker's higher room rate, not the staffer's lower room rate.

Although it is best to resolve billing differences while they are still fresh, it may not be possible to do so before the group departs. Agreed-upon items should be resolved and billed promptly without waiting to reach accord on the few differences. Otherwise, a small sum keeps thousands of master-account dollars unpaid.

Groups and Packages

Master accounts are used whenever one account receivable is responsible for the charges of an entire group. Such is the case with single entities such as traveling athletic teams and prepaid tour packages. Names and rooms numbers of group members are available at the desk. Further identification of the membership is shown on the room rack: with color on older manual racks; with code on newer computer racks.

The hotel may be told to post every member's charge to the master account. That's rare. Split folios are the more likely design. Major items such as VIP rooms and group meals are posted to the A folio, the master account, for which the entity pays. Personal incidentals are charged to B folios and paid as the individual guests checkout. They may be reminded of that arrangement when they arrive. Sometimes the alert comes while they're on the bus, sometimes by computer-generated notices included with the room keys (see Exhibit 12–5).

Who pays for what is more clearly understood with tour packages. The package has been marketed and sold with certain services included or not. Services that are not

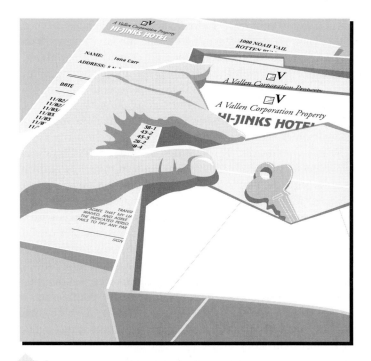

Exhibit 12–5   Room key envelopes are readied for distribution to an arriving group. Discount or tour group coupons, convention information, and instructions about settling personal expenses (B folio charges) may also be included.

included are posted to the guest's individual folio. Coupons are issued to the guests for those services included in the package. The coupons are color-coded and dated to limit their use to the particular package. Guests pay for breakfast, drinks, tennis—whatever is part of the prepaid package—with the appropriate coupon. Cashiers in the various hotel departments treat the coupons as part of their turn-in (see Chapter 11).

Coupons are charged to the tour operator's master account, so breakage accrues to the tour operator. That is, the tour operator collects from the guest for the entire tour but pays the hotel only for actual tickets returned to the master account. By not using the services they have purchased, guests create additional profit for the promoter. The hotel also creates additional profits for the promoter if it handles the vouchers carelessly. Vouchers are not just colored slips of paper that can be lost or thrown away; they are debts that the promoter must pay if the hotel can account for them.

In the hotel's own inclusive tour (IT) package, breakages accrues to the hotel. The package is sold to the guest and the money is collected in advance (minus commissions if it goes through a travel agency). If the guest fails to use the coupon, the hotel has gained. Accountingwise, the hotel distributes the single payment received from the guest among the departments, allocating a portion to room sales, food sales, bar sales, and so on.

Individual City-Ledger Receivables

Hotels have accounts receivable that originate with individuals as well as with groups. The former are not as large in dollar volume as the latter, but in some ways they are more difficult to manage.

►*Travel Agencies.*   Hotels and travel agencies have a strong love–hate relationship. That antipathy springs from the industry's view that travel agents (T/As), as third parties in the reservation process, get paid for supplying hotels with the hotels' own customers. Travel agents complain about not getting paid, which lodging's spokespersons deny vehemently. If hotel payments are sporadic, at least they're there. Airlines have stopped paying commissions altogether. In contrast, hotel chains have consolidated payments to assure that individual properties honor the commission structure. Some chains have outsourced commissions to payment-processing companies. Pegasus Solutions, Perot Systems, and Utell's Pay-Com are representative of these. Processors consolidate commissions from hotels and other commission-paying industries. For that, they take fees out of the travel agencies' fees.

Not all travel agents are small, corner proprietorships. American Express's travel agency volume is probably larger than that of the hotels with which it deals. But even the big guys are fighting the likes of online bookings and rate-cutting competitors. Size aside, travel agents complain that they are heavily solicited when the lodging business is slow, but neglected when occupancy improves. Front-office managers do turn away commissionable business during peak occupancies, just as they increase room rates at that time. Notwithstanding industry-to-industry complaints, individual agencies and individual hotels, particularly Hawaiian hotels, develop strong profitable relationships. For the most part, hotels are pleased to take travel agency business and pay the 10 to 15% commission.

A travel agency can become an account receivable in the city ledger. The process starts if the agency collects for the room in advance of the guest's arrival. Later, the guest arrives. When checking out, the guest pays the first night's room charge with the agency's coupon. That coupon appears on the folio as a transfer and becomes a city-ledger account receivable.

Increases in assets, including *accounts receivable* and cash, are made with debits. Decreases in assets, including *accounts receivable* and cash, are made with credits.

Debit: Accounts Receivable/City Ledger, Travel Agency Account   100.00
Credit: Accounts Receivable/Guest ledger, Front-office Folio   100.00
Explanation: Guest checks out and settles room charge with travel agency's voucher.

Eventually, the agency pays the hotel, less commission.

Increases in assets, including accounts receivable and *cash,* are made with debits. Increases in expenses, including salaries, *commissions,* and utilities, are made with debits.
Decreases in assets, including *accounts receivable* and cash, are made with credits.

Debit: Cash   85.00
Debit: Rooms Commissions   15.00
   Credit: Accounts Receivable/City Ledger, Travel Agency Account 100.00
Explanation: Travel agency settles prepaid guest's room charge, less commission.

Travel agents are entitled to commission even if they don't collect in advance. Then, the agency waits for the hotel to compute the amount and forward the check. There may be delay while the hotel waits for the credit card to clear.

Increases in expenses, including salaries, *commissions* and utilities, are made with debits.

Decreases in assets, including accounts receivable and *cash*, are made with credits.

Debit: Rooms Commissions   15.00
  Credit: Cash   15.00
Explanation: Hotel pays travel agency's commission for room charge settled by the guest.

The status of the nation's travel agencies is unclear. They are threatened by Web shopping, satellite ticket purchases (convenience stores in Japan sell domestic airline tickets), and ticketless travel. Agencies must find new revenue sources or face extinction. Commissions alone no longer sustain them. Agencies are consolidating, diversifying, charging new fees to customers, servicing commercial accounts, or disappearing from the hotel's city ledger.

▶*The Original City-Ledger Accounts.*   Local individuals and companies were the original nonregistered accounts receivable. Hence came the term *city* ledger. Individual accounts still exist, but they have been replaced in the main by the widespread use of credit cards. Hotels hunger for individual city accounts with good credit—payment is made in full without credit-card fees.

What accounts there are may not be local and may not originate at the front desk. Standard city accounts include individuals and companies that preestablish credit in order to use the hotel's facilities. A distant company may send employees to the hotel on a regular basis. A local business might use guest rooms for visitors and public rooms for business meetings and social affairs. Once credit has been established, the authorized user merely signs for the charges. Bills go out monthly, sometimes more frequently.

Airline crews are a good example of the standard city-ledger account. They are much sought after by hotels as basic occupancy even though the average daily rate is very low. Layover crews charge rooms to the airline's city account, and once a month the hotel bills. Airline contracts sometimes require the hotel to accommodate stranded travelers as well as crews. Typically, the airline pays for the facilities by giving the passenger a miscellaneous charge order (MCO). The stranded passenger pays with the MCO, which the hotel uses to balance the front-office folio. The account receivable is transferred to the city ledger and the airline is billed. MCOs are also used when the airline acts as a travel agency and books the guest into a prepaid room. The MCO becomes a travel agency voucher, as previously explained.

▶*Banquet Charges.*   Credit cards have also replaced open-book credit (based solely on a signature) that was once the norm for banquet charges. Party givers and banquet chairpersons once expected to sign for the party leaving the hotel waiting for collection. Catering managers still give open-book credit in limited cases. When open credit has not been cleared beforehand, collection is arranged in advance with a credit card or check. When open credit has been cleared beforehand, a bill is presented and signed at the close of the event. The value of the function is charged to a one-use, city-ledger account and billed within three days. Three days is also the billing pattern from the city ledger for speedy check-outs and master accounts.

Pay-as-you-go functions are much riskier affairs. The group may be known, but there is no financial security behind it. Included in this category are school proms, political dinners, charitable fundraisers, and other speculative functions that base payment on ticket sales. A portion of the estimated bill should be collected in advance, and a ticket accounting system should be part of the up-front agreement. The credit department should review the contract and establish the identity and creditworthiness of the responsible individual.

▶*Late Charges.*   Late charges are departmental charges (food, beverage, spa) that appear on the folio after the guest has checked out. These postings were late getting into the system either from the point-of-sale terminal or from the front-desk terminal.

Late charges are irritants to both the guest and the hotel. Guests may need to modify expense accounts after the late charge arrives in the mail. Hotels may need to absorb the costs because guests often refuse to pay after the fact. If the charge is small, the hotel might not even bill. The cost of processing and the loss of guest goodwill might cost more than the amount sought.

Collections are easier when the folio of the departed guest has been transferred to the city ledger with a credit card. Then the front-office folio is retrieved, updated with the late charge, and transferred to the city ledger along with the earlier folio charges. The process is not even noticeable with express check outs. Accurate folios arrive when the guest is copied by mail some three days later and the total shown agrees with the amount submitted to the credit-card company.

The discrepancy is sharper if the guest settled at the cashier's window with a signed credit-card voucher. Then the copy that the guest carries away will be smaller than the amount that the credit-card company bills. If the card company does not permit after-the-fact additions to a signed charge slip, the hotel bills the guest directly using the reg card's address. The hotel has a second chance at collection, but that doesn't minimize the guest's anger. Direct billing of late charges is the only option for guests who settle with cash, checks, or traveler's checks. There is no option at all if there is a corrected or dishonored charge from a nonregistered guest who used the bar or dining room. Not registered means the guest's address is not known to the hotel. Credit-card companies will not release the cardholder's address nor allow altered charge slips.

Late Charge Procedures.   Late charges are abbreviated by LC or AD (after departure). Small late charges, say, $15 and under, are wiped off with an allowance. First, the departed guest's folio is reopened and the charge—now, a late charge—is posted in the regular manner. Immediately, the new balance is zeroed out by means of an allowance (see Chapter 10). This procedures creates a permanent record of the charge.

A separate late-charge folio is an alternative approach. All small late charges are posted there rather than individually to each folio. Daily, the day's total late charges are cleared with one allowance, which is obviously less burdensome for the desk. Either way, management should get a daily allowance report, which is one of the exception reports prepared during the night audit (see Chapter 13).

Notwithstanding these provisions for allowancing late charges, efforts to collect them should be conscientiously pursued. In that case, the late charge could be posted to the guest's closed folio and immediately transferred to the city ledger for billing.

Increases in assets, including *accounts receivable* and cash, are made with debits. Increases in incomes (food, beverage, spa, etc.) are made with credits.

> Debit: Accounts Receivable/Guest's Folio
> Credit: Proper Departmental (food, beverage, spa, etc.) Sale
> *Explanation:* Late-charge income posted to reopened folio.

Decreases in incomes (food, beverage, spa, etc.) are made with debits. Decreases in assets, including *accounts receivable* and cash, are made with credits.

> Debit: Proper Departmental (food, beverage, spa, etc.) Allowance
> Credit: Accounts Receivable/Guest's Folio
> *Explanation:* Allowance issued for late charge to zero out the folio balance.

▶*Delinquent Accounts.* Into the delinquent (or bad debt) division of the city ledger go all receivables that are awaiting final disposition. Such is the case with large, uncollectible late charges, which were not treated as allowances. They, and other unrecoverable debts, are eventually written off the books as bad.

Returned checks (bounced checks) also account for a portion of delinquent receivables. Rather than reestablishing the customer's old records, returned checks are viewed as new debt and tracked separately. Checks come back for many reasons. Chief among them are insufficient funds, no such account, account closed, illegible signature, and incorrect date. Since passing bad checks is a criminal offense, hotels should support the police in prosecuting offenders even when restitution is made.

Credit-card chargebacks, guests who skip (intentionally leave without paying), and judgmental mistakes in extending open credit comprise the remainder of the delinquent division. For most hotels, credit-card chargebacks, skips, bad checks, and open credit errors represent a negligible operating cost. Hotels that show significant costs in these areas should reevaluate their credit policies.

▶*Executive Accounts.* Hotel executives can be city ledger receivables in their own hotel. Management people use the hotel for personal pleasure as well as for house business. Company policy dictates how charges are to be made. House entertainment might be distinguished from personal charges on the guest check by an "H" (house business) or an "E" (entertainment) added under the signature. Without the symbol, the accounting department bills the person as a regular city account. Many times, though, the billing is only a percentage of the actual menu price, depending on the employment agreement.

▶*Due Bills.* Hotels have traded room-nights for products since the great depression of the 1930s. Swaps with radio and television stations, billboards, newspapers, and magazines involve free rooms for free advertising. Trades with manufacturers for capital goods such as beds, carpets, and televisions are a later development. Evidence of the hotel's obligation to meets its half of the bargain is a contract called a *due bill. Trade advertising contacts, trade-outs,* and *reciprocal trade agreements* are other names for due bills. Temporary accounts receivable in the city ledger are needed when the other party to the agreement checks in to take advantage of the "free" facilities.

Rationale for Due Bills. Airlines, theaters, arenas, and the media deal in highly perishable products. There is no means of recapturing an unsold airline seat or an unused television spot for resale another day. The same is true with the lodging industry.

All of these businesses have the same problem: no means of inventorying the product for resale at a later time. Once the newspaper is printed, that day's advertising space is lost. Once the night has passed, that empty hotel room cannot be sold again. Trading the lost inventory for something useful is mutually beneficial when both parties have unsold, perishable products.

The hotel would like to restrict the products it trades to its most profitable item, rooms, and have the occupant pay in cash for the less profitable items, food and beverage. This is understandable from the hotel's point of view. The cost of providing an otherwise empty room is minimal; the cost of food and beverage is high. Moreover, unused food and beverage, unlike unused rooms, can be sold the following day. The advertising media set restrictions too, making no promise as to where the hotel's ad will appear in print or at what time it will be heard on the airwaves.

Whereas the hotel would like to limit the due bill to rooms, to use by certain individuals, and to given days of the week with advance reservations required, the facts of life may be otherwise. It is a matter of negotiation.

Some due bills are so negotiable that they are traded on an open market. Discount brokers buy the bills from the original receiver, or negotiate directly with the hotel, at reduced prices. The due bills are resold to a third, or even a fourth party, each time with an additional markup. In due course, they are used at the hotel by the final buyer in lieu of cash. The hotel accepts the bills at face value, which is still greater than the price paid by the user.

The concept works, and so does the series of marked-up resales, because two prices are involved. Both the hotel and the media (or other swapping party) deliver the due bill at retail prices but deliver the goods or services at cost. If the media accepts a $100 room for a $100 TV spot that costs $40, the TV station can resell the room at $60 and still make $20. There is even greater impetus when we remember that the room and the air time would have gone unused anyway.

Due bills are favored during periods of low or moderate occupancy and are less popular during busy periods. The oil embargo of the 1970s and the poor economy of the early 1980s and early 2000s brought a rebirth of due bill usage.

Processing the Due Bill.   Due bill users must present the actual due bill agreement at the time of registration. This permits the guest–service agent to assign the most expensive accommodations. (The hotel's cost of delivering an expensive room is almost the same as delivering an inexpensive one.) The clerk also verifies the expiration date of the agreement. Amounts unused after that date are lost to the due bill holder. When that happens—and it does frequently—the hotel gets the advertising (or product), but the media company never gets to use all of its due bill.

The due bill is attached to the registration card and the rate is marked "Due Bill" along with the dollar room charge. A standard guest folio, or sometimes one specially colored or coded, is used. The actual due bill is filed at the front desk during the guest's stay. After the value of the accommodations used has been recorded on the due bill, it is returned to the holder at check out.

The transient folio, which was used to accumulate charges during the due bill user's stay, is transferred to the city ledger in the usual manner. However, the city ledger account is treated differently. There is no billing. Instead, the account is charged off against the liability incurred by the contract. At the time of the agreement, a liability was created by the hotel's promise to furnish accommodations to the media or other trader. As hotel accommodations are furnished, that liability is decreased. It is balanced off against the city ledger account that was created from the transfer of the guest folio at the time of check out.

Increases in assets, including *prepaid advertising* and cash, are made with debits. Increases in liabilities, including *due bills* and taxes *payable,* are made with credits.

> Debit: Prepaid Advertising
>   Credit: Due Bills Payable
> *Explanation:* Negotiated a swap of rooms for advertising.

Increases in assets, including accounts receivable and cash, are made with debits. Increases in incomes (*rooms,* food, beverage, spa) are made with credits.

> Debit: Accounts Receivable/Guest's Folio
>   Credit: Room Sales
> *Explanation:* Due-bill guest occupies accommodations.

Decreases in liabilities, including *due bills payable,* are made with debits. Decreases in assets including *accounts receivable* and cash are made with credits.

> Debit: Due Bills Payable
>   Credit: Accounts Receivable/Guest's Folio
> *Explanation:* Due-bill guest pays transient folio with a trade-out via the City Ledger.

➤ MANAGING CREDIT

Organizing and processing credit charges through the city ledger, the first segment of this chapter, is but one component of credit. Management must attend to a long list of other functions, including bad-debt management, check processing, internal procedures, and collections. But first of all, management must decide what are its credit policies.

Cost-Benefit Decision.   There is no perfect credit policy. Any business that extends credit is vulnerable to loss. Each credit decision weighs immediate, determinable benefits against possible, uncertain costs. Recognizing that, the hotel industry has reduced its level of open credit. More reliance is now placed on credit cards and credit investigations. Open credit still has traditional uses—for advances to concessionaires, outlays for tips, payments for C.O.D. packages, and even some convention/banquet sales.

Successful credit policy cannot be measured by accounting figures alone. Hotels with small amounts of bad debts (or small ratios of bad debts to accounts receivable) are not necessarily the best managed ones. A conservative credit policy will mean few credit losses, but it may also cause substantial losses from business that was turned away. Low credit losses are easily measured on the books; lost business has no entry. Profits might have been improved by taking the business that an ultraconservative credit policy denied. The conundrum is that the increase might not have been achieved; there's no way to know.

The issue is not black and white—always credit/never credit. Every full-service hotel offers some amount of credit. The question focuses on how much, when, and under what circumstances credit is offered. The answer is not always the same, even for the same credit manager in the same hotel. With different conditions, credit could be severely curtailed, moderately administered, or liberally issued, even to the same customer with the same credit standing (see Exhibit 12–6).

Severely Curtailed	Moderately Administered	Liberally Issued
High occupancy	. . .	Low occupancy
In-season	. . .	Off-season
No competition	. . .	Price cutting
Established property	. . .	New hotel
Interest rates are high	. . .	Interest rates are low
Reputable hotel	. . .	Disreputable hotel
Item of high variable cost	. . .	Item of low variable cost
Inexperienced lender	. . .	Low losses from debt-recovery
Hotel's credit overextended	. . .	Hotel has good credit rating

Exhibit 12–6   Factors other than the creditworthiness of the guest explain why credit is tightened and and eased over time even for the same guest at the same hotel. Likewise, credit may be denied by one hotel and granted by another a short distance away.

Good occupancy, the first item of Exhibit 12–6, permits the hotel to adopt a conservative credit policy. There is no reason to replace low-risk guests with those of uncertain credit standing. When occupancy is high, a bad debt loss is the sum of full rack rate plus administrative costs, not just the marginal cost of providing a room during low occupancy.

Food and beverage sales, which have a high variable cost, are different. Far more caution is needed to justify banquet sales during a low period than room sales during a low period. A banquet bad debt may well cost the hotel two-thirds or more of the bill (food, call-in labor, flowers, special cake, favors, etc.). Room losses are substantially less, both in percentage (about 25% marginal cost) and in absolute dollars.

Hotels reduce rates when occupancies are low. These would also be the times for a more liberal credit policy. In fact, the more liberal credit policy might be traded for the lower room rates. Too dismal a circumstance, and the hotel will need to give both to get the business. Fighting for market share or competing with better appointed properties are additional reasons for liberalizing credit (see Exhibit 12–6).

The most obvious cost of poor credit is the out-and-out loss from nonpayment. Bank charges, attorney fees, and collection expenses are heavy additional costs. So too are several hidden expenses that are not usually added on. Rarely charged against the debtor are inhouse administrative costs, forms, printing, credit checks, postage and telephone, and employee time. To the whole package must be added the permanent loss of a customer.

Expanded sales volume is the offsetting benefit to credit risk. Hotels also gain from a spread in interest rates. If the hotel's credit rating is good, it borrows at low rates or self-finances. Extending credit at 18% (1.5% per month) represents a measurable benefit, provided, of course, that it eventually collects.

The Management Function

Establishing and monitoring credit is a broad-based management function coordinated by the credit manager. If there is no credit manager, the controller takes on the task. Some responsibilities are handed off to other managers, who then form a credit committee. The rooms manager assumes an active role in front-office credit, and the sales/catering executives do the same for banquets and group business.

The credit manager/controller must support a credit policy that encourages a healthy marketing approach even as it strives for prompt payment and bottom-line returns. Otherwise, the drive to collect legitimate debt will offset the principles of customer relations management (see Chapter 7).

> I've never seen an organizational chart or read a job description for accounts receivable that included guest-relations and sales components. I've never heard of a director of sales and marketing routinely being invited to participate in the training of accounts receivable personnel.[6] [Implying, of course, that they should.]

➤*Extending Credit.*   Collecting from overdue accounts begins with identifying them. This can be done at the time of registration or earlier. Very few reservations come directly to the hotel as they once did. Prescreening to verify credit is just not possible, and it's certainly not doable with walk-in guests. Thus, after-the-fact collections depend on procedures in place during registration.

Identification was more reliable when guests had reservations that involved correspondence. Then, the name and address, and perhaps even the company name, was verified by mail. This must now be done at registration with complete name, not just initials; complete address, not just post-office box, office building, or city. Scribbled, illegible signatures must be translated. Early suspicions can be confirmed quickly. ZIP code directories uncover false addresses. Some hotels have the bell staff record car license numbers on rooming slips. Telephone calls to the guest's supposed office puts many issues in perspective.

Unheard of a generation ago, guests are expected to announce their method of settlement as they register. Strange as it seems, hotels prefer credit cards with their costly merchant fees over cash or checks. This shifts some credit issues to the credit-card companies and provides the hotel with help from the fraud divisions of the credit-card companies.

Credit procedures put stress on the clerk–guest interchange. Specific information must be elicited but done under the customer relations umbrella. Tact in selecting the right words and care in applying voice intonations—often ignored in training programs—must be taught and practiced. Many factors, such as a tired guest or a misplaced reservation, exacerbate an already awkward situation. If baggage is missing or light, the clerk will need to press for more complete details. If the guest is nervous or poorly dressed, the clerk may insist on photocopying a driver's license. The line between information gathering and invasion is a thin one, as is the line between guest understanding and anger. Front-office clerks need to be masters of diplomacy.

No magic formula separates safe risks from poor ones. But collection is possible only if the hotel can identify the person and the address. Returned checks, late charges, credit-card chargebacks, and other open accounts cannot be collected, regardless of the guest's sincerity, without these essential facts. Unlike most industries, innkeeping has the opportunity to get the data. Procedures should be in place to ensure its collection.

Because walk-ins pose additional credit risks, they are flagged with special identifications. NR (no reservation), OS (off-the-street), and WI (walk-in) are common abbreviations (see Chapter 10, Exhibit 10–9). The reg cards of walk-ins are not always

---

[6]"Accounts receivable and guest relations: An imperfect mix." Anthony Marshall. *Hotel & Motel Management*, March 20, 2000, p. 16.

filed immediately. Some properties have their credit managers inspect them. Credit managers use telephone directories, credit-card companies, city directories, colleagues, and direct-dial telephone calls to verify information about questionable guests, be they walk-ins or otherwise.

Suspicious guests can be required to pay in advance—credit card or not. Paid-in-advance guests are usually denied credit throughout the house. Extreme measures like these do not build guest loyalty. Few walk-ins intend to defraud the hotel. The extra caution needed to protect against some should not disintegrate into antiservice for all.

➤*Managing the Specifics.*   Credit is an issue for every operating department, but the heaviest burden falls on the front desk. The guest and the staff stand face-to-face at the front desk, increasing the tension and hardening the positions. Credit issues must be resolved firmly and yet with courtesy even though the pressure of time often demands instantaneous decisions. Poorly conceived and poorly implemented credit policies undermine even the best guest-service programs.

Early departure fees was one horrible example that gained momentum during the heady occupancy that closed the 1990s. Guests who left earlier than their original reservation were charged an early departure fee of as much as $50. Try standing across the desk and explaining that fee to an early departure with hundreds of dollars in folio charges. As one would expect, the practice did not survive the steep downturn in occupancy that followed.

Minimizing Chargebacks.   Hotels work hard to find and to service customers. Large costs are incurred in marketing and in training employees. In light of the efforts and the costs, the hotel's failure to collect the bill—never to collect the bill—is beyond understanding. But that is what happens with an estimated 50% of all chargebacks. Chargebacks are credit-card charges disallowed by the card company because (1) the guest refuses to pay, or (2) a procedural error makes the charge unacceptable to the card company.

By federal law, credit-card companies allow hotels 30 days to respond to and submit evidence about chargebacks. Hotel credit offices simply fail to answer. Reservation no-shows are the most common chargebacks. Guests guarantee the reservation using a credit card and then refuse to pay the first night when they don't show. With the credit-card number and no record of a cancellation number, the hotel has a strong argument, especially if the card company advertises its guarantee of this type of reservation. However, there can be no collection if the credit office fails to complete the inquiry. Of course, not pushing for payment may be more about guest relations than about credit. If that's the case, early check-out fees have no footing at all.

Credit-card companies keep announcing shifts in the burden of proof, from hotels to cardholders, even as hotels keep changing their positions. Losing room revenue to unclaimed "guaranteed" reservations demands one response when occupancy is high and another when occupancy collapses. Besides, not all chargebacks come from unclaimed reservations. About 10% originate in efforts to recover room damages and property theft. Smoking in nonsmoking rooms, theft of pictures and towels, and damage during conventions and prom nights are high on the list of charges that bounce back. Guests simply protest such discretionary postings.

Mistakes in procedure account for another group of chargebacks. Procedural chargebacks originate more with departmental cashiers than with accounting offices. Training programs, often undertaken with help from card companies, concentrate on the do's and don'ts of taking and processing cards (see Exhibit 12–7).

1. Be aware that every business is assigned a floor limit, which is the maximum dollar volume allowed on a single credit card without additional authorization.

2. Insist that employees know that limit, for, once exceeded, all charges, including those below the floor, are voided.

3. Do not split charges on two or more vouchers to avoid floor limits.

4. Never give a cash refund if an unused advance deposit was made through a credit-card charge (or travel agency voucher, for that matter).

5. Bill credit-card companies promptly.

6. Refuse to post fictitious items in order to give cash against the credit card.

7. Watch for altered cards, rearranged numbers, or replaced digits that will make a hot card usable. Clues are glue on the card, blurred holograms, color variations, or misaligned numbers. Compare numbers on the back and front sides. Watch for altered signature panels, which are made tamper-evident by repetitive designs on the panels.

8. Adhere to the recommendations of the credit-card companies: Do not place telephone numbers on credit-card slips.

9. Question credit-card signatures made with a felt-tip pen that could be used to cover an original signature.

10. Compare the signature on the departmental voucher with the signature on the credit card. If uncertain still, compare with the registration card signature.

11. Make certain that manual cards imprint completely on all copies of the voucher; check the clarity of the signature.

12. Use the proper voucher form if a manual system is still in place. Each company has its own and may not accept its competitors.

13. Anticipate employee misuse—changed figures or additional charges that permit the employee to pocket some cash.

14. Answer promptly chargeback inquiries from the card companies.

15. Instruct employees not to apprehend anyone suspected of using an invalid card, nor to exercise any force in retrieving a card. Since the card remains the property of the credit-card company, cardholders agree to surrender it on request. Agents of the hotel should not destroy the card nor publicly humiliate the guests.

16. Carry insurance against false arrest based on incorrect information furnished by the credit-card company.

17. Refuse credit cards whose expiration date has passed the last day of the month specified. Watch on some cards for "from" dates; charges before that time will be rejected.

18. Compare the credit card and driver's license signatures when suspicious of the individual or the card. (Many states are treating their driver's licenses with a chemical process that disintegrates, changing the graphics if the data on the card have been tampered with.)

19. Teach cashiers that MasterCard uses numbers that begin with 5; Visa numbers begin with 4; American Express numbers begin with 3; and Discover numbers begin with 6.

20. Maximize recovery by retaining original documents such as signed outlet or room service vouchers.

Exhibit 12–7   Reducing losses from credit-card transactions begins with the staff's knowledge of the law and the procedures established by the credit-card companies.

➤*Monitoring Credit.*   Credit is only checked twice for most guests. It happens once on arrival and again at departure. A small number of guests is tracked more closely if early signs suggest possible problems. Two restrictions need watching. Every hotel has a credit limit or floor limit for the premises. The floor limit is the maximum credit that the hotel can extend to any one guest without getting prior approval from the credit-card company. Obviously, the initial floor limit should be as high as the hotel can negotiate. Just as obvious, that limit is a function of the hotel's average daily rate. If the card is approved at registration, the credit-card company guarantees payment up to that floor—actually, a ceiling. In case of default, credit-card charges above that ceiling void the entire guarantee even the amount below the ceiling if prior approval wasn't obtained.

Hotels also need to monitor the ceiling of the guest's own credit line. Each credit-card holder has a personal maximum. Therefore, a freeze is put on the guest's card for the amount that he or she is apt to spend. If less is spent, and usually it is, the hotel is supposed to release the difference at check out. This allows the guest to make other purchases elsewhere. Few hotels bother, which restricts the guest because the personal ceiling is reached before the expenditure has actually been made. New York was the first state to outlaw this practice.

Losses can be substantial if floor limits are breached without prior clearance. But it is a problem with only a small number of guests, and only if those guests fail to pay. Only then does the hotel turn to the credit-card company for reimbursement. The danger is minimized if folio balances are constantly monitored. The job is usually assigned to the swing or graveyard shifts to make certain that an examination takes place at least once daily. In a manual system, the clerk flips through the bucket scrutinizing each folio by noting the daily charges and the cumulative balance of each account receivable. With a computer, an overlimit report, which is an exception report (see Chapter 13), can be screened quickly several times during the day. Whether done manually or electronically, the monitor must project the rate of spending as the folio nears the floor thresholds.

Questionable folios, and even some picked at random, are examined in detail. Is there a credit card for the room? Are the numbers legible? Is the expiration date still valid? Is the balance below the floor? Has preapproval been obtained? The total charges are examined, but especially the pattern of charges. Suspicious accounts are listed by the night clerk in a report, which the credit manager examines first thing in the morning.

Several situations mandate immediate action. The most serious is the credit-card company's refusal to increase the floor limit on a suspect folio. Paid-in-advance guests who exceed the deposit limit and guests with preapproved direct billing who exceed the agreed limit are additional examples. Actions that portend a skipper are probably the most immediate problem.

If discovered during the day, or as a result of the night clerk's report, the credit manager acts immediately to collect. If unable to collect, the credit manager may take the guest's luggage, lock the guest out of the room, or call the police in case of fraud. (State laws make skipping and bad-check passing prima facie cases of fraud.)

If the credit alert is discovered during the wee hours of the morning, common sense dictates waiting until a more reasonable hour. (Courts have ruled against hotels that lock out guests at unreasonable hours.) Wait too long, however, and the hotel might have a skip.

Credit Alerts and Skippers.   Intentional skippers can often be identified by the pattern of their actions. Indeed, the credit manager should develop a standard description much like airlines have done for the typical hijacker. The average skipper is male, 30 to 35 years old, a late walk-in with light baggage and vague identification. He is a heavy tipper and a quick new friend of the bartender. The skipper makes no telephone calls that can be used to trace him. His address is usually a well-known one in a large city, but it proves to be false. He writes his name and address poorly and offers no business identification.

Skipper alarms begin ringing when baggage is light or worthless. Guests arouse additional suspicion when they charge their folios with small items (candy bar, tube of toothpaste) that are normally paid for in cash. Skippers compound the hotel's costs by passing bad checks or using stolen credit cards. Bad-check passers concentrate on weekends or holidays when commercial hotels are understaffed and banks are closed. With ATM machines readily available, fewer and fewer hotels are cashing checks. Those that do should maintain a check-cashing record to alert other shifts of ongoing activities. Then a check-cashing report becomes part of the night–audit activities.

Skippers and bad-check passers frequently work one area before moving on. A telephone or fax network among local hotels does much to identify the culprit even before his or her arrival. Photographs of suspects and identifying information, perhaps from the police, will undoubtedly be displayed someday on computer terminals.

Something needs to be done because crime has moved from the street into the hotel. Frustrating the criminal takes the combined efforts of all employees. Clerks, bellpersons, house police, cashiers, housekeepers, engineers, and room service waiters, too, must watch for and report the telltale signs. Large quantities of blank checks or money orders, firearms and burglary tools, keys from other hotels, unusual amounts of cash or gems, or just heavy traffic or loitering about a room indicate serious trouble is brewing.

➤*Collecting Receivables.*   Accounts receivable are what the city ledger is all about. Some receivables enter the city ledger directly, credit-card charges in the food and beverage outlets, for example. Most receivables come to the back office from the front office as transfers from the guest ledger to the city ledger. Here is accumulated every category of debt: master accounts, travel agency coupons, wholesaler settlements, skippers, credit cards, direct billings, convention and association activities, due bills, delinquent accounts, executive accounts, and banquet charges. How these debts are collected and by whom reflects on the hotel's cash flow and its profit picture. Having gone to the trouble of marketing, servicing, and charging the account, the hotel can be no less diligent in collecting what's due.

Billing and Chasing.   Like many other retailers, hotels bill their receivables monthly. If the guest charges services early in the 30-day cycle and the hotel allows an additional 30 days before payment, 60 plus days elapse before the hotel realizes that there is a possible collection problem. Switching to a 15-day billing cycle improves collections because the longer a bill is unpaid, the less likely it is ever to be paid (see Exhibit 12–8). Similarly, convention and banquet billing must be speeded up to three to five days after the function, direct company billing and express check outs to one to three days after departure. To meet these recommendations, management needs to allocate adequate resources to the credit/accounting department.

Second notices should follow soon after the first billing, usually at the end of the month. Routine notices twice during the next 30 days and telephone calls thereafter should inquire whether the statement has come, whether it is accurate, and when payment can be expected. Each notice should point up the additional interest charges that late payments accrue.

Chasing unpaid debts should not be a random assignment. It must be in someone's job description. Otherwise, customers get the impression that the hotel has forgotten. Nor should the collector be apologetic—the late payer is the wrongdoer.

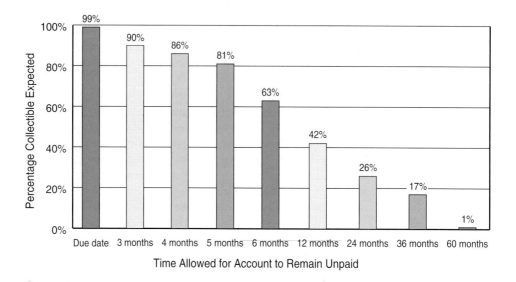

Time is the Enemy of Debt Collection

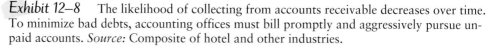

Exhibit 12–8   The likelihood of collecting from accounts receivable decreases over time. To minimize bad debts, accounting offices must bill promptly and aggressively pursue unpaid accounts. *Source:* Composite of hotel and other industries.

Payment arrangements should be specific in both amounts and dates. Partial payments may be accepted, even encouraged, provided that details (when and how much) are fixed and enforced. Small payments should be avoided since they are costly to administer and tend to be overlooked as insignificant when payments are missed.

What Next?   No matter how carefully credit requests are screened, some bad debts will materialize. Faced with a delinquent account, the manager responsible for credit has two main courses of action. Either the hotel can continue its own internal efforts at collection or it can employ a third party, an attorney or a collection agency, that specializes in bad-debt collections. Either way, there are substantial collection costs that must be reckoned with.

Hotels that choose the internal option must be prepared to invest in the process. In addition to outright fees, there are many hidden administrative costs. Credit collection is not a sometimes affair. To be effective, collection must be systematic and thorough, not a passing effort. It takes a flow of information and a stack of records, manual or computerized, to track debtors. Yet the job is one more task added to the office of controller when there is no full-time credit manager. Knowledge of federal and state legislation is another hurdle. If the in-house staff is insensitive to the rights of the debtor (and they have many legally protected rights), the process might best be left to a third party that has the legal expertise.

The worst of the bad debts ends up with collection agencies. Oddly enough, their basic technique is writing letters, much like the hotel does. More than 90% of their collections are generated by simple dunning letters. Still, collections are light, especially for small accounts, which have the lowest priority with the collection agencies.

Less than 25% of accounts turned over are collected. If no collection is made, there is no fee, but the fee takes 30 to 40% of what is collected.

What success collection agencies have is probably due to psychological effects on the debtor as much as to techniques employed by the agency. For a start, the customer realizes that the matter has grown more serious, more intense, seeing the agency as a more relentless and threatening force than the hotel. Whatever softening existed through the customer–client relationship has dissolved with the appearance of this third party. The debtor is aware that the agency knows more about his entire credit record than the hotel knew. Credit ratings may suddenly be in jeopardy. Sometimes the debtor simply tires of the battle and willingly makes arrangements. *Arrangements* is a good word for any collector to use because it says that some kind of settlement can be negotiated and worked out. That is, after all, the intent of the collection effort.

➤ MECHANICS OF THE ENTRY

Some guests, but very few, settle their front-office folios with cash. They are not accounts receivable. Some guests, a somewhat larger number, settle their food and beverage purchases with cash. Neither are they accounts receivable. With those two exceptions, all hotel customers are accounts receivable. Hotels bill and collect these receivables through the city ledger.

Two methods are used to get the information to the city ledger in the first place. Under one system, the one used for registered guests, charges are accumulated on the front-office folio and transferred to the city ledger. Chapter 10 assigned many pages to this procedure. Purchases by credit card or open credit are the second source of city-ledger transactions. The front-office folio is not involved, charges are made from the outlets directly to the city ledger. There are no ledger-to-ledger transfers with credit-card purchases. This happens when guests, registered or not, use credit cards or open credit to pay for services throughout the hotel. Obviously, registered guests can use either option when buying food and beverage services. They can charge the folio or they can use a credit card and have it charged directly. Nonregistered customers, who do not pay with cash, have charges posted to the credit card because they have no front-office folio.

Transfers from Guest Folios

Transfers *from* the guest ledger *to* the city ledger increase the city-ledger receivable and decrease the guest-ledger receivable, the folio. (See the final line of Exhibit 10–1.)

Increases in assets, including *accounts receivable* and cash, are made with debits. Decreases in assets, including *accounts receivable* and cash, are made with credits.

    Debit: Accounts Receivable, City Ledger/Credit Card Company
        Credit: Accounts Receivable, Guest Ledger (Folio)/Guest Name
    Explanation: Folio settled with a credit card.

OR

    Debit: Accounts Receivable, City Ledger/Personal or Company Account
        Credit: Accounts Receivable, Guest Ledger (Folio)/Guest Name
    Explanation: Folio to be settled by direct billing.

Total debits to the city ledger must equal total credits from the guest ledger both daily and cumulatively. Once the transfer is made, billing takes place from the city ledger. When settlement is received (from an individual, company, organization, or credit-card issuer), the debt (the city-ledger account receivable) is cleared and the check (cash) is deposited. For some receivables, such as an association's master account or a bridal shower, the one-time city-ledger account is closed. Other receivables, such as the credit-card companies, are continuing records with new charges and new payments continually flowing in and out.

Increases in assets, including accounts receivable and *cash,* are made with debits. Decreases in assets, including *accounts receivable* and cash, are made with credits.

> Debit: Cash
>   Credit: Accounts Receivable, City Ledger/Personal or Credit-Card Co.
> *Explanation:* Any city-ledger account receivable settled its account

---

The procedure just described applies to almost every city-ledger account. Travel agency records and FGPs are two exceptions. With bank cards, the merchant/hotel gets an almost instantaneous deposit in its bank account, but that deposit is reduced by the amount of the merchant fees, as it is with T&E cards. Accounting for those fees is similar to accounting for travel agency commissions.

▶ *Travel-Agency Records.*   A good share of the antipathy between hotels and travel agencies can be ascribed to poor recordkeeping on both sides. Accounting for the travel agency commission starts with the reservation. Commissionable reservations are flagged, and that identification is carried onto the registration card and the folio. Computer systems capture and track the travel agency guest more efficiently than manual systems. Whichever system is used, commissionable folios are segregated from noncommissionable folios, and immediate attention given to DNAs (did not arrive). A notice of nonarrival, frequently a postcard, is mailed to the travel agency. This forestalls a claim and the endless correspondence that follows.

How It Is Supposed to Work.   There are so many hotels and so many travel agents in the world that there is no way for each to know another. Therefore, the best working relationship is a prepaid reservation. The agency confirms its reservation with a check or company credit card for the full amount less commission. Accompanying the payment is a reservation form similar to Exhibit 12–9. By returning one copy of the form, the hotel confirms the reservation and awaits the guest. The travel agency's check, which arrives before the guest, is deposited. Now the hotel owes the travel agency pending the guest's arrival.

Increases in assets, including accounts receivable and *cash,* are made with debits. Increases in expenses, including fees and *commissions,* are made with debits. Increases in liabilities, including *accounts* and taxes *payable,* are made with credits.

> Debit: Cash   90
> Debit: Rooms Expenses/Travel Agency Commissions   10
>   Credit: Accounts Payable/City Ledger/ABC Travel Agency   100
> *Explanation:* Received advanced payment, less commission, for reservation.

Step 1. Agency types out as much of form as it can.
Step 2. Agency faxes Parts 2 and 3 to hotel or completes form by phone.
Step 3. If Step 2 was done by fax, hotel fills out balance of form on both parts and returns

Part 3 to agency. If Step 2 was completed by phone, agency throws away Part 2.
Step 4. When form has been all filled out, remittance is attached to Part 4 and mailed to hotel.

Step 5. Part 3 is filed in client's folder and Part 1 is mailed or delivered to client.
Step 6. Part 5 is filed in date tickler for commission collection and/or is thrown out when commission has been collected.

AGENCY REQUEST FOR HOTEL/MOTEL ACCOMMODATIONS

Date_____ ☐ INITIAL REQUEST ☐ CANCELLATION ☐ CHANGE

CONFIRM TO AGENCY VIA ☐ RETURN FAX ☐ E-MAIL ☐ TELE-PHONE
CATEGORY ☐ MINIMUM ☐ MODERATE ☐ DELUXE

CLIENT

AGT.
HOTEL/MOTEL

TEL. NO.
AGENCY LIABILITY SUBJECT TO CONDITIONS ON REVERSE SIDE HEREOF

CONFIRMED RESERVATIONS FOR:
_____ ROOMS _____ PERSONS _____ NIGHTS
HOUR   DAY   DATE   VIA   FROM
ARRIVE
DEPART
_____ SINGLE _____ TWIN _____ DOUBLE _____ STUDIO _____ SUITE

☐ NO MEALS(EP) ☐ CONTINENTAL BREAKFAST ☐ AMERICAN BREAKFAST
☐ DEMI PENSION (MAP) ☐ FULL PENSION(AP)

CONFIRMED FOR HOTEL BY _____ DATE _____

ROOM RATE $_____

NO. OF NIGHTS _____

WHEN VALIDATED THIS VOUCHER HAS A VALUE OF
$_____
EXCLUDING TAXES AND CHARGES FOR SERVICE AND PERSONAL INCIDENTALS

PLEASE REPLY BELOW AND RETURN GREEN COPY TO TRAVEL AGENCY
☐ Quote rates in U.S. Dollars or specify currency exchange rate_____
☐ Advise cancellation date without penalty_____
☐ State if reservations are guaranteed _____ YES _____ NO
☐ May agency deduct commission if fully prepaid _____ YES _____ NO

COMM. $_____
DEPOSIT $_____
HOTEL/MOTEL TO COLLECT FROM CLIENT $_____

Reply by Hotel/Motel:

THIS BOX FOR AGENCY USE ONLY
CK.   DATE
NO.   SENT

By_____ Date _____

Exhibit 12–9   Hotel/travel-agency relationships are smoothest when an agency's request for room reservations is accompanied by check or company credit card. The system fails— hotels require payment from the arriving guest—when unknown agencies expect the hotel to accommodate unknown guests based on paper work without payment. *Courtesy of Willow Press, Syosset, New York.*

The cash received is less than the room rate because the travel agency has kept its commission. The difference is an expense of operation like salaries, utilities, cleaning supplies, or credit-card fees.

The arriving guest presents a copy of the same reservation form (Exhibit 12–9) now called a *coupon* or *travel agency voucher.*[7] Full credit is given against this voucher, although the hotel received less cash from the travel agent. So, the room has been prepaid (often just for one night); the hotel has its money; the travel agency has its commission. Most important, the guest is welcomed and accommodated even if the agency is unknown to the hotel or is on the other side of the globe.

To check out, the coupon-carrying guests pays for incidentals as any other guest would do by using cash, allowances, or transfers (see Chapter 10). An additional commission check is mailed to the travel agency if the guest stays longer than the time covered by the original reservation. At settlement, the room portion of the folio is transferred from the guest ledger to the city ledger. Unlike other transfers, it is not billed

[7]Travel agency coupons (or vouchers) differ from marketing coupons (discount incentives) and tour group coupons (used as tickets for admissions and meals).

from the city ledger because it was prepaid by the travel agency. The prepaid amount is charged off against the liability that was created when the funds were received. Room nights in excess of the reservation are billed and collected in the normal manner.

Decreases in liabilities, including *accounts* and taxes *payable*, are made with debits. Decreases in assets, including *accounts receivable* and cash, are made with credits.

Debit: Accounts Payable/City Ledger/ABC Travel Agency   100
Credit: Accounts Receivable, Guest Ledger (Folio)/Guest Name   100
Explanation: Prepaid room rate offsets room charges of current folio.

Although it is poor management of money and records, small hotels sometimes hold the travel agency's check at the front desk rather than depositing it. That's not advisable if the sum is large or the reputation of the travel agency questionable. But clerical savings can be significant if the check is held. There is no need to maintain and post agency accounts in the back office. Cancellation of the reservation requires nothing more than returning the original check. Accounting is reduced because the paperwork and the check are processed together when the guest arrives.

Why It Doesn't Always Work.   Rarely does the agency reservation work as well in practice as it does in theory. First of all, the agency may not send the check. There may not be time if the reservation was made by telephone. Even if there were time, the agency may not have the check to send. A corporate account, for example, is customarily settled after the trip, not before. So rather than being prepaid, the guest tenders an IOU (the agency's coupon), naively expecting hotel credit for payment that has not yet been made to the agency, let alone to the hotel.

This arrangement is not to the hotel's liking. The hotel finds itself in the position of servicing the guest while attempting to collect from a third party. Quite naturally, the agency's voucher is refused unless a credit relationship exists beforehand. To accommodate the guest, the room clerk takes the guest's personal credit card, leaving the guest and the travel agency to resolve the voucher issue later.

A full house presents special problems even if the credit relationship is well established. Without a prepaid reservation, the guest finds himself without a room and without a refund. The deposit, if any, is still with the travel agency. Similarly, a guest who stays fewer days than the reservation stated gets no refund even if the room was prepaid; the excess is rebated to the agency.

Situations grow more intense when the guest is carrying a coupon from an overseas agency. International tourists present foreign vouchers that front-office staffers are often unprepared to deal with. Help is available from the International Hotel Association (IHA), which publishes the World Directory of Travel Agencies. The IHA also circulates a list of problematic and late-pay agencies. Members who rely on the IHA's material can recover some debt through the association if an agency proves unwilling to pay.

Foreign-exchange companies such as Deak-Perera have clearinghouses that facilitate international exchanges. For a fee (in addition to the foreign funds exchange fee), they will handle the conversion of foreign agency deposits into U.S. funds and commissions paid with U.S. currency into foreign funds. A few international reps (representatives) and even some airlines will also assist with foreign-currency conversions.

Helping to Make It Work.   The clash between agencies and hotels is about upfront money. If the agency prepays the reservation, the system works as designed. If the reservation is not prepaid, everything depends on whether or not the hotel accepts the agency's coupon (voucher). That involves two issues. First, does the guest-service agent recognize the voucher? They are not standardized, even within the United States. Unfamiliar forms, formats, colors, designs, and languages raise questions, which a busy desk finds easier to reject than to answer. Attempts at standardization, even by companies as big as Hilton and Holiday, have floundered on the second issue: the creditworthiness of the travel agency. Credit is simply not granted willy-nilly to unknown customers or unknown agencies.

Enter the credit-card companies. They interposed their financial credibility between hotels and travel agencies just as they did between hotels and guests. Before corporate credit cards were introduced, travel agencies would pay the credit-card company and receive a reservation voucher. Hotels accepted that voucher because it was backed by the credit-card company, not by some unknown agency thousands of miles away. The form was standardized, and payment was in local currency. Of course, fees were charged, but transferring accounts to the city ledger and cutting commission checks to travel agencies also involve costs. The process was short-lived because corporate credit cards were introduced for travel agencies, and overseas visitors grew more receptive to personal cards.

For a long time, international travelers to the United States preferred vouchers to credit cards. To accommodate that cultural difference, several chains sold their own vouchers abroad. Foreign travelers bought them in packets of, say, 25, at a substantial discount. Besides the bargain, the guest felt more secure. The chain captured the business, since the vouchers were good only at their branded properties. Moreover, the chain had interest-free loans from the prepayments and the possibility of breakage if all of the vouchers were not used.

Individual properties accepted the prepaid vouchers, transferred them to the city ledger, and billed the parent company for remittance in the same manner that frequent-guest vouchers are still processed.

▶*Frequent-Guest Programs.*   The rationale for FGPs has been discussed several times throughout the book. The mechanics of the programs are equally clear. Guests earn points toward free room nights and sometimes airline points as well. Each stay is validated electronically or, rarely now, manually. Points are earned in every type and class of hotel within the chain, but are usually cashed in at resort destinations. The resort accepts payment with a FGP coupon and looks to the parent company for reimbursement.

Split folios are used to process the award coupons that frequent guests tender. Onto the B folio are posted all the incidental charges. The guest is responsible for

---

Increases in assets, including *accounts receivable* and cash, are made with debits.
Increases in incomes (sales of *room*, food, and beverage) are made with credits.

> Debit: Accounts Receivable/Folio/Guest Account   100
> Credit: Rooms Sales   100
> *Explanation:* Guest with FGP voucher charges accommodations on the A folio.

Increases in assets, including *accounts receivable* and cash, are made with debits.
Decreases in assets, including *accounts receivable* and cash, are made with credits.

> Debit: Accounts Receivable/City Ledger/FGP Account   100
> Credit: Accounts Receivable/Folio/Guest Account   100
> *Explanation:* FGP guest checks out and room charge is transferred to city ledger.

these and pays them at check out. The A folio, which contains the room charge, is transferred at check out to the FGP account, a receivable in the city ledger.

The chain is billed either for the full rack rate or at a reduced rate agreed to in the FGP contract. Only rarely does the hotel get reimbursement at the rack rate. Rooms have a high profit margin and the parent company knows that. Besides, sales from guest purchases of food and beverage are additional incomes since they are not covered by the voucher. A rooms allowance reduces the amount between the rack rate and the rate reimbursed by the parent company. That allowance can be made when the bill is sent to the chain or when payment is received.

Increases in assets, including accounts receivable and *cash,* are made with debits.
Decreases in sales, including *allowances,* are made with debits.
Decreases in assets, including *accounts receivable* and cash, are made with credits.

Debit: Cash   40
Debit: Room Allowances/Frequent Guest Program   60
   Credit: Accounts Receivable/City Ledger/FGP Account with Chain   100
Explanation: FGP account is settled at rate agreed to in FGP contract.

FGPs are marketing programs, so every hotel of the chain contributes on a per room basis towards the costs. From the fund come payments for rooms used as well as the sales and administrative expenses. Reimbursement for bad checks is one such expense. FGPs offer check-cashing privileges. Should the check bounce, the hotel transfers the unpaid amount to the chain's city ledger account and bills along with the reimbursable room charge.

Under some FGPs, the monthly amount due the hotel from the chain is offset against the monthly amount due the chain from the hotel: FGP fees and franchise fees. Others keep the several accounts separate, collecting from the FGP on the normal 30-day cycle of city-ledger billing.

Transfers to Guest Folios

Occasionally, though not often, guests with unpaid city-ledger balances return to the hotel. The balance owed is then transferred *from* the city ledger *to* the guest ledger at the front desk. Shifting accounts in that direction is the opposite of all the other ledger-to-ledger transfers that have been discussed. When this guest checks out, the total debt (that incurred during the current stay and that transferred *to* from the previous stay) is due. Settlement may simply mean another transfer: that of the new total in the usual manner from the guest ledger back to the city ledger. The most frequent use of these *from*-city ledger *to*-guest ledger transfers are advanced deposits, which are discussed in depth at the close of Chapter 10.

City-Ledger Postings Without Transfers

Many guests, whether registered or not, use credit cards to pay for food and beverage services. These credit-card charges become part of the departmental cashiers' daily turn-in (see Chapter 11). As such, they go directly to the accounting office, bypassing the front office and bypassing the ledger-to-ledger transfers that have been discussed.

How the accounting office processes these credit-card charges depends on the type of credit-card system in place. Most hotels have replaced the manual slips with electronic capture.

➤*Manual Charge Slips.*   If the hotel still uses the manual credit-card form (see Exhibit 12–10), departmental cashiers in the food and beverage outlets process each on an imprinter; get the guest's signature, and include the signed slips as part of the turn-in. These signed slips are separated by type (MasterCard, Visa, etc.) in the accounting office. Then they are batched and bundled, usually in groups of 100 vouchers. As a total, the bundle is posted to the credit-card company's account receivable and forwarded with a transmittal form (see Exhibit 12–10). The accounting entry charges the credit-card company and records the income from the departmental outlet:

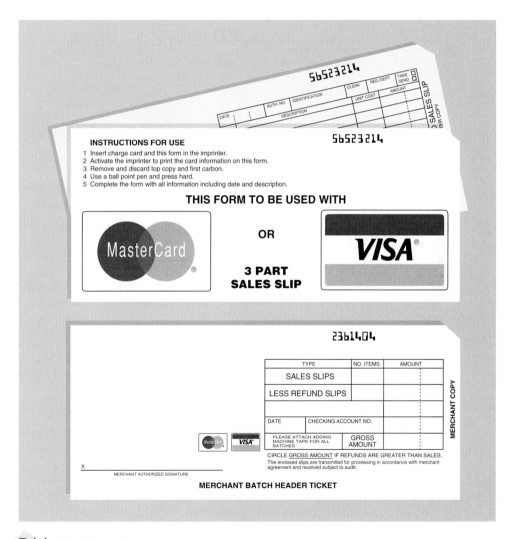

Exhibit 12–10   Using manual charge slips increases the cost of credit-card processing. The top copy is taken away by the guest. The merchant/hotel retains one copy and the third is bundled along with the batch header ticket (bottom form) and shipped to the credit card company. Rarely used today when even bank checks are being processed digitally.

> Increases in assets, including *accounts receivable* and cash, are made with debits. Increases in incomes (sales of *food* and *beverage*) are made with credits.
>
>   Debit: Accounts Receivable/City Ledger/Credit Card Company   65
>   Credit: Food Sales, Beverage Sales, etc.   65
>   *Explanation:* Guest paid for services with a credit card.

Periodically, the T&E companies reimburse the hotel, minus fees. With bank cards, the slips are deposited the next day—no need to mail them off—so the funds are available sooner. That may soon be the case with T&E cards, depending on the outcome of current litigation that allows T&E cards to use banks. In both cases, the cash received is reduced by the discount fees.

> This illustration is for one card, but the process is batched in hundreds of cards.
>
> Increases in assets, including accounts receivable and *cash,* are made with debits.
> Increases in expenses, including *discount fees* and commissions, are made with debits.
> Decreases in assets, including *accounts receivable* and cash, are made with credits.
>
>   Debit: Cash   63.50
>   Debit: Discount Fees   1.50
>   Credit: Accounts Receivable/City Ledger/Credit Card Company   65
>   *Explanation:* Credit-card company paid its account, less commission.

Credit-card chargebacks, charges that are refused by the card company for one of several reasons, are separated from the original receivables. Doing so highlights the difference and focuses the accounting department on a remedy. If the hotel fails to act within 30 days, and even if it does act, the new account often becomes a bad debt.

> Increases in assets, including *accounts receivable* and cash, are made with debits. Decreases in assets, including *accounts receivable* and cash, are made with credits.
>
>   Debit: Accounts Receivable/City Ledger/Chargebacks
>   Credit: Accounts Receivable/City Ledger/Credit Card Company
>   *Explanation:* Chargebacks moved from regular charges to a separate account.

▶*Electronic Draft Capture.*   The communications highway has brought significant changes in the handling of credit-card charges. Guests encounter manual charge slips less and less. Instead, the electronic verification of the card's authenticity (swiping the card through the reader) is followed by an electronic printout of the charges. A slip of paper (see Exhibit 12–11), looking much like the tape of an old-fashioned adding machine, is presented for signature. One copy goes to the guest; the second copy remains with the hotel or merchant as part of the cashier's departmental turn-in.

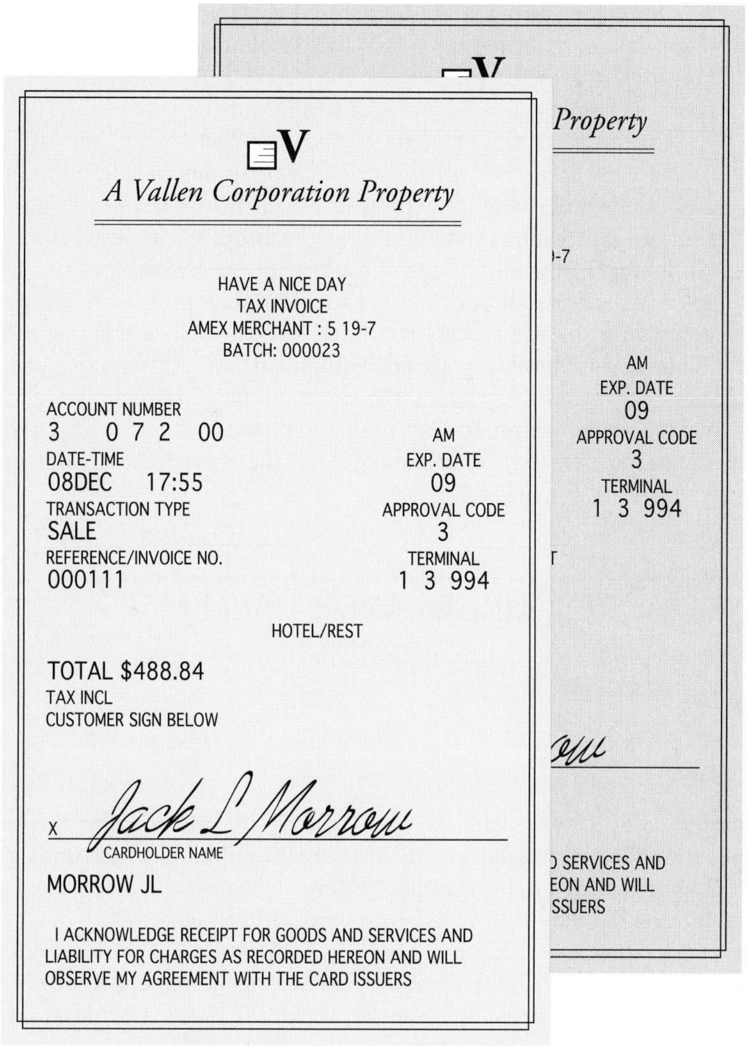

▢**V**

A Vallen Corporation Property

HAVE A NICE DAY
TAX INVOICE
AMEX MERCHANT : 5 19-7
BATCH: 000023

ACCOUNT NUMBER
3   0 7 2   00
DATE-TIME
08DEC   17:55
TRANSACTION TYPE
SALE
REFERENCE/INVOICE NO.
000111

AM
EXP. DATE
09
APPROVAL CODE
3
TERMINAL
1 3 994

HOTEL/REST

TOTAL $488.84
TAX INCL
CUSTOMER SIGN BELOW

X *Jack L Morrow*
CARDHOLDER NAME

MORROW JL

I ACKNOWLEDGE RECEIPT FOR GOODS AND SERVICES AND
LIABILITY FOR CHARGES AS RECORDED HEREON AND WILL
OBSERVE MY AGREEMENT WITH THE CARD ISSUERS

Exhibit 12–11   Pencil-and-paper forms for credit cards (Exhibit 12-10) have been replaced almost entirely by electronic terminals that verify the card and record the transaction. Although the charge is recorded electronically, both the hotel and the guest get receipts that look like old-fashioned adding machine tapes.

What happens during the processing is less visible, but more important, than what happens with the copies of the charge slips. The charge is captured electronically (EDT, electronic draft capture) by the credit-card company. Simultaneously, the status of the card is validated, approval to proceed is granted, and the card's ceiling is cleared. EDT eliminates paper sales drafts and the sorting, postage, and manual posting that batch handling involves. Communicating with the financial institution through an electronic process means quicker access to the funds. Funds could be transferred immediately by EFT or delayed until the records are transmitted overnight to the clearing center. Either way, funds are accessed more rapidly than through the manual system. Moreover, credit-card companies reduce the merchant discount fees when EDT is used.

Speedy electronic data, much of it by laser imaging, represents additional float for the credit-card company. The earlier that the charge appears on the customer's monthly statement, the sooner the credit-card company gets paid. All credit cards have electronic capture by one of several means.

In the early stages, manual-dial telephones and then touch-tone terminals were used to get card authorization. EFT with point-of-sale online processing is the other end of the technology. Swiping the card through the terminal obtains the authorization at registration and interfaces the hotel's computer (PMS) with the credit-card computer. Electronic billing and ultimate collection from the card issuer then follows. In between the dial and the on-line interface options are a series of electronic choices depending on what costs the hotel can absorb or counterbalance through savings. Whether purchased or leased, equipment and software costs must be absorbed, perhaps negotiated as part of the discount fee. Maintenance and repairs must be provided, but by whom and for how much is also at issue. In general, the more automatic the procedure, the higher the costs but the greater the savings in discount fees.

RESOURCES AND CHALLENGES
Resources

► SUMMARY

Today's travelers prefer credit over cash. So do hotelkeepers, who accommodate this business fact while keeping a keen eye toward credit management. Assigning some credit responsibilities to credit-card companies reduces credit risks, but not without costs. The credit-card industry has the same objectives (increasing sales and decreasing credit losses) as the lodging industry and, despite some operational irritations, works closely with it.

Hotels track and bill their credit guests (accounts receivable) through the city ledger. *City ledger* is an easy way of referring to a group of records that contains information about nonregistered persons who owe the hotel for services. Hotels provide rooms, food, beverages, and other services to a variety of city-ledger identities. Among them are banquet and convention groups, travel agents, companies, individuals, including the hotel's own executives, and frequent-guest participants. Most city-ledger records start out as front-office folios. They become city-ledger accounts when guests

check out and transfer the amounts owed to credit cards. Other city accounts come directly into the city ledger from credit-card charges in the hotel's various outlets.

Modern electronic communication has replaced much of the paper recordkeeping that once plagued the front desk. The development of this capability has been undertaken by a variety of third-party intermediaries. Lodging now has numerous credit partners, including national credit-card companies and banking institutions. They issue two classes of credit card. Travel and entertainment cards (T&Es) are used heavily by businesses and individuals with better credit ratings. Bank cards are in more widespread use. The two types continue to borrow ideas from one another, so their differences are blurring. They will blur even more so if a series of court cases helps the T&Es locate within the banking system.

Credit and credit cards have become essential to and inseparable from the lodging industry's management of credit through the city ledger.

➤ WEB SITES

American Express–Financial corporation with a long history in travel and tourism: http://www.americanexpress.com

Buyers' Zone–Provides multiple purveyor quotes for merchants seeking card-processing installations: http://www.buyerszone.com

Card Web–News and information about credit cards: http://www.cardweb.com

Federal Trade Commission–Guide to e-payment protection: http://www.ftc.gov

UATP–Universal Air Travel Plan issues travel cards but not consumer cards: http://www.uatp.com

Web Site Assignment

Report on the first story in Card Web for the 12th day of this month and year.

➤ INTERESTING TIDBITS

➤ A 1963 film, *The Man from Diner's Club,* starring Danny Kaye, played off the one-time popularity of the Diners Club card, an icon of early credit-card history.

➤ BankAmericard selected Visa as its new name (1977) because Visa is pronounced the same in many languages around the world.

➤ Footnote 7 explains some differences in the use of the word "coupon." Another type of coupon is issued by Hawaii's Aloha and Hawaiian Airlines. Available from the airlines, from wholesalers, even from ATMs, these coupons, which sell at a discount, are used as currency when purchasing inter–island travel.

➤ READING REFERENCES

"Accounting for Liabilities Vacated by Provision of Service." Barry Wexler. *The Trusted Professional* (New York Society of Certified Public Accountants), January 2001. Deals with credit cards and a form of trade-outs.

Credit Card Glossary, 3 Delta Systems. Fairfax, Virginia. http://www.3deltasystems.com. Manages credit-card processing.

"Credit Card Policies." *Lodging.* May 1996. For guaranteed reservations.

"The Future of Electronic Payments, From Paper to Plastic and Beyond." J. Dave Oder. *Hospitality Upgrade Magazine,* Summer 2000.

Challenges

➤ TRUE/FALSE

Questions that are partially false should be marked false. (F).

___ 1. A roadside motel would most likely have credit cards as its only city-ledger receivable.

___ 2. Chargebacks, charges returned to the merchant by the credit-card company, are so easily remedied that almost all of them are eventually recovered.

___ 3. All accounts receivable enter the city ledger by way of the front office, which transfers the folio balance as the guest checks out.

___ 4. As an incentive to accept frequent-guest points as room payments, resort hotels collect for frequent-guest stays from the chain's headquarters at 150% of room rate.

___ 5. Hotels may fail to press for collection of no-show reservations that have been guaranteed with a credit card because they fear to lose potential customers.

➤ PROBLEMS

1. Write two dialogues for a training manual that is to be used by guest-service agents at the front desk. Include the questions posed by a room clerk seeking additional credit information and the responses made by a guest. What disposition does the room clerk make when (a) a walk-in guest arrives with no baggage?, (b) a same-day reservation arrives, but no information has been provided previously?

2. Explain how the following transfers should be handled. Be specific, citing the location of the entry, the ledger or ledgers involved, and the debit or credit requirements.
   a. A transient guest checks out using a national credit card.
   b. The president and treasurer of a small company check in for a business meeting. The hotel has been carrying the unpaid balance of a charge generated by these officers at their last business meeting about three months ago.
   c. A couple departs and requests that the balance of the folio be charged to the couple's parents, who are registered in another room. The parents concur.
   d. An association completes its meeting and the association executive, after reviewing the balance due, requests billing to the group's headquarters.

3. In terms of the front office and of the city ledger, explain the quick check-out system used by numerous hotels.

4. Many older hotels in the area in which your resort is located have suffered for years from a seasonal influx of skippers and room burglary gangs operating with stolen keys. (Few of these old properties have modern locks.) The local hotel association has asked you to draft a plan for a security network that could be implemented before the next season. Prepare the plan, providing details of the procedure by explaining the roles of the individuals or groups involved.

5. In terms of the front office and of the city ledger, explain how a reservation request from a travel agent is processed if (a) the agency has a good credit relationship with the hotel and the guest pays the agency; (b) the agency has no credit rating with the hotel, and the guest pays the agency; and (c) the guest makes no payment to the agency.

6. A noticeable squeeze on profits had brought the management team to a brainstorming session. One idea is put forth by the controller. Noting the large amount of credit-card business that the hotel is doing, the controller suggests that each tip charged to a credit card be reduced by 4.77% when paid to the employee. (That amount is the average discount fee the hotel is paying to all the credit-card companies.) The controller further suggests that an additional 1.1% be subtracted, representing the percentage of credit-card charges that prove uncollectible. What comments would the food and beverage manager be apt to make? The rooms manager?

➤ ANSWERS TO TRUE/FALSE QUIZ

1. True. Lacking food and beverage facilities, motels are unlikely to have any type of charges (accounts receivable) except for rooms from registered guests.

2. False. Lack of staff and the great probability that there is no signature supporting the charge (a ghost card) means the charge-back will not receive accounting attention within the 30 day period to act.

3. False. Nonguests, for example, may charge services (food and beverage) on credit cards. Banquets and room rentals are other receivables that enter the city ledger without first passing through a front-office folio. (See also question 1.)

4. False. Just the contrary—hotels that accept guests on frequent-guest points are reimbursed at less than rack rates.

5. True. The statement is true as it stands. Besides, such reservations are made without a signature on file (ghost cards), which makes collection less likely. (See also question 2.)

PART V

Technology

America's ever-increasing rate of national productivity is due in large measure to the shift from labor-intensive work to electronic equipment. Lodging is a significant participant, although certainly not at the forefront of the movement. New devices are being tested and older ones refined as the industry strives to better serve its clientele and manage its operating costs. Automated elevators, direct-dial telephones, and electronic keys were the forerunners of what will certainly come to be an all-electronic hotel.

Property management systems (PMSs) were among the early efforts. As hotels grew larger, new approaches were needed to offset the increases in billing errors caused by paper-and-pencil folios. The first hotel PMSs borrowed applications from other industries. They failed to meet the lodging industry's unique needs. Vision didn't become reality until suppliers recognized the size of the potential market. Only then did manufacturers invest the research dollars needed to develop hotel-specific software. Although the lodging industry invested very little in research, reliable, inexpensive, and easy-to-use systems gradually emerged. The paper jam disappeared, employee accuracy increased, and management reporting improved. Costs fell so dramatically that even the smallest property replaced the hand-prepared folio with the electronic one.

The first chapter of this final unit examines the PMS in terms of the night audit. Users cannot see into electronic equipment, so glimpses of the old pencil-

and-paper audit are also included. These pencil-and-paper segments help explain both the purpose and procedure of the night audit, as they did in Chapter 10 with folio billing. Night audits uncover and correct errors in guest billing and prepare reports for management's use the following day. Error detection and correction were the main thrust of the pencil-and-paper audits; management reporting is the driving force of the electronic audit.

Property management systems gather, store, and quickly retrieve information. Their ability to handle vast amounts of data has made possible the industry's important frequent-guest programs. Technology is ready now to move beyond the routine posting of room rates and taxes and data manipulation. The next generation of electronic solutions will focus beyond clerical labor savings. What about computerized vacuum cleaners?

Chapter 14 looks at some of the first results of this emerging technology. Among them are call-accounting systems, in-room television, on-demand films, safe-deposit accessibility, in-room vending, and telecommunications. Guests who once selected hotels on the basis of swimming pools and bath amenities are starting to choose on the basis of sophisticated television-based entertainment and in-room business centers. There soon will be other criteria that we cannot even foresee at this time. And the speed of change will be, indeed, as rapid as it is always forecasted to be. Just a brief few years ago, the centralized business center was the ultimate for commercial hotels; today the equipment is in the guest's own room, and the center is no more.

The Night Audit

Outline

➤ *THE AUDIT AND THE AUDITOR*

The night audit ends the hotel's day. All records of accounts receivable (A/R) are collected, corrected, and summarized by the night-audit crew—in a small hotel, no more than a single person. Closing the day's accounting records validates the work of the previous shifts and provides information for the issues of the upcoming day.

What night auditors do and how they do it have changed dramatically since the introduction of electronic data processing (EDP), which has altered the focus and changed the procedure. Pre-computer audits concentrated on uncovering the errors of pencil-and-paper systems. Fewer errors occur with property management systems (PMSs), so management reporting has become the new emphasis.

The Night Auditor

Despite the title, the night auditor is rarely a trained accountant and is an auditor only by the broadest definition. In general terms, an *auditor* is an appraiser–reporter of the accuracy and integrity of records and financial statements. One type of auditing, internal auditing, involves procedural control and an accounting review of operations and records. Internal auditing also reports on the activities of other employees. It is this final definition that best explains the role of the hotel night auditor.

No special knowledge of accounting or even of bookkeeping's debits and credits is required of the night auditor. That's why this and previous chapters identify accounting explanations in a different format and font. Having this knowledge is helpful and desirable, but it is sufficient for the auditor to have good arithmetic skills, self-discipline, and a penchant for detailed work. Auditors must be careful, accurate, and reliable. The latter trait is an especially redeeming one because the unattractive working hours make replacements difficult to recruit and almost impossible to find on short notice.

➤**Work Shift.**   The audit crew works the graveyard shift, arriving sometime between 11 PM and midnight and finishing some 8 hours later, at 7 or 8 in the morning. Since the audit reconciles records needed to start the new day, night auditors remain on the job until the audit is complete, regardless of the hour.

➤*General Duties.*   For a large hotel, the audit staff consists of a senior auditor and assistants. Guest-service agents and even cashiers may also be on hand. Their presence frees the auditors to do their job without interruption. In smaller hotels, the audit team relieves the entire desk, filling the jobs of reservationist, guest-service agent, cashier, telephone operator, and auditor. Whether or not the auditors assume these jobs, they must be conversant with them. It is those very duties that the night audit audits.

When the actual tasks are taken on, the night auditor is likely to be the only responsible employee on duty. The auditor assumes the position of night manager whether the title is there or not. The same range of problems faced by the day manager is involved, but to a lesser degree. Emergencies, credit, mechanical breakdowns, accidents, and deaths are some of the situations encountered by the night manager.

Security and incident reports must be filed by either the night auditor/manager alone or cooperatively with the security staff. Without a security contingent, the auditor may be the one who walks security rounds and fire watch.

Few hotels of less than 150 rooms employ a night engineer. Yet management has generally been lax in preparing the night auditor/manager for the problems that arise in this area of responsibility. Fire, plumbing problems, power failures, elevator mishaps, and boiler troubles are matters that may take the auditor's time.

Equally time consuming are guest relations: a noisy party going into the early hours of the morning; the victorious football team shouting in the lobby; a sick guest; visiting conventioneers in the 11th-floor suite; paid reservations yet to arrive and the hotel 100% occupied. Such are the nonaccounting matters for which the night auditor might be responsible.

Mature judgment and experience are needed to carry out these nonaudit functions. The combination of audit skills, working hours, and responsibility merit a higher salary for the night auditor than for the average guest–service agent, but the spread is not noticeably larger.

The Audit

The night audit is an audit of accounts receivable, of folios. Cash sales in food, beverage, and other outlets of the hotel are not included in the night audit because they are not posted to folios. Instead, cash sales are audited by the income auditor, sometimes called the day auditor, in conjunction with the general cashier. Folio sales to accounts receivable pass through the night audit to the same income or day audit, which takes place the next morning. There, both types of sales (cash and credit) are combined. From that total comes the daily report to the manager and the ultimate entries in the hotel's sales journal.

➤ *Reconciling Accounts Receivable.* Every business authenticates its accounts receivable periodically. Whereas other retailers balance and close their accounts monthly, hotels do the job nightly. The night audit verifies the accuracy and completeness of each guest folio each night.

Hotel auditors lack the luxury of time because hotelkeeping is a very transient business. Arrivals and departures keep coming and going without notice at all hours of the day and night. Each new day brings more charges and more credits whether or not the previous day has been reconciled. There is no holding a departing guest until the folio is ready. The night audit must make certain that it always is ready.

The pressure of immediacy is missing with city-ledger guests. City-ledger guests are not registered, so their billing cycle is more like the accounts receivable of other businesses. Depending on the nature of the original charge, city receivables are billed for the first time three days—sometimes 10 days—after the charge is incurred.

➤ *The Closeout Hour.* The night audit reviews the records of a single day. Since hotels never close, management selects an arbitrary hour, the *closeout hour* (also called the *close of the day*), to officially end one day and start the next. The actual time selected depends on the operating hours of the lounges, restaurants, and room service of the particular hotel. Each new charge changes the folio, so the audit is prepared when changes are infrequent—in the early morning hours when guests are abed. Departmental charges before the closeout hour are included in today's records. Departmental charges after the closeout hour are posted to the folio on the following date after the night audit has been completed.

A late closeout hour captures the last of the day's charges, but it puts pressure on the auditing staff, which needs to finish the job before the early departures begin leaving. On the other hand, too early a closeout hour throws all the charges of the late evening into the following day, in effect, delaying their audit for 24 hours. Standardized stationery forms list midnight as the closeout hour (see Exhibit 10–7), but the actual time is set by management.

Posting Room Charges

➤*Posting Room Charges Manually.*   Posting (recording) room charges is one of the night auditor's major tasks. Before the advent of the PMS, room charges were posted manually. That required each folio to be removed one by one from the cashier's well (see Chapter 10, Exhibit 10–3). The room charge and the room tax were recorded in pencil, the column totaled, and the folio returned to the well in room number sequence. Exhibit 13–1 illustrates the results on a manual folio: $60 recorded on the horizontal line labeled "rooms" and $3 for the tax. The $78 and $6.24 posted in Exhibit 10–2 offers a second illustration.

Once the room charge and tax are posted, the night auditor adds the column, which includes the previous day's total. (The second columns of Exhibits 13–1 and 10–2

<table>
<tr><td colspan="8" align="center">**THE CITY HOTEL**
ANYWHERE, U.S.A.</td><td>#8001</td></tr>
</table>

NAME _____ *B. M. Oncampus* _____
ADDRESS _____ *1 Campus Rd., University City* _____
ROOM NUMBER _____ *1406* _____   RATE _____ *60* _____
NUMBER IN THE PARTY _____ *1* _____   CLERK _____ *ABC* _____
DATE OF ARRIVAL _____ *10/5* _____   DATE OF DEPARTURE _____ *10/7* _____
CHANGES: ROOM NO. _____   TO ROOM NO. _____   NEW RATE _____

DATE	10/5	10/6	10/7				
BAL.FWD		(19)	70				
ROOMS	60	60					
TAX	3	3					
FOOD	10	12					
BAR		6					
TELEPH							
LAUNDRY							
CASH DISBR GARAGE	8	8					
TRANSFERS							
TOT CHRG	81	70					
CASH							
ALLOWANCES							
TRANSFERS	100						
TOT CRDS	100						
BAL DUE	(19)	70					

Exhibit 13–1   Pencil-and-paper folios (see also Exhibit 10–2) accumulate daily charges in separate columns. Figures in the appropriate day's column are copied onto a transcript sheet for balancing during that night's audit. Column 10/6 has been copied to line 1 of Exhibit 13–10. Note the credit balance of ($19) that opens October 6. (*For ease in reading, all illustrations use small dollar values, which may not seem realistic.*)

illustrate the addition.) The new balance is carried forward from the bottom of the column to the top of the column of the following day. In this manner a cumulative balance is maintained, and the manual folio is ready at any time for the departing guest.

Included in the cumulative total are departmental charges other than room. These are posted throughout the day by the front-office staff as the charges arrive at the front desk from the operating departments. Exhibit 13–1 shows these as food, bar, and garage. Garage is a cash paid-out made by the hotel to the garage for the guest.

Manual System Errors.   With a manual system, the same values are written repeatedly. Guests' names, room numbers, and dollar values are recorded many times by different individuals on reg cards and folios, vouchers and control sheets. The night auditor rewrites the figures once more: room rates, departmental charges, credits, and others. Writing, rewriting, and adding columns manually create numerous human errors that PMSs avoid. Point-of-sale (POS) terminals (see Exhibit 13–2) communicate electronically, bypassing the need for written vouchers between the department and the desk.

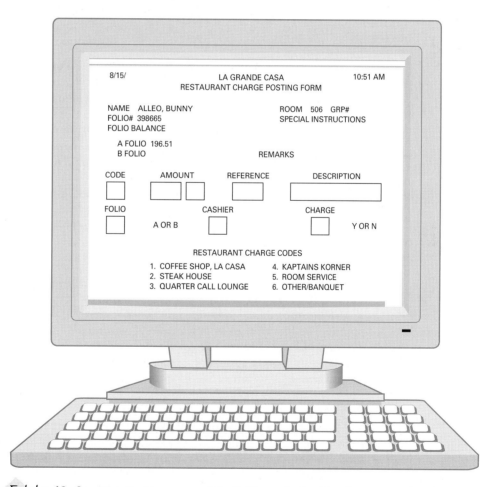

Exhibit 13–2   The display screen of the POS terminal guides departmental cashiers (see Exhibit 10–8) through the posting sequence. POS charges are recorded instantaneously on the folios in the PMS. Without a POS, cashiers communicate with pencil-and-paper vouchers, so posting, either manually or with a POS, is done at the desk. Poor handwriting and frequent handling increase the number of errors.

Additional errors are inherent in the manual system. Poor handwriting is the most obvious one. When handwritten, figures 1 and 7, 4 and 9, and 3 and 8 are often confused. Recopying also causes slides and transpositions. Slides are misplaced units, which may involve decimals. Saying 53 21 mentally or aloud may result in either 53.21 or 5,321 being recorded. Transpositions are similar errors, but the digits are re-ordered—53.21 may become 35.21.

Even simple addition causes problems. The auditor may create errors by incorrectly totaling the folios, the control sheet, or the packets of vouchers. Adding machines help, but there is no guarantee that the figures are accurately entered. Hand audits still require adding-machine tapes to allow comparison between the actual figures and those entered into the calculator.

Subtracting one total from another highlights the error. Errors of addition usually appear as differences of 1 in the unit columns. If the difference in the totals is 1 cent, 10 cents, $1, $10, and so on, the culprit is likely to be an error of addition. If not an error of addition, it might be a slide or transposition. Slides and transpositions are flagged when the difference in the total is evenly divisible by 9. For example, the difference between 53.21 and 35.21 is 18, evenly divisible by 9. Searching for mistakes begins by looking for errors of addition or transpositions and slides.

▶**Posting Room Charges Electronically.**   Posting room charges electronically is easier and far faster than posting manually. There are no folios, and there is no bucket or well (see Exhibit 10–3). Time is saved in simply not removing and replacing 100 or 300 or 1,000 folios from a cashier's bucket. Room rates are not posted individually, and hundreds of folios are not added up. Room charges with the appropriate taxes have been programmed into the computer. Memory knows how much each room is to be billed and how much tax to be added. No math errors here. Activating the audit program brings all the accounts receivable up to date in memory. Folios containing the new information are printed on demand, illustrated by any of the folio exhibits in Chapter 10.

Computers do crash! so a hard copy, a nightly printout, for emergency backup is part of every night audit (see Exhibit 13–3).

▶**Room Charges Not Posted By the Auditor.**   Room charges are normally posted by the night auditor. Infrequently, and then only because of special circumstances, room and tax are posted by the day crew, not by the night auditor. In two of the instances, the auditor is simply not there at the time the charge is to be posted. The first of these involves guests who arrive and depart the same day, called *day rate, use rate,* or *part day rate guests*. These guests arrive during the day after the previous night's audit has been finished. They depart before the night audit of the following day. Since the folio is opened and closed without any intervening audit, the room charge, which is often less than a full night's rate, must be posted by the day watch.

Extra room charges for late check outs are the second special case. Brief extensions to the check-out hour are usually accommodated without charge when space allows. Extraordinary delays, or even brief occupancy when demand is high, incur late-departure charges, occasionally as much as a full night's rate. During the heady days of the late 1990s, when hotels thought they could do no wrong, guests were charged another type of penalty. Special room charges were levied on guests who failed to stay through the reservation period. Whatever the reason, excess room charges that occur between shifts of the night audit must be posted and collected by the front-office cashier.

Room #	Name	Folio #	Open Bal	Charges	Credits	Close Bal

THE CITY HOTEL, ANYWHERE, U.S.A.   Page 1
03/16   Guest Ledger Summary Report

Room #	Name	Folio #	Open Bal	Charges	Credits	Close Bal
3004	Huent	0457	–0–	81.30	.00	81.30
3005	Wanake	0398	65.72	91.44	.00	157.16
3008	Lee	0431	132.00	101.01	.00	233.01
3110	Langden	0420	–0–	99.87	100.00	0.13–
3111	Nelston	0408	233.65	145.61	.00	379.26
3117	O'Harra	0461	789.75	121.10	.00	910.85
6121	Chiu	0444	32.60–	99.87	.00	67.27
6133	Valex	0335	–0–	165.30	.00	165.30
7003	Roberts	0428	336.66	109.55	.00	446.21
7009	Haittenberg	0454	19.45	87.43	.00	106.88
Totals			44,651.07	18,632.98	950.00	62,334.05

Exhibit 13–3 A hard copy (printed copy) of closing folio balances is prepared nightly as part of the PMS audit and left at the desk the following day. The new day's opening balances (last night's closing balances) are then available in case of computer failure. Each column of this computer report corresponds to a column on the hand-prepared transcript. For example, the counterpart of the Charges column of Exhibit 13–3 is column 16, Total Debits, of Exhibit 13–10.

Revenue Verification

There are two major objectives to the audit. The discussion has already focused on one: reconciling accounts receivable. Each folio needs to be updated nightly so an accurate bill can be presented on demand. By the time the audit begins, hundreds of postings will have been made on guest accounts. Among them are charges for food; beverage; local and long-distance telephone calls; laundry and valet; cash advances; in-room charges for films, safes, and bars; greens fees; saunas; ski-tows; and more. Added to the day's list are the room charges and local taxes just completed by the night auditor. The audit must prove the accuracy of all.

Chapter 10 emphasized that every departmental charge has equal debits and credits. Thus each time a guest buys service, the guest account is charged and the departmental income is recorded.

What takes place individually—one folio being increased and one sale being recorded—has application to the audit. A rule of mathematics—the total is equal to the sum of the parts—plays a fundamental role in balancing the audit. All the income earned by any one department, say, room service, must equal the total of all the individual room-service charges posted to guest folios. If each individual room-service event increases a guest's folio and simultaneously increases income to the room-service

> The accounting rules apply:
>
> Increases in assets, including *accounts receivable* and cash, are made with debits. Increases in incomes (sales of rooms, *food*, beverage, etc.) are made with credits.
>
> Debit: Accounts Receivable/Guest's Folio   50
>   Credit: Proper Departmental (room, *food*, beverage, spa, etc.) Sale   50
> *Explanation:* Guest charged food in the coffee shop.

department, then the totals of each should agree, that is, be in balance. Since there are hundreds of posting and hundreds of folios, this simple fact is not evident immediately. The night audit reconciles the two by making evident this equality: The total income earned by each department from accounts receivable is the same total charged to guest folios.

➤ RECONCILING USING A PROPERTY MANAGEMENT SYSTEM

The night audit provides the most spectacular demonstration of the PMS in action. Only those who have machine-posted using the NCR (National Cash Register) system or hand-copied pages of transcript sheets can appreciate the savings in time and efficiency. Labor savings, the often touted but seldom delivered advantage of computer installations, is certainly evident in the PMS night audit. Since a minimum crew is always needed, the greatest labor savings are at the largest hotels.

The computer has altered the mechanics of the audit, its purpose, and its scope. Traditionally, the night audit concentrated on finding and correcting errors—except the errors were caused by the system. Initial errors, transmittal errors, posting errors, and errors of addition are inherent in the hand audit. The entire thrust of the hand audit is discovery and repair. The computer audit has no such problems. The information that is input with the departmental POS appears everywhere, and everywhere it appears the same. Of course, there are errors of input, and these are discussed shortly.

Interfacing Different Systems

There are also problems with the PMS—computer bugs. When the situation becomes very serious, the bug is upgraded to a virus. Viruses or glitches (misplaced decimals is a very simple example) are errors of equipment, not errors of audit. Increases in the number of such incidents can usually be traced to additional interfaces, linkages between equipment pieces of various manufacturers. An interface is a third system used to link two unrelated systems. Hotels have as many as eight or ten such linkages. Common links to the property management system are POS terminals and call accounting systems (see Chapter 14).

Interface problems are created when systems differently designed by different manufacturers are purchased to be used with an already existing PMS. In addition to POS and call accounting (CA), there might be interfaces for in-room minibars, in-room films, reservation programs, housekeeping room status and others. Recent efforts by the American Hotel & Lodging Association have focused on developing integration standards.[1] These will ensure the compatibility of different products by different manufacturers and not require the special interface programs that bring grief to many hotel systems.

A second wave of integration is being driven by the large franchise companies. To increase seamless communications, particularly reservations between the parent and the franchisee, several large franchisors are now insisting on a particular PMS for each franchisee.[2] Once in place, last-room availability (see Chapter 4) will be accessible across a wide range of channels, including the Web. Consolidation, so apparent in the hotel business, is a likely outcome of technology standardization. The number of technology vendors has declined from the 100 plus that once competed.

Verifying Basic Data

The PMS is closed and updated daily at the closeout hour in a process akin to the manual night audit. Although the PMS closeout could be done at any time—as could the manual night audit, for that matter—the quiet hours of the early morning are favored for both. The PMS shuts down during the closeout. Departmental POS terminals cannot interface with the system. Charges to guest accounts must wait until the audit is complete. Manual audits are not quite as dramatic. With lots of erasing and rewriting, manual audits can accommodate changes during the process.

➤*Closing Routine.*   Updating the PMS requires the night auditor to monitor the progress of the audit rather than perform the work. Room charges and room taxes are posted automatically. It is an internal function that the auditor does not see until the job is complete and the hard copy is printed. In contrast, the auditor actually records the rate and tax during the manual audit (see Exhibit 13–1). A summary printout is prepared immediately, showing the folio balances that open the new day (see Exhibit 13–3). This hard-copy recap enables the hotel to settle guest accounts even if the computer crashes. (The upcoming discussion of the manual audit stresses that the opening balances of the new day are the same as the closing balances of the previous day.)

Departmental verifications of revenues are another part of the audit. Unlike manual audits, discrepancies are unusual. Point-of-sale terminals post the same figure both to the account receivable on the folio and to the revenue of the departmental sale. Rare differences are corrected by comparing departmental incomes reported by the PMS to account receivable records such as registered readings and/or vouchers. Vouchers come into play because POS terminals are not used by every hotel. Even those that have them may operate some departments manually. If so, the manual system of vouchers, control sheets, and folios may be partially in place. Even if this is so,

---

[1]The AH&LA has been developing integration standards in cooperation with several large chains, notably Holiday and Microsoft. Vendors who adopt the Hospitality Information Technology Integration Standards (HITIS) offer systems that interface with all others who comply with HITIS. Hotels that specify HITIS in their bid solicitations will enjoy reduced risks, lower costs, and savings in installation time. The first set of standards is the interface between POS and PMS.

[2]Cendant Corporation is installing chain-mandated property management systems free of charge in all franchise properties because it believes that 60% of hotels at the midtier or lower levels operate with only racks, cigar boxes, and cash registers. *Lodging Hospitality,* June 1998, pp. 26, 28. (Because the authors concur, this edition of *Check-In, Check-Out* continues to include sections on the hand-prepared folio and audit.)

the night audit is simplified tremendously with the PMS. The property management system creates the folios and the spreadsheet electronically and ensures the accuracy of the mathematics.

The night auditor finishes the PMS audit with an end-of-the-day routine much like that of the hand audit. A trial balance of debits and credits is made. Debits are charges to the receivable folios; credits are earnings in the several departments. The day and date are closed and the next day opened. The POS terminals are put back on-line. Monthly and annual totals are accumulated as part of the reporting process that follows next. The sequence varies at each hotel. At some properties, the routine is pre-programmed; at others, the update proceeds by prompts from the system to which the auditor responds.

Folios of guests who are departing the following day may be printed as part of the audit procedure. Preprinting folios speeds the check outs. Copies are filed by room number sequence in the cashier's well and produced without delay when the departing guest appears at the desk. If subsequent charges—breakfast, for example—alter the previous night's balance, the old folio is merely discarded and a new one printed.

A copy of the preprinted folio might be left under the guest-room door for use in express check outs. This wouldn't be necessary if the hotel provides express check out by means of the TV set.

Express Check Out.   Express check out is one of the exciting stories of PMS installations. Standing in line to check out has been the bane of hotel guests, who are always in a hurry. Flexible terminals able to quickly shift from registration to departure status, and vice versa, were one of the first PMS innovations to focus on the problem. This increased the number of front-office stations when demand was greatest. Lines were shortened, but not enough.

Because early output printers were slow, many operations began printing the folios of expected departures during the previous night's audit. From printing them to delivering them to the room wasn't a large conceptual jump, but it created *zip-out check out*, also called *speedy check out, no-wait check out*, or *VIP check out*.

Zip-out check out is only for guests using direct billing or credit cards—but that is almost everyone. At first, guests who wanted the service completed a request card. Later, every departure using a credit card had a folio under the door. If the folio was accurate, the guests left after completing one additional step: They either telephoned an extension to give notice, or they dropped a form with the key in a lobby box (see Exhibit 13–4). The final folio was mailed to the guest within a day or two, and the charges were processed through the credit-card company.

Express check out leaped ahead with the interface of Spectradyne's TV pay-movie system into the hotel's PMS. Delivering folios to the room was necessary no longer. The folio appeared on the TV set any time the guest wanted it. From then on, the procedure was the same. With a click of the remote control, the guest signaled departure. As with zip-out check out, the folio followed in the mail, and the credit-card charges were processed. An integrated PMS transfers the charges, which have been accumulated in the front-office folio, to the city ledger module.

Another great leap forward was taken when self-check-in/check-out terminals were interfaced with the ever-expanding PMS. At freestanding locations within the lobby, self-check-out terminals present guests with their folios and accept their credit cards to speed them on their way. This completes the PMS cycle, which was started when the guest registered at the same terminal (see Chapter 8, Exhibit 8–14). It is another step closer to the fully electronic hotel.

▣**V**

A Vallen Corporation Property

EXPRESS CHECK OUT

DO NOT DEPOSIT CASH
IN THIS ENVELOPE

To expedite departure, we are pleased to offer you
EXPRESS CHECK OUT privileges. Please complete
the information below and deposit the envelope, with
your room key enclosed, at the front desk in the key
drop box.

Room Number ——————— Date ———

Name ————————————————————

Address ————————————————————

City ——————— State —— Zip ———

Do you require a copy of your account? ————

**VIDEO CHECK OUT IS ALSO AVAILABLE
THROUGH THE IN-ROOM TELEVISION SET!**

➤*PMS Posting Errors.*   Property management systems are not guaranteed to
be error free! Staff members make mistakes whether the system is manual or electronic. The PMS provides consistent figures throughout, but those values will be in
error if the wrong keys are struck. Human errors are not offset by equipment. Computerized front offices minimize system errors and facilitate error discovery, but they
do not create error-free environments.

The night auditor prints a detailed list of transactions as the first step in pinpointing errors. The hard copy itemizes transactions by register keys or by reference codes.
Reference codes are illustrated on the folio figures throughout Chapter 10. Departmental cashiers need authority to post charges to someone's folio. A source document,

such as a signed departmental voucher, provides that authority. Since most source documents are maintained in numerical sequence, the voucher number becomes the reference code. The POS program doesn't post until the cashier inputs that reference number or code.

A different code is used to validate the identity of the guest who is making the charge. The cashier inputs the guest's room number, which the guest provides, and on prompt, enters the first several letters of the guest's surname, which the guest also provides. The charge is processed, but not before the system matches the POS information with the registration data in the file of the PMS. Exhibit 13–2 illustrates the computer screen that a dining room cashier uses to post a charge.

Matching the guest-room keycard (with its magnetic strip) to the PMS's registration data file is another means of verifying a guest's identity. The guest inserts the keycard into a POS and the system verifies the identification. Implementation of this system has already begun, but it may be replaced before it even goes into general use. The smart cards of Chapter 12 suggest that one's own credit card may become the keycard for the next generation of electronic locks.

The POS reduces receivable losses by rejecting invalid postings. The guest may have checked out already; be a paid-in-advance customer with no charges permitted; or have exceeded the credit-card floor or other credit ceiling set by the hotel. Late charges are reduced dramatically when POS terminals are in place.

Departing guests sometimes challenge the accuracy of departmental postings. Denying that the charges were ever made, they ask for offsetting allowances from the front desk. Obtaining a copy of the check (voucher) signed by the guest to show its accuracy is a slow process with a pencil-and-paper system. So time consuming is it that the front-office cashier simply grants the allowance without further investigation. Until recently, the results were the same with a PMS. Now disputed charges are being met with proof in a test program introduced at the Boca Raton Resort and Beach Club. The PMS is able to display the protested voucher despite the range of operating departments at the Boca: 84 revenue sources, 23 different voucher forms, and 13 different sizes of paper![3]

Reports from the Night Audit

An unlimited number of reports can be generated by the PMS once it captures the information. Data can be arranged and reordered in a variety of ways. The registration card is a good example. From it, several different reports can be generated: geographic origin of guests; membership in groups; credit limits; company affiliations; average length of stay; and rate level preference.

The ease of obtaining reports undoubtedly contributed to the vast numbers that were demanded when PMSs were first introduced. Much of that has shaken out. Management took control and pared the numbers by emphasizing exception reports. One no longer sees piles of reports prepared by the night auditor trashed, unread by the recipient the next day.

Still, the night audit produces a wide range of reports for all departments of the front office. Many of these are day-end summaries, since unit managers use (through display terminals or hard-copy print) the same data several times throughout the day. Some reports are traditional from the days of the pencil-and-paper audit: the balancing of accounts receivable, credit alerts, and statistical reports to the manager.

[3] *CKC Report,* May 1988, p. 14.

►*Turnkey Systems.* In a turnkey installation, the buyer merely "turns the key" to activate the PMS. The vendor has programmed the system including the reports. Nothing is ever quite that easy, but it is unlikely that the industry would be so far along if the burden of development had not shifted from individual hotel companies to industrywide vendors.

Prior to the turnkey concept, each hotel shopped among manufacturers for its own hardware. Then it developed its own software by employing computer specialists, who at that time knew nothing about the business of keeping a hotel. The large data processing departments that appeared as a result of inhouse programming disappeared quickly with the introduction of the turnkey package.

Now systems are purchased off-the-shelf, shopping among suppliers for an existing system that is close to what the hotel needs. And systems are close to what is needed. Generic programs are much alike because hotels are much alike. What differences there are in off-the-shelf products diminish as third- and fourth-generation programs are developed. Each generation improves flow and screening, new or missing functions being added to remain competitive. Most recently, the push has been toward a Windows/Intel environment.

Turnkey companies now dominate the field. Single suppliers furnish both the hardware and the software. If the supplier specializes in one segment, other vendors supply the missing parts. Responsibility remains with the primary vendor, who puts together the package, gets it up and running, trains the staff, and services the installation—not without some major grief for the hotel, of course. Vendors who adopt the Hospitality Information Technology Integration Standards (HITIS) that the AH&LA is encouraging will offer systems that interface with all others who comply with HITIS. Hotels that specify HITIS in their bid solicitations will enjoy reduced risks, lower costs, and savings in installation time. Access to the World Wide Web will also change the hotel's PMS from one with dedicated hardware to one that uses Web technology. As that happens, the front-office workstation will become a general-purpose rather than a specific-purpose screen.

Currently, vendors are modifying their off-the-shelf systems to meet special needs. Just as often, however, hotels modify their special needs to conform to the standardized product. Products are almost identical among hotels with the same vendor and very similar among hotels with different vendors. It is difficult to say whether a uniform need created the turnkey system or whether mass production created consistency across the industry. Nowhere is this standardization more apparent than in the reports prepared nightly by the PMS.

►*Kinds of Reports.* Reports prepared by the night audit fall into several categories: reservation reports; rooms management reports, including reports of room status; accounting reports; and reports to the manager. Unless management remains selective, an excessive number of reports involving expensive machine time, labor, storage, and paper costs is spewed out nightly. Since a good deal of the information keeps changing, viewing it on screens is just as effective and far more economical. Reporting by exception is another approach to the issue.

Exception Reports. Exception reports highlight situations that digress from the norm. Reporting everything that is as it should be serves no purpose. Reports by exception alert the reader to problem areas without requiring the time-consuming inspection of normal data. A report on credit limits is a good example. Listing the folio balance of every guest against the credit ceiling is unnecessary. It is unduly long and requires a tedious search to find the important information. An exception report lists only those folios that are at, above, or close to the hotel's limit. The size of the report is reduced and the important data is emphasized.

Some common exception reports are listed here:

Allowance Report: identifies who authorized each allowance, who received the allowance, the amount, and the reasons.

Cashier's Overage and Shortage Report: pinpoints by stations overages and shortages that exceed predetermined norms.

Comps Report: similar to an allowance report; identifies who authorized each comp, who received the comp, the amount, and the reasons.

No Luggage Report: lists occupied rooms in which there is no baggage (see Exhibit 13–15); a credit report.

Room Rate Variance Report: compares actual rates to standard rate schedule and identifies the authority for granting the variance (not meaningful if the hotel is discounting frequently and deeply).

Skipper Report: provides room identification, dollar amount, and purported name and address.

Write-off Report: lists daily write-offs, usually late charges, whose account balances are less than a specified amount.

Downtime Reports. Downtime reports, for use when the computer crashes, provide insurance against disaster. Like a great deal of insurance, the reports usually go unused because emergencies rarely materialize. Downtime reports are dumped 24 hours later when the contingency has passed and the backup reports of the following day have been printed.

Basic downtime reports include the following:

Folio Balance Report: itemizes in room number sequence the balances due from receivables; comparable to columns 2, 1, 4 and 5, 16, 20, 21 and 22 of a manual transcript (compare Exhibits 13–3 and 13–11).

Guest-List Report: alphabetizes registered guests with their room numbers; computer version of a manual information rack.

Room Status Report: identifies vacant, out-of-order, on change, and occupied rooms at the beginning of the new day; a computerized room count sheet (see Exhibit 13–12).

Disk Backup: not a report, but part of the closing sequence of the auditor's shift; data is replicated onto another disk to be retrieved if a malfunction erases the working disk.

Credit Reports. The night auditor is the credit manager's first line of defense. In that capacity, the night auditor handles both routine matters and special credit situations.

Mention has already been made of the auditor's responsibility to preprint the folios of expected check-outs. Although not nearly as numerous, folios must also be prepared for guests who remain longer than one week. On the guest's seventh night, the auditor prints the folio (or prepares a new folio if the system is manual) for delivery to the guest the next day.

The night auditor also makes an analysis of guest account balances. With a manual system, the auditor scans the last column of the transcript (see Exhibit 13–11, column 21) and itemizes those rooms with balances at or near the hotel's limit. The computer makes the same list. If the audit team has time, additional credit duties may be assigned.

All credit reports are sensitive and may be viewed as exception reports:

Credit Alert: list of rooms whose folio charges exceed a given amount in a single day. That amount varies with the class of hotel.

Cumulative Charges Report: similar to the credit alert except a cumulative figure for the guest's entire stay.

Floor Report: list of guests whose folio balances approach the maximum allowed the hotel by the credit-card company (the hotel's floor), or the maximum the credit-card allows on the guest's own card.

Three-Day Report: weekly statements that remain unpaid three days after billing.

Reservation Reports.   Computerizing reservations added a new dimension to the process. The toll-free WATS number globalized the reservation network. Instant confirmation was given for dates that were months away to persons who were miles apart. In so doing, reams of information—fodder for reports—was generated.

Information is the power to decide. Reservation managers must know the number of rooms sold and the number available, by type, rate, and accommodations. They must know the number of arrivals, departures, stayovers, cancellations, out of orders, and walk-ins for a start. This information comes to the reservation department in a variety of reports.

Supplemental information flows from the same database. Which rooms are most popular and at which rates? Do no-show factors vary with the season and the day of the week? If so, by how much? How many rooms in which categories are turnaways? How many reservations were walked? How many in-WATS calls were there? How many were initiated by travel agents? Questions of this type illustrate again the dual management–operations capability of the computer.

An alphabetical list of arrivals is an example of the computer in operations. It reduces the number of lost reservations and facilitates the recognition of VIPs. It helps the bellcaptain schedule a crew. It identifies group affiliation, which improves reservation and billing procedures.

Reservation data can be displayed on a monitor or preserved on hard copy for slower digestion and evaluation. A permanent copy turns the data into a report. Then it serves more as a management tool than an operational one. Although different vendors format reports differently, there is a common grouping for the reservation department, which includes the following:

Arrivals Report: alphabetical list of the day's expected arrivals, individually and by groups.

Cancellation and Change Report: list of reservation cancellations for the day or reservation changes and cancellations for a later date.

Central Reservations Report: analysis of reservations made through the central reservations system, including numbers, kinds, rates, and fees paid.

Convention (Group) Delegates Report: compilation of group (and tour) room blocks; the number of rooms booked, and the number still available by rate category and name of group. Also called a **Group Pickup Report**.

Daily Analysis Report: one or more reports on the number and percentage of reservations, arrivals, no-shows, walk-ins, and so on, by source (travel agent, housing bureau, etc.) and by type of guest (full rack, corporate rate, etc.).

Deposit Report: reservations by deposit status—deposits requested and received, deposits requested and not received, deposits not requested. Could be treated as an exception report.

Forecast Report: one of a variety of names (**Extended Arrival Report, Future Availability Report**) for projecting reservation data forward over short or long durations (see Exhibit 6–6).

Occupancy Report: projection within the computer's horizon of expected occupancy by category of room.

Overbooking (Walk) Report: list of reservations walked, including their identification; the number of walk-ins denied; and the number farmed out to other properties.

Regrets Report: report on the number of room requests denied.

Rooms Management Reports.   The PMS has brought major procedural changes to the front office but not to the functions that need doing. Comparisons of the old and the new are best illustrated through the room rack. Unlike manual room racks, which one can see and physically manipulate, computerized racks are in computer memory, viewable only on the monitor screen (see Exhibits 13–5 and 13–6). Whether the clerk turns to one rack type or the other, the information is the same: room rates, location, connecting and adjoining rooms, bed types, and room status.

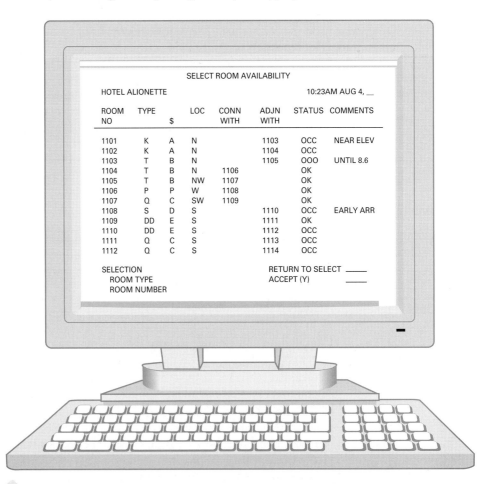

SELECT ROOM AVAILABILITY

HOTEL ALIONETTE   10:23AM AUG 4, __

ROOM NO	TYPE	$	LOC	CONN WITH	ADJN WITH	STATUS	COMMENTS
1101	K	A	N		1103	OCC	NEAR ELEV
1102	K	A	N		1104	OCC	
1103	T	B	N		1105	OOO	UNTIL 8.6
1104	T	B	N	1106		OK	
1105	T	B	NW	1107		OK	
1106	P	P	W	1108		OK	
1107	Q	C	SW	1109		OK	
1108	S	D	S		1110	OCC	EARLY ARR
1109	DD	E	S		1111	OK	
1110	DD	E	S		1112	OCC	
1111	Q	C	S		1113	OCC	
1112	Q	C	S		1114	OCC	

SELECTION   RETURN TO SELECT _____
    ROOM TYPE   ACCEPT (Y)   _____
    ROOM NUMBER

Exhibit 13–5   A computer display of the room rack lists room availability by room type, location, rate, and status. The clerk's selection (lower left) must agree with previous input of room type requested by the arriving guest. If so, the clerk exits with Y (yes), lower right corner, and the assignment is complete. Compare the PMS display with that of the manual rack, Exhibit 13–7.

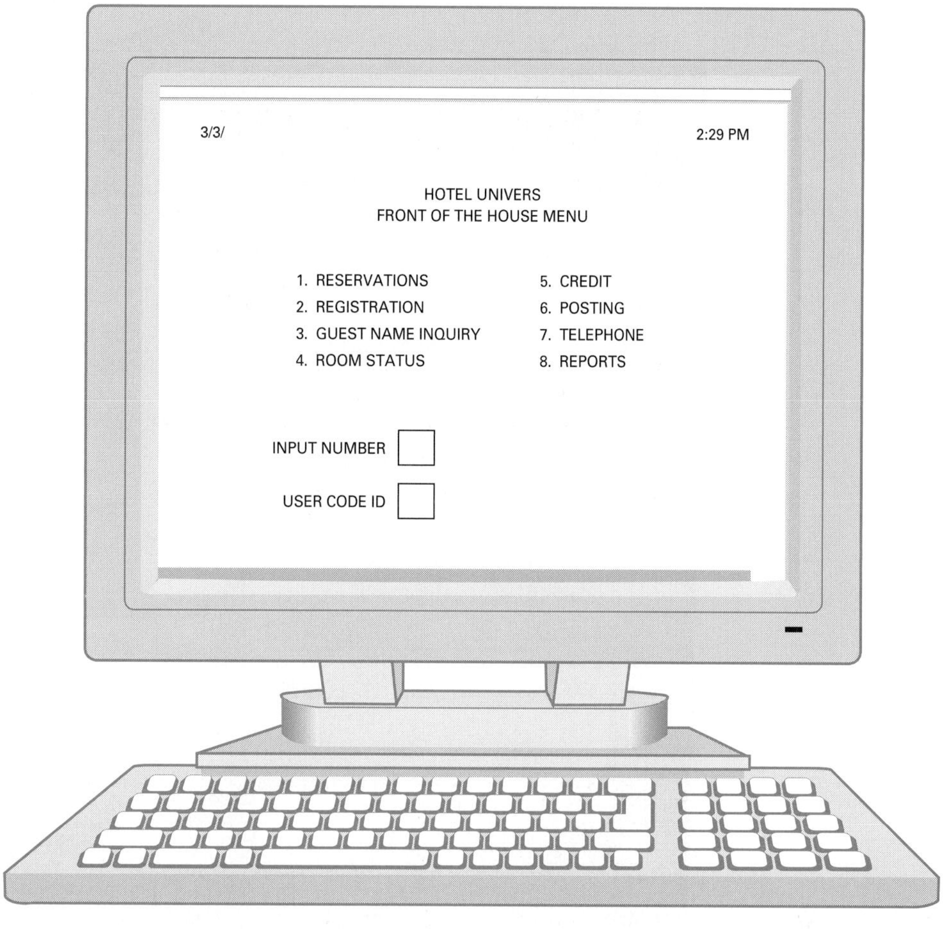

Exhibit 13–6
Each function per-
formed by the
guest-service agent,
Exhibit 13–5, for
example, requires a
different computer
screen, which is
called up from this
main menu. Two or
three masks may be
required before the
task is completed.

```
3/3/                                                  2:29 PM


                         HOTEL UNIVERS
                     FRONT OF THE HOUSE MENU


              1. RESERVATIONS          5. CREDIT
              2. REGISTRATION          6. POSTING
              3. GUEST NAME INQUIRY    7. TELEPHONE
              4. ROOM STATUS           8. REPORTS



         INPUT NUMBER    [   ]

         USER CODE ID    [   ]
```

The computer restructures the data. It separates into different windows what is visible with one glance to the user of the manual rack (see Exhibit 13–7). Separate menus (see Exhibit 13–6) are needed to view what the manual rack identifies as one class of information. With a glance at the manual rack, one sees the rooms vacant and occupied, the rooms out of order and on change, the names of the guests and their city of residence, the number in the party and their company or group affilia-tion, the rate on the room and the anticipated check-out date. It doesn't work that way with an electronic system, where separate programs are needed for each func-tion. Room identification (see Exhibit 13–5) is different from guest identification (see Exhibit 13–8).

Far more information is available from the computer rack than from the manual rack of Exhibit 13–7, but the information has to be manipulated to provide the data. For example, the computerized rack can display all the vacant rooms on a given floor. All the king rooms in the tower or all the connecting rooms in the lanai building can be listed. Facts that would take many minutes to ascertain, if at all, from the manual rack are flashed onto the screen in seconds.

Information is more complete and can be processed more rapidly with the com-puterized rack than with the manual one. This is true for the whole, although a greater amount of time may be required for the computer to process a single fact. In a contest to identify a guest whose name begins with either "Mac" or "Mc," for exam-ple, the manual user may be able to beat out the computer user.

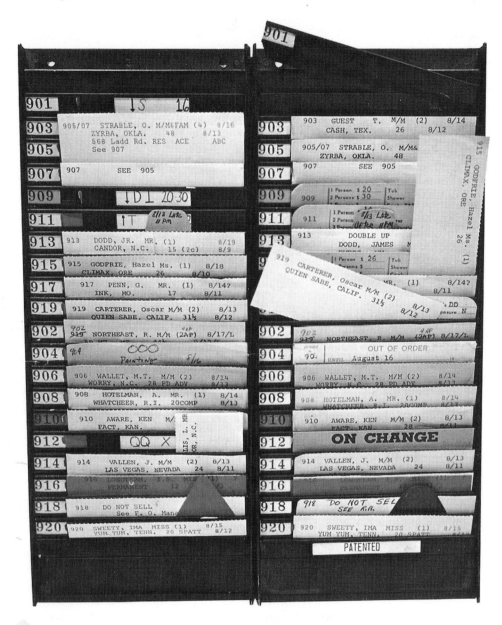

Exhibit 13–7   A manual room rack, circa 1960. With one glance, the guest-service agent determines which rooms are vacant and which occupied; who the occupants are and their home towns; rates paid; arrival and anticipated departure dates. It would take several computer screens to obtain the same information. Colors furnish additional facts: members of a tour group; paid-in-advance; permanent guest and so on. (*For ease in reading, all illustrations use small dollar values, which may not seem realistic.*)

Computer reports for the rooms function include the following:

Change Report: identification of room changes, rate changes, and the number in the party.

Convention Use Report: summary of the room use by different convention groups in order to justify the number of complimentary rooms.

Exhibit 13–8
Code 3 of Exhibit 13–6 leads to the screen that identifies a particular guest in a particular room. Compare the guest information here with that shown on the room rack slips of Exhibit 13–7.

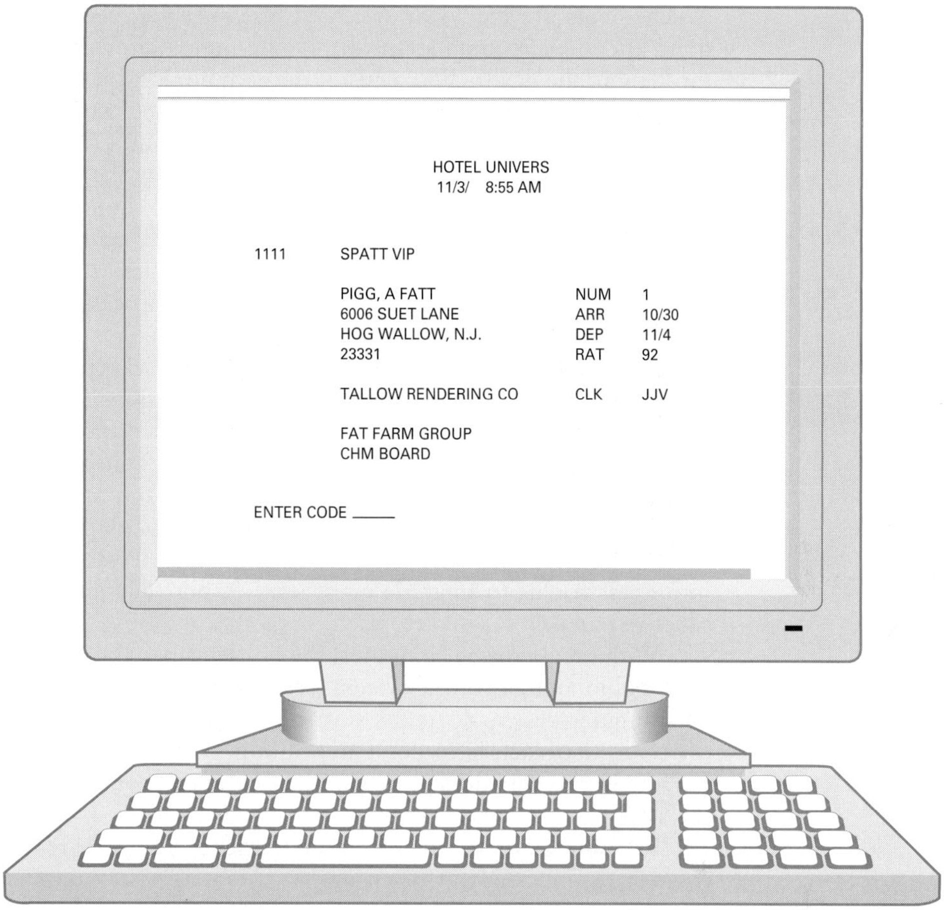

```
                          HOTEL UNIVERS
                          11/3/   8:55 AM


        1111        SPATT VIP

                    PIGG, A FATT            NUM    1
                    6006 SUET LANE          ARR    10/30
                    HOG WALLOW, N.J.         DEP    11/4
                    23331                   RAT    92

                    TALLOW RENDERING CO     CLK    JJV

                    FAT FARM GROUP
                    CHM BOARD


        ENTER CODE _____
```

Expected to Depart Report: list of anticipated departures. The converse would be a Stayover Report.

Flag Report: list of rooms flagged for special attention by the desk.

House Use Report: list of rooms occupied by hotel personnel.

Out-of-Order Report: list of rooms that are out of order or out of inventory with reasons.

Pickup Report: names and room numbers picked up by members of a specific group against its block.

Rate Analysis Report: display of distribution of rates by sources—reservations, walk-ins, travel-agency made, res system, hotel sales department, packages, company-made.

Room Productivity Report: evaluation of housekeeping's productivity in total and by individual room attendant.

VIP Report: list of distinguished guests and very important persons, including casino high rollers.

Rooms Status Reports.   Rooms status offers what is probably the best example of an old function with a new face. Whether the hotel uses a manual rack or a computer, room status (on change, vacant and ready, out-of-order, or occupied rooms) must be communicated between the desk and housekeeping. Clerks need to know which rooms are ready for sale, and housekeeping needs to know which rooms require attention. A room status display on the monitor is called up innumerable times throughout the day by both ends of the communication link.

The communication procedure hasn't changed with the computer. The cashier still puts the room on change as the guest checks out. (This is done electronically if the guest uses the speedy check-out option.) That's how the room clerk learns that a given room will be available soon. On-change status tells housekeeping that the room needs attention. When the room is clean, the housekeeper updates the system, switching the on-change room to ready. Immediately, the desk clerk has the information. The room is sold and the cycle begins anew. The faster the process goes around, the quicker the new guest is settled and the room sale consummated.

Prior to the computer, the cashier–desk–housekeeping link was direct conversation person to person; by means of paper notations; by telephone calls; and, frequently, not at all. The floor housekeeper wasn't included in the communication loop. Although the critical link, she couldn't be reached at all. Today's housekeepers communicate by telephone, not by conversation, but as an electronic input device to the computer. The message is tapped in either through the telephone or by means of a terminal located in the linen closet on each floor. Personal PCs are being introduced into guest rooms to upgrade guest service, but they also provide the staff with another terminal.

With access to the computer, the housekeeper's office tracks room attendants as they dial in and out of the system (see Exhibit 13–9). Daily job assignments can also be computer designed. At the start of the shift, each employee gets a hard-copy list of rooms that each is to do. The printout also includes special assignments such as mirrors in the corridors, attention to sick guests, or messages from management to the staff.

In addition to the reports that housekeeping uses to manage the department, room status includes the following:

ROOM ATTENDANT'S SCHEDULE						01:53 PM NOV 11						
NAME					NUMBER	DUTY H		MESSAGE SIGNAL OFF				
	NUMBER OF ROOMS ASSIGNED				0			BEGINNING ROOM NUMBER				
ROOM	U-R	IN	OUT	SL	HK	CO	ROOM	U-R	IN	OUT	SL	HK	CO
1200	A	9:35A	9:49A	SG	OK	SO	1209	A			SD	D	SO
1201	A	9:50A	10:14A	SS	OK	SO	1210	A	8:44A	9:02A	SD	OK	SO
1202	A	11:50A	12:12P	SS	OK	SO	1211	A	1:13P	1:48P	OK	I	OK
1203	A	9:20A	9:35A	SS	OK	SO	1212	A	9:03A	9:19A	SG	OK	SO
1204	A	10:54A	11:17A	SM	OK	SO	1213	A	1:48		OK	57	DO
1205	A	11:17A	11:50A	SD	OK	SO	1214	A			OK	D	DO
1206	A	10:31A	10:54A	SS	OK	SO	1215	A			OK	D	DO
1207	A	10:14A	10:31A	SS	OK	SO							
1208	A	12:12P	1:13P	OK	OK	OK							

END DISPLAY

Exhibit 13–9   Property management systems track each room attendant, permitting management to monitor productivity and locate the employee if direct communication is required. By the time of this display, 1:53 PM (top right), the housekeeper has serviced almost all the rooms.

ADA Report: Lists rooms occupied by handicapped guests. Copies to bell department and desk, but especially to security in case evacuation of the building is required.

Out-of-Order Report: special focus on out-of-order or out-of-inventory rooms, includes dates the rooms went down, expected ready dates, and the causes of each OOO or OOI room.

Permanent Guest Report: list of permanent guests by room number and name.

Room Status List: room-by-room identification of occupied and vacant rooms, made-up and not-ready rooms, out-of-order rooms, and on-change rooms. (This report also appears among the downtime reports.)

Sick Guest Report: list of sick guests by room number and name.

Accounts Receivable Reports.   The PMS prepares electronically what the manual audit prepares with pencil and paper. Both audit the same thing: front-office folios, accounts receivable. Viewed at its simplest, the night audit is nothing more than a cumulative inventory of accounts receivable. Comparing accounts receivable to food items, say, canned peas on a storeroom shelf, helps clarify the point.

Each day's computation starts with the opening balance of accounts receivable (cans of peas on the shelf). This opening balance is the amount already owed to (peas on hand) the hotel. New charges (account receivable debits) made by guests (new pea purchases) that day are added to the opening balance:

	Of Accounts Receivable in Dollars	Of Peas in Cans
Opening Balance	$ 186,000.00	186
Today's Charges (Purchases)	24,000.00	24
Total	$ 210,000.00	210

From that sum are subtracted payments (credits) made by guests (cans opened and consumed) that day. The new (closing) balance is thus obtained for both accounts receivable and peas. This closing becomes the opening balance of the following day, and the sequence begins anew.

	Of Accounts Receivable in Dollars	Of Peas in Cans
Total (See Above)	$ 210,000.00	210
Today's Payments (Consumption)	60,000.00	60
A/R owed at day's close	$ 150,000.00[*]	
Peas on the shelf at day's end		150[*]
[*]Opening balance tomorrow.		

The accounts receivable reports include the following:

Alpha List: alphabetically lists the entire guest (accounts receivable) population and the amount each owes (this would be comparable to a list of each can of peas on the shelf).

City-ledger Transfers: itemizes all the accounts transferred from the front-office ledger to the city ledger that day; a journal of city-ledger transfers. (Identifies specific cans of peas shipped to the kitchen from the storeroom).

Credit-Card Report: reports amounts and identities of credit-card charges by both registered and nonregistered guests.

Daily Revenue Report: analyzes revenue totals from all sources by outlet and means of payment. Comparable to the old NCR machine audit D report (and sometimes called a D report).

Departmental Sales Journal: shows the individual transactions of each department (comparable to the vertical columns of a hand transcript, see Exhibit 13–11).

Guest Ledger Summary: displays the daily activity for both the A and B folios of individual guest accounts—opening balance, charges and credits, and closing balance (comparable to the horizontal lines of a hand transcript, see Exhibits 13–3 and 13–11).

THE CITY HOTEL, ANYWHERE, U.S.A.   Page 1
03/16   Night Auditor's Report

SALES		ROOM STATISTICS	
Rooms	$12,900.00	Total Rooms	320
Coffee Shop	1,524.80	House Use	–0–
Steak House	CLOSED	Out of Order	–0–
Cap'tn Bar	896.00	Complimentary	–0–
Telephone	990.76	Permanent	2
Laundry	100.51	Room Count	180
Total Sales	$16,412.07	Vacant	140
		House Count	210

Other Charges:	
Cash Advance	987.76
Taxes Payable	540.00
Transfers	693.15
	$18,632.98

ACCOUNTS RECEIVABLE		ROOM RATIOS	
Opening Balance	$44,651.07	% Occupancy	56.3
		% Double Occupancy	16.7
Charges	18,632.98	Average Daily Rate	$71.67
Total	$63,284.05	RevPar	$40.35
Credits	950.00		
Closing Balance	$62,334.05		

Exhibit 13–10   A night auditor's report is prepared for the manager under both manual and computerized systems. Basic information includes charge sales for the day (left top), a cumulative balance of accounts receivable (left bottom), and room statistics and ratios. This report is incorporated into the daily report to the manager, which includes cash sales as well as charge sales.

Late-Charge Report: identifies late charges that were transferred to city ledger that day.

Posting Report: displays posting activity by individual POS terminal (comparable to a departmental control sheet, see Exhibit 10–7).

Room Revenue (Posting) Report: displays room, rate, and tax posted at the day's close. In that room revenue can be obtained floor by floor, it is comparable to a room count sheet without the taxes also called an occupancy and room revenue report (see Exhibit 13–12).

DAILY TRANSCRIPT OF

ACCOUNTS RECEIVABLE

DATE 10/6 20 ___

1 ACCOUNT NO.	2 ROOM NO.	3 NUMBER OF GUESTS	OPENING BALANCE 4 DEBIT	OPENING BALANCE 5 CREDIT	DEBITS 6 ROOMS	7 RESTAURANT	8 BEVERAGES	TELEPHONE 9 LOCAL CALLS	TELEPHONE 10 LONG DISTANCE	11 LAUNDRY	12 VALET	13 CASH DISBURSEMENTS	14 TRANSFERS	15 ROOM TAX	16 TOTAL DEBITS	CREDITS 17 CASH RECEIPTS	18 ALLOWANCES	19 TRANSFERS	20	CLOSING BALANCE 21 DEBIT	CLOSING BALANCE 22 CREDIT
8001	1406	1		19 —	60 —	12 —	6 —					8 —		3 —	70 —					70 —	
8811	1817	2	63 60		30 —	5 —			4 —					60	39 60					103 20	
8123	1824	1			18 50	6 40						1 —		37	26 27	37 —					10 73
7188	1906	2	21 93		21 56									43	21 99					43 92	
7913	1907	2	39 96		30 —		6 —						47 96	60	84 56					124 52	
TOTAL	40	51	768 20	25 32	676 50	52 10	61 70	7 20	18 40		4 —	17 —	47 96	13 53	898 39	167 50	2 10			1488 70	17 03
								DEPARTURES													
8106	1616	3	46 20			4 40									4 40			50 60			
8007	1649	1	18 87													18 57	30				
7992	1824	2	39 96															39 96			
8282	1600	1	– 0 –				4 —	40	3 60						8 —	8 —					
TOTAL			105 03			4 40	4 —	— 40	3 60						12 40	26 57	30	90 56			
								CITY LEDGER													
Cum			500 —			40 —	30 —						90 56		160 56			47 96		612 60	
TOTALS			1373 23	25 32	676 50	96 50	95 70	7 60	22 —		4 —	17 —	138 52	13 53	1071 35	194 07	2 40	138 52		2101 30	17 03

Courtesy: American Hotel Register Co., Northbrook, IL.

Exhibit 13–11 The transcript is a summary of accounts receivable. The vertical daily column of each folio is copied here as a horizontal line. This separates departmental incomes by columns. Column totals are then compared to departmental control sheets to verify account receivable sales.

Two methods of recording the folios are illustrated, but only one would be used at one time. Line 1 (the folio of Exhibit 13–1) includes the opening balance of columns 4 minus 5 in the total of column 16. The remaining exhibit illustrates the second method in which column 16 represents only the sum of the day's charges, columns 6 through 15. The cumulative balance of accounts receivable (column 21 minus 22) is the same with both methods. (*For ease in reading, all illustrations use small dollar values, which may not seem realistic.*)

▶**Reports to the Manager.**　The night auditor furnishes information about accounts receivable sales to the income (or day) auditor. The income audit, which includes both cash and accounts receivable sales, casts a wider net than the night audit, which is limited to accounts receivable. Sometimes the income audit and its corresponding report to the manager is delayed, just as the night audit is at times. To offset the delay, the night auditor leaves a preliminary report for the manager. It is abbreviated, of course, because it contains accounts receivable sales only. Still, most hotel sales are accounts receivable sales. Room sales, the hotel's largest revenue source, is sold only on account. There are no cash sales in the rooms department.

Exhibit 13–10 illustrates a *night auditor's report to the manager*. Three items are reported: (1) accounts receivable sales in the several departments appear in the upper left. These figures are identical to columns 6 through 16 of the manual transcript (see Exhibit 13–11); (2) a cumulative balance of accounts receivable, the pea illustration above, is at the bottom left of Exhibit 13–10; (3) room statistics and their corresponding ratios, which were introduced in Chapter 1, appear on the right side of this abbreviated night auditor's report. One or all of the values may be changed by the day audit, which could uncover mistakes in any of the sections. There aren't many changes, but new information (cash sales among them) modifies the night auditor's report into the daily report to the manager.

Room Count, House Count, and Room Income.　Room count, the number of rooms sold (occupied); house count, the number of guests (persons) registered; and room income (room sales) are computed during the night audit. These three values are verified by the income audit using a formula exactly like the cans-of-peas illustration above.

OCCUPANCY AND ROOM REVENUE REPORT　**Hotel Gary**　DAY _Monday_　DATE _9-18-_

EAST WING

ROOM	No Guests	RATE	ROOM	No Guests	RATE	ROOM	No Guests	RATE	ROOM	No Guests	RATE	ROOM	No Guests	RATE	ROOM	No Guests	RATE
3101			3319			3615			3910			4206			4501		
3102			3320			3616			3912			4207			4502		
3103			S3322	4	80	3617			3914			4208			4503		
3104			3401			3618			3915			4210			4504		
3105			3402	2	66	3619			3916			4212			4505		
3106			3403	2	66	3620			3917			4214			4506		
3107			3404			S3622			3918			4215			4507		
3108			3405	2	68	3701			3919			4216			4508		
3110			3406			3702			3920			4217			4510		
3112			3407			3703			S3922			4218			4512		
3114			3408	1	58 —	3704			4001			4219			4514		
3115			3410			3705			4002			4220			4515		
3116			3412	3	72	3706			4003			S4222			4516		
3117			3414	1	59 50	3707			4004			4301			4517		
3118			3415	3	66 —	3708			4005			4302			4518		

ROOM	No Guests	RATE	ROOM	No Guests	RATE	ROOM	No Guests	RATE	ROOM	No Guests	RATE	ROOM	No Guests	RATE	ROOM	No Guests	RATE
3312			3606	2	66	3903			S4122			4418			4712		
3314			3607	2	66	3904			4201			4419			4714		
3315			3608	3	71	3905			4202			4420			4715		
3316			3610	1	66	3906			4203			S4422			4716		
3317			3612			3907			4204						4717		
3318			3614			3908			4205						4718		
TOTAL			TOTAL	57	3,731 00	TOTAL			TOTAL			TOTAL			TOTAL		

Exhibit 13–12　A paper-and-pencil room count sheet is prepared at the closeout hour of each day. It is a snapshot of the room rack at that time. Included are the number of rooms occupied, the number of guests, and the total room revenue. These figures should agree with columns 2, 3, and 6 respectively of the transcript, Exhibit 13–11. The comparable PMS report is the room status list.

First, arrivals are added to the opening balance. Today's opening balance is yesterday's closing balance. This opening/closing balance idea applies to every running-balance computation, be it accounts receivable, rooms occupied, or bottles of scotch at the bar. Consider the scotch. When the bar closes at 2 AM, there are six bottles of scotch. Twelve hours later, when the bar reopens, the same six bottles of scotch are there. The closing balance of one day is the opening balance of the following day. The rule is the same for room statistics. The number of rooms, persons, and dollar income from yesterday's close is increased by today's arrivals and decreased by today's departures. The values determined by the day audit's approach should be the same as those counted by the night audit.

Occasional changes that do not involve arrivals or departures are also added in or subtracted out. These might be room-count changes (guest shifts from a three-room suite to a single room), house-count changes (a spouse departs from a two-person occupancy with a single folio), or rate changes (caused by a room change or by any of the other two changes). The simple mathematics is illustrated so:

	Room Count	House Count	Room Income
Opening balance	840	1,062	$174,200
+ Arrivals	316	391	80,100
= Total	1,156	1,453	$254,300
− Departures	88	122	16,400
= Total	1,068	1,331	$237,900
± Changes	+ 6	− 2	+ 1,730
= Closing balance	1,074	1,329	$239,630

Room Statistics.   Both the night auditor's report to the manager and the income auditor's daily report to the manager contain statistics. Statistics are merely special ways of grouping data in an orderly and usable manner. Statistics are the facts expressed in dollars, cents, or numbers. For example, instead of itemizing

Guest A	Room 597	$150
Guest B	Room 643	$130
Guest C	Room 842	$160

and so on, one might say there are 220 guests in 189 rooms paying a total of $27,198. A great deal of information has been grouped, classified, and presented to become a statistic.

Taking the next step, these room figures are expressed in ratios, which are more meaningful than the simple statistic. So the 189 rooms sold is expressed in relation to the number of rooms available for sale, 270. The result is a percentage of occupancy, a mathematical expression of how many rooms were sold in relation to how many could have been sold. The occupancy percent is a widely quoted figure and one discussed as early as Chapter 1. Using the illustration, the percentage of occupancy is

$$\frac{\text{number of rooms sold (room count)}}{\text{number of rooms available for sale}} = \frac{189}{270} = 70\%$$

A frequent companion to the percentage of occupancy computation is the average daily rate (ADR). Both ratios appear in the night auditor's report to the manager. Sales per occupied room, as this figure is sometimes called, is the income from room sales divided by the number of rooms sold.

$$\frac{\text{room income}}{\text{number of rooms sold (room count)}} = \frac{\$27,198}{189} = \$143.90$$

A similar computation, RevPar, once called *sales per available room*, is derived by dividing room income by the number of rooms available for sale rather than by the actual number of rooms sold.

$$\frac{\text{room income}}{\text{number of rooms available for sale}} = \frac{\$27,198}{270} = \$100.73$$

The fourth most frequently cited ratio in the manager's daily report is the percentage of double occupancy. Double occupancy is the relationship of rooms occupied by more than one guest to the total number of rooms occupied. That is what the following ratio expresses:

$$\frac{\text{number of guests} - \text{number of rooms sold}}{\text{number of rooms sold}} = \frac{220 - 189}{189} = 16.4\%$$

Having finished the audit with the preparation of the night auditor's report to the manager, the night auditor lays aside the pencils and erasers—or more likely, rubs some stiff shoulders from working at the keyboard—and, at the end of the shift, goes home to bed.

The following discussion explains the pencil-and-paper audit using a hand transcript. Except for a segment on the housekeeper's report, the content is more historical than contemporary. Readers may choose to study the housekeeping material of pages 543–544 and then skip ahead to the chapter summary.

➤ RECONCILING USING A HAND AUDIT

The purpose of the manual night audit (by hand with pencil and paper) is the same as the purpose of the computerized audit. Each aims to validate folio balances, the accounts receivable, and to verify simultaneously the accurate posting of departmental sales. (Those are charge sales; cash sales do not pass through the night audit.)

Property management systems record the two events simultaneously. When accounts receivable guests buy services (food, beverage, spa, etc.), the PMS records (posts) the charges on the guest's folio. That posting simultaneously accumulates the value of the service with similar sales made to other guests. Not so with pencil-and-paper systems. When a departmental charge arrives at the front desk by way of a voucher, it is posted to the guest's folio only. There is no means of accumulating all the charges made by all the guests to that particular department. That must await the manual night audit.

The manual night audit proves that the total accounts receivable sales in each department (food, beverage, spa, etc.) is the same as the total charged on all the folios. This work is done with the hand transcript (see Exhibit 13–11).

The Hand Transcript

The PMS accumulates a running total of departmental charge sales as each sale takes place. The manual system waits until night to obtain the same totals. Auditors use a *daily transcript of accounts receivable* to distribute folio posting into separate columns. Each column represents the charge sales earned by a particular department. Once separated, the total sales of each department, obtained from the departmental control sheets (see Chapter 10), can be compared to the total sales posted to all the folios, obtained from the appropriate column of the transcript. "Once separated" is the operative phrase.

Let's review the steps of the manual audit. The night auditors post all vouchers that arrive before the closeout hour. They record room rates and taxes on each folio. They add the folios and carry the balances forward (see Exhibit 13–1). Next comes the transcript.

Each folio is removed from the well and copied in room-number sequence onto a large spreadsheet, the transcript (Exhibit 13–11). The horizontal lines of the folios (room, food, beverage, spa, etc.) appear as vertical columns on the transcript. This procedures separates the charges of each folio. Doing so allows the capture of the folio totals by departments.

➤*The Premise.*   When all the folios, including the day's departures, are copied onto the transcript—and that may take several transcript sheets—the night audit is back to the basic premise: Do the totals of the columns, which are the sum of the postings to the individual folios, agree to the charges originating in the departments, as shown on the control sheets?

Although the form of the control sheet differs somewhat in the several departments (in some instances, only the cash register tape is available), the method of proving departmental charges is identical department to department.

Vouchers from the various departments arrive at the desk all during the day. After being posted, each voucher is marked to lessen the chance of duplicating the charge. Next, the checks (vouchers) are sorted by departments—a job made easier with different colors for each department—and filed into pigeonholes. There they remain for the night auditor, who totals them on an adding machine. The adding machine tape is then attached to the pile of vouchers.

Three different totals are available to the auditor for each department:

1. The total derived from the departmental control sheet. Each time a guest charges a departmental service to the folio, the departmental cashier makes an entry on the control sheet. At the end of the day, this sheet is totaled and forwarded to the night auditor.

2. The total on the adding machine tape of the individual vouchers, which have arrived at the desk one at a time. These are the communicative devices between the departmental cashier and the front-office billing clerk.

3. The total posted to the folio for that department. This total is the sum of the postings made to the folios. The auditor gets that value from the departmental column of the transcript.

If the system is in balance, the departmental control sheet (which records the event) has a total equal to the tape of the vouchers (which communicate the event) and to the sum of the folios (the ultimate record of the event). If the three totals agree, the auditors move to the next department. There, the three comparisons are made again.

➤*The Search.*   The audit begins in earnest when any one of the values fails to reconcile. If two of the three agree, the search concentrates on the unequal total. There are several likely causes.

Mathematical mistakes account for a very large portion of the errors. The major ones—slides, transpositions, and additions—were explained earlier in the chapter.

A control sheet total larger than the other two totals suggests a voucher (check) was lost enroute from the department to the desk. It was never posted. Had the voucher been posted and then lost, the voucher total would be the smallest of the three.

Sometimes several columns of the transcript (food and beverage, for example) are smaller than the corresponding control sheets and vouchers, which are in agreement. Most likely a folio was stuck in the well and never appeared on the transcript. Such an omission impacts several departments. Simple oversights like this seem less simple in the early morning hours. Then, a check omitted from the departmental control sheet or a voucher filed before it was posted means long minutes of searching by the weary auditor.

Vouchers posted to the correct department but to the wrong guest account will not be evident to the auditor. All three totals will agree even though the wrong guest account is charged. This is not so with the reverse situation—when the charge is made to the proper folio but posted to the wrong department. Let's use a food-and-beverage example again. Assume a restaurant charge appears on the transcript in the beverage column. (The error might originate with the clerk's original folio posting, or the auditors might mistakenly copy from the folio to the wrong transcript column.) The food column total of the transcript would be smaller than the voucher and control sheet totals, which would be in agreement. The total of the beverage column is the clue to the error. That total will be larger than the voucher and control sheet totals by the same difference as the restaurant column was smaller.

One error special to the manual audit is particularly difficult to find. It occurs when the original voucher is misposted by the desk. The charge is recorded on the folio of a stayover guest but in a previous date's column. That's what would happen if the $6 bar charge of Exhibit 13–1 had been posted in the October 5 (10/5) column instead of in the 10/6 column. The figure never makes it to the transcript because it doesn't even appear as that day's business. Transcript totals that are smaller than voucher and control sheet totals highlight the problem. Finding it requires the auditor to sort vouchers by room-number sequence and compare each voucher to the transcript column, which is also by room-number sequence. Matching vouchers and transcript entries uncovers the mistake.

Finding and correcting errors is difficult because manual audits have numerous flubs. Mistakes are compounded, so simple column differences are often no clue at all.

It's easy to forget that reconciling the three balances is not the purpose of the audit. Reconciling balances is only a means to the end. As each error is uncovered, the record must be corrected. Either the folio is changed or departmental sales are restated, or both. Making the corrections ensures the guest of an accurate billing and determines the exact revenues of each department. As errors are uncovered, corrections are made and the audit moves to the next department.

▶**Proving Room Charges.**   Room charges originate at the front desk. That's different from other departmental charges (food, beverage, spas, etc.), which originate some distance from the desk. Vouchers are not needed to communicate room charges, so there is no departmental control sheet. The room columns of the transcript (income, occupancy, and house count—columns 6, 2, and 3 of Exhibit 13–11) are tested against the room rack, not against vouchers and control sheets.

Basic information that appears on the folios, and thus eventually on the transcript, is identical to that contained in the room rack. Both the rack and the hand-prepared folio have their origins in the same registration card. That duplication enables the auditors to prove the three transcript columns from the room rack. A *room count sheet*, which is a manual version of the computerized *room status list*, is prepared from the room rack (see Exhibit 13–12). This form goes by other names, including *daily rooms report* or *night clerk's report*. From the room count sheet, the auditor obtains a list of occupied rooms, the number of persons in each room, and the rate charged. Grand totals from the room count sheet are compared to grand totals on the transcript, columns 2, 3, and 6.

The Housekeeper's Report.   Further verification of room status comes from the housekeeper's report. Housekeeping forwards that report to the desk once or twice daily. Using generally accepted abbreviations (see Exhibit 13–13), housekeeping reports room status to the desk. Occupied rooms are reported with checkmarks (✓). Sleep-outs, rooms with baggage but no occupants, are flagged with a B. Occupied rooms with no baggage or light baggage get an X mark. Other codes mix handwritten and alphanumeric symbols.

The housekeeper's report to the desk (see Exhibit 13–14) is a composite report. Each floor housekeeper reports on the status of his or her floor (see Exhibit 13–15) from actual visits to the rooms. Discrepancies between room status at the desk and the final housekeeper's report must be resolved. If they cannot be resolved easily by telephone, someone (bellperson, housekeeper, credit manager) must be dispatched to the room. Credit managers are especially interested in reports of light luggage, in discrepancies in the number of occupants and in potential skippers—X-marked rooms.

The second report of the day, the afternoon report, is the chief means of uncovering sleepers, skippers, and whos. *Sleepers* are guests who have checked out, but are still being carried as if the room were occupied. *Skippers* are guests who have left without checking out, without paying. *Whos* are unknown guests—someone is occupying a room but the desk doesn't know who it is.

Exhibit 13–13
Communication between the front desk and housekeeping use alphabetic and numeric symbols to report on the status of rooms (see Exhibit 13–14).

Baggage: no occupant (sleep-out)	B
Check out: room on change	c/o
Cot	C
Do not disturb	DND
Double-locked room	DL
Early arrival	EA
No service wanted (Do not disturb)	NS
Occupied	✓
Occupied, but dirty	OD
Occupied, with light baggage or no baggage	X
OK	ok
Out of order	O (also OOO)
Out of inventory	OOI
Permanent guest	P
Ready for sale	/
Refused service	RS
Stayover	s/o
Stayover, no service	SNS
Vacant	V (also no symbol at all)
Vacant and dirty (on change)	VD

Exhibit 13–14
The housekeeper's office (the linen room) uses the symbols of Exhibit 13–13 to report room status to the desk. The housekeeper's report is compiled from the floor reports (see Exhibit 13–15) submitted to the linen room by the room attendants.

HOUSEKEEPER'S DAILY REPORT

Kayco Form No. 1209   DATE _10-6_____ 19 ___

ROOM NO.	OCCUPIED	VACANT	BAGGAGE	BED USED	ROOM NO.	OCCUPIED	VACANT	BAGGAGE	BED USED	ROOM NO.	OCCUPIED	VACANT	BAGGAGE	BED USED
2529	/				3517		/			4211	%			
2530	/				3518	/				4212	%			
2531		%			3519	/				4213		/		
2532					3520	/				4214	ρ			
2533			B		3521	/				4215				/
2534	/				3522		%			4216		/		
2535	/													

The housekeeper's report is used even if room status is maintained electronically with a PMS. Internal control is difficult in a small hotel, where the desk is staffed by one person who sells the room, collects the money, and posts the record. The housekeeper's report was originally furnished to the income auditor. Having a second party compare the room status at the front office to the independently prepared housekeeper's report established a degree of internal control. It is still important for the small hotel! As front offices grow larger and departmentalize, the internal control function of the housekeeper's report diminishes.

Property management systems have helped eliminate the old and irritating way of verifying occupancy by banging on the guest-room door. Indeed, the PMS has actually reversed the flow of the housekeeper's report. *A room occupancy status report* is prepared during the night audit for housekeeping, which gets its copy early in the morning. This preworkday report on the status of rooms speeds the work of the housekeeper. Room attendants are assigned early in the day, so they begin work immediately. With early knowledge of the room count, the housekeeper refines the work schedule, calling in extras or scheduling days off for full-time staff. This reverse housekeeper's report also communicates guest complaints, ensuring that they get attention early in the day.

The housekeeper's report alerts the desk to special circumstances. Among these are double-locked rooms (DL) and do not disturb rooms (DND) that remain unchanged between the morning and afternoon reports. Floor attendants mark these rooms NS, not serviced, or RS, guest refused service (see Exhibit 13–13). Wise hotel managers telephone such rooms before the day has passed to verify the condition of the occupant. If no one answers the call, the room is entered in the company of security or housekeeping.

▶*Balancing the Transcript's Mathematics.*   Property management systems monitor their own mathematics, but a manual, pencil-and-paper transcript requires a mathematical check of additions and subtractions. *Crossfooting,* which is adding horizontally across the transcript totals, ensures the mathematical accuracy of all lines of the transcript. A review of the several steps in the manual audit will explain why crossfooting works.

Exhibit 13–15
The room attendants of the housekeeping department complete floor reports, which are consolidated into the housekeeper's report (see Exhibit 13–14).

Floor Report

Floor # _16_

01	V	28	RS
02	V	29	✓
03	✓	30	✓
04	✓	31	OOO
05	B	32	V
06	✓	33	X
07	✓	34	C
08	V	35	✓
09	V	36	✓
10	DND	37	✓

27	✓	54	✓

Code:
V = Vacant	RS = Refuse Service
B = Baggage	DND = Do Not Disturb
X = No Baggage	C = Cot
✓ = Occupied	EA = Early Arrival

Step 1: The night auditor posts room charges and taxes to the folios.

Step 2: The folios are totaled and the balances carried forward to the next day.

Step 3: Folios are copied onto the transcript. Within the figures are errors created by steps 1 and 2 and errors made during the day by the desk cashiers. Among the mathematical errors will be slides and transpositions, inaccurate figures, oversights, duplications, and mistakes in addition and subtraction. The audit is designed to uncover all these errors.

Step 4: The total of each transcript column is proved against other documents, as explained earlier, chiefly control sheets, vouchers, cash sheets, and the room count sheet. Corrections are made on the transcript and on the folio as errors are uncovered. This verification ensures the mathematical accuracy of all the departmental columns, which are vertical columns 6 through 19, except column 16 (see Exhibit 13–11).

Step 5: The opening balance columns, vertical columns 4 and 5, are now verified. Unlike columns 6 to 15, columns 4 and 5 are not income columns, so there are neither control sheets nor vouchers. The opening balance of each folio is the guest's cumulative debt, carried forward from yesterday. Therefore, the opening balances of today (columns 4 and 5, debit and credit) are compared to the closing balances of yesterday, yesterday's transcript columns 21 and 22.

The guest goes to bed the previous night owing columns 21 and 22 of yesterday's transcript and awakens the following morning owing the same exact amounts, now reflected in columns 4 and 5 of the new day. If today's opening balance does not agree with yesterday's closing balance—perhaps a folio has been left off today's transcript—a search begins for the discrepancy.

Step 6: Crossfoot (horizontally add) the totals of columns 6 to 15 to obtain a value. If the transcript is in balance, that value will equal the total of vertical column 16. This can be understood by doing the very same thing on any one horizontal line. Columns 6 to 15 on any horizontal line must equal column 16 of that line. Therefore, crossfooting the grand totals of columns 6 to 15 should equal the sum obtained by vertically adding column 16. (The total should equal the sum of its parts.)

If the sum of all the columns does not equal the total of column 16, there is an error on one or more of the horizontal lines, which is, of course, someone's folio. [That folio was added by the night auditor (step 2) and copied onto the transcript (step 3). Obviously, it was added or copied incorrectly.] Each horizontal line must be crossfooted until the mathematical error or errors that contributed to the total error is uncovered. Once uncovered, column 16 of that line will be changed, and since that line represents a folio—the line of figures was copied from the folio—the folio itself must also be corrected.

Step 7: Verify the three credits. Previous discussions have stressed the three methods of settling folios: cash, allowances, and transfers. Credit column 17 is the cash settlement and that transcript total is compared to the receipts reported on the cashiers' front-office cash sheets. (Similarly, disbursements on those sheets must agree to the cash disbursement column, column 13 of Exhibit 13–11.)

Column 18, allowances, is compared to the sum of the allowance vouchers granted at the desk that day. Column 19 is the most common credit, since it includes credit-card transfers. It is tested against column 14, transfer debits, because transfer credits and debits must always equal. Since most of column 19's transfers (transfers credit) are to the city ledger, balancing with column 14 (transfers debit) requires that the cumulative balance of the city ledger also be reported on the transcript. Exhibit 13–11 shows the equality, but the city ledger is abbreviated at the bottom of the exhibit.

Column 20, which is blank in Exhibit 13–11, is missing on many transcripts. It might be used for advanced deposit credits if the hotel's clientele commonly used them, but that's very rare. More likely, it would be used to total credit columns 17, 18, and 19. As such, it would represent the sum of all credits as column 16 represents the sum of the day's debits (charges).

Step 8: Crossfoot and mathematically balance the entire transcript. First obtain the net opening balance by subtracting column 5, opening credit balance, from column 4, opening debit balance. To that difference add the total of column 16, which was tested by step 6. These total charges are next reduced by payments (credits), the sum of columns 17, 18, and 19 (or perhaps column 20; see step 7). The result is the net amount owed by accounts receivable.

Recall the pea analogy. Opening inventory (column 4 minus column 5) plus new purchases (column 16) minus peas used (columns 17, 18, 19) equals peas still on hand—or accounts receivable owed; that is, column 21 minus column 22.

The transcript is a summary of accounts receivable, a summary of folios. The closing balance represents the total amount that all accounts receivable owe the hotel at the close of the day. It's possible for the hotel to owe one or more guests temporarily, so some lines (folios) will have credit balances, probably as a result of advanced deposits. For two different examples, see column 2 (10/6) of Exhibit 13–1 and the third horizontal line of Exhibit 13–11, column 22.

Step 9: Vertical addition is easier to visualize than horizontal crossfooting. It's just a more traditional way to do the mathematics. Then the proof, or the formula as it is sometimes called, looks like this (see Exhibit 13–11, line 2):

Opening balance, column 4 minus 5 (debit minus credit)	$63.60
+Charges and services used by guests, column 16 (debits)	39.60
−Payments made by guests, columns 17 to 19 (credits)	−0−
=Closing balance, column 21 minus 22 (debit minus credit)	$103.20

The closing balance is the cumulative balance of guests' debt to the hotel and is a debit balance.

The math can also be done by having column 16 represent the running total (see Exhibit 13–11, line 1). Then the formula would look different:

Opening balance, column 4 minus 5 (debit minus credit)	$19.00CR
+ Charges and services used by guests, columns 6 to 15 (debits)	89.00DR
= Total, column 16 (cumulative debit balance before payments of the day)	70.00DR
– Payments made by guests, column 17 to 19 (credits)	–0–
= Closing balance, column 21 minus 22 (debit minus credit)	70.00

The result of the two approaches is the same. The difference is the handling of column 16. Some auditors use column 16 to reflect only the day's debits, as the top formula illustrates. Other auditors use column 16 to reflect the cumulative balance, including the balances of yesterday, the bottom illustration. Whichever is selected reflects the procedure used on the folios because the transcript is a copy of the folios.

RESOURCES AND CHALLENGES
Resources

➤ SUMMARY

Accounts receivable, what guests owe the hotel, grow larger or smaller as guests buy new services or pay down debt. Hotels verify the balances of these accounts receivable (front-office folios) nightly. That procedure is known as the night audit. The audit provides a snapshot of values at the closeout hour—midnight, more or less—of each hotel's day.

Since every accounting transaction has equal debits and credits, each service purchased or debt payment made has an offsetting record. The offset is an equal and opposite entry. Two things happen if, for example, a guest charges a bar drink to the folio. The guest owes more and the bar earned more. An audit focusing on the accuracy of the guest's debt (account receivable) must obviously consider the value of the bar charge. The night audit is designed to prove that each transaction was recorded on a guest folio and that each folio entry is accounted for by some transaction.

Cash sales in the various outlets (restaurants, lounges, and gift shops, for example) do not affect accounts receivable. Only charge sales appear on folios. Cash sales are combined with charge sales by the income (or day) auditors, and the total is reported on the daily report to the manager. Night auditors report charge sales, but only charge sales, in the night auditor's report to the manager.

Hotels maintain a cumulative value of receivables, tracking them just as they inventory other assets—cans of peas, for example. The opening balance of accounts receivable is increased by guest purchases and decreased by guest payments. This closing balance becomes the start of the next day's computation. Thus comes a rolling balance of receivables: some days larger, some days smaller.

Computerized property management systems (PMSs) have replaced manual paper-and-pencil night audits. The result has been improved speed and accuracy both at the desk and during the audit, but especially when posting nightly room charges. Property management systems have done the job so well that additional tasks have been added to what started out as a bookkeeping system. Other technological linkups are being added as the industry adopts a standardized system, Hospitality Information Technology Integration Standards (HITIS). Chapter 14 enlarges on the increasing capacity of the PMS and hints of robotics yet to come.

➤ WEB SITES

Micros Fidelity–PMS provider: http://www.micros.com

Springer-Miller Systems–PMS provider: http://www.smshost.com

Execu/Tech–PMS provider: www.execu-tech.com

HVS International–A wide variety of readings, including executive reports, global reports, and the Rushmore Letter: http://www.hvsinternational.com

Web Site Assignment

Using the Web sites of three different PMS providers, either those given or others, prepare a list of accessory programs that electronic systems support besides that of the night audit. Identify both the product and the supplier.

➤ INTERESTING TIDBITS

➤ An electronic audit for a 1,000-room hotel takes less than one hour. A mechanical audit with the NCR 4200 (the last of the mechanical machines) took a crew of five persons the better part of an eight-hour shift.

➤ "We print out every night 5,000 pages of reports out of our systems, and let me tell you how much of that is used: the bare minimum. . . ." Dominic Van Nes, Director of Information Services, Pebble Beach Resorts. *H&MM*, November 16, 1998, p. 29.

➤ Lucius Boomer, president of the Hotel Waldorf-Astoria Corporation, explained the application of the earliest National Cash Register equipment to the night audit in Appendix D "Machine Bookkeeping," *Hotel Management* (New York: Harper & Brothers, 1925). Ralph Hitz, president of the National Hotel Management Company, did the same in *Standard Practice Manuals for Hotel Operation*, v. vi, "Audit and Control Division," p. 21. (New York: Harper & Brothers Publishers, 1935).

➤ Installing a PMS was a great uncertainty when the MGM Grand (now Bally's) opened in Las Vegas. Management was so uncertain of its reliability that a dozen NCR 4200 machines were purchased as backup. They were never used. Similarly, electronic locks were rejected initially, but installed later at extra cost.

➤ READING REFERENCES

CKC Report, The Hotel Technology Newsletter. Published 10 times annually by Chervenak, Keane & Company, New York, CKCWorld@aol.com.

Hospitality Information Technology: Learning How To Use It. Galen Collins and Tarum Malik. Dubuque, Iowa: Kendall/Hunt, 2004.

Managing Computers in the Hospitality Industry. Michael Kasavana and John Cahill. East Lansing, Michigan: Educational Institute of the AH&LA, 2001.

Challenges

➤ TRUE/FALSE

Questions that are partially false should be marked false (F).

___ 1. *Hard copy* is part of the professional language, referring to the tough stance taken by late-arriving guests when they discover their reservations have been given away and will not be honored.

___ 2. *Exception reporting* highlights issues that veer from the norm, saving management precious time that would otherwise be spent in reviewing normal data.

___ 3. *Turnkey* is a reference to prison guards; hence, turnkey computer systems are those with special protection from hackers.

___ 4. *Zip-out check-out* is available only if guests use credit cards or direct billing.

___ 5. *On change* indicates bed linens in the room of a permanent guest are to be changed; permanent guests have linens changed every three days, not daily.

➤ PROBLEMS

1. Explain how the three backup reports discussed in the section "Downtime Reports" would be used in the event of a computer malfunction.

2. A guest checks in at 4:30 AM on Tuesday, January 8. Under hotel policy, the guest is to be charged for the room-night of Monday, January 7. The closeout hour of Monday, January 7, was 12:30 AM, January 8, and the room charge postings were handled automatically by the PMS at approximately 3 AM on that morning. The room rate is $72 and the tax is 5%; no other charges were incurred. Sketch a computer-prepared folio as it would appear when the guest departs on Wednesday, January 9, at 10 AM. Identify each posting by day and hour and briefly explain who made which posting.

3. **Given**

Rooms occupied	440
Rooms vacant	160
Total rooms sales	$32,330
House count	500

   Required

The percentage of occupancy	_____
The percentage of double occupancy	_____
ADR	_____
RevPar	_____

4. Use Exhibits 13–3 and 13–11, and identify your answers by room numbers.
   a. Which guests, if any, arrived today?
   b. Which guests, if any, had advanced deposits?
   c. Which guests, if any, checked out today?

d. Which guests, if any, used credit cards at departure?

e. Which guests, if any, had amounts due from the hotel?

5. The discussion on reservation reports cites a central reservation report that includes fees. Explain who pays what fees and to whom. About how much might those fees be? (Refer to earlier chapters if necessary.)

6. Is the transcript in balance? If not, what error or errors might account for the discrepancy? What percentage of sales tax is being charged in this community?

Allowances	$ 100.00
Telephone	670.70
Transfers to	395.05
Rooms	9,072.00
Cash advance	444.25
Debit transfer	395.50
Beverage	1,920.00
Credit-card charges	14,482.07
Cash	10,071.22
Closing balance	3,670.41
Opening balance	48,341.50
Rooms tax	725.76
Food	3,000.10
Closing balance	43,007.33
Opening balance	185.00
Total charges	$64,384.81

➤ ANSWERS TO TRUE/FALSE QUIZ

1. False. *Hard copy* refers to a printed form or report in contrast to one that appears on a computer screen. Paper file copies made from a computer are hard copies.

2. True. *Exception reporting* is just what the question says: Special cases (rather than every case) that differ from the standard are reported to management for further investigation and action.

3. False. *Turnkey* systems are those ready to be used without additional work or pro-gramming. Users have merely to turn the key to get started.

4. True. *Zip-out check-out* is completed without the service of hotel personnel, so payment has to be on account: by credit card or company-direct billing. Payment by cash or check isn't possible.

5. False. *On change* refers to the status of a guest room awaiting service from housekeeping after a previous guest has checked out. When housekeeping is finished, room status changes to "ready."

CHAPTER 14

Technology and the Hotel Industry

Outline

From wireless handheld terminals and ASP-software at the front desk to high-speed Internet access and improved smart-card doorlock security in the guest room, the industry is experiencing nothing less than a revolution in lodging technology applications. Successful managers are necessarily adding another skill to their laundry list of tasks and abilities. Along with customer service, resource management, industry and company public relations, employee relations, and the like, today's managers also need to be techno-savvy users and investors.

The hospitality industry is maturing in its use and investment in technology. What used to be considered "technology for the sake of technology" (because hotels were notorious buyers of products that either failed to work as promised or simply provided no benefit to the operation) has changed over the last few years. Many products foisted on hotels in the mid- to late 1990s are now represented by companies that are either out of business or simply no longer support a product they once sold. As revenues are negatively impacted by stiff competition and increasing use of the Internet, energy and related operating costs continue to rise, and profits are squeezed at every property, hotel operators need to make the most out of every dollar invested in technology.

As such, industry experts are generally advising managers to maximize their existing technologies before looking and investing elsewhere. This advice is especially appropriate for novice managers who have unrealized potential residing on their existing software applications. Talking with current providers about enhanced capabilities related to their property management, call accounting, energy management, electronic locking, and other interfaced systems is an important first step toward saving money and maximizing efficiencies.

Additional recommendations suggest any new technological application must ultimately impact the guest. Technologies visible to the guest or those that provide a higher level of service should top any list when investment dollars are scarce. In addition to impacting the guest experience, new applications should enhance revenues or boost bottom-line profits. And standalone applications are out of favor—new technologies must interface with existing applications and provide some level of synergy to their current use.

This chapter offers a look at some of the major categories of software and hardware applications found at almost any hotel in America.

➤ INTEGRATED CALL ACCOUNTING SYSTEMS

Not so many years ago, hotel operators viewed guest-room telephones as profit centers. The in-room telephone was a convenience for which the guest was expected to pay. In order to stay in touch with the office, home, family, and friends, the guest depended on the in-room guest telephone.

Today, with close to 65% of all business travelers carrying a laptop computer, the in-room telephone is more than just something to talk through. Unfortunately, many hoteliers have not understood this subtle change in the role of the guest-room telephone, so not all hotel guests are getting what they need inside the room. What they need is a connectivity solution—what they get is an old-fashioned telecommunications solution. We are witnessing that change in purpose and product across the industry today.

With the prevalence of wide-range cellular phones and discounted long-distance calling cards, hotels are lucky if the guest even touches the in-room telephone. Oh, they'll use it to call another in-house department, another guest room, or maybe even a toll-free access number. But certainly they are not using the in-room telephone to the extent (and profitability) of yesteryear.

To understand the dynamics of in-house PBX and guest room telephone departments today, let's take a look back over the evolution of the guest room telephone.

Telephones have been used in hotel rooms since the first were installed in New York City's Netherland Hotel in 1894.[1] Initially, they were manual systems requiring hotel operators to physically connect incoming analog signals via a PBX switchboard system. In 1930, the New Yorker hotel employed 92 manual switchboard telephone operators. That was expensive labor, but full-service hotels correctly viewed the telephone department as a crucial service, and the labor cost was usually offset by telephone department profits.

Years later, manual telephone switchboards gave way to automated call accounting systems, which not only route calls automatically, but identify long-distance and access charges for outgoing calls and interface the entire system with the hotel's property management system (PMS). Automated call accounting systems (CAS) allow a hotel like the New Yorker (today it is the Ramada Inn & Plaza New Yorker Hotel) to reduce its telephone operator workforce from a high of 92 in 1930 to just 9 operators today.

Communications Architecture

The CAS, energy management system (EMS), and electronic locking system (ELS) are the three most common interfaces that operate in conjunction with the PMS. Although such systems can readily stand alone, the synergies gained through an interface with the PMS are so great that almost all hotels (especially larger properties) have such interfaces. In-room movies or entertainment, self-check-in and self-check-out systems, in-room safes, and in-room minibar or beverage units are additional examples of PMS interfaces.

In most cases, each of these interfaced systems stands alone with its own processing capabilities. The interface or connection between the standalone system (for example, the EMS) and the PMS provides an uninterrupted flow of guest information. An EMS interface, for example, allows the front-desk PMS to monitor room activity; shut off heating systems and nonessential lighting in unoccupied rooms; and adjust water temperatures as a function of occupancy. Although the EMS is a complete system with its own input, output, and processing, it functions better with a communication interface to the PMS.

▶ *Uniform Connectivity.* The history of interface connectivity is one of hit and miss, trial and error. In the 1970s, there were close to 100 vendors of PMSs and numerous manufacturers of point-of-sale (POS) systems, call accounting systems, back-office accounting systems, and guest history databases.

An unsophisticated hotel operator could easily purchase a PMS, POS, and CAS from three separate vendors. Of course, each salesperson promised his or her system would interface with the other systems. Yet months later, the frustrated hotel operator could find no company willing to take responsibility for the interface. The POS vendor blamed the PMS vendor who blamed the CAS vendor, and so on.

There are plenty of horror stories about hotel operators who spent thousands of dollars on software programming to get one system to electronically interface with an-

[1]Donald E. Lundberg, *Inside Innkeeping* (Dubuque, IA: William C. Brown Company, Publishers, 1956), p. 91.

other. Many times, however, the hotel was left with a dysfunctional system. Downtime was common, the interface slowed the processing speed of each system, and valuable data was lost between the source system and the PMS. This last problem was the worst of all, because hotel revenue (say, from a CAS) was forever lost between systems!

The problem of incompatible interfaces has mostly been eradicated with today's state-of-the-art technologies. Practically every PMS has the capacity to interface with almost every auxiliary system. Indeed, if a property has a standalone system that has never been previously interfaced to a particular brand of PMS, the PMS vendor will often provide free interface software programming. This is a marketing approach many PMS vendors use to enable them to add another system to their list of compatible products. This has been so successful that there are few PMS system–auxiliary system incompatibilities anymore.

New properties have the best of all worlds. Technology managers can choose various interface systems (CAS, EMS, etc.) based on the beneficial synergy each may offer (price, support, guest history, or some other operational feature) without being overly concerned with the interface compatibility between systems.

Standardization.   In 1994, a consortium of hospitality vendors began establishing a standard platform against which all hardware, software, databases, and communication formats must conform. Although conformity is voluntary, such standardization platforms have performed well in other industries.

Unfortunately, the lodging industry, with its myriad of competitors, has had less success bringing standardization to market than other industries. The problem is that standardization is only as strong as the number of vendors who comply voluntarily. In fact, since 1994, three separate attempts have been made to bring standardization to the lodging industry. In 1994, the Integrating Technology Consortium (ITC) was created. In 1996, Microsoft started the Windows Hospitality Interface Standards (WHIS) initiative. And in 1997, the AH&LA convened the Hospitality Industry Technology Interface Standards (HITIS) committee.

Once HITIS is fully introduced, it will become the standard for industry purchases of technological hardware and software. By joining the voluntary consortium, vendors will be entitled to promote their products as complying with industry standards. That's a powerful message because hoteliers who purchase noncomplying products would be at risk.

Data Browsing.   Standardization may reach the industry from an unusual direction: It may be market driven. The increasing consolidation of major chains, which we noted in Chapter 1, has accelerated the standardization of PMSs. How long this trend will continue is hard to know, but the results are already evident. In terms of technological capacity, the hospitality industry is quite mature. Hundreds of millions of dollars have been invested year after year to ensure that individual and chain properties are wired. They have successfully automated every stage from check-in to check-out. That's the problem—too much "data" but not enough "information."

The successful competitor of the future will be the chain that strategically utilizes guest history information (generated by the PMS and its interfaces) and turns it into worthwhile and marketable information. To that end, a standardization of PMSs makes good sense. Chains have an easier time browsing warehoused data (corporate data browsers are usually Internet-based) when each property in the organization stores information in a like manner—standardization.

Cendant, the world's largest franchising organization (Amerihost Inns, Days Inn, Fairfield, Howard Johnson, Knights Inn, Ramada, Super 8, Travelodge, Villager

Lodge, and Wingate Inns), implemented a 75 million dollar standardization program across all properties several years ago. The new standardized property management system—at no charge to the individual franchisees—replaced over 60 different PMS systems in use chainwide at that time.

Once the standardized systems are completely installed, the parent organization will uniformly be able to

➤ Ensure that all revenues are reported accurately

➤ Browse data at the property, regional, national, and international levels

➤ Display like rooms inventory screens and last-room availability information to central reservationists

➤ Create central databases for warehousing such programs as guest history, frequent-guest and frequent-flyer programs, corporate and group activity, and travel agent accounts

A Brief History of Hotel Telephone Service

Bear with us—we think you'll find this brief history of hotel telephone service as interesting as we do. While reading it, consider the players involved—big business (AT&T, OCCs, and the like), the guest, and the hotel—and ask yourself how certain hotel telephone department profitability decisions negatively impacted the guest. With hindsight, would you have made the same decision? Do you think past mistakes are to blame for today's current plight (most guests only use in-room telephones to get onto the Internet via a local access number or for nonrevenue inhouse calls)?

In 1944, the Federal Communications Commission (FCC) approved a proposal that was to structure the economic relationship between the hotel industry and the telephone industry for almost four decades. The ruling required telephone companies to pay hotels a 15% commission for all long-distance calls originating in hotel rooms. As expected, this rule expedited the general introduction of telephones into American hotels. Despite the success, the two industries battled about the size of the commission almost from the start. Hotels argued that the fee was too low to offset costs and earn a fair profit. AT&T countered by arguing that the department was really a customer amenity and shouldn't be considered a profit center.

The year 1981 was another critical date. Once again, the federal government acted to restructure the system. Within a short time, three traumas rocked the telephone industry. First, the large, integrated Bell system was dissolved, its long-distance service separated from its local operations. Second, competition from other manufacturers and service companies was invited in, weakening the monopoly still further. And third, hotels were permitted once again to levy their own fees on calls originating from their premises. The 1944 commission schedule had been rescinded.

On June 1, 1981, the FCC ruled that hotels could make their own surcharges on interstate calls, just as they had done prior to 1944. A stroke of the pen undid a 37-year experiment. Before the year was out, the Bell system had an announcement of its own: Commissions (estimated in 1981 at $230 million annually) would no longer be paid. Bell's decision was not mandated by the FCC. It was a business decision, and it was a gutsy one at that, since the new federal policy encouraged competition against the Bell system.

A series of court pronouncements destroyed once and for all the concept of the telephone as a utility. Competition was encouraged, and it appeared on the scene with some appealing deals. By an earlier court decision, the Carterfone Case allowed non-Bell equipment to be interconnected with Bell equipment.[2]

Motivated by a great deal of uncertainty and an equal lack of information, the AH&LA negotiated a year's delay with the Bell system. The 15% commission, which had caused such strident arguments earlier, looked awfully good in the face of uncertainty. Commissions were paid until December 31, 1982, while the hotel industry shopped for alternatives.

▶ ***Historical Billing Procedures.***   Before automation, the guest's telephone request was completed by the hotel's operator, who dialed the local call. Long-distance numbers were passed on to the telephone company operator, who dialed that connection. The front office posted to the guest folio from a voucher forwarded by the hotel's telephone operator. Local calls were billed at a fixed amount per state regulations. Long-distance charges were called in by the telephone company operator after the call was completed.

Long-Distance Billing.   Semiautomation came first to long-distance (LD) billing. The first development allowed guests to bypass the hotel operator and dial the telephone company's long-distance operator directly. This system also allowed the telephone company to send room charges directly to the hotel by way of teletype.

Hobic.   HOBIC (Hotel Outward Bound Information Center) is an acronym for the telephone company's long-distance network. Even today, HOBIC is the system that guests encounter when they use AT&T's traditional service. HOBIC, the workhorse of the precomputerized system, is still an option for certain hotels (see Exhibit 14–1).

With HOBIC, the guest direct-dials long-distance calls from the room telephone. The first digit dialed, 8, tells the system that long distance is going through. Digit 1, or digit 0 to get the operator, follows; then comes the number to be called. Zero-digit operator intercepts are for person-to-person calls, third-party calls, credit-card calls, and collect calls. The distinction between digit 1 and digit 0 is critical. It dictated the strategy of AT&T following deregulation. The pursuit of that strategy accounted in large measure for the appearance of the alternative operator services (AOS).

Hotel Options Following Deregulation

Following deregulation of the telephone industry in 1981, hoteliers settled down to the task of choosing among several alternatives. That choice sums up the intent of deregulation. Alternatives could be pursued, new telephone companies could be tried, special equipment could be tested, and profits could be made.

With AT&T out of the commission business, the scramble for a viable replacement began. The one-year delay negotiated with the telephone company passed quickly as one plan after the other was suggested. Three options faced the hotel industry.

---

[2]Another landmark case was decided in 1968, when the FCC ruled in favor of Carterfone. In this case, the FCC reversed AT&T's policy which prevented the interconnection of private telephones to AT&T equipment. This opened the door to a new industry of equipment sales as opposed to the lease-only policy that AT&T was trying to protect.

PBX Market Share in Hospitality Industry

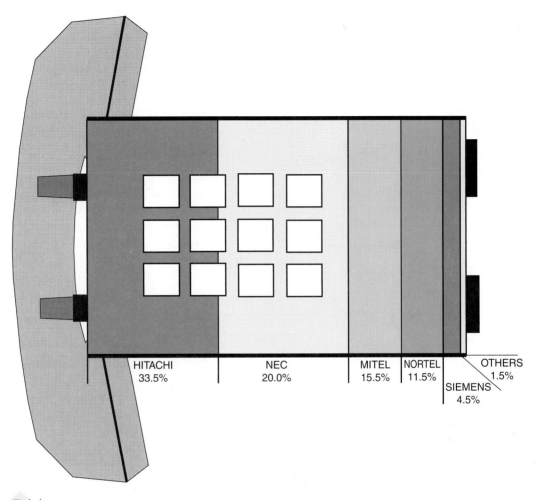

Exhibit 14–1   When purchasing PBX systems, hotels look for a system life cycle of 8 to 12 years. Therefore, successful vendors (like those shown here) have a history of providing support, software interfaces, and upgrades to current platforms for years and years.

First and foremost, PBX systems must provide seamless integration to existing property management systems. When guests check in, the hotel wants their telephone and voice-messaging services to activate automatically. Likewise, upon check-out, such services need to deactivate. In that way, telephones in unoccupied rooms will allow internal calls only. This restricts the potential for housekeeping employees to waste time and money making local and long-distance telephone calls in unoccupied rooms. *Source: Hotel & Motel Management. January 15, 2001.*

➤*First Option: Status Quo.*   A very workable option, but one that was initially ignored, was to maintain the status quo. Keeping the HOBIC system of AT&T, which was in place and working very well, would cost nothing. No heavy investment in capital equipment, no new training for front-office personnel, and no change in guest habits would be required. The equipment and procedures were still

Bell's, so the infrastructure and support of the telephone company were still there. This plan required the hotel to levy its own commission.

The do-nothing decision proved a wise one for the small hotel. It provided the luxury of time to examine what was happening elsewhere. After the fact, many larger hotels wished they, too, had waited. Some decisions proved disastrous.

▶*Second Option: Install a Call Accounting System.*   The same technology that AT&T was using—HOBIC—was available for hotel use in the form of a microprocessor called AIOD. AIOD, *automatic identification of outward dialing*, enabled the hotel to identify the calling guest's room number without an operator intercept from the telephone company. Charges went through at direct-distance dialing (DDD) rates rather than operator-assisted rates. AIOD was installed on hotel switchboards, but not without difficulty.

Through a number of trunk lines, the PBX (private branch exchange) connects the numerous internal lines to various outside telephone systems. But PBX switchboards are not all created equal; some are smart and others are dumb.

With smart switches in place, additional equipment, such as AIOD or least cost routers (LCR), could be installed with little cost and difficulty (see Exhibit 14–2).

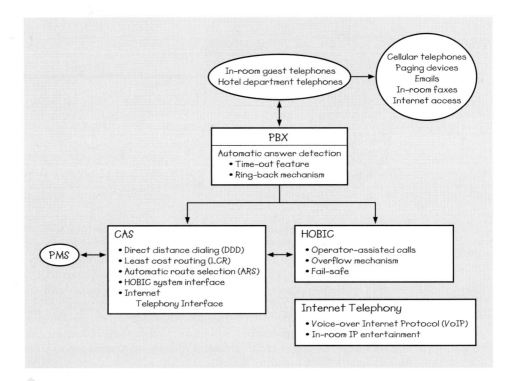

Exhibit 14–2   A graphical representation of the call accounting system. Note the increasing role of Internet telephony, in-room faxes, emails, and Internet access.

By the way, the automatic answer-detection function offers two distinct possibilities. The time-out feature (found in older systems) cannot detect when the placed call connects, and it begins charging automatically in 30 to 60 seconds after a standard grace period (usually), even if the placed call is still ringing. In more sophisticated systems, the ring-back mechanism only begins charging after the placed call has actually been answered.

Smart switches allowed the newest PBXs to function with AIOD and LCR as integral parts of the equipment. Additional property management capability could also be handled through the smart boards.

After committing to AIOD, however, many hoteliers learned that they had dumb switchboards. Because dumb switches cannot handle sophisticated functions such as AIOD and LCR, managers now faced a whole series of new decisions about which boards to acquire, from which company, with what options, and with whose money.

▶*Third Option: Shop the Competition.*   Some hotels elected to move beyond call accounting by shopping among other common carriers (OCC), such as MCI and GTE (Sprint), as well as AT&T, for the least expensive long-distance lines (see Exhibit 14–3). To do this, more technology was needed—least cost routing (LCR) equipment. Here the emphasis is on the cost of the call rather than the resale price. With reduced costs, small surcharges, which maintain the hotel's competitiveness, could produce substantial profit gains.

The smart switches of the LCR equipment work in tandem with the smart switches of the call accounting equipment to evaluate each call and to route it over the most economical trunk line. Eventually, the charge finds its way to the folio (see Exhibit 14–4). With this technology in place, the cost of calls has come down, and gross income has gone up.

Exhibit 14–3   An AT&T promotional tent designed to stand near each guest-room telephone. This document informs guests which common carrier (AT&T, in this example) the hotel has selected. Notice that the tent reads "You have the right to reach other long distance carriers from this telephone." *Courtesy of AT&T, Basking Ridge, New Jersey.*

	ROOM	PLACE CALLED		NUMBER	TIME	MIN	TYP	CLASS	RATE
A 2-22	103	LOS ANGELES	CA	213 555-7784	2245	6	1	S	1.51
A 2-22	104	HUNTITNBCH	CA	714 555-7711	1317	3	1	K	1.36
A 2-22	107	WICHITA	KS	316 555-5020	0747	2	1	B	.43
A 2-22	107	VAN NUYS	CA	213 555-7487	0916	2	1	K	.97
A 2-22	107	LEWISTON	ME	207 555-6141	1628	12	1	K	6.13
A 2-22	107	CHICAGO	IL	312 555-5134	1832	7	1	S	1.96
A 2-22	107	CANOGAPARK	CA	213 555-4815	1935	14	1	S	3.39
A 2-22	108	PHOENIX	AZ	602 555-4958	0810	2	1	K	.97
A 2-22	111	ROOPVILLE	GA	404 555-4422	0806	3	1	K	1.52
A 2-22	111	NO HOLLYWD	CA	213 555-9540	0908	1	1	K	.58
A 2-22	114	GREELEY	CO	303 555-5876	1750	38	1	S	9.91
A 2-22	117	STPETERSBG	FL	813 555-1411	1620	4	1	K	2.21
A 2-22	118	OCILLA	GA	912 555-7464	1238	1	1	K	.64
A 2-22	118	HUNTITNBCH	CA	714 555-7243	1801	5	1	S	1.28
A 2-22	125	CANOGAPARK	CA	213 555-4815	1114	8	1	K	3.31
A 2-22	125	CODY	WY	307 555-2245	1131	5	1	K	2.34
A 2-22	202	DRAPER	UT	801 555-5093	1745	3	1	S	.85
A 2-22	203	BOULDER	CO	303 555-1181	0902	7	1	K	3.20
A 2-22	203	LONG BEACH	CA	213 555-8832	1747	8	1	S	1.98
A 2-22	206	BAMMEL	TX	713 555-7580	0811	7	1	K	3.28
A 2-22	206	GREELEY	CO	303 555-7067	1723	10	1	S	2.69
A 2-22	209	FORD CITY	PA	412 555-9600	1656	12	1	K	4.56
A 2-22	210	LITTLETON	CO	303 555-9999	1331	2	1	K	1.05

* * * N24 * * *

Exhibit 14–4   Printout of long-distance charges generated by the call accounting system. Although this printout was produced in numerical room order, it could just as easily have been printed in chronological order beginning with the first call of the day. Note the shift (A, B, or C), the date, and the room number from which the call was placed. Additionally, this printout (sometimes called an on-the-fly call record) shows location and number called, time of day the call was placed, and duration of the call. The system then evaluates the type and class of call to determine the charge assessed the guest. Also note the 555 exchange used to mask actual telephone numbers—you've probably heard it used in television and movies. *Courtesy of Centel, Las Vegas, Nevada.*

►*Wats.*   Like the entire telecommunications industry, wide area telephone (also sometimes transmission) service (WATS) has changed since its introduction. The original concept of one flat monthly fee, for which the user could talk indefinitely at any time, has been modified. Charges are now based on increments of time. Rates vary according to the time of the day and the day of the week.

Hundreds of companies have gone into the resale of WATS lines. They buy long-distance lines from AT&T and other OCCs at quantity discounts and resell to customers at a lower charge than that of the common carriers.

In-WATS (incoming toll-free numbers) have a critical role in the development of central reservation offices, as explained in Chapter 4. It has become quite fashionable to substitute catchy phrases for traditional telephone numbers in an attempt to retain the number in the user's memory (see Exhibit 14–5).

Company Name	Dial the Toll Free Area Code (800, 888, 877, 866, etc.)
Clarion Hotels	Clarion
Club Med	Club Med
Colonial Williamsburg	History
Embassy Suites	Embassy
Harrah's (Atlantic City)	2 Harrah
Hilton Hotels	Hiltons
Marriott Hotels & Resorts	USA WKND
National Car Rental	Car Rent
Nikko Hotels International	Nikko US
Omni Hotels	The Omni
Ramada Hotels	2 Ramada
Renaissance Hotels	Hotels 1
Southwest Airlines	I Fly SWA

Exhibit 14–5   Here is a baker's dozen of some of the more creative toll-free numbers found in the hospitality industry. Replacing telephone numbers with catchy words and phrases makes the chains' phone numbers more memorable and hopefully creates a higher level of repeat business.

Out-WATS have a critical role in call accounting system profitability. Hotels that route guest long-distance calls over WATS lines may save substantially over normal long-distance costs. These savings may be returned to the guest or are more likely converted into additional hotel profit.

➤*Alternative Operator Services.*   The rise in AOSs began in the late 1980s. It came as a direct result of the first stage of deregulation in 1981. As hotels found themselves free to levy higher fees to their guests for telephone use, the guests themselves turned toward services for which the hotel did not charge—0-digit dialing. And though AT&T offered hotels a commission for all 0-digit calls originating from their rooms, a new third-party, the alternative operator service, paid far higher commissions.

High commissions from AOSs meant that guests were paying high fees to get the service. That is the negative side of AOS. Although high rates can be explained, hotels didn't bother to do so. Guests were shocked when the charges arrived by way of their monthly business or residential bill. That sometimes took weeks, because the charges for 0-digit calls were run through the local or regional telephone companies. And the fees were high—as much as 10 times the prevailing AT&T rate!

Ticking off the reasons for the high rates does little to appease guests. Here they are, anyway. Hotels want their commission, the bigger the better. AOS companies have their own expenses and profits. The cost of the call still has to be paid, even with discounted lines that may be greater than AT&T rates. The call needs to go to the operator center of the AOS. That's the first charge. The call is then forwarded to the AOS connection center, which might actually be in the direction opposite to the direction in which the call is headed, ("back-hauling"). Tack on another charge. When the call is completed through AT&T or an OCC, another cost is added. Finally, there is a fee to get the local telephone companies to include the charge and collect the billing.

AOS Regulations.   The biggest and loudest complaints came from guests who were unaware of how the system worked and how much it cost. Hotels never told their guests things like: "If there is no answer in 10 rings (or 45 seconds), you will be charged nevertheless"; "If you use our convenient in-room AOS, the charge might be 10 times the AT&T operator-assisted rate"; "If you prefer to 'splash off' the AOS and use AT&T, here's how to do it."

Companies such as Hampton Inns heard the complaints and eliminated all 8–0 service charges. Others didn't hear and left the listening to the FCC and various states. On April 27, 1989, the FCC followed the lead of several states (Exhibit 14–3) and required that notice be posted. Moreover, it required that *call blocking*, which prevents a caller from reaching a competitive carrier, be halted.

Recognition of Area Codes.   Surprising as it may sound, not all PBX systems recognize all possible area codes. This issue was first brought to light in 1995, when a number of new area codes were introduced to supplement the 144 existing codes. Prior to 1995, all 144 area codes used either the numbers 1 or 0 as the middle digit.

As the increasing surge in various technologies (for example, fax machines, pagers, cell phones, and modems) created a need for new area codes, Bellcore's North American Numbering Plan Administrative Group found it necessary to begin introducing the numbers 2 through 9 in the middle digit of new area codes. Introducing these new digits caused a number of difficulties with older hotel PBX systems. Guests would often receive a fast busy signal or a recording stating that the number dialed is not working.

The problem was fixed just in time for the new 888 and 877 toll-free area codes. Many hotel phone systems were not programmed to recognize these new toll-free numbers. As such, for the first several months following their introduction, guests were being charged exorbitant long-distance charges because the PBX system recognized the new numbers as toll calls rather than toll-free calls.

Recent Developments in the Telephone Department

The deregulation of the telephone industry and other issues discussed above are still not fully resolved. The latest and most wide-reaching step occurred in 1996 with passage of the Telecommunications Act. This latest tale in the deregulation saga supposedly removed all remaining barriers to competition, freeing long-distance carriers, local telephone companies, and cable companies to compete head-on with one another. In recent years, other telephone department issues have developed about which hotel managers should be aware.

▶*Emergency 9-1-1 Calls.*   One critical telephone-related issue is the risk caused the hotel from in-house emergency 9-1-1 (E 9-1-1) calls. Many E 9-1-1 calls that pass through the hotel's PBX systems are routed over normal telephone trunk lines to the Public Safety Answering Point assigned to that jurisdiction. If the caller is unable to talk to the PSAP operator, or cannot remember the room number from which he or she is calling, valuable time is lost in the emergency response. That's because the PSAP will only see the name and physical address of the hotel, not the number of the room from which the call is being made. Upon arrival, there may be hundreds of rooms to choose from. Indeed, even if the front desk is able to look up which room made the E 9-1-1 call, chances are the hotel will not be aware of the emergency until the vehicles are pulling up out front. Again, valuable time will be lost.

In this age of increasing technological sophistication, only those hotels boasting a PBX system equipped with enhanced 9-1-1 capabilities are safe from potential litigation. With enhanced 9-1-1 capabilities, not only will the PSAP be given the guest's room number, but the hotel front office and/or security staff will also be alerted to the

Exhibit 14–6   Feature phones, such as this one from Teledex Corporation, offer safety, convenience, and revenue-generating options to the hotel: Safety because they clearly display the emergency button (especially attractive to hotels with large international markets); convenience because common guest services, marked with appropriate icons, are available at the touch of a button; revenue-generating because some hotels lease telephone buttons to local merchants (proximate restaurants, exercise clubs, and dry-cleaning, for example). *Courtesy of Teledex Corporation, San Jose, California.*

emergency (see Exhibit 14–6). In many cases, faster hotel staff response time can make a significant difference in the guest's well-being.

Although legislation mandating enhanced 9-1-1 information for PBX-generated calls has been proposed at the federal level, no regulations have yet been established. At the state level, however, PBX E 9-1-1 enhancements have been passed in such states as Colorado, Illinois, Mississippi, Texas, and Washington.

➤*Mandatory and Voluntary System Upgrades.*   The hotel industry has begun providing increasing varieties of telephone services to appeal to guests. Sometimes the law mandates such telephone services (as with volume-control features). In other cases, it is as much a marketing decision as anything else. For example, dual lines to data ports may serve corporate hotel guests' needs, but they may represent an unnecessary investment for leisure guests.

Volume Controls.   The FCC passed a ruling that volume control features on guest-room telephones are required for all new telephones installed after January 1, 2000. Although the ruling applies only to new telephones, it affects existing hotels planning to renovate rooms and replace existing phones. Because guest-room telephones are replaced often in the course of regular room renovations and enhancements, it won't be long before the majority of all hotel rooms are equipped with volume-control features.

This ruling is an attempt by the FCC to make the hotel industry friendlier to guests who are hearing-impaired. Although it falls under a different implementation schedule, the FCC has also required the installation of hearing-aid-compatible telephones in hotel guest rooms.

Cordless and Battery-Operated Telephones.   In an effort to differentiate their lodging product, a number of hotel chains (especially extended-stay and all-suite brands) are introducing cordless guest-room telephones. During their visit, guests expect all the comforts of home, including walk-around, cordless freedom when talking on the telephone.

The problem with cordless telephones, however, has been twofold. They are battery-operated, and so the battery needs to be replaced every so often (about every four years). The replacement of the battery is not the time-consuming element. Rather, when the battery is replaced, the telephone requires reprogramming of information. Today's newest telephones feature an on-board computer chip that keeps phone information stored even when the battery wears down (see Exhibit 14–7).

The other problem with cordless telephones is "crosstalk" and "channel-hopping." You may have experienced similar interference at home if you own more than one cordless telephone. Imagine how exacerbated the problem could be in a hotel with hundreds of cordless guest-room telephones operating in a relatively narrow transmission space. Several telecommunications companies have successfully adopted digital spread spectrum technology to avoid such interference (Exhibit 14–7). Today, cordless telephones are the latest amenity for new properties and those undergoing extensive guest-room renovation!

➤**Supplemental Guest Services.**   Some of the most exciting new innovations come in the form of supplemental guest services. Supplemental or *auxiliary* guest services are clearly designed with the guest in mind. They have a positive impact on the perception of quality service by providing the guest with some of the comforts of home or office. Examples of supplemental guest services—commonly viewed as additions to the call accounting system—include electronic voice messaging and automated wake-up systems.

Electronic Voice Messaging.   Guest telephone messages have historically been a cumbersome affair. Some callers wish to leave lengthy messages, operator-transcribed return telephone numbers are often incorrect, and the growing number of international travelers adds a non-English-speaking component to many of the calls. Today's hotels have answered most of these issues with the introduction of electronic voice messaging.

Electronic voice messaging or voice mailboxes are quite similar to the standard answering machine found in a person's home. However, rather than servicing one incoming telephone line, electronic mailbox systems may be capable of handling thousands of extensions. Mailboxes are usually designed to handle hotel executive office extensions as well as guest-room telephone lines.

Many systems allow newly arrived hotel guests a chance to record their own personalized messages. This is an especially powerful feature in an international market. Guests can leave customized messages in whichever language they speak, and the hotel does not need to translate their incoming messages.

Furthermore, these systems also allow various hotel departments to prerecord messages. An interested guest can call the main dining room mailbox and learn the special entrée of the night or the hours of operation. Another mailbox might be re-

Exhibit 14–7   Cordless in-room telephones are the latest high-end guest amenity. Designed for use in high-density hotel settings where hundreds of such cordless telephones may be operating in limited transmission space, they usually offer a multitude of features. Most, for example, provide state-of-the-art channel security (to prevent crosstalk and channel-hopping), up to 10 preprogrammed guest-service buttons, three-way conference calling, volume control, base/handset message waiting, and of course a readily accessible data port. Oh, yes—Teledex cordless phones (like the one displayed here) offer one additional feature exclusive to Teledex: their exclusive lifetime warranty! *Courtesy of Teledex Corporation, San Jose, California.*

served for use by the concierge staff to promote certain activities in the hotel or across town. The possibilities from such a service are endless.

Automated Attendant Services. Automated attendant services actually relieve the PBX department from answering the telephone at all. Instead, the caller is asked to select from a series of choices and to press the corresponding telephone digit accordingly.

Automated attendant systems are gaining popularity across the world. Most high-volume telephone centers sport some form of this service. In the hospitality industry, however, there are some guest-service purists who believe automated attendant systems are too impersonal and mechanical to find a home in such a customer-oriented business. Although they raise a good point, let's remember that practically every national central reservation office currently operates some type of automated attendant system.

Automated Wake-up Systems.   Automated wake-up systems are consistent with other auxiliary guest services because they both save labor and provide higher levels of customer service. Not only do automated wake-up systems remove the front-desk department from the repetitive early morning task of phoning each guest room and waking the occupant, they also offer a number of unique features.

Although some automated wake-up systems still require the front-desk employee to enter the room number and time of the wake-up call, most systems allow guests to directly input the wake-up time themselves. In addition, systems produce reports identifying which rooms were called, the time of the calls, and the guest's wake-up status. Wake-up status—call was answered, call was not answered the first time but was eventually answered during one of the routine system callbacks, or phone was never answered—is an important tool for addressing potential guest complaints.

Automated wake-up systems also serve as a unique marketing medium because the groggy guest makes for a wonderful captive audience. In this regard, hotels not only inform guests about the day's weather conditions, they also describe the breakfast specials in the dining room. Some automated wake-up systems even provide an option for guests to self-design their own personalized wake-up calls!

▶*Telephone Department Revenues.*   Telephone system upgrades, cordless guest-room phones, and the addition of second or third lines in each room are expensive enhancements for any hotel. But when such investment is made for a department experiencing shrinking revenues, the costs seem even more extravagant. Yet that is exactly what has happened to telephone revenues over the past 10 years.

Historically, telephone department revenues consistently contributed to almost every hotel's bottom line. Representing 3 to 5% of gross revenues for the average hotel, any investment in telecommunications paid for itself over time. However, changing guest-room telephone use patterns have negatively impacted these historical revenues. Here is a broad look at the reasons behind shrinking telephone department revenues and some ideas toward enhancing future profitability.

Deteriorating Revenues.   The average guest-room telephone call used to be 2 to 5 minutes in duration. Today, with Internet access, email, modem transmissions, and the like, the average corporate phone call lasts 45 to 90 minutes. And with Marriott estimating that 76% of all its corporate guests carry laptop computers, the problem will only worsen.

The result of this new lifestyle is a growing need for increased hotel telephone capacity. Where one phone line per room was the norm 10 years ago, the trend is to two or even three lines for each guest room (hotels that offer in-room fax machines often provide three separate lines for each room). That is an expensive enhancement.

Guest dialing patterns may be the single biggest culprit causing the deterioration of telephone department revenues. Where guests historically used 0+ dialing to place their calling card or operator-assisted long-distance calls, today that traffic is routed over toll-free lines. Indeed, 1-800-CALL-ATT is the most frequently dialed number in every hotel in the United States! And toll-free calls placed over either AT&T or MCI carriers represent better than 75% of all toll-free calls placed at hotels.

Unfortunately for hotel operators, the commissions, surcharges, and profits associated with 0+ calls have all but disappeared as toll-free calls have gained favor. Many hotels receive no revenue whatsoever for toll-free calls. Others attach a moderate fee to the convenience of placing such calls from the room—maybe $.75 or $1.00 per call.

This change in dialing patterns has had another negative impact on hotel telephone department bottom lines: increased investment in local trunk lines. Historical trunk configurations no longer serve the modern hotel. Few outgoing calls are long distance, so many long-distance trunks sit idle while toll-free calls are routed through the local telephone company. Because of this new demand for local trunk lines, hotels have experienced increasing trunk congestion and guest dissatisfaction. Guests who simply cannot get a line out of the hotel are forced to wait and try again. And remember, the average corporate telephone call—primarily due to modem use—ranges from 45 to 90 minutes in length! As a result, hotels have found themselves investing in more and more local trunk lines.

Excessive and Fraudulent Telephone Charges.   There are two additional factors not to be overlooked when understanding the deterioration of telephone department revenues. One is the increased use of personal cellular phones. With the introduction of one-rate or no-roaming-fee plans, most corporate guests choose this convenient form of communication when traveling. This goes hand in hand with the second factor leading to reduced guest room telephone usage—the perception that hotel telephone fees are exorbitant. Possibly the shortsighted decisions of yesteryear (the use of AOSs charging as much as 10 times the prevailing AT&T rates) have come back to haunt the lodging industry. Who can blame guests for using their cheaper (if not free) cellular phones in lieu of receiving a surprisingly high phone charge on the guest folio?

One guest vacationing at a major resort in Las Vegas decided to place a few in-room telephone calls back to his home office in San Francisco. He called to check his email, chatted a time or two with his boss, and stayed in touch with his secretary. In total, he made seven separate in-room telephone calls back to San Francisco. The seven calls totaled just 15 minutes. What would you expect to pay for 15 minutes worth of long-distance calls? Well, upon check-out, this guest was shocked to see his telephone usage totaling $167.00. A mistake? A clerical error? Unfortunately, no. As one expert aptly noted, guest room telephone charges seem to be on par with $8 mini-bar sodas!

Wyndham International is one chain that understands the average guest's perception that hotels can be unscrupulous (e.g., $167 for 15 minutes worth of calls) when it comes to setting telephone call rates. Wyndham now offers free unlimited local and long-distance calls (that's right, free long-distance calls "limited to ordinary personal and business requirements in the 48 contiguous United States") and free high-speed Internet access to members of its ByRequest guest-recognition program (see Exhibit 14–8).

So, who can blame guests for using toll-free calling cards to avoid excessive long-distance charges? Indeed, there is now a company that even helps guests avoid the $1 access fee charged by many hotels for toll-free calls. The company, Kallback, has a unique solution to avoiding such charges: Call its toll-free number but only let the phone ring once, then hang up. Moments later, Kallback's computer will ring you back and enter you into its system—free of any access charge. And you'll see no charge from the hotel for the interrupted single ring. Neat idea!

A Few Ideas for Enhancing Telephone Department Revenues.   The answer to continuing deterioration of telephone revenues is not to simply raise long-distance rates. This was the culprit in the first place. Rather, consider implementing extended call pricing on toll-free, 0+, and local calls. This will generate revenue from those guests who dial a local access number, log onto the Internet, and use their computer for hours on end. Give them a generous period at no charge (say, one hour), but then levy a per-minute fee after that. Of course, such charges are only as good as your in-house disclosure program. Be fair and inform guests about your extended call pricing.

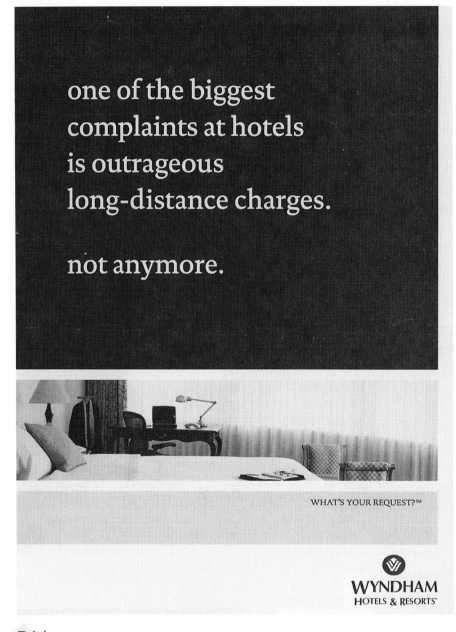

Exhibit 14–8   Taking advantage of least-cost routing technologies affords hotels the unique opportunity of reducing long-distance call costs. Most hotels turn these lower costs into greater profits for their telephone department. Wyndham Hotels & Resorts, however, may have a better idea. Wyndham believes that in an age of increasing scrutiny of corporate travel costs, free local and long-distance calls, high-speed Internet access, faxes, and copies may go a long way toward attracting and retaining valuable customers. *Courtesy of Wyndham Hotels & Resorts, Dallas, Texas.*

Many other new venues for generating telecommunications revenues are gaining popularity. Certainly hotels profit from incoming and outgoing fax services, but other options should be considered as well. For example, there is a growing expectation that hotels be able to provide corporate guests with cellular phones for use during their visit. In addition, wireless pagers are also an option. In fact, a number of hotels now provide integrated service from guest room to cellular telephone—after the guest-room phone rings for the guest a predetermined number of times, the caller is provided the option of leaving a message or ringing through to the guest's cellular line. Now that's first-class service!

This service is especially worthwhile overseas. Although most corporate guests carry domestic cellular telephones when traveling in the United States, few use their cellular telephones on overseas trips. The idea of renting local cellular service at overseas hotels is catching on and may someday be an expected amenity at higher-end international properties.

Feature Phones. Today's in-room guest telephones can perform a multitude of functions not generally associated with telephones. These feature phones have met with outstanding approval from hotel guests. Feature phones offer one-button speed dialing to inhouse departments or local merchants, who pay for the convenience of a captive audience (see Exhibit 14–6). In addition, they usually offer a hold button and call-waiting function. Such phones are commonly found with a built-in speakerphone, alarm clock, and even an AM/FM radio.

Telephones of a higher (and more expensive) class are commonly called *hard-wired multipurpose phones.* These phones may cost the property $500 or more per unit but are easily justified from an energy-savings standpoint. Hard-wired telephones are available that can regulate temperature levels in the room; control as many as six remote lighting fixtures; turn the television set on, change the channels, and adjust the volume; open and close the curtains; and even change the room status to "do not disturb."

Many hard-wired telephones require the guest to activate the room by inserting a keycard in a specially designed slot. When the room is unoccupied, the system automatically disengages most lights, the television, and even heating and air conditioning units, thereby saving the hotel wasted utility costs.

Internet Protocol Telephony. Aside from generating new methods to raise telephone department revenues, another way to increase net profits is to simply reduce variable costs. Voice-over Internet Protocol (VoIP) offers this approach, to literally reduce variable long-distance and Internet access costs to zero.

We have all heard stories of people making free long-distance telephone calls over the Internet. The technology, however, has not been well accepted by the public. Fraught with problems like low-quality voice transmissions, poor caller security, and the like, this technology is not popular with individual users. Hotels, however, can use this technology to gain advantage in two ways: They can save money on inhouse departmental telephone and Internet use (telephone calls made by employees working on hotel business) and save money on guest-room telephone use as well.

What this means for hoteliers is huge cost savings that can either be passed on to guests or used to increase telephone department profits. This technology also integrates email, fax, pagers, and voice mail, allowing hotel guests (and employees) to receive multiple message types over one connection.

Of course, the downside is the initial investment, which represents a large capital outlay for hotels facing lean earnings projections. Still, most major telecommunications companies—Mitel, Nortel, 3Com, Cisco Systems, NEC, and Siemens, to name a few (see Exhibit 14–1)—have been introducing new telephone systems that are VoIP-compatible. According to many experts, it is only a matter of time before most major hotels have this technology in place.

➤ GUEST-ROOM LOCKING SYSTEMS

Looking back at hotels from a historical standpoint, one realizes how far we've come in terms of guest-room security. From today's post–September 11 vantage, it is hard to believe that guest rooms at one time in our history didn't even have door locks:

> Yet, roughly two hundred years ago, in the United States's infancy, this was exactly the case. Guests staying at inns and taverns would drop off their footwear and outer garments in the common boot room on the main floor (with no guarantee of safekeeping) and adjourn to the second floor, where a sheet draped down the middle of the sleeping room segregated the sexes. Outfitted with only a candle from the innkeeper, the guests sauntered over to their designated side of the room and searched for the least crowded bed.[3]

Without question, today's guest demands far more safety and security than ever before in history. Certain guest markets (for example, corporate female travelers) place hotel security near the very top of their list when selecting a chain or independent property. And guests are not alone in their quest for enhanced security.

Hotel employees, managers, and owners are equally concerned with providing high levels of guest security. In the wake of numerous lawsuits charging hotels with inadequate standards of security, a heightened awareness has ensued. This awareness has not been lost on the insurance companies, either. Most insurers of lodging properties offer deep discounts for modern electronic security improvements such as ELSs, property surveillance systems, and fire-system monitoring devices.

Major chains have taken guest security to heart in recent years. A number of chains recommend, and some (such as Hilton Hotels, with its 100% ELS compliance in all hotels) require, that electronic security devices be installed in all new construction. Indeed, even AAA includes guest security protection as part of its property rating system!

Although security involves surveillance, intrusion detection, fire prevention, employee screening, and numerous other concerns, initial efforts have been directed toward lock and key security. It's here that some of today's technological advances hold the greatest promise.

The Room Key Revolution

In recent years, the historical tasks of maintaining key security, tracking lost guest-room keys, managing the distribution of master keys, rekeying locks, and inventorying several keys for each of hundreds of rooms have given way to a simple electronic interface. You see, with ELSs there are no keys to track. The key is disposable or renewable, and each guest gets a new key and a new key combination. With traditional keys, the types that are still used in homes, key loss is staggering. Estimates put the number at one key per room each month. Many hotels have four or five lost keys per day. Lock replacement for Holiday Inns, for example, was pegged at $1 million annually.

---

[3]An except from a historical piece on hotel guest-room locks written by Stephen Rushmore and Carolyn Malone. "Keys and Hotel Security," *Cornell Hotel and Restaurant Administration Quarterly*, December 1998, pp. 91–96.

Not so many years ago, there was a strong black market for stolen hotel keys (up to $1,000 for a master key), and many hotel employees knew about it. Forced entry into guest rooms was almost unknown, because access through stolen, duplicated, or master key blanks was so easy. One group of blitzers (6- to 10-person units) "did" nearly 200 rooms in Anaheim, California, in one morning. And *Los Angeles Magazine* reported the capture of a person who had master keys for 17 hotels.

Those kinds of statistics, and the potential liability they represented, made ELS technology especially attractive to hoteliers. The first magnetic-strip ELS installed in the United States was placed at the Hilton New York in 1985.

▶*Levels of Access.*   Control of keys begins with an understanding of the type and number of keys available. Most key systems consist of four or five levels of access. Although modern ELSs have changed the format of that access, the terminology and functions performed by each level remain roughly the same as the traditional locking systems of yesteryear.

For the most part, each level of the hierarchy exceeds the level below. The guest-room key level (and the fail-safe level) can access only one room. The next level, the maid or housekeeping level, can access an entire wing of rooms. The third level, the general manager or master level, can access the entire hotel property. And the final level, the emergency or E-key level, can access the entire property even when the guest-room deadbolt has been activated (see additional discussion related to the deadbolt later in this section).

Although the levels of hierarchy are much the same with both ELS and standard hardware locking systems, ELSs add a new dimension of security. The electronic key-card is designed to override and invalidate previous keycard combination codes.

For example, Daniel Adams checks into room 1111 on Monday evening. On Tuesday morning, Adams checks out of the hotel. Because the ELS keycard is disposable, he keeps the card as a souvenir for his daughter. Later in the morning, Adams realizes that he has left his wallet hidden in the room. Retrieving the keycard from his pocket, Adams is able to enter the room and find his wallet. That's because the hotel front desk has not yet rented room 1111 to a new guest.

Later in the morning, a maid inserts her housekeeping keycard and enters room 1111. Although she accessed the room after Adams, inserting a housekeeping card in the lock does not invalidate the guest's (Adams's) card. That's because the maid's card is on a separate level of the hierarchy. At this point, Adams could still access the room. Still later in the day, room 1111 is rented to Elizabeth Brown. Her insertion of the new guest-level keycard into the lock electronically invalidates Adams's card. In fact, Brown's card is designed to invalidate all guest-level keycards with lower code sequences than her own. Similarly, Brown's card can only be overridden with a higher-coded card inserted by the next new guest to check in to room 1111.

Microfitted Versus Hard-Wired ELS.   The Adams/Brown scenario above is generally true for all hotels using microfitted ELSs. It is probably not as true for hotels using more sophisticated hard-wired ELSs. The difference between microfitted versus hard-wired is the manner in which the key control center (the front desk's ELS computer and keycard-encoder) communicates with each room. With microfitted ELSs, the only way the room lock communicates with the key-control center is through the keycard. When an arriving guest inserts a newly written keycard, the lock at the guest-room door is told to accept this key and any code higher, but to reject all previous key codes.

Microfitted electronic locks are popular because they are less expensive than hard-wired systems. Primarily, they are used in hotel retrofit situations where hard-wiring an existing hotel would make little sense. Refer to "Categories of Locking Systems" later in this chapter.

With a hard-wired ELS, Mr. Adams would likely not have been able to access his room after he checked out. That's because the key-control center is in constant communication with each guest-room doorlock. After all, there is physical hardware (the hard wire) connecting each guest-room doorlock to the key-control center (in some cases locks may use infrared technology to form continual communication without the presence of a hard-wire). And because the key-control center is interfaced with the PMS, most guest-room keys are invalidated at the time of check-out. At check-out, guests who perhaps left luggage in their room usually have their key codes extended for a brief period of time. Likewise, should Mr. Adams have found his keycard invalidated at the guest-room door, he needed simply to return to the front desk. The front-desk guest-service representative would have handed him a new temporary or single-access keycard. With a temporary keycard, he would have been given, say, 15 minutes, to return to his room, open the door, and retrieve whatever he had left behind (his wallet).

Hard-wired ELSs are the standard in new hotel construction. That's because so much technology now interfaces with the guest room. And much of this new technology uses the electronic lock's hard-wired feature to connect with the front-desk PMS. Such interfaces as energy management systems, guestroom minibars, and in-room safes commonly use hard-wired technology to improve their functionality.

Online Locking Systems.   The trend in coming years will be toward increased integration between other hotel systems and the PMS through the hard-wired ELS. As communication from other systems travels to the PMS via the ELS hard-wire, the system becomes known as an online locking system. Any hard-wired (or those using infrared, radio waves, or pager technology) ELS can be converted to an online system. For many properties, the enhanced capabilities of an online ELS more than compensate for the added cost.

Probably the most valuable enhancement in terms of the hotel's bottom line lies with energy management. Tying EMSs to the guest-room doorlock allows the system to monitor when the guest is in the room. Certainly when the room is occupied, all air conditioning, lighting, television, and related functions must be operational. But the moment the guest leaves the room, many systems can be shut down or reset to an unoccupied energy-savings status. Integrating the EMS through the ELS to the PMS saves the average hotel $10,000 per month or better. A more thorough discussion of the integration of the EMS is provided later in this chapter.

Other benefits of online systems include increased guest-related information. For example, every time a guest enters a certain area (say, the health club), the door-lock card reader automatically sends a record of who accessed the area, the time, and date. This log can provide management valuable information about the movement of guests in and around the hotel. Online systems also aid housekeeping efficiencies by alerting room attendants when guests depart their rooms. Hotel security is enhanced as well, because the system can warn management when a guest-room door has been left open or if there has been forced entry. Management can also track the minute-by-minute whereabouts of all employees who use an electronic keycard to access guest-room and other secured locks.

The Guest-Room Key Level.   The single guest key, which fits a standard lock and deadbolt (see Exhibit 14–9), an electronic lock (see Exhibit 14–10), or a nonelectronic lock (see Exhibit 14–11), gives the guest access to the room. In some hotels, the same key that fits the guest-room door may also unlock connecting doors between

Exhibit 14–9
Even traditional mechanical locks have improved with technology. This one can easily be rekeyed. Using a special control key, the interchangeable core is quickly removed and replaced with a new one. *Courtesy of Schlage Lock Company, San Francisco, California.*

Exhibit 14–10
Some guests prefer traditional-looking room keys (possibly, they feel more secure than with a simple plastic keycard). Those shown here have a reprogrammable magnetic strip embedded in them. They are really just a variation of the keycard. Other, more creative variations, are displayed in Exhibit 14–16. *Courtesy of ILCO Unican, Inc., Montreal, Quebec, Canada.*

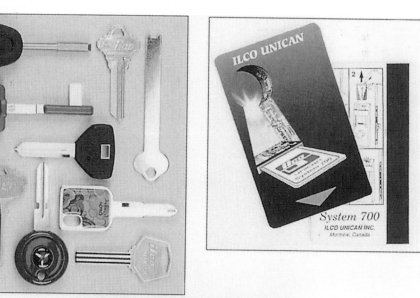

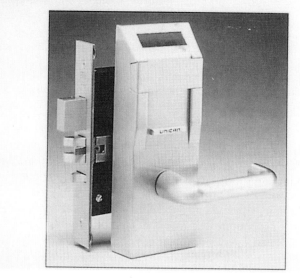

Exhibit 14–11   A nonelectronic locking system utilizes mechanical hardware. As a result, they are less costly than ELSs and require no batteries, electrical connections, or dedicated computers (see Exhibit 14–16). Yet the code of nonelectronic locks can still be changed with each new guest key. *Courtesy of CORKEY Control Systems, Hayward, California.*

rooms (when such access is warranted), open spa or health club facilities, and even open lobby entrance doors. With ELSs, a single keycard can be programmed to open an almost unlimited variety of doors. A meeting planner who wishes to leave a welcoming gift in the rooms of arriving guests, for example, would probably be given one key programmed to access all arriving rooms. The key would have an expiration time on it, so the meeting planner could leave gifts between, say 2 and 4 PM, but it would become invalid as guests began arriving after 4 PM.

Once inside the room, virtually all types of hotel locks (traditional, electronic, or nonelectronic) provide guests with deadbolts for added security. However, locking the door from inside sometimes trips a signal, which tells the room attendant the room is occupied. In this age of enhanced security and concern for potential litigation, such signal devices may be questionable. You see, signal systems of all types—Do Not Disturb signs, lock signals, light systems, room service trays left in the corridor, signals on latches, and message notes on the door—tell the thief as well as the room attendant whether the room is occupied.

Burglars have been known to enter a room marked by the guest to be made up, change the sign to Do Not Disturb, and finish their business in peace. Thieves will also enter when they hear the shower running or when the guest is asleep. Burglars have an edge when they know where their victims are. Estimates suggest that one in every three guests fails to use the deadbolt (see discussion related to deadbolts later in this section).

The Fail-Safe Key Level. The second level in the key distribution hierarchy is only found with ELSs. The fail-safe level provides a preestablished option for use during computer downtime. Most hotels create at least two fail-safe keys for each guest room. Once created, fail-safe keys are secured by management until they are needed.

When the host ELS computer is down (inoperative), either due to a power outage or a hardware/software operations problem, the hotel reverts to the use of fail-safe keys. Just like a new guest keycard, fail-safe keys invalidate previous guest-level keycards. Yet fail-safe keys do not alter the normal sequence of guest-level key codes. They temporarily interrupt the stream of codes, but once the ELS computer is operational again, the new guest-level keycard will invalidate the fail-safe key and everything will be back to normal.

Hotels create two fail-safe keys to gain plenty of time. Two fail-safe keys are good for two new sequences. That's at least two days of fail-safe operation. Once the ELS computer comes back online, front-office management will create new back-up fail-safe keys, always keeping at least two such keys in storage for another down period.

The Maid or Pass Key Level. The next level in the key hierarchy is the maid level, also known as the housekeeping level, the pass key level, the submaster level, the section level, or even the area key level. Each maid-level key controls the room attendant's section of the floor, usually 12 to 18 rooms. Since the pass key fits no other subset, both the hotel and the individual room attendant are protected. Well-trained employees of every department refuse guests' requests to be admitted to rooms. Pass keys are used for this purpose only after proper authorization is obtained from the desk.

Room attendants must not permit guests without identification—that is, a room key—to enter open rooms where they are working. Similarly, rooms must not be left unlocked if the room attendant is called away before the room is completed. Obviously, then, the room attendant's own keys should not be hung on the cart or left in the door. That's why a plastic ELS keycard hung around the room attendant's neck proves both secure and convenient.

The Master Key Level. The master or general manager level may be next in the key hierarchy. However, depending on the design of the hotel, there are a number of key hierarchy possibilities between the maid level and the master level. For example, some properties may wish to create an inspector- or floor-level key. This level would exceed the maid's key (which opens something like 12 to 18 rooms) by opening all rooms on a given floor or section (probably 60 to 100 rooms). One vendor, SAFLOK, currently offers an ELS with 14 separate levels of hierarchy!

Another possibility is an executive housekeeping–level key that would probably open every room in the hotel. The difference between the executive housekeeping level and the general manager or master level is that the executive housekeeper is restricted from access to certain high-security areas. While the general manager level will access all locks in the hotel, the executive housekeeper may be denied access to such areas as the accounting office, the food and beverage department, and other administrative offices.

The Emergency Key.   The highest level in the hierarchy is the emergency or E-key (sometimes called the grand master). Like the general manager-level key, the E-key can access every lock in the hotel. The difference is that the emergency key can access all rooms regardless of lock status. In other words, even when the guest has activated the deadbolt from inside the room, the E-key can still gain access. During periods of extreme emergency—for example, a guest has taken ill and cannot answer the door, or the fire department needs to enter a guest room—the E-key can literally be the difference between life or death!

►*Enhanced ELS Security.*   The loss of guests' personal belongings from their rooms can be traced to three causes: outsiders (intruders), insiders (employees), and the guests themselves. The smart-switch locks of modern technology have affected primarily the outsiders. However, there have been important spin-offs protecting the hotel from insiders and even from guests. Careless guests lose, misplace, forget, and accuse. Dishonest guests manipulate their hotel stays to bring claims against the property or against their own insurance companies.

The director of research and security for the AH&LA maintains that 30% of employees are honest; 30% are dishonest; and 40% must be protected from themselves— as opportunists, they will take advantage of weaknesses in the system.

ELS Identification Database.   Electronic locking systems provide the best line of defense against unethical guests, employees, and even outsiders. That is because the ELS maintains a simple database capable of communicating critical information to management.

Many a manager has dealt with an upset guest accusing a hotel employee of theft. In some cases, guests are correct about the employee who has wronged them; in other instances, guests are incorrect. Maybe the "stolen" wristwatch was merely misplaced, lost, or never packed with their luggage in the first place.

Answers to such questions and accusations are ready and waiting inside the microprocessor of the ELS. Hotel management need merely download the information to a handheld computer (or, in the case of a hard-wired online locking system, the front-desk computer can access the information) to learn which keycards have accessed the guest's room during the period in question. Even the least-expensive microfitted systems hold at least the last dozen keycard entries—other systems hold substantially more. In many cases, the ELS keycard–access database provides enough information to solve the "crime."

Distribution Control.   Control must be established over the numbers of employees who have legitimate access to keys. That includes all the front-office and uniformed services personnel, the housekeeping staff, and the maintenance crews—well over half of all the employees in the hotel. Control must be established on the distribution of keys to the vast number of guests who make legitimate demands for access to their rooms.

An earlier discussion pointed out what the room attendants and the housekeeping department must and must not do with keys on the guest-room floors. Good key security invariably focuses back on the front desk. Clerks must never issue keys without verifying the guest's identity, a procedure that takes but seconds. Still, in the pressure of the rush hours, many keys are issued with abandon. Almost anyone can request a key and get it (see Exhibit 14–12).

Well-publicized lawsuits with huge settlements have pounded security into the minds of every hotel manager. Security is a serious matter. That's the attitude that must be instilled in the staff, who may otherwise treat the subject rather nonchalantly.

Automatic Deadbolt Locks.   In spite of highly publicized guest-room break-ins, some percentage of hotel guests forget to engage the deadbolt lock upon entering the guest room. They leave themselves substantially more vulnerable than when the deadbolt has been activated. To answer this problem, a number of ELS vendors have begun offering automatic deadbolt locks.

Although automatic deadbolt locks have been on the market since the early 1990s, they were initially plagued with problems. Probably the biggest single issue was the noise associated with the automatic deadbolt. Guests felt trapped after hearing a loud click and thud as the deadbolt was engaged and seated. Additionally, there were stories of guests being locked in their rooms because the deadbolt automatically engaged but then malfunctioned and would not disengage. Today's automatic deadbolt systems are quieter and more reliable.

Without the deadbolt in place, burglars easily use spreaders to separate the door latch from the frame. It takes little effort to spread the frame enough to open the door when just the latch is seated. It takes substantially more effort, and usually breaks the frame, to spread it wide enough when the one-inch deadbolt has been engaged. Therefore, it is in everyone's best interest—the guests', the hotel's, and the hotel's insurance company's—to automatically engage deadbolts for those guests who forget or don't understand the importance of this protective feature.

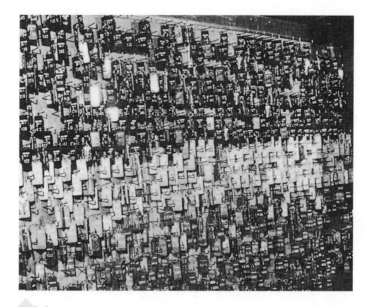

Exhibit 14–12   This exhibit says it all. Protection from litigation aside, electronic locking systems are so much simpler than managing the inventory of thousands of keys required with a traditional locking approach. And just imagine the nightmare for the maintenance and engineering department should a traditional master key become lost or stolen and the entire hotel have to be rekeyed. With a hard-wired electronic locking system, rekeying for a lost master is a matter of a few simple keystrokes to invalidate the missing master key, create new masters in its place, and never disturb the existing guest-level keys in the process.

Exhibit 14–13   Major providers of ELSs, such as Timelox, Onity, ILCO Unican, and SAFLOK, offer automatic deadbolt features on their current systems and some even offer inexpensive upgrades to existing systems. See Exhibit 14–10.

Categories of Locking Systems

There are three categories of guest-room doorlocks available in the marketplace. The most basic of these locks is the standard mechanical keyed doorlock found in older lodging properties and personal residences. Next in line in terms of sophistication is the nonelectronic locking system doorlock. Nonelectronic locking systems offer many of the positive attributes found in ELS locks but cost substantially less. Electronic locking systems are the third type of doorlock available. As discussed, ELSs come in both microfitted and hard-wired systems.

➤*Traditional Mechanical Locks.*   Although the handwriting is on the wall, mechanical locks are still widely used. They are more appropriate for the small property, which can track the history of the individual room lock. Rekeying mechanical locks can be done only by going from door to door and only by keeping good records. That's not feasible with large hotels, which favor ELSs and their remote rekeying capability.

Changing Mechanical Locks.   Changing locks originally meant just that: moving the entire lock from one room to another. With new technology, the method of rotating mechanical locks has changed.

One system uses a removable lock core. With a twist, a control key removes the whole pin–tumbler combination, allowing it to be used in some other housing. The key core is replaced with a different core requiring a different room key. The lock housing remains intact. It is a rapid and effective means of rotating locks for either emergency situations or periodic replacements (see Exhibit 14–9).

The other innovation, changeable tumblers, is even simpler. The change is made in the tumblers without removing the core. It is the key, not the tumbler, that is replaced (see Exhibit 14–14).

Exhibit 14–14   Unlike the lock in Exhibit 14–9, which requires tumbler core replacement, rekeying this deadbolt lock is done externally by changing the key. Making the change requires a master key along with the old and new guestroom keys. *Courtesy of Winfield Locks, Inc., Costa Mesa, California.*

Rekeying time is less than one minute for both the guest key and the master key, according to the manufacturer. Keys are not discarded; they are reused. A removable, colored room number disk snaps in and out of the key, which permits the key to be used in other rooms. Changing disk colors distinguishes previously used keys from the combination currently in use.

➤ *Nonelectronic Locking Systems.*   Nonelectronic locking systems are really just sophisticated mechanical locks. However, because a card is used instead of a key, there is often confusion between electronic and nonelectronic locking systems. Nonelectronic locks use a snap-off card with holes in the plastic (see Exhibit 14–11). According to one manufacturer, 4 billion combinations are possible. Both sides of the card have the same configuration. The door opens when the configuration of holes on the guest card, inserted from the corridor, coincides with the configuration on the control card, which is inserted from the room side.

One variation employs a separate cylinder lock for access by employees and management. Changes can be made in the cylinder lock for the maid, master, and E-keys without altering the guest card entry.

The whole system is like all the other mechanical systems. Someone needs to come to the door and change the card. The change could be done by the bellperson each and every time a new guest is roomed. The bellperson, who gains access through the cylinder lock, breaks off the card parts and completes the rekeying. Rekeying need not be done with each guest, provided the previous guest returned the key(s) at check out.

Benefits of Nonelectronic Locking Systems.   There are several reasons a hotel might select a nonelectronic locking system. First, when compared to standard mechanical locks, nonelectronic locking systems are superior. Their rapid rekeying feature is foremost on the list of advantages over the traditional keyed lock.

In addition, nonelectronic locking systems offer many of the security advantages associated with ELSs. Similar to an ELS, a new guest keycard inserted in the lock will invalidate the previous guest's card. Indeed, hotel managers who select nonelectronic locking systems can provide a strong defense in court that their hotels are providing reasonable care and proper levels of guest security. However, the biggest reason newly constructed properties choose nonelectronic locking systems is cost—they are significantly less expensive than even the least costly ELSs.

▶*Electronic Locking Systems.*   Although ELSs are the best of all guest-room door-locking systems, they are expensive. Average costs range in the neighborhood of $150 to $350 per door plus the cost of the dedicated computer processor, one or more key-writing terminals, an audit trail interrogator, a printer, software, and programming. Yet most newly constructed properties have ELSs. The price only seems high until you analyze the alternatives.

Electronic locks save direct expenses in two ways: labor and key cost. They also provide less direct monetary savings in terms of lower insurance premiums, reduced liability risk, happier guests, and less property theft. In terms of direct expenses, let's look at the experience of the San Diego Marriott Hotel and Marina.

This property was originally constructed with a standard mechanical locking system in all 682 rooms. Today, this property has retrofitted an ELS in its original rooms, and here's why. Guests were constantly losing or misplacing room keys. According to the property's chief engineer, it was not uncommon for the Marriott to rekey up to 40 rooms per day! Each lost room key required the maintenance person to rekey the lock, make four copies of the key, and log in each one. Key blanks cost $2 each (compared to electronic keycards, which cost only about $0.10 each). But the real expense was not key blanks; it was labor. The maintenance department spent upwards of 30 hours per week rekeying doorlocks. Today, that same property spends less than three hours per week maintaining its electronic locks.

Power Sources.   The system is energized either by a hard-wire hookup using utility power or by a battery power pack on the door. The hard-wire installations have

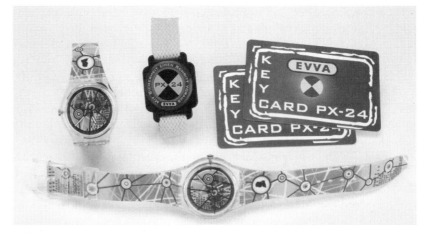

Exhibit 14–15   Electronic locking systems are flexible in terms of where (or on what) the magnetic strip is attached. Creative companies have left the keycard behind as they seek new innovations. Shown here are TESA's new programmable watches, which eliminate the need to carry a keycard. Another company (Sphinx Dialock) has introduced programmable clips, which conveniently hook to the guest's pocket or belt. Another variation requires carrying nothing at all; the guest simply enters a custom-designed PIN number to access the guest room (see also Exhibit 14–10). *Courtesy of Onity, Norcross, Georgia.*

more capability, but they are far more costly. Each door must be cabled to the console at the front desk (or as discussed previously, some systems use radio waves, paging, and infrared technology to communicate with the front desk). This proves too expensive for retrofits, which tend toward the microfitted electronic systems.

Hard-wire installations need to provide for power failures, which make the locks inoperable. One seldom-used option is a battery pack on each door. The batteries have a life of one to three years. Large, centralized power packs are generally used, unless the hotel has emergency generators that back up the entire hotel during power failures.

The Control Center. The control center is at the front desk, where the key is issued as part of the registration process (see Exhibit 14–16). What happens there depends on whether the system is hard-wired or microfitted.

If the system is hard-wired, then the code in the card that is processed at the time of registration is forwarded over the wires (or radio waves) to the lock in the door.

Exhibit 14–16   Combination codes for individual room keycards are processed at the main ELS console located at the front office. Each guest receives a disposable keycard (other options are available as displayed in Exhibits 14–10 and 14–15).

Notice the key-read/write hardware (lower center of photo) through which a blank keycard is encoded for the new guest. Notice also the sample door lock (at far left of photo and another in the back right corner) with which the front-desk receptionist can demonstrate the functions of the guestroom doorlock. *Courtesy of ILCO Unican, Inc. Montreal, Quebec, Canada.*

Exhibit 14–17   Keyless locks have recently gained a foothold in the hospitality industry. Active guests who engage in water sports and other recreational activities often misplace their keycards. Additionally, those hotels which check guests in from remote locations or kiosk front desks can simply provide the guest a 4- or 6-digit number without the added hassle of physically delivering them a key. This Onity Keypad Lock offers access with both a keycard and a combination code. *Courtesy of Onity, Inc. Norcross, Georgia.*

Hard-wiring makes the door code and the console code at the desk one and the same. A self-correcting feature verifies the accuracy of the keycard, saving the guest from a duplicate trip to the desk because the card doesn't work.

As previously discussed in the scenario with Adams and Brown, microfitted ELSs communicate with the desk by way of the keycard. Physically inserting the keycard in the lock updates the code sequence in the doorlock with the code sequence maintained at the front-desk control center.

➤ OTHER COMMON INTERFACES

As the hotel industry continues its trek and investment toward fully automated and fully integrated properties, a number of decisions face management. Depending on the size, type, age, and market of the property, certain applications and potential interfaces become more or less necessary. Whenever management seeks to enhance its current system, it must ask itself a series of questions.

Prior to the Investment in New Automation

Although the questions below are designed around investing in new automated systems, they are appropriate for any hotel investment—management should ask the questions and analyze the answers before making investments.

➤*Degradation.*   Management should first ask, Will integrating a new system degrade the speed of my existing PMS? Interfaced applications have a dedicated central processing unit that "polls," that is, communicates, with the host PMS. Still, interfaces act as "phantom" users, and there are limits to the numbers and types of interfaces appropriate for each PMS. When degradation occurs, the speed of the host PMS slows down. This slower operating time may affect service levels as well as guest and employee satisfaction.

It is critical to assess the degree of degradation that will occur prior to performing any type of interface. If the PMS is appreciably slowed, significant new hardware and software investment may be necessary. Management should apprise itself of this additional potential cost well in advance of performing the interface.

➤ *Synergy.* Another question management should ask itself is, What is the synergistic value gained from this investment in new hardware and software? Most interfaces provide added value (synergy) to the existing property management system. For example, rather than manually turning on guest-room telephones and tracking, pricing, and posting calls, the electronic interface between the CAS and the PMS performs those functions automatically. However, if there is little or no synergy to be gained, management would be wise to forgo the interface.

➤ *Cost–Benefit Relationship.* Another question that must be addressed asks, Is there a positive cost–benefit relationship? Management needs to clearly understand the purpose for the investment, the value added from this new application, and the cost of installing the system. If long-term employee and/or guest benefits are something less than the investment required, management might reconsider the venture.

There is currently a trend to automate everything in sight. Rather than analyzing the cost–benefit relationship, many properties merely follow the industry trend. Yet the reasons for interfacing applications are different for each property. If management cannot answer the cost–benefit question, it should not make the investment.

Matching Technology to Guest Expectations. Another key factor to consider before jumping into an investment in technology is, How will this new automation affect the guest's experience? (see Exhibit 14–18). Today's sophisticated travelers are receiving more and more from their hotels in the way of technological toys, gadgets, and services. Therefore, when prioritizing their computer applications "wish-list," hotels should consider the guests' expectations as well as management's needs.

Corporate hotels are competing on many fronts these days. "Location, location, location" has been augmented by a number of other factors, and a hotel's technological sophistication has become a major selling point for today's frequent business travelers. Indeed, some lodging chains have designed their entire product around the technologically savvy business traveler. Chains like Matrix eSuites Hotels and InternetInns.com offer a variety of standard amenities with a technological slant, including high-speed Internet access, in-room computers, ergonomic workstations, and wireless technology.

To understand why this has become such a valuable market, listen to these surprising statistics developed in part by the Hospitality Sales and Marketing Association International (HSMAI):

➤ Business travelers are more likely than leisure travelers to have a wireless device (PDA, laptop, wireless phone).

➤ Mobile phones are increasingly being used to wirelessly access the Internet.

➤ Smaller devices are favored for wireless access on the go; mobile phones and PDAs are far more commonly used in airports and hotels than are laptop computers.

➤ Some 91% of frequent business travelers use a mobile phone.

➤ Some 88% of frequent business travelers use a laptop computer.

➤ Some 41% of frequent business travelers use a PDA.

➤ Some 48% of frequent business travelers use high-speed Internet connections in the hotel guest room.

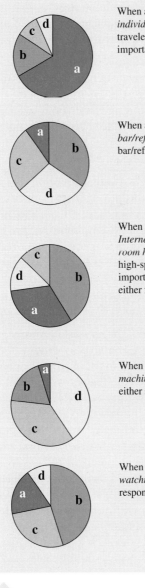

When asked, *How important is it that your guest room has individualized climate control (your own thermostat)?* 84% of frequent travelers said individualized climate control was either somewhat important or very important.
    a. 67% very important
    b. 17% somewhat important
    c. 9% of little importance
    d. 7% not at all important

When asked, *How important is it that your guest room has an in-room bar/refreshment center?* 44% of frequent travelers said an in-room bar/refreshment center was either somewhat important or very important.
    a. 10% very important
    b. 34% somewhat important
    c. 26% of little importance
    d. 29% not at all important

When asked, *How important is it that your guest room has high-speed Internet? And if available, how much would you be willing to pay for in-room high-speed Internet access?* 73% of frequent travelers said in-room high-speed Internet access was either somewhat important or very important. Most respondents think high-speed Internet access should be either free of charge or about $2 to $3 per session.
    a. 32% very important
    b. 41% somewhat important
    c. 13% of little importance
    d. 14% not at all important

When asked, *How important is the availability of an in-room fax machine?* 23% of frequent travelers said an in-room fax machine was either somewhat important or very important.
    a. 5% very important
    b. 18% somewhat important
    c. 36% of little importance
    d. 40% not at all important

When asked, *Other than watching movies, how much time do you spend watching TV in the hotel guest room?* the average frequent traveler responded with 53.7 minutes watching TV (not including movies).
    a. 18% watch 0–30 minutes of TV
    b. 45% watch 30–60 minutes of TV
    c. 27% watch 60–90 minutes of TV
    d. 10% watch 90+ minutes of TV

Exhibit 14–18   A survey of 2,500 frequent travelers conducted by *Lodging Hospitality* and sponsored by ESPN shares some insight about guest preferences. Before investing in guest-operated interfaces, the hotel needs to understand how much value the guests place on the module in question. For example, a hotel would be far better advised to install individualized climate controls (84% of frequent travelers said individualized climate controls were either somewhat important or very important) as opposed to in-room fax machines (just 23% of frequent travelers said an in-room fax machine was either somewhat important or very important). *Source: Lodging Hospitality Magazine.*

Armed with this information, no wonder hotels are reexamining their technological priorities and adopting certain programs that fit their guests' needs. Probably the best example of an investment that benefits both the hotel and the guest is wireless technology. Today, better than 135 million Americans carry some type of wireless device. An investment in wireless technology does more than allow guests to access the Internet. Hotels can gain substantial synergy by implementing their own wireless applications, like PMS (for check-in and check-out functions in remote locations), POS (for handheld ordering in restaurants and lounges), managerial modules (so managers can check vital hotel data and emails without having to return to their offices), and so on.

Common PMS Interfaces

Aside from the call accounting and electronic locking systems already discussed, there are several other common PMS interfaces. A fully automated property might also boast an integrated POS, EMS, and guest-operated interfaces.

▶*Point-of-Sale.* POS systems provide true synergy to the hotel operation in terms of labor savings, lower transcription error rates, and reduced late charges. That is because the POS communicates directly with the host PMS. No matter how distant from the front desk, a computer located at the point of sale (for example, restaurants, lounges, gift shops, and health club centers) is electronically integrated with the front-office PMS.

A POS system removes the hotel from the labor-intensive, error-ridden, manually posted room charge process of yesteryear. The interface poses electronically the same questions the nonautomated system asked manually. Before accepting the room charge, the system polls the front-desk PMS and asks, Is the guest registered under that name and in that room? Is the amount of this charge acceptable to the guest's current credit status? After the PMS validates the guest's ability to charge, the POS accepts the transaction and transmits the data directly to the guest folio. At the POS, the cashier merely inputs the guest name, guest-room number, amount of transaction, and check voucher or reference code number (see Exhibit 13–3).

There are no late charges because a cashier forgot to bring the check to the front desk. There are no errors of fact from posting the wrong amount to the wrong room. And labor is minimal because the POS interfaces directly with the PMS.

▶*Energy Management Systems.* Energy management is another common interface to the property management system. By effectively controlling energy (for example, heating, airconditioning, lights, and power to run equipment), the hotel can provide a full level of services and comfort to the guest while effectively minimizing utility-related costs. An EMS conserves electricity, gas, and water by electronically monitoring the property's mechanical equipment.

An EMS saves money in three ways. First, it conserves overall energy utilization by turning down or shutting off nonessential equipment. It also prevents premium charges on utility bills by shedding energy loads during otherwise peak demand periods. And it enhances the useful life of equipment by duty-cycling machines on and off.

Guest-Room Consumption. Although some 19% of the energy used in full-service properties is used in guest rooms (see Exhibit 14–19), guest-room consumption increases to as much as 80% for limited service properties. An EMS/PMS interface can provide substantial savings in terms of guest-room energy utilization. As discussed earlier in this chapter, such interfaces often function around hard-wired electronic locking systems. That's because the hotel already has a physical (hard-wired) connection between every guest room and the front desk; the EMS simply adds a new dimension to electronic equipment already functioning.

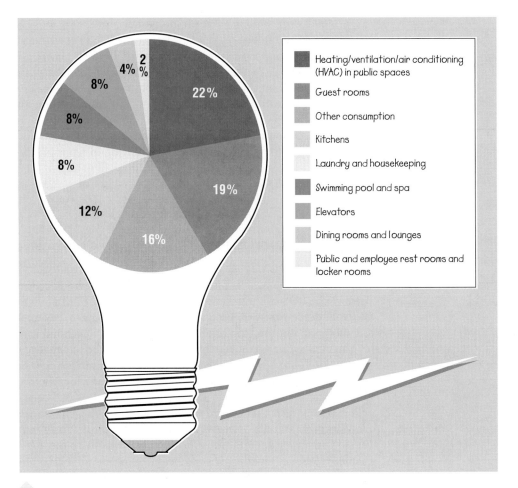

Exhibit 14–19   Breakdown of energy consumption in a full-service, 300-room hotel. A small effort in reducing HVAC, water, and electrical usage can produce significant annual savings. Even without an automated energy management system, properties can benefit by implementing a voluntary compliance program. Guests can be reminded to turn off lights and television when exiting the room, hang up towels that are wet but not dirty, and turn off water when brushing their teeth.

Some EMSs route the flow of guest-room information through the minibar in those hotels where the minibar system is hard-wired to the PMS.

Through an EMS, the property management system reduces energy consumption in unoccupied rooms. Depending on the time of day, the temperature, and forecasted room demand, the EMS may decide to curtail heating and cooling by a few degrees, or it may substantially reduce energy consumption by closing everything down. Even in occupied rooms, the EMS may override the in-room thermostat by a few degrees when faced with peak-demand energy utilization. The industry generally views a few degrees warmer or colder than the desired temperature as a fair trade—a minimal impact on guest comfort in order for the hotel to substantially save on energy costs. Peak-demand periods usually abate within a few minutes, after which time the EMS ceases the override and the guest's room temperature returns to the desired level.

Through the use of computer algorithms, the EMS may actually control the property management system by determining which rooms should be sold and which rooms should remain unoccupied. A guest checking into a 60% occupied house may be routed (through the room availability screen of the PMS) to a well-occupied floor. This would leave other floors or wings of the hotel totally empty. In such cases, the computer could then shut down hallway ventilation systems, turn off every other ceiling light in the hallway, and reduce the temperature of the water heater(s).

An EMS interface might also incorporate in-room occupancy sensors. Tied to the ELS, these sensors use either infrared heat-sensing technology or ultrasonic motion detection equipment to register occupancy in the guest room. A door that has been opened from the inside (without using a keycard to gain access) probably indicates the occupant has left the guest room. This information is validated against the occupancy sensor technology, and if the room is truly unoccupied, the EMS reduces or turns off nonessential energy consumption.

Some less-sophisticated in-room occupancy sensors are not connected to the doorlock and merely sense body heat (infrared detection) or body movement (ultrasonic motion detection) without verification. Such equipment works fine except in those instances where a heavy sleeper pulls the blankets up over his head. In these situations, neither heat nor movement registers the room as occupied. The guest may be surprised to wake up and find the TV set turned off and the room temperature somewhat less than comfortable.

➤ ***The Wired Room.***   In addition to the integrated applications discussed in the preceding section, today's wired rooms provide a number of additional guest-operated interfaces. The following section provides a brief overview of the more popular guest-operated interfaces. Included here are in-room safes, in-room beverage or minibar systems, fire-safety systems, and in-room entertainment systems (See Exhibit 14–20).

In-room Safes.   Modern safes boast two features viewed as essential by today's managers: size and automatic override features. In terms of size, smaller is better—but not too small! In-room safes must be large enough to provide safekeeping for most common articles carried by guests, yet they should be small enough to be concealed in attractive case goods with finishes that match the room's decor. In terms of size, the safe should be just large enough to secure a guest's laptop computer or briefcase.

Digital safes (see Exhibit 14–20) are superior to keycard or traditional lock and key safes. Digital safes work best because there is no secondary element (the key or keycard) to be lost. Some safes work with a swipe of the guest's personal credit card. That doesn't work so well when the guest wants to lock up the credit card before going down to the pool.

Digital safes use a code programmed by each new guest. Everyone has a few digits stored in their brains: birthdates, bank PIN codes, and so on. With a simple "code and close" safe, the guest places the secured items inside and shuts the door, enters a unique PIN code, punches the "close" button, and walks away. It is as simple as that. By the way, some of the newest products on the market feature biometrics (electronic fingerprint readers) rather than digital codes!

Automatic override is another feature of a digital safe. Guests can conceivably forget their code combination, maybe their spouse programmed it and then left, or possibly they thought they had entered one code but pushed the wrong buttons by mistake. Should this occur, hotel management has the ability to open the safe by overriding the current combination code. Usually, such an override requires two inputs: some type of handheld unit, key, or device as well as a secure override access code. Most digital in-room safes maintain an override audit trail.

Exhibit 14–20   In-room safes reduce guest losses as well as guest demands on front-desk personnel to open safe-deposit boxes. Although in-room safes are sometimes provided as a complimentary amenity, many hotels charge between $1 and $5 or more per day for this guest-operated convenience. Digital safes, similar to the one shown, allow guests to program their own unique combination codes. *Courtesy of Elsafe International, Vanvikan, Norway.*

Electronic safes may be hard-wired to an interfaced central processing unit. If the PMS is interfaced, daily charges are posted automatically to the electronic folio. Manual systems charge guests for the use of the safe in a number of creative ways. Some ask the housekeeping attendant to document whether or not the safe was used. Another approach is to simply ask the guest at check-in or check-out. Other properties charge a fee for the safe—usually $1 to $5 per day—whether it was used or not (obviously, this approach causes a few guest complaints at check-out). And a recent growing trend is to charge all guests a small "resort fee" for the use of the guest-room safe, in-room coffee, and free local phone calls (see Chapter 9).

Of course, the hotel can provide the safe without charge, as it does other amenities. Charging came about because vendors developed quick payback schemes by which management could justify installing in-room safes.

Other than direct cost recovery, there are economic arguments for not charging. The safes reduce the number of thefts, and that should reduce the cost of insurance. Traffic at safe deposit boxes falls dramatically, reducing front-office labor costs. Fewer claims means even larger savings in security and management time. Investigations, guest relations, reports, police inquiries, and correspondence may represent days of lost work. Legal fees, court costs, settlements, and more management time must be factored in if the case goes to trial. Thus, a safe reduces losses, which reduces costs.

Evidence suggests that safes do reduce theft. Electronic doorlocks do battle with external theft and in-room safes with internal theft. Experts say that internal theft by employees is usually an impulsive act caused by temptation (laptop computers are proving to be one of the most tempting items of all). The safe reduces employee opportunity. It also undermines guest moves to defraud the hotel or the insurance company.

►*In-room Minibars.*   In-room beverage, minibar, or vending systems may be automatically interfaced to the PMS, semiautomatically interfaced (with a handheld microprocessor), or fully manual in design (see Exhibit 14–21). Both manual and semiautomated minibars rely on a guest honor system. At the time of check-out, front-desk clerks ask departing guests if they had occasion to utilize the minibar in the last 24 hours. Although some departing guests will invariably fleece the hotel, minibar profits are significant enough to cover a sizable number of losses.

Minibars are extremely convenient—that's their attraction. And guests are often willing to pay a premium for the convenience of having snacks and drinks available in the room. As a result, some hotels have realized rapid payback (sometimes in less than 12 months) from their in-room minibar systems.

With semiautomated minibars, changes in inventory are recorded on a handheld microprocessor by the room attendant or minibar employee. The microprocessor is capable of storing inventory information from a number of guest rooms before being downloaded via the telephone directly into the property management system interface (see Exhibit 14–22).

Exhibit 14–21   Electronic in-room minibar systems can easily support 75 to 100 items. By design, some sections remain at room temperature (nuts and candy) while other sections are refrigerated (soda and champagne). A new trend offers healthier snacks and personal toiletries in addition to the obligatory liquor and soda. *Courtesy of Minibar North America, Inc., Bethesda, Maryland.*

ROBOBAR COMMUNICATION SCHEMATIC

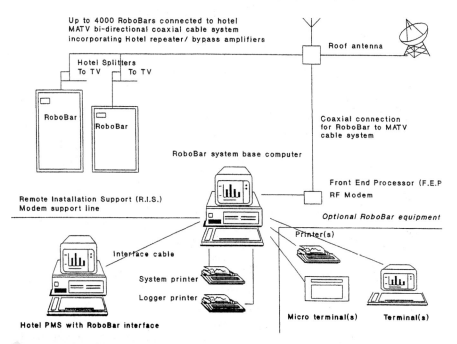

Exhibit 14–22   Advanced systems, such as this one from Robobar, deliver in-room amenities with maximum efficiency. It has several notable features: Purchases are posted to the folio electronically as the guest removes the product; bars can be locked remotely to comply with local regulatory requirements; and restocking reports are prepared automatically—no need for a physical count. *Courtesy of Minibar North America, Inc., Bethesda, Maryland.*

Some delay in installing honor bars was caused by jurisdictions such as New York State. Without control of consumption by minors, liquor was not permitted in the rooms. Automatically interfaced minibars have changed that: The system can be turned off at certain hours or whenever children are registered.

Interfaced minibars brought additional benefits: eliminating the frequent late charge of the honor system, for one. The most sophisticated minibars utilize fiber-optic sensors to identify when a product has been removed for consumption. These sensors are often programmed with a slight delay to allow for those guests who wish to handle, look at, and then possibly return the product to the refrigerator. Once the product has been removed for a period of time, the sensor alerts the interface, which then charges the guest folio for the minibar item. Not only does this minimize cheating and late charges, it also produces a restocking report that simplifies the job of the minibar employee. There is no longer any reason for the minibar employee to enter and check every guest room—only those from which an item was removed.

Aside from the recent technological advances in minibars, there has been a revolution of purpose as well. Gone are the days when minibars were stocked exclusively with liquor and stale snacks. The new purpose has minibars stocking a multitude of items ranging from healthier snacks and beverages to indispensable products such as toiletry items. Imagine the relief of the guest who doesn't discover until morning that he has forgotten his razor, and finds one conveniently located in the minibar (that's far better than walking downstairs in pajamas).

Even the pricing of minibar products has become somewhat more user friendly in recent years. A grand opening special at the Nikko Hotel in Hanoi included the entire original content of the in-room minibar free of charge. Who knows, the future may see more hotel minibar promotions and creative uses (even complimentary continental breakfast) in years to come.

▶*In-room Entertainment Systems.* In-room movie or entertainment systems hold a great deal of promise for the years to come. Recent trends suggest continued investments in guest-room televisions. The rule of thumb is to provide guests with in-room televisions equal to or surpassing the size and quality of the sets they have at home. Therefore, as home electronics grow more high-tech, so must guest-room electronics. One mid-sized chain now provides 42-inch flat-panel plasma televisions in all its luxury and upscale rooms!

The television remains the guest-room entertainment center for now. Better televisions and more amenities featuring the television are the standard for the day. The three major vendors of guest-room televisions, Philips, Zenith, and RCA, are all experiencing revenue growth in the hotel sector.

Another trend is to increase the number of cable channels available to the average guest. Guests grow frustrated channel-surfing through the few (10 or so) channels found at many hotels. They expect to find 40 or 50 channels (again, similar to what they might have at home), so hotels are complying by providing greater viewing selection. The three most popularly viewed cable channels in hotel rooms are HBO, Showtime, and Disney.

The availability of in-room movies, for which most hotels charge (using the electronic folio), is another popular amenity (see Exhibit 14–23). Videocassette viewing is another. Some hotels charge, and some don't; some rent films via electronic vending machines, and some supply them gratis on the concierge floors.

Although not exactly entertainment, the proceedings taking place in the conference area of the hotel can be viewed on the TV screen in some hotels. Other TV channels offer airline schedules; news, sports, and stock market reports; local restaurant guides; the guest folio; weather reports; advertising; and personal messages left for the guest.

When some of the capabilities of the telephone and personal computer are added in, television broadens its service offerings. Express check-out and room status are two common functions. A room-service menu can be viewed (changes are easier to make and less costly than printed menus) and orders placed. Other orders can also be placed: a morning wake-up call; a reservation in a dining room that hasn't opened; goods from shops in the hotel (or mall merchants, if the hotel is so located). Even airline tickets can be ordered. With a remote printer at the desk—eventually, perhaps, in the guest room—the tickets can also be picked up.

The trend by the big three lodging pay-per-view companies—SpectraVision, LodgeNet Entertainment, and On Command Video—has changed in recent years. Where a signed pay-per-view contract once guaranteed the hotel a free TV set in every room, today's contracts provide more information technology without the free sets. Less sophisticated hotels can still get the free TV sets, but more advanced properties are opting to buy the sets themselves in order to get the pay-per-view company to include a wider range of differentiated services in the contract.

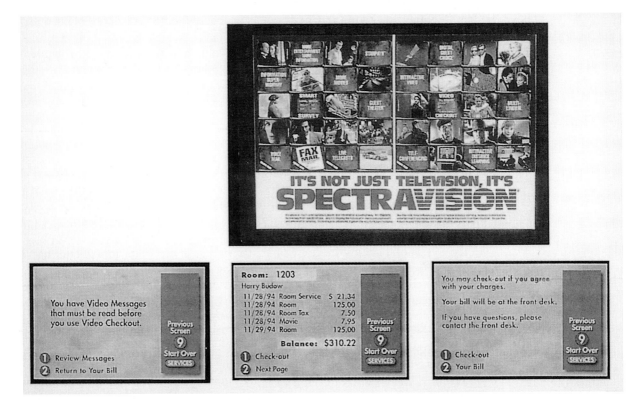

Exhibit 14–23   SpectraVision is one of the big-three lodging pay-per view and in-room technology companies (along with LodgeNet Entertainment and On Command Video). The top photo promotes many of the services available in a fully integrated system. The bottom photos show how simple it is for the guest to read messages, review the folio, and check out from the room. *Courtesy of SpectraVision, Richardson, Texas.*

➤*Fire-Safety Systems.*   Although fire-safety systems are not truly guest-operated devices, they do monitor and detect activities occurring in the guest room. Like most interfaced functions, fire-safety systems began as stand-alone devices. An example is a single smoke detector in the corridor. Change came quickly after several widely publicized fires occurred. In quick response, many municipalities passed retrofit legislation. The emphasis was toward interfacing fire technology and the PMS, using the hard wires of the call accounting or locking systems, or through wireless broadcasting. Some jurisdictions mandated hard-wiring—integrating the control panels and the room communication systems.

Hard-wire systems tie each room sensor to a fire-control panel on the premises. In-room smoke detectors and sprinkler-head sensors can also be included to provide an early-warning network. An annunciator on the panel pinpoints the source of the smoke or fire. The interfaced system then does several things automatically:

➤ It releases the magnetic locks that hold open the fire doors.
➤ It adjusts the ventilation and air-handling (HVAC) systems to minimize the spread of fire and externally vent smoke as necessary.

> ➤ It automatically notifies guests in their rooms through the activation of horns or speakers, it may dial each guest-room telephone and play a prerecorded message, and it notifies the local fire department. On arrival at the scene, the fire department takes control of the speakers and announces specific instructions.

> ➤ It automatically overrides all affected elevators and returns them to the ground floor.

Codes require evacuation routes in corridors and rooms to be clearly marked. In-room signage now identifies that route and the closest exit. Lighted, phosphorescent signs in the corridors at crawling height have gained popularity since their introduction in the Far East over a decade ago.

Instead of ignoring the reality of the danger, which had been the stance for a long time, hotel companies have begun communicating their concerns. Written booklets and evacuation instructions have been prepared. With electronic systems, audio instructions are also being offered. Other emergency systems use the music channels or the television speakers. The voice comes through even if the switch is off. Special hard-wired systems and in-room sprinklers are legislated in several places that have experienced especially deadly fires, such as Las Vegas and San Juan.

A message that is recorded tends to be more calming and informative than a live one made during the excitement of the emergency. Several hotels have gotten the local fire marshal to tape the message.

➤*The Electronic Concierge.*   In an effort to provide guests with additional information while easing the strain on the concierge desk (or eliminating the position altogether), hotels have heartily embraced electronic concierge technology. Through either the guest-room television, a dedicated kiosk or a computer terminal in the lobby, or even a phone-based system (where guests interact by pushing the appropriate phone buttons), guests receive answers to questions about local attractions, restaurants, museums, shows, and so on. Some of the more sophisticated systems even provide maps (which can be printed at the front desk or to the guest-room fax machine when available) and recommended routes.

Hotels are not the only venue that supports electronic concierge systems. They are also commonly found at bus depots, airline terminals, city halls, and other public or quasipublic buildings. Hotels, however, benefit tremendously from this new technology, which is usually installed free of charge. Whether the electronic service replaces or merely supplements a live concierge desk, the guest saves time and gains an overview of community attractions from the information available through the electronic concierge.

However, the guest is not always provided a full and accurate picture. You see, electronic concierge services are provided by businesses that profit from advertising included at the site. Large communication companies (Bell Atlantic and U.S. West are two such examples) often fund the investment necessary to start such services. To be listed at the site, local merchants pay rates ranging from $100 to $1,000 per month. Not all merchants choose to participate, and that's where the picture gets muddled. Asking the concierge desk where the nearest Italian restaurant is located may point you to a lovely place right next door. The electronic concierge, however, will highlight only those Italian restaurants that pay the monthly fee. As such, the guest may drive miles out of the way seeking the closest Italian restaurant, having been provided something less than full disclosure.

RESOURCES AND CHALLENGES
Resources

➤ SUMMARY

The lodging industry lagged behind most other businesses in terms of adopting computer automation in the 1970s. As a result, most hotel operations avoided the first generations of computer development, choosing instead to wait for the faster, cheaper, more perfected systems that were soon to follow. The waiting is over, and hospitality computer applications have gained acceptance at a dizzying rate. Today, technology prevails across all spectrums of the lodging industry.

Few properties operate without a computerized call accounting system (CAS). The CAS performs many tasks that historically belonged to the hotel telephone operator: It identifies when a guest call is made, the originating room, the duration, the destination, and the cost of the call. Once the long-distance carrier cost of the call is determined, most properties add a profit margin to help defray CAS equipment costs and to make a reasonable return on investment for the hotel. Some chains, however, choose to make no profit on either long-distance or local guest phone calls. Functioning in concert with the CAS are sophisticated guest-room telephones. These feature telephones are actually capable of serving as a remote control for a number of in-room services. Pressing a few buttons on the phone may close the drapes, dim the lights, adjust the temperature, or lower the television volume.

Another common technological interface found in hotels is the electronic locking system (ELS). Few newly constructed hotels are built without some form of locking system technology. This technology may include nonelectronic locking systems that utilize specially encoded keys, but more often than not it will be an electronic locking system. The ELS may be microfitted (that is, battery-operated) or hard-wired. Though more expensive, the hard-wired systems are capable of a number of enhancements. Since each hard-wired lock is actually wired directly to the front-desk PMS, the hotel can integrate fire safety, occupancy sensors, and energy management components directly through the door lock.

In addition to the CAS and ELS, a number of guest-room or guest-service interfaces are also available in full-service, technologically sophisticated properties. Common guest-service interfaces include point-of-sale and energy management systems. In the guest room, there may be electronic-safe, mini-bar, entertainment, and fire-safety system interfaces.

➤ WEB SITES

Contemporary locking systems are as diverse as the lodging industry. Even product lines developed by the same manufacturer may offer substantially different features. Besides the structural differences we've discussed between microfitted and hard-wired installations, there are numerous other distinctions between brands and models. After all, not all locks are for all properties; some properties have budget constraints, others require extreme outdoor conditions (as with an exterior-entry hotel located at a ski resort), and some are thinking ahead to the growing popularity of smart cards and need a dual reader technology (one that can read both magnetic strip cards as well as smartcards). Additionally, locking systems are designed for specific property sizes; a smaller, 75-room property can work well with an entry-level key encoder and key control system; larger properties need systems with greater capabilities. Even questions of warranty and adaptability to existing technologies come into play.

Look at these ELS company Web sites and answer the following questions:

1. How many different lines of ELS door locks do you see for each company?
2. Can you readily tell which of those lines are hard-wired and which are microfitted?

3. Pick one line of locks from each of the five companies; list three key features for the lock selected from each company.

4. Can you find any features boasted by one company that are not offered by other companies? In other words, can you see any competitive distinction between brands?

5. Try to identify the price of at least one line of products for each listed company.

➤ http://www.uniqey.com

➤ http://www.tesalocks.com

➤ http://www.vingcard.com

➤ http://www.saflok.com

➤ http://www.kaba-ilco.com (formerly ILCO Unican)

➤ INTERESTING TIDBITS

➤ With increasing use of personal cell phones, guest-room telephones have become more a cost center than a revenue center. That may change with the introduction of Voice over Internet Protocol (also known as Internet telephony). With Internet telephony, per-call costs are substantially reduced, and the technology allows for video conferencing, email, Web surfing, and much more. Watch for it soon!

➤ If you find today's innovative locking systems fascinating, consider delving into the past. Antique locks are the *key* items (get it—ha ha) you'll find at the unique Lock Museum of Orange County located in Garden Grove, California. You'll have to *restrain* yourself from going crazy over all the classic prison locking hardware like handcuffs, leg irons, and a full-scale jail cell (they even have some of Harry Houdini's handcuffs). Looking for something more appropriate to hospitality industry students? How about the lock from Elvis Presley's dressing room at the MGM Grand in Las Vegas. Or maybe the snack bar serves *locks and bagels*?!

➤ READING REFERENCES

Hospitality Information Technology: Learning How to Use It. G. Collins, C. Cobanoglu, and T. Malik. Dubuque, Iowa: Kendall/Hunt, 2003.

"Keys and Hotel Security." S. Rushmore and C. Malone. *Cornell Hotel and Restaurant Administration Quarterly,* December 1998, pp. 91–96.

Challenges

➤ TRUE/FALSE

___ 1. Surprisingly, the rise of cellular telephone usage has corresponded with a rise in guest-room telephone long-distance calls. Most experts suggest that even though many corporate guests carry cellular telephones, they hesitate to use them when making long-distance telephone calls and still prefer using their in-room guest telephone.

___ 2. Due to increased in-room computer modem usage, the average corporate guest's telephone call now lasts 45 to 90 minutes.

___ 3. Although more expensive, microfitted ELSs are superior to hardwired ELSs for a number of reasons. Microfitted ELSs can be integrated to an energy management system, room occupancy sensors, and the PMS. Hard-wired

ELSs, however, are actually standalone micro-processors, which are not physically capable of such sophisticated integration.

___ 4. Although energy management systems can temporarily override the guests' desired in-room temperature settings (in order to reduce power demand for several minutes during peak-demand usage periods), it has been challenged in court and determined to be against the law in almost every state.

___ 5. The most sophisticated in-room minibar systems are integrated to the PMS. Using fiber-optic sensors, the minibar can actually sense when the guest removes an item. After a delay of several minutes (in case the guest changes his or her mind and returns the item to the minibar), the guest folio is automatically charged for the item.

➤ ANSWERS TO TRUE/FALSE QUIZ

1. False. Telephone departments have faced dramatic decreases in long-distance revenues due to proliferating use of mobile cellular telephones. What used to be a certain profit center has thus become a costly department in many hotels.

2. True. Due primarily to their need for access to the Internet through their laptop computer modems, corporate hotel guests spend 45 to 90 minutes on the average in-room telephone call.

3. False. Exactly the opposite is true. Microfitted ELSs are actually standalone microprocessors incapable of sophisticated integration. Hard-wired ELSs are the superior systems able to integrate energy management, room occupancy sensors, and the PMS.

4. False. EMSs can temporarily override the guests' desired in-room temperature settings—that is true. But this has not been challenged in court and is not an illegal procedure—that part is false. The EMS only overrides the guest's room setting for a few critical minutes during periods when the hotel is facing peak demand. After that, the EMS allows the guest-room temperature to return to its desired setting.

5. True. Minibars can be hard-wired through the guest-room locking system or telephone system to the PMS. Then, using fiber-optic technology, it can sense which item locations have been vacated (an item has been removed) and perform two functions: It can charge the guest folio, and it can make an inventory restocking report for the minibar attendant staff.

➤ PROBLEMS

1. The relationship of the telephone and hotel industries has changed significantly since the 1960s. List three major pieces of legislation, court rulings, findings by the FCC, or decisions by members of either industry that caused or contributed to the changes. How did each alter the way in which the hotel's telephone department operates?

2. Undoubtedly, some PMS vendors will comply with the new HITIS standards and oth-

ers will not. What are the benefits and disadvantages to a hotel manager who purchases software from a vendor in compliance?

3. Most hotel operations charge a premium for the convenience of placing long-distance phone calls directly from the room. This premium may range from 10 to 25% above the cost of the call. Other properties charge as much as 10 or more times the

cost of the call. Assuming that the hotel announces its surcharge with a notice similar to the one shown in Exhibit 14–3, discuss the fairness of charging the guest such a premium. Is it ethical to charge a small premium (say, 10 to 25%)? Is it ethical to charge a large premium (say, 10 times the cost)? At what point does the hotel overstep the limits of "fairness"?

4. Using professional terminology correctly is important to understanding and being understood. Identify the following acronyms and briefly discuss what they represent:

a. HOBIC	i. PBX
b. AOS	j. AIOD
c. WATS	k. POS
d. PMS	l. CAS
e. FCC	m. AH&LA
f. ELS	n. LCR
g. OCC	o. PPC
h. AT&T	p. VoIP

5. Identify by name the levels of keys that comprise the locking systems of most hotels. Explain who has access to which keys and what purpose is served by each level. How does the system work if the mechanical lock and key are replaced by the computer and the computer keycard?

6. Be creative and imagine the hotel room of the future. Describe several guest-operated interfaces or devices that might be available in your fictitious hotel room of tomorrow.

Glossary

● ● ●

Words in *italic* in each definition are themselves defined elsewhere in the Glossary. (Words not listed might be found in the Index.) cf. means "compare."

A card   A form once used with the *NCR front-office posting machines* to reconcile and report cash at the close of the first shift and alternate shifts thereafter; see also *B card.*

account balance   The difference between the *debit* (charge) and *credit* (payment) values of the *guest bill.*

account card   See *guest bill.*

account receivable   A company, organization, or individual, *registered* or not, who has an outstanding bill with the hotel.

accounts receivable ledger   The aggregate of individual *account receivable* records.

acknowledgment   Notice of a *confirmed reservation* by telephone, fax, Email, letter, postcard, or preprinted form.

ADA   See *Americans with Disabilities Act.*

adds   Last minute *reservations* added to the reservation list on the day of arrival.

ADR   See *average daily rate.*

adjoining rooms   Rooms that abut along the corridor but do not connect through private doors; cf. *connecting rooms.*

advance deposit   A deposit furnished by the guest on a room *reservation* that the hotel is holding.

advances   See *cash paid-outs.*

affiliated hotel   One of a chain, *franchise,* or *referral* system, the membership of which provides special advantages, particularly a national reservation system.

after departure (AD)   A *late charge.*

afternoon tea   A light snack comprising delicate sandwiches and small sweets served with tea, or even sherry; cf. *high tea.*

agency ledger   A division of the *city ledger* dealing with *travel agent* (agency) accounts.

agent   Representative of an individual or business; term that is a popular substitute for clerk, as in guest-service agent rather than room clerk.

AIOD   Telephone equipment that provides *Automatic Identification of Outward Dialing* for billing purposes.

All-inclusive   *Plan* that includes all hotel services: room, food, beverages, entertainment for one price.

allowance   A reduction to the *folio,* as an adjustment either for unsatisfactory service or for a posting error. Also called a *rebate.*

amenities   Literally any extra product or service found in the hotel. A swimming pool, *concierge* desk, health spa, and so on, are all technically known as amenities. However, this term is used primarily for in-room guest products: as soap, shampoo, suntan lotion, mouthwash, and the like.

amenity creep   The proliferation of all guest products and services when hotels compete by offering more extensive *amenities.*

American Hotel & Lodging Association (AH&LA)   A federation of regional and state associations that are composed of individual hotel and motel properties throughout the Americas.

American plan (AP)   A method of quoting room *rates* where the charge includes room and three meals.

American Resort Development Association (ARDA)   A professional association of *timeshare* developers.

American Society of Association Executives (ASAE)   An organization of the professional executives who head the business and *SMERF* associations in the United States.

American Society of Travel Agents (ASTA)   A professional association of retail *travel agents* and wholesale tour operators.

Americans with Disabilities Act (ADA)   Established in 1990, the ADA prohibits discrimination against any guest or employee because of his or her disability.

application service provider   Supports *central reservation system* and *global reservation system* with hardware and software.

arrival, departure, and change sheet   A pencil-and-paper form to record guest *check ins, check outs,* and *changes* under a hand audit system; sometimes three separate forms.

arrival time   The hour which the guest specifies as the time that he or she will arrive to claim the *reservation.*

attrition   The failure of a convention *group* to fill its reserved *block* of rooms.

authorization code   (1) Response from a credit-card issuer that approves the credit-card transaction and provides a numbered code referral if problems arise; (2) a code for entry to a computer program.

available   The room is ready.

available basis only   (1) Convention *reservations* that have no claim against the *block* of convention rooms (see *blanket reservation*) because the request arrived after the *cutoff date;* (2) no reservations permitted because the rate being granted is too low to guarantee space, employee *reservations,* for example.

available rooms   The number of guest rooms the hotel has for sale—either the total in the hotel or the number unoccupied on a given day.

average daily rate (ADR)   The average daily *rate* paid by guests; computed by dividing room revenue by the number of rooms occupied. More recently called *sales per occupied room.*

back to back   (1) A sequence of consecutive *group* departures and arrivals usually arranged by tour operators so that rooms are never vacant; (2) a floor plan design that brings the piping of adjacent baths into a common shaft.

bank   Coins and small bills given to the cashier for making change.

bank cards   Credit cards issued by banks, usually for a smaller fee than that charged by *travel and entertainment cards.*

batch processing   A computer procedure that collects and codes data, entering it into memory in batches; cf. *online computer.*

B card   A form once used with the *NCR's front-office posting machines* to reconcile and report cash at the close of the second shift and alternative shifts thereafter; see also *A card.*

bed and board   Another term for the *American plan.*

bed and breakfast (B&B) Lodging and breakfast offered in a domestic setting by families in their own homes; less frequently, the *Continental plan*.

bed board A board placed under the mattress to make a firmer sleeping surface.

bed night See *guest day (night)*.

bed occupancy A ratio relating the number of beds sold to the number of beds available for sale; *occupancy* measured in available beds rather than in *available rooms*.

bellcaptain (1) The supervisor of the bellpersons and other uniformed service personnel; (2) a proprietary in-room vending machine.

bellcaptain's log See *callbook*.

bellstand The bellperson's desk located in the lobby close to and visible from the front desk.

Bermuda plan A method of quoting room *rates*, where the charge includes a full breakfast as well as the room.

best available A *reservation* requesting (or a confirmation promising) the best room available or the best room to open prior to arrival; cf. *available basis only*.

B folio The second *folio* (the individual's folio) used with a *master account*.

blanket reservation A *block* of rooms held for a particular *group*, with individual members requesting assignments from that *block*.

block (1) A number of rooms reserved for one *group*; (2) a restriction placed in the *room rack* to limit the clerk's discretion in assigning the room.

book To sell hotel space, either to a person or to a *group* needing a *block* of rooms.

bottom line The final line of a profit-and-loss statement: either net profit or net loss.

box Reservation term that allows no *reservations* from either side of the boxed dates to spill through; cf. *sell through*.

breakage The gain that accrues to the hotel or tour operator when meals or other services included in a *package* are not used by the guest.

brunch A meal served after breakfast but before lunch and taking the place of both.

bucket See *cashier's well*.

budget motel See *limited service*.

building cost rate formula A rule-of-thumb formula stating that the average room rate should equal $1 for every $1,000 of construction cost; see also *rule-of-thumb rate*.

C-corporation Used to distinguish standard corporations from nonstandard corporations, such as non-taxpaying *REITs*.

cabana A room on the beach (or by the pool) separated from the main *house*; may even be furnished as a sleeping room.

café complet Coffee snack at midmorning or midafternoon.

California length An extra-long bed, about 80 to 85 inches instead of the usual 75 inches. Same as *Hollywood length*.

call accounting system (CAS) Computerized program that prices and records telephone calls on the guest's electronic *folio* through a *property management system (PMS) interface*.

callbook The bellperson's record of calls and activities.

call sheet The form used by the telephone operator to record the room and hour of the *morning call*; replaced by automatic systems.

cancellation A guest's request to the hotel to void a *reservation* previously made.

cancellation number Coded number provided by the hotel or *central reservations office* to a guest who cancels a *reservation*.

cash advance See *cash paid-outs*.

cash disbursement See *cash paid-outs*.

cashier's drop A depository located in the front-desk area where others can witness cashiers depositing their *turn-ins*.

cashier's report The cash *turn-in* form completed by a departmental cashier at the close of the *watch*.

cashier's well The file that holds paper-and-pencil *folios*, often recessed in the countertop; also known as *tub*, *bucket*, or *pit*.

cash paid-outs Monies disbursed for guests, either advances or loans, and charged to their accounts like other departmental services.

cash sheet The *departmental control sheet* maintained by the front-office cashier.

casualty factor The number of individual or *group reservations* (*cancellations* plus *no-shows*) that fail to appear.

cathode ray tube (CRT) A television or computer screen that displays information; also called a VDT, *video display terminal*.

central processing unit (CPU) The *hardware/software* nucleus of the computer.

central reservations office (CRO) A private or chain-operated office that accepts and processes *reservations* on behalf of its membership.

central reservations system (CRS) The sophisticated *hardware* and *software* used by a *central reservations office* to accurately track and manage *reservations* requests for member properties.

change Moving a party from one guest room to another; any change in room, *rate*, or number of occupants.

chargeback Credit-card charges refused by the credit-card company.

check-in All the procedures involved in receiving the guest and completing the *registration* sequence.

check out All the procedures involved in the departure of the guest and the settlement of the *account*.

check out hour That time by which guests must vacate rooms or be charged an additional day.

city ledger An *accounts receivable ledger* of nonregistered guests.

city-ledger journal The form used to record transactions that affect the *city ledger*.

class The quality of hotel, with *average daily rate* the usual criterion.

closeout hour Also called *close of the day*.

close of the day An arbitrary hour that management designates to separate the records of one day from those of the next.

closet bed See *Murphy bed*.

collar hotel   Identifies location of a hotel on the collar (outside rings) of a city.

colored transparency   A colored celluloid strip placed in the *room rack pocket* as a *flag* or indicator of room status.

commercial hotel   A *transient hotel* catering to a business clientele.

commercial rate   A reduced room *rate* given to businesspersons to promote *occupancy*.

commissionable   Indicates the hotel will pay *travel agents* the standard fee for business placed.

comp   Short for "complimentary" accommodations—and occasionally food and beverage—furnished without charge.

company-made (reservation)   A *reservation* guaranteed by the arriving guest's company.

concession   A hotel tenant (concessionaire) whose facilities and services are indistinguishable from those owned and operated by the hotel.

concierge   (1) A European position, increasingly found in U.S. hotels, responsible for handling guests' needs, particularly those relating to out-of-hotel services; (2) designation of the sleeping floor where these services are offered.

condominium   A multiunit dwelling wherein each owner maintains separate title to the unit while sharing ownership rights and responsibilities for the public space.

conference center   A *property* that caters to business meetings, corporate retreats and conferences. Generally considered smaller in size and more personable in nature than a convention property.

confirmed reservation   The hotel's *acknowledgment*, usually in writing, to the guest's *reservation* request.

connecting rooms   *Adjoining rooms* with direct, private access, making use of the corridor unnecessary.

consortium   A new organization, formed by existing organizations (banks, developers, hotels) to carry out a particular enterprise.

continental breakfast   A small meal including some combination of: bread, rolls, sweet rolls, juice, or coffee. Often set up in bulk by the innkeeper or host; continental breakfasts are usually self-service.

Continental plan   A method of quoting room *rates* where the charge includes a *continental breakfast* as well as the room rate.

convention rate   See *run-of-the-house rate.*

convertible bed   See *sofa bed.*

corner (room)   An *outside room* on a corner of the building having two *exposures.*

Corporate Meeting Package (CMP)   An *all-inclusive plan* quoted by *conference centers* and hotels for corporate meetings.

correction sheet   A form once used with *NCR front-office machines* to record posting errors for later reconciliation by the *night auditor.*

cot   See *rollaway bed.*

coupon   (1) A checklike form issued by *travel agents* to their clients and used by the clients to settle their hotel accounts; (2) a ticket issued by *tour groups* for the purchase of meals and other services to be charged against the *master account.* Also called a *voucher.*

credit   An accounting term that indicates a decrease in the *account receivable;* the opposite of *debit.*

cutoff date   The date on which unsold rooms from within a convention's *block* of reserved rooms are released for sale.

cutoff hour   That time at which the day's unclaimed *reservations* are released for sale to the general public.

daily rooms report   See *room count sheet.*

day rate   A reduced charge for occupancy of less than overnight; used when the *party* arrives and departs the same day. Also *part day rate* or *use rate.*

D card   A form once used with the *NCR front-office posting machines* as the machine equivalent of the *transcript;* the term is still used for the daily revenue report prepared now by the *property management system.*

dead room change   A physical change of rooms made by the hotel in the guest's absence so no tip is earned by the *last* bellperson.

debit   An accounting term that indicates an increase in the *account receivable;* the opposite of *credit.*

deluxe   A non-U.S. designation implying the best accommodations; unreliable unless part of an official rating system.

demi-pension (DP)   A non-U.S. method of quoting room *rates* similar to the *modified American plan (MAP)* but allowing the guest to select either luncheon or dinner along with breakfast and room; also called *half pension.*

density board (chart)   A noncomputerized *reservation* system where the number of rooms committed is controlled by type: *single, twin, queen,* etc.

departmental control sheet   A form maintained by each *operating department* for recording data from departmental *vouchers* before forwarding them to the front desk for *posting.* Replaced by *point-of-sale* terminals.

departure   *Check out.*

deposit reservation   See *advance deposit.*

destination hotel   The objective of—and often the sole purpose for—the guest's trip; cf. *transient hotel.*

did not stay (DNS)   Means the guest left almost immediately after *registering.*

difference returnable   See *exchange.*

dine-around plan   A method of quoting *AP* or *MAP* room rates that allows guests to dine at any of several different but cooperating hotels.

display room   See *sample room.*

D.I.T.   Domestic independent tour or domestic inclusive tour; cf. *F.I.T.*

double   (1) A bed approximately 54 by 75 inches; (2) the *rate* charged for two persons occupying one room; (3) a room with a double bed.

double–double   See *twin–double.*

double occupancy   (1) Room occupancy by two persons; (2) a ratio relating the number of rooms double occupied to the number of rooms sold.

double-occupancy rate   A *rate* used for tours where the per person charge is based on two to a room.

double-up   A designation of *double occupancy* by unrelated parties necessitating two *room rack* identifications and/or two *folios.*

downgrade   Move a *reservation* or registered guest to a lesser accommodation or *class* of service; cf. *upgrade*.

downtime   That time span during which the computer is inoperative because of malfunction or preemptive operations.

ducat   See *stock card*.

due back   See *exchange*.

due bank   See *exchange*.

due bill   See *trade advertising contract*.

dump   To *check out* early; with reference to *groups*.

duplex   A two-story *suite* with a connecting stairwell.

duvet   A cover for a bed comforter, much like a large pillowcase.

early arrival   A guest who arrives a day or two earlier than the *reservation* calls for.

EBITDA   See *house profit*.

economy class   See *tourist class*.

efficiency   Accommodations that include kitchen facilities.

elderhostel   Study programs for senior citizens that include travel and classes, often held on college campuses.

electronic data processing (EDP)   A data handling system that relies on electronic (computer) equipment.

ell   A wing of a building usually at right angles to the main structure.

emergency key (E-key)   One key that opens all guest rooms, including those locked from within, even those with the room key still in the lock; also called the great *grandmaster*.

English breakfast   A hearty breakfast of fruit, cereal, meat, eggs, toast, and beverage generally served in the United Kingdom and Ireland, but less often of late.

en pension   See *full pension*.

European plan (EP)   A method of quoting room *rates* where the charge includes room accommodations only.

exchange   The excess of cash *turn-in* over *net receipts*; the difference is returnable (due back) to the front-office cashier; also called *due back*, *due bank*, or *difference returnable*.

executive floor   See *concierge* (floor).

executive room   See *studio*.

exposure   The direction (north, south, east, or west) or view (ocean, mountain) that the guest room faces.

express check out   Mechanical or electronic methods of *check out* that expedite *departures* and eliminates the need to stop at the desk; also called *zip-out*.

extra meals   An *American plan* charge made for dining room service over and above that to which the guest is entitled.

family plan   A special room *rate* that allows children to occupy their parent's room at no additional charge.

family room   See *twin–double*.

fam trip   Familiarization trip taken by (offered to) *travel agents* at little or no cost to acquaint them with *properties* and destinations.

farm out   Assignment of guests to other *properties* when a *full house* precludes their accommodation.

fenced rates   One of several tools used by the reservations department to maximize room revenues under *yield management* systems, including nonrefundable, prepaid *reservations* and *reservations* not subject to change.

first class   A non-U.S. designation for medium-priced accommodations with corresponding facilities and services.

F.I.T.   Foreign independent tour, but has come to mean free independent tour, a traveler who is not *group* affiliated; by extension, frequent independent traveler, or full inclusive tour; cf. *D.I.T.*

flag   (1) A device for calling the room clerk's attention to a particular room in the *room rack*; (2) designating a hotel's membership in a chain or franchise.

flat rate   (1) See *run-of-the-house rate*; (2) same price for *single* or *double occupancy*.

float   The free use of outstanding funds during the period that checks and credit-card charges are in transition for payment.

floor key   See *master key*.

floor (release) limit   The maximum amount of charges permitted a credit-card user at a given *property* without clearance; the limit is established for the property, not for the user.

folio   See *guest bill*; also called an *account card*.

force majeure (forz mazhoei)   An unexpected and disruptive event that frees parties from contractual obligations; an act of God.

forecast   A future projection of estimated business volume.

forecast scheduling   Work schedules established on the basis of sales projections.

forfeited deposit   A *deposit reservation* kept by the hotel when a *no-show* fails to cancel the reservation; also called a lost deposit.

franchise   (1) An independently owned hotel or motel that appears to be part of a chain and pays a fee for that right and for the right to participate in the chain's advertising and reservation systems; (2) the chain's right (its franchise) to sell such permission; or the permission itself, or both.

franchisee   One who buys a *franchise*.

franchisor   One who sells a *franchise*.

free sale   Occurs when a *travel agent*, airline, or other agency commits hotel space without specific prior confirmation from the *property*. See also *sell and report*.

from bill number . . . to bill number   A cross-reference of *account* numbers when the bill of a guest who remains beyond one week is transferred to a new *folio*.

front   The next bellperson eligible for a *rooming* assignment or other errand apt to produce a *gratuity*; cf. *last*.

front office   A broad term that includes the physical front desk as well as the duties and functions involved in the sale and service of guest rooms.

front of the house   (1) The area of the hotel visible to guests in contrast to the back-of-the-house, which is not in the public view; (2) all of the functions that are part of the *front office*.

full day   The measure of a chargeable day for accounting purposes; three meals for an *AP* hotel, overnight for an *EP*.

full house   Means 100% *occupancy*, all guest rooms sold.

full pension   A European term for the *American plan*.

full service   Means a complete line of hotel services and departments are provided, in contrast to a *limited-service property*.

futon   A Japanese sleeping arrangement made of many layers of cotton-quilted batting that is rolled up when not in use.

garni   A non-U.S. designation for hotels without restaurant service except for *continental breakfast*.

general cashier   The chief cashier with whom deposits are made and from whom *banks* are drawn.

general manager (GM)   The hotel's chief executive.

ghost card   Nonexistent credit card or credit-card charges not supported by a signature.

global distribution system (GDS)   The *hardware, software,* and computer lines over which *travel agents,* airlines, on-line subscription networks, and others access *central reservations systems* and individual *property management systems*.

grande dame   French for an aristocratic lady; hence, an elegant, grand hotel.

grandmaster   One key that opens all guest rooms except those locked from within; see also *emergency key*.

gratuity   A tip given to an employee by a guest, sometimes willingly and sometimes automatically added to the charges; see also *plus, plus*.

graveyard   A work shift beginning about midnight.

greens fee   A charge for the use of the golf course.

group   A number of persons with whom the hotel deals (reservation, billing, etc.) as if they were one party.

guaranteed rate   The assurance of a fixed *rate* regardless of the hotel's *occupancy,* often given in consideration of a large number of *room-nights* per year pledged by a company.

guaranteed reservation   Payment for the room is promised even if the occupant fails to arrive.

guest account   See *guest bill*.

guest bill   An accounting statement used to record and display the charges and payments made by registered guests *(accounts receivable)* during their hotel stay. Different formats are used for hand-prepared bills and bills prepared by *property management systems;* also known as *folio* or *account card*.

guest check   The bill presented to patrons of the dining rooms and bars and, when signed, often used as the departmental *voucher*.

guest day (night)   The stay of one guest for one day (night); also called *room night* or *bed night*.

guest elevators   Lobby elevators for guest use exclusively; employees are permitted only during guest service, as bellpersons *rooming (a guest);* cf. *service elevators*.

guest history   A record of the guest's visits including rooms assigned, *rates* paid, special needs, credit rating and personal information; used to provide better guest service and better marketing approaches.

guest ledger   All the *guest bills* owed by registered guests *(accounts receivable)* and maintained in the *front office,* in contrast to the group of *city-ledger* bills (nonregistered guests) maintained in the accounting or back office.

guest night   See *guest day*.

guest occupancy   See *bed occupancy*.

guest-service area   See *front office*.

half-board   See *modified American plan*.

half-pension   See *demi-pension*.

handicap(ped) room   A guest room furnished with special devices and built large enough to accommodate guests with physical handicaps.

hard copy   Computer term for material that has been printed rather than merely displayed.

hard goods   Guest-room furniture: beds, chairs, etc.; cf. *soft goods*.

hardware   The physical equipment (electronic and mechanical) of a computer installation and its peripheral components; cf. *software*.

HFTP   Hospitality Financial and Technology Professionals, an association specializing in hotel accounting, finance, and technology; formerly the IAHA, International Association of Hospitality Accountants.

hide-a-bed   See *sofa bed*.

high season   See *in-season rate*.

high tea   A fairly substantial late afternoon or early evening meal; cf. *afternoon tea*.

HITIS   An acronym for Hospitality Industry Technology Integration Standards, which are computer *interface* standards developed to facilitate the *interface* of computer systems from various vendors onto the hotel's *property management system*.

HOBIC   An acronym for Hotel Outward Bound Information Center, the telephone company's long-distance hotel network.

holdover   See *overstay*.

Hollywood bed   *Twin* beds joined by a common headboard.

Hollywood length   An extra-long bed of 80 to 85 inches instead of the usual 75 inches. Same as *California length*.

Hospitality Sales and Marketing Association International (HSMAI)   An international association of hotel sales and marketing managers.

hospitality suite (room)   A facility used for entertaining, usually at conventions, trade shows and similar meetings.

hostel   An inexpensive but supervised facility with limited services catering to young travelers on foot or bicycle; cf. *elderhostel*.

hotelier   Innkeeper or hotelkeeper.

hotel manager   Hotel executive responsible for the front of the house, including *front office,* housekeeping, and uniformed services; sometimes called rooms manager, house manager or guest-services manager.

hotel operating hours   Twenty-four hours per day; 7 days per week; 365 days per year.

hotel rep   See *rep(resentative)*.

hot list   A list of lost or stolen credit cards furnished to hotels and other retailers by the credit-card companies.

house   A synonym for hotel, as in *house bank, house count, house laundry;* see also *property*.

house bank   See *bank*.

house call   Telephone call made to the outside of the hotel by a member of the staff doing company business; not subject to a *posting* charge as guest calls are.

house count   The number of registered guests; cf. *room count*.

housekeeper's report   A report on the status of guest rooms, prepared by the *linen room* and used by the front desk to verify the accuracy of the *room rack*.

house laundry   A hotel-operated facility, usually on premises, in contrast to an *outside laundry* that contracts with the hotel to handle *house* and/or guest laundry.

house profit   Net profit before income taxes from all *operating departments* except *store rentals* and before provision for rent, interest, taxes, depreciation, and amortization; renamed as "earnings before interest, taxes, depreciation, and amortization (EBITDA)" by the 1977 edition and subsequent editions of the *Uniform System of Accounts* for hotels; see also *bottom line*.

house rooms   Guest rooms set aside for hotel use and excluded, therefore, from *available rooms*.

housing bureau   A citywide reservation office, usually run by the convention bureau, for assigning *reservation* requests to participating hotels during a citywide convention.

Hubbart room rate formula   A basis for determining room *rates* developed by Roy Hubbart and distributed by the *American Hotel & Lodging Association*.

HVAC   Acronym for heating, ventilation and airconditioning.

ideal average room rate   This formula assumes a hotel sells an equal number of rooms from both the least expensive upward and from the most expensive downward. The resulting average rate is a theoretical benchmark against which to compare actual operating results.

imprest petty cash   A technique for controlling petty cash disbursements by which a special, small cash fund is used for minor cash payments and periodically reimbursed.

incentive (group, guest, tour, or trip)   Persons who have won a hotel stay (usually with transportation included) as a reward for meeting and excelling sales quotas or other company-established standards.

inclusive terms   (1) Phrase that is sometimes used in Europe to designate the *American plan*; (2) indicates that a price *quote* includes tax and *gratuity*.

independent   A *property* with no chain or *franchise* affiliation, although one proprietor might own several such properties.

information rack   An alphabetic listing of registered guests with a room number cross-reference.

in-house   On the premises, such as an inhouse laundry; cf. *off premises*.

in-season rate   A *resort's* maximum rate, charged when the demand is heaviest, as it is during the middle of the summer or winter; cf. *off-season rate, low season, shoulder*.

inside call   A telephone call that enters the switchboard from inside the hotel; a telephone call that remains within the hotel; cf. *outside call*.

inside room   A guest room that faces an inner courtyard or light court enclosed by three or four sides of the building; cf. *outside room*.

inspector   Supervisory position in the housekeeping department responsible for releasing *on change* rooms to ready status.

interface   Computer term designating the ability of one computer to communicate with another; see *HITIS*.

International Association of Travel Agents (IATA)   A professional affiliation which both lobbies on behalf of the travel industry and identifies/verifies legitimate *travel agents* to other vendors.

Internet telephony   Telephone capability on Internet access; also called VoIP, Voice-over Internet Protocol.

interstate call   A long-distance call that crosses state lines.

interval ownership   See *timeshare*.

intrastate call   A long-distance telephone call that originates and terminates within the same state.

in-WATS   See *wide area telephone service*.

IT number   The code assigned to an inclusive tour for identification and *booking*.

joiner   A guest who joins another guest or *party* already *registered*.

junior suite   One large room, sometimes with a half partition, furnished as both a *parlor* and a bedroom.

king   An extra-long, extra-wide *double* bed at least 78 by 82 inches.

lanai   A Hawaiian term for "veranda"; a room with a porch or balcony usually overlooking gardens or water.

last   The designation for the bellperson who most recently completed a *front*; cf. *front*.

last-room availability   A sophisticated reservations system that provides real-time access between the chain's *central reservations system* and the hotel's *in-house property management system*.

late arrival   A guest with a *reservation* who expects to arrive after the *cutoff hour* and so notifies the hotel.

late charge   A departmental charge that arrives at the *front office* for billing after the guest has *checked out*.

late check out   A departing guest who remains beyond the *check-out hour* with permission of the desk and thus without charge.

least cost router (LCR)   Telephone equipment that routes the call over the least expensive lines available. Also called automatic route selector (ARS).

light baggage   Insufficient luggage in quantity or quality on which to extend credit; the guest pays in advance.

limited service   A hotel or motel that provides little or no services other than the room; a *budget hotel (motel)*; cf. *full service*.

linen closet   A storage closet for linens and other housekeeping supplies usually located conveniently along the corridor for the use of the housekeeping staff.

linen room   The housekeeper's office and the center of operations for that department, including the storage of linens and uniforms.

lockout   (1) Denying the guest access to the room, usually because of an unpaid bill; (2) a key of that name.

log   A record of activities maintained by several *operating departments*.

lost and found   An area, usually under the housekeeper's jurisdiction, for the control and storage of lost-and-found items.

low season   See *off-season rate*.

maid's report   A status-of-rooms report prepared by individual room attendants and consolidated with other reports by the *linen room* into the *housekeeper's report*.

mail and key rack   An antiquated piece of *front-office* equipment where both guest mail and room keys were stored by room number.

maitre d' The shortened form of maitre d'hotel, the head-waiter.

market mix The variety and percentage distribution of hotel guests—conventioneer, tourist, businessperson, and so on.

master account One *folio* prepared for a *group* (convention, company, tour) on which all group charges are accumulated.

master key One key controlling several *pass keys* and opening all the guests rooms on one floor; also called a *floor key*.

master franchise A *franchisee's* right to resell pieces of the *franchise* to other *franchisees*.

menu An array of function choices displayed to the computer user who selects the appropriate function.

message lamp A light on the telephone, used to notify an occupant that the telephone system has a message to relay.

meters See *square meters*.

minisuite See *junior suite*.

minor departments The less important *operating departments* (excluding room, food, and beverage) such as valet, laundry, and gift shop.

miscellaneous charge order (MCO) Airline *voucher* authorizing the sale of services to the guest named on the form, with payment due from the airline.

modified American plan (MAP) A method of quoting room *rates* in which the charge includes breakfast and dinner as well as the room.

mom-and-pop A small, family-owned business with limited capitalization in which the family, rather than paid employees, furnishes the bulk of the labor.

moment of truth A popular term describing the interaction between a guest and a member of the staff, when all of the advertising and representations made by the hotel come down to the quality of the service delivered at that moment.

morning call A *wake-up call* made by the telephone operator or automatically by the *property management system* at the guest's request.

move-in date The date that a group, convention or trade show arrives to begin preparing for their meeting or exhibit; cf. *move-out date*.

move-out date The date that a group, convention or trade show vacates the *property* after a meeting or exhibit; cf. *move-in date*.

Ms An abbreviation used to indicate a female guest without consideration of marital status.

Murphy bed A standard bed that folds or swings into a wall or cabinet in a closet-like fashion, trademarked.

NCR front-office posting machine A mechanical device used to *post folios* and automatically accumulate *account receivable* and revenue balances; two popular models, the NCR (National Cash Register Company) 2000 and the NCR 42(00), neither of which are manufactured today, were replaced by electronic *property management systems*.

NCR paper No carbon required; paper is specially treated to produce copies without carbon.

net rate A room *rate quote* that indicates no additional commissions or fees are to be paid to *travel agents* or other third parties.

net receipts The difference between cash taken in and *cash paid-outs*.

night audit A daily reconciliation, which is completed during the *graveyard* shift, of both *accounts receivable* and incomes from the *operating departments*.

night auditor The person or persons responsible for the *night audit*.

night auditor's report An interim report of *accounts receivable*, room statistics, and incomes earned; prepared by the *night auditor* for the *general manager*.

nightbird Euphemism for prostitute.

night clerk's report Another name for the *room count sheet*.

no reservation (NR) See *walk-in*.

no-show A *reservation* that fails to arrive.

occupancy (percentage of occupancy, occupancy percentage) A ratio relating the number of rooms sold *(room count)* to the number of *rooms available* for sale.

occupied (1) A room that is sold or taken and is not available for sale; (2) someone is physically in the room at this time.

ocean front A front room with an *exposure* facing directly on the ocean; cf. *ocean view*.

ocean view Other than a front room, but with some view of the ocean; cf. *ocean front*.

off line See *batch processing*.

off premises Not on the *property*; cf. *in-house*.

off-season rate A reduced room *rate* charged by *resort hotels* when demand is lowest; cf. *in-season rate*, *shoulder*.

off the shelf Standardized, not customized, computer software.

off the street (OS) See *walk-in*.

on change The status of a room recently vacated but not yet available for new occupants.

one- (two-) pull dialing One (two)-digit telephone dialing (or Touch-Tone) that connects the caller to hotel services such as room service and bellstand.

online (computer) Computer facilities hooked directly to input and output devices for instantaneous communication; cf. *batch processing*.

open credit Credit based only on a guest's signature.

operating departments Those divisions of the hotel directly involved with the service of the guest, in contrast to support divisions such as personnel and accounting.

out of inventory (OOI) A significant problem has removed this room from availability. Although *out of order (OOO)* rooms are usually available in only a matter of hours, OOI rooms may be unavailable for days or weeks.

out of order (OOO) The room is not available for sale because of some planned or unexpected temporary shutdown of facilities.

outside call A telephone call that enters the switchboard from outside the hotel; a call that terminates outside the hotel; cf. *inside call*.

outside laundry (valet) A nonhotel laundry or valet service contracted by the hotel in order to offer a full line of services; cf. *house laundry*.

outside room A room on the perimeter of the building facing outward with an *exposure* more desirable than that of an *inside* room.

out-WATS   See *wide area telephone service*.

over or short   A discrepancy between the cash on hand and the amount that should be on hand.

overbooking   Committing more rooms to possible guest occupancy than are actually available.

override   (1) Extra commission above standard percentage to encourage or reward quantity bookings; (2) process by which the operator bypasses certain limits built into the computer program.

overstay   A guest who remains beyond the expiration of the anticipated stay.

package   A number of services (transportation, room, food, entertainment) normally purchased separately but put together and marketed at a reduced price made possible by volume and *breakage*.

paid in advance   A room charge that is collected prior to occupancy, which is the usual procedure when a guest has *light baggage*; with some motels, it is standard procedure for every guest.

paid-outs   See *cash paid-outs*.

parlor   The living room portion of a *suite*.

part day rate (guest)   See *day rate*.

party   *Front-office* term that references either the individual guest ("Who's the party in room 100?") or several members of the group ("When will your party arrive?").

pass key   (1) A sub *master key* capable of opening all the locks within a limited, single set of 12 to 18 rooms, but no other; (2) guest key for access to public space (spa, pool).

PBX   See *private branch exchange*.

penthouse   Accommodations, almost always *suites*, located on the top floor of the hotel, theoretically on the roof.

percentage of occupancy   See *occupancy*.

permanent guest   A resident of long-term duration whose stay may or may not be formalized with a lease.

personal digital assistant (PDA)   Hand-held computer, often with wireless capability.

petite suite   See *junior suite*.

petty cash   See *imprest petty cash*.

pickup   (1) The procedure once used with *NCR front-office posting machines* to accumulate the *folio* balance by entering the previous balance into the machine before posting the new charges; (2) the figure so entered.

pit   See *cashier's well*.

plan   The basis on which room *rate* charges are made; see *American plan* and *European plan*.

plus, plus   Shorthand for the addition of tax and tip to the check or price per cover.

pocket   A portion of a manual *room rack* made to accept the *room rack slips* and provide a permanent record of accommodations and *rates*.

point-of-sale (POS) terminal   An electronic "cash register" providing *on-line* communications to the *property management system* from remote sales locations, in contrast to an input device at the *front office*.

porte–cochère   The covered entryway that provides shelter for those entering and leaving a hotel; French: coach gate [port-ko-shâr].

porterage   (1) Arrangements made to handle luggage; (2) the charge for luggage handling.

posting   The process of recording items in an accounting record, such as a *folio*.

power of the pen   Right to *comp* guest services.

preassign   *Reservations* are assigned to specific rooms that are *blocked* before the guests arrive; cf. *prereg(istration)*.

prereg(istration)   Registration is done by the hotel before the guest arrives, although the actual *(reg)istration card* is not completed; used with groups and tours to reduce *front-office* congestion, since individual guests need not then approach the desk; cf. *preassign*.

private branch exchange (PBX)   A telephone switchboard.

projection   See *forecast scheduling*.

property   Another way to reference a hotel, includes physical facilities and personnel.

property management system (PMS)   A hotel's, that is a *property's*, basic computer installation designed for a variety of functions in both the back office and *front office*.

published rate   The full *rack rate* quoted or published for public information; the rate quoted without discounts.

quad   Accommodations for four persons; see also *twin–double*.

quality assurance   A managerial and operational approach that enlists employee support in delivering a consistently high level of service.

quality circle   A group of persons from different but related departments who meet on a regular basis for dialogue and problem resolutions as part of a *quality assurance* program.

quality management   See *total quality management* and *quality assurance*.

quality of the reservation   Differentiates *reservations* on how likely they are to be honored by the guest: *paid in advance reservation* vs. *guaranteed reservation* vs. 6 PM *cutoff hour*, etc.

queen   An extra-long, extra-wide *double* bed, about 80 to 85 inches long by 60 inches wide; see *California length*; see *king*.

queuing theory   The management of lines (queues of persons waiting their turn) in order to maximize the flow and minimize the inconvenience, but doing so with attention to operating costs. Also called *waiting-line theory*.

quote   To state the cost of an item, room *rates* in particular.

rack   See *room rack*.

rack rate   The full *rate*, without discounts, that one *quotes* as a room charge; so called because the *room rack* is the source of the information.

rate   The charge made by a hotel for its rooms.

rate cutting   A reduction in *rate* that attracts business away from competitors rather than creating new customers or new markets.

real estate investment trust (REIT)   A form of real estate ownership (public corporation) that became popular during the real estate recovery of the mid-1990s because of income tax advantages at that time.

rebate   See *allowance*.

recap   A summary or recap(itulation) of several *transcript* sheets in order to obtain the day's grand totals.

referral A *central reservation system* operated by *independent* properties in contrast to that operated by chains and *franchisors* for their *affiliated hotels.*

registered, not assigned (RNA) The guest has *registered,* but is awaiting assignment to a specific room until space becomes available; see *on change.*

register (ing), registration (1) Indication (completing and signing the *registration card*) by a new arrival of intent to become a guest; (2) register: the name for a book that served at one time as the registration record.

(reg)istration card A form completed during *registration* to provide the hotel with information about the guest, including name and address, and to provide the guest with information about the hotel, including legal issues.

REIT See *real estate investment trust.*

reminder clock A special alarm clock that can be set at 5-minute intervals across a 24-hour day; used by the *front office* chiefly for *wake-up calls.*

rep(resentative) Short for *hotel representative:* An agent under contract, rather than an employee under salary, who represents the hotel in distant cities or for special activities, chiefly marketing activities, but sometimes gaming related.

reservation A mutual agreement between the guest and the hotel, the former to take accommodations on a given date for a given period of time, and the latter to furnish the same.

reservation rack A piece of *front-office* equipment, largely replaced by the *property management system,* providing an alphabetic list of anticipated arrivals with a summary of their needs, filed chronologically by anticipated date of arrival.

residential hotel A hotel catering to long-stay guests who have made the *property* their home and residence; see also *permanent guest.*

resident manager See *hotel manager.*

resort hotel A hotel that caters to vacationing guests by providing recreational and entertainment facilities; usually a *destination hotel.*

RevPar Short for revenue per available room, a ratio of room revenue to the number of *available rooms.*

road warrior Slang for a frequent traveler battling the hardships and indignities of being on the road, that is, of traveling, for long periods of time.

rollaway bed A portable utility bed approximately 30 by 72 inches; also called a *cot.*

rondoval A *suite* in the round, special to honeymoon *resorts.*

room charge sheet See *room count sheet.*

room count The number of occupied rooms; cf. *house count.*

room count sheet A permanent record of the *room rack* prepared nightly and used to verify the accuracy of room statistics; also called a *night clerk's report.*

rooming (a guest) The entire procedure during which the desk greets, *registers,* and assigns new arrivals, and the bell staff accompanies them to their rooms (rooms them).

rooming slip A form issued by the desk during the *rooming* procedure to the bellperson for guest identification, and left by the bellperson with the guest to give the guest an opportunity to verify name, *rate,* and room number.

room inspection report A checklist of the condition of the guest room prepared by the *inspector* when the room attendant has finished cleaning.

room night See *guest day (night).*

room rack A piece of *front-office* equipment, largely replaced by the *property management system,* in which each guest room is represented by a metal *pocket* with colors and symbols to aid the room clerk in identifying the accommodations.

room rack slip (card) A form prepared from the *registration card* identifying the occupant of each room and filed in the *pocket* of the *room rack* assigned to that guest; cf. *room rack.*

rooms available See *available rooms.*

room service Food and beverage service provided in the privacy of the guest room.

rooms ledger See *guest ledger.*

rule-of-thumb rate A guideline for setting room rates with the hotel charging $1 in rate for each $1,000 per room construction costs; see also *building cost rate formula.*

run-of-the-house rate A special *group* rate generally the midpoint of the *rack rate* with a single, flat price applying to any room, *suites* excepted, assigned on a *best available* basis.

ryokan A traditional Japanese inn.

safe deposit boxes Individual sections of the vault where guests store valuables and cashiers keep house *banks.*

sales per occupied room See *average daily rate.*

sales rack A piece of *front-office* equipment, now replaced by the *property management system,* used for the storage and control of *stock cards* (*ducats* or *sales tickets*).

sales ticket See *stock card.*

salon The European designation for *parlor.*

sample room A guest room used to merchandise and display goods, usually in combination with sleeping accommodations.

Scottish breakfast See *English breakfast.*

seamless connectivity The next step beyond *last room availability. Travel agents,* airlines, on-line subscription networks, and others can access a *property*'s room availability right down to the last room.

season rate See *in-season rate.*

segmentation The proliferation of many hotel types as the lodging industry attempts to target its facilities to smaller and smaller market niches (segments).

sell and report *Wholesalers,* tour operators, *reps,* airlines, and *central reservation systems free sell* rooms, periodically reporting the sale to the hotel; also called status control.

sell through Denoting days for which no *reservation* arrivals are accepted; reservations for previous days will be accepted and allowed to stay through the date; cf. *box* date.

sell up Convince the arriving guest to take a higher priced room than was planned or reserved.

service charge A percentage (usually from 10 to 20%) added to the bill for distribution to service employees in lieu of direct tipping; see also *plus, plus.*

service elevators Back elevators for use by employees (room service, housekeeping, maintenance, etc.) on hotel business and not readily visible to the guests; cf. *guest elevator.*

share   More than one person occupying the guest room.

shoulder   Marketing term designating the period between peaks and valleys; the time on either side of the *in-season rate* or the leveling off between two sales peaks.

Siberia   Jargon for a very undesirable room, one sold only after the *house* fills and then only after the guest has been alerted to its location or condition.

single   (1) A bed approximately 36 by 75 inches; (2) a room with accommodations for one; (3) occupancy by one person; (4) the *rate* charged for one person.

single supplement   An extra charge over the tour *package* price assessed for *single* occupancy when the total price was based on a *double-occupancy rate*.

sitting room   See *parlor*.

size   The capacity of the hotel as measured by the number of guest rooms.

skip   See *skipper*.

skipper   A guest who departs surreptitiously, leaving an unpaid bill.

sleeper   A departed guest whose record remains active giving the appearance of an *occupied* room.

sleeper occupancy   See *bed occupancy*.

sleep out   A room that is taken, *occupied,* and paid for but not slept in.

slide   The transcription error caused by a misplaced decimal, as when 36.20 is written 3.62.

smart card   A credit card or other card containing a microprocessor capable of interfacing with the *PMS* or other computer configurations.

SMERF   Marketing reference to Society, Military, Educational, Religious and Fraternal organizations.

sofa bed   A sofa with fixed back and arms that unfolds into a standard *single* or *double* bed; also called a *hide-a-bed*.

soft goods   Linens; cf. *hard goods*.

software   The programs and routines that give instructions to the computer; cf. *hardware*.

special attention (SPATT)   A label assigned to important guests designated for special treatment; see *very important person*.

split rate   Division of the total room *rate* charge among the room's several occupants; see *share*.

split shift   A work pattern divided into two work segments with an unusually long period (more than a rest or mealtime) between.

spread rate   Assignment of *group* members or conventioneers using the standard *rate* distribution, although prices might be less than *rack rates*; cf. *run-of-the-house rate*.

square meters   Measurement used in the metric system: 0.093 square meters equal 1 square foot; 10.76 square feet equals 1 square meter.

star rating   An unreliable ranking (except for some well-known exceptions) of hotel facilities both in the United States and abroad.

star reservation   Indicates the arrival of a *very important person, SPATT*.

stay   See *stayover*.

stayover   (1) Any guest who remains overnight; (2) an anticipated check out who fails to depart; also called *holdover* or *overstay*.

stock card   Once used with a *sales rack* to represent the content of the *room rack pocket* when the room rack was distant and therefore inaccessible to the room clerk; also called a *ducat*.

store rentals   Income earned from shop leases; cf. *concession*.

studio   (1) A bed approximately 36 inches wide by 75 inches long without headboard or footboard that serves as a sofa during the day; (2) the room containing such a bed; cf. *sofa bed*.

suite   A series of *connecting rooms* with one or more bedrooms and a *parlor;* very large suites occasionally include additional rooms such as dining rooms; see *hospitality suite*.

summary transcript sheet   See *recap*.

supper   (1) A late-night meal; (2) the evening meal when midday service is designated as dinner.

swing   The work shift between the day *watch* and the *graveyard* shift; usually starts between 3 and 4 PM.

T&T   See *trash and towels*.

take down   Cancel *reservations* that are without an *advance deposit* after the *cutoff hour*.

tally sheet   See *density board*.

TelAutograph   A historical piece of communication equipment that transcribes written messages.

timeshare   (1) A method of acquiring vacation accommodations by which each occupant purchases the right to use the facility (room or apartment) for a specified period, an interval; partial ownership of the real estate, which was not possible initially, has broadened the market; (2) term for users who share computer facilities.

time stamp   A clock mechanism that prints date and time when activated.

to-date   Designates a cumulative amount; the sum of all figures in the current period (usually monthly or annually) including the day or date in question.

total quality management (TQM)   A way to continuously improve performance at every level of operation, in every functional area of an organization, using all available human and capital resources. See also *quality assurance*.

tour group   See *package*.

tourist class   A non-U.S. designation for *limited-service* hotels whose accommodations frequently lack private baths; also called *economy class*.

trade advertising contract   An agreement by which hotel accommodations are swapped for advertising space or broadcast time; also called a *due bill*.

traffic sheet   A *departmental control sheet* used by the telephone department before *call accounting systems*.

transcript   A pencil-and-paper form used by the *night auditor* to accumulate and separate the day's charges by departments and guests.

transcript ruler   The headings of a *transcript* sheet attached to a straightedge and used as a column guide at the bottom of the long *transcript* sheet.

transfer   (1) An accounting technique used to move a figure from one form to another, usually between *folios*; (2) the movement of guests and/or luggage from one point to another (e.g., from the airline terminal to the hotel); see *porterage*.

transfer folio A special unnumbered *folio* used to carry noncomputerized guest accounts beyond the first week's stay when the original folio was numbered and cross referenced to the *registration card.*

transfer from The *debit* portion of a *transfer* between accounts or ledgers.

transfer journal A *front-office* form once used to record *transfer* entries between different accounts or different ledgers.

transfer to The *credit* portion of a *transfer* between accounts or ledgers.

transient guest A short-term guest; see *transient hotel.*

transient hotel A hotel catering to short-stay guests who sometimes stop en route to other destinations; cf. *destination hotel.*

transient ledger See *guest ledger.*

transmittal form The form provided by national credit-card companies for recording and remitting nonelectronic credit-card charges accumulated by the hotel.

transposition A transcription error caused by reordering the sequence of digits, as when 389 is written as 398.

trash and towels References basic service fee paid for each stay by occupants of *timeshares.*

travel agent (TA) An entrepreneur who *books* space and facilities for clients in hotels and public carriers for which hotels usually pay a 10 percent commission.

travel and entertainment card (T&E) A credit card issued by a proprietary company, or bank, for which the user pays an annual fee; cf. *bank card.*

Travel Industry Association of America (TIAA) A nonprofit association of many travel-related agencies and private businesses working to develop travel and tourism in the United States.

tray service The fee charged *American plan* guests for *room service.*

tub See *cashier's well.*

turn-away (1) To refuse *walk-in* business because rooms are unavailable; (2) the guest so refused.

turn-downs An evening service rendered by the housekeeping department, which replaces soiled bathroom linen and prepares the bed for use.

turn-in The sum deposited with the *general cashier* by the departmental cashier at the close of each shift.

turnkey A facility (computer, *franchise*, entire hotel) so complete that it is ready for use at the turn of a key.

twin (1) A bed approximately 39 inches wide by 75 inches long to sleep a single occupant; (2) a room with two such beds, *twins.*

twin–double (1) Two double beds; (2) a room with two such beds capable of accommodating 4 persons; see *quad.*

twins Two *twin* beds.

type The kind of market toward which the hotel is directed, traditionally: *commercial, residential,* and *resort.*

understay A guest who leaves before the expiration of the anticipated stay.

Uniform System of Accounts for the Lodging Industry A manual and dictionary of accounting terms, primarily incomes and expenses, to ensure industry-wide uniformity in terminology and use.

United States Travel and Tourism Administration (USTTA) A division of the Department of Commerce responsible for promoting travel to the United States; successor to the U.S. Travel Service (USTS).

unoccupied (1) An unsold room; (2) a room that is *occupied,* but is temporarily vacant, the guest is out.

u-owe-me See *exchange.*

upgrade Move a *reservation* or a currently registered guest to a better accommodation or class of service; cf. *downgrade.*

use rate See *day rate.*

user-friendly Computer design, application, or implementation that minimizes the user's fears, encouraging purchase and use of the equipment.

vacancy The hotel is not fully *occupied,* so there are rooms available for sale.

very important person (VIP) A reservation or guest who warrants *special attention (SPATT)* and handling.

video display terminal (VDT) See *cathode ray tube.*

VoIP Voice-over Internet Protocol. See *internet telephony.*

voucher (1) The form used by the *operating departments* to notify the front desk of charges incurred by a particular guest; (2) form furnished by a *travel agent* as a receipt for a client's advance *reservation* payment; see *coupon.*

waiting-line theory See *queuing theory.*

wake-up call See *morning call.*

walk (a guest) To turn away guests holding confirmed *reservations* due to a lack of available rooms.

walk-in A guest without a *reservation* who requests and receives accommodations.

walk-through A thorough examination of the *property* by a hotel executive, *franchise* inspector, prospective buyer, etc.

watch Another term for the work shift.

WATS See *wide area telephone service.*

who An unidentified guest in a room that appears vacant in the *room rack.*

wholesaler An entrepreneur who conceives, finances, and services *group* and *package* tours that he or she promotes (often through *travel agents*) to the general public.

wide area telephone service (WATS) Long-distance telephone lines provided at special rates to large users; separate charges are levied for incoming and outgoing WATS lines.

worldwide travel vouchers (WTVs) Form of payments drawn against a well-known financial institution (usually a major credit-card company).

xenodogheionology The study of the history, lore, and stories associated with inns, hotels, and motels (zeno-dog-hi-on-ology).

yield The product of *occupancy* times *average daily rate.*

yield management (1) Controlling room *rates* and restricting *occupancy* in order to maximize gross revenue *(yield)* from all sources; (2) a computerized program using artificial intelligence.

youth hostel See *hostel.*

zero out To balance the *guest bill* as the guest *checks out* and makes settlement.

zip-out See *express check out.*

Web Sites

• • •

Categories are representative; they are not intended to be complete.

Listings are abbreviated because http: //www. **has been dropped.**

Americans With Disabilities Act (ADA)

Catalog of assistive technology: listen-up.org/edu/assist.htm

Compliance and checklists: usdoj.gov/crt/ada/hsurvey.pdf

Legal action taken by Department of Justice: usdoj.gov/crt/ada/pubs/reg9rpt.htm

Proposed rule changes: usdj.gov/crt/ada/t2nprm94.htm

Report on ADA activities: usdoj.gov/crt/ada/civicfac.htm

Consortia and Affiliates

American Resort Development Association–Fractional ownerships: arda.org

Anti-Counterfeiting Coalition: iacc.org

Boutique Hotels–Bookings for independently owned and operated: boutiquelodging.com

Historic Hotels of America: historichotels.org

International Association of Conference Centers: iacconline.com

International Spa Association: ispa.com

Interval International–Exchange of times and periods: resortdeveloper.com

Society for Accessible Travel & Hospitality–Handicapped travel: sath.org

Timeshare Users Group–Self-help membership association: tug2.net

Utell International–Rep for 5,000 hotels worldwide: utell.com

Credit Cards

American Express–Has a long history in travel and tourism: americanexpress.com

Buyers' Zone–Multiple quotes for card processing installations: buyerszone.com

Card Web–News and information about credit cards: cardweb.com

Federal Trade Commission–Guide to e-payment protection: ftc.gov

3 Delta Systems–A Merchant Service Provider: 3deltasystems.com

UATP (Universal Air Travel Plan)–travel cards, but not consumer cards: uatp.com

Environment

Design magazine: isdesignet.com

Environmental magazine: greenatworkmag.com

Environmental News Network: enn.com

Hotels offering environmental friendly facilities: greenhotels.com

Frequent Guest Programs

Preferred Guest (Starwood Hotels): starwood.com/preferredguest/terms_conditions.html

Priority Club Rewards (Six Continents Hotels): priorityclub.com

Hotels
All-suites

Homestead Studio Suites (studio rooms): homesteadhotels.com

Staybridge Suites (extended stay): staybridge.com

Boutiques

W Hotels (division of Starwood Hotel): whotels.com

Chains

Cendant: cendant.com

Choice Hotels: choicehotels.com

Hilton: hilton.com

Red Lion or WestCoast Family of Hotels: redlion.com or westcoasthotels.com

Red Roof (part of the French chain, Accor): redroof.com

Jobs

Hilton–One company's effort: hilton.com [click job search]

Hospitality careers: hcareers.net

Hyatt–One company's effort: careers.hyatt.com

Monsterboard–Openings listed by geography, career or interest: monster.com

Net-temps.com (enter hotels)

Locks and Keys (Access control)

kaba-ilco.com

saflok.com

tesalocks.com

uniqey.com

vingcard.com

Maps

For plotting adventures: away.com

Road trip planner: bestwestern.com

Maps for any place: mapquest.com

Miscellaneous

Booklet on Hotel Crib Safety: cpsc.gov/cpscpub/pubs/cribsafe.html

Feng Shui (for hotel design): hotelfengshui.com

SafePlace Corporation (hotel safety accreditation by private company): safeplace.com

State of Texas (sales tax procedure for hotels): window.state.tx.us/taxinfo/taxforms/00-forms.html

U.S. Government (click per diem): policyworks.gov/org/main/mt/homepage/mtt/

Professional Associations and Public Interest Groups

Asian American Hotel Owners Association (AAHOA): aahoa.org

American Hotel & Lodging Association (affiliation of state associations): ahla.com

American Society of Association Executives (ASAE): asaenet.org

CHRIE (affiliation of hotel and restaurant educators): chrie.org

Convention Industry Council (formerly Convention Liaison Council): conventionindustry.org

Green Seal (giving environmental approval): greenseal.org

Hospitality Financial and Technology Professionals (HFTP) (formerly, International Association of Hospitality Accountants; previously Hotel/Motel Accountants): hftp.org

International Executive Housekeepers Association, Inc.: ieha.org.

National Sleep Foundation (sleep research and sleep aids): sleepfoundation.org

Travel Industry Association of America (association of travel interests): tia.org

United States Tour Operators Association (USTOA): ustoa.com

Publications

Credit Card News–Trade publication for credit card users: creditnews.com

Hotels–International coverage: hotelsmag.com

Hotel & Motel Management (H&MM): hotelmotel.com

Hotel & Travel Index–Lists 75,000 hotels: htihotelink.com

Journal of Hospitality & Tourism Education: publications@chrie.org

Lodging (publication of the AH&LA): lodgingnews.com

Lodging/Hospitality Magazine (need to register): lhonline.com

Meetings & Conventions Magazine: meetings-conventions@ntmllc.com

Spas: spamagazine.com

Travel Weekly–More travel issues than hotel matters: travelweekly.com

USA Today (General newspaper): usatoday.com

Wall Street Journal (International business news): WSJ.com

Research and Resources

American Hotel & Lodging Association (AH&LA): ahla.com (click information center)

Findarticles.com

(click hotels, hotel management, etc.)

Globalhospitalityresources.com
(membership required)
Globalhotelnetwork.com
(news releases about hotels wordwide)
Glossary of travel terms (Iowa State University):
adp.ia state.edn/vpbf/accounting/
tr_glossary.htm
Thehighlandgroup.com
(click hotels)
HVS International (worldwide reports):
hvsinternational.com
Hotel real estate: lodgingeconometrics.com
Meetings and Conventions Guide to Facilities:
mcgavel.com
Meetings West/South and East Magazine (database
of facilities): meetings411.com
Michigan State University:
tourismcenter.msu.edu/MTVTA
Phocuswright.com
(research reports for sale)
PKF Consulting: (research reports for sale)
headline.com
PricewaterhouseCoopers: (research reports for sale)
pwcglobal.com
Realtime Hotel Reports LLC (lodging industry
research): hotelreports.com
R. K. Miller & Associates, Inc. (lodging industry
research): rkmillerInc.com
Rushmore Letter: hvsinternational.com
Articles by Ron Kaufman: ronkaufman.com
Smith Travel Research: (research reports for sale)
smithtravelresearch.com
U.S. Census–Counts the nation's lodging
establishments: census.gov

Reservations and Exchanges

Bidding for Travel: bidding for travel.com
Discount reservation service: expedia.com
Innlink, LLC (wholly owned subsidiary of
ShoLodge, Inc.): innlink.com
Timeshare trading of Marriott properties:
ownertrades.com

Discount reservation service: priceline.com
Travelocity (discount reservation service):
travelocity.com
Timeshare trading:
vacationsonly.com/trading_timeshares_tradefor
.jsp
Walked guest (rights of): findlaw.com (search for
"walked guest")

Technology

CSS Hotel Systems (PMS purveyor):
csshotelsystems.com
Data Plus, Inc. (PMS purveyor): dphs.com
(Technology modeling and best practices) Host.com
Registration and software services: event411.com
Registration and software services:
eventbookings.com
Registration and software services:
eventregistration.com
Execu/Tech PMS purveyor: execu-tech.com
Galaxy Hotel Systems (subsidiary of Starwood
Hotels): galaxyhotelsystems.com
Micros Fidelity (PMS purveyor): micros.com
Registration and software services: register123.com
Registration and software services: seeuthere.com
Springer-Miller Systems (PMS purveyor):
smshost.com

Tourism & Travel

Guide to sites (worldwide): concierge.com
National Center for Infectious Diseases (traveler's
health): cdc.gov/travel
Pet-friendly hotels (hotels willing to accept pets):
petswelcome.com
Travel routing (from American Automobile
Association): aaa.com
Travel tips (and business etiquette): a-zoftourism.com
Travel warnings (Foreign & Commonwealth Office
of U.K. government): fco.gov.uk
Travel warnings (U.S. government):
travel.state.gov/travel_warnings.html

Bibliography

• • •

A Hospitality Guide to the Americans with Disabilities Act. Horsham, PA: LPR Publications, 1999.

Abbot, P. *Front Office: Procedures, Special Skills and Management,* 2nd ed. Oxford: Butterworth-Heinemann, 1999.

Abramson, Susan, and Stuchin, Marcie. *The Boutique Hotel.* Weimar, TX: Culinary and Hospitality Industry Publications Service, 2001.

The ABCs of Travel. New York: Public Transportation and Travel Division, Ziff-Davis, 1972.

Anolik, Alexander. *Travel, Tourism and Hospitality Law.* Elmsford, NY: National Publishers of the Black Hills, 1988.

Arthur, Roland, and Gladwell, Derek. *The Hotel Assistant Manager,* 3rd ed. London: Barrie & Rockliff, 1975.

Astroff, Milton, and Abbey, James. *Convention Sales and Services,* 5th ed. Cranbury, NJ: Waterbury Press, 1998.

Axler, Bruce. *Room Care for Hotels and Motels.* Indianapolis, IN: ITT Educational Publishing, 1974.

Baird, C., and Carla, L. *Front Office Assignment.* London: Pitman Publishing Ltd., 1988.

Baker, Sue, Bradley, Pam, and Huyton, Jeremy. *Principles of Hotel Front Office Operations,* 2nd ed. London: Cassell PLC, 2000.

Barba, Stephen. "Operating the Traditional American Plan Resort," in *The Practices of Hospitality Management,* editors Pizam, Lewis, and Manning. Westport, CT: AVI Publishing, 1982.

Bardi, James A. *Hotel Front Office Management,* 3rd ed. New York: John Wiley & Sons, 2002.

Barth, Stephen. *Hospitality Law: Managing Legal Issues in the Hospitality Industry.* New York: John Wiley & Sons, 2001.

Baum, Tom, and Mudambi, Ram. *Economic and Management Methods for Tourism and Hospitality Research.* New York: John Wiley & Sons, 1999.

Be Our Guest, Perfecting the Art of Customer Service. Lake Buena Vista, FL: Disney Institute [no date].

Beavis, J. R. S., and Medlik, S. *A Manual of Hotel Reception,* 3rd ed. London: William Heinemann Ltd., 1981.

Berman, Shelley. *A Hotel Is a Place. . . .* Los Angeles: Price/Stern/Sloan Publishers, 1972.

Boomer, Lucius. *Hotel Management.* New York: Harper & Row, 1938.

Borsenik, Frank and Stutts, Alan. *The Management of Maintenance and Engineering Systems in the Hospitality Industry,* 4th ed. New York: John Wiley & Sons, 1997.

Braham, Bruce. *Computer Systems in the Hotel and Catering Industry.* London: Cassell Educational Ltd., 1988.

——. *Hotel Front Office,* 2nd ed. Gloucestershire, England: Stanley Thornes, 1993.

Brotherton, Bob (Ed.). *The Handbook of Contemporary Hospitality Management Research.* New York: John Wiley & Sons, 1999.

Browning, Marjorie. *Night Audit Procedure.* Columbus, OH: The Christopher Inn, March 1, 1969.

Bryson, McDowell, and Ziminski, Adele. *The Concierge: Key to Hospitality.* New York: John Wiley & Sons, 1992.

Bucher, A. F. *101 Tips on Check Cashing.* New York: Ahrens Publishing Co., circa 1930.

Burstein, Harvey. *Hotel Security Management.* New York: Praeger Publishers, 1975.

Buzby, Walter J. *Hotel and Motel Security Management.* Los Angeles: Security World Publishing Co., 1976.

Cabot, Anthony. *Casino Gaming Policy, Economics and Regulation.* Las Vegas, NV: UNLV International Gaming Institute, 1996.

Casado, Matt. *Housekeeping Management.* New York: John Wiley & Sons, 2000.

Chandler, Raymond. *Trouble Is My Business.* New York: Ballantine Books, 1972.

Check and Credit-Card Fraud Prevention Manual. New York: The Atlantic Institute, Atcom Publishing, 1984.

Collins, Galen, and Malik, Tarun. *Hospitality Information Technology: Learning How to Use It,* 5th ed. Dubuque, IA: Kendall/Hunt Publishing, 2004.

Convention Liaison Council Manual, 6th ed. Washington, DC: Convention Industry Council, 1994.

The Credit Card Industry. National Education Program of Discover Card. Riverwoods, IL: Novus Network Services, 1996.

Cournoyer, Norman, Marshall, Anthony, and Morris, Karen. *Hotel, Restaurant and Travel Law: A Preventive Approach,* 5th ed. Albany, NY: Delmar, 1999.

Dahl, J. O. *Bellman and Elevator Operator.* Revised by Crete Dahl. Stamford, CT: The Dahls, 1993.

——. *Room Clerk's Manual.* Revised by Crete Dahl. Stamford, CT: The Dahls, 1993.

DeFranco, Agnes, and Noriega, Pender. *Cost Control in the Hospitality Industry.* Upper Saddle River, NJ: Prentice-Hall, 1999.

Dervaes, C. *The Travel Dictionary.* Tampa, FL: Solitaire Publishing, 1992.

Deveau, Jack, and Penraat, Jaap. *The Efficient Room Clerk.* New York: Learning Information, 1968.

DeVeau, Linsley, and DeVeau, Patricia. *Front Office Management and Operations.* Upper Saddle River, NJ: Prentice Hall, 1996.

Directory of Hotel & Lodging Companies. Waldorf, MD: American Hotel & Lodging Association, Annually.

Dittmer, Paul. *Dimensions of the Hospitality Industry: An Introduction,* 3rd ed. New York: John Wiley & Sons, 2001.

Dix, Colin, and Baird, Chris. *Front Office Operations,* 4th ed. London: Longman Group United Kingdom, 1998.

Drury, Tony, and Ferrier, Charles. *Credit Cards.* London: Butterworth, 1984.

Dukas, Peter. *Hotel Front Office Management and Operations,* 3rd ed. Dubuque, IA: William C. Brown Company, Publishers, 1970.

Dunn, David. "Front Office Accounting Machines in Hotels," unpublished master's thesis, Cornell University, Ithaca, NY, June 1965.

Dunseath, M., and Ransom, J. *The Hotel Bookkeeper Receptionist.* London: Barrie & Rockliff, 1967.

Fidel, John. *Hotel Data Systems,* rev. ed. Albuquerque, NM: September 1972.

Ford, Robert, and Heaton, Cherrill. *Managing the Guest Experience in Hospitality.* Albany, NY: Delmar, 2000.

Foster, Dennis. *Rooms at the Inn: Front Office Operations and Administration.* Peoria, IL: Glencoe, 1992.

——. *The Business of Hospitality: Back Office Operations and Administration.* Peoria, IL: Glencoe, 1992.

Front Office and Reservations. Burlingame, CA: Hyatt Corporation, 1978.

Front Office Courtesy Pays. Small Business Administration. Washington, DC: U.S. Government Printing Office, 1956.

Front Office Manual. New York: New Yorker Hotel, 1931.

Front Office Manual: Franchise Division. Sheraton Hotels & Inns, Worldwide [no date].

Front Office Operations Manual (of the) Hotel McCurdy, Evansville, Indiana. Research Bureau of the American Hotel Association, April 1923.

Front Office Selling. East Lansing, MI: Educational Institute of the American Hotel & Motel Association [no date].

Front Office Selling "Tips." New York: Hotel Sales Management Association, 1960.

Gathje, Curtis. *At the Plaza: An Illustrated History of the World's Most Famous Hotel.* New York: St. Martin's Press, 2000.

Gatiss, Gordon. *Total Quality Management.* London: Cassell PLC, 1996.

Giroux, Sharon. *Hosting the Disabled: Crossing the Communication Barrier.* Albany, NY: Delmar, 1994 (video).

Godowski, S. *Microcomputers in the Hotel and Catering Industry.* London: William Heinemann Ltd., 1988.

Goldblatt, Joe. *Special Events.* New York: John Wiley & Sons, 2002.

Gomes, Albert. *Hospitality in Transition.* Houston, TX: Pannell Kerr Foster, 1985.

Goodwin, John, and Gaston, Jolie. *Hotel, Hospitality and Tourism Law,* 5th ed. Scottsdale, AZ: Gorsuch Scarisbrick, Publishers, 1997.

Gray, William S., and Liguori, Salvatore C. *Hotel and Motel Management and Operations,* 4th ed. Upper Saddle River, NJ: Prentice Hall, 2002.

Guest Relations Training for Front Office Cashiers. Boston: Sheraton Corporation of America, 1961.

A Guide to Terminology in the Leisure Time Industries. Philadelphia: Laventhol & Horwath [no date].

Hall, Orrin. *Motel–Hotel Front Office Procedures.* Hollywood Beach, FL: circa 1971.

Hall, S. S. J. *Quality Assurance in the Hospitality Industry.* Milwaukee, WI: ASQC Quality Press, 1990.

Hamilton, Francis. *Hotel Front Office Management.* Miami, FL: 1947.

Hanson, Bjorn. *Price Elasticity of Lodging Demand.* New York: PricewaterhouseCoopers, January 20, 2000.

Haszonics, Joseph. *Front Office Operation.* New York: ITT Educational Services, 1971.

Heldenbrand, H. V. *Front Office Psychology.* Evanston, IL: John Wiley & Sons, 1944. Republished by American Hotel Register Company, Chicago, circa 1982.

Hilton, Conrad. *Be My Guest.* Englewood Cliffs, NJ: Prentice Hall, 1957.

Hitz, Ralph. *Standard Practice Manuals for Hotel Operation, I, Front Service Division.,* 2nd ed. New York: Harper & Row, 1936.

Hotel and Travel Index. Secaucus, NJ: Cahners Travel Group, Quarterly.

The Hotelman Looks at the Business of Meetings. St. Paul, MN: 3M Business Press, 1968.

Hsu, Cathy, and Powers, Tom. *Marketing Hospitality,* 3rd ed. New York: John Wiley & Sons, 2001.

Hubbart, Roy. *The Hubbart Formula for Evaluating Rate Structures of Hotel Rooms.* New York: American Hotel & Motel Association, 1952.

Hyatt Travel Futures Project Report on Business Travelers. New York: prepared for Hyatt Hotels and Resorts by Research & Forecasts, December 1988.

Implications of Microcomputers in Small and Medium Hotel and Catering Firms. Prepared for the Hotel and Catering Industry Training Board by the Department of Hotel, Catering, and Tourism Management, University of Surrey, Guildford, Surrey, England, November 1980.

Ingold, Anthony, McMahon-Beattie, Una, and Yeoman, Ian (Eds.). *Yield Management,* 2nd ed. Washington, D.C.: Continuum, 2001.

Ismail, Ahmed. *Front Office Operations & Management.* Albany, NY: Delmar, 2001.

Ismail, Ahmed. *Hotel Sales & Operations.* Albany, NY: Delmar, 1999.

Iverson, Kathleen M. *Introduction to Hospitality Management.* New York: Van Nostrand Reinhold, 1997.

Iverson, Kathleen. *Managing Human Resources in the Hospitality Industry: An Experiential Approach,* 1st ed. Upper Saddle River, NJ: Prentice Hall, 2001.

Jones, Christine, and Paul, Val. *Accommodations Management.* London: Botsford Academic and Education, 1985.

Kaplan, Michael. *The New Hotel, International and Resort Designs.* Weimer, TX: Culinary and Hospitality Industry Publications Services, 2002.

Kasavana, Michael, and Brooks, Richard. *Managing Front Office Operations,* 6th ed. East Lansing, MI: Educational Institute, 2001.

Kasavana, Michael, and Cahill, John J. *Managing Technology in the Hospitality Indusustry,* 4th ed. Orlando, FL: Educational Institute of the American Hotel & Lodging Industry, 2003.

Kline, Sheryl, and Sullivan, William. *Hotel Front Office Simulation.* New York: John Wiley & Sons, 2002.

Lawrence, Janet. *Room Sales and Reception Management.* Boston: The Innkeeping Institute of America, 1970.

Leask, Anna, and Yeoman, Ian. *Heritage Visitor Attractions: An Operations Management Perspective.* London: Cassell Academic, 1999.

Lefler, Janet, and Calanese, Salvatore. *The Correct Cashier.* New York: Ahrens Publishing Co., 1960.

Link Hospitality Consultants, Ltd. *Canadian Job Strategy: Hotel Front Office Specialist.* Calgary, Alberta, Canada: Southern Alberta Institute of Technology, 1986.

Lundberg, Donald. *Front Office Human Relations.* Distributed by NU:PAK, San Marcos, CA, 1970.

Martin, Robert, and Jones, Tom. *Professional Management of Housekeeping Operations,* 3rd ed. New York: John Wiley & Sons, 1998.

MasterCard International Frequent Business Traveler Study. Presented at the American Hotel & Motel Association Annual Meeting, November 14, 1983.

Medlik, S. and Ingram, Hadyn. *The Business of Hotels,* 4th ed. London: Butterworth-Heinemann Medical Ltd., 2000.

——. *Dictionary of Travel and Tourism Hospitality,* 3rd ed. Oxford: Butterworth-Heinemann Medical, 2003.

——. *Profile of the Hotel and Catering Industry,* 2nd ed. London: William Heinemann Ltd., 1978.

Meek, Howard B. *A Theory of Room Rates.* Ithaca, NY: Cornell University, Department of Hotel Administration, June 1938.

A Meeting Planner's Guide to Master Account Billing. Developed by the Insurance Conference Planners, and published by The Educational Institute of the American Hotel & Motel Association, May 1980.

Metelka, Charles J. *The Dictionary of Hospitality, Travel and Tourism,* 3rd ed. Albany, NY: Delmar, 1989.

Michael, Angie. *Best Impressions in Hospitality.* Albany, NY: Delmar, 2000.

Ministry of Tourism. *The Front Desk Business.* Toronto, Ontario, Canada: Ontario Ministry of Tourism, 1978.

Moreo, Patrick, Sammons, Gail, and Beck, Jeff. *Front Office Operations and Auditing Work Book,* 2nd ed. Upper Saddle River, NJ: Prentice Hall, 2001.

Nebel, Eddystone. *Managing Hotels Effectively: Lessons from Outstanding General Managers.* New York: John Wiley & Sons, 1991.

O'Connor, Peter. *Using Computers in Hospitality and Tourism,* 2nd ed. London: Cassell PLC, 2000.

Ogilvie, A. W. T. *Lecture Outline in Front Office.* American Hotel Association, 1923.

Paananen, Donna. *Selling Out: A How-to Manual on Reservations Management.* East Lansing, MI: Educational Institute, 1985.

Paige, Grace, and Paige, Jane. *The Hotel Receptionist,* 3rd ed. London: Holt, Rinehart and Winston, 1988.

——. *Hotel Front Desk Personnel,* rev. ed. New York: Van Nostrand Reinhold, 1988.

Pfeiffer, W., Voegele, M., and Wolley, G. *The Correct Service Department for Hotels, Motor Hotels, Motels and Resorts.* New York: Ahrens Publishing Co., 1962.

Picot, Derek. *Hotel Reservations.* Jersey City, NJ: Parkwest Publications, 1997.

Powers, Tom, and Barrows, Clayton. *Introduction to the Hospitality Industry,* New York: John Wiley & Sons, 2003.

Poynter, James. *Foreign Independent Tours.* Albany, NY: Delmar Publishers, 1989.

Poynter, James. *Mystery Shopping.* Dubuque, IA: Kendall/Hunt Publishing, 1996.

Property Management and Point of Sale Systems: Guide to Selection. New York: American Hotel & Motel Association.

Raleigh, Lori, and Roginsky, Rachel (Eds.). *Hotel Investments: Issues & Perspectives,* 2nd ed. Orlando, FL: Educational Institute of the American Hotel & Lodging Industry, 1999.

Ransley, Josef, and Ingram, Hadyn (Eds.). *Developing Hospitality Properties and Facilities.* London: Butterworth-Heinemann, 2000.

Relieving Reservation Headaches. East Lansing, MI: Educational Institute of the American Hotel & Motel Association, 1979.

Renner, Peter. *Basic Hotel Front Office Procedures,* 3rd ed. New York: Van Nostrand Reinhold, 1993.

"Resale in the Lodging Industry: A Bell System Perspective." American Hotel & Motel Association, Mid-year Meeting, Nashville, TN, April 1982.

"Room Clerk, The Man Up Front." *Motel/Motor Inn Journal,* 1977.

Roper, A. J. *Hotel Consortia and Structures: An Analyses of the Emergence of Hotel Consortia as Transorganizational Forms.* Oxford University [no date].

Rosenzweig, Stan. *Hotel/Motel Telephone Systems: Opportunities through Deregulation.* East Lansing, MI: Educational Institute of the American Hotel & Motel Association, 1982.

Ross, Bruce. "Hotel Reservation Systems Present and Future." Unpublished master's monograph, Cornell University, Ithaca, NY, May 1977.

Rushmore, Stephen, and Baum, Erich. *Hotels & Motels: Valuations and Market Studies.* Addison, IL: Appraisal Institute, 2001.

——. *Hotel Investments: A Guide for Lenders and Owners.* New York: Warren, Gorham & Lamont, 1990.

Rutes, Walter, Penner, Richard, and Adams, Lawrence. *Hotel Design, Planning, and Development.* New York: W. W. Norton, 2001.

Rutherford, Denney. *Hotel Management and Operations,* 3rd ed. New York: John Wiley & Sons, 2001.

Saunders, K. C. *Head Hall Porter.* London: Catering Education Research Institute, 1980.

——, and Pullen, R. *An Occupational Study of Room Maids in Hotels.* Middlesex, England: Middlesex Polytechnic, 1987.

Scatchard, Bill. *Upsetting the Applecart: A Common Sense Approach to Successful Hotel Operations for the '90s.* Box 19156, Tampa, FL 33686; 1994.

Schneider, Madelin, and Georgina Tucker. *The Professional Housekeeper.* New York: Van Nostrand Reinhold, Inc., 1989.

Self, Robert. *Long Distance for Less.* New York: Telecom Library, 1982.

Shaw, Margaret, and Morris, Susan. *Hospitality Sales: A Marketing Approach.* New York: John Wiley & Sons, 1999.

Sherry, John. *How to Exclude and Eject Undesirable Guests.* Stamford, CT: The Dahls, 1943.

Sicherman, Irving. *The Investment in the Lodging Business.* Scranton, PA: Sicherman, 1977.

Starting and Managing a Small Motel. Small Business Administration. Washington, DC: U.S. Government Printing Office, 1963.

The State of Technology in the Lodging Industry. New York: American Hotel & Motel Association, 1980.

Stiel, Holly. *Ultimate Service: The Complete Handbook to the World of the Concierge.* Upper Saddle River, NJ: Prentice Hall, 1994.

Stutts, Alan, and Borsenik, Frank. *Maintenance Handbook for Hotels, Motels and Resorts,* 4th ed. New York: John Wiley & Sons, 1997.

Successful Credit and Collection Techniques. East Lansing, MI: Educational Institute of the American Hotel & Motel Association, 1981.

Tarbet, J. R. *A Handbook of Hotel Front Office Procedure.* Pullman, WA: Student Book Corporation, circa 1955.

Taylor, Derek, and Thomason, Richard. *Profitable Hotel Reception.* Elmsford, NY: Pergamon Press, 1982.

Trends in the Hotel-Motel Business. New York: Pannell Kerr Forster & Co., various years.

Uniform-Service Training. Boston: Sheraton Corporation of America, 1960.

Uniform System of Accounts for the Lodging Industry, 9th ed. New York: Hotel Association of New York City, 1996.

Vallen, Jerome, and Abbey, James. *The Art and Science of Hospitality Management.* East Lansing, MI: Educational Institute, 1987.

Van Hoof, H., McDonald, M., Yu, L., and Vallen, G. *A Host of Opportunities: An Introduction to Hospitality Management,* 2nd ed. Chicago: Richard D. Irwin, 2004.

VanStrien, Kimberly, et al. *Front Office Management and Operations.* Upper Saddle River, NJ: Prentice Hall, 1998.

Walker, Terri, and Miller, Richard. *The 2000 Hotel & Lodging Market Research Handbook,* 3rd ed. Norcross, GA: Richard K. Miller, 1999.

Weissinger, Suzanne S. *Hotel/Motel Operations.* Cincinnati, OH: South-Western Publishing Co., 1989.

White, Paul, and Beckley, Helen. *Hotel Reception,* 4th ed. London: Edward Arnold (Publishers) Ltd., 1982.

Wingenter, Tom, et al. *The Relationship of Lodging Prices to Occupancy: A Study of Accommodations in Northern Wisconsin.* Madison, WI: University of Wisconsin Cooperative Extension Service, 1982–83.

Wittemann, Ad. *Hotel Room Clerk.* Las Vegas, NV: Camelot Consultants, 1986.

Wolosz, Joe. *Hotel & Motel Sales, Marketing & Promotion: Strategies to Impact Revenue & Increase Occupancy for Smaller Lodging Properties.* San Francisco, CA: Infinite Corridor Publishers, 1997.

Woods, Robert, and King, Judith. *Managing for Quality in the Hospitality Industry.* East Lansing, MI: Educational Institute, 1996.

——, Heck, William, and Sciarini, Michael. *Turnover and Diversity in the Lodging Industry.* New York: American Hotel Foundation, 1998.

Yellowstone Park Company Cashier Training Program. Yellowstone: Yellowstone Park Co., 1978.

Yeoman, Ian, and McMahon-Beattie, Una (Eds.). *Revenue Management and Pricing: Case Studies and Applications.* Washington, D.C.: Continuum International Publishing Group, 2003.

Yu, Lawrence. *The International Hospitality Business: Management and Operations.* Binghamton, NY: Haworth Hospitality Press, 1999.

Index

• • •